IVOR·GUEST HISTORY·PRIZE

Rebecca Sebborn

July·1993

JULES PERROT

Also by Ivor Guest

Napoleon III in England
The Ballet of the Second Empire
The Romantic Ballet in England
Fanny Cerrito
Victorian Ballet Girl
Adeline Genée
The Alhambra Ballet
La Fille mal gardée (editor)
The Dancer's Heritage
The Empire Ballet
A Gallery of Romantic Ballet
The Romantic Ballet in Paris
Dandies and Dancers
Carlotta Zambelli
Two Coppélias
Fanny Elssler
The Pas de Quatre
Le Ballet de l'Opéra de Paris
The Divine Virginia
Letters from a Ballet-master
Adeline Genée : a pictorial record
Designing for the Dancer (contributor)
Adventures of a Ballet Historian

JULES PERROT

Master of the Romantic Ballet

Ivor Guest

[signature: Ivor Guest]

Dance Books Ltd.
9 Cecil Court London WC2

This book is dedicated
to the memory of
YURI SLONIMSKY (1902–78)
who suggested that it should be written,
and unstintingly provided encouragement,
advice and practical assistance.

© 1984 Ivor Guest

First published in 1984 by Dance Books Ltd.,
9 Cecil Court, London WC2N 4EZ.

ISBN 0 903102 77 3

Designed by Kate Hughes-Stanton
Design and production in association with
Book Production Consultants, Cambridge

Typeset by Glyn Davies, Cambridge
Printed by The Alden Press, Osney Mead, Oxford.

Frontispiece
La Esmeralda *at the Scala, Milan. Act I, with Fanny Elssler as
Esmeralda, and other characters at the front of the stage –
Quasimodo by the goat, Phoebus with plumed headdress, Frollo
and Gringoire to the right. Oil painting by Carlo Bossoli.
Collection of Cav. Ugo Rivoiro Pellegrini.*

Contents

Preface i
1 The Child Polichinelle 1
2 Apprenticeship on the Boulevard 7
3 Le Vrai Danseur 17
4 Enter a Muse 30
5 First Steps in Choreography 38
6 A Paris Triumph 50
7 Gestation of a Masterpiece 60
8 On Trial at Her Majesty's 78
9 The Turning Point 90
10 An Essay in Dance Drama 112
11 The Championing of Lucile Grahn 138
12 The Season of the Golden Apple 155
13 The Unfinished Masterpiece 182
14 The Year of 'Faust' 206
15 The Lure of Russia 224
16 Carlotta's Indian Summer 250
17 The Emergence of Russian Talent 275
18 Last Years in Russia 297
19 Frustrations of Retirement 320
The Survival of Jules Perrot's ballets after his retirement 347
The Choreographic Works of Jules Perrot 352
Genealogical Tables 358
Bibliography 360
Notes 368
Index 375

Illustrations

Frontispiece
   1. *La Esmeralda* at the Scala, Milan. Painting by Carlo Bossoli.

Between pages 80 and 81
   2. Charles Mazurier.
   3. Frédérick Lemaître.
   4. The Boulevard du Temple.
   5. Mazurier in *Jocko*.
   6. The Théâtre de la Porte-Saint-Martin.
   7. Frédérick Lemaître and Mme Zélie in the *valse de fascination* in *Faust*.
   8. Auguste Vestris.
   9. August Bournonville.
  10. Louis Véron.
  11. Benjamin Lumley.
  12. Jules Perrot in *Robert le Diable*. Drawing by Le Faget.
  13. Jules Perrot in *La Révolte au sérail*.
  14. Jules Perrot and Pauline Leroux in *Nathalie*. Drawing by Le Faget.
  15. Carlotta Grisi and Jules Perrot in *Le Rossignol*.
  16. Jules Perrot and Carlotta Grisi in *Der Kobold*.
  17. Carlotta Grisi in *Zingaro*.
  18. Jules Perrot in *Zingaro*.
  19. Carlotta Grisi in *Zingaro*.
  20. Jules Perrot and Carlotta Grisi dancing the *valse saxonne* in *Zingaro*.
  21.
  22. } Carlotta Grisi and Jules Perrot in the *pas de deux* in Act I of *Giselle*.
  23. Carlotta Grisi and Jules Perrot in Act I of *Giselle*.
  24. Carlotta Grisi in Act II of *Giselle*.
  25.
  26. } Moments from Act II of *Giselle*, with Carlotta Grisi and Lucien Petipa.
  27. Jules Perrot, Fanny Cerrito and Marie Guy-Stéphan in *L'Elève d'Amour*.
  28. Fanny Cerrito in *Une Soirée du Carnaval*.
  29. Jules Perrot in *Alma*.
  30.
  31. } *Ondine*, Scene 1.

Illustrations

32.\
33. } *Ondine*, Scene 2.
34.\
35. } *Ondine*, Scene 4.

Between pages 176 and 177
36. *Ondine*, Scene 4.
37. *Ondine*, Scene 5.
38. Silk programme for the Command Performance at Her Majesty's Theatre in 1843.
39. Fanny Cerrito and Fanny Elssler in their *pas de deux*.
40. Jules Perrot and Fanny Elssler in *Le Délire d'un peintre*.
41. Jules Perrot. Caricature bust by Jean-Pierre Dantan.
42. Jules Perrot. Bust by Claude-François Lequine.
43. Adèle Dumilâtre in the *pas de Diane chasseresse*.
44. Jules Perrot and Fanny Elssler in *La Castilliana Bolero*.
45. Jules Perrot and Carlotta Grisi in the *truandaise* in *La Esmeralda*.
46. Arthur Saint-Léon in Scene 3 of *La Esmeralda*.
47. Jules Perrot and Carlotta Grisi in the dance lesson scene in *La Esmeralda*.
48. The Festival of Fools in *La Esmeralda*.
49.\
50. } Jules Perrot and Carlotta Grisi in *The Polka*.
51. Carlotta Grisi in *The Polka*.
52. *Eoline*, Scene 4.
53. Lucile Grahn in *Eoline*.
54. Jules Perrot and Lucile Grahn in the *mazurka d'extase* in *Eoline*.
55. Cesare Pugni's manuscript score of the *Pas de Quatre*.
56. The *Pas de Quatre*.
57. Cesare Pugni.
58. Lucile Grahn in the *pas stratégique* in *Catarina*.
59. Lucile Grahn and Jules Perrot in the *valse à cinq temps* in *Catarina*.
60. *Brigand on the Watch*, by Léopold Robert.
61. *Catarina*, Scene 2.
62. *Catarina*, Scene 5.
63. Dwarkanath Tagore.
64. Fanny Cerrito and Arthur Saint-Léon in the *pas de chibouk* in *Lalla Rookh*.
65. The *pas de neuf* in *Lalla Rookh*.
66. The *pas de neuf* in *Lalla Rookh*. Water colour by A.E. Chalon.
67.\
68. } *Le Jugement de Pâris*.

Between pages 272 and 273
69.\
70. } The influence of Léopold Robert on Jules Perrot: *Le Retour du pèlerinage à la Madonne de l'Arc* and *L'Improvisateur napolitain*.
71.\
72.\
73. } Mephistopheles, as seen by Moritz Retzsch, Eugène Delacroix and Tony Johannot.
74. *Les Eléments*.

Illustrations

75. *Les Quatre Saisons*.
76. Fanny Elssler and Gustave Carey in the Dance of the Seven Deadly Sins in *Faust*.
77. Amalia Ferraris in *Odetta*.
78.
79. } *Esmeralda* in St. Petersburg. Drawings by D. Timmo and Adolphe
80. } Charlemagne.
81.
82. } *Esmeralda* in St. Petersburg. Drawings by Adolphe Charlemagne.
83. Carlotta Grisi in Act I of *La Filleule des fées*.
84. Carlotta Grisi in Act II of *La Filleule des fées*.
85. Jules Perrot in *La Filleule des fées*.
86.
87. } *La Filleule des fées*, Act II.
88. Carlotta Grisi and Jules Perrot in *La Filleule des fées*.
89. Jules Perrot in rehearsal, with Cesare Pugni. Drawing by Adolphe Charlemagne.
90. Carlotta Grisi in *The Naiad and the Fisherman*.
91. Carlotta Grisi and Jules Perrot in an open-air performance of *The Naiad and the Fisherman* at Peterhof.
92. Nadezhda Bogdanova in *Esmeralda*.
93. Katrine Friedberg in *Catarina*.
94. Jules Perrot in his first years in Russia.
95. Gabriele Yella.
96. Praskovia Lebedeva as Marguerite in *Faust*.
97. Louis and Zina Mérante.
98. Martha Muravieva in *Giselle*.
99. Jules Perrot in rehearsal attire.
100. Jules Perrot in morning dress, 1856.
101. Page from Jules Perrot's annotated copy of Noverre's Letters.
102. Carlotta Grisi in her Esmeralda costume, with Aleksander Tarnowski.
103. *La Classe de danse de M. Perrot*, by Degas.
104. *La Classe de danse, adage*, by Degas.
105. *Le Danseur Perrot, assis*, by Degas.

Illustrations in the text
Page   2 Birth certificate of Jules Perrot.
         19 Playbill of Jules Perrot's début at the Paris Opéra.
         25 Playbill of the King's Theatre, London, for a performance of *Faust*.
         42 Baptism entry of Marie-Julie Perrot.
         62 Playbill of Carlotta Grisi's début at the Paris Opéra.
         85 Jules Perrot and Fanny Cerrito in the *valse de fascination* in *Alma*.
        103 *Ondine*, Scene 3: Cerrito's shawl dance
        103 *Ondine*, finale: the coloured fountains.
        117 Playbill of Her Majesty's Theatre, London, for *La Esmeralda* and the polka.
        156 Playbill of Her Majesty's Theatre, London, for *Catarina*.
        175 A caricaturist's view of *Le Jugement de Pâris*.

Illustrations

204 Playbill of Her Majesty's Theatre, London, for Taglioni's last performance as the Sylphide.
238 Playbill of the Paris Opéra for *La Filleule des fées*.
239 *La Filleule des fées*, Act I.
240 *La Filleule des fées*, Act I.
287 Playbill of the Bolshoi Theatre, St. Petersburg, for *Armida*.
331 Caricatures of *Gazelda* at the Scala, Milan.
343 Invitation to the funeral of Jules Perrot.

Preface

Of all the choreographers who contributed to the extraordinary flowering of ballet around the middle of the nineteenth century, none enjoyed a more extensive or more influential reputation than Jules Perrot. Although very little of his choreography has survived, his works form a significant part of the bedrock of tradition on which ballet, as we know and enjoy it nearly a century and a half later, rests.

To today's ballet-goers the name of Petipa is much more widely known because several important ballets which he staged during his long career in St Petersburg have survived as classics, thanks partly to his good fortune in working with a composer of genius, Tchaikovsky. However, just as Petipa has been revered by later generations of choreographers, so did he himself look back to honour a past master. In the course of his development as a maker of ballets there was no more potent influence than his predecessor, Jules Perrot, whose originality and method he had been privileged to observe at first hand during his formative years as a creative artist, and many of whose ballets he had himself revived, revising them in the process to suit the developing technique of his dancers, but always respecting their dramatic structure.

The innovative quality of Perrot's work was fully recognised in his own day, and still stands out clearly in historical perspective in spite of the ephemeral nature of the material of choreography in days before cinematography and video-recording, or even the action photograph. Essentially he was a dramatic author working in movement. His ballets, with only one or two exceptions, were in the full sense of the term products of his own imagination, being conceived and set on stage under his sole direction. Mercifully, he was seldom subjected to the restraints of an imposed scenario – the bane of choreographers working at the Paris Opéra – and was free to select his subjects and construct his own plots. To enjoy this freedom, as he did during his most productive years in London, and later, with an occasional tussle with the censorship, in St Petersburg, was a priceless boon, for it enabled him to respond directly to the undercurrents of Romanticism, the new wave of ideas that flooded the arts during the impressionable years of his youth and early

Preface

adulthood. The literary sources of his ballets show most clearly how responsive he was to these new trends, and at another level, how extensively he must have read and educated himself, for his schooling, which had to be fitted into a theatrical career that began when he was a young boy, must by any standard have been fragmentary. His apprenticeship in the Boulevard theatres of Paris was an education in itself, bringing him into early touch not only with the actors and dancers, but with the playwrights, journalists, artists, speculators and men of fashion who haunted the world of the theatre. Later, his association with Théophile Gautier during the gestation of *Giselle* must have brought an acquaintance with the literary circle of Victor Hugo, perhaps even a personal contact with the great poet and dramatist himself. As his ballets bear witness, his imagination was fed by the works of a wide spectrum of writers of the Romantic school: Gautier first of all, with whom he was privileged to collaborate in *Giselle*; Victor Hugo, from whose novel *Notre Dame de Paris* came the plot of *Esmeralda*; Thomas Moore, whose lush poem *Lalla Rookh* provided the theme of the ballet of the same name; La Motte Fouqué, whose story of Undine inspired the poetic ballet of *Ondine*; the historian Michelet, whose vivid evocation of France's past was undoubtedly a main source of *Odetta*; and most significant of all, Gœthe, whose *Faust* fascinated Perrot throughout his career, suggesting the rôle of the sardonic demon which he played in so many of his ballets, and inspiring his most ambitious, though unhappily ill-starred, ballet. Perrot was also influenced by artists. His conception of Mephistopheles may have partly derived from the illustrations by Retzsch and Delacroix for Gœthe's *Faust*; two of Léopold Robert's canvases were recognised as having inspired important passages in *Ondine* and its derivative, *The Naiad and the Fisherman*; while a supposed incident in the life of Salvator Rosa – his capture by *banditti* in the picturesque mountain landscape which he painted so vividly – inspired the action-filled ballet of *Catarina*. All these sources, so essentially Romantic, were moulded by Jules Perrot into ballets that were never mere translations into another medium, but each one a creation of true inspiration in which the source was transmuted into a work of art with an identity of its own. Thus, to a degree achieved by no other choreographer of his time, Jules Perrot established himself as an original artist of supreme eminence, as fundamentally Romantic in spirit as the greatest exponents in other fields of art.

The secret of his genius was to be found in his choreographic method: his skill in peopling the stage, setting the scenes in movement and breathing life into the narrative, and an ability, quite novel in his time, to weave the dances into the action. Analysis of his ballets from the choreographic viewpoint reveals that his supremacy rested on two exceptional abilities. The first was his development of the *pas d'action*, a dance scene envisaged as an integral part of the dramatic action that progressed or assisted the narrative in terms of dance. In his ballets, passages of this nature reduced the reliance on long stretches of mime, which so frequently provoked tedium, and added new depths of meaning and mood. Although other choreographers before him – notably, in his experience, Coralli and Deshayes – had tentatively shown the way, the *pas d'action* was developed by him to such an extent that it was virtually his own invention. His other achievement was his mastery in composing passages of pure dance, whether variations for individual dancers or *pas* for groups of dancers. His nurturing of Carlotta Grisi from a mere promising child to the creator of the rôle of Giselle must have initiated him into the arcane secret of perceiving the essence of a dancer's style and technical potential and creating movement out of a dancer's body much as a great sculptor can draw out a masterpeice from a particular block of fine stone. This discovery led him to his most sublime achievements, that series of divertissements which reached a peak of perfection in the *Pas de Quatre*, staged in London when his invention was in its fullest flow. To produce not one but several such works in which none of the performers ever complained of partiality was little short of miraculous.

It is a sad reminder of the ephemeral nature of ballet in times past that little of his choreography has survived to this day. *Giselle* has come down through the revising hand of Petipa, although it is fair to assume that much of Perrot's choreography has been preserved in the rôle of Giselle and the, alas, truncated rôle of Albert, even if one gem – Giselle's original variation in the first act – has long been forgotten. What remains, however, is convincing evidence of the sensitivity of his inventive power, not only in the choice of steps, often effective by their very simplicity, but in his understanding of mood and sudden flashes of genius that could lift the dance to a peak of exaltation such as is achieved in the greatest works of music and poetry. Passages of *Esmeralda* and *The Naiad and the Fisherman* no doubt remain in the recesses of memory of old dancers and ballet-masters in Russia, and are to be found, in scrappy form, having passed through the revising process of Petipa and others, in the rough pencil-written scores in Stepanov notation which Nicolai Sergueyev spirited out of Russia after the Revolution and which are now in the Harvard Theatre Collection. So we have to be content with the descriptions written by Perrot's contemporaries, on which the accounts of his ballets in this book are primarily based, and grateful to the critics of his time who often recorded their impressions in gratifying detail. But although so much first-hand evidence of his work has vanished beyond recall, enough remains for us to recognise Jules Perrot as the most influential figure of his time, standing head and shoulders above his fellow choreographers like a Praxiteles of the dance – indisputably the master of the Romantic ballet.

What of Perrot the man? We glimpse him only occasionally, for he was absorbed in a medium that is mute by definition, and by his own confession was incorrigibly reluctant to take up a pen. He seems to have kept no diary, written no memoirs, recorded no reflections on the practice of his art, and his

Preface

correspondence was desultory, although when he did write, he showed that he could express himself with felicity and wit. Across a span of nearly a century he emerges as a powerful personality, able of course to dominate and command a large body of dancers, temperamental and quick to show his feelings, a man with a great pride in his art and a full consciousness of his worth; yet a very private man, unpretentious and refreshingly free of arrogance, with simple tastes and frugal habits; a man who respected himself and was respected by others, surrounded by a wide circle of friends of all ages, and blessed with a devoted family who cherished him as – a little impatiently, one imagines – he passed from the vigour of middle life into the frailty of old age.

This was the man whom I came to know ever more intimately as this book took shape. I had realised the significant part he played in the ballet of his time quite early in my researches as a historian, but it needed an outside stimulus to spur me into writing a detailed study of his life and work. This eventually came from Yuri Slonimsky, my Russian colleague and pen friend, with whom I corresponded almost weekly for some twenty years, but never met. Yuri Iosifovitch's last years were clouded by an illness which reduced the hours when he could write to the barest minimum; a book on Perrot was one of his projects that he knew he could never fulfil, and he urged me to undertake it in his stead. The research and the writing took six or seven years, and sadly, as he foretold would happen, he did not live to see it in print or even in draft. This book must therefore be dedicated to his memory, and it is his encouragement, advice and active assistance in supplying me with much of the Russian material on which the later chapters are based, that I must acknowledge first of all.

Many others have patiently answered my enquiries, undertaken tasks of research or helped in other ways in the course of this book's preparation: in the Soviet Union, the historians Vera Krasovskaya and Elizabeth Souritz; in France, Marie-Françoise Christout, Etienne Grafe, Josette Gruss, Marie-France Gurney, Lydia Joffé, Pierre Lacotte, Véronique Martin-Payen, and the late Marian Hannah Winter; in the USA, Edwin Binney 3rd and Parmenia Migel Ekstrom; in Italy, Mercedes Ferrero-Viale and Lisa Finzi; in Denmark, Knud Jürgensen; in Austria, Clara Thiel and Gunter Brosche; in Switzerland, Fanny Bonzon; in England, Edward Kelland-Espinosa. My thanks are due too to those who helped me with translations, notably J. Stuart Barker, Christian Barreault, Mervyn and Mila Matthews and Mme Anne de Merindol, and to those who have allowed me to reproduce pictures in their possession and whose names are recorded in the list of illustrations, also to the photographers who have produced the plates for the illustrations, particularly Godfrey New Photographics Ltd of Sidcup, Kent, John R. Freeman & Co of London, the late Max Erlanger de Rosen of Paris, Jonathan S. Winslow of South Orleans, Mass. and Tadeusz Kazimierski of Warsaw.

I also owe an incalculable debt to the numerous archives and libraries from

Preface

which I have been privileged to draw material, and in particular to the individual librarians who have so willingly and efficiently smoothed my way. Without the help of the following institutions this book would have been sadly impoverished: in the United Kingdom, the British Library, the Theatre Museum, the Royal Acadamy of Dancing, the Cambridge University Library, the Brighton Public Library; in the USA, the Dance Collection of the Museum and Library of the Performing Arts, the Harvard Theatre Collection, the Stravinsky-Diaghilev Foundation, and the libraries of Yale University and Indiana University; in France, the Bibliothèque Nationale, the Archives Nationales, the Bibliothèque de l'Opéra, and the Bibliothèque de l'Arsenal in Paris, and the Archives Départementales and the Bibliothèque de la Ville in Lyon; in Italy, the Biblioteca Braidense, the Museo alla Scala and the Museo Storico Civico, all of Milan; in the Soviet Union, the Bakhrushin Theatre Museum, the Soviet Archives, the Lunacharsky Theatre Museum, the Leningrad Theatre Museum; in Austria, the Theatre Collection of the Osterr. Nationalbibliothek, the Universitätsbibliothek, and the Wiener Stadtbibliothek, all of Vienna, and the Derra de Moroda Dance Archive, now at the University of Salzburg; in Germany, the Theatermuseum in Munich; and in Denmark the Royal Library and the Theatre Museum in Copenhagen.

If Yuri Slonimsky was this book's godfather, then credit must also be given to its nursemaids – above all to my wife, Ann, who put up with yet another lodger in our household and helped in his upbringing in so many ways, solving points of technical detail and being the first to read the text in draft; and to Sandy Mitchell, who helped with secretarial assistance, coping with the considerable correspondence that the preparation of this book entailed.

Finally, a few words are necessary about the dating of events in Russia. The old-style calendar in use in Russia in the nineteenth century was twelve days behind the Gregorian calendar adopted elsewhere. To avoid confusion I have transposed all Russian dates into the new style in the text, but have given both styles in dates of issue of Russian newspapers listed in the notes.

Goose Pond,
Lee, Massachusetts   IVOR GUEST
July 1982

1

The Child Polichinelle

At the unconscionable hour of four o'clock in the morning of August 18th, 1810, in a modest room on the fourth floor of No. 195 Cours Napoléon in the city of Lyon, Laurence Perrot gave birth to her first-born – a son. Later that same day, as the law required, the proud father, Jean Perrot, presented himself at the office of the Mayor in the company of his father-in-law André Rochas and a friend, Joseph Delorge, to register the birth. He announced the boy's name to be Joseph, after a cousin; the name Jules was to be a later addition. Jean Perrot, describing himself as a carpenter, and his father-in-law then signed the entry in the register. M. Delorge did not do so, for he could not write.

The Perrots were a working-class family. The child's paternal grandfather, Jean-Claude Perrot, a manufacturer of silk goods, was already dead when his son Jean married. Jean Perrot had been born not long before the Revolution, on October 22nd, 1788, and had fallen in love with Laurence Rochas, the daughter of a dyer in the hat trade, who lived a few doors away in the Rue Bourgchanin. The two young people were as well matched in age as they were in background, for Laurence was only fifteen days younger than Jean. They were married on October 1st, 1807, and moved into their first home at No. 195 Cours Napoléon, where their elder son was born a little less than three years later. The local census records of 1811 reveal that each of the rooms on the fourth floor of this tenement building was separately occupied. Jean Perrot, whose occupation was recorded as that of a cabinet-maker, lived in one of the smallest of these rooms, sharing it with Laurence, who supplemented the family income by working at home weaving gauze, and two children, his infant son and a baby girl whom Laurence was suckling as a wet-nurse. In another room on the same floor lived Jean's widowed mother, a satin-worker, and his sister who earned her living repairing old clothes. Life must have been a continual struggle for this obscure and humble family who, except for the baby Jules, were destined to spend almost their entire lives in the same district of Lyon.

The fame that Jules was later to achieve in the theatre must at times have

Jules Perrot

Birth certificate of Jules Perrot. Archives Départementales, Lyon.

prompted his friends to enquire whether there were any theatrical or artistic traditions in his family. Eighteenth-century records in Lyon are scanty, but the name Perrot occasionally emerges in such a context. A list of theatrical employees in a legal document records a Perrot as being on the staff of the Lyon opera house in 1718, and somewhat later, in the middle of the century, there was a bassoonist by the name of Benoît Perrot living in the city, but whether any of these were ancestors or relatives of the choreographer is probably beyond verification.

The Perrot family was too busy scratching an existence to leave any record of the impact that the Revolution made on their lives, even had their education allowed them to do so. Jean and Laurence would have had no memories of the *ancien régime*, but in the impressionable years of their childhood they had experienced the terror, excitement and hardships of the Revolution, which had struck Lyon with devastating savagery, and their tales of those troubled times must have ingrained themselves very deeply into the highly charged imagination of their son. For they had both been young children when the bitter conflict between Jacobins and moderates had raged, a conflict that had culminated in the short-lived victory of the moderate faction before bringing upon the city the wrath of the Revolutionary government in Paris. Lyon had then been besieged and partially destroyed, and the vengeance of the Red Terror had been followed, after the fall of Robespierre, by the no less brutal retaliation of the White Terror. The children must have witnessed the hysterical mobs on the rampage, wreaking their savage justice on counter-revolutionaries and Jacobins in turn. Their innocent eyes may have gazed upon horrifying scenes of brutality and death such as inevitably follow in the wake of civil strife, and they must have been caught up in the extraordinary passions of the time. And from them, in turn, must have been handed down to their son Jules an identification with the less fortunate strata of society which he was to project into the humbly-born heroes of his most successful ballets.

Other questions may be asked in the context of the Revolution. In that period of confusion, when families were often riven by divided loyalties and sundered by denunciations, how did the Perrots fare? Did any of them mount the scaffold to the guillotine? Again it is impossible to establish any definite links, but the departmental archives record two Perrots as having been tried by the Revolutionary Committee of Lyon – Jean-Marie Perrot or Perrault, a lace-maker, and Jean-Baptiste Perraud or Perrot, an architect,* while in a list of those who denounced their fellow-citizens during the Red Terror, the name of an F. Rochat appears. It may be that there was no direct connection between these unfortunates and Jean and Laurence Perrot, but the record is not entirely irrelevant, for it emphasises the undercurrents of terror, suspicion and sometimes private revenge that poisoned society during the 1790s, when Jules' parents were children.

Of Jules' early childhood nothing is known. His father may have already been working in the theatre – perhaps as a stage-hand in the Grand Théâtre – for the boy was directed towards a theatrical career at a very early age. While he no doubt attended a local school, learning to read and write and having lessons in history, arithmetic, geography and the catechism, his education had an unconventional side to it, as he later recalled when telling the writer Eugène Briffault about his early days. As soon as he could stand on his feet and shake his legs, he said, he was handed over to a dancing master, and at the age of nine he began to study dancing in earnest.[1] In a note in his own hand he recorded that 'he began his career at the Dancing School of the Lyons theatres,'[2] and it is reasonable to assume that while he may not have been directly taught by the *maître de ballet* Roger, his training was at least supervised by him.

He began to be useful almost at once, making his first stage appearance at the Grand Théâtre in 1818 in Boïeldieu's opera, *Le Petit Chaperon rouge*. However, he played only a supernumerary part in the production, and was to date his performing career from his début, shortly afterwards, in a *pas seul* in *Les Meuniers*, a comedy ballet by Jean-Baptiste Blache that enjoyed a popularity second only to *La Fille mal gardée*. In those early days he might well have chosen an acting career, for drama was presented at the Grand Théâtre as well as opera and ballet, but the enthusiasm of an actor called Saint-Elme after seeing him in a harvest dance opened his eyes to where his future lay.[3] From that moment on he dedicated his life to the dance.

By now Jules was a regular member of the company, earning a salary of 12 francs a month, and gaining valuable experience by observing the other dancers while striving in class to improve his technique and build up his strength. The regular ballet company of the Grand Théâtre was modest both in numbers and in talent. Roger, the *maître de ballet*, was a conscientious and hard-

* It is of some interest to record that Jules' younger brother François-Marie, born in 1813, became an architect, though of somewhat modest accomplishments, judging from two of his plans deposited in the municipal archives – a plan for a dye-factory, and a project for a latrine to be built in the Bas Port.

working man who did what he could with the meagre resources at his disposal. During the years of young Jules' apprenticeship he produced a number of ballets, the most celebrated being *Le Bazar d'Ispahan*, which he staged for Fanny Bias, a star of the Paris Opéra who came to Lyon to give a series of performances in the autumn of 1819.

Fanny Bias was to be the first of many ballerinas whom Jules Perrot was to observe in his career. And he could have had no better vantage point than his place on the stage or in the wings to appreciate her brilliant technique and, in particular, the extraordinary speciality, still limited to a select few, of rising on to the very tips of the toes as she performed some of the jewels from the contemporary Paris repertory – Pierre Gardel's *Psyché* and *La Dansomanie*, Louis Milon's *L'Epreuve villageoise*, Louis Duport's *Le Volage fixé* and Jean Dauberval's *La Fille mal gardée*.

It was during Fanny Bias' visit to Lyon that Jules became aware of the existence of a handsome young dancer, some ten years older than himself, Joseph Mazilier. Although still lacking in assurance, Mazilier was rapidly wining favour with his natural and graceful style. On the evening of Fanny Bias' last appearance he was selected to take over a leading rôle at the last minute, and would have doubtless excelled himself if the performance had not ended, through no fault of his own, in a riot. To Jules the incident was a useful lesson on the reactions of the public to any breach of good manners on the part of an artist. In the first ballet Fanny Bias' partner, Henri Jacotin from Brussels, was hissed for a rather vulgar display of virtuosity, and in a fit of pique refused to appear in the final work of the evening, *La Dansomanie*. When the audience saw that Mazilier had taken his place, their indignation at Jacotin's lack of respect knew no bounds. The house erupted into such a violent uproar that most of the spectators went home, leaving only a hard core of demonstrators who finally had to be forcibly evicted by the Commissioner of Police and a squad of soldiers.

Fanny Bias was succeeded by another distinguished visitor from Paris – Antoine Paul, known as '*Paul l'aérien*,' a dancer of seemingly inexhaustible vigour and effortless lightness, who brought with him his fourteen-year-old sister Pauline. Paul, who had made his first stage appearances at the Grand Théâtre before seeking and finding fame in Paris, had time for only one performance in Lyon, but this must have been enough to leave a strong impression on Jules, whose ambition to attain such heights of virtuosity burned all the more strongly as a result. As for the great man's sister, who was only five years older than the boy, she was already displaying a prodigious technique that Jules was to have the opportunity of observing at closer quarters in later years.

At this time Jules Perrot was still a wide-eyed child, and while he was thrilled by feats of daring virtuosity, the artistic niceties of the ballet probably meant less to him than some of the entertainments to be found on the more popular stages of the city. Together with other children he no doubt slipped into the Théâtre Mécanique de la Crèche in the Rue Noire, and sat fascinated by the Panorama of the World and performances by a troupe of pygmies. Equally appealing to a nine-year-old would have been the performing monkeys presented in a theatre on the Quai Bon Rencontre. One of these animals was trained to perform acrobatic tricks after the maner of Félix Mayer, a comic dancer from Paris who had appeared at the Théâtre des Célestins in 1818.

But an even greater influence was now to appear on the expanding horizon of Jules' experience in the person of a dancer whom he was openly to acknowledge as the model on which he consciously based his style. Charles Mazurier was a Lyonnais by birth, born in the troubled times of the Revolution, but he had built up his reputation in Bordeaux, where he had danced for a number of years. Engaged at last in his native city, he made his first appearance there at the Grand Théâtre in Milon's *Le Carnaval de Venise* on May 30th, 1820. Since its creation in Paris four years earlier, this ballet had become a universal favourite, but the revival in Lyon was given added distinction by the astonishing interpretation of the rôle of Polichinelle by Mazurier, who elaborated it with many brilliant tricks of his own devising. 'It contains,' wrote one critic, 'a Polichinelle so funny as to make the most melancholy gentleman split his sides with laughter. Mazurier gives such an original performance that, when you have seen him, your interest is entirely concentrated on the scenes in which he appears. In this part he carries comedy and the grotesque style to their utmost limits, performing so naturally that you are convinced you are seeing a marionette controlled by wires from a thousand different directions, manipulated by some exterior agency. The word "*désossé*," the boneless, describes Mazurier marvellously, for one can easily imagine that his limbs are activated by elastic.'[4]

Another critic wrote of 'the suppleness and mobility of his poses . . . and the unbelievable agility with which he performs his *tours de force*. His head seems to disappear at a stroke of Harlequin's scimitar, then suddenly pops out of his shoulders again, breaking into a thousand grimaces that are so comical and extraordinary as to raise the buffooneries of this actor to the level of genius.'[5]

Jules was fascinated by the antics and contortions of Mazurier, and in talking of his early years, remembered him as 'the darling of Lyon, the delight of the silk-weavers who in their sedentary toil would dream of his marvellous perilous leaps, the *grand écart* of his Polichinelle, and his miraculous *saut de carpe*.'[6] Fundamentally Mazurier's style was not novel – Félix Mayer could be said to belong to the same school – but it was touched by that indefinable quality that transforms a skilled performance into an act of genius. Bridging the gap between the acrobats of the fairground and the classically trained dancers of the opera house, the technique that Mazurier practised had developed out of the 'grotesque' style that had originated in Italy. It lent itself particularly to comedy of the knock-about variety, and was to find a place in English pantomime. The *grand écart* or the splits – then a comparatively rare feat, and not yet performed by women. for the *cancan* was still to be invented – was one of Mazurier's most famous stunts. Another of his specialities was the *saut de carpe* – or, in the language of the English acrobatic dancers, the 'nip up' – in which the dancer falls back onto his shoulder blades and smartly springs to his feet again by thrusting off the floor, repeating the sequence in rapid succession as often as desired. It had been performed by grotesque dancers in the eighteenth century, being listed in Compan's *Dictionnaire de la Danse* of 1787, and it became part of the dance vocabulary of Clown in the nineneenth century.

Bursting with vitality, and discovering a precocious control over his movements that astonished even himself, Jules burned to emulate this astonishing dancer. Full of self-confidence, he wearied of hearing Mazurier praised as 'inimitable.' His strong little legs shook with indignation, and he vowed to show the world that there was nothing Mazurier did that he could not. He seized every opportunity of observing the great comic dancer. He worked out for himself the secrets of his technique, and practised his feats and tricks until they became second nature. Soon he could give an imitation of the famous Polichinelle with all the gestures, poses, jumps, turns and *tours de force*, even the very personality of Mazurier himself, copied with uncanny accuracy.

The theatrical milieu of Lyon was small and compact, and this unusual feat of mimicry soon reached the ears of Singier, the director of the city's theatres. There could be no question, of course, of the boy understudying Mazurier on the stage of the Grand Théâtre, but Singier also managed the Théâtre des Célestins. Built during the Revolution on the site of a convent of Celestine nuns, it was a dingy, ill-lit playhouse that presented popular entertainment, but its lack of elegance passed unnoticed by a boy bursting with excitement at the prospect of showing off his prowess.

Wearing the costume of the Neapolitan Pulcinella, and adopting the traditional crooked stance with a false double hump strapped to his back beneath his jacket, he came on to the stage to parody the great Mazurier in a piece called *Le Petit Carnaval de Venise*. As if instinctively realising that it had another comic genius on its hands, the boisterous, good-natured audience roared its approval. There could now be no doubt that Jules Perrot was well and truly launched on a career in the theatre, but the direction in which his gifts were to develop still lay hidden in the future.

2

Apprenticeship on the Boulevard

To ambitious performers such as Mazurier and his young impersonator, Lyon could never offer the ultimate satisfaction. Theatre managers from Paris were continually on the look-out for budding talent in the provinces, and one after the other in the same year, 1823, the two acrobatic dancers were enticed to the capital to seek fame and fortune – Mazurier with an engagement at the Théâtre de la Porte-Saint-Martin, and Jules to join the company of the Théâtre de la Gaîté.

These two theatres stood at opposite extremes of that stretch of the Boulevard where the people of Paris sought their pleasures. Scattered along its length was a great variety of amusements: itinerant entertainers, cafés and restaurants, and especially theatres presenting the popular forms of melodrama, comedy and pantomime. The Porte-Saint-Martin was the most prestigious of these; the Gaîté, sandwiched between the Ambigu-Comique and the Funambules, a more modest house.

By the time Jules arrived in Paris, Mazurier had already established himself at the Porte-Saint-Martin, having made his début in May in a pantomime entitled *Polichinel Vampire, ou l'Ile des muets*, with dances arranged by Frédéric-Auguste Blache. The piece itself had little merit, but Mazurier's Polichinelle caused a sensation and, after two weeks, he was filling the house at every performance. Later he consolidated his success by appearing 'with his face unmasked'[1] in a revival of Jean Petipa's ballet, *Les Six Ingénues*, revealing another side to his talent.

When the twelve-year-old Jules Perrot crossed the threshold of the Gaîté for the first time, he was fully aware that he owed the 1,200 francs a year that Mme. Bourguignon had offered him entirely to his uncanny imitation of the celebrated Mazurier. And indeed, when he made his first appearance on a Parisian stage on December 29th, 1823, it was in the costume of Polichinelle. The Paris public first saw him in the culminating scenes of a pantomime called *Polichinelle avalé par le baleine*, produced by the theatre's ballet-master, Lefebvre. As befitted a New Year presentation, its components were skilfully calculated to appeal to children: a beautiful heroine in love with a handsome hero but desired by a wicked king, a series of adventures in which the girl is continually at the mercy of the villain, and the introduction of such fantastic creatures as a sea-monster and a great bird of prey that carries the hero to an island inhabited by dwarves. There he is befriended by the dwarves, whose humps he throws into a fountain. This was the cue for Jules' first entrance, rising from the fountain as a little Polichinelle. For the rest of the piece he acted as a sort of good genie to the lovers, much to the fury of the wicked king. At one stage he is taken prisoner and sentenced to be beheaded, but he escapes, only to be captured again and to be thrown into the sea, where he is swallowed by a whale. All had to end happily, and the curtain came down on the lovers reunited at last through the agency of the sprightly little Polichinelle.

The boy's triumph was as immediate as had been that of Mazurier a few months earlier. 'Young Perrault *(sic)*,' recorded the *Journal de Paris*, 'performs all the leaps and feats of suppleness, dislocation and strength for which Mazurier is so famous, and these leaps and feats are attached to situations much more amusing than those of that miserable farce of *Polichinel Vampire*, which has been brought out by the Porte-Saint-Martin as a masterpiece.'[2] Perhaps it was to his advantage that he was appearing in more modest surroundings, for 'while the auditorium of the Porte-Saint-Martin was ten times too large for the small number of peasants who just wander in out of curiosity, that of the Gaîté was much too small for the crowd that besieged its doors every evening to see young Perrault *(sic)* . . . With his stage presence, suppleness and lightness, this child of only twelve is already far superior to the Mazuriers and other jumpers and performers of *tours de force*.'[3]

He was already a thorough professional, as was proved by an incident that might have had the most serious consequences. At a certain point in the piece he was enclosed in a wicker frame to which fireworks were attached to surround him in a blaze of sparks at a given moment. One evening one of these fireworks had been carelessly fitted, and discharged its fiery cascade on to the boy's body. Without the slightest indication that he was in pain, Jules continued the performance to the end, but when the curtain fell, he collapsed and had to be carried home. Fortunately the burns were not too serious, but it had been a disturbing experience.[4]

Mazurier bore no ill feelings towards his young rival. His was a generous nature, and he was sensible enough not to consider Jules a threat – indeed, even regarding his efforts as a sort of personal compliment to himself. One evening, when the boy was appearing in a ballet-pantomime by Lefebvre, *Le Tonnelier*, Mazurier conspicuously made his presence in the audience known. The ballet was a wretched piece, and was redeemed, it was reported, 'solely by young Perrot, who amused the audience by the originality of his capers and frequently silenced the hissing to be received with applause.'[5] Mazurier's cries of 'bravo' were genuine expressions of pleasure at the sight of a young dancer who seemed destined to follow in his own footsteps.

Apprenticeship on the Boulevard

There was no doubt that Jules was beginning to make his mark, and a few months later, at the end of 1824, he was rewarded with a more testing challenge, the rôle of Philps *(sic)* the jockey in a '*folie-pantomime-féerie*' entitled *Le Rameau d'or*. For the first time he found himself given a character into which he could grow, and with obvious relish he revealed a natural gift for comic acting alongside the obligatory feats of physical agility. It was only a minor part in the piece, the main rôle being played by a German grotesque dancer, Gottlieb, whose antics no doubt seemed to Jules crude and contrived by comparison with the art of Mazurier.

Gottlieb's engagement at the Gaîté was predictably brief, and his departure was to open the way for another test of Jules' acrobatic skill and interpretative gifts against the genius of his model. This time, however, the contest was to be on more equal terms, for Jules was fast growing up, gaining in strength, and accumulating an impressive fund of stage experience. In August he would be fifteen, and already he had been performing for seven years – nearly half his young life.

In March 1825 Mazurier appeared in a new rôle at the Porte-Saint-Martin – that of the monkey Jocko in the melodrama *Jocko, ou le Singe de Brésil*. Inspired by an affecting tale by Charles-Marie de Pougens about a monkey with almost human characteristics of devotion and gratitude, the part had been fashioned so as to make full use of Mazurier's extraordinary suppleness and his great range of expressive movements. Jocko is a monkey whose life has been saved by Fernandez, a wealthy Portuguese settler. Since then Fernandez has won its affection and confidence, and taught it to obey his orders. It is, however, a mischievous animal that has been creating havoc among the crops, but it is too clever to be deceived by a trap, which it manages to release so as to ensnare two of Fernandez's servants instead. In the second act Fernandez discovers Jocko playing with some diamonds. His endeavours to ascertain where the monkey found them are interrupted by the appearance on the horizon of the ship bringing Fernandez's wife and child from Europe. But a storm breaks, and the vessel is wrecked. Happily Fernandez's wife is saved. Jocko, who has witnessed her rescue, then sees the child clinging to the mast and, imitating the manner of the previous rescue, brings the boy ashore and takes him to his lair. The child's fear soon gives way to trust. He plays with the monkey, who saves him once again – this time from a venomous snake. A band of sailors arrive in search of the child, who has been seen in the clutches of a monkey, and one of them, seeing Jocko with the boy in his arms, shoots the animal. The wounded Jocko crawls to his lair, and in his dying moments drags himself out to lay the diamonds at his master's feet.

This naive and sentimental tale was transformed by Mazurier's uncannily observed impersonation of the monkey. Not only did he bring to the part his exceptional physical elasticity, but he was sufficient of an artist to touch the hearts of the audience by conveying the purity of the animal's devotion to its master. The effect of his miming was enhanced by the expressive music of Alexandre Piccinni and by the brilliant colours of Pierre Ciceri's scenery, which was lauded as being as beautiful as anything to be seen at the Opéra. *Jocko* became the theatrical sensation of the summer, and the public flocked to see it, filling the vast auditorium for several months. Dancers in particular found much in it to interest them, and among those who saw it was a young Danish dance student, August Bournonville. Writing to his father in July, he reported that it had so far had ninety-five performances in four months, each of which earned the fortunate Mazurier a bonus of 200 francs.[6]

Quick to capitalise on the talents of young Perrot, the management of the Gaîté responded, on August 9th, with a '*folie*, interspersed with pantomime and dance,' written by one Dupetit-Méré under the pseudonym of M. Monkey, entitled *Sapajou, ou le Naufrage des singes*. 'Sapajou' is another name for the capuchin monkey, the small agile animal that was much sought after as a pet and was frequently to be seen as the companion of street pedlars and organ-grinders. Jocko himself had been conceived as a sapajou, and the Sapajou of the Gaîté's parody was an obvious reflection. It proved to be an ideal part for Jules, who added depth and conviction to his interpretation as the result of many hours spent at the Jardin des Plantes, observing the behaviour and antics of the monkeys there.

The piece itself made no pretensions to be taken seriously, and the libretto's only interest now lies in the descriptions of the pantomime passages for Sapajou which were acted to music by Henri Darondeau. As in *Jocko*, the central character was a colonial land-owner, Cabas, who is planning to marry his daughter Rose to a rich nincompoop, Riboulet. But Rose is in love with Cabas's nephew Jules, who has left the homestead to seek his fortune elsewhere, taking with him his uncle's favourite pet monkey, Sapajou. On the very day of Rose's wedding Jules returns, swimming ashore after his ship has been wrecked, bemoaning the loss of his fortune and his troupe of performing animals. But as the storm abates, a whale comes into view, bearing Sapajou on its back. In his first mime scene Sapajou 'jumps nimbly on to the beach and leaps around his master to express his joy at finding him. Sapajou performs a number of monkey tricks, pointing alternately to the sea and to the whale, vexed that his master does not understand him. The furious monkey then leaps on to the back of the whale and angrily stamps his feet as if to ask it something. At that moment the plaintive cry of Polichinelle is heard. Sapajou stamps harder, and after some heaving, the whale disgorges Polichinelle on the beach and disappears into the water. Polichinelle is lying motionless on the sand. Sapajou lifts him up as if he were a broken marionette and carries him to the front of the stage, holding him in his arms and rocking him as if he were a child.' While Rose brings biscuits and clothes to Jules, 'Sapajou continues his *lazzi*. He takes the biscuits and eats ravenously, then tries to feed Polichinelle like a baby.'[7] The act closes with the arrival of the rest of the performing monkeys, who have happily survived the wreck.

In the second act Cabas's old servant Jacques proudly boasts of his monster catch ... which turns out to be Jules' performing bear! Sapajou, who has been performing tricks in a tree, jumps to the ground to help his old friend, the bear, who is helplessly rolling about in the net. Released by Sapajou, the bear is greeted by Jules, who is delighted to find all his animals safe. The monkeys play havoc with the fine clothes which Riboulet has brought for Rose, and have to be chased away. Finally, Cabas's reluctance to give his blessing to Jules and Rose is overcome when Sapajou unbuttons Polichinelle's jacket and produces, out of the hump, Jules' wallet, which he places in Cabas's hands. Cabas is duly impressed by Jules' fortune, and the piece closes with a divertissement in which Sapajou gives a hilariously simian imitation of Polichinelle.

In his rôle as the monkey, Jules had an excellent foil in Bouffé, the actor who played the part of the servant Jacques and who had a richly comical scene when he put on a monkey costume to impersonate Sapajou, with the intention of raising his master's spirits. Bouffé was then at the beginning of his distinguished career as a comedian. Brought up in the school of melodrama, he had already shown himself to be a very versatile actor with a natural touch who could equally effectively assume a mime rôle in a ballet, as was evidenced by his performances as Mother Simone in *La Fille mal gardée* and the Grand-Cousin in another Dauberval ballet, *Le Déserteur*.

Bouffé and Jules Perrot shared not only the laughs but also the discomforts of *Sapajou*, which was produced during a heat-wave. The two of them perspired so heavily in their monkey-costumes that the process of stripping after the performance seemed like skinning rabbits. They had to spread their costumes out in the sunshine so that they could wear them the next day, and although they eventually had spare costumes, there were occasions when they had to put them on still wet. Bouffé was convinced that this was the cause of the rheumatism that crippled him later in life, and it may be more than coincidence that Jules Perrot was to suffer from the same ailment.

At the time of *Sapajou*, Jules' ambitions had undergone a significant shift. He had made his Paris début as a dancer – as distinct from his appearances as a comic mime – in a graceful divertissement which Lefebvre had arranged for the spectacular melodrama, *L'Etrangère*, first given on April 28th, 1825, and had decided that it was time to put an end to his imitations of Mazurier and to become an artist in his own right. The realisation that his destiny lay in the classical school had come to him some time before his visits to the Jardin des Plantes. Obsessed by his new-found ambition, he began to fill every spare moment of his day with dance classes and practice, breaking off only for his sessions in front of the monkey cages and his attendance at the theatre in the evening. As he put it, all the time he was watching the monkeys, his thoughts were on the wings of birds.

Only the most eminent teacher in Paris would satisfy him. Auguste Vestris, the son of the greatest *danseur noble* of the eighteenth century, had done much in a long career as a dancer at the Opéra to promote the brilliant *demi-caractère* style, and after retiring as a performer, had devoted his energies to teaching at a time when the style of classical dancing was undergoing a significant transformation. Essentially, this amounted to a relaxation of rules that in former days had been considered sacrosanct. Jules' contemporary, August Bournonville, gave an illuminating example of Vestris's novel teaching method by citing the old rule that the head must always be turned towards the raised arm in the *effacé* position. 'Any position which broke this rule was condemned by the older teachers and called a false "opposition,"' he explained, 'but Vestris, *the creator of the new school*,[*] discovered partly by studying antiquity, partly by his own inspiration, that it was possible to deviate from the strict rule without ceasing to be graceful. While not foreshortening the older, beautiful "oppositions," he enriched the dance with innumerable others, and thus proved that head and shoulders in different positions enable the arms to form delightful curves which, even though not in opposition to the legs, far from hampering such movements, give them added grace.'[8]

Vestris quickly recognised Jules' exceptional qualities, and bent his mind to guiding him on his way to the ultimate achievement of an engagement at the Opéra. The fulfilment of such an ambition still lay some years ahead, however, and at this moment it was difficult to see how such an ugly boy could ever hope to appear alongside the current stars of the Opéra, the brilliant Paul and the majestic Albert. Vestris was faced with a formidable task, as Bournonville remembered in his memoirs.

'While Paul's realm was the air, and Albert belonged, if not to the earth, to the salon, what was to be the domain of Perrot?' he wrote. 'He belongs to the realm of gnomes, and our mutual teacher Vestris capitalised his ugliness by forbidding him to take up picturesque attitudes. "Keep jumping from one spot to another, turn and sway, and never give the public time to observe you closely." With these words the maestro created the "Perrot style" – that of a zephyr with the winds of a bat, a divinity belonging not to mythology but to the occult, a whimsical being with an indescribable lightness and suppleness and a brilliance that was almost phosphorescent. He really made history at a time when the demonic was the most important element on the French stage. He became the ideal in male dancing, but can it be wondered at that connoisseurs of beauty and elegance turned their attention to the ballerinas?'[9]

Bournonville's admiration for Jules Perrot was unbounded, and he used to refer to a certain combined step that was characteristic of Jules' style as the '*sissonne Perrot.*' In Bournonville's own words this consisted of '*sissonne doublée, battue de la jambe de derrière, le corps penché de côté, pied dessous, et assemblé enlevé de côté,*'[10] a sequence that must have been engrained in his

---

[*] *Author's italics.*

memory and even used in many of the male variations he was to devise in the course of his choreographic career.

The Gaîté could no longer contain a young dancer with the talent and ambition that Jules now possessed. So he moved on, as in a natural progression, to the Théâtre de la Porte-Saint-Martin, where he was offered a salary of 2,200 francs a year – a considerable advance on the 1,600 francs he had been receiving at the Gaîté. His début at the Porte-Saint-Martin took place in April 1827, and he made a good impression with 'the good taste of his dancing and his aplomb.'[11] His imitations of Mazurier and his animal impersonations had now been put behind him, and sadly this transition in his career was to be accompanied by the disappearance of his model. Towards the end of 1827 Charles Mazurier was stricken with tuberculosis. He lingered through the winter, becoming progressively weaker, and died in the early days of February the following year. In common with several other theatrical artists of his time he suffered a final indignity when his parish priest refused to receive his body in his church, and it had to be taken directly from his humble home to the cemetery. Many of his fellow artists and admirers came to pay their last respects, and Jules was no doubt among them, reflecting sadly on his indebtedness to the departed as the rolling phrases of Frédérick Lemaître's oration sounded in his ears.

The presence of Lemaître at this turning-point in Jules' career was highly significant, for he personified the wider world of the theatre which the young dancer was now entering. He dominated the actors and the dancers at the Porte-Saint-Martin, inspiring them no less than the public by the energy of his performances. In addition he had the good fortune to be paired with an actress of the most delicate sensitivity, Marie Dorval. These two were almost perfectly matched, and in the following decade were to play together in some of the greatest dramas of the Romantic theatre. The benefit that Jules derived from close contact with two such remarkable artists was incalculable.

During his years at the Gaîté and the Porte-Saint-Martin Jules gained his stage experience within the framework of melodrama, which made up the staple fare of these two stages. With its clear-cut distinction between good and evil, the melodrama appealed strongly to the naive and unsophisticated public that frequented the popular theatres. Literary niceties that were considered essential by the *habitués* of the Comédie-Française meant nothing to the majority of the audiences at the Gaîté, who only asked to be thrilled and moved by a story of innocence imperilled and virtue triumphant. At the Porte-Saint-Martin the standards were higher. A sizeable proportion of its public was drawn from the diverse elements of well-to-do society, not merely the aristocracy, but also the industrialists and the wealthy *bourgeoisie*. The pieces were correspondingly less naive than those presented at the smaller theatres, and heralded the new form of drama with which the younger generation of dramatists was experimenting, with a real attempt at depicting character and moving the audience without offending against good sense. Spectacular staging was an essential element in the productions there, and during the 1820s designers such as Pierre Ciceri enjoyed greater freedom and opportunity on the Boulevard than at the Opéra, satisfying the public demand for realism and illusion with the aid of improved methods of scenery construction and the novelty of gas-lighting.

Another lesson which melodrama held for a future choreographer lay in the use of music, not only for the dances but also to accompany entrances and exits of the characters and to heighten the effect of dramatic or pathetic situations. When skilfully composed, music could add enormously to the theatrical effect, here underlining a moment of suspense, there emphasising the mood of a scene or the motive of a character. 'To give some examples,' wrote a commentator of the time, 'a blind man, lacking a guide and in danger or falling from a rock, or a tyrant treacherously preparing to stab his victim, is seldom presented without a well-aimed stroke of a violin bow, causing hearts to flutter in the pit and the boxes, particularly if accompanied by the note of a horn or the funereal tolling of a bell.'[12] Writing this kind of music required a special talent which, it was not difficult to see, had an affinity with the composition of music for a ballet, and in Alexandre Piccinni, who produced most of the music for the Porte-Saint-Martin at this time, Jules had an admirable example before him. The natural son of the operatic composer who had been set up as the rival of Gluck, Piccinni was astonishingly industrious, producing music to order that, by all accounts, was remarkably consistent in quality and – unlike the work of many other melodrama composers – was almost wholly original.

As a training ground for a choreographer melodrama was exceptionally rich because of the variety of its content. 'The moving theatrical effects employed in melodrama,' remarked the same commentator, 'do not exclude the comic element, and it is the happy mixture, ranging from the solemn to the sentimental, from the amusing to the serious, that makes the performances of the Boulevard very much an entertainment of the people – and even of a section of high society. The premières in particular attract a large number of elegant folk who, while protesting to decry them, find much enjoyment in the rages of the tyrant, the imbecilities of the simpleton, and the dancing of dwarves and hunchbacks.'[13]

To appear in the melodramas and the ballets the Porte-Saint-Martin maintained a ballet company that, in number and quality, was second only to that of the Opéra. It was under the direction of Jean Coralli, an experienced ballet-master who, although of Italian extraction, was Parisian by birth and training, having passed through the School of Dance of the Opéra during the last decade of the previous century. His career as a choreographer, however, had been largely centred abroad – principally in Vienna, Milan and Lisbon – until he came to the Porte-Saint-Martin in 1825, but his style of composition was,

Apprenticeship on the Boulevard

in the words of Saint-Léon, 'essentially French, that is to say, delicate and poetic,'[14] and since an aspiring choreographer can only gain experience by observation, his work must have taken as a model in Jules' early development.

Among the other dancers of the company was a companion from Jules' years in Lyon, Joseph Mazilier, while the women included Mimi Dupuis, Zélie Paul, and a young dancer whom he was frequently to partner, Florentine Dufour, a pupil of Coulon, much admired for her grace and assured technique.

It was not long before Jules had an opportunity of proving his worth in a ballet. On June 10th, 1828, he appeared in Coralli's *Léocadie* and was praised as 'a correct dancer possessing aplomb and strength, whose talent is based on a good training.'[15] This success was sealed a few days later when he and Florentine were honoured with a royal command to dance before King Charles X at Versailles.

Almost immediately Jules had to take an enforced leave of absence, for the theatre was closed for repairs – works long over-due, for the plaster-work in the ceiling had begun to crumble on to the heads of the audience. It did not reopen until the end of October, but the public was then amply compensated by an important new production, the drama of *Faust*, imitated, as the libretto expressed it, from Goethe by Antony Béraud with the anonymous collaboration of Charles Nodier and J.-T. Merle.

Apart from an opera produced at the Théâtre des Nouveautés a year earlier, this was the first adaptation of Goethe's masterpiece to be seen on the Paris stage. It was admittedly a popularisation of no real literary merit, but it was to have a profound influence in Jules' artistic education – an education largely self-acquired – by drawing his attention to a theme that he was later to adapt for one of his most famous ballets. Although Marie Dorval obtained what was called a '*succès de mouchoirs*' by her affecting acting as Marguerite, the production was dominated by Frédérick Lemaître's extraordinary interpretation of Mephistopheles. His demonic laugh echoed in the memory of everyone who heard it. It was an effect that had been obtained only after much toil and heartache. At one moment during rehearsals he had almost abandoned his attempt to achieve what he wanted and decided to replace it with a facial contortion. But as he was seeking the right expression before a mirror at his home, he became conscious of being watched by some curious neighbours. So he quickly closed the blinds, and with the sharp rattle of the slats came the inspiration he had been seeking for the sinister, inhuman laugh. Another highlight of his performance, which Jules must have observed with particular interest, was his impressive use of mime in the waltz scene with Martha – a minor character played by Zélie Paul – in which Mephistopheles 'exerts all his infernal magnetism to bend her to his will, and she, all-a-tremble with terror and pleasure, finally succumbs.'[16] This dance scene, which

Jules Perrot

Lemaître himself arranged with assistance from Coralli, was the most applauded episode in the whole play. For Jules it was to have a special significance, for it was a seed from which grew, in later years, the concept of the *pas d'action* that would be one of the hallmarks of his choreographic style.

The next two productions, *Sept Heures*, in which Frédérick created a frightening study of a ruthless political tyrant, and Casimir Delavigne's drama, *Marino Falieri*, contained very little dancing, but if they did nothing to advance Jules' reputation, they added to his stage experience, whether he played a small unannounced part or watched from a seat in the auditorium.

In the summer of 1829 the affairs of the Porte-Saint-Martin began to disintegrate. The management was insolvent, and the courts became so heavily occupied with the legal wrangles that ensued that the actors might have wondered if they were working for the sole benefit of the lawyers. Coralli had decided not to renew his engagement, and on July 30th produced his last ballet before departing. *Les Artistes* followed the conventional pattern of a ballet-pantomime, with the plot acted out in mime and a divertissement tacked on at the end. The story told of three impecunious young artists, a painter, a sculptor and a choreographer, who are unable to pay their rent, and a wealthy patron who saves them in the nick of time. Mazilier took the rôle of the choreographer, the heroine was Aimée Gauthier and the landlord was played by a well-known comic dancer, Laurençon. Jules had to be content with appearing in the final divertissement, dancing in a *pas de trois* with Aimée Gauthier and Florentine, and again in the general finale.

Coralli's successor was Anatole, a ballet-master of lesser repute whose first task was to produce the dances for a new production of *Macbeth* in November. The divertissement in which Jules was featured was of no particular consequence, but the production itself, which he saw nightly from the wings, was another landmark in his education, introducing him to Shakespeare, whom the Romantic dramatists worshipped for the expressive power and the freedom of his writing.

Jules' days at the Porte-Saint-Martin were now numbered, for he had already been officially notified that he was to be engaged at the Opéra from April 1st, 1830, when his contract with the Porte-Saint-Martin was due to expire. It must have seemed the ultimate achievement, but it also came at a fortuitous moment, for the management of the Porte-Saint-Martin was on the verge of collapse. The theatre closed in January, and Jules can have had few regrets when he walked out of its stage door for the last time.

3

Le Vrai Danseur

In the seeming maturity of his nineteen years, Jules' apprenticeship lay behind him and he could take stock of his progress with considerable pride and satisfaction. Contemplating the solid pile of the opera house in the Rue Le Peletier, where he was shortly to be inducted into the world's most illustrious ballet company, he must have sensed that he would be entering an establishment that was a world apart from the free and easy theatres of the Boulevard. Yet he had no cause for anxiety, for he could feel fully confident of his technical skill while realising the advantages of his years in the Boulevard theatres, where he had rubbed shoulders with authors, artists and actors who were responding to the latest trends and seeking new means of expression. They saw themselves as representatives of a new school, which they called Romanticism, and no doubt Jules felt himself to be one of them.

His two years at the Porte-Saint-Martin had also given him a revealing insight into the devious ways of theatre management. He had been engaged by François-Louis Crosnier, one of the sharpest men in the business, who seemed to have a masterly flair for selling his theatre and buying it back more cheaply when his purchasers in turn found themselves in financial difficulty. In fact it was in the course of one of these operations that the theatre closed down early in 1830 and Jules found himself on the street with a worthless contract that still had several months to run. As it happened, this unexpected release from his contractual obligations came at an opportune moment, enabling him to accept an offer from London that would conveniently fill the interval before his début at the Opéra.

The London opera house – the King's Theatre in the Haymarket – relied heavily on Paris for its supply of leading dancers. Unlike the Paris Opéra, though, it operated on a seasonal basis, the company being assembled afresh each year for a season that lasted only about six months. Another difference was that it received no government subsidy, the lessee relying for support on generous advance subscriptions from the aristocracy to secure prominent places in what was, for most of them, as much a social meeting-place as a temple of the lyric and choreographic arts. On arriving in London, Jules

Jules Perrot

found that a number of his French colleagues had preceded him and were already preparing for the opening of the season. Prominent among them were two of the ballerinas of the Opéra – Pauline Montessu, the sister of Paul, whom Jules had first seen during his early years in Lyon, and Julia de Varennes. Another was Joséphine Hullin, who came from a well-known dancing family and, like him, had begun her performing career as a child.

The world of fashion, seated elegantly in their boxes, and the more modest lovers of opera and ballet accommodated less comfortably in the pit and the upper tiers saw Jules make his first appearance in London on February 6th, 1830, in Milon's ballet, *Le Carnaval de Venise*. He commanded attention literally at his first bound. 'Perrot shines conspicuously,' recorded the *Morning Post*, 'and is evidently destined to be the star of the season. The wonderful ease and agility with which he performs surpasses anything that has hitherto been witnessed on these boards.'[1]

His next triumph was in Arnaud Léon's ballet *Guillaume Tell*, to music from Rossini's opera arranged by Costa and Nadaud. His was only a dancing role, but he 'exhibited his wondrous agility'[2] in a *pas de trois* with Julia and Joséphine Hullin. But all too soon he had to return to Paris, and he was replaced by Antoine Coulon, to whom was to fall the honour, in June, of partnering Marie Taglioni in *Flore et Zéphire* on her London début.

Echoes of Jules' 'complete'[3] success in London had reached Paris in advance of his home-coming in April. The time had now come to prepare himself seriously for his début at the Opéra, and he spent many hours in the somewhat cramped studio that the Opéra allocated to Auguste Vestris for his perfection class. Most of his pupils were attached to the Opéra, but Jules was admitted exceptionally by the old teacher's choice. In a survey of the class made for the Direction, he was specifically mentioned: 'Perault (*sic*) – M. Vestris asks that this paying pupil should not be taken from him because he does not belong to the Opéra.'[4]

As a teacher Vestris was the link between the old world and the new and had done much to adapt the style of the *ancien régime* to suit the rapidly changing tastes of the new France that had emerged in the nineteenth century. His efforts were not appreciated in every quarter. Just two weeks before Jules' début, the old teacher had launched another pupil, Giovanni Casati, and Charles Maurice in the *Courrier des Théâtres* had been sternly critical. 'We would have liked to seen less movement and more correctness,' he had written, 'less skipping about and more grace, a strength that does not exclude elegance, and results which appear to derive from the study of an art rather than fairground tricks. This last remark should always be kept in mind by our dancers, for without taste dancing tends to degenerate into feats of suppleness and strength which are to dance what the pun is to true wit.'[5] These strictures might well have made Jules apprehensive, but happily he had friends to watch over his interests. 'Yesterday's rumour at the Opéra,' reported the *Courrier*

Le Vrai Danseur

Playbill of the Paris Opéra for June 23rd, 1830, the evening of Jules Perrot's début. Bibliothèque de l'Opéra, Paris.

des Théâtres, 'was that the great-grandfather of the Zephyrs had been reprimanded over a young pupil whose accomplishments he is spoiling by his ridiculous advice. The enlightened management, which regards the acquisition of new talent as of great importance, exerted its authority wisely on this occasion, so hopes should not be disappointed.'[6]

Jules made his début at the Opéra on June 23rd in a *pas de deux* arranged by Vestris himself and inserted in Le Brun's one-act opera, *Le Rossignol*. His companion was Pauline Montessu, the diminutive ballerina whose star was very much in the ascendent after creating the leading rôles in two important and successful ballets by Jean Aumer, *La Somnambule* and *Manon Lescaut*. The ordeal passed satisfactorily, and the next day Jules read in his *Courrier des Théâtres* that he had not been found wanting. 'His dancing,' wrote Maurice, 'is in good taste and has an elegant simplicity, and all in all his style is suitable for the Opéra. He has elevation, softness and grace. If the expressiveness of his features had matched these accomplishments, one might have hoped for another mime. But with his talent as a dancer, Perrot will be sure to find a place for himself.'[7]

The Opéra had deliberately played down Vestris's part in preparing Jules for his début, and it was only at his second appearance, when he was no

Jules Perrot

longer at risk, that this was stated on the playbills. Charles Maurice, smarting perhaps from being deceived, devoted a long piece a few days later to the antiquated style of 'Grandpapa Zéphyre,' in which, to save his face, he explained that Jules was 'too good to have come out of the class to which people went for dancing lessons when they were released from the Bastille.'[8]

In spite of this back-biting, which happily had little effect, the arrangements for a formal engagement proceeded leisurely. Although Jules had been at the Opéra's disposal since April 1st, it was not until June 10th that his engagement as a *double* – the lowest grade of soloist – was reported to the minister responsible. By the end of August no reply had been received, and the Director of the Opéra sent a reminder that, for want of confirmation, he had not been able to place Jules on the establishment, and that, since he had been working at the Opéra since April 1st, he was expecting to be paid from that date. This plea produced a prompt response, and early in September Jules was notified that he had been engaged as a *double* from April 1st at a salary of 2,500 francs a year. It was a little disappointing that this was 100 francs below the salary he had been receiving in his last year at the Porte-Saint-Martin, but how infinitely greater were the prospects!

In the meantime Jules had been an eye-witness of the three glorious days of the July Revolution, which had overthrown the Bourbon monarchy, and with his working-class background, he must have sympathised with the forces of change. When the excitement subsided France found itself with a middle-of-the-road régime, a constitutional monarchy under the Duc d'Orléans, who took the title of Louis-Philippe, King of the French. Much more to the point, so far as Jules was concerned, was the effect on the Opéra, which was no longer to be dependent on the Royal Household, but was henceforth to be run as a private enterprise, supported by a government subsidy. The following spring it was announced that the new Director was to be Dr. Louis Véron, who, as must have been clear from the beginning, was unlikely to follow slavishly the policies of his predecessors. In fact his term was to witness the ultimate triumph of Romanticism, not only in opera, but to an even greater degree in ballet.

Dr Véron was more than the embodiment of the *bourgeois* class that was gaining increasing prominence in Parisian society; he seemed, in both his physical appearance and his demeanour, to be a caricature of it. His qualifications as Director of the Opéra had nothing to do with music. He had made his fortune by launching a patent medicine for sore throats, an enterprise that had taught him the value of publicity through the newspaper press. Cynical, self-seeking and indulgent, he was not an attractive personality, but he was essentially a man of his time, and therein lay the secret of his success. For in his four years at the Opéra he was to show how accurately he felt the public's pulse and how uncannily effective was his prescription for the financial, if not artistic, success of his theatre.

Le Vrai Danseur

This was the man whom Jules now had for a master. He probably regarded him with less animosity than the German poet, Heinrich Heine, but in all truth Véron was not a likeable man and Heine's portrait, for all its dramatic overtones, shows the extent of the revulsion which the man could arouse in a sensitive soul. 'The great Véron and the great public understood one another,' Heine observed. 'He knew how to make music harmless, and gave under the name of "opera" nothing but show-and-splendour pieces; while It – the public – could go with its wives and daughters as became genteelly cultured people, without being bored to death . . . Did you ever see M. Véron? It must have often happened that you met on the Boulevard Coblence* or in the Café de Paris this bulky, caricature-like form, with a hat drawn deeply down on the head, which was entirely buried below in an immense white cravat, while the shirt collars rose above his ears so as to conceal a great scar, while very little of the red jolly face with its small blinking eyes is visible. In the full consciousness of his superior knowledge of mankind and of his success, he rolls about insolently at his ease, surrounded with a cortège of young, and here and there of older, dandies of literature, whom he usually treats to champagne, or beautiful dancing-girls. He is the god of sheer sensuous materialism, and his glance, sneering at all spirit or soul, cut to my heart painfully when I met him. It often seemed to me as if there crept from his eyes swarms of little sticky shining worms.'[9]

Strangely enough, the first new work to be staged during the new régime was a revival of an anacreontic ballet from the turn of the century – Charles Didelot's *Flore et Zéphire*. Didelot had originally produced this ballet in London in 1796, and had later taken several opportunities to revise it. He had arrived in Paris in 1815 in the wake of the allied armies to produce it at the Opéra, where it enjoyed great success, but he had then returned to Russia, where he devoted himself to raising the prestige and standards of the Tsar's ballet. In those pre-railway times it was unthinkable to bring the old ballet-master out of Russia, and so a producer had to be sought closer at hand who could revive this old work as well as memories could achieve. There was talk of commissioning Jean Coralli, but he declined, it was said, out of modesty, and in the end the revival was staged by Albert, who taught the rôles, and Aumer, who arranged the ensembles.

This relic from a bygone age would have attracted little notice if the title-rôles had not been played by Taglioni and Perrot. 'Mlle Taglioni,' wrote Castil-Blaze in his chronicles of the Opéra, 'had a partner who was worthy of her. The way his style conformed to hers made him an ideal match for the favourite virtuoso.'[10] The same writer, in his review of the first performance on March 14th, 1831, clearly considered them to be of equal status, coupling them together as 'Mlle Taglioni, charming and graceful, and Perrot, holder of

* During the Directoire part of the Boulevard des Italiens was known as 'le Petit Coblentz' by being a favourite meeting place of emigrés returning from Koblenz.

21

the title of "*l'aérien*," which was bestowed on him when he entered the Opéra,' and again, writing of 'the magical influence of our bayadère and the presence of Perrot, the young dancer of whom the public is so fond . . .'[11] And Jules Janin, one of the most eminent of the younger critics, praised the new administration for 'having daringly selected the light and graceful Taglioni and this young Perrot, so lissom and agile, who if the regulations had been applied strictly, would not have danced this rôle for another twenty years.'[12]

Jules' unprepossessing appearance served merely to emphasise his extraordinary talent. In her memoirs the Comtesse Dash recalled Taglioni, dancing in *Flore et Zéphire* 'with Perrot, the only male dancer who truly had charm in spite of his repulsive features. They did not dance, they flew among the flowers without touching them. A wit said of Perrot that if he had lived in the time of Molière, and had taken part in one of his divertissements, he would have been called "A Dancing Frog." Frog or not, I repeat, Perrot had a talent that no one else possessed.'[13]

By succeeding in sharing the honours with Taglioni, Jules was unwittingly sowing seeds of trouble, for Taglioni was accustomed to shine in solitude. Charles Maurice observed that while both she and her partner shared a brilliant triumph, it was Jules who drew the greater applause – 'a circumstance which many people noticed.'[14] And at the second performance Jules 'monopolised the applause even more.'[15] Such praise was not likely to ingratiate him in the eyes of his partner.

To Dr. Véron, who was now in full command, Jules' pre-eminence among the male dancers was not in doubt, and instructions were issued for a new contract to be drawn up for one year starting on April 1st, 1831, at a salary of 10,000 francs plus *feux* – bonus payments given for each performance – of 30 francs, eight of these being guaranteed each month except during a period of illness. Not only was a fourfold increase in salary in itself a staggering recognition of Jules' gifts, but the figure at which it now stood confirmed his standing as the most important male dancer at the Opéra. Ten thousand francs a year was the maximum basic salary that a dancer could earn there. It was true that in the past male stars had received more by the addition of a special '*gratification*' – Auguste Vestris and Louis Duport had each been paid 15,000 francs a year at the height of their rivalry during the First Empire, and Albert, Paul, Ferdinand and Antoine Coulon had attained a figure of 14,000 francs – but all these belonged to earlier generations. When Jules entered this select company, his friend Mazilier was left far behind with only 4,500 francs a year. But even 10,000 francs seemed modest when the terms of Taglioni's new engagement were announced, for Véron had agreed to give her 30,000 francs a year in salary, guaranteed benefit and *feux*.

Surprisingly, Jules' assignments during the year of his new engagement were relatively modest. He assisted a terrified newcomer, Pauline Duvernay, through her six début performances; in the summer he partnered Pauline

Montessu, with signal success, in a *pas de deux* in Coralli's new ballet, *L'Orgie*; and at the end of the year he danced in the divertissement in Meyerbeer's new opera, *Robert le Diable*.

The Ballet of the Nuns in *Robert le Diable* was a work of momentous consequence in the progress of Romanticism. In the moonlit setting of a ruined cloister, Marie Taglioni emerged, wraith-like, from a tomb as the ghost of an impure abbess, creating, at a single stroke, a new image that etched itself into the imagination of the time – the white-clad ballerina, symbol of purity and the unattainable. For Jules Perrot this was to be a mixed blessing. As a dancer he was forced to recognise the supremacy of the ballerina and the growing disfavour with which the public viewed male dancers, but in the years to come, as a choreographer, he was to reap the full benefit of the unprecedented vogue for ballet that was to be generated by the appeal of an extraordinarily gifted generation of ballerinas.

For the moment his own position as a dancer seemed secure, for when his contract expired, he was given a new two-year engagement from April 1st, 1832, at a salary of 15,000 francs.

It was at this stage in his career, this moment of supreme achievement, that he struck a bad patch. In April the *Courrier des Théâtres* criticised him for not working hard enough. Aplombs and pirouettes, it was alleged, were being fluffed, and people were noticing a deterioration in his precision and finish. 'Perrot is not falling, but he seems to be slipping.'[16] Could he have been discouraged at being passed over in the casting of the new ballet, *La Sylphide*, which had created such a sensation only a few weeks earlier? After his reception as Zephyr, he might well have considered it his due to become Taglioni's regular partner, but it was Mazilier who was chosen for the rôle of James Reuben. Perhaps, too, he had become disheartened at the lack of opportunities, for he had to content himself with such trifles as a *pas de deux* with Duvernay in the opera *Fernand Cortez*, which drew from Janin the doubtful comment that he 'had the great misfortune of being a man.'[17] He did, it is true, have the opportunity, that autumn, of trying his hand at choreography with a *pas de deux*, inserted in Rossini's *Moïse*, which he danced with Pauline Montessu, but his first creative effort made little impression.

Poor Jules had to learn to live with his ugliness, which even seemed to endear himself to the public. The artist Jean-Pierre Dantan was fascinated by his features, and used him as a model for one of his caricature busts. In it he caught that likeness to a frog on which the Comtesse Dash had remarked, exaggerating the protruding eyes and the sinews of his neck which, as one writer put it, seemed to invite 'those experiments in electricity which are normally conducted on the green inhabitants of the marshes.' 'Perrot's agility must be most extraordinary,' this same commentator continued, 'for the *habitués* of the Opéra to have such an affection for this dancer. The appearance of Perrot in a short pink or sky-blue jacket in the midst of the charming sylphides of the Opéra was the most fantastic sight you could imagine. Happily he did not stay still for very long, and was soon spinning away like a German top.'[18]

Those who made his acquaintance at this time found him a strange personality. His sudden rise to fame and his equally sudden wealth seemed to have made no difference to his way of life, and he continued to travel to and from the Opéra by omnibus – a habit that some interpreted as a praiseworthy lack of affectation, others, less generously, as an excessive display of parsimony. He mixed well enough with his fellow artists, but he was essentially a private man who lived modestly and decently with his parents. If ever it happened that a young dancer conceived a weakness for him, he handled the situation with tact and discretion. No hint of scandal sullied his name. His existence was wholly bound up in the dance.

* * *

His growing reputation had not escaped the notice of foreign theatre managers, and Laporte, for whom he had danced at the King's Theatre, London, three years before, made him an attractive offer for the season of 1833. His colleague Pauline Montessu was also engaged, and they may have shared the unpleasant experience of the journey. The English Channel in February could be decidedly hostile, and the London papers reported that it took Mme Montessu fifteen hours to make the crossing from Calais to Dover, where she arrived, not surprisingly, prostrate with sea-sickness.

After recovering from the journey, Jules began rehearsing for the opening performance of the season, which was to include a new ballet based on a theme familiar to him from his Porte-Saint-Martin days – *Faust*. The choreographer was André-Jean-Jacques Deshayes, a man of great experience who was to become a close friend and to give Jules a wealth of useful advice. Deshayes had received his training at the Paris Opéra, and, as a boy, had danced before Louis XVI and Marie-Antoinette at Versailles in the year the Revolution had broken out. When he reached maturity he had danced for a time at the Opéra, but he had not stayed and spent most of his dancing career in Milan, London and Vienna. The only ballet he managed to produce at the Opéra – *Zémire et Azor* in 1824 – had unluckily been a failure, and he was never invited back. Bur he enjoyed better fortune in London, and this new ballet, *Faust*, was to have more than a score of performances at the King's Theatre during the season of 1833.

Laporte had given his son-in-law, Adolphe Adam, the opportunity of writing the music for this ballet. Until then Adam's work for the ballet had been confined to arranging the music of *La Sylphide* for the London production of the year before. His contribution to *Faust* was to pass unnoticed by the critics, but it was good enough for three numbers to be published in a piano reduction, including the *pas du sylphe* which Jules and Pauline Montessu danced in

Le Vrai Danseur

Playbill of the King's Theatre, London, for a performance of Faust, featuring Jules Perrot in a dancing rôle. Theatre Museum, London.

the first act. The meeting of the young musician and the future choreographer was to have happy consequences for them both in years to come.

The centrepiece of Deshayes' ballet was a reproduction of the famous orgy scene from the opera-ballet *Le Tentation*. The previous summer this had created a sensation at the Paris Opéra with its gigantic staircase, ablaze with flame, down which had rushed helter-skelter a riot of demonic creatures. The score of the opera-ballet had been composed by Fromental Halévy, with additional ballet music by Casimir Gide, but whether Adam used any of this in his score for *Faust* was not recorded. Deshayes preceded this interpolation with the opening scene in Faust's study, in which the doctor, in his quest for eternal youth, conjures up Mephistopheles to help him. After the orgy scene the action continued with Faust, now in his rejuvenated form, meeting Marguerite. With Mephistopheles' aid Faust presses his suit by leaving a casket of jewels in Marguerite's chamber, but is interrupted by the arrival of her mother Bertha and her brother Valentin. Bertha is shocked to learn of the appearance of the casket, and persuades Marguerite to make an offering of it to the Holy Virgin. Mephistopheles, however, exerts his infernal power to make it appear that the Madonna rejects the gift. Finally Bertha consents to her daughter's marriage to Faust, but Valentin is less compliant. After an evening of gambling, Faust kills Valentin in a duel. Marguerite is condemned for the murder. Doomed, Faust falls into the abyss, while in an apotheosis the Genius of Virtue is shown extending her hand to Marguerite.

Jules was cast only in a dancing rôle, but with his early memories of *Faust* at the Porte-Saint-Martin, he must have been duly impressed by the manner in which Deshayes conveyed Gœthe's narrative in mime and gesture. The *Court Journal* called it 'a splendid *ballet d'action*,' praised the 'highly poetic pantomime' of Albert and Coulon as Mephistopheles and Faust, and made special mention of the *allemande*, 'an animated picture of the highest class,' which those two men danced with Pauline Montessu and Therese Heberle as Marguerite and Martha. Pauline Montessu made a very moving Marguerite, but Jules created an even greater impression. This same critic could not help wondering 'whether the demons of the Brocken created Perrot out of a caoutchouc ball,' and felt that it was inhumane of the audience to demand an encore. 'On Saturday last,' he recorded, 'we observed Perrot breathless and almost disabled after a repetition of one of his exquisite performances.'[19]

The progress which Jules had made since his first visit to London three years before was self-evident. 'On his former visit,' wrote another critic in the *Court Journal*, 'we did not consider him by any means equal to the situation of first dancer; he has, however, greatly improved, and is now one of the first *artistes* we have seen on these boards for several seasons. The chief characteristics of his dancing are lightness, vigour and activity; he bounds about the stage like an India-rubber ball, and is not deficient in elegance. His pirouette is always given with finished neatness. He was frequently, warmly and deser-

Le Vrai Danseur

vedly applauded, and will, we are of opinion, become a great favourite with the admirers of good dancing.'[20]

A few weeks later two young dancers from Vienna, sisters by the name of Elssler, made their début at the King's. The success of the younger and more talented of the two, Fanny, seemed to have an electrifying effect on Jules, who redoubled his efforts to impress the public. 'Perrot,' reported the *Court Journal*, 'was, as usual, here, there and everywhere; he is a wonderful little fellow. In endeavouring to accomplish one of his difficult double turns, however, he lost his balance and fell forward, but saved himself by falling onto his hands; he repeated the passage as soon as he recovered and was greeted with enthusiastic approbation.'[21] This was just the sort of courageous spirit that appealed to the sporting instincts of the English.

* * *

Jules' first task on returning to the Paris Opéra after his vacation was to partner a visiting ballerina. Elise Vaque-Moulin had made a considerable reputation in Italy, and her principal accomplishment was an unusual skill, for those times, of rising on to her *pointes*. Four years earlier, when she was dancing in London, Coulon had described her, in a letter to his friend Deshayes, as being 'extremely small . . . She has *pointes* of iron, astonishing vivacity, and an excessive articulation of the hips, for she lifts her legs, and even her arms, too high.'[22] The evening of her début at the Opéra was not a happy one for her partner, who was very much out of form. His right knee had been giving him trouble, and the doctors were mystified. Not knowing that he was in pain, the public expressed its displeasure in no uncertain terms. He was so upset by this that he left the stage, but his sense of duty prevailed and he reappeared, indicating that he was feeling unwell. The audience responded by applauding him warmly, and thus encouraged, he danced on as if in perfect form. Happily his leg quickly recovered, and by August the *Courrier des Théâtres* was hailing him as '*le vrai danseur.*'[23]

Meanwhile Marie Taglioni's father was preparing a new ballet for her, *La Révolte au sérail*. Once again it was Mazilier who was chosen for the leading male rôle, but Jules was given the privilege of partnering the ballerina in a *pas de deux*. It proved to be the highlight of the ballet. The two dancers bounded 'like balloons, skimming the ground . . . and shooting into the air like those virtuosi which a painter's fancy has depicted on the walls of Pompeii, performing the most exacting and difficult feats with prodigious grace and agility.'[24] Taglioni was as matchless as ever, but Jules once again proved a match for her. 'You forget he is a male dancer,' remarked Janin. 'I do not think that the oldest and most rabid flatterers of Vestris ever saw Vestris dance like Perrot danced, and Perrot must have danced superlatively well for me to speak of him like this.'[25]

Marie Taglioni was less than generous in her view of Jules' success.

Overwrought at the end of the first performance, she flew into a tantrum.

'It is too bad,' she cried, 'that a male dancer should obtain more applause than I. It is monstrous!'

Véron tried to pacify her. He summoned the head of the claque, and demanded an explanation. The reply was a shrug of the shoulders. He could not restrain his men, he said, let alone prevent the public from applauding Perrot.

'Get out!' Véron shouted at him.

Duponchel and her father tried their best to console the ballerina, but she wept uncontrollably, crying: 'It is very hard to have sacrificed so much for such a result.'[26]

So perhaps it was hardly surprising that although Talioni and Jules were both engaged for the London season of 1834, they never danced together. The ballerina appeared on the opening night in *La Sylphide*, but with a very inexperienced dancer called Emile in the rôle of James. In any event the part was not really suitable for Jules on account of his build, nor at that time had he begun to play rôles with a mime content. So when he arrived in London and made his first appearance, it was to partner the beautiful young Pauline Duvernay. 'His amazing elasticity of limb and facility in bounding are still as great as ever,' reported the *Morning Herald*. 'In addition to some of those double whirls, for which he was so distinguished last season, he executed on this occasion admirably that favourite movement of the *premières danseuses* of passing buoyantly from one side of the stage to the other on the right leg, while the left is swaying gracefully pendulous. Perrot was almost exhausted with his chief effort in this ballet.'[27]

On May 10th he was given another partner. In Therese Elssler's short ballet *Armide*, he was given the task of partnering her sister Fanny in one of her two *pas de deux*. This had been arranged with the express purpose of displaying the young ballerina's bewitching charms, but Jules was well served too. 'As for Perrot,' added the *Morning Post*, 'he bounded about the stage with so much elasticity that we begin to fancy that his flesh must be some sort of caoutchouc.'[28]

Jules returned to Paris at the end of June with high hopes of renewing his engagement at the Opéra on favourable terms. The warmth of the public's reception encouraged him to believe that he was the '*danseur à la mode*.' Certainly he was now at the peak of his powers, 'full of elegance, suppleness and lightness, his style a little reminiscent of Paul but perhaps with less strength, although with more grace and expression,'[29] and his lack of good looks was apparently no disadvantage. Confident that he could have no serious rival, he set his sights high, but the negotiations soon ran into difficulties. He wanted at least 20,000 francs, but Véron was only prepared to engage him at a reduced salary. One factor in the Director's ungenerous attitude may have been the disappointing performances he had been giving because of his knee trouble, another, the growing prejudice against male dancers. Also Véron may

Le Vrai Danseur

have been counting on replacing Jules by Edouard Carey, an enormously strong, though still somewhat unpolished, dancer, who was receiving only 8,000 francs, but then Carey himself demanded an increase and departed. Finally the Opéra seemed prepared to increase its offer to 17,000 francs, but this was unacceptable. The gap proved unbridgeable, and Jules found himself without employment.

Charles Maurice disclosed more of the background in his paper the *Courrier des Théâtres*. Reporting the break-down of the negotiations, he explained that 'the need for a male dancer who can also play rôles' had been strongly pressed by the influential *abonnés*.[30] The matter may not have been quite so simple. Although the breaking-point had been a question of money, the resentment that Taglioni expressed, perhaps in an unguarded moment, at having to share her triumph with him may have awakened a response in the minds of some of her influential admirers. She may have understandably preferred a partner with a nobler appearance, but it was unlikely that she had any part in Jules' departure from the Opéra, for he was to partner her, seemingly quite happily, in *La Sylphide* in London a few months later, and they were to remain on affectionate terms for the rest of their lives.

4

Enter a Muse

Jules' contract with the Opéra was due to expire on March 31st, 1835, but since he had not taken his three months vacation, he found himself free of obligations at the end of the previous December. He had no difficulty in obtaining employment, and before January was out he had left Paris to give a series of performances at the Grand Théâtre in Bordeaux. This was a theatre with a considerable ballet tradition, for Dauberval had been its ballet-master half a century before and had produced there his evergreen *Fille mal gardée*. It was therefore an appropriate setting for a modest advance in Jules' career in the direction of choreography. He was allowed to arrange a *pas*, which impressed the local critic as being 'most graceful and deserving of the bravos it received.'[1] This was probably the *pas de quatre* which he danced with Mlles Ancellin, Louise and Martin in an anacreontic divertissement; the *Courrier des Théâtres* reported that it was from *La Tempête*, presumably referring to the music that was used.[2]

Another step forward in Bordeaux was his first appearance in a mime rôle. His portrayal of Figaro in Milon's *Le Carnaval de Venise* revealed a natural gift for interpretation which anyone remembering his early appearances at the Gaîté would have recognised, but which, ironically, the Opéra had failed to detect.

He was back in Paris early in March, when his presence was noted at the Opéra, but a few days later he was off again, this time to London, to dance throughout the 1835 season at the King's Theatre. He found lodgings at No. 60 Haymarket, just up the street from the theatre, and where his friend Antoine Coulon was also staying. Deshayes was still ballet-master, and it was in his production of *Nina* that Jules made his appearance on the season's opening night on March 21st. He was in as good form as ever; in the words of the *Morning Post*, 'he outrivalled himself' and 'his pirouettes and *tours de force* were really astonishing.'[3] His performance, particularly in an interpolated *pas* from Coralli's ballet *L'Orgie*, was distinguished, according to one critic, by 'movements which he originated and which have stayed with us.'[4] A month later, on April 25th, he repeated his success in Deshayes' production of *Paul et Virginie*, and on the 30th, at Coulon's benefit, he took part in a new ballet, *Zéphir Berger*, which Deshayes was said to have 'concocted for the purpose of showing to advantage that prince of dancers, Perrot, who fully succeeded in displaying all that was graceful and brilliant.'[5]

Marie Taglioni, who was the only leading ballerina to be engaged that season, arrived during May and, on the 28th, made her first appearance in a one-act compression of *La Sylphide*, in which Jules played the part of James Reuben for the first time. In their *pas de deux*, which *The Times* described as 'such a masterpiece of dancing as is rarely witnessed,' they showed themselves to be as evenly matched as ever. 'Each seemed to emulate the other, and both *se sont surpassés*. The applause was nearly equally divided in favour of the two, and was equally deserved.'[6] They produced the same magic in the famous *Tyrolienne* from *Guillaume Tell*, and again on June 5th, when they appeared in a hurriedly put-together ballet called *La Chasse des nymphes*. According to one observer, the occupants of the omnibus boxes that were situated at the side of the stage had never been in such rapture.

Further proof that Taglioni no longer harboured any resentment against her brilliant young partner seemed to be provided when her father produced a new one-act ballet for Jules' benefit on June 29th, even if the sub-title sounded somewhat like a declaration of war. *Mazila, ou Haine aux hommes* was little more than a frame for two new *pas de deux* for the principals. As its title hinted, it bore a slight resemblance to a ballet which Filippo Taglioni had staged for his daughter at the Paris Opéra in April, *Brézila*, but to judge from the somewhat ironical account in the *Morning Herald*, no one was expected to take the plot very seriously. 'Mazila is the chief of a community of nymphs who have a sovereign contempt for mankind. Therefore they live apart and become mighty huntresses. A wight, however, who is chief of a troop of bachelors, strays into the domains of these rustical amazons, and finding the Diana asleep in a hammock, falls in love, and so forth. The lady awakes and soon detects the intruder, and is on the point of sending a grey goose quill through his ribs, when she thinks better, and entertains a penchant for him. Both tell their emotions through the eloquent medium of a *pas de deux*. Meanwhile the bevy of inferior nymphs return from the chase and detect their Princess in the act of making love *à la pirouette*. They one and all draw their bows on the solitary beau. His death appears pretty much a matter of certainty, when fortunately the whole *corps d'armée* of his bachelors come upon the scene, and, encountering the opposite host, soon bring about a suspension of arms and an amicable adjustment. There ensues a general capering, and the whole transaction winds up by another *pas de deux*.'[7]

Four days later Jules gave his services for Taglioni's benefit, joining her and Mlle Clara in the *Tyrolienne*. After the ballerina's departure he stayed in London until the season ended in the middle of August, partnering Elise Varin in *La Sylphide* and *La Somnambule*.

Jules Perrot

After a short stay in Paris Jules was able to set off for warmer climes. He had signed an engagement with Domenico Barbaja to dance at the Teatro di San Carlo in Naples, one of the most celebrated opera houses in Italy, where numerous operas by Rossini and Donizetti had been given their first performance, and where the ballet enjoyed considerable prestige under its veteran ballet-master Salvatore Taglioni, uncle of the ballerina. His journey was not without incident. An epidemic of cholera had broken out and it was necessary to take a circuitous route by way of Lyon, Geneva, the Simplon pass, the plains of Lombardy and Milan. On the way to Lyon he descended to lighten the load of the horses as they pulled the lumbering diligence up a steep hill, and when the carriage gathered speed again at the summit, he leapt on to the running board but missed his footing and found himself hanging from the straps. It was only his exceptional agility that saved him from serious injury. As it was, he sprained his left foot so badly that he had to decline an invitation to dance en route in his birthplace. When he eventually reached Naples, he was welcomed there with all the respect that was due to a former principal dancer of the Paris Opéra, and publicised as '*il famoso* Perrot,' but it was not until December 1st that he was able to make his first appearance there as Zephyr in *Zeffiro*, a production probably based on Didelot's famous ballet. A few weeks later, on January 12th, 1836, he partnered Amalia Brugnoli, an early virtuoso of *pointe* work, in Salvatore Taglioni's new ballet, *Il Ritorno di Ulisse*, with music by Pietro Romani. But it was not the experienced Brugnoli who caught Jules' attention, but a golden-haired girl of sixteen summers and exciting promise called Carlotta Grisi, whom destiny had marked to be his muse.

He soon became an intimate friend of her family, hearing the story of Carlotta's early life from her own lips. The name of Grisi was already celebrated in the world of opera, for Giulia Grisi and her elder sister Giuditta were two of the greatest singers of the day. Carlotta was their cousin. For a reason which history seems, tantalisingly, not to have preserved, she had been brought into the world – on June 28th, 1819 – in what she described as a palace built by the Emperor Franz I near the village of Visinada in the forests of Upper Istria. In reality it may have been a building that comprised government offices, for Carlotta's father had been employed in the public surveyor's department. Certainly there was nothing palatial about the amenities or surroundings, for Carlotta's memories were of a wild habitation with mice scuttling on the tables in search of food and wild bears prowling near the roads. Carlotta's sister Ernesta chose to follow the profession of their famous cousins, while she herself, at the age of seven, was placed in the ballet school of the Scala, Milan. Her natural gift for dancing was apparent almost from the moment she began her training in the class of Claude Guillet. Within a few years she had been selected by Auguste Lefebvre to take part in a children's *pas*, and she became the darling of the public, who called her 'the little

Heberle' after the popular Viennese ballerina of that name. It was doubly fortunate that her talent developed so early, for her father was then dead and without her earnings the family would have been in desperate straits, since Ernesta was as yet unable to make any contribution to the expenses of the household.

At this point in her career there was a real danger of Carlotta being spoilt by success. The public clamoured so much to see her that she overtaxed her strength and was forced to rest. A friend suggested that a singing career might be physically less demanding, for she had a pleasing voice and she did not lack encouragement in this direction, not only from her two famous cousins and her sister Ernesta, but also from the celebrated Giuditta Pasta, creator of Bellini's Norma. Pasta had once heard her singing in the wings and, seeking the owner of the voice, had been surprised to find it issuing from a dancer. She had foretold a brilliant career in opera and even offered to take the child to London with her. But neither Carlotta nor her mother were to be moved. Carlotta loved music and seldom missed a performance of opera, but the dance was her abiding passion.

A permanent place in the ballet company of the Scala would no doubt have followed as a matter of course if Ernesta had not been engaged by the impresario Alessandro Lanari to join a touring opera company. Signora Grisi insisted on accompanying her daughter, and that meant taking Carlotta as well. There was no difficulty in obtaining an engagement for her, but because she had received free training at the Scala, it was necessary to obtain permission to leave Milan. The letter of request was carefully worded and written out by Carlotta in her neatest hand. 'The unfortunate circumstances in which I and my family find ourselves,' she explained, 'forces me to beg Your Excellency most earnestly to be kind enough to grant me two years leave of absence, because my elder sister is obliged to leave on the 20th of the current month of September. In anticipation of Your Excellency's kindness, I thank you in advance and most fervently pray God to grant you and all your family prosperity. Your most humble servant, Carlotta Grisi,'[8]

Lanari had assembled a distinguished company for his new enterprise, including the brilliant young French tenor, Gilbert Duprez. The elegant Teatro della Pergola in Florence became their base, and the repertoire was distinguished by two new operas by Donizetti. The company was large enough to be divided into two groups, and Carlotta was assigned to the group that went first to Venice and then, for the 1834 Carnival season, to the Teatro Apollo in Rome. In the summer of that year she found herself seconded to the Royal Theatres in Naples in a relatively humble position. The two principal ballerinas, Amalia Brugnoli and Elise Vaque-Moulin, were paid four or five times as much as she, but for all their renown it was not their performances that inspired Carlotta so much as the rivalry of another young dancer, whose promise she sensed was equal to her own – Francesca Cerrito.

Jules Perrot

The two girls, both still virtually unknown, frequently danced together, but Cerrito had already moved on by the time that Jules arrived in Naples. Carlotta's position in the ballet seemed secure, but she had not finally discarded the possibility of becoming an opera singer. She could well have attended the first performance of *Lucia di Lammermoor* in September 1835, and certainly she learnt some of the arias which she had heard Fanny Persiani sing as Lucia. Also, like everyone else, she must have been overwhelmed by the powerful voice of Duprez, who created such a sensation in the rôle of Edgardo that many music lovers put off their departure to hear him again and steamers were leaving Naples with empty berths. Jules too was to be drawn to Duprez, and the two men became firm friends, finding a common bond in their desire to be recognised in their native land.

Jules had only to see Carlotta dance to recognise her exceptional promise. He pressed her to become his pupil, and dissuaded her once and for all from any thought of becoming a singer.

'Dance, Carlotta, dance,' he urged. 'You are too pretty for a singer. There are already two Grisis whom you would have to match, let alone surpass. Taglioni,' he went on somewhat uncharitably, 'is no longer able to flap both wings, and Fanny Elssler is growing old. Besides, at fifteen or sixteen a ballerina can earn money, while a budding prima donna has to starve.'[9]

During these months in Naples Carlotta made astonishing progress under his tutelage. 'To her own natural gifts he added qualities that were acquired through hard study,' wrote Gautier, who was to know them well a few years later, 'He gave strength to her grace, precision to her vivacity, assurance to her boldness, and to top it all, he instilled a rhythmical harmony of movement, an attention to detail, an elegance and clarity of pose – secrets which he has revealed to Carlotta alone.'[10]

Their meeting in Naples was to be a turning-point for both of them. In spite of their difference in age – he was twenty-five and she was sixteen – they were strongly attracted to one another. To Carlotta the extraordinary physical skill of the young Frenchman made up for his lack of good looks, while her own attractions spoke for themselves. Her youthful beauty was just beginning to unfold in its fresh femininity. Her figure was gently rounded, her complexion perfect – like a tea-rose, Gautier would say – and her hair seemed to sparkle with glints of gold. By the end of the season at the San Carlo, Jules was not only wooing her, but had persuaded her mother that the careers of himself and her daughter were inextricably intertwined.

The couple returned to Paris together in March, pausing there just long enough for Jules to arrange a puff in the *Courrier des Théâtres,* announcing his discovery, 'in the modest ranks of the ballet in Naples, of a young Grisi, whose name itself is a recommendation. Impressed by her talent, he developed it under his guidance, and the pupil was soon able to appear alongside the master with real success. Accompanied by her mother, this young person is now on her way to London where she will join her teacher, who will graciously share the ovations with her. If she perseveres with her studies, Mlle Grisi II will one day make a pretty gift for our Opéra.'[11]

A few days later master and pupil fell into each other's arms in London. They took rooms at No. 51 Quadrant, in Regent Street, and soon Jules was presenting his cherished *protégée* to his friends, old Deshayes, the principal ballet-master, and Coulon, the director of the ballet, while Carlotta for her part had the pleasure of introducing Jules to her first teacher, Claude Guillet, whom they found in the company.

They appeared together on the King's Theatre stage on April 12th, 1836, dancing a *pas de deux* inserted in Deshayes' *Le Rossignol*. Considerable interest had been aroused in the début of 'the dancing Grisi,' and her very name assured her of notice. 'She came, curtsied and conquered,' reported the *Morning Herald*. Although she was noticeably nervous at her ordeal, the audience warmed to her beauty at once. 'She is tall and delicately moulded... Her head... is of a Medician smallness, and sits lightly and airily on a lithe neck and gently sloping shoulders... In her dancing we observed no trace of imitation, although in many respects it was of the true Taglioni school. It was full of life, vivacity, and a daring boldness, thoroughly imbued with grace... It was characterised by a delightful freshness, novelty and unerring *abandon*... exceedingly various in detail, showing a peculiar sympathy... with the changeful expression of her guiding music.'[12] The *Morning Post* spoke of her 'great force and bounding ability.'[13] Meanwhile, her mentor, who gallantly allowed her to receive the honours of the evening, seemed to have put on a little weight, but the *Morning Herald* thought he was still 'the miracle of human machinery, which moves without effort, and threatens perpetual motion.'[14]

Carlotta endeared herself to the public more and more as the season progressed. When Jules took his benefit on July 7th, she not only danced but she sang, choosing an aria from *Lucia di Lammermoor*. The opera had not then been heard in London, and the melody of '*Regnava nel silenzio*' came across quite fresh in the high tones of her soprano voice and the delicate notes of Bochsa, the harpist. For her it was a nerve-wracking ordeal, but the genial, rotund bass, Luigi Lablache, lent her his comforting presence, leading her on to the stage and standing protectively by her side while she sang. Later in the evening she was able to relax when she joined Jules in the 'original *Tarantella*, as imported from Naples,' after which the evening ended with the rousing galop from Auber's opera *Gustave*, which Jules had arranged.

Just three weeks later it was Carlotta's turn to take a benefit, and she repeated her aria and again danced the *Tarantella* with Jules. All trace of nervousness seemed to have gone, and the public was entranced. 'Her vivacity is the very elixir of youth,' wrote the *Morning Herald*, 'her grace the inspiration of nature. Smiles almost breaking into laughter are ever on her cheek, and she

Jules Perrot

evidently cares less for the admiration of her beholder than for the pleasure she derives from the efforts that are but recreation. She is a wild faun before our eyes, or an Esmeralda, or as one of those spirits of some bright particular star which the Roman painters represented as dancing down through the skies and rejoicing in their course.'[15]

Jules was continually discovering new facets of her talent, but he returned to Paris a rather disappointed man. Rumours had been circulating that he and Carlotta were to be married at the close of the London season, but the girl was reluctant, as the *Courrier des Théâtres* discovered. 'Perrot's marriage with Carlotta Grisi has not taken place, as has been said, nor is it even fixed,' it was reported. 'The young person is only seventeen. At that age one can take a good year to make up one's mind.'[16] However, they decided that while the wedding would be postponed, they should, for appearances' sake, 'become provisionally married,'[17] and Carlotta adopted the name of Madame Perrot.

They now threw themselves into the preparations for Carlotta's first appearance before a Paris audience, the opportunity having arisen in the form of an invitation to take part in Mme Paradol's benefit at the Théâtre Français on August 30th. Jules recognised the importance of the occasion for both of their careers, and wrote a careful letter to the chief conductor of the Opéra, François Habeneck, who was to be in charge of the orchestra for the third act of Rossini's *Moïse*, in which the dances were to be inserted. 'My dear Monsieur Habeneck,' he wrote, 'Would you be so kind as to comply with the request of a beautiful girl and myself and come to the Théâtre Italien to rehearse us and note the movements in the *pas* which you are having us dance at the Français for Mme Paradol and which we must repeat tomorrow at midday at the Foyer of the Opéra. Please leave a reply, for which I will send to your home tomorrow morning, and believe me, your devoted and affectionate Jules Perrot. P.S. Please let me know what time will be convenient.'[18]

The 'repeat' performance of the *pas* at the Opéra on the 29th may have been an audition. If it was, nothing came of it. The next day they appeared at the Théâtre Français, and Carlotta came before the scrutiny of the Paris public for the first time. Jules Janin devoted considerable space to recording the event. Jules, he thought, 'danced with much lightness in a *pas* which he composed . . . and composed rather badly. This *pas* is just like any other. There is a great deal of coming and going, *pointes*, and displaying of self and partner. Considering that he is far from good-looking, Perrot was particularly inept in not avoiding those risky anacreontic poses in which the male dancer does nothing but attract the attention of the ballerina. For her part, Carlotta, who is light and young, appeared before us in a wretched costume: tawdry satin, dreadful ribbons, an off-white skirt, and a touch of that dreadful Italian negligence in dress which clever Italian women manage to avoid.'

'The *tarantella*, as performed in Italy, showed Perrot and Mlle Grisi in a new light. When Perrot puts a bonnet on his head and a jacket over his shoulders, he becomes very acceptable. Mlle Grisi, for her part, danced with a truly national ardour. She circles and turns, stops in her tracks and pauses, all very wonderfully. Indeed the Italian flavour of this *tarantella* comes across in the very manner in which this Italian girl performs it. But again Mlle Grisi was poorly costumed. There is something haphazard about her dress, as there is in her performance, but it is a haphazardness that is not artistically contrived.'[19]

There was no need for Jules to feel disappointed. He cannot have expected more from this occasion than to make a sounding of French taste, and this had confirmed what he must have known already, that Carlotta was not yet ready to be launched in Paris. But he was aware of the potential that still remained untapped. And she was only just seventeen.

5

First Steps in Choreography

Assuming responsibility for Carlotta gave Jules a new outlook. Winning personal laurels as a dancer now seemed less important, and his thoughts began to turn to creating the framework in which his art and hers together might best be displayed. Until now his attempts at choreography had gone no farther than arranging *pas de deux*, a natural extension from inventing *enchaînements* for Carlotta in class, but an endeavour that, under the inspiration she gave him, would almost inevitably lead to working on a larger canvas when opportunity offered, as it did when he signed a six month engagement in Vienna.

He and Carlotta left Paris at five o'clock in the morning of September 1st, 1836, so as to take full advantage of the hours of daylight, for it would take them several days to reach Vienna by coach. Having arrived at their destination and recovered from the journey, they took stock of the elegant opera house that stood alongside the city gate where the road to Carinthia emerged, and paid their first courtesy call on the Director, Carlo Balocchino. It was a pleasant interview, and for Jules – as he realised later – an important turning point, brought about by a chance remark of the Director.

'You know,' he said, 'if you do not want your *protégée* to be presented in isolated *pas*, you should arrange a ballet for her.'

'I?' exclaimed Jules in amazement. 'I have never composed a ballet in my life. I am a dancer, not a ballet-master.'

'Come now, have a try,' urged Balocchino. 'Why not arrange some little trifle?'[1]

So Jules began to think, and sketched out a scenario for a short ballet, in which he ventured to arrange the *pas* for the principals but, whether hesitant about his abilities or diplomatically not wishing to tread on sensitive toes, left the corps de ballet work to the theatre's ballet-master, Pietro Campilli.

No record has survived of the action, which was divided into two scenes, and the theme of the ballet, which was presented on September 29th, can only be conjectured from the title, *Die Nymphe und der Schmetterling*. Carlotta played the nymph Thisbe, and Jules was a sylph. How the butterfly was introduced passed unrecorded, possibly as a metamorphosis of the sylph. The public had paid increased prices not to see a new ballet, but to judge the two new dancers. Their reactions were reflected in the enthusiasm of the critics, who were lyrical in their praise, directing their attention mainly to Jules. The *Allgemeine Theaterzeitung* talked of his 'inner motivation,' seeing his exceptional grace as a step towards complete artistic fulfilment. In an unusually detailed analysis he spoke of 'an indescribable lightness and freedom, a graceful development both in attitude and movement which is most enchanting. Characteristics which are not sufficient by themselves combine to form a pleasing artistic personality whose performance must be counted as one of the most extraordinary in this field of art – a performance of such delicacy as has not been seen since Duport and Albert, for dancers since their day have been noted more for exertions that bring to mind the words of Schiller in *Cabale und Liebe*, "When I appear, the whole kingdom trembles." Perrot sails in with a lightness and a manner which is almost apologetic. You see none of the flailing arms of his predecessors, but a small figure who owes much to nature, yet is an artist who has added much to nature. There is grace in every arm movement, every inclination. You only have to see him offer his hand to his partner to realise that he is a true artist of the dance. Seeing him actually dancing in a graceful *pas* of the true French style with light rhythmic pirouettes and turns that are effortless yet firm and finished, you are filled with astonishment and delight. A beautiful step *en avant* in which his body reminds you of a flower swaying in the breeze is an expression of pleasure, as dancing at its best should be, and not an exercise or a triumph over difficulty. With such artistic understanding and sensitive appreciation of the beauty of line Perrot flatters his partner, melting into the background as he supports her in delicate groups, and finally joining her, arm in arm, in a jubilant coda which might well be called the most effective moment of the evening.'[2]

Jules and Carlotta exerted an inspiring influence on the Viennese company by demonstrating how close and intimate was their mutual understanding of rhythm and line in their *pas de deux*. 'With Perrot you do not admire isolated details,' wrote this same critic a few weeks later after seeing them in another *pas de deux* that was a gem of humour and charm. 'Their entire bodies are united in their dancing . . . All is graceful and in harmony, melting into lines of great beauty. Some details stand out because we have not seen them before – Perrot's wonderful balances and quick movements in the air, and the beauty of Grisi's footwork.'[3]

The rustic ballet, *Das Stelldichein* (The Assignation), which followed on November 23rd, was entirely Jules' own creation. The chief conductor, Engelbert Aigner, a composer of some experience who had written operettas as well as ballet music, provided a score. The production was modest, but the action was admirably simple and easy to follow. Julien, a young peasant, and Colas, a timid musician, are both in love with a farmer's daughter, Lise.

Jules Perrot

By chance Colas witnesses an assignation between Lise and Julien, whom she favours, and sends for the girl's father, who is finally persuaded to give his consent to the marriage of the young lovers. A series of meetings and partings, quarrels and reconciliations take place, brought to life by the passionately felt acting of Jules and Carlotta, who danced a *pas de deux* of great beauty and then joined in a galop of astonishing precision that brought the ballet to a close.

Rapturous accounts in the press echoed the delight of the public, which did not tire of seeing this unassuming yet near-perfect work. One critic descriptively recorded that the audience 'wallowed in it,' and two weeks after its first performance it was still drawing full houses. It was given fourteen times during Jules' first season in Vienna, and eight more when he and Carlotta returned the following year. Its charm was then undimmed, and the critic Tuvora called it 'one of the most beautiful and attractive poems,' in which Jules and Carlotta 'lift the veil from Arcadia before our eyes, and we see reflected in the clear mirror of their mime the unspoiled magic of a vanished world, in which Cupid hides in the bushes and sharpens his arrows and Apollo wanders through the meadows. Everywhere is love, merriment, happiness and life.'[4]

Jules and Carlotta were kept busy by the management, with *pas de deux* inserted in Mozart's *Don Giovanni* and in another ballet by Campilli, *Liebe, stärker als Zaubermacht*, and on January 5th, 1837, a revival of *La Sylphide*. When it had been first revived in Vienna nearly a year before – not, it must be explained, with Taglioni – *La Sylphide* had not been particularly successful, but now the production had been revised and the appearance of Jules and Carlotta in the principal rôles ensured its success. The climax of their performance was a *pas de deux* in which they were accompanied on the violin by Josef Mayseder. The extraordinary accord they attained when they danced together seemed, to Heinrich Adami, to invest their dancing with an 'inner meaning' and to approach the very ideal of beauty of movement. 'From Perrot,' Adami went on, 'our public has received a completely new idea of the art of dance . . . We admire not only his strength and bravura, but also the nobility and grace of his movements and the quite unostentatious ease with which he surmounts every difficulty.'[5]

For some reason, which the press discreetly glossed over, Carlotta's appearances ceased some weeks earlier than those of her partner. She was last seen that season on February 2nd, while Jules himself continued to appear until March 17th. During these last few weeks he assumed two rôles from the Paris repertory, Figaro in *Le Carnaval de Venise* on February 5th, and Edmund in *La Somnambule* on March 7th. Strangely, Carlotta's absence was hardly noticed, and he prepared Aimée Gauthier, who played the rôle of the sleepwalker in the latter ballet, so well that the audience unprecedentedly demanded an encore in the middle of their *pas de deux*.

First Steps in Choreography

In this first season Jules had impressed Vienna mainly as a performer, and in summing up his visit Heinrich Adami made no mention of his success as the choreographer of *Das Stelldichein*. He had been unanimously acknowledged, Adami declared, as a phenomenon such as had never been seen before, and had projected a completely new image of the dance as an art that was both noble and beautiful. 'Perrot,' he wrote, 'is entitled, without any reservation, to the honourable title of artist.'[6]

He was shortly to add another accomplishment to his name, that of a father. Carlotta's pregnancy was already well advanced when she stopped dancing early in February, and she and her mother returned to their retreat in the village of Auteuil, west of Paris, where Jules joined them only two or three weeks before the child was born, probably prematurely, on April 8th. It was a daughter, and two days later the child was baptised at the parish church of Notre Dame d'Auteuil in the presence of Jules, his father and Carlotta's mother.*

Jules did not forget his career in the excitement of parenthood. Paris was only a short drive away, and his thoughts inevitably turned to the Opéra. There was a new Director there now, Henri Duponchel, who lent a sympathetic ear when Jules approached him about the possibility of being re-engaged. Jules desperately wanted to return to the theatre of his early triumphs, but his loyalty to Carlotta was stronger than his personal ambition, and when Duponchel refused to consider engaging Carlotta as well, he allowed the negotiations to lapse. He was not to know it at the time, but by this act of self-denial he sacrificed his last chance of achieving his ambition.

As a result the couple danced in Paris only once during the summer of 1837, taking part in a benefit performance at the Opéra-Comique on September 5th for Madame Adolphe, an actress who had been a comrade of Jules in his days at the Gaîté. The *pas* which he arranged specially for this occasion showed how much his choreographic skill had improved. Charles Maurice found it elegant and graceful, with a welcome touch of humour, and recognised an emerging talent that held promise of better things to come.

They were looking forward to returning to Naples, the scene of their first

---

* The baptismal entry reads: 'On April 10th, 1837, by me the undersigned was baptised Marie Julie, born on the 8th instant, daughter of M. Joseph Perrot and Dlle Adélaïde Joséphine Grisi, artiste, he being resident in this parish. The godfather is M. Jean Perrot, paternal grandfather of the child, and the godmother is Dame Marie Grisi, who have signed with the father and me.'

Lillian Moore (in *Artists of the Dance*, p. 131) gives Carlotta Grisi's baptismal names as Caronne Adele Josephine Marie. She does not state her source, which may have been a baptismal certificate formerly in the possession of the Archives Internationales de la Danse, which its director, Dr. Pierre Tugal, showed to the present writer in July 1947.

Jules Perrot

The record of the baptism of Marie-Julie Perrot, daughter of Jules Perrot and Carlotta Grisi, in the Asnières parish register.

meeting, but the news that cholera had broken out there caused them to change their plans. The wisdom of this decision was soon confirmed by the tragedy that befell their colleague, Antonio Guerra, who lost his mother, his two sisters and an aunt in the epidemic. They toyed with the idea of dancing in Lyon and Marseille, but nothing came of it and they spent the rest of the summer and the autumn preparing for their second engagement in Vienna, where they were expected in the middle of November.

This engagement, like the previous one, was for six months, but with the difference that Jules' standing as a choreographer was now officially recognised. His ballet, *Das Stelldichein*, was greeted as an old favourite when he and Carlotta made their reappearance on December 9th. A month later, on January 10th, 1838, he presented another work – a slight divertissement, described as a 'character sketch,' entitled *Die neapolitanischen Fischer*. The action needed no printed synopsis to explain it. Jules appeared as Pietro, a young fisherman who arouses the jealousy of his sweetheart Zanetta – Carlotta's part – by dancing with two fishergirls. Zanetta's fit of sulks is only temporary, and the reconciled lovers end by dancing a fiery tarantella. The whole divertissement lasted scarcely more than half an hour, and its success rested largely on the talents of the two principals. Of the choreography there is virtually no record, but one of the notices in the press mentioned a dance with a net that was pronounced 'very attractive.'[7] It was performed to the strains of Mayseder's violin, and thirteen years later its theme was to be taken up again and developed in one of Jules' major ballets, *The Naiad and the Fisherman*.

Die neapolitanischen Fischer, together with a revival of *Die Nymphe und der Schmetterling* and isolated *pas* – among them two new numbers, a Swiss *pas de trois*, in which they were joined by Mme Crombé, and a Sicilian dance inserted in Pierre Aniel's ballet, *Oberon* – held the public's attention throughout the first two months of 1838. During this time Jules was hard at work preparing his first important ballet, which was presented under the title of *Der Kobold* on March 2nd.

This 'faery ballet' in two acts and five scenes was the most ambitious work he had so far attempted. The score, which incorporated a number of melodies from well-known operas, was skilfully compiled and composed by the conductor, J. Wilhelm Reuling, and help was also forthcoming from the French ballet-master, Pierre Aniel, who had recently been engaged in Vienna and may have served Jules as a sounding-board for his ideas and generally given advice and assistance from time to time.

The seed from which this ballet developed had been sown some months previously in Paris, in the small theatre on the Boulevard du Temple, the Folies-Dramatiques. Jules had gone there to see *La Fille de l'air*, a faery spectacle interspersed with music and dancing, which had been presented in August 1837, and had come away with his imagination fired with ideas, some of which would still be surfacing several years later. The action of *Der Kobold* was directly derived from this piece, although Jules had considerably adapted the original story to transform it into a ballet for himself and Carlotta. He was indebted to the script by the Cogniard brothers and Raymond not only for the underlying idea, but also for several of the principal characters. In both works the action turned on the adventures of a supernatural being – female in the play, male in the ballet – who is sent to earth to be tested against the power of love and, succumbing, sacrifices immortality in order to marry a mortal. Among the human characters who appear in both pieces were the gauche young peasant Rutland and Mathias, his scheming uncle in the play and his father in the ballet, while Azurine, the daughter of the air of the play's title became the 'kobold,' the goblin, of the ballet – the character which Jules conceived and fashioned for himself, half spirit, half mortal, and was ideally suited to his personality, appearance and style.

As in the play, the ballet opened with a prologue that explained the purpose of Follet's visit to earth. The scene was set in the volcanic waste-land of the underworld, where Follet's father, Astaroth, is condemned to bear the consequences of having fathered a son by a mortal woman. It is Fate's implacable decree that Follet must go to earth and prove that he can resist the charms of women before being granted immortality.

In the next scene Follet makes his appearance on earth by emerging from a well close by a humble cottage in the Tyrol just as Iola – played by Carlotta – is drawing water for the garden. To calm her fright and explain who he is, he plucks a rose, which opens and sheds its petals in his hand as he tells her that while she must wither and die like the flower, he will live for ever. But when she asks whether he has a heart, he recalls his father's warning and flies away. Shortly afterwards he returns to find Iola reading aloud while her grandmother works at her spinning wheel. Being invisible, he bounds lightly on the arms and back of the old lady's chair and the spinning wheel, teasing her by breaking her thread, and making his presence known to Iola by kissing her. It is Iola's wedding day, and soon there arrive her intended husband, Rutland, and his father, Mathias. Follet continues his pranks, his object now being the hapless Rutland, whom he regards with a mischievous jealousy. At the end of the scene Astaroth is seen in a vision, expressing his chagrin at his son's growing interest in Iola.

His concern is all too well founded. As the second act opens, Follet is discovered dancing along a leaf-covered stream before the cottage. He is determined to prevent the marriage, and when Rutland arrives in his wedding suit, he appears before him out of nowhere, and the youg man flees in terror into the forest. When the wedding guests arrive, he is nowhere to be found, and while his father goes to look for him, the dancing begins. A mysterious stranger then arrives – 'a stranger whose presence fills everyone with a kind of stupor. He goes straight to the bride, whom he asks to dance with him. She dares not, and cannot, refuse, for the sight of the stranger fascinates her, and she feels herself under the influence of some sort of magnetism. To calm her fear, she asks one of her friends to dance with her. After this dance the stranger, who is Follet himself in human form, vanishes.'[8] Eventually Rutland reappears, still suffering from fright. His troubles are not yet over, for as he prepares to join Iola in the wedding procession, Follet uses his magic powers to effect a transformation and takes Rutland's place by the bride. But entering the consecrated portals of the church is too much for him. Overcome by giddiness, he takes to his heels and, to everyone's amazement, is swallowed up by the earth.

Iola returns to her cottage. Alone in her room, she sees a vision of Follet hovering above her and prays for guidance. Suddenly the window flies open to reveal Follet, 'his eyes fixed upon her in a satanic stare.' Although realising the risk he is running, he takes her into his arms, beseeching her to love him. She yields to his entreaties, but as their lips touch in a kiss, Follet's fate is sealed and he falls lifeless at her feet.

Astaroth now arrives to claim his son, but an angel descends and insists that Follet's soul belongs to Heaven, for it has been purified through his love for

Iola. The scene then changes to show the wedding procession returning from the church with Iola arm in arm with her bridegroom. Rutland appears, but he is too late. It is Follet whom the girl has married. The ballet then ended with general rejoicing in a divertissement evoking the Spirit of Wine.

To judge from the verdict of the critics, the dramatic structure of the ballet was not completely satisfactory. Because its theme treated of a spirit's interference with a betrothal of two mortals, it was compared by several critics with *La Sylphide*. Heinrich Adami, Jules' warmest supporter, even found *Der Kobold* the more interesting of the two ballets, approving of the happy ending as being more theatrical, even if less poetic, than the sad note of the Sylphide's death.[9] Another critic, however, considered the happy ending to be a 'sacrifice of a beautiful and poetic idea which gave *La Sylphide* a deeper meaning than is usually found in ballets,' although he conceded that this was made up for by the 'visual jollity' of the final divertissement.[10] Ferdinand Bernstein of *Der Sammler* thought Jules would have done better to have translated the Cogniard play directly into a ballet instead of inserting scenes after the manner of *La Sylphide* and *Das Stelldichein*,[11] and this criticism was echoed by *Der Humorist* who called it a hodge-podge of *La Sylphide*, *Le Diable boiteux* (Coralli's ballet for Fanny Elssler), and *Das Stelldichein*.[12]

But if, through inexperience and zeal, Jules had tried to cram too many ideas into his work, he was at least successful in holding the interest of the public throughout a performance lasting more than two hours. No one could complain of boredom. It was not just his own performance, inspired though that was, but the cumulative effect of the whole production, and not least his work for the corps de ballet, that roused the public to recall him fourteen times at the end of the first performance and earned the ballet a tally of twenty performances in three months.* Further proof of its success was to be afforded within a few weeks of its production, when it was parodied on two of Vienna's popular stages, one of these parodies coming from the pen of the witty, irreverent satirist, Johann Nestroy.**

In spite of its faults it was a remarkable work. Adami was impressed by its originality, crediting Jules with a 'happy gift for composition' and approving the way in which he had 'carefully avoided any comparison with earlier treatment of similar material.' 'Not for a very long time has a new ballet been so universally popular as this one,' he wrote. 'It offers an unbroken series of

---

* Only four ballets before *Der Kobold* had reached their 20th performance in Vienna in a shorter time: *Die Fee und der Ritter* (1823) and *Die Maskerade im Theater* (1832) in 40 days, *Danina* (1826) in 48, *Ottavio Pinelli* (1827) in 64. *Der Kobold* took 90 days.

** *Der Kobold*, a fairy play in 2 acts, book by F.X. Told, music by M. Hebenstreit, first performed at the Leopoldstadt-Theater on April 17th, 1838, and *Der Kobold, oder Staberl im Feendienste*, a farce in 3 acts, book by Johann Nestroy, music by Adolf Müller, first performed at the Theater an der Wien on April 19th, 1838.

Jules Perrot

fascinating images that surprise both the eye and the heart. In inventing such scenes Perrot is indefatigable. The end of the third scene, when the goblin is swallowed up by the earth, was extraordinarily effective. Of the ensembles the final galop, in which several novel dance figures were displayed, is quite outstanding. The dance of the goblins in the first scene seemed less characteristic, although it contained many pretty groupings. The whole treatment of the ballet is very simple, making the customary synopsis quite superfluous. It moves progressively forward, is never boring, and holds the interest of the spectator throughout. In spite of its simplicity, though, it is rich in variety. Scenes are never long-drawn-out, and repetitions are ingeniously avoided . . . If any adjustment is needed, it is only in the third scene, where too many dance numbers follow without a break.'[13]

Der Sammler spoke of Jules' 'taste and talent,'[14] but the critic of *Der Humorist* considered the choreography to be uneven. 'One must admit,' he wrote, 'that Perrot is an accomplished choreographer "in mosaic," in producing individual moments that are extraordinarily successful and enliven the whole work. But in spite of the skilful way in which it is arranged, this ballet is only a torso, without head or feet, for the introductory dances of the goblins lack character and resemble military exercises, which are perhaps not without their own value. The conclusion is also unpoetic, particularly the "Spirit of Wine."'[15]

Unfortunately the reviews threw no light on the quality which, in his maturity, was to place Jules in a category apart among choreographers – his unique gift of weaving dance and mime to express some aspect of the action or the interrelation of characters. However, two passages can be recognised from the scenario that foreshadow important scenes in Jules' later ballets: the blooming and fading of a rose to convey the idea of mortality was to be used again in *Ondine*, and Follet's appearance as a 'mysterious stanger' among the wedding guests was to be developed into the *mazurka d'extase* in *Eoline*.

No praise, it seemed, could be too fulsome for Jules' performance as Follet. He sustained his part, which was full of the most varied and demanding virtuosity, without the least sign of exhaustion. He seemed to be everywhere, and subject to no physical laws. As one critic put it, 'he appears out of caves, he flies through the air, he disappears into the ground and hovers like a dragonfly over a waterfall. You have to see all this to have any conception of his incomparable art . . . Perrot's dancing is poetry, an idyll. His body is free, like the spirit.' By his side, Carlotta was a 'fitting companion,' still taking second place to the extraordinary display of stamina and virtuosity that Jules could produce at this stage of his career. They made an incomparable team. 'His performances are poems to his wife, in which both live and love to the full. Alas that such poetry can exist only in their hands.'[16]

During the preparation of *Der Kobold* Jules had found Pierre Aniel obligingly helpful, but not long afterwards their relationship was soured by a

First Steps in Choreography

dispute which has to be judged in the context of the lack of protection afforded at that time to choreographers. In 1840 Jules became aware that Aniel was planning to produce *Der Kobold* at the Grand Théâtre in Lyon, where he had become *maître de ballet*. Always prickly when his rights were at stake, he wrote both to Aniel and the director of the theatre, putting them on notice that the work was his exclusive property and that, if necessary, he would take legal proceedings to protect his rights. Aniel retorted by submitting the dispute to the Committee of Dramatic Authors in Paris, and Jules and Aniel met in Charles Maurice's office, in the presence of Joseph Mazilier and Louis Brétin, to try and reach an understanding. Jules was forced to concede that Aniel had made a contribution to the work, and that he had assured Aniel in Vienna that his name would be added to his own on the playbill.

So that there should be no misunderstanding, Aniel wrote to Mazilier on January 5th, 1841: 'I beg you to inform Perrot that I have deemed it desirable to produce the ballet in three acts, altering the title from *Le Lutin* to *Le Follet, ou le Fils de l'enfer*, and changing the *dénouement* entirely. Ask him if he consents to his name appearing alongside mine on the playbill. If he refuses, I shall be obliged to take positive action: the playbill will state that the ballet is by MM.***, arranged and produced by me. If, on the other hand, Perrot acquiesces in my just demands, I shall approach the administration of our theatres to ensure that he receives his half share of the royalty, although I am not obliged to do so for a work that originated outside France.'

There was little that Jules could do. He could not prevent the ballet being performed because, as Aniel had pointed out, a theatre director was free to present a work created abroad without its author's consent. All Jules could do was to write an angry letter to Maurice's paper, the *Courrier des Théâtres*, protesting against 'the most blatant violation of an author's rights, of which I am the victim.' He mentioned that he alone had composed the work, and pointed out that Aniel had considered his claim so slight when he was in Vienna that he had made no objection when the playbills and the synopsis omitted his name altogether.[17]

However, no sign of this future unpleasantness marred the remainder of their Viennese season, which Jules and Carlotta brought triumphantly to a close on June 4th with two rousing *pas de deux*, one of them – *El Zapateado* – in the Spanish style. A busy year now lay ahead of them. Within a few days they were in Munich, giving four performances, two each of *Die Nymphe und der Schmetterling* and *Das Stelldichein*. Then, after a short rest, they crossed the Alps to give fifteen performances at the Scala, Milan, at the beginning of the autumn season. Here Jules had another personal triumph, while Carlotta, who was returning to the city where she had received her childhood training, was honoured as 'one of the most distinguished ballerinas of our day.'[18] From Milan they journeyed south to Naples, to the San Carlo, where their paths had first crossed. To celebrate their return Jules produced a new *pas de deux*,

Jules Perrot

which was inserted in Salvatore Taglioni's new ballet, *Il Rajah di Benares*, and revived his *Stelldichein* under the Italian title of *L'Appuntamento* for the Teatro Fondo.

Their reputation was growing, but at the same time their partnership was undergoing a subtle metamorphosis that would inevitably change the basis of their relationship. In the three years they had spent together each had developed greatly as an artist; Jules had discovered his creative potential as a choreographer, while Carlotta was emerging from his tutelage to establish herself as an artistic personality in her own right and an equal partner with her former mentor. Jules may have found it hard to adjust to this development, which, he may have sensed, bore the possibility of an eventual parting of their ways.

This must have strained their relationship, which had begun as one of master and pupil rather than of lovers, and apparently remained so until they separated. 'You ought to hear Carlotta describing the sort of life she led with Perrot,' wrote Charles de Boigne, who was as well acquainted as anyone with the Paris dance world. 'Love played a very small part in it. It was an unusual household in which work was the order of the day and the night. The master had one goal with which the husband never thought of interfering, while the pupil secretly dreamed of glory, fortune and above all, freedom. So our two turtle doves wasted no time in loving which they could employ, more usefully, in dancing.'[19]

A more intimate glimpse of their life together was vouchsafed to Alexandre Dumas by Carlotta herself, who confessed that 'the most ardent caress was when Jules stood on my hips like the Colossus of Rhodes while I was lying flat on the floor, face downwards. It was to strengthen my hips.'[20]

Being of a like mind about the purpose of their existence, they were apparently content in their life together. Jules certainly taught Carlotta much else beside the technique of dancing. Exceptionally for a dancer who must have had a fragmented education, he was a man of varied interests, and imparted much of his wide knowledge to Carlotta. She for her part was by nature very industrious, and possessed a keen mind that absorbed facts and ideas easily. He must have found her an enchanting companion. Always ready to help her friends, she was completely devoid of pettiness and jealousy, and lacked also two qualities that de Boigne associated particularly with dancers – laziness of mind, and an aversion to physical effort when off the stage. Carlotta, on the other hand, always seemed busy with one thing or another. If she was not dancing, she was singing, and if she was not singing, she was occupied with her needlework, at which she excelled. She sang now more for relaxation, for she was irrevocably committed to her career as a dancer, although Jules had encouraged her to continue with her singing lessons and insisted that she should study under the best teachers.

Carlotta's feelings for Jules were perhaps founded more on gratitude and respect than on any profound stirring of the passions. She fully recognised the unique value of her years of apprenticeship as his pupil and partner, without which she would have never developed into the great artist she became. As for Jules himself, he was certainly deeply in love with her – it was perhaps his first serious involvement, and certainly the great love of his life – but more and more he was being driven by a compulsive urge to create, and while his moulding of Carlotta was partly motivated by a genuine dedication to her interests, it was, at a deeper level, a supreme act of creation.

6

A Paris Triumph

After pausing in Paris just long enough to inspire a news paragraph in the *Courrier des Théâtres*, Jules and Carlotta continued their journey to London, arriving there in the last days of March with the expectation of appearing at Drury Lane Theatre in *Der Kobold*. The manager, Alfred Bunn, had extravagant plans to present a season of opera and ballet, and had already made overtures to Carlotta's cousin Giulia and other renowned opera stars. Ballet was to have an important place, and his choice of Jules and Carlotta showed a keen instinct for promising talent. For Jules this might have seemed a heaven-sent opportunity to extend his experience as a choreographer, but as the weeks passed it became all too clear that Bunn's enterprise was doomed before it could begin. At last the two dancers could wait no longer and returned to Paris disappointed.

Viewed in proportion, however, this was only a minor set-back, for Jules' ambition was fixed on returning to the Opéra, and he would have been more concerned by the news he learnt when he arrived in Paris. A contender for the position of principal male dancer, Lucien Petipa, had been engaged by the Opéra after a successful début. The critics had been impressed by his elevation and grace, which no doubt Jules could emulate and even surpass, and in addition were much taken by his handsome appearance, an advantage that could only be conceded.

Perhaps he was never more sensitive than now of nature's cruel trick of refusing him good looks, although he was sufficiently balanced to take his friends' raillery in good part. The tenor, Gilbert Duprez, who was no less unprepossessing to look at, used to tease him unmercifully, and one day when strolling along the Boulevard with another singer, Paul Barriolhet, hailed Jules with the words: '*Mon Dieu*, my poor Perrot, how ugly you are!'

'Bah!' Jules retorted, 'you and Barriolhet are no beauties either.'

'Steady on,' cried Barriolhet, 'I certainly do not consider myself good-looking, but both of you are even less so than I.'

The three of them seemed on the point of quarreling when Duprez stopped a passer-by. 'Can you spare a moment, monsieur,' he said. 'Will you settle a little difference that has arisen between us and, in the manner of Paris of ancient mythology, award the apple to whichever of us you consider the ugliest?'

The passer-by stared at them in disbelief. Then, hardly able to contain himself, he blurted out, '*Ma foi*, gentlemen, I am too embarrassed to make a choice,' and turned away shaking with laughter.[1]

Being very conscious of his undistinguished appearance, Jules no doubt saw the unintended irony in the remark of a blind man who was introduced to him. 'Have pity on me,' this man said, 'for I am unable to see you.' Jules retained his composure. 'And I shall see that you do not hear me either,' he retorted with a laugh.[2]

Any frustration which he must have felt at the collapse of the London venture and Lucien Petipa's engagement at the Opéra was soon dispelled when he succeeded in securing an engagement for himself and Carlotta at the Théâtre de la Renaissance. It was an imposing enough setting for them to appear before the Paris public and, for him, to stake a claim to be restored to his former position at the Opéra.* The Renaissance had once served as a temporary home for the Opéra-Comique, and more recently had been converted for the production of drama and comedy, vaudevilles and two-act operas in French. Within these carefully defined limitations – prescribed so as not to encroach upon the rights of the Opéra-Comique – the management had been entrusted to Anténor Joly, a man with an extensive knowledge of the theatre and a vast network of contacts which he had built up through owning the theatrical paper, *Le Vert-Vert*. Joly's management had been launched under the most favourable auspices by Victor Hugo's colourful drama, *Ruy Blas*, with Frédérick Lemaître. Later, when Joly ventured to introduce music into the pieces he presented, he had a few brushes with the Opéra-Comique, and even one with the Opéra, but he had held his ground and early in 1840 he was emboldened to present a two-act opera entitled *Zingaro*, written expressly for Jules and Carlotta.

The name of the composer was unlikely to cause any flutters at the Opéra-Comique, for Uranio Fortuna was completely unknown in Paris, and indeed had only had one work publicly performed before, in Rome. He seemed to have no particular qualification to be chosen as the composer of *Zingaro* unless he happened to be a friend of Jules and Carlotta, or perhaps Joly, and certainly his music made little impression on Jules, who was never to use him again.

Thomas Sauvage, the author of the libretto, was no doubt chosen by Joly, for he had been one of the signatories of the application that had led to Joly's

---

* The theatre was also known as the Salle Ventadour from the street of that name. From 1841 to 1870 it housed the Italian opera and was called the Théâtre Italien. It ceased to be a theatre in 1879, but the building still exists as offices of the Banque de France.

Jules Perrot

Joly's appointment and had already written several works for the theatre. The narrative, however, was worked out in close collaboration with Jules, who was credited with the arrangement of the pantomime and the divertissements and always considered himself as a part-author of the piece.[3] In fact the content of the mime passages that were interspersed among the songs and the dialogue was the most distinctive feature of the opera, revealing the care and attention to detail that Jules devoted to the relationship between his characters.

The conception of his own rôle of Zingaro, the young gypsy who has lost his power of speech as a result of a shock received in childhood, was no doubt largely his own. He made his first entrance shortly after the curtain rose on the prologue, 'bounding like a deer from rock to rock,' at the summons of the rascally chief, Hayraddin. The gypsies implore him to dance some of the folk dances of the countries they have passed through, but he appears downcast. Asked the reason for his melancholy, Zingaro mimes his reply. Shuddering at some memory, he puts his hand to his forehead and looks about him. He indicates that he recognises this spot, and suddenly Hayraddin remembers having buried here a chest of loot to avoid capture. Zingaro is agitated by the memory of a girl. He tries to deny it, but Hayraddin is too astute to be deceived, and discovers that the young gypsy is wearing a silver medallion around his neck as a sentimental memento. Forget the girl, Hayraddin tells Zingaro, for in time you will fall in love with, and marry, a gypsy girl.

The foppish Casimir de Rosenthal, who owns the neighbouring castle, then appears to seek the gypsies' help in abducting a girl on whom he has designs. Hayraddin strikes a hard bargain, but the plot is overheard by Zingaro. Bursting through the foliage, he demands that the attempt be abandoned and, kissing his medallion, he announces that he will risk his life to save the girl. Hayraddin is forced to have him seized. The carriage is then heard approaching, and soon it appears on the bridge at the back of the stage. As the gypsies prepare to strike, Zingaro breaks free and, with incredible nimbleness, scales the rocks to the bridge. Seizing the horse's bridle, he brings the carriage to a halt. One of the two occupants – Goldmann, the guardian of the girl at his side – takes Zingaro for a bandit and fires his pistol. Wounded, Zingaro tumbles into the torrent below. The girl, Gianina – Carlotta Grisi – seems to recognise the young man. She leaps out of the carriage to call for help, and the gypsies are foiled by the arrival of some woodcutters. Zingaro is dragged out of the water. On regaining consciousness, his first reaction is to protect Gianina, but he is reassured by the sight of the woodcutters. He smiles and faints, and Goldmann and Gianina insist on taking him to their home.

The first act opens in Goldmann's cottage, which he shares with his housekeeper Dorothée. Soon several interesting facts are revealed. Dorothée is secretly in love with Casimir, who seduced her some years before. And Goldmann was once the intendant of the castle, before it was burnt and pillaged by gypsies. His wife had then been killed trying to save the old Baron's niece, who had never been heard of since. Goldman was dismissed by the Baron, and had found Dorothée as a child abandoned by the roadside. Before his death, however, the Baron realised that Goldmann was innocent, and gave him the cottage. Now Goldmann has become the guardian of a cousin's child, Gianina, and has fallen in love with her. Gianina is indifferent to him, and she has fallen in love with Zingaro. She conveys her feelings in a cavatina, which Carlotta sang charmingly in Italian, and this was followed by the first important scene between her and Jules. Gautier's description of it as one of 'three great *pas*'[4] reveals that it was not a conventional passage of pantomime, but was conceived with elements of dance woven into the mime to form a danced scene:

> Towards the end of the cavatina Zingaro enters softly. He has heard Gianina's gentle words and is happy, though he does not show it.
> Gianina sits in the large armchair. She seems troubled and pensive.
> Zingaro climbs on to the back of the chair and looks down at her lovingly.
> She raises her head, and seeing him, is overcome by shame at being surprised and letting him guess the secret of her heart. Annoyed by Zingaro's indiscretion, she scolds him and sulks.
> It is now Zingaro's turn to be sad. They walk about the room without speaking, but casting glances at one another.
> Suddenly Gianina notices the bouquet which Zingaro has brought for her, but which he still has in his hand. She wants to take it.
> No, it is not for you.
> Who is it for then?
> Ah, for someone who is gracious, pretty and kind. (He mimes a description of her.)
> Gianina smiles and turns aside, still coveting the bouquet.
> Zingaro, holding the bouquet away from her, asks if she will love him.
> Gianina's only answer is to try and snatch it from him.
> Zingaro offers it to her, whisks it away, holds it over her head, throws it into Gianina's apron and snatches it back again.
> After a while Gianina loses patience and becomes angry.
> Zingaro falls to his knees and implores her forgiveness.[5]

They are interrupted by Dorothée, who comes to announce the arrival of Casimir. Gianina imitates his affected walk, but Zingaro does not conceal his distrust of the man. Dorothée believes that Casimir is about to seek her hand, but it is Gianina whom he has come to see. Gianina plays him along, trying on the jewels he has brought and finally refusing them and taking up Zingaro's bouquet. It is time for the local fête to begin, and Zingaro is left behind to guard the cottage. In his frustration at not being able to follow his beloved, he suddenly decides to bolt the doors and follow the others.

The scene changes to the village square. Zingaro hides among the musicians of the band so as to keep an eye on Casimir, who, after instructing

Jules Perrot

Hayraddin to steal the paper that establishes Goldmann's ownership of his cottage, turns his attentions to Gianina. He begs her to dance. At first she is reluctant and pretends to be lame. Then the clatter of Zingaro's castanets resounds across the square and she bursts into action as he darts forward to dance with her. Their *pas de deux*, *La Bohémischka*, was followed by *La Valse saxonne*, arranged for the company, an outburst of general happiness which was quelled by Goldmann's discovery that he has been robbed of his title to his home. Zingaro is filled with remorse at leaving the cottage unoccupied, and rushes into the forest.

The second and last act opens in the cottage, where Dorothée is reading to Gianina a story about a girl whose lover, who has been plying her with rich gifts, turns out to be an evil goblin. Just when Gianina's imagination is absorbed by the poor girl's fate, Zingaro appears carrying a heavy chest full of jewels, which he offers to Dorothée so that she can save her unfortunate master. Zingaro and Gianina find themselves alone, and their relationship is developed by another long mime scene, which draws a parallel with the story of the goblin:

Happy to think that, thanks to his efforts, Goldmann will soon be set at liberty, Zingaro approaches Gianina.

Gianina is still preoccupied with the story that Dorothée has just read to her. She turns it over in her mind and shudders. Could he be a goblin?

Seeing her turn away from him, Zingaro goes up to her and takes her hand.

Gianina pulls her hand away with a shiver. She recoils, and withdraws to the far corner of the room.

Zingaro drops to his knees in surprise, and begs her to treat him less severely.

Gianina begins to look at him. No, he has no horns, no cloven feet, no wings, but yet . . . the devil can change his form. In the old tale he took the shape of a young man, lively, light and nimble . . . And he made gifts of gold.

Still on his knees, Zingaro cannot understand why Gianina is annoyed with him. Of course it was wrong of him to leave the cottage and expose his benefactor to being robbed. But then he had been shut in . . . while she was going to dance and display her grace with him not there! Gianina's presence was his very existence, and life was unthinkable without her. He could not help himself. Although he was the cause of Goldmann's imprisonment and Gianina's sadness, he has made amends. Goldmann will now be set free. The wrong he did, and what he did to repair it, were both caused by his love for Gianina. It was at first sight that he fell in love with her, when he was dancing in a tavern. He still wears next to his heart the silver medallion she gave him. He shows it to her and presses it rapturously to his lips.

Timidly, Gianina takes a step towards him.

Zingaro continues to talk about his love, and tells how he overheard Casimir secretly giving orders to the gypsies to abduct her, and how it was for her sake that he ran in the path of the horse and was wounded.

Moved, but still a little afraid, Gianina comes closer.

Zingaro is under the impression that Gianina is indifferent. She does not love me, perhaps she despises me? How clear it all is. How can I, a wretched gypsy without country or family, expect her to be interested in me? No, she cannot love me.

Gianina looks at him tenderly.

Zingaro does not want pity. For the sake of her own happiness, she must forget him.

Gianina is aghast. 'Forget you! Is it possible?'

Zingaro is determined to go away.

Gianina stretches out her arms in disbelief. 'You are leaving!'

Zingaro tells her he is leaving, not to forget, but to seek death which alone can put an end to his love and his suffering.

Gianina, no longer able to contain her distress, runs to him and holds him back. 'Stop!'[6]

Their reconciliation is followed by the appearance of Hayraddin. Zingaro places himself protectively before Gianina, and declares his intention of breaking with the gypsies. Once again the attempt to abduct Gianina is foiled, this time by the arrival of Goldmann, Dorothée and the Baron. Goldmann, recognising the jewels as having belonged to his former master, accuses Zingaro of theft. Zingaro then explains how the jewels came into his possession in another complex mime passage:

When he was young he happily followed the gypsy tribe. One evening they came to a castle. The night was cold and dark. Someone kindled a fire. Zingaro thought it was to warm them as they set up camp and settled down for the night. But not so. Cutting branches from the trees, the gypsies made themselves torches with which they forced their way, armed with daggers, into the castle grounds. They broke into the castle. The servants who resisted were killed. Terrified, Zingaro watched them pile jewels, gold and silver into a chest. Finally he found himself in a room with a woman and a little girl. Here Zingaro's horror seems to redouble and he bursts into tears. ('My poor wife,' exclaims Goldmann, while Hayraddin shakes with fear.) At the sight of the gypsies the woman took the child into her arms. A gypsy tried to snatch it from her. The woman resisted, and a terrible struggle ensued. The gypsy, unable to seize the girl, stabbed both woman and child. Struck by terror, Zingaro fled and fainted in the courtyard. The next day, revived by the fresh morning air, he was about to leave the pillaged castle when he heard a feeble moan. He looked around him and saw a little girl in the rubble; she was not dead, but wounded in the arm. Making sure that no one was watching, he dragged her free and, as she was cold, wrapped her in his cloak. He then carried her, a heavy enough burden for a little boy, to the road, where he laid her near a stream, and after saying a prayer for her safety, kissed her and hurried away, for he could hear the gypsies approaching. The gypsies were being pursued by soldiers, and only just had time to bury the chest with their loot near a tree, which they marked with a cross. Soon afterwards they left the district. Today, the sight of Goldmann's misery reminded Zingaro of the chest. He went and found the tree, dug the earth with his bare hands and eventually discovered the treasure, which he brought back for the old man whom he had ruined by negligence. (During this scene Gianina and Dorothée run to a cupboard and bring out a piece of material.) Zingaro recognises it as the child's cloak. With an expression of joy he runs to Dorothée, seizes her hand and points to a scar. She is the child he saved![7]

Jules Perrot

Recognised as the heiress of the estate, Dorothée offers to share it with Casimir, whom she has loved all along. In this way all ended happily, and the opera concluded with a divertissement containing a rousing *Forlana* and a final *pas de deux* by Jules and Carlotta entitled *La Ziguerrerina*.

Judged solely on its literary and dramatic merits, the piece was obviously artificial and contrived, yet its first performance on February 29th, 1840, was seen as an event of special significance. Strangely enough, it was not the appearance of a new ballerina that stirred the public's interest so much as the return of a popular male dancer whose departure from the Opéra had been generally deplored and, at a deeper level, a timely restatement of man's place in ballet. As the title made clear, it was around Jules' rôle, with its demands on his pantomimic talent, that the narrative revolved, and his triumph was all the greater for overcoming, momentarily, the indifference, if not distaste, which was fast becoming the male dancer's lot. Though this prejudice was too deeply ingrained to be vanquished by one man's efforts in a single evening, the public was at least given pause to reflect.

One critic, who surprised himself by admiring Jules that evening, was Jules Janin, who admitted that he was 'hardly a supporter of what are called the *grands danseurs*. The *grand danseur*,' he went on, 'seems so sad and heavy, so miserable and yet so pleased with himself. He responds to nothing, he represents nothing, he is nothing . . . Nowadays the dancing man is no longer tolerated except as a useful accessory; he is the shading in the picture, the green box hedging that surrounds the flowers in their bed, the obligatory foil . . . Yet, while not changing my opinion, you can take my word that Perrot is the most admirable male dancer you could ever see. He possesses a lightness that even those who have seen the queen of lightness, Mlle Taglioni, at close quarters find unbelievable. We raised no objection when Perrot left the Opéra when he was already its master, and so terrified were we by male dancers, we were even glad to see him go. But today this same dancer has made marvellous progress. He has returned as an excellent mime and an ingenious choreographer, and his success is greater than we can express.'[8] The last word was said by the *Courrier des Théâtres*: 'Perrot has brought about a revolution.'[9]

The most vivid account of *Zingaro* came from the pen of Théophile Gautier, who was to become a close friend of Jules and Carlotta – particularly the latter, whom he adored with a devotion that would not falter until the day he died. Gautier was a poet of the youthful Romantic school that acknowledged Victor Hugo as its leader. His mastery of words had already been revealed in his early poems, and was now being put to use in the dramatic criticism he was writing for the newspaper, *La Presse*. His review appeared in the issue that was on the streets two days after the opening performance. Although written to a deadline, it combines the vivid imagery of his poet's pen with an immediacy that still has power to bring the performance to life more than a century later.

A Paris Triumph

'A success at last, a real success! M. Anténor Joly deserved it, for he has striven for it a long time with unprecedented zeal. It was not a matter of a hundred *claqueurs* or so. The whole audience participated, clapping, stamping their feet, and even throwing bouquets . . . M. Sauvage's dialogue and M. Fontana's music played no part in this – Perrot's legs did it all. And what legs!

'Perrot is not good-looking, he is even extremely ugly. Above the waist he has the physique of a tenor – there is no need to say more – but from there down he is a pleasure to look at. It is not exactly in good taste nowadays to be concerned with the perfection of a male body, but we cannot keep silent about Perrot's legs. So imagine that I am speaking of a statue of the mime Bathyllus or the actor Paris that has just been excavated from Nero's gardens or Herculaneum. The feet and the knees are extremely delicately formed, and counterbalance the feminine roundness of contour of his legs which are both soft and pliable, elegant and supple. The legs of the young man in red hose breaking the symbolic wand across his knee in Raphael's painting of *The Marriage of the Virgin* are in exactly the same style. Let me add that Perrot, in a costume by Gavarni, has nothing of that feeble and inane manner which usually makes male dancers so insufferable. His success was assured even before he began to dance. Seeing his quiet agility, his perfect rhythm, the supple movement of his miming, it was not hard to recognise the aerial Perrot, Perrot the sylph, the male Taglioni! And in the *grand pas de deux* of the divertissement, cries of bravo exploded like thunderclaps.

'This *pas* is charming, the idea behind it very pretty, and – unusually for a *pas* – it had a meaning. The Cassandre of the story wishes to make his ward Gianina dance before the nobleman, but because he has just locked up the girl's sweetheart, she consents with very ill grace. Suddenly she raises her head, her eyes gleam, her features break into a sparkling smile, and her steps grow livelier. She has heard the distant chatter of castanets. The sound comes nearer – it is Perrot, Zingaro, who has leapt through the window and alighted on the tip of his elegant foot to take part in the village festivities (comic opera style), and there begins one of the most charming *pas* you could possibly behold. In it Perrot displays a perfect grace, purity and lightness. It is music made visible, and if one can express it so, his legs sing most harmoniously to the eye.

'Such praise is all the more suspect coming from me because I do not like male dancing at all. A male dancer performing anything other than *pas de caractère* or pantomime has always seemed to me something of a monstrosity. Until now I have only been able to support men in mazurkas, saltarellas and cachuchas. With the exception of Mabille and Petipa, the male dancers of the Opéra only reinforce my view that women alone should be admitted into the corps de ballet.

'Mme Carlotta Grisi supports her husband admirably. She knows how to dance, a rare quality. She has fire, although lacking a little in originality. Her dancing is not very distinctive. It is good, but not superlative. As well as being a good dancer, she is an accomplished singer – two talents that are difficult to combine. Her voice is supple, clear, a little shrill, and weak in the middle register, but she manages it with skill and method. It is a very good voice for a dancer. Many singers who do not dance cannot do as well. As for her features, they are not typically Italian and do not conform to the image that is evoked by the name Grisi . . . She has chestnut-coloured hair, blond rather than dark, quite regular features, and so far as can be seen under her make-up, a natural complexion. She is of medium height, slender, quite well proportioned; she is not too slim for a dancer, but the shape of her foot is somewhat Italian – or English, if you prefer . . .

'It has just occurred to me that I have not said a word about the libretto. I must confess that I did not understand it at all, which is a tribute to my sagacity, for I should be very worried about my intelligence if I could understand such things. The prologue seemed to be all about a chest and a young girl, in the style of *saltimbanques*. I espied a sort of bridge . . . over which passed a carriage that was attached to it, and then there was a pistol shot that kills Perrot-Zingaro. This idea of killing off in the prologue a man who is going to dance three great *pas* in the following acts seemed a little premature to me, but it was no doubt a toy pistol. For in the next act Perrot-Zingaro, who a moment before had been a corpse, dances a charming *pas de bouquet* with his wife. Then the chest reappears, and Perrot goes into an explanation about it . . . which is not very easy to understand considering that it was expressed with his hands and feet and that miming can hardly convey anything outside the present tense. In his capacity as a dancer Perrot is as dumb as Fenella in Auber's opera.* Added to which, Carlotta Grisi sings with such a strong accent that it is impossible to know if she is expressing herself in Italian or French, and is equally unintelligible to those of either nation, so you will excuse me for not being very clear in my review. In the end the ridiculous nobleman marries a woman in a yellow and green skirt whom I thought was Mlle Ozy, though I am not sure.** Perrot married his own wife, who wore a blue skirt. He came off best.

'The divertissements are arranged and staged with great taste and clarity. The groups are well disposed, the evolutions perfectly performed and easy to distinguish. The *pas des Bohémiens* and the styrian rondo*** gave great pleasure.'[10]

The fortunes of *Zingaro* during its short run were chronicled in the col-

---

* *La Muette de Portici*, in which the leading rôle was mimed.
** He was correct. Caroline Ozy played Dorothée.
*** It is not wholly clear to which dances Gautier is referring: the first is probably the *Bohémischka* in Act 1, Scene 2, but he seems to have been confused about the geographical provenance of the second, which may have been the *valse Saxonne*.

umns of the *Courrier des Théâtres*, which left its readers in no doubt about the extent of Jules' triumph. It was his dancing that had 'made it a delirious success,'[11] and 'everyone [was] asking why [he had] not been engaged at the Opéra.'[12] It was explained that the production had been put on in just six weeks, and that Jules and Carlotta had been so exhausted after the first performance that they had requested two days' rest. It was clear that Jules' success was far greater than Carlotta's, and this remained so at the second performance, when 'Perrot transported, delighted and subjugated the entire audience, which showered him with bravos.'[13]

The performance of March 31st was announced as the last, but a few more were to follow in April, including one at the Odéon. At the end of that month Jules took Carlotta to his birthplace, Lyon, where they danced at the Grand Théâtre throughout the summer in *Der Kobold* and *Zingaro*. One of the first people with whom they got in touch on their return to Paris at the end of August was Charles Maurice of the *Courrier des Théâtres*, and the result was a curiously worded but useful puff that 'Perrot is the Mlle Taglioni who is addressed as "monsieur."'[14] It was all part of a determined effort to prepare the ground for a return to the Opéra, and in the first flush of his triumph, success must have seemed almost within his grasp.

7

Gestation of a Masterpiece

'How is it,' asked the critic J. Chaudes-Aigues, after seeing Jules Perrot in *Zingaro*, 'that an artist of such power is not enthroned alongside his wife at the Opéra?'[1] To many the answer was clear: it lay in the indifference of Léon Pillet, the Director, who was so besotted with the soprano Rosine Stoltz that he was quite shamefully neglecting the ballet. Taglioni had left the Opéra some years before, and with Fanny Elssler on the point of sailing for America, the burden of leading the company was now about to descend on the frail shoulders of Pauline Leroux. There would be lean years ahead if Pillet could not be shaken into activity to strengthen the ballet company at the top, and it was here that Jules saw his chance. It was no secret that he was manoeuvring to be re-engaged at the Opéra, if not as a dancer – for he had to accept Lucien Petipa's engagement as an established fact – then as a choreographer, and his aim was now to interest the Opéra in Carlotta, for whom there was obviously an opening, and to convince Pillet of the advantage of taking him as well.

Unknown to Jules however, other pressures were at work directed to securing an engagement for Carlotta alone. Through the contacts of her cousins, Giulia and Giuditta, the Grisi family could command enormous influence in the highest quarters, and seeing that Jules' efforts were having little effect, they took matters into their own hands with Machiavellian guile. Not only did Jules play no part in their plans, but he was completely unaware of them. Early in December a letter of recommendation that could not be ignored arrived on Pillet's desk. It was initiated by Edouard Monnais, the Royal Commissioner whose task it was to supervise the financial affairs of the Opéra. At his behest the head of the Theatre Section of the Department of Fine Arts – ironically, a man bearing Jules' own surname, although no relation, Louis Perrot – wrote to Pillet on November 30th, 1840: 'I am taking the liberty of introducing you to Mme Carlotta Grisi, of whom Monnais has already spoken to you. He has told you what influence is interested in her being engaged by you. So far as I am concerned, I assure you that she deserves to be, and is, a charming dancer, and that her talent and her name are good recommendations for the public, and I believe I may say that in more ways than one your interests will be well served by this. After the recommendations to which I refer, my own is little.'[2]

Even Carlotta was unaware of what was going on, and the family had to adopt a deceitful stratagem – no doubt convincing themselves that they were acting in her best interests – to get her to sign the contract. The terms had apparently been negotiated by Giulia Grisi and Carlotta's mother, who one day, when they knew Jules would be out, called unexpectedly for Carlotta under the pretence of taking her shopping. Innocently Carlotta put on her cloak and bonnet, and to her surprise found herself being taken to the Opéra and ushered into the Director's office. Giulia Grisi was a formidable personage, and Carlotta meekly signed the contract that was placed before her, flattered no doubt by this sudden stroke of luck and probably unmindful that she was destroying Jules' own hopes of returning to the Opéra. The contract, which was dated that fateful day, December 10th, was essentially a débutante's engagement, carrying the possibility of more advantageous terms for the future if public favour warranted it; it bound her for one year from January 1st, 1841, at the modest salary of 5,000 francs without performance bonuses.

When Jules learnt what had happened, there was a frightful scene. He raged and screamed at Mme Grisi, accusing her of base treachery and abduction, but there was nothing he could do. He was well and truly tricked; the deed was done, and not being Carlotta's husband he had no legal standing in the matter of the contract. He demanded an explanation from Carlotta, who certainly knew how to calm him down, for he accepted that she herself was not at fault.

Nor was this the full extent of his troubles. For several years he had been earning good money, much of which he had saved and invested at a satisfactory rate of interest that would provide him with a comfortable income when the time came for him to retire, but unwisely he had allowed all his income to remain under his father's control. This had been arranged as a precaution, but he had discovered that his trust was misplaced when he wanted to legitimise his relationship with Carlotta after the birth of Julie. His father had a vested interest in his remaining unmarried, for Jules was the principal support of his parents and his good-for-nothing brother, all of whom lived with him and on him. There was consternation, therefore, when Jules announced his intention of marrying Carlotta, and the father retorted that if he went ahead with his plan, he could not expect him to give up a penny of the money that had been put into his name. The Grisis were equally opposed to the marriage for reasons of their own, for the absence of the matrimonial bond was an essential factor in their plan to conclude Carlotta's contract with the Opéra without his knowledge.

Poor Jules felt he was the unluckiest of men, and the atmosphere of his home, with parents who had betrayed him and a 'mother-in-law' he could not

Jules Perrot

stand, must have become well nigh unbearable. Some months later August Bournonville, who had been a fellow pupil in Vestris's perfection class, came to Paris on a visit, and into his sympathetic ear Jules poured his troubles. Bournonville did what he could to cheer him up, but Jules was shattered and defeated. His despair was all the deeper for his having given up taking class and allowed his skill as a dancer to deteriorate. Now, as Bournonville told his wife in a letter, he had 'nothing left save his ugliness and his bad temper . . . He [had] never been a religious man, in spite of his other virtues, but he [thought] about God and the immortality of his soul just like his honourable father.'[3]

What hurt him as much as anything else was the blow that Carlotta's engagement dealt to his own prospects. He 'would have sold his soul to the devil for a year's restoration'[4] at the Opéra, but with three ballet-masters already on the pay-roll – Coralli, Mazilier and Albert – it became doubly difficult to gain a foothold. He was, however, still useful to Carlotta, and although their relationship could never have been the same after the affair of the contract, he continued to teach her and arrange her *pas*.

Playbill of the Paris Opéra for February 12th, 1841, the evening of Carlotta Grisi's début. Bibliothèque de l'Opéra, Paris.

Although it must have been galling to relinquish his accustomed rôle as her partner, he was grateful for small mercies when he was allowed to arrange the *pas* to be interpolated in Donizetti's opera, *La Favorite*, for her début on February 12th, 1841. Lucien Petipa was chosen to accompany her, and she found it strange to accommodate herself to someone other than Jules. 'Something was missing,' noticed the percipient Jules Janin. 'Even when she is in the air, she is anxious and looks up to see if someone is at her side. The missing someone is Perrot, her lord and master, that light male Sylphide, that fine dancer for whom we have made such a great concession in permitting him to be a dancer.'[5]

Jules was meanwhile beginning to realise that he would have to consider his own career apart from Carlotta, and while continuing to press his case for an engagement as a *maître de ballet* at the Opéra, he was investigating other openings for employment. A few days after Carlotta's début the *Moniteur des Théâtres* reported that he was having difficulty in coming to an arrangement with the Opéra, and might shortly be producing and dancing in a work at the Porte-Saint-Martin.[6] This prospect did not materialise, possibly because the door had by no means been closed to him at the Opéra.

Although Gautier called it 'ravishing,' Jules' choreography for the *pas* in *La Favorite* received little attention from the press, but the Opéra recognised his contribution to Carlotta's success and also his position as her mentor. Plans for her future were therefore discussed with him, and to give her a more substantial rôle, a revival of *La Sylphide* was contemplated to which he was to add a distinctive flavour in the form of a new *pas*. This was to be a *pas de trois* in the first act in which the Sylphide was to be seen dancing with the hero James and his fiancée Effie, both of whom were unaware of her presence. Unfortunately this project was abandoned when another ballerina, Adèle Dumilâtre, claimed that *La Sylphide* had been promised to her. The Opéra gave in to her, and the proposed new *pas* was given to Mazilier to arrange. Jules could only hope that he was slowly consolidating his position at the Opéra, as in April he seemed to be doing, for during that month he arranged two more *pas* for Carlotta, one inserted in *La Juive* and another in *Don Juan*.

Carlotta's success had had one result of consequence. The Director, Léon Pillet, at last realised that he had a ballet, and turned his thoughts to exploiting the interest which the young dancer had awakened. A new ballet scenario by the dramatist Saint-Georges, entitled *La Rosière de Gand*, had been accepted in January, and this was now offered to Carlotta. The choreography was to be by Albert, who, in spite of his age – he was fifty-four – had reserved for himself the rôle of a young seducer. When she read it, however, Carlotta found it too long and asked to be given 'a more danceable subject'[7] for her first creation at the Opéra.

Probably this 'more danceable subject' had already been suggested to her by a new admirer, Théophile Gautier, who came with an idea that was soon to germinate into *Giselle*, the most enduring of all the ballets created during these richly productive years of Romanticism. In the gestation of this masterpiece both Jules and Carlotta were to be intimately concerned, Carlotta to become the first Giselle and Jules to make the major, though anonymous, contribution to the choreography. The benefit of this experience to Jules as a creative artist was incalculable. Not only was he given an insight into a multiple act of creation virtually from the initial conception, but his artistic education was to be broadened immeasurably by his friendship with Gautier.

A more engaging companion could hardly have been found. Gautier still revelled in the physical pleasures of life, in spite of the demands of his journalistic chores, which he was finding increasingly irksome. He was a natural athlete, a fine swimmer and a good horseman, and an enthusiastic dancer. But one suspects that it was not his physical accomplishments that appealed to Jules so much as the artistic and intellectual stimulation that his friendship offered. Gautier was a gregarious man, a fluent and vivid talker with an infectious sense of humour, a man whose company delighted his friends with whom he would discuss poetry and art for hours on end. On the occasions that Jules was drawn into his circle, he could not fail to absorb the ideas that were reshaping literature and art under the banner of Romanticism. The leader whom these young Romantics revered was Victor Hugo, but there were many other gifted celebrities to be met in that circle – writers such as Alexandre Dumas, Gérard de Nerval, Arsène Houssaye and Delphine Gay, whose husband owned the newspaper *La Presse*, for which Gautier wrote, and among the artists Eugène Delacroix, Théodore Chassériau, the Devéria brothers, Célestin Nanteuil, Gavarni, who had designed the costumes for *Zingaro*, and Lorentz, who was to draw a brilliant series of caricatures of the first production of *Giselle*.

Gautier had an absorbing passion for the dance, and had begun writing notices of ballet performances, as well as other theatrical events, at an early stage in his journalistic career. No other critic could match the verbal imagery with which he could capture the essence of a dancer's style or the fleeting beauty of a movement. Warm-blooded and sensitive to women's charms, Gautier made no attempt to conceal his enthusiasms. At the height of the rivalry of Taglioni and Elssler, he openly avowed his preference for the Viennese dancer, and now – since seeing her at the Renaissance – he was a devoted worshipper of Carlotta.

Gautier claimed that the original idea for *Giselle* came to him while he was thinking of Carlotta in the quiet of his study. According to his own account, he was leafing through Heinrich Heine's book, *De l'Allemagne*, when his eye alighted on a passage about the wilis, nocturnal spirits of Slavonic folklore who haunt the forests and lure young men to their deaths by drawing them into their pitiless dance. In a flash of inspiration he conceived an idea for a

Charles Mazurier, and, below, a scene from Polichinel Vampire. *Engraving by Cardon from a drawing by Duboulez. Bibliothèque de l'Opéra, Paris.*

Frédérick Lemaître. Lithograph by Léon Noël. Bibliothèque de l'Opéra, Paris.

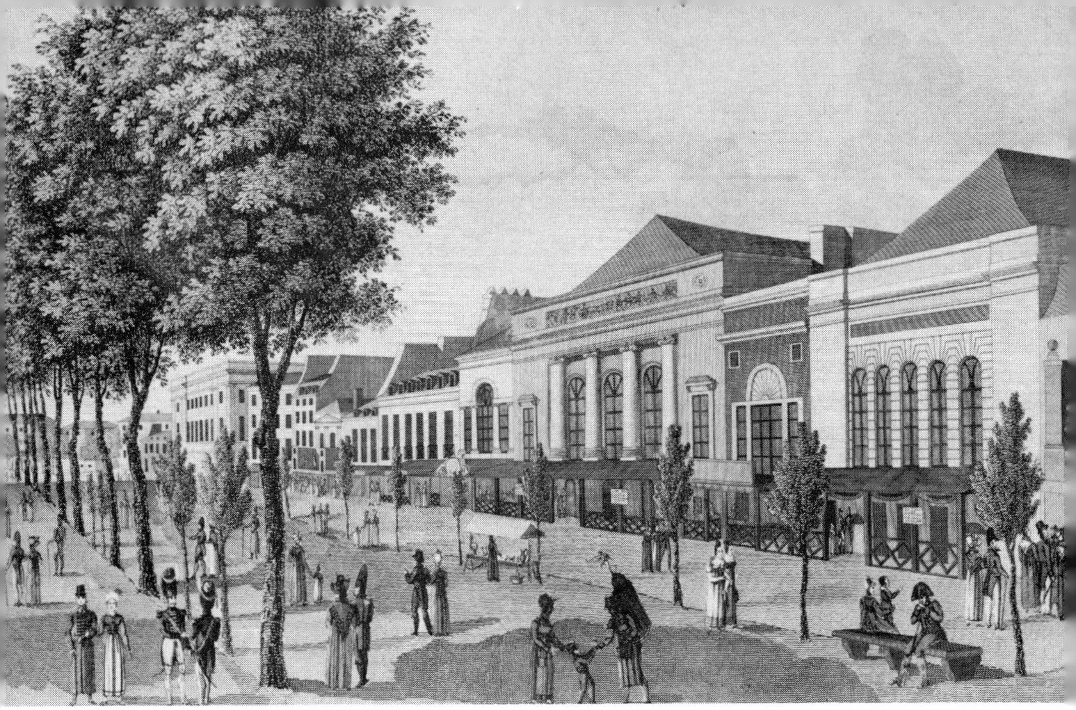

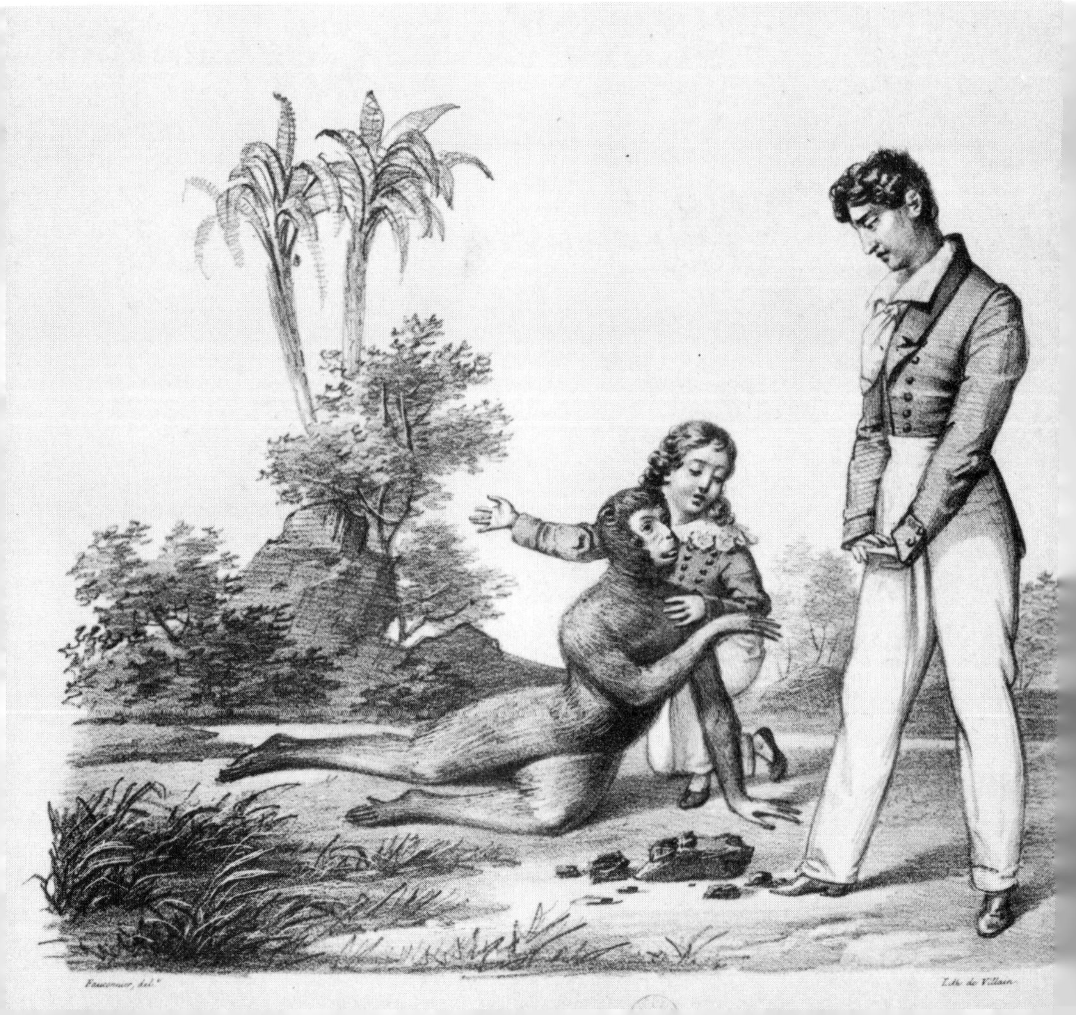
Fauconnier, del.t
Lith de Villain

Above left *The Boulevard du Temple, with the Théâtre de la Gaîté, where Jules Perrot made his first appearance in Paris, on the right. Engraving by Eugène Aubert from a drawing by Courvoisier. Bibliothèque de l'Opéra, Paris.*

Left *The final scene of* Jocko, *with Mazurier as Jocko. Lithograph by Villain from a drawing by Fauconnier. Bibliothèque de l'Opéra, Paris.*

Above *The Théâtre de la Porte-Saint-Martin, Paris. Engraving by Guignet from a drawing by Courvoisier. Bibliothèque de l'Opéra, Paris.*

Right *Frédérick Lemaître and Mme Zélie as Mephistopheles and Martha in the* valse de fascination *in the Porte-Saint-Martin production of* Faust, *1828. Engraving by Maleuvre. (Petite Galerie Dramatique, No. 637) Bibliothèque de l'Opéra, Paris.*

Miniature portrait of Auguste Vestris, given to Jules Perrot by his friend, August Bournonville. Collection of Serge Lifar.

August Bournonville in 1841. Lithograph by Em. Baerentzen. Bibliothèque de l'Opéra, Paris.

Louis Véron, Director of the Paris Opéra, who promoted Jules Perrot to the position of star dancer. Engraving by Carey from a drawing by J.A. Beauce. Bibliothèque Nationale, Paris.

Benjamin Lumley, Manager and Lessee of Her Majesty's Theatre, London, who gave Jules Perrot his greatest opportunities as a choreographer. Engraving from a drawing by Count d'Orsay. Collection of the author.

Above left *Jules Perrot in the divertissement in* Robert le Diable. *Drawing by Le Faget. Bibliothèque de l'Opéra, Paris.*

Above right *Jules Perrot in* La Révolte au sérail. *Engraving by Maleuvre. (Petite Galerie Dramatique, No. 834) Bibliothèque de l'Opéra, Paris.*

Below *Jules Perrot and Pauline Leroux in* Nathalie. *Drawing by Le Faget. Bibliothèque de l'Opéra, Paris.*

Carlotta Grisi and Jules Perrot in Le Rossignol. *Etching by T. Jones. Theatre Museum, London.*

Jules Perrot and Carlotta Grisi in a scene from Der Kobold. *Engraving by Andreas Geiger from a drawing by Johann Christian Schoeller. (Prämien Bilder zur Theaterzeitung, No. 57) Collection of Edwin Binney 3rd.*

Carlotta Grisi as Gianina in Zingaro. Raccolta di Stampe, Castello Sforzesco, Milan.

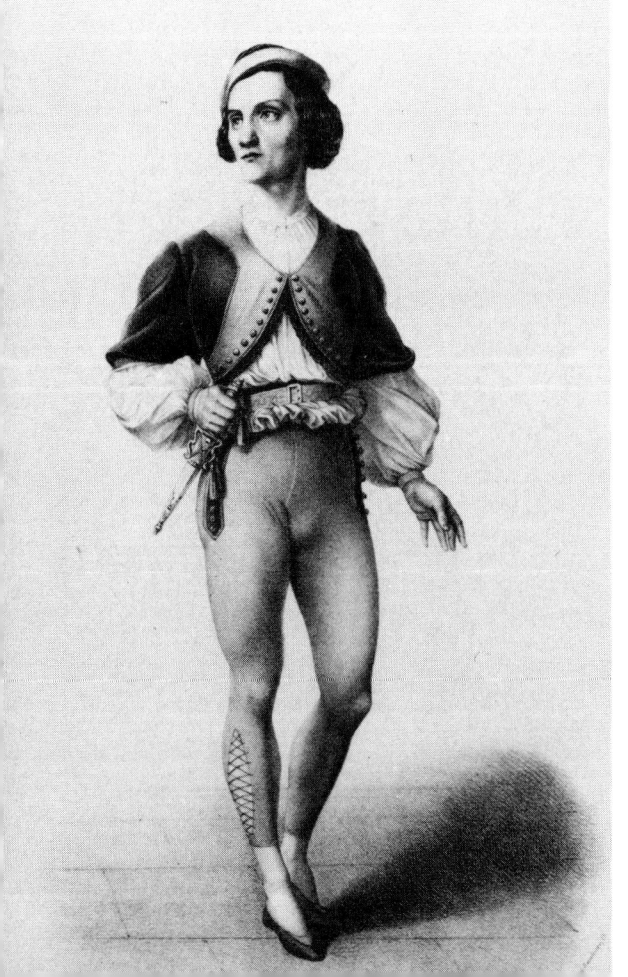

Jules Perrot in the title-rôle of Zingaro. Lithograph by Alexandre Lacauchie. Collection of the author.

Carlotta Grisi in Zingaro. (Petite Galerie Dramatique, No. 1377) Bibliothèque de l'Opéra, Paris.

Jules Perrot and Carlotta Grisi dancing the valse saxonne in Zingaro. (Petite Galerie Dramatique, No. 1379) Bibliothèque de l'Opéra, Paris.

Above Carlotta Grisi and Jules Perrot in Act I of Giselle. Collection of Stanislav Buzek and Otto Zajik.

Right Carlotta Grisi in Act II of Giselle. Lithograph by John Brandard. Theatre Museum, London.

Left Two moments in the pas de deux in Act I of Giselle danced by Carlotta Grisi and Lucien Petipa. Lithographs by Victor Coindre. **Above:** Harvard Theatre Collection. **Below:** Bibliothèque de l'Opéra, Paris.

Two moments from Act II of Giselle, with Carlotta Grisi and Lucien Petipa as Giselle and Albert. **Above:** Lithograph by Victor Dollel. Collection of Mary Clarke. **Left:** Lithograph by Célestin Nanteuil.

Above *Jules Perrot, Fanny Cerrito and Marie Guy-Stéphan in the* pas de trois *in* L'Elève d'Amour *at Her Majesty's Theatre, London.* (Illustrated London News, *June 25th, 1842*).

Below *Fanny Cerrito's entrance in* Une Soirée du Carnaval *to dance the Double Cachucha, with Jules Perrot in the background. Lithograph by Joseph Bouvier. Theatre Museum, London.*

Right *Jules Perrot in* Alma. *Detail from a drawing, probably by R.J. Hamerton. New York Public Library.*

Above Ondine, *Scene 1: Ondine appearing to Matteo.* Engraving by Thomas Williams from a drawing by H. Warren.

Left Ondine, *Scene 1: Ondine disappearing into the water, beckoning Matteo to follow her.* Engraving by I. Andrew from a drawing by E. Courbould.

Ondine, *Scene 2: Ondine playing pranks in Matteo's hut, with Matteo, his mother and Giannina.* Engraving by S.W. from a drawing by H. Warren.

Ondine, *Scene 2: Ondine flying out through the window of Matteo's hut.* Engraving by Timms.

Ondine, *Scene 4: Ondine appearing to Matteo among the praying villagers. Engraving by M. Easom from a drawing by H. Warren.*

Ondine, *Scene 4: Matteo and Giannina rowing across the bay, with the naiads below the surface of the water. Engraving by Measom.*

ballet, and seizing a large sheet of paper, he wrote down 'in superb capitals' – the title: '*Les Wilis*, a ballet.' But then the absurdity of translating 'such misty, nocturnal poetry . . . such richly sinister phantasmagoria' into theatrical terms struck him, and he threw the sheet of paper away.[8]

That was the story he recorded for posterity in his celebrated review of the ballet, written in the form of a letter to Heine. No one ever contradicted him, but there may have been an earlier experience in his theatre-going, as there certainly was for Jules, that could have contributed to that first moment of inspiration. This was the melodrama, *La Fille de l'air*, which had been produced at the Folies-Dramatiques in 1837. Jules had certainly seen it, for he had adapted its story for his ballet, *Der Kobold*. Gautier was already being drawn to dramatic criticism at the time, and although he did not review it, he may yet have seen it, or if he did not, he probably heard about it from Jules, and in particular learnt of a scene, which Jules did not use in *Der Kobold* but was just the sort of scene that a choreographer would store in the back of his mind for future use. It was none other than a dance scene, introducing a band of wilis, headed by their queen. The action of the melodrama had reached the point where the efforts of those protecting the aerial spirit were directed towards recovering a magic talisman which had fallen into the mortal hero's hands. To music selected from *Les Huguenots*, the wilis are summoned from their tombs, and in a dance scene form groups and attitudes as they swirl around him in a fantastic round. The hero falls to the ground exhausted, and is on the point of expiring when the spirit of the air calls upon the wilis to desist. As they advance upon their intended victim, she protects him with one arm while commanding them to disperse with the other. She overcomes their power with an imperious look, and one by one they return to their tombs.

The doubt which Gautier at first felt that the legend of the wilis might prove impossible of transposing into a ballet soon vanished, and that evening at the Opéra, meeting his friend Saint-Georges, the idea came pouring forth from his lips.

Saint-Georges, despite his stylish dandyism and perfumed elegance, was a highly professional dramatist who had been turning out theatrical pieces of all kinds for years – vaudevilles, libretti for operas both serious and comic, and more recently a couple of ballet scenarios. He was quick to recognise a promising theme, and in no time transformed Gautier's poetic fancy into a well-fashioned and craftsmanlike scenario. Gautier had never written a ballet scenario before, and although he was to write his later ballets unaided, Saint-Georges' skill and experience were indispensable, for this first effort, to shape his ideas into a produceable form for the ballet-master.

Perhaps Gautier spoke to Jules and Carlotta about his friend Heine – 'a charming god, malicious as a devil, and a good fellow'[9] – and pointed out the passage in *De l'Allemagne* which had struck the first spark. It came in a long essay describing the elemental spirits that recur in so many varied forms in

65

German folklore. 'In a part of Austria,' the passage ran, 'there is a legend which has much in common with [that of the elves], although it is of Slavic origin. This is the legend of the nocturnal dancer known in Slav countries as the wili. The wilis are betrothed girls who have died before their wedding day. The poor young creatures are unable to rest in their graves. In their stilled hearts and lifeless feet the passion for dancing, which they could not satisfy in their lifetime, still burns. So at midnight they rise and gather in bands by the roadside, and woe betide any young man who crosses their path! He is compelled to dance with them; they surround him with unbridled desire, and he must dance with them until he falls dead. Adorned in their wedding dresses, with crowns of flowers on their heads, and flashing rings on their fingers, the wilis dance, like the elves, in the moonlight. Their faces, though white as snow, have the beauty of youth. They laugh with a terrible joy, and they beckon seductively, with the promise of sweet rewards. These lifeless bacchantes are irresistible! When a bride has died in the fullness of youth, it is impossible to believe that beauty in all its brilliance can vanish beyond recall, and so the belief arose, easily enough, that the girl continued, after death, to seek the joys of which she had been deprived.'[10]

The legend of the vengeful wilis, with its macabre and sinister overtones, fascinated the Romantics, and in fact Heine had woven it into another of his works, *Les Nuits florentines*. The tale he told in the 'Second Night' would have made a deep impression on Jules' receptive imagination, if he read it. In it the story-teller recounts his obsession with a beautiful girl he first sees dancing on Waterloo Bridge with a small troupe of itinerant players – an old woman beating a drum, a performing dog and a dwarf. After they had moved on, he remained spellbound by the dancing of the girl. 'Was it some national dance from the South of France or Spain? These were recalled by the violence with which the dancer threw her body to and fro, and the abandon with which she tossed back her head like a bold bacchante . . . Her dancing had a spontaneous and intoxicating quality, something darkly inevitable or fatalistic, for she danced like Fate itself. Or was it a fragment of some age-old, forgotten pantomime? Or an expression in motion of some personal experience? Often the girl bent towards the ground with listening ear, as if hearing a voice calling to her. Then she trembled like an aspen leaf, twisted aside and threw herself into the wildest bounding. Again she bent her ear to the ground, listening more anxiously than before, then nodded her head, shuddered and stood awhile, upright, as if frozen, and finally made a motion *as if washing her hands*! Was it blood she was so carefully, and with such dread, washing away? While doing this she cast a glance, side-long, so pitifully imploring as to melt one's very soul.' It was surely not mere coincidence that this hand-washing motif was to be used as a salient feature in the choreography of Giselle's mad scene at the end of the first act.

After losing sight of the little troupe for some time, the teller of the tale chanced across the girl again in very different surroundings in Paris society, and at this point of the story Heine was reminded of the legend of the wilis as he discoursed on the beauty and charm of Parisian women. 'A Parisienne must be studied,' he wrote, 'not in the house, but in the salon, at soirées and balls, where she flutters freely with wings of gauze and silk under the joyous sparkle of crystal chandeliers. It is then that a burning joy in life and a longing for sweet sensuous oblivion are revealed, and she becomes almost terrible in her beauty and acquires a charm that intoxicates and thrills the soul. This thirst for the enjoyment of life, as if in the next hour death might snatch them from the sparkling fountain of enjoyment, or this fountain were to run dry – this haste, this fury, this madness of the Parisiennes, revealing itself most clearly at balls, always reminds me of the legend of the dead dancers whom we call wilis. These are young brides who have died before their wedding day, but still have the unsatisfied mania for dancing so deeply ingrained in their hearts that they rise from their graves at night and gather in bands on highways where at midnight they give themselves up to the wildest dances. In their bridal gowns, with wreaths of flowers in their heads and sparkling rings on their pale white hands, laughing terribly, irresistibly beautiful, the wilis dance in the moonlight ever more impetuously and wildly as they feel the short hour allotted to them drawing to an end and the moment approaching when they must descend again to the icy cold of the grave.'[11]

The impression which these readings from Heine had made on Gautier's soaring imagination had been reinforced by a poem by his friend Victor Hugo. It was called *Fantômes*, and had been written in 1828 and published the following year in the collection, *Les Orientales*. From its very opening lines it breathed the Romantics' obsession with the decay of beauty:

> Hélas! que j'en ai vu mourir de jeunes filles!
> C'est le destin. Il faut une proie au trépas.

'Death must have its prey,' and so profoundly poignant was the thought of youth and beauty for ever stilled that the poet sought their phantoms in the solitude of a forest:

> Doux fantômes! c'est là, quand je rêve dans l'ombre:
> Qu'ils viennent tour à tour m'entendre et me parler.

These sweet phantoms appeared to the poet's imagination like young girls dancing, an image which lingered in Gautier's mind and would find its expression in the second act of the ballet that was taking shape in his imagination:

> Elles prêtent leur forme à toutes mes pensées.
> Je les vois! je les vois! Elles me disent: Viens!
> Puis autour d'un tombeau dansent entrelacées;
> Puis s'en vont lentement, par degrés éclipsées:
> Alors je songe et me souviens.

Jules Perrot

One of these sweet phantoms, '*une ange, une jeune Espagnole,*' had died, not of a broken heart but from an excessive love of dancing:

> Elle aimait trop le bal, c'est ce qui l'a tuée.
> Le bal éblouissant! le bal délicieux!
> Sa cendre encor frémit, doucement remuée,
> Quand dans la nuit sereine, une blanche nuée
>   Danse autour du croissant des cieux.

Losing herself in the frenzy of the ball, the girl had danced, untiringly, until the first light of day, but stepping into the world outside, had shivered at the touch of the cold morning air on her shoulders. Death was claiming her '*pour danser d'autres bals,*' to dance at other balls beneath a pale full moon and clouds silver-fringed.

Gautier originally conceived the first act simply as Hugo's poem set into action. The curtain would rise on an empty ballroom, to which the wilis are drawn irresistibly in the hope of claiming a new victim. Shadowy phantoms that they are, they vanish at the approach of the mortal dancers, but when the ball is over and Giselle emerges into the chill morning air, tired but exhilarated, their queen places her icy hand on the girl's heart. It was a poetic conception, but lacking the dramatic interest that was conventionally necessary to hold the audience's attention for half an hour or more. After Saint-Georges had worked the idea into a detailed scenario, Gautier freely admitted that his own *dénouement* at the end of the first act did not compare with the 'touching and well acted scene'[12] that closed the act in its final form. He recognised, too, that he had not developed the character of Giselle as Saint-Georges did, and that his idea of introducing the wilis in the first act would have taken away the element of surprise that was achieved by their appearance in the second act. Even in its final form, though, the debt to Hugo's poem was easily recognised, and Janin and several other critics referred to it in their reviews.

For the second act, Gautier imagined a moonlit forest glade where, in the dead of night, the wilis foregather – not a ghostly band all dressed in white, but a colourful array of wraiths, including a gypsy girl, a Hungarian dancer, a bayadere and a *petit rat* from the Opéra. The wraiths would then be joined by the ghost of Giselle, who emerges from her grave to fulfil her tragic destiny of luring her lover to his death, the young man still believing, in their final embrace, that he can feel the beating of her heart.

The finished scenario preserved the two-scene structure that Gautier had envisaged. Giselle, a young peasant girl, lives with her mother Berthe among the vineyards on the hillsides of Thuringia. She is loved by Hilarion, a gamekeeper, and a handsome stranger, whom she prefers and knows only as Loys. She is innocently unaware that Loys is the young Duke Albert of Silesia in disguise – a deception that Hilarion begins to suspect when he observes his rival dismissing a respectful attendant – his companion Wilfrid –

before knocking on the door of Giselle's cottage. Hilarion interrupts the lovers' tryst, but Giselle refuses to listen to him, despite having dreamt of Loys preferring a beautiful lady to herself. A group of peasant girls comes to take Giselle to the vintage, and Giselle persuades them to dance with her. Her mother comes out of the cottage to chide her and warn her of the legend of the wilis. The sound of distant horns then announces the approach of a hunting party, and Loys, becoming suddenly uneasy, gives the signal for the girls to disperse and runs into the wood. Hilarion seizes the opportunity to slip, unseen, into Loys' cabin. The hunting party of the Prince of Courland and his daughter Bathilde arrives and is welcomed respectfully by Giselle's mother. Bathilde is struck by the beauty of Giselle, and learning that she is in love, makes her a gift of a necklace. The prince and his daughter are invited to enter the cottage, and Loys and Giselle, finding themselves alone, fall into each other's arms. To the sound of joyful music, the vintagers arrive, and Giselle is proclaimed Queen of the Vintage. But her happiness is short-lived, for Hilarion emerges from Loys' cabin, carrying a sword and cloak he has found there. He accuses Loys of duplicity. Sounding the horn that has been left hanging on a tree, he summons the hunting party. The prince and Bathilde are astonished to see Albert* in peasant costume. At the sight of Albert's discomfiture, Giselle realises that he is betrothed to Bathilde and that she has been deceived. Her mind gives way under the shock. In her madness she seizes Albert's sword, and before it can be snatched from her hands, she falls on to its point.** Her last movements then become more and more confused until, with a last despairing look at her lover, she falls dead in her mother's arms. Bathilde is in tears. Albert vainly tries to revive Giselle with caresses. He seizes his sword to kill himself, but is disarmed and led away in his grief.

* Albert or Albrecht? I have preferred to adopt the original French version of the name, as given in the published scenario and in general use during the period covered by this book. The variant of Albrecht came into use in England in the present century, being justified by Gautier's use of it in the article on *Giselle* in *Les Beautés de l'Opéra*.

** The cause of Giselle's death, whether it was due to shock resulting from her betrayal, or to a self-inflicted wound with Albert's sword, has been the subject of some controversy. While the scenario states that it is Giselle's mother who snatches the weapon away at the moment she falls on its point, Gautier's description of the action in *Les Beautés de l'Opéra* has Albert dashing the weapon aside, 'but not before a deep and fatal wound had pierced the young and innocent maiden's heart,' and this was no doubt how the incident was produced. It seems that the scenarists envisaged an accidental self-inflicted wound, but that the scene was produced, for dramatic effect, with split-second timing that left spectators in doubt as to whether Albert's action was in time. The importance of timing in this scene is confirmed by a report of a later performance when Petipa 'fluffed the dramatic movement with the sword.' (*Moniteur des Théâtres*, May 11th, 1842)

Jules Perrot

The second act is set by a lake in the heart of the forest, where Giselle has been buried. It is an accursed spot, for it is there, as Hilarion tells his comrades, that the wilis are reputed to dance their fatal round. The men depart hastily as midnight strikes. Then, in the mysterious light, Myrtha, Queen of the Wilis, appears and summons up her ghostly subjects. This night a new sister is to be admitted to the band. The flowers on Giselle's grave part, and the figure of Giselle appears. At a touch of Myrtha's wand, Giselle's shroud falls away, wings unfold from her shoulders, and she gives herself up to a wild dance. Some passing villagers are surrounded by the wilis, but being guided by a wise old peasant, manage to escape. Albert then appears, distraught at the loss of Giselle. As he weeps by the grave, he sees an apparition of Giselle; he tries to grasp her but his hands pass through the empty air. She vanishes, leaving him with the memory of a loving glance. He falls to his knees before the grave, and, as though moved by his sorrow, Giselle momentarily appears to him once again. He is about to flee when the wilis return. Concealing himself behind a tree, he sees the unfortunate Hilarion brought before the Queen and forced to dance to his destruction. Albert is then discovered, but as the Queen is about to condemn him to a similar fate, Giselle comes forward and stays her hand. She draws Albert towards the cross above the grave, which protects them against Myrtha's evil powers. The Queen forces Giselle to dance, and Albert is irresistibly drawn towards her. They dance together until his strength falters. Conscious that she is inexorably fated to be the instrument of his death, Giselle is powerless before the commands of the Queen. But Albert is saved, for a vestige of life still remains in him when the first rays of the sun penetrate the trees and the wilis vanish. Albert carries the form of Giselle to a grassy mound, and as he gently lays her down, flowers rise up to cover her.* At that moment Wilfrid leads Bathilde and her suite into the glade. Before disappearing from view, Giselle stretches out her arm in a gesture of entreaty, and as the curtain falls, Albert collapses into the arms of his companions, reaching his arms out to Bathilde.

Because the scenario was destined by its principal author expressly for Carlotta, it was not offered to the Opéra in the usual way. Instead the ground was carefully prepared to ensure that it was substituted for *La Rosière de Gand* to become Carlotta's first Paris creation. Perhaps indeed Gautier may have had an ulterior motive when selecting Saint-Georges and Adam to be his

---

* In modern productions Giselle disappears into her grave whence she had been summoned by the Queen of the Wilis. The original 1841 production was careful to show her sinking into the earth *on the other side of the stage*. She made her first entrance rising on a trap in front of the cross on the O.P. side, and vanished at the end by being laid down on a mound on the prompt side and covered by artificial flowers which, by some mechanism, closed over her body from the back and the front. (Scenery inventory, Archives Nationales, AJ^{13} 207.)

collaborators, for both of them were involved, in the same capacities, in *La Rosière de Gand* and the danger of one of them objecting to the desired substitution would therefore be greatly diminished. Jules and Carlotta were no doubt shown the scenario before anyone else, and it was Jules who was entrusted with the task of interesting Adolphe Adam, who already had several ballets to his credit, in composing the music. Jules, of course, knew him from his London visit of 1833, when he had danced to his music in Deshayes' *Faust*. They discussed the scenario in the fantastic surroundings of Adam's apartment, which was always filled with a profusion of flowers, plants and pets, and Adam was immediately captivated by what he recognised as a 'true ballet scenario.' Willingly falling in with the plot that was being hatched, he secured an appointment with Léon Pillet and had little difficulty in persuading him to suspend the preparation of *La Rosière de Gand* to give *Giselle* priority, arguing that *La Rosière de Gand* – 'our grand ballet,' as he described it[13] – could only benefit by being preceded by the success that Carlotta was bound to obtain in the more modest *Giselle*.*

Adam then threw himself into the task of composing the score with unusual enthusiasm. Working to a time limit always stimulated his imagination, and in the case of *Giselle* there was the added incentive that he was working with, and for, friends. 'I was on terms of very close friendship with Perrot and Carlotta,' he wrote, 'and the work took shape, so to speak, in my drawing-room.'[14] Years later, when he came to write his memoirs, he seemed to remember that he had written the music in about a week, but he was probably thinking of the time it took to sketch it out, for the autograph score, on which he recorded the date he completed each number, shows that the work took somewhat longer. The earliest date, April 11th, relates to the opening section ending with the 'Retour de la Vendange et Valse' in Act I, and the rest of that act was finished by the 28th of the same month. The *Courrier des Théâtres* reported on May 11th that the music for Act I was ready. By this time Adam was already working on Act II: the latest date inscribed on his autograph score was June 8th. The overture had been finished just a week earlier.[15]

Any hope that Jules may have had of producing *Giselle* for Carlotta were to be dashed, for when it was formally accepted for production in the first days of April, the task of staging it was given to Jean Coralli, the *maître de ballet en chef*, under whom Jules had worked during his years at the Porte-Saint-Martin. It would have been a very unusual, though not entirely unprecedented, departure for the Opéra to bring in a choreographer from outside, but judging from de Boigne's remark that the choice of Coralli had struck Jules like a 'bolt from the blue,'[16] he may have been expecting an exception to be made. However, he was not without influence at the Opéra, and the

---

* *La Jolie Fille de Gand*, as it was eventually called, became Carlotta's second creation at the Opéra, being first performed on June 22nd, 1842.

combination of Carlotta's wishes and representations made by Gautier and Adam resulted in an understanding that he would, without remuneration or acknowledgment, produce Carlotta's part in the new ballet. Coralli raised no objection to being assisted in this way. He was, as Maurice explained to his readers, a man of established reputation who could not be prejudiced by 'the presence of Perrot giving advice to Carlotta.'[17] There was also the pressure of urgency if the ballet was to be ready by May, as originally planned, and what with his other duties, he was happy, it seems, to be relieved of some of the burden of what he may then have regarded as a work of minor importance.

For the fortunes of *Giselle* this was just as well, for Coralli, though a very competent and experienced ballet-master, had produced very little that was memorable on its own merits. His greatest successes at the Opéra had been due more to the talent of Fanny Elssler, for whom they were created, than for any originality in their composition. He was above all a producer with a special skill for presenting a narrative in carefully worked out mime, with the interpolation of well designed dances. In the judgment of Charles de Boigne, he was 'a ballet-master of the old school. He *tutoyé*-ed and bullied his slaves. The rages of M. Coralli were legendary. He ruled his regiment of *danseuses* with his cane, and frequently exercised his *droit de seigneur*.'[18] *Giselle*'s poetic subtleties may not have been fully appreciated by him, but he was not unaffected by them and perhaps he was even stimulated by the energetic young choreographer working anonymously by his side. During the rehearsal period, Pillet wrote to the Marquis Aguado, his financial backer, that '*Giselle* seems destined to make a fortune. Coralli has discovered a freshness of ideas of which I never thought him capable.'[19]

Pillet may, of course, have been unaware of Jules' contribution to the new ballet, but happily for the record there was a more knowledgeable observer on the scene. August Bournonville had arrived in Paris in Jules' hour of need. For many a long hour Jules confided his troubles to his Danish friend, telling him of the crisis in his private life, and bemoaning the obstacles that stood in the way of his being engaged as a *maître de ballet* at the Opéra. It was his one ambition now to compose, and for that he had given up his classes completely. But Coralli and Mazilier were so firmly in possession, and with Albert there too, there seemed little prospect of his achieving his heart's desire. Bournonville did his best to console him by pointing out that conditions at the Opéra were far from ideal for a choreographer of his taste and creative force, particularly with the restricting practice of accepting scenarios from literary men, a practice not followed in Copenhagen, and his presence must have come as a godsend at the moment when Jules was in the throes of creating the rôle of Giselle for Carlotta and, at the same time, wondering whether it was all worthwhile.

Bournonville was on his way to Italy, but had decided to break his journey to see what was new in Paris. In his diary Jules' name appeared in about half the daily entries during the five weeks of his stay. The two men met nearly every day, sometimes at the Opéra, sometimes sitting over a drink at a café or taking a stroll along the Boulevard, where one day Jules greeted Donizetti and introduced him to his Danish friend. Bournonville was also a frequent visitor at the apartment which Jules shared with Carlotta. 'I am enjoying a pleasant acquaintance with Perrot and his wife, who likes me very much, and whose little girl reminds me of my own tots,' he told his wife in one of his letters home.[20] They took him to the theatre to see Lemaître in a 'detestable drama' called *Zacharie*, and on the two public holidays early in May – one, the King's fête-day and the other, celebrating the baptism of the Comte de Paris – they went to a concert in the Tuileries and watched the fireworks in the Champs Elysées.

Bournonville neglected no opportunity of adding to his professional experience. He went regularly to the Opéra, and was frequently there during the day, being particularly interested in the activities of Jules and Carlotta, as his diary bears witness:

April 14th. Opéra, benefit of Duprez . . . *Pas de deux*, Petipa and Carlotta Grisi (the latter excellent, strength, precision, grace, a great combination of qualities).
April 26th. To the Opéra, *La Juive* . . . *Pas de deux* by Carlotta Grisi with Mabille, danced like an angel, extraordinary lightness.
April 27th. To the Foyer of the Opéra, rehearsal of *Giselle*, talked to Adam.
April 30th. To the Opéra, *Don Juan*. Mabille & Carlotta Grisi, 2nd *pas* very good, great success. Walked in the Foyer with Albert and the painter Lepaulle. Congratulated Perrot at his home.
May 1st. Went to the Opéra to speak to Coraly (*sic*) about my début (evasive and unfriendly), saw Mme Perrot working.
May 5th. Opéra, *La Favorite* . . . Carlotta and Petipa's 1st *pas de deux*, divinely good.
May 9th. Opéra, *La Favorite*, Carlotta dancing, success.[21]

The following day Bournonville left Paris by the diligence that departed from the Rue Croix des Petits Champs at half past one, sitting on top with his friend, Edouard Carey. In the past weeks he had been entranced by what he had seen of Carlotta, and equally interested in the choreography that Jules was devising for *Giselle*. He was to miss the ballet's first performance by many weeks, but the experience of watching those early rehearsals made a lasting impression, and when he wrote his memoirs some years later he carefully recorded the contributions of those who were responsible for the ballet, not forgetting his friend Jules, whom he mentioned first of all. 'I have seen with my own eyes,' he wrote, 'how, for *Giselle*, Perrot rehearsed fragments from the main part of another ballet for Carlotta, while the idea for the action, which was taken from Heine's *Les Wilis*, came from Théophile Gautier, being arranged and revised by Saint-Georges, and finally staged – or, as one might say, composed – by the ballet-master Coralli.'[22] Unfortunately Bournonville did not specify from what ballet Jules was inserting passages into *Giselle*, but it is hardly conceivable that it would have been another choreographer's work, and probably it was one of his recent productons in Vienna, perhaps *Das Stelldichein*, which contained situations that could have been fitted very appropriately into the first act of *Giselle*.

As Adam put it in the account of the first performance he sent to Saint-Georges, Jules 'has a big finger in the pie,'[23] being responsible for all Carlotta's dances and scenes.[24] Taking this statement at its face value, Jules would have arranged Giselle's first entrance, her part in the *pas de deux*, and the mad scene in the first act, and in the second, Giselle's entrance and dance, her scene with Albert, and her part in the *pas de deux*. In addition his contribution must have included part of Albert's rôle, certainly in the *pas de deux* and his scenes with Giselle. How much Jules' contribution extended beyond this remains a matter for conjecture, but a news item that appeared in *Le Monde dramatique* suggests that he was very much in charge at the rehearsals.

'What caused Gautier the greatest astonishment during the rehearsals, which have been conducted with unparalleled speed,' ran this report, 'was the ferocity of Perrot's invention as a choreographer. Not wishing to abdicate his position completely, this inimitable dancer has married a pair of very graceful, supple, modest and obedient legs that go under the name of Carlotta Grisi. Thus Perrot dances on the legs of his wife, and since he was never afraid of risking his own, he is even more reckless in exposing those of his spouse. For her he has conceived some extremely dangerous exercises, and has made her perch on some fantastically high wires. For *Giselle* he invented some aerial "rails" that are projected with the velocity of an Indian arrow ... and by means of a certain see-saw mechanism, gave Carlotta the charming prospect of being quartered and blown into the air like an ammunition waggon if she made the slightest misjudgment of balance. In spite of her fright, the poor gazelle, trembling under her tulle skirt, was on the point of climbing on to the rail when the Director decided to try it out first on an ordinary mortal. A stage-hand was used for this perilous exercise, and despite every precaution bruised his forehead and broke his nose on the wing-flats. Perrot was still not satisfied, but the authors then declared that, speaking as philanthropists rather than scenarists, they wanted *Giselle* to have at least a second performance, and their desire could not be accomplished if Mme Perrot was to be allowed to perform this sort of *pas*. If such a thing was permitted the playbill might just as well announce: "Today, Monday, Mlle Carlotta will be guillotined at the Opéra," for the guillotine is less dangerous than the rails and quicker in its effect.'[25]

As summer advanced, the pressure mounted. Ciceri, who was responsible for the scenery, was an old hand, and was able to meet his deadline by augmenting his new sets with odd pieces he had painted for earlier productions. The cottages on the prompt side in Act I were taken from the stock of *La Fille du Danube*, while other flats and sky-cloths had been originally designed for the opera *Pharamond* in 1825 and had even been re-used before, in the naiad scene of Aumer's ballet, *La Belle au bois dormant*. He also borrowed a trolley from the *Flore et Zéphire* material to carry the Queen of the Wilis across the lake at the beginning of Act II.

The strain on Carlotta in the frantic weeks leading up to the first performance was considerable. She was indisposed for about a week in the beginning of June, and so as not to overtax her strength, a *pas* and about forty measures were cut from the first act just before the first performance. Adam's music had been ready in the middle of June, and was arousing great interest. François Habeneck, the principal conductor of the Opéra, who had read it and heard it in rehearsal, exclaimed that it was too good to be entrusted to an assistant conductor and that he would conduct the first performance himself. This was an exceptional honour, for Habeneck never conducted for the ballet. He was the most distinguished orchestral conductor in Paris. He was the founder of the Concerts du Conservatoire, for which he had created an orchestra that was renowned for its precision, and with these musicians he had introduced Beethoven's symphonies to Paris. At the time of *Giselle*, however, he was recovering from a serious illness, and when he appeared for the orchestral rehearsal, 'his strength failed to match his intentions and he had to give up half way through the first act,'[26] and the rehearsal had to be adjourned to the next day.

At the first performance on June 28th, 1841, Carlotta's twenty-second birthday, the ballet was received with rapturous applause. All anxieties about Carlotta's stamina were dispelled, the stage effects worked (even if the chief machinist's frantic commands in the second act were clearly audible), and Habeneck's conducting apparently offended only Adam himself. As the box-office receipts showed, the Opéra found itself with both a commercial and an artistic success on its hands.

It was the second act that produced the greater impression of the two. By comparison with the first act, whose rusticity and the interpolated peasant *pas de deux*, arranged by Coralli to music by Burgmüller, gave it an old-fashioned look, it attained a mystical quality that had never been achieved in ballet before, even though the act bore a superficial resemblance to the second act of *La Sylphide*. This magical illusion resulted from an almost perfect harmony of intention between those responsible for the production – scenarists, composer, choreographers and designers – thanks to whose efforts the principal interpreters, Carlotta and Lucien Petipa, who created the rôle of Albert, were able, as Gautier expressed it, 'to make this last act into a true poem, a choreographic elegy full of charm and tenderness. More than one spectator, expecting to see only *ronds de jambe* and *pointes*, was surprised to find his eyes filling with tears – something that does not often happen at the ballet.'[27]

The part Jules played in the success of *Giselle* was to be measured by

Jules Perrot

Carlotta's own triumph. Overnight she found herself hailed as one of the supreme ballerinas of her time, and for this she was indebted to her choreographer as much as to Gautier himself. In a phrase which Heine was to use after seeing the ballet a few months later, she stood out 'like an orange among potatoes,' transporting the public to a 'fairyland over which she reigns as queen' and conveying his conception of the elemental character of the wilis to perfection.[28] Jules had fashioned her rôle with love as well as genius, creating it with an economical vocabulary of classical technique that enabled her never to stray outside the character of her part. The entire rôle, even the mad scene at the end of the first act, was conceived in terms of dance and simple movement rather than the conventional mime or histrionic gesture to which most other choreographers of that time would have resorted. While it is impossible to be precise, much of the choreography of Giselle's part has probably been handed down with little change. Certainly some of the simple details have survived: the *glissades* with which Giselle and Loys move to the bench in the first act, the use of the *arabesque* as they blow kisses to one another, the choreographic leitmotiv of *ballonnés piqués* followed by *pas de basque* that characterises Giselle's rôle throughout the first act – in her first entrance at the end of the *pas d'amour* and in Giselle's scene with Bathilde – and, in the second act, the simple crossing of the hands over the breasts with palms inward, used for the wilis as well as for Giselle, to denote their spectral condition. It was a near-perfect translation into movement of Gautier's conception, capturing its essential qualities of melancholy and mystery. The only moment when technical virtuosity was admitted was in the variation in the first act – today no longer included, and long since forgotten – in which Carlotta was allowed to display the quick-silver speed and delicacy of her *pointe* work to a rippling melody on the flute.

Jules' choreography for *Giselle* was mainly concerned with Carlotta's part, but the rôle of Albert could not be wholly separated from it, either dramatically or choreographically. Having himself been a virtuoso performer, he must have arranged the male part as if for himself, giving it a prominence that was unusual for its time, and enabling Lucien Petipa to appear not only as a partner and a mime, but as a dancer in his own right.

Although Jules had been forced to agree that his name would not appear on the bills, his contribution to the choreography was no secret. Surprisingly the major critics who could review the ballet at length made no mention of him, as if they were part of some conspiracy of silence, but the critics of the theatrical papers were not so reticent. The *Moniteur des Théâtres* openly named him as the 'author, in large part, of the new ballet,'[29] giving him praise for 'the remarkable choreographic talent of which he gave proof in his wife's *pas*,'[30] while the theatrical paper, *La Sylphide*, considered his work to be infinitely superior to that of Coralli, which 'almost inevitably reminds one of the choreography of *La Sylphide*, *La Fille du Danube* and *La Tarentule*.'[31]

Seemingly Jules had accepted the anonymity of his contribution with certain vague assurances for the future on which he pinned his hopes, but his was a bitter triumph. For her reward Carlotta received a new contract on terms appropriate to her new status, but for Jules there was nothing. 'Envy and base jealousy'[32] had effectively kept him out, Coralli no doubt recognising all too clearly the threat to his own position that Jules could pose. Jules lacked the political cunning and the support to counter the built-in advantage of the man in possession, and not surprisingly no more was heard of his being invited to stage a ballet on his own.

Perhaps there was a modicum of consolation in the sympathy of the dancers themselves. They could appreciate his gifts much better than the dark-suited men who made the decisions, for the neglected male dancers in particular could remember the time, not long before, when Jules aroused the audience's enthusiasm by his own extraordinary efforts. Now, inspired by his presence, they began to recall his technique to penetrate what seemed almost to be a lost secret. Their efforts gave birth to a new word. 'The best male dancers of the Opéra,' reported Charles Maurice, 'are making a good resolution to assure their success by what they call "perrot-ing." A number of steps are known to have been invented by Perrot, who initiated many developments in this area of his art. It is not for want of trying that the vacancy caused by his departure has not been filled by his successors, and the verb "to perrot" – analagous to the phrase, "*poitriner*," as applied to singers – is being used to indicate following the new method.'[33] But the incentive was to vanish when Jules departed from the Opéra, and the new word slipped into oblivion.

8

On Trial at Her Majesty's

That winter Jules had come to terms with the disappointment of seeing the doors closed to him at the Opéra. Happily for his self-esteem, and his future, his services were in demand elsewhere, and a meeting with Benjamin Lumley, who had just taken over the management of Her Majesty's Theatre, the opera house of London, quickly resulted in an agreement. Lumley was in Paris planning his first season, which he wished to open with *Giselle*. He had undoubtedly seen the ballet for himself and taken the advice of his ballet-master, Deshayes, a man of vast experience who spent the winters between seasons in Paris and kept in close touch with developments at the Opéra. It took no unusual perception to discern the artistic quality of *Giselle* and, from the size of the audiences, its commercial potential, and Lumley was also astute enough to realise that the contributions of Jules and Carlotta were essential elements in its success. He therefore engaged them both, Carlotta for the period of her contractual leave during March and April, and Jules, who was free of commitments, for the whole season. Their names were prominently listed among the dancers in Lumley's prospectus, but Jules was engaged also as a ballet-master, and given the task of staging *Giselle*, with the assistance of old Deshayes, for the opening night of the season.

London may have appeared an unwelcome exile to an artist whose heart was in Paris, and indeed in the operatic firmament it occupied a relatively lowly place. Although it could boast of traditions that extended back for more than a century, the opera house in the Haymarket was managed from season to season on foundations that, financially at least, could only be described as unstable. Lacking any government or municipal subsidy, and unsupported by any civil list grant, its director could hardly hope to vie with the well-endowed opera houses on the continent. He had to shoulder the entire risk of a vast speculation, committing himself to an enormous expenditure in the anticipation of recouping himself, during a season of four or five months, from advance subscriptions paid by the aristocracy for the seasonal hire of their boxes and from the nightly box-office takings. In the past successive managers had been defeated by such conditions, and it was hardly surprising that the London opera house had established no great reputation for the splendour of its productions. However, the previous manager, Pierre Laporte, had unexpectedly died in the summer of 1841, and the succession of his assistant, Lumley, had aroused hopes for better times. Experienced observers were no doubt right to be sceptical, but for once they were to be proved wrong, for Lumley's enterprise would be crowned with success, achieving in the realm of ballet a prestige that was not exceeded even in Paris. Very soon Jules was to realise the benefits of hitching his fortune to the star of the new manager.

Benjamin Lumley was by birth a Jew. The son of a wealthy merchant who had immigrated from Canada, he had been educated at King Edward's School, Birmingham, and started his career as a solicitor. Having become a parliamentary agent, he was studying for the bar when Laporte happened to employ him on some legal business for the theatre. His services were so appreciated that he was persuaded to abandon his profession and join the staff of Her Majesty's, first to superintend the finances and later becoming Laporte's right hand man. To his surprise he was offered the management when Laporte died. He accepted, and now, full of energy and confidence, he was determined to overcome the difficulties that had defeated his predecessor. Combining firmness of character with a winning charm and a natural sympathy with artists, he was already justifying the faith of those who had supported him. And Jules, who had considerable experience of theatre managers, must have been quick to appreciate his exceptional qualities when, early in February 1842, he arrived in London for the rehearsals of *Giselle*.

He had already been communicating with Deshayes by letter about the production, which the old ballet-master was to supervise. This time, however, there was to be no difficulty about crediting Jules with the choreography, for it had been settled that the ballet would be announced as 'by MM. Deshayes and Perrot.' Nor was there any question of mentioning the name of Coralli. This may have indicated the relative unimportance, at least in Jules' mind, of his contribution, but it did not necessarily imply that Jules and Deshayes produced the ballet completely without reference to Coralli's production. With Coralli out of the way, however, Jules would have been freer to suggest changes in the production, and the London version was a revision, a second state, of a ballet on which he was to continue to work intermittently throughout his career.

Jules established a good working arrangement with Deshayes, to whom, on February 5th, the eve of his departure for London, he wrote a brief but witty letter:

My dear Monsieur Deshayes,

Thank you very much for what you say in your letter. I am, however, equally proud to be able to assure you that I shall do everything that you ask of me, and I am very obliged to you for this. It [i.e. Deshayes' letter] could not be unhelpful with a wretched

Jules Perrot

hare like me who loses his memory when he runs. I hope everything will be settled. I leave by carriage tomorrow at 3 o'clock. I go by way of Boulogne and count on going directly to the Court [by which he presumably meant Her Majesty's Theatre]. So farewell, my dear Monsieur Deshayes, Your affectionate and respectful servant,

Jules Perrot.[1]

With no performances interrupting the course of the rehearsals, the preparations for *Giselle* progressed smoothly, and were already well advanced when Carlotta arrived in London later in the month. With her came her family – her formidable mother and her sister, Ernesta, who was engaged for the opera – and they all settled in lodgings at No. 71 Opera Colonnade, alongside the theatre. A few days later another friend turned up – Théophile Gautier, who came to attend the final rehearsals and the first performance. '*Le bon Théo*' was already accepted almost as a member of the family, his adoration of Carlotta unconcealed and not unwelcome, but perhaps beginning to realise that his destiny lay not with her but with Ernesta.

This was Théo's first visit to England, and he was busily marshalling his impressions for an article in the *Revue des Deux Mondes* which would help defray the cost of his journey. How different it all seemed to Paris! A host of images jostled one another in his imagination: the forest of masts that met his eye in the port of London, the speed of the traffic and width of the London streets, the pollution of the air by the factories and the patina of black soot that covered buildings and monuments alike, the lugubrious emptiness of London on the Sabbath, the gin temples, the appalling poverty in the 'rookery' of St. Giles. All these, and many others, must have been subjects of discussion when they were not talking about the progress of the rehearsals. This, of course, was the subject they always came back to, as he did himself in his letters to his mother. 'I lunch in the English house [presumably where he was lodging] or with Vabre,' he wrote a few days before the season was to open, 'and I dine at Carlotta's. It is no more difficult than that. My ballet was rehearsed yesterday at Her Majesty's Theatre . . . It will be given on Saturday because Perrot has had a cramp in his leg.'[2]

Shortly after seven o'clock in the evening of March 12th, Gautier, with Ernesta and her mother, were to be found, one may imagine, in a box at Her Majesty's, surveying the auditorium as it slowly filled. His practised journalist's eye took in the scene around him – the dim lighting, the rather gloomy aspect of the boxes with their crimson hangings, the 'elegant, frail figures' and 'mannered graces' of the aristocratic ladies who filled them – but it was the stage itself that interested him most of all, different in so many ways from the familiar Opéra in Paris. He was surprised to find it so small and shallow, and was fascinated by the fore-stage that jutted out so far in front of the curtain that several boxes on either side actually abutted on the stage. The chorus and supers were forbidden to advance beyond the line of the proscenium so as not to obstruct the view of the gentlemen in the side boxes, but this rule did not apply to the leading singers. This produced some unusual effects, particularly when an act concluded with a death scene. Then some members of the cast had to be delegated to pick up the body and carry it back so that the star performer would not be left stranded in front of the curtain.

The programme on the opening night opened uninspiringly with Donizetti's opera *Gemma di Vergy*, but after the National Anthem had been sung by the whole company, the atmosphere changed as the strains of Adam's overture to *Giselle* rose from the orchestra pit under the baton of Jean-Baptiste Nadaud. An interesting cast had been assembled for the first London performance of this ballet. Carlotta would be repeating her interpretation of Giselle that, until then, had been seen only in Paris. Jules himself was to partner her as Albert, hoping that there would be no recurrence of the cramp. He had in fact taken the precaution to post notices craving the audience's indulgence, but *The Times* thought that nevertheless 'he sprang about with his usual rapidity . . . and his apology seemed altogether superfluous.'[3] The part of Hilarion had been learnt by Jules' old friend Antoine-Louis Coulon, for long a stalwart of the company at Her Majesty's and a personage there of some influence – the confidant of Deshayes, a close friend of the previous manager, Laporte, who had in fact died in his arms, and a teacher who was much in demand at his studio at No. 20 Brook Street. The part of Giselle's mother had been entrusted to Mme Copère, another member of long standing, while in the rôle of the Queen of the Wilis, a tall, reserved girl of sixteen, dancing under the name of Louise Fleury, was making her début. Louis Gosselin, whose sister Geneviève had been one of the earliest virtuosos of *pointe* work, was to play the Prince of Courland, and Augustine Proche was cast at Bathilde. The peasant *pas de deux*, which had been inserted in the first act of the Paris production, was omitted, no doubt because Jules considered it superfluous to the action.

The audience's response to the poetic quality of the ballet was reflected in the descriptions, some of considerable length, that appeared in the daily and weekly papers. The *Morning Herald* called it one of 'the most felicitous creations of its class.'[4] *The Times* remarked on Carlotta's 'joyous carelessness' (perhaps 'carefreeness' was meant) at the moment of her first entrance, when she bounded from her cottage on to the stage. This critic also spoke of the 'easy voluptuousness' that was such a pleasing characteristic of her dancing; 'her indolent fall into the arms of Perrot, without an effort to sustain herself, was one of her happiest achievements.' The mad scene, which in time was to develop into a histrionic highlight, was still in an embryo form, for Carlotta was not primarily a dramatic dancer. *The Times* described it as 'a short *pas seul*' preceding Giselle's death, and complimented the choreographer by saying that it was 'exceedingly well devised. The fling of the arms, the joyous movement was supernatural; it was an anticipation of the ghostly scene of the

Jules Perrot

second act.'⁵ In its original conception the purport of this scene was conveyed mainly in terms of dance; the strong mimetic overtones were to come later.

The rustic simplicity of the first act was found very engaging, but the second act made the greater impression. The materialisation of the wilis in the moonlit forest and the ensuing conflict between Giselle's love for Albert and the implacable urge to drive him to his destruction evoked a special response from the Victorians' obsessive fascination with death, particularly that of young people, a tragedy from which few families were then spared. Also, the conception of the wilis was ideally suited to ballet because, as *The Times* remarked, dance was used in the choreography not as 'the mere casual illustration of an independent drama' but as 'part and parcel of the drama itself.' Giselle's predicament of being forced against her will to be the instrument of her lover's death introduced a psychological insight that was something quite novel in ballet, while the concluding scene, when Giselle vanishes slowly from sight, after pausing for a last lingering look at the grieving Albert, was 'heart-rending'⁶ and hauntingly poetic.* Everything accorded perfectly with the romantic mood that had been established so successfully during the act, and the audience was left spell-bound by an image that was 'melancholy as a souvenir of death, but beauteous as a dream of love.'⁷

Both stage designer and composer had played their part in this triumph. Although lacking the resources that the Paris Opéra could command, Lumley had on his pay-roll a highly skilled designer, William Grieve, whose sets for *Giselle* were, in a more modest way, as evocative as those that Ciceri had produced in Paris. Gautier noticed the excellence of the lighting – in marked contrast to the niggardly illumination of the auditorium – and was enchanted by the effect of the sunrise that brought the ballet to its close. Adam's music also made a favourable impression, the erudite music critic, H.F. Chorley, finding it superior to any of his earlier ballet scores and praising it for its fund of melody, the liveliness of the dance tunes, and its orchestration which, 'if somewhat coarse, is sparkling and provocative (a first requisite in dance music).'⁸

Gautier stayed in London long enough to see the first two performances,** and returned to Paris in a state of euphoria. '*Giselle* had an enormous success,' he told his mother in a letter. 'According to the Director it is the greatest

---

* It is probably too much to infer from the descriptions of the ballet in the press, which conclude without exception with Giselle sinking slowly into the bed of flowers, that Bathilde's reappearance at the end was cut in this London production.

** Queen Victoria attended the second performance, but she may have seen Henri Desplaces as Albert. The *Morning Post* (March 16th, 1842) reported that Jules had fully recovered and 'bounded about as if . . . made of india rubber,' but the *Courrier des Théâtres* (March 20th) reported that Desplaces took over the rôle at this performance.

ballet success he has ever seen. I have been pampered, hugged, coddled, stuffed in London in the most charming fashion by Carlotta, Ernesta Grisi, Mother Grisi and Perrot – they did not want to let me go.'9

Giselle was presented at eleven successive performances – nine times in its entirety, and on the last two occasions the second act alone. The omission of the first act made room, on the first occasion, for the *pas de deux* from *La Favorite*, which Carlotta danced with Henri Desplaces, and on the second, which was the evening of her benefit, for a revival of *Le Pêcheur napolitain* with its rousing tarantella.

Both Lumley and Carlotta had hoped she would be allowed to remain in London beyond the expiration of her leave of absence from Paris, but the Opéra was obdurate and she had to be replaced at Her Majesty's, during the few weeks that remained before Cerrito was due to arrive, by Marie Guy-Stéphan. Whether because of the haste which this necessitated, or because of his failing powers, the two pieces that Deshayes produced for Guy-Stéphan were unremarkable. In one of them, an inconsequential divertissement called *La Fête des nymphes*, Jules partnered her in a *pas de deux*, and in the other, a wretched ballet version of Auber's opera, *La Fiancée*, he accompanied her in a Spanish number, *Las Boleras de Cadiz*.

The performances during these two weeks lacked lustre, as if everyone's thoughts were on the imminent reappearance of Fanny Cerrito. Cerrito, a Neapolitan ballerina possessing great physical charm and an infectiously buoyant style, was now, at the age of twenty-five, at the peak of her powers. She had conquered London two years earlier at a single bound, so to speak, gaining immense popularity among the masculine section of the fashionable public, led vociferously by the swells who occupied the omnibus boxes that flanked the fore-stage. At their first meeting Jules and Cerrito no doubt observed one another with professional curiosity, he sizing up her personality and style of dancing as a sculptor might examine a model, and she, aware no doubt of his contribution to *Giselle*, regarding him not only as a prospective partner but also as a creator who might serve her as he had served Carlotta.

Cerrito had pretensions to choreography herself, and for her first appearance on May 14th she revived her divertissement, *L'Elève d'Amour*. Jules partnered her on this occasion, accompanying her in a *pas de trois* and in one of her most celebrated numbers, the *pas de quatre* from *Le Lac des fées*. Clearly each passed the other's test, for they were almost at once involved in a closer collaboration – the production of a new ballet, *Alma*, that was scheduled for performance in June.

The theatre was a hive of activity during the next few weeks, every effort being concentrated on this new work. Deshayes was in nominal charge of the production, with instructions to arrange Cerrito's part so that the main pantomimic burden would fall on Jules, while Cerrito and Jules were entrusted with the task of arranging the principal *pas*, a decision to which Deshayes,

Jules Perrot

who was growing old, raised no objection. Michael Costa, the musical director who conducted for the opera, had produced an impressively orchestrated score that was full of lively melodies. The experienced William Grieve was responsible for the scenery, in collaboration with Mr. Hall who was to make the properties, Mr. Sloman who was in charge of the mechanical effects, and the Misses Glover and Bradley, the costumiers.

Who was primarily responsible for the scenario of *Alma, ou la Fille de feu* history has not recorded, but it may be significant that the idea of a supernatural creature coming to earth to be tempted by the fatal power of human love had been used not long before by Jules himself in *Der Kobold*. Also, his own part was so ideally suited to his personality and style that it is difficult to avoid the conclusion that it was the fruit of his own imagination. This was the evil genius, Periphite, who accompanies Alma, the daughter of fire, on her mission to the world to enchant mankind, and who has promised himself to bring about her downfall by encouraging her to yield to the temptation of love. In a series of brilliant scenes, their travels encompass a town in Germany, a glittering ballroom in France, and finally the city of Granada during the struggle between the Spaniards and the Moors. At the ball Alma bewitches the knight Emazor, who is a Moorish prince in disguise. In the final scene Emazor vanquishes the Spaniards and, revealing his true identity, seizes the crown. Alma finally yields to his passionate declarations, but as she mounts the steps of the throne to become his queen, her fate is accomplished and she is turned to stone.

At the first performance on June 23rd, the critic of *The Times* was fascinated by Jules' conception of Alma's companion. The sinuous quality of his movements reminded him of the acrobatic dancer, George Wieland, and on a different level, of the sly but elegant Mephistopheles in Moritz Retzsch's well-known engravings for Gœthe's *Faust*. Jules presented the rôle, not as a stock demon of melodrama, but as 'a curious sort of gentleman . . . looking something like a skinned eel, and threading his way among things in a very eel-like fashion,'[10] with a layer of mordant humour that threw into relief Cerrito's naturally happy presence.

But even more striking was the manner in which he brought out the relationship between the two characters in the choreography of the *valse de fascination* which he arranged in the second scene. It was undoubtedly derived from the waltz scene which Frédérick Lemaître had performed many years before in *Faust* at the Porte-Saint-Martin, but Jules had developed the idea in a manner that was entirely his own. He produced it as a *pas d'action* in the literal sense of the term, taking its place not as an interpolated dance but as an ingredient of the narrative. By a nicely balanced combination of dance and expressive gesture he managed to convey the hypnotic power of Alma's charms and Periphite's influence over her so effectively that it was remembered as the most conspicuous feature of the ballet.

On Trial at Her Majesty's

Perrot, your name is punless, or, if pun
　　Could over-take it, you would go to pot,
And we should speak of your decay as one
　　Who, like a sheep was ruined quite, *per rot*.

Whereas, no ruin e'er can catch you, for
　　You tread with steps that much too lightly go;
And, as you raise your pretty freight, *O lor!*
　　You raise your eye, your leg, your *Cherrytoe!*

And she is wondrous fair with whom you fly;
　　For when you dance it is but flight, I ween:
Man sees you with the *apple* of his eye,
　　And says, " Sure such a *pair* was never seen !"

Jules Perrot and Fanny Cerrito in the valse de fascination *in* Alma. (Illustrated London News, *August 17th, 1842*)

Jules Perrot

The Times devoted many lines of its review to a description of it. 'The *valse de fascination*,' observed its critic, 'when the strange little demon and the daughter of fire lure the German maidens to dance, was composed by Perrot, and the conception is worthy of a Retzsch. Perrot has made a finished portrait of the frolicsome Mephistopheles; the saucy turn of his hat, the insolent strut, the half-insolent, half-terrific look of defiance which he casts round him, produce an effect which the odd expression of his features tends greatly to heighten. There is a fine want of courtesy in his mode of asking the three reluctant damsels to dance, in his holding up his finger with a sneer of superiority, fully aware that come they *must*. But his power is incomplete without the aid of his fair coadjutor, the *fille de feu* – Cerrito. He must invite her to join in the temptation, and then it is irresistible. Here the *pas* brings out very prominently an element in Cerrito's dancing, with which the public have been less familiar. It is not the exhibition of physical force, but power subdued down to its easiest expression. Here is a sort of quiet witchery; it is playful yet malicious – almost demoniac. Nothing can be more perfect as a dramatic *pas*, both in its idea and the delicacy with which it is worked out.'[11]

There was also another level of achievement. At a time when male dancers had to struggle to win favour, Jules demonstrated how a striking portrayal of a male part could be given a prominence and a meaning that conquered prejudice. Here his ugliness of feature was a decided advantage, for one criticism that could never be levelled at him was that he was effeminate. 'Perrot,' *The Times* was to record at the end of the season, 'has infused a new spirit into ballets, and threatens to scowl away the unmeaning herd of gentlemen in white tunics who are usually such awful "bores." Perrot is a true artiste, a real genius, there is a meaning in his dancing. If he could paint his own Mephistopheles – so we call his devil in *Alma* – he would be immortalised. Let M. Claudet secure him with the daguerreotype.'[12]

The other *pas* which Jules contributed to *Alma* was of a more conventional form, a *pas de trois* in which the personal attributes of each of the ballerinas he partnered were skilfully exploited. *The Times* was impressed by this too, finding it 'excellently adapted for the display of those rising *danseuses*, Guy-Stéphan and Fleury, the former bounding along with energy and animation, her face beaming with excitement, the tall figure of the latter springing with equal force, yet apparently less excited, and more calmly trusting to her physical strength.'[13]

To Lumley the triumph of *Alma* in the first year of his management was immensely encouraging, and he basked in the contented reflection that 'the majestic bark of Her Majesty's Theatre seemed to be floating down the agitated stream towards its haven of rest, with favouring breezes, and with gilded banners.' These effusive words were the measure of his gratitude to Jules, both for his contribution to *Alma*'s success and for resolving the problem of the succession to the ageing Deshayes, who was not to be re-engaged for 1843. 'It was,' wrote Lumley in his memoirs, 'the talent displayed by Perrot in the composition and execution of the *pas de fascination* in this ballet which induced me to fix on him as my future *maître de ballet*.'[14]

Three weeks later Jules gave further proof of his skill, arranging, for his benefit performance on July 14th, a sparkling divertissement called *Une Soirée de Carnaval*. The curtain rose on a colourful, bustling scene of a ballroom alive with revellers in carnival costume. Gliding through their midst, wrapped in a black domino, appeared Cerrito, exuding an air of mystery that drew admiring glances from the menfolk. Then, suddenly throwing off her cloak, she darted forward in a superb Andalusian costume, to be joined by Jules in a *Double Cachucha*, a variation on Fanny Elssler's celebrated solo. 'A sort of introduction to this dance was exceedingly graceful,' described *The Times*. 'Cerrito appeared intimidated at the impetuosity of Perrot; she shrank back; it was as if she would avoid the fascinations of the dance. At length it seems as if the voluptuous character of the music has its effect upon her. She is forced to glide into the dance, and at last resigns herself entirely to its influence. Then, when the cachucha really does begin, it is an inspiration; she is a creature of fire. It is in the Spanish spirit of defiance that she and Perrot dance *at* each other. The fury, as it were, of this part of the dance is beautifully relieved by those exquisite attitudes, where Cerrito falls on one knee, and leans back with languishing expression, while Perrot stands over her.'[15]

This was followed by the *Cracovienne* – another of Elssler's dances – which Guy-Stéphan performed. Then a quieter note was struck by a *pas de deux* by Louise Fleury and Desplaces, giving Jules and Carlotta time to change their costumes for the galop from Deshayes' ballet, *Beniowsky*. Finally the corps de ballet and the other principals came on for the grand galop, whirling round the stage in a kaleidoscope of colour. According to the newspaper announcements, the intention had been to include a *Furlana* by the corps de ballet and also the original *tarantella*, danced by Jules and Guy-Stéphan, but these two dances were omitted to keep the divertissement to a manageable length.

The *Double Cachucha* was not, however, to everyone's liking 'Cerrito spoiled the *Cachucha*,' complained the *Morning Post*, 'by allowing Perrot to jump about with her . . . The national characteristic of the dance is annihilated by this desecration, and we trust that for the future the male dancer may not be permitted to obtrude his *pas* upon us, while Cerrito is bounding about the stage like a gazelle.'[16] Whether by design or not, it was omitted from the programme on July 30th, when the two most famous exponents of this dance – Fanny Elssler, who had created it, and Pauline Duvernay, who had been the first to dance it in London – both happened to be in the audience, Elssler thin and tired from her exhausting triumph in America, and Duvernay, in contrast, putting on weight comfortably now that she had retired to enjoy the material benefits of living with a millionaire.

The last and most important benefit of the season was Cerrito's, which the honour of the omnibus boxes demanded should be marked by a display of that unrestrained adulation which Lumley scornfully referred to as Cerritomania. To stand by the ballerina's side during such an outburst was a real trial for a self-respecting male dancer, and Jules found it impossible to assume the proper attitude of servility without inwardly viewing the proceedings with a wry detachment. In an unguarded moment he allowed his sense of fun to obtrude. Bouquets were falling fast at the ballerina's feet, and she was gathering them up and pressing them to her heart with a show of gratitude and delight when an ardent youth leaned forward from one of the boxes and flung an enormous bundle of flowers that 'fortunately missed Cerrito's head, but fell on the stage at her feet with a *whap* that made her start. Perrot, with some difficulty, lifted this mighty offering in his arms, and poised it with an air of ludicrous solemnity over Cerrito's brow, that threw the whole house into fits of laughter, to the infinite annoyance of the disconcerted *danseuse*.'[17]

When Jules returned to Paris after the London season closed, he found the Opéra still giving *Giselle* to packed houses. He may have seen a new Giselle, for Elisa Bellon gave two performances in September which, if they lacked the special magic that Carlotta brought to the part she had created, at least showed that it was capable of more than one interpretation. For she was unusually musical, she danced with a gentle grace that made up for her lack of technical brilliance, and she gave an intelligent rendering of the mad scene that earned her 'unanimous applause.'[18]

This was a difficult time for Jules, for during the summer Carlotta's affair with Lucien Petipa had become an open secret. With his mane of flying hair and dark, handsome features, Petipa was a strikingly attractive young man, and to many it had seemed almost inevitable that his professional partnership with Carlotta would develop into a more intimate relationship. While Jules was in London they were reported to be 'inseparable.'[19] On one occasion, while they were dancing in *La Jolie Fille de Gand*, a clumsy movement by Petipa undid the hook on Carlotta's skirt, which she hurriedly had to refasten in view of the audience, an incident, reported the *Moniteur des Théâtres*, 'that gave rise to some ribald remarks in our vicinity. We do not know whether they were well founded. We merely report what we heard.'[20] A few days later the same paper published a more significant item that must have wounded Jules' feelings if he had read it. 'It is said that Mme Perrot is planning to change her name in the immediate future, and to prepare herself for this, she is more particular than ever about calling herself *Mademoiselle* Carlotta Grisi. We will not go into greater detail, which has no bearing on choreography. We prefer to wait and see. We refuse to believe in ingratitude, and will only speak when we have proof before us.'[21]

The final break was imminent. At about this time Carlotta and her mother moved out of the apartment at No. 42 Rue Richer, which had been Jules' home too, and took another apartment at No. 13 Rue de Trévise, where they were already installed when Carlotta signed her next contract with the Opéra the following May. For Jules it was the end of an idyll, but he could not have been unprepared for the blow, which he accepted with exemplary resignation. He harboured no grudge against Carlotta, and in the years to come would continue to work for her with undimmed devotion.

At the end of that year another sorrow was to follow. His old teacher, Auguste Vestris, who had followed his career with an almost paternal solicitude, sickened from a chill and died in his lonely apartment in the Rue des Martyrs. Jules, who had loved the old man dearly, was so heart-broken that Charles Maurice thought 'anyone would have taken him for the deceased's son.'[22] He was the ideal choice to deliver the funeral oration, for of all the young dancers who had passed through the hands of the old master he more than any other had caught something of that irresistible yet inimitable artistry that very old men could still recall. If anyone was Vestris's artistic heir, it was he, for he had established himself as 'the true model' of the *demi-caractère* style that his master had virtually created, excelling, as the teacher Adice recorded, 'instinctively and with equal perfection in *terre-à-terre*, feats of strength and *grand ballon*.'[23] So it was both appropriate and just that it should have been Jules who stepped forward on that cold winter's day in the Montmartre cemetery to review, with all proper solemnity, 'the great saltatory talents and Christian virtues of the deceased.'[24] There was also something very symbolic about the occasion. It was as if the torch of tradition was being passed on, to burn with renewed brilliance in the years that lay ahead.

9

The Turning Point

For Jules and Carlotta the end of their intimate personal relationship marked a turning point in both their lives. In Jules' case it brought a change of direction, with the focus of his activity shifting from Paris to London and his choreographic genius coming into flower with the opportunities that Lumley afforded him at Her Majesty's Theatre. The transformation of the dancer into the choreographer, for which he had been preparing himself for more than a year, was to compensate for the emotional shock he had received. For Carlotta, on the other hand, the break seemed to have more serious consequences. It meant perhaps the end of innocence, and brought on an inner stress that those who saw her dance could hardly fail to notice. The *Coureur des Spectacles* became openly critical of her performances, referring to failing powers and technical shortcomings. Its editor, Charles Maurice, doubtless relied on advice from outside when treating of such details, and it is possible that some of Jules' own feelings came to his ear and transferred themselves to the printed page. Maurice certainly seems to have taken sides, if only to suggest that Carlotta was the loser by recalling the imperfections of her technique when she had first appeared in Paris, at the Renaissance, and how Jules had 'transformed an unpolished stone into a diamond.'[1]

Now that their ways had parted, Jules was making plans for the London season while Carlotta was becoming involved at the Opéra in the preparation of a new ballet. Entitled *La Péri*, its scenario was being written by Gautier, this time unaided by a collaborator. However, in his determination to make his offering to Carlotta as perfect as possible, the poet needed advice, and it was an indication that the two dancers had separated on amicable terms that he felt able to turn to Jules, perhaps even hoping that he would make a positive contribution to the choreography. The peri of the title was to appear to the hero in a dream, and remembering, from the rehearsals of *Giselle*, Jules' flair for designing novel stage effects, Gautier sought his opinion on how to give this scene a really spectacular impact. 'At this point,' he explained, 'there has to be arranged a dance such as only you can design. The peri comes up quite close to him, as if to tempt and provoke him, but when he moves towards her, she hurls herself a great distance away from him, with a single bound.'[2] Jules' response to this request has not survived; he certainly did not arrange a *pas*, but he may have suggested the sensational leap with which Carlotta made her first entrance in the finished ballet, launching herself from a raised platform in the wings to fall, dead-weight, into Lucien Petipa's arms. What Gautier had asked for, a great backward leap, was somewhat different, and although this did not find its way into *La Péri*, it registered in Jules' mind to be used a few months later for Ondine's disappearance into the water in the first scene of *Ondine*.

Jules' presence was meanwhile required in London, where Lumley was impatiently waiting to discuss plans for the forthcoming season. The manager had spent the winter in Italy and Paris negotiating engagements with singers and dancers, and now, in the few weeks before the theatre opened, there were new productions to be planned, set on stage and rehearsed. Jules could not have imagined the demands that were to be made on his time, for never was a choreographer worked so hard as he was to be during his seasons in London. Ballet was to be featured more prominently than ever before. There was a hope that Fanny Elssler would grace the opening night, returning to the stage for the first time since her return from America, but because there was some doubt whether her agent was acting with her authority, Lumley had taken the precaution of engaging a ballerina from Paris, Adèle Dumilâtre, who had created the rôle of the Queen of the Wilis in *Giselle* and would be appearing in London for the first time. As in the previous year the season would reach its climax with the arrival of Cerrito in May. Also engaged was a young male dancer who had the reputation of being as astonishing a virtuoso on the violin as on his feet, Arthur Saint-Léon.

Jules now began to work with a composer who was to remain his musical collaborator throughout the rest of his career. Cesare Pugni was a man after Jules' own heart, dedicated to composing for the ballet, possessing a vast fund of experience and a selfless understanding of a choreographer's needs, and willing to produce music to order and adjust it at short notice to meet requirements during the rehearsal period. Some eight years older than Jules, Pugni had gained his early experience at the Scala, Milan, where he had served some of the most celebrated choreographers working in Italy, including Gaetano Gioja and Louis Henry. He had risen to a post of some eminence there, but he had left Milan somewhat precipitously and for the past ten years had been living in straightened circumstances in Paris, where Lumley – or possibly, Jules himself – had found him. This coming together of choreographer and composer was to have fruitful consequences for them both. Pugni was rescued from obscurity and poverty, while Jules gained a valued collaborator brought up in the atmosphere of a great opera house and possessing an unusual insight into the art of constructing a ballet in the Italian manner, with its reliance on strong dramatic action conveyed by specialised mimes.

Jules Perrot

Pugni's first task at Her Majesty's was to provide the music for the grand ballet that was planned for Adèle Dumilâtre's first appearance in London on the opening night of the season – a balletic version of Victor Hugo's novel, *Notre Dame de Paris*. The original idea for this ballet, which was to be given the title of *La Esmeralda*, had come from Lumley himself. Jules' first reaction had been to dismiss it as impracticable, but Lumley had persisted and gradually Jules had come round to seeing its possibilities. Reducing the vast panorama of the novel to the dimensions of a ballet scenario was a formidable undertaking, in which he must have been grateful for Lumley's help. 'I frequently sat up with him the greater part of the night,' the manager remembered, 'in order to assist and encourage him in his labours,' and Pugni 'was always present ready to seize any idea that might suggest itself for a "situation" or a *pas*.'[3]

Not surprisingly the plan to produce *La Esmeralda* in the space of little more than a month proved over-sanguine and in the event the ballet was to be deferred until the following year. It would not have been presented at the opening performance on March 11th in any event because it so happened that Fanny Elssler was available after all and it was she, not Dumilâtre, who had to be featured in the concluding ballet. The young French dancer, therefore, had to take second place, making her London début in a divertissement of minor importance called *L'Aurore*, inserted between two of the acts of Donizetti's opera, *Adelia*. When the curtain rose William Grieve's set was hidden behind banks of property clouds and the stage was dimly lit. A group of huntsmen, led by Jules, emerge from the shadows. The outer clouds were then drawn off, revealing Dumilâtre as Dawn reclining gracefully on a small white cloud at the back. The lighting was turned up to show the colours of Grieve's backcloth, a bright seascape with some dark arched rocks in the foreground. This skilfully contrived introduction of the new ballerina was matched by what followed when, in a few brief *enchaînements*, Jules showed off the essence of Dumilâtre's style as she gracefully rose to her full height and then seemed to take flight, skimming across the stage with the ease and rapidity of a bird. 'So ethereal was the effect,' described *The Times*, 'that she almost looked transparent.' After summoning her attendants – seven soloists in light blue and the rest of the corps de ballet in white – she came face to face with the chief huntsman. Love at first sight was the idea behind their mime scene, with 'the youth offering the goddess a bouquet and she teasingly withdrawing it, a succession of graceful groups being obtained by the various modes in which this was done.' The huntsmen then pair off with Dawn's blue-clad attendants, and the three principal soloists – Mlle C. Camille, Elisa Scheffer and Adeline Plunkett (a newcomer to London and disguised under the name of Planquet) – performed a *pas de trois*, Scheffer 'displaying great energy and vigour' and Camille ('clever little Camille,' as *The Times* affectionately called her), 'the best of the three, executing with the most perfect neatness, and doing wonders with her slight figure.'[4] This was the prelude to the *grand pas de deux*, the moment for which everyone, from Jules and Dumilâtre to the eager audience across the footlights, were waiting.

Suddenly, while Jules was performing one of his most graceful steps, a sound was heard like the crack of a whip. He stopped in his tracks, his features twisted in an expression of great agony. Holding his leg off the ground with his two hands, he hopped towards the wings, where several of the corps de ballet girls rushed forward and almost carried him out of sight. The curtain fell amid a stunned silence. The Earl of Pembroke and his doctor, who happened to be in the audience with him, hurried backstage to attend the injured dancer. The sight of Jules in such pain had cast a gloom over a performance that had opened so propitiously, and when the curtain rose for the continuation of the opera, Lumley had to reassure the audience by reporting on Jules' condition. There was little he could say, for it was too early to judge the extent of the injury.

Happily the injury was not quite as serious as had been feared, and later that evening the two doctors who attended Jules were able to issue a reasonably reassuring bulletin:

> We have examined the leg of M. Perrot, and are glad to find the tendon Achilles safe; but it is probable some fibres of a minor muscle have given way, and so to have caused the sudden incapability of supporting himself.
>
> John S. Gascoin, Thomas Stone M.D.[5]

For Adèle Dumilâtre, whose great moment had been so brutally interrupted, this accident came as a double blow. The abrupt termination of *L'Aurore* had robbed her of an ovation, and the public had to wait until the second performance three days later to judge her properly. For that occasion the divertissement had to be adjusted, the huntsmen being removed entirely and a new *pas de trois* being substituted for the *pas de deux*. The spectacular conclusion of Dawn departing in a chariot amid a burst of pink fire* remained, and Dumilâtre came forward to receive a creditable ovation, for Jules had done well by her in his choreography, showing off her strong technique and turning her unusual height to good advantage by devising passages that emphasised the natural elegance of her line.

Her greatest disappointment was to lose the opportunity of creating the grand ballet that had been conceived for her, *La Esmeralda*. The requirements of Fanny Elssler may have necessitated this in any event, but Jules' enforced absence was the deciding factor in postponing this ballet to the next season. Although his injury had proved less serious than at first feared, his

---

* Coloured fire was a theatrical effect in constant demand in the nineteenth century. Fundamentally it was a firework used in a controlled manner, the colour depending on the choice of chemicals that were ignited.

activities were very considerably curtailed. Even a month later, he could only put his injured foot to the ground to take a few steps in his room, and he had to go everywhere by carriage. The production of a new ballet involving the choreographer in continual physical activity was out of the question in such circumstances. However, Jules was not completely out of action, for he gallantly turned up, presumably hobbling on crutches, to coach Fanny Elssler in *Giselle* and to produce the framework of a divertissement for her benefit performance.

Under his guidance Elssler was to add dramatic meaning to the rôle of Giselle so effectively that it was to be her interpretation rather than Carlotta Grisi's that became the model to which future generations looked back. She came to the ballet completely fresh, for she could not have seen it in performance. She had returned to Europe the previous summer too late to see any of Carlotta's performances in London; the ballet was not in the repertory when she was in Vienna, and she avoided visiting Paris, where she would have been in danger of being served with legal proceedings issued against her by the Opéra for breach of contract.

When she appeared in the rôle for the first time on March 30th, 1843, the audience was overwhelmed by the power of her portrayal. 'We had expected a remarkable execution,' wrote *The Times*, 'but certainly we did not anticipate such a *chef d'œuvre*, such a grand conception and perfect execution.'[6] The *Morning Post* echoed this view. 'To compare the performance of Fanny Elssler with that of last season would be doing her a gross injustice. She breathes a passion and a beauty into the village girl which would have been vainly emulated by her predecessor in the character.'[7] By shifting the emphasis of the ballet to the first act Elssler gave it a different balance. Her interpretation contrasted sharply with the impression that Carlotta gave of 'melancholy sweetness' and 'fleeting unearthly sentiment.' Her mad scene was a *tour de force*. The shock at realising Albert's deception was dagger-sharp. 'A face beaming with joy is one moment rigid with the deepest grief,' described *The Times*, 'the mouth is fixed, the eyes have lost their lustre. From this position of despair she recovers, but it seems that she has a sort of intermediate existence – that she has half become a "wili," while yet wearing a mortal frame. She is approaching towards an ethereal state, and her hands move swimmingly along the air. The last act in which the mere mortal shows itself is where the unhappy girl flings herself weeping upon the ground. But from this paroxysm she is soon aroused; she dances with something like joy, but it is joy of a terrible character; the lips smile while the eyes are fixed. There is something of a cold malice in her mirth. While dancing she dies, and the drop scene falls to rise again and introduce the audience to the "Wilis," the Queen of whom raises Giselle from her tomb, and makes her one of their body. She appears worn with sorrow, the grief of earth adheres even to her shade, but at a touch of the Queen's wand wings spring out of her shoulders, and she whirls round with a maniac delight. But the task of luring her lover to destruction she cannot bear, and while she makes him join in the fascinating *pas de deux* she is in despair at his approaching fate. The steps she executes are wonderful – *Elsslerisch* steps – exhibitions of force and skill such as are in the power of none but Fanny, and throughout them all there is the cold unwilling countenance. It is the attractiveness of terror, and it seems as if the lover were led on by something that should repel him; the farce is unearthly; the very dance has something strange and chilling in its voluptuousness; and yet on he must go. This Giselle of Fanny Elssler's is a work of the greatest genius.'[8]

This new dimension which Elssler gave to *Giselle* under the guidance of its choreographer prompted some interesting reflections from the music critic of the *Morning Post* (probably C.L. Gruneisen) on the significant development of the ballet department under the new ballet-master. 'We have always been jealous of the influence of the ballet,' he began, 'and at all events felt quite convinced that dancing addressed itself to the senses and not to the mind. But now *c'est fini*, we acknowledge that such dancing as was displayed in *Giselle* is an affair of art, poetry, nay, even genius. This is owing to a total revolution in the empire of Terpsichore. Formerly dancers' evolutions were as precise as those of soldiers – in their feats they bounded and leapt in the perpendicular line. How greatly did his contemporaries eulogise the perpendiculars of the great Vestris . . . when at his début he made his three bounding *entrechats* amidst a thunder of applause – which by the bye was not diminished by his disappearing at the the third bound through a trap-door on the stage the last ghost that had descended had left open. Now dancers have discovered that the line of beauty in dancing is like that of Hogarth in painting – and that the more it is waving, undulatory, and inclined, the more it is graceful and captivating. They have gone one step further and laid down this axiom – that dancing excels in proportion as it resembles flying. That is the source of all the present triumphs.'[9] And therein too, he might have added, lay ballet's debt to the spirit of Romanticism.

It was one of the ballet-master's duties to arrange occasional divertissements to show off the principal ballerinas, and an interlude of this nature – *Un Bal sous Louis XIV* – was brought out for Elssler's benefit a week later, on April 6th. In spite of the implication in its title, which was suggested by just one of the dances it contained, it made no claim to historical authenticity. Indeed, while it opened to show the corps de ballet strolling in a ballroom in period costume, the atmosphere was broken almost at once by the introductory quadrille and *pas de huit* by dancers wearing modern-style dresses. The title of the divertissement was explained by the following number – the *Menuet de la Cour* and the *Gavotte de Vestris*, danced by Elssler and Dumilâtre. This pair of dances, traditionally given together, had survived as a popular example of the style of the previous century. They had been arranged

Jules Perrot

by Maximilien Gardel for the ballet *Ninette à la cour* in 1778, the Vestris of the gavotte's title being Gaétan, who had danced it in that ballet. Within recent memory, in 1835, Gaétan's son Auguste had come out of his retirement to partner Taglioni in these same dances at the Paris Opéra. Both Jules and Fanny Elssler had been pupils of Auguste Vestris, but the playbills and reviews give no indication which of them was responsible for this revival, which from all accounts was coloured by the condescension with which the eighteenth century was generally regarded at that time. Although this divertissement was billed as being by him, Jules did not include it in his list of works, and since he was still recovering from his accident, it may well have been staged mainly by another hand, with Jules being involved merely to stitch the various numbers together to make a tidy sequence. In later performances its content, apart from the Minuet and Gavotte, was continually being changed, and in fact the dances that were inserted in it from time to time included only one that Jules specifically claimed as his own.

This was the *pas de Diane chasseresse*, first given on April 20th, which he arranged for Adèle Dumilâtre and a group of supporting dancers dressed as huntresses in leopard skins. It was notable for the skilful way in which he exploited the soaring quality of Dumilâtre's leaps, and the moment when the ballerina held an arabesque on *pointe* with bow in hand was frozen for posterity by the artist Joseph Bouvier in one of the most elegant ballet prints of the time. It may be this dance which is referred to in Jules' list of works, for a reason which is obscure, as *Atalante*.

A somewhat more substantial, although still minor, work followed on April 27th, when Dumilâtre took her benefit – a Turkish divertissement called *Les Houris*. It opened with a scene showing 'a party of evil-minded Turks . . . sitting on ottomans smoking pipes,' expressing their dissatisfaction with the dancing girls and indulging in the forbidden vice of alcohol. They are interrupted by a good son of Islam who dashes the goblets from their hands and is stabbed for his pains. He expires on the sofa, but receives his reward in the after-life for sacrificing his life in the service of the Prophet. A scene change reveals the Mohammedan paradise, 'one of those shining scenes, half temple, half cloud,' inhabited by houris, 'the most ethereal creatures that ever Caliph dreamed of, with white muslin frocks and the thinnest pink veils.'[10] Against this setting Dumilâtre made her entrance, and in a few short minutes Jules again encapsulated her special qualities, taking advantage of her height, devising soft languorous falls into the arms of her partner, and in the more rapid passages displaying her graceful lightness in long floating bounds across the stage.

No less well served was her partner, Arthur Saint-Léon, who had made his London début only a week before. Jules had been much impressed by his phenomenal technique and provided him with such splendid opportunities to show off his strength and control, and in particular the astonishing rapidity and steadiness of his turns, that he was rewarded with an ovation such as no other male dancer had received for some years. In its original form *Les Houris* contained only one other dance, a *pas de trois* by Mlles Camille, Scheffer and Plunkett, but like other divertissements of this kind, it was not considered sacrosanct, and a few weeks later it was adapted for Fanny Cerrito to include a new *grand pas*, featuring her and Saint-Léon, with Mlles Benard and Galby in support.

By the middle of May Jules had recovered sufficiently to contemplate appearing on the stage again. Performing was in his blood, and whatever the doctors said, he was determined to take part in the benefit performance to which he was entitled. *Alma* was to be revived for the occasion, and to excuse his disability, the name of the character Periphite was changed to Asmodeus, the limping devil of Le Sage's novel – a wry allusion to his lameness. He must have been very anxious about the chances of complete recovery, for dancing was still his livelihood and he could not be certain that he would earn an acceptable living as a choreographer. His 'somewhat melancholy appearance,' therefore, was understandable, but *The Times* found 'his grimaces ... as humorous as ever,' and could not help admiring 'the honest determination of the artist in thus boldly making head against a severe calamity.'[11]

The *Spectator* gave a vivid description of his performance. 'Though scarcely able to put his hurt leg to the ground, he went through the part ... and made it something better than a lame affair; supporting some *danseuse* round the waist while she formed an angle of 120 degrees with her legs, or giving her a lift to achieve some otherwise impossible feat of agility, and even managing to turn a pirouette himself on his sound limb. He hovered haltingly about the stage, looking with quaint significance at the dancers, as if [he were] the daemon of lameness threatening them with his spells; and altogether was as amusing as when he turned round like a teetotum, twiddled his calves in the air, turned his back on himself, and performed other incredible achievements. It would not have been out of character had he come in on crutches, with his lame leg in a sling; and he would have had more fun in this way. So it turns out, after all, that a disabled dancer can be efficient in a ballet – that is, if he be an expert pantomimist.'[12]

Jules' friend Coulon wrote to old Deshayes about the performance. 'Yesterday evening *Alma* was revived for Perrot's benefit, with the last scene omitted as was agreed with you in Paris. It was Saint-Léon who played my rôle. He danced a *pas* with Cerrito in the ball scene. I myself played your part. Perrot made his reappearance (amid bravos). He changed the character of his rôle. He turned it into a sort of Devil on Two Sticks so that he could support himself on a cane, for he is getting much better, being able to hold his place in the *pas de fascination* in the German act and even take part in a *pas de trois* in the ball scene, but he will have to be careful [if he is to play] all his other rôles as last year. In the evening, after supper, I drank your health with Perrot and

Jules Perrot

Dubourg, and we were truly sorry that you were not with us. Our theatre is doing well. It is making a lot of money, and everything leads us to hope that this will continue. You have probably heard about M. Saint-Léon as a violinist. He played at Perrot's benefit, and is certainly very talented.'[13]

* * *

In fact the rest that was imposed on Jules by his injury had wonderfully concentrated his imagination, and in a remarkable burst of creative activity spread over a few summer weeks he and Pugni, no doubt in close collaboration with Lumley and Cerrito, devised and shaped a new grand ballet for the Neapolitan ballerina, *Ondine, ou la Naïade*.

The source of the scenario was immediately evident from the title. Friedrich de la Motte Fouqué's fairy-tale of *Undine*, written more than thirty years before, had long been popular in England, much more so in fact than in France. However, it underwent a radical transformation in the process of being adapted for the ballet. Fouqué's story contained elements which Jules found unacceptable, for in the final result, the narrative of his ballet owed little more to this source than the basic idea of a naiad falling in love with a mortal and facing a conflict with a human rival. The mediaeval trappings with which the original work was heavily overladen were rejected, the setting was transposed from the Danube to a sunnier, Mediterranean clime and – reflecting, significantly, Jules' vision of the hero as a common man – the knight errant hero was turned into a Sicilian fisherman. Somewhat surprisingly, Jules omitted from his *dramatis personae* Fouqué's mysterious lord of the waters, Kühleborn, the vengeful power that watches over Undine, who could have been made into a much more impressive character than the Queen of the Naiads of the ballet, particularly if the choreographer had played it himself. But Jules had chosen to cast himself in the rôle of the hero; he had not yet come to accept the limitations that his injury was to impose on his activity as a dancer.

In working out his scenario it is unlikely that Jules was influenced by earlier ballets on the same theme. In fact, he could not have seen either of the *Undine* ballets produced by Louis Henry in Vienna in 1825 and Paul Taglioni in Berlin in 1836, although he was in Paris in 1834 when Henry presented, at the Théâtre Nautique, his one-act ballet-pantomime called *Les Ondines*, which might have suggested some of the effects he was later to incorporate in his underwater scenes. A more likely influence was a *féerie* by Guilbert de Pixerécourt and Thomas Sauvage, *Ondine, ou la Nymphe des eaux*, which was running at the Gaîté when Jules had returned from his first London engagement in 1830. Its authors had taken considerable liberties with Fouqué's story, setting the action in Sicily, and introducing two spectacular underwater scenes. The Italian setting and the underwater scenes were to reappear in Jules' ballet, in which the hero was given the same name, Matteo, with only the slightest variation, as Ondine's fisherman father Mathéo in the *féerie*.

The Turning Point

Another point of similarity was the use of a shell to convey Ondine through the water.

Another possible influence was much more recent, dating only from the previous summer, in 1842, when Edward Fitzball's romantic drama, *The Kiss, or Bertha's Bridal*, was produced at the English Opera House (Lyceum). It was not based on Fouqué's tale, but among its characters was Undine, Queen of the Waters, and it included an incident that might have suggested the idea for the *pas de la rose flétrie*, one of the highlights of Jules' ballet. The heroine gives her fiancé a pair of rosebuds which wither and lose their petals, providing the cue for a sentimental duet:

> The brightest and rarest must perish,
> Be they ever so blooming and gay –
> As friends whom we love most to cherish,
> The earliest sink to decay.

Did the association of the name of Undine recall to Jules the theme of this song?

Certainly the ballet scenario was the result of much imaginative thought, for without denying the debt to Fouqué for the original inspiration, it was in its final form a work of originality and brilliance, as well as a model of balletic construction. The plot was narrated in six scenes that followed one another without intervals in a performance lasting about an hour and a half. The continuity that Jules achieved outweighed the fatigue of sitting for such a long stretch, and the critic of the *Examiner*, for one, was glad not to be 'balked by a tiresome act-drop . . . If our readers recollect the length of time during which the drop generally remains down when it does descend, they will fully appreciate this merit in *Ondine*.'[14]

An original touch in the scenario was the titling of each scene after some significant feature, as if the choreographer saw the ballet as a series of narrative paintings. The first scene was called 'La Coquille,' the scallop shell, a title that was explained when the scene reached its climax. After the overture the curtain rose on a lively gathering of peasants and fishermen by the sea-shore, making preparations for the Festival of the Madonna. For this opening scene William Grieve had painted a 'fine distant landscape,' seen across a stretch of water.[15] Matteo and Giannina are to be married the next day, and the young fisherman is happily inviting his friends to the wedding, while his fiancée blushingly receives congratulations. The introduction of these two principal characters was skilfully woven into a striking *ballabile*, which was followed by a *pas de cinq* for Giannina and her companions.* The stage then empties,

---

* According to the announcement in *The Times* on the day of the première, this dance was a *pas de cinq* by Mlles Guy-Stéphan (Giannina), Galby, Benard, Chevalier and Ducie, but the list of numbers set out in the piano score, published in August 1843, refers to it as a *pas de trois* by Mlles Guy-Stéphan, Camille and Galby. The explanation may be that Jules substituted a new *pas* shortly after the first few performances.

Jules Perrot

leaving Matteo on his own. He is about to cast his net when, to his amazement, a shell rises slowly out of the water, bearing the naiad Ondine, whom he recognises as a spirit that has been haunting his dreams. The naiad has fallen in love with him, and is determined to bring him under her spell in spite of the danger of associating with a mortal. Matteo, struggling against the supernatural force of her attraction, turns to the hut where he lives with his mother, but the naiad's power restrains him and, step by step, he is drawn after her along the shore and up a rocky slope. On reaching the summit, Ondine gives him a long loving look and sinks slowly and gracefully into the water, beckoning him to follow. Only the fortuitous arrival of some peasants prevent him from plunging after her. Ondine's power is momentarily dispelled, and realising what has happened, he falls to his knees to give thanks for his deliverance.

The second part of this scene, the *pas de la coquille, scène dansante d'entraînement*, was a masterly example of Jules' developing skill at creating atmosphere and conveying a relationship between two characters in a dance. 'Nothing can surpass the poetry of this scene,' wrote the author of the account in *Beauties of the Opera and Ballet*, 'whether we consider the idea, effect or the skill of the artistes. Matteo (admirably played by Perrot) delineates the progress of his fascination – his spell enthralment – with the evident anxiety, but entire disability, to shake off the spell that surrounds him, and at each moment binds him the more inextricably; and wrapt in the full wonder and ecstasy of his infatuation, he has no sensation of fear, no thought of danger. His *entraînement* is complete. The spirit of the waters is evidently deeply enamoured; but there is, besides, an evident display of, and delight in, her power of enchantment beyond the attraction of her unearthly loveliness. She knows the fullness of her charms, but she also evinces the delight of possessing and exercising influences more than mortal; and there is hardly a situation more effective on the stage than the moment when the Naiad (to whom the power of floating in the air is given equally with that of gliding upon, through, or beneath the waters) – having gained the pinnacle of the precipice upon which she has tempted Matteo to follow her, after the pause of a moment, during which her countenance and figure express the utmost endearment, mingled with the confidence of success and triumph – sinks gently from the rocky point, and is gradually enveloped in the transparent waves, which enclasp her in their bosom as a fond mother welcomes back a loved and truant child! Had the ballet consisted of this scene only it must have been popular.'[16]

To achieve the effect he desired, Jules was ably assisted by the scene painter Grieve and the chief machinist D. Sloman, who between them contrived the appearance and disappearance of Cerrito. Her emergence from the sea was effected by means of a simple trap, but her slow gliding fall into the water at the end was a more complicated effect, probably accomplished by her slipping into a harness concealed by the pointed rock at the top of the slope and being lowered through the trap on a wire.

A cloth depicting a rustic interior was then lowered near the front of the stage for the scene of 'The Fisherman's Hut and the Pranks of Ondine,' while the orchestra played an introduction intended to mask the sounds of stage hands bringing on the properties and changing the scenery behind. The action opened with Matteo's mother and Giannina anxiously awaiting the fisherman's return. When at last he appears he is still haunted by his vision, but Giannina calms him and he tells them of his strange adventure. His mother dismisses it as a hallucination and sits down at her spindle, while Matteo begins helping Giannina unwind a skein of thread. This domestic scene is suddenly interrupted as the window bursts open and Ondine darts into the room. She is visible only to Giannina, whose confusion mystifies the other two. At length Ondine becomes invisible again, and the mortals resume their occupations. But their contentment somehow seems to offend Ondine, who mischievously vents her spite by snapping Giannina's thread, striking the distaff out of the old woman's hand, and other pranks. Then she becomes visible to Matteo, who vainly tries to seize her. Giannina then sees her too, but her attempts to grasp her are no more successful, and in no time Ondine has flown out of the room, beckoning Matteo to follow – a spectacular exit with a series of brilliant turns characteristic of Cerrito's style leading into a leap through the window, contrived perhaps, as in the previous scene, with the aid of a wire. Her summons is irresistible, and Matteo has to be restrained by Giannina from leaping through the window after her. Giannina chides him for his faithlessness, but he tells her not to worry, for all will be well on the morrow when they will be united for ever. The mother joins their hands and gives them her blessing.

Left alone, Matteo throws himself on to his couch, and overcome by sleep, again comes under the influence of Ondine. At this point the machinist Sloman showed great ingenuity in achieving the transformation Jules required. With remarkable smoothness the cottage walls disappeared and the fisherman on his couch was transported to the underwater abode of the naiads, a marine cave reminiscent, thought *The Times*, of the Dropping Well at Knaresborough. He stirs to find himself surrounded by long-haired naiads, dressed in light blue and adorned with coral branches. Before his bewildered gaze the whole corps de ballet dance a *pas des ondes*, in which Jules achieved an ingenious effect by making them 'rise and sink with a wave-like motion,'[17] before vanishing as mysteriously as they appeared, leaving the stage clear for the entrance of Ondine. Accompanied by a male partner – Saint-Léon – and four supporting soloists (Mlles Camille, Scheffer, Galby and Benard) the naiad displays her bewitching allurements in a shawl dance that was to set a fashion among ladies of society for white or pink scarfs of Iris or Zephyr Gauze worn over their evening dresses. This *pas de vision*, choreographed by

Cerrito herself, included a bravura variation for Saint-Léon, who performed wonders of strength, 'flinging his legs back as he bounced in the air in a manner we have never seen before.'[18] When this interpolated dance was over, the ballet continued, as devised by Jules, with a *scène de la vision* in which Ondine, carried away by her love, throws herself at Matteo's feet. In this situation she is discovered by Hydrola, Queen of the River, Lake and Fountain, who warns her of the danger of losing her immortality should she choose to marry a mortal. But Ondine's love is too intense for this warning to be heeded, and in her overpowering desire to possess the mortal fisherman, decay and death lose their dread. Plucking a rose from a tree, she declares her readiness to wither like the flower if only Matteo can be hers. As Hydrola sadly leads her away, the scene changes again.

'The Festival of the Madonna' has begun. The music has broken into a march, and the peasants and fisherfolk are advancing in a colourful procession to lay offerings at the foot of the Madonna's statue. This was one of the most striking moments in the ballet, for Jules had produced an immediately recognisable representation of Léopold Robert's famous painting in the Louvre, *La Fête de la Madonne*, employing the whole corps de ballet. With 'castanets cracking on the ear and echoing the coarser clatter of the tambourines,'[19] the procession dissolved into a fiery tarantella, 'as spirited and as characteristic as if it were danced on the chiaja by the real *contadini* when the lachryma Christi is getting into their noodles.'[20] 'All is wild, animated, and in picturesque disorder, and the colours of the various dresses, rapidly intermingled, flash upon the eye most brilliantly.'[21] 'The picturesqueness of the Italian costume, and the varieties of colour which floated on the view at every change, contrasted prettily with the placid landscape in the background; and the groups of children squatting in front, smartly sounding their *vielles* and tambours, and laughing in sharp, merry concert, completed a broad and comprehensive effect.'[22] Suddenly this turbulent merriment dies down as the bell of the angelus rings out, and in an impressive change of mood everyone kneels down for the evening prayer. During this moment of quiet Ondine emerges from a fountain, visible only to Matteo, who springs to his feet to follow her. Giannina, noticing Matteo's agitation, leads him back to the shrine, but no sooner is he on his knees before it than the figure of Ondine has taken the place of the Madonna's statue. He turns to his fiancée, but when they look back the naiad has vanished. The prayers over, the tarentella is resumed, followed by a *pas de quatre* by Giannina and Matteo with two supporting soloists (Mlles Camille and Plunkett) and finally a rollicking galop to an infectious bouncy tune.

The festivities have now come to an end, and Matteo and Giannina find themselves alone by the shore. Night is falling, ' a fine dioramic effect' which attained a high degree of realism, thanks to the skill of Grieve and Sloman. 'The mountains in the background, which shone with the light of day,

The Turning Point

become red with the tints of sunset, and at last the moon rises, and a full blue light is thrown upon the stage.'[23] It is time to return home, and while Matteo is away unmooring his boat, Giannina's attention is caught by something glinting in the water. She bends down and before she realises what is happening, is pulled beneath the waves by the naiads, while Ondine, having assumed her form, rises to take her place. Stepping on the shore, the naiad sees her shadow for the first time. At first she thinks it must be Giannina pursuing her, but when she realises that it is an attribute of her new mortality, her fear vanishes and she gives expression to all the capricious vivacity of her naiad temperament, bounding on the shore in an ecstasy of childish delight and exaltation.

Choreographically the shadow dance was the centre-piece of the ballet, a beautifully conceived solo for Cerrito that established Ondine's character entirely in dance. Fanny Cerrito was not the remarkable interpreter that Elssler was, but in these years of her prime, that lack was amply compensated for by an infectious *joie de vivre* that Jules exploited to the full in this dance. Darting to and fro in the bright glare of the hydro-oxygen light that threw her shadow on to the stage before her, she brought out its wealth of detail so clearly that the impressions of no two spectators were the same. One recalled the opening

Ondine, *Scene 3. Fanny Cerrito's shawl dance.* (Pictorial Times, *July 15th, 1843*)
Ondine, *finale. The coloured fountains effect. Engraving by A. Henning.*

103

Jules Perrot

when, 'bewildered with the novelty of her existance, [Ondine] for a moment believes the shadow to be her rival, and plunges into the lake to convince herself of her error.'[24] Another was left with the memory of the passage where 'she clutches the shadow on the ground and like an infant is innocently astonished at the dark, elongated monster which perseveringly mimics her movements.'[25] And yet another was reminded of 'a kitten . . . beholding for the first time its likeness in a mirror' and wrote of her amused delight at seeing her shadow mocking her movements and of 'her playful gambols and graceful attempts' to catch it.[26] It was an exquisite dance, criticised only for not being long enough – a merit in itself. Presented in a *chiar'oscuro* which gave it a haunting atmosphere, it conveyed, through its choreography and its interpretation, an exquisite beauty that was quite beyond description.

At length Matteo returns with his boat. Ondine has put on Giannina's hat and cloak, and Matteo helps her into the boat under the belief that she is his fiancée. As the boat makes its way across the bay, the unfortunate Giannina is seen beneath the surface being borne to the underwater regions of the naiads – 'a *coup d'œil* of most startling effect'[27] that brought the scene to a close.

This was followed by another scene set in the front of the stage, 'The Withered Rose.' Ondine is asleep in Giannina's room, watched over by Hydrola, who vanishes as she wakes. The lovesick naiad is already feeling the burden of mortality, and disturbed by the weakness that is stealing over her, she kneels down to pray. Hydrola reappears, repeating the warning that Ondine is fading like the rose-bud that has already begun to wither, and begging her to reconsider her foolish attachment before it is too late. But Ondine is obdurate, and sorrowfully Hydrola leaves her to her fate. Day is breaking, and Matteo and his mother enter the room. At this point Jules inserted another expressive *pas d'action* – the *pas de la rose flétrie*. Using the form of the saltarello, he depicted Ondine continually faltering and recovering herself as an increasing languor spreads through her body, and all the time trying to reassure her beloved with a pale, brave smile. She seems to be fading away before his eyes, and despairingly he realises that the hand of death has fallen on the girl for whom, so he believes, he has sacrificed the affection of a divine spirit. The dying Ondine has now but one purpose, to go through with her marriage to Matteo so that in death she will possess him for evermore.

On this unhappy note the final scene opens with 'The Departure for the Wedding,' a sad procession with Ondine leaning heavily on Matteo's arm and walking with faltering steps. As if in sympathy with the withered rose, Ondine is herself at the point of death when Hydrola and her naiads make a last effort to recover her. She is in no state to resist, and the Queen restores Giannina, full of health and joy, to Matteo, who can hardly believe the miraculous recovery which, to him, Giannina seems to have made. Meanwhile, Ondine, having resumed her immortal condition, is borne away to her home in the deep in an apotheosis on which Grieve and Sloman lavished a

The Turning Point

plethora of scenic effects – rainbows, 'transparent walls of rippling water,'[28] and coloured fountains, each enclosing a naiad, rising up from below the stage.

So ended a truly remarkable production that was the fruit of a close collaboration between choreographer, scene painter and machinist. For Jules it probably seemed a natural development from his experience in the boulevard theatres in Paris, where spectacle was an important element, but for the London critics it appeared as something extraordinary. 'We defy even Mr. Lumley, with his Prime Minister Perrot, to devise anything more exquisite than *Ondine*,' challenged the *Morning Post*,[29] while the *Examiner* called it 'a spectacle ... perhaps without a parallel in the annals of the Italian Opera.'[30]

How exceptional it was emerges unequivocally from the perceptive account published in the *Morning Post* the day after the first performance. 'We have,' wrote its critic, 'beheld ballets for thirty years at Her Majesty's Theatre – we have seen the most successful of such performances in some of the most celebrated theatres in the greatest capitals of Europe – and we must in justice place *Ondine* far above them all. Music and dancing, painting and poetry – in this ballet all four are comprised. We could never have believed that such a *mise en scène* could be effected; such scenic illusion produced in the few yards square that form the scanty stage at Her Majesty's Theatre. We should feel greatly at a loss to apportion to the ballet-master, Perrot, the scene painter Grieve, etc., the share of praise each may justly claim. Good as the music is – sprightly, characteristic and descriptive – it is the least extraordinary portion of the ballet. Perrot's *maestria* is perceptible in the minutest detail of the action of the ballet. The scenes are as varied as they are fascinating; at one moment representing nature with surpassing truth; at another embodying the poet's imaginings in fairyland.'[31]

If it lacked the poetic fancy of *Giselle*, *Ondine* was a superb demonstration of Jules' all-round skill as a producer, with its changing moods conveyed by a skilful admixture of dance forms and an understanding of human nature that brought the characters to life before the audience's eyes. His mastery as a choreographer was many-sided. Equally at ease when composing for large groups as for individual dancers, his palette contained a rich variety of dance material from the formal *enchaînements* in the classical technique to national dances, and in *Ondine* he made the most imaginative use of Italian material. His tarantella was an impressive set-piece for the corps de ballet, but its interruption for the evening prayer was a masterly stroke which doubled the effect of the reprise that followed, while later in the ballet, his adaptation of the saltarello to convey Ondine's faltering strength was a prime example of his use of dance to advance the narrative. His ability to maintain the dramatic flow and his use of dancers as interpretative artists enabled him to hold the interest of the audience for an hour and a half, unbroken by any interval. Not

105

Jules Perrot

all the dances were *pas d'action*, but the atmosphere of the ballet was never disturbed by the sort of pointless divertissement which critics so often complained about: even Cerrito's *pas de la vision* was skilfully woven into the rest of the work. The experienced Gruneisen had seen so many ballets that had been ruined for him by the appearances of dancers going through, 'with monstrous regularity . . . the prescribed *jetés battus, voltes* and *pirouettes de rigueur*' and finishing out of breath, with 'petrified grins' that he rejoiced to discover, in *Ondine*, a ballet in which 'all the *pas* [were] interwoven with the subject, and generally all the personages on the stage [were] engaged in the moving incidents of the scene – an immense improvement.'[32]

No less remarkable a quality of Jules' choreography was his sense of plastic form, which was strikingly revealed in his ensemble dances, which Gruneisen described as 'mazes of exquisite and varied intricacy, and still symmetrical, like the designs of a kaleidoscope.'[33] This was specially evident in the opening of the fourth scene, the Festival of the Madonna, but the *pas des ondes*, 'in which a wavy undulation is carried through all its varying movements,'[34] was equally imaginative in a gentler way.

More than one critic equated Jules' art with other forms. Gruneisen praised his groups as 'models for a painter,'[35] while his colleague of the *Morning Herald* advanced the analogy of sculpture. 'The tableaux,' he wrote, 'are composed with an inventiveness extremely creditable to Perrot, and they not only merit extraordinary eulogy for the mechanical artifices which demonstrate them, but for the better artistic qualities which belong to them as artistic designs. In all his compositions of this kind Perrot evinces a fine sense of the beautiful, and independently of the characteristic properties they have as pantomimic illustrations they are frequently constructed with a classic feeling, which, in another sphere of art, would be estimated by a much higher standard. Many of his configurations are worthy of being arrested and made permanent. Pity they are so fleeting. They come like shadows and so depart, but they leave a distinct impression on the mind of a novel and ingenious form of beauty. Perrot is the Flaxman of the ballet; he would compose admirable *bas reliefs* for the frieze of a temple; and in olden times he would have wielded the mallet of the sculptor rather than the baton of the ballet-master.'[36]

Pugni's score, his first major work for Jules Perrot, was more than a skilfully written accompaniment. In its original form it can only be judged from the composer's piano transcription, published that summer by Charles Ollivier of No. 41 New Bond Street at a price of one guinea and dedicated to the Duchess of Cambridge. In feeling and rhythmical structure it was Italian rather than French, being full of lilting danceable melodies, introducing some national dance forms from the composer's native land, and containing many expressive pages to accompany the action. Particularly effective, for example, was the interruption of the tarentella when the angelus calls the peasants to their prayers. Certainly the music lacked the inspiration that characterised

Adam's *Giselle*, but its light texture was what was expected of ballet music at that time. Bearing in mind that it was written to order, as was usual, and also at great speed – in three weeks, according to one source – it is hardly surprising that it did not find favour with everyone. The *Athenæum*, for instance, dismissed it as 'very poor,' and regretted that Sterndale Bennett's overture to the Naiads had not been used instead of Pugni's 'nonsensical and meagre prelude.'[37] The overture was also criticised by Gruneisen in the *Morning Post*, but that having been said, he gave the score serious consideration, devoting a considerable proportion of his notice to discussing it.

'The only thing to which [the overture] appears to us to resemble,' he began, 'is the contention of rival bands at a fair. Such an absence of motifs and melody, such a scrambling race of string instruments, and din of trumpets, ophicleides, kettle and double drums, seems to have been invented to make one enjoy the more the softer strains of the ballet . . . The music of the ballet itself is worthy of the highest commendation – not consisting, as customary in a *pasticcio*, [of] broken snatches of stolen melodies, enveloped and disguised in overwrought harmony. The music of a *ballet d'action* should constantly supply a voice to render intelligible the mute pantomime of the dancers. Signor Pugni's composition is true to this precept; it is highly descriptive, and it has even the *couleur locale*, as for example in the dance in the "bosom of the deep," where a sound like the falling of the waves marks the rhythm of the music.'[38]

Gruneisen's remarks found an echo in the description in *Beauties of the Opera and Ballet* of the end of the third scene, when Matteo is conveyed to the watery kingdom and the naiads 'dance their mazy fascinations around him.' 'The musical accompaniments which describe the rise and fall of the waves are eminently characteristic and beautiful: the very ripple of the flow, and the rushing sound of the ebb over the pebbly strand, are heard, and fully satisfy the ear; whilst the eye is filled and delighted with gorgeous scenery and exquisite dancing.'[39]

In fact the idea of water was woven into the texture of the score at several points. It was very effectively suggested in the 'Coquille' scene when Matteo is left alone fishing and Ondine appears to him for the first time, and again in the slow movement of Cerrito's *pas de six* and the closing passage of the *scène de la vision*, and in the final scene. And by juxtaposing 'the seraphic music "of the deep"' and 'the characteristic Neapolitan strains of the world above,' the composer reinforced the contrast between the fantasy and realism which lay at the heart of Jules' conception. 'In the former,' Gruneisen continued, 'every strain is mellowed, and even the dashing of the waves imitated, whilst in the latter you have all the *couleur locale* of the prayer of the *Pifferari* and the wild passions of *Lazzaroni* and *Contadini*, and the still wilder *Tarantella*.'[40]

Pugni's experience of ballet construction in Milan was particularly evident in the passages he wrote for transitions between the scenes. For the first

Jules Perrot

interlude, to give time for the properties for the scene in the hut to be put into position, he composed a bridging passage containing a lilting melody, typically Italian in flavour, played *forte* so as to cover up any noise made by the stage hands. Later, the transition from the fifth to the sixth scene was accompanied by a passage of an almost Lisztian rhapsodical character, again marked *forte*. Another effective transition accompanied the transformation scene preceding Matteo's dream in the underwater realm of the naiads. Here Pugni introduced melodies he had used earlier in the score, one that had accompanied the passage preceding Ondine's first appearance to Matteo, and another a melody from the second scene. It was a skilful piece of bridging which also produced the change of mood for the *pas des ondes*.

Ondine was a triumph for all concerned, but mostly for the choreographer. Apart from his early productions in Vienna, it was the first major ballet for which Jules had been solely responsible, and it sealed his reputation in the eyes of Europe as the most original choreographer of his time. Its triumph must also have come as a balm, to ease the difficult adjustment he had to make now that his days as a bravura dancer were clearly at an end. Performing was in his blood, and he had designed his own rôle of Matteo with the limitations of his physical powers very much in mind. His incapacity was still very apparent. He joined in the tarantella 'with spirit, despite his limping gait,'[41] but apart from that he exerted himself as little as possible. The relief of the *Athenæum*'s critic must have been shared by many others. 'To the comfort of our nerves,' he recorded, 'he hardly danced at all.'[42]

* * *

Jules was now to be presented with a new challenge. Among Lumley's many preoccupations at this time was the arrangement of a state visit by Queen Victoria. Although she was a frequent visitor to the Opera, it was as a private box-holder; there had been no Command Performance since the previous reign, in 1834. Lumley's approach to the Palace met with a positive response, a date was fixed – July 20th – and the programme approved. Rossini's *Il Barbiere di Siviglia*, with Mario, Grisi and Lablache, and *Ondine* with Cerrito were to be the main works, but also to be included, at Her Majesty's express wish, was an intriguing *bonne bouche* in the form a *pas de deux* by Elssler and Cerrito.

The Queen's wish presented Jules with a formidable task. Never before had two ballerinas of such standing danced together, and there were only a few days in which to arrange their *pas*. The two ladies had not even met one another, and it fell to Jules to effect the introduction. At this first contact they eyed one another warily, each equally reluctant to make any concession in the ensuing discussion of how the *pas* should be presented. Almost at once the first difficulty arose. It concerned the order of their variations, each seeing the second variation as conferring superiority. Elssler considered she had the right to it on grounds of age and experience, while Cerrito staked her claim on the fact that she was engaged as the leading ballerina of the season. Neither would give way, although Cerrito suggested drawing lots as a way out of the difficulty. It was Elssler who yielded in the end, grasping the hand of poor Jules, who by that time was in a pitiable state of despair, and saying: 'Come, let us begin.' All went well after this contretemps, and on the night of the Command Performance the *pas de deux* proved a sensation – as one onlooker put it, 'worth walking barefoot to Loretto to witness.'[43]

Before a backcloth of a verdant landscape, with groups of *danseuses* standing motionless at either side, the two ballerinas entered together and began to dance in unison, with arms round each other's waists, to a slow melody. This was a condition that Lumley had imposed so that neither would start at a disadvantage. It was a concession to their susceptibilities which in ordinary circumstances Jules might have been unwilling to accept, for the two dancers were very different in height, Elssler appearing almost a giantess alongside the petite Cerrito, and the artistic effect was undeniably somewhat marred.

Elssler's *pas seul* followed, beginning with a profusion of delicate *pointe* work, and this was followed by a variation of a very different kind for Cerrito. The Neapolitan dancer bounded about with exhilarating vitality, circling the stage with extraordinary speed, and after a brilliant series of *ronds de jambe en l'air*, came to rest with an air of *insouciance* that seemed to suggest that such exertions were a natural expression of her temperament.

Elssler then rejoined her and more marvels followed. 'At one moment Elssler stood in marvellous equilibrium on the point of her toe, whilst Cerrito gracefully bent her form to the ground, and then they both leapt into the air together, performing simultaneously at a tangent the quickest repeated and most marvellous *jetés battus*. Then Elssler glided along the stage with invisible movement of her toes in the most fascinating attitude, with the flutters of a bird, and Cerrito soon followed, flying through the air and revolving on herself with a rapidity indescribable.'[44]

It was a remarkable tribute to Jules' skill and tact that the two ballerinas appeared together, not just once in obedience to the Queen's command, but ten times more before the season closed in August, in an atmosphere that was charged with the most partisan excitement. Whenever the *pas de deux* was performed, it took on the appearance of a contest in which the honours went to the dancer who excited the longest and loudest applause. Each must have felt that she was well served by the choreographer, and so even was the contest that only at the end of the season was it possible to pass a balanced judgment. Jules of course would have been careful to express no preference, but Lumley awarded the palm not to the younger dancer whose physical charms and strength were at their peak, but to her who possessed the greater experience. 'Captivating as were both the danseuses on this occasion – much as Cerrito exerted all her powers – different as were the styles of the two rivals,

Jules Perrot

and strong as both were in their partisans and supporters, there can be no doubt that, in the eyes of connoisseurs, the victory remained with Elssler.'[45]

Just one more task now remained, the production of a short divertissement for Fanny Elssler, *Le Délire d'un peintre*. To introduce the three dances it was to contain, and to provide himself with an interesting mime rôle, Jules devised a simple plot which, 'further elaborated, might have extended itself into an excellent ballet with less of the all-pervading sameness of action with which the whole race of ballets seems inevitably characterised.'[46] At the rise of the curtain, Jules, in the guise of the artist Stephano, is discovered sitting alone, pale and distraught, before a painting concealed by a covering. His mother enters and tries to console him, but he shuns her embraces. 'He makes odd gestures, stamps violently with his foot, and commits other desperate acts, which indicate plainly that he is possessed of a monomania of some kind – the veiled frame having an indistinct reference to his frenzy.'[47] The cause of his madness is then explained. Beneath the covering is a portrait which he has painted from memory of a young Spanish widow, Blanche d'Oviedo, whom he has fallen in love with at first sight but met only once. He is so obsessed by the portrait that he spends his days gazing at it. While he is momemtarily out of the studio, the real Blanche arrives and learns of his extraordinary passion. Deciding to cure him, she hides beneath the covering and awaits his return. When he kneels before the portrait to resume his adoration, she steps out from the frame. He starts back in amazement, gazing in ecstasy at what he takes to be a vision of his beloved, as she hovers languorously over him and seems to float around the studio. Then, hearing footsteps, she springs back into the frame, leaving the artist more agitated than ever. At last he cannot resist tearing aside the covering. She has changed back into her every-day attire, and he realises that she is no vision but the real object of his passion, standing before him with love in her eyes. The restoration of his sanity is celebrated by three dances – a *pas de deux* by Elssler and James Sylvain, a *pas de deux* arranged by Gosselin for Elisa Scheffer and Adeline Plunkett, and finally a Spanish bolero, *La Castilliana*, which Jules composed expressly for Elssler with himself as her cavalier.

This slight work was held together by the sensitive interpretations of Jules and Fanny Elssler. Elssler was unrivalled as a dramatic dancer, but Jules was at no disadvantage by her side. His acting as the love-sick artist was praised as 'alike expressive of emotion and full of meaning; in intensity and variety he surpasses all pantomimists.' Although he had to curtail the technical demands of his rôle, he conceived his part in the bolero as more than a mere support for the ballerina, although this aspect could not be appreciated until the following summer, when his leg was better. His dancing was then found to be 'exquisite,' 'the extreme lightness and elasticity of his movements, and the precision combined with freedom of his execution [giving] a fiery impulse to this passionate dance.'[48]

The Turning Point

The last night of the season was a celebration, with Elssler and Cerrito honouring him by appearing together in the *Menuet de la Cour* and the *Gavotte de Vestris*. A few days later he returned to Paris, secure in the knowledge that he was re-engaged for next year's season. His imagination was bursting with ideas. He had been toying with an ambitious project, unfortunately to be unrealised, of staging a ballet version of Shakespeare's *Hamlet,* with Cerrito playing Ophelia to his prince, Louis Gosselin as Polonius, Mme Copère as Gertrude, and Coulon as the ghost. But foremost in his mind was *La Esmeralda*, on which he was to work during the following months in preparation for the opening of the 1844 season, with his muse of former years – Carlotta – in the rôle of Hugo's heroine.

He also found time that winter to visit the studio of the sculptor, Claude-François Lequine, who caught him in a moment of calm repose and portrayed him, not as the bustling, commanding figure he must have cut in the rehearsal room, but as a sensitive observer of life, an artist absorbed in his dreams.

10

An Essay in Dance Drama

When he arrived in London in the beginning of February 1844, Jules could hardly wait to begin work on *La Esmeralda*, which had been taking shape in his mind for nearly a year. Quite forgotten were the doubts he had originally expressed to Lumley; he had read and re-read Victor Hugo's novel, absorbing its powerful narrative until the characters had become as real as if he had known them in the flesh, and he now saw clearly how it should be presented on the stage. The long period of gestation, forced upon him by his accident a year before, had so concentrated his mind on the dramatic events that swept the street dancer Esmeralda along to her death that the ballet had already taken shape in his imagination as a sequence of powerful and vivid scenes in which the interplay of characters and some of the dramatic situations of the novel would be presented in a canvas of mime and movement, with dances emerging naturally and appositely out of the action.

The few weeks before Carlotta arrived in London would have enabled him to sketch out the five scenes with the corps de ballet and his two colleagues, Louis Gosselin, the *sous-maître de ballet*, and Antoine Coulon, the *régisseur de la danse*, whom he had cast respectively as the archdeacon Claude Frollo and the hunchbacked bell-ringer of Notre Dame, Quasimodo. Carlotta arrived to find him bursting with energy. Having no doubt already coached her privately in the part of Esmeralda, he now began to weave it into the main fabric of the ballet. Rehearsing daily without respite, he drilled the company to achieve the result he desired, and was presumably well pleased when the day of the first performance – the opening night of the season, Saturday, March 9th – arrived. All was as ready as it could be. The orchestra was thoroughly familiar with the score that Cesare Pugni had composed, William Grieve's splendidly evocative scenary, fresh from his workshop, was hanging in place, the costumes that Miss Bradley and Mr. Palmer had made under the supervision of Mme Copère were laid out in the dressing rooms, and the stock of scenarios had arrived from the Nassau Steam Press in Soho for distribution, gratis, to the audience.

When the carriages began to arrive and the audience came in from the chill

An Essay in Dance Drama

evening air to take their places, there was a sense of expectancy and excitement. Some important party elsewhere that evening had deprived Her Majesty's Theatre of some of its distinguished subscribers, and others were still out of town enjoying the last days of the hunting season at Badminton, Melton and other great estates, but the audience was nonetheless 'highly animated, and on the *qui vive* to discover, as they successively arrived, friends and well-known faces, particularly those fair owners of the boxes who are the chief ornaments of the house.'[1]

How to open the season effectively early in March was a perennial and unavoidable problem for the manager because most of the great opera singers were under contract for the Carnival season in Italy until the end of Lent, and this year there had been an added complication in that Lumley had been forced at the last minute to replace the opera he had announced, Herold's *Zampa*, with the mediocre work by Donizetti, *Adelia*, with which he had opened the previous season. Consequently the main interest of the evening centred on the new ballet, which exceeded everyone's expectations, proving to be 'of surpassing magnificence and ingenuity' and removing 'all remembrance of the insipidity of the foregoing opera.'[2] This reversal of the relative importance of opera and ballet was commented upon by several critics, and was a striking testimony to the remarkable impact which Jules, with Lumley's support, had made on the London ballet scene in the course of just two seasons. The critic of the *Morning Post* touched on the thoroughness with which the new ballet had been prepared. 'As long as the ballet mania prevails,' he wrote, 'vain are our protests in favour of the superior rights of the lyrical drama. If, however, thousands out of the operatic exchequer and the talents of first-rate composers are bestowed on ballets, it is but just to confess that the results are incalculably superior to all we beheld in our early days. At that period the dancing department presented scarce anything but the most inane and affected mythological absurdities. One very striking circumstance in the ballets in former days was that all the general dances and all the pantomimic portions of the performance were intolerable, or only borne by the public because they allowed the chief dancers to rest, whilst the dancers of lesser note were, beyond measure, offensive. In the present ballet the secondary *dramatis personae* are admirably grouped; their motions are full of life and spirit, and the intricate dances which they execute most justly draw down, from time to time, the loudest plaudits.'[3]

The distinctive feature of *La Esmeralda*, however, was not that it had been produced with extraordinary attention to detail – in fact, although it had been taking shape in Jules' mind for so long, the actual rehearsal period could not have been much longer than usual – but the fundamental originality of its conception. The prominence which Jules gave to the secondary characters resulted from the new formula on which the whole production was based. For the ballet had been conceived as a dance drama, opening up new possibilities in the use of dance to express dramatic narrative, background atmosphere and the study of character. Of all his works, *La Esmeralda* marked the farthest advance in the development of ballet as a theatrical spectacle. It was, as few other ballets can claim to be, a seminal work. Noverre would have approved it as a demonstration of the principles he had laid down for the *ballet d'action*, Dauberval would have admired the skilful balance between the characters and above all the manner in which they came to life and 'spoke to the heart,' and choreographers such as Gioja and Henry would have appreciated the attempt to reproduce a literary masterpiece. However, Jules had dared to go further than any of his predecessors, for instead of breaking into the action to interpolate dances which had little relevance to the theme, or presenting an Italian-style mime drama, he chose to use the dance as an integral part of the dramatic action. Consequently there were no great set pieces, every dance having a significance within the context of the situation out of which it arose.

In preparing this work Jules must have been deeply conscious of the responsibility he had accepted when yielding to Lumley's persuasive suggestion to base a ballet on Hugo's *Notre Dame de Paris*. Hitherto – with the exception of *Giselle*, for which he had worked to a ready-made scenario – he had constructed his ballets as his imagination had led him, but now he had chosen to set upon the stage a drama with which many of the audience would have been familiar, written by France's greatest living poet. The shadow of Victor Hugo cast itself awesomely in his path. Once the choice of subject had been made, there was no question of treating it lightly, for he knew he would be judged not merely on the superficial qualities of his ballet as an entertaining and brilliant spectacle, but on its fidelity to the original, on the extent to which it caught the atmosphere, spirit and magic of a novel that was a consecrated classic. He therefore found himself assuming the mantle of a dramatic author to an extent that no other choreographer – even in Italy, where literary subjects were frequently used for mime dramas – had assumed before.

There is no evidence that Hugo was in any way involved in the adaptation of his novel as a ballet, but he must have been aware of the preparations, for several of Jules' friends, notably Gautier, moved in his circle and Jules may have himself been acquainted with the great man. Even if there had been no such contact, the ballet was likely to come under Hugo's scrutiny. These considerations apart, however, Jules was too sensitive an artist not to recognise a duty to remain true to the author of the original source, as both the scenario and the resultant production showed.

Compressing the novel's vast canvas into a compact five-scene ballet scenario – designed to occupy somewhat more than an hour of continuous performance time – demanded much judicious selection and pruning, but the story it told was inherently suitable for theatrical representation. Hugo was himself a master of the dramatic idiom, having led the struggle of the Romantics against the restrictive conventions of classical tragedy and written some of the most powerful dramas in the vivid, full-blooded manner of the new school. His novel, *Notre Dame de Paris*, cried out for theatrical treatment, with its colourful setting of Paris emerging from the Middle Ages, its insight into different strata of society from the underworld of the truands to the aristocracy, and above all its vividly drawn characters, caught up in an interplay of events that lead to the final tragedy – the hounding and hanging of Esmeralda – which was not a histrionic climax so much as a consequence of heartrending pathos that was specially affecting in an unashamedly sentimental age.

The change of title from *Notre Dame de Paris* to *La Esmeralda* denoted a significant shift of emphasis from the great cathedral, which from being the symbolic focus of the novel receded into a mere background feature in the ballet, to the tribulations of the street dancer Esmeralda, on which the ballet's action was concentrated. In this Jules was following the precedent set by Hugo himself, who in 1836 had reduced the story to an opera libretto for Louise Bertin, the daughter of his friend, Armand Bertin, owner of the influential newspaper, *Journal des Débats*. For reasons that were not entirely musical, the opera has sunk almost without trace, but Hugo's libretto* was printed and shortly afterwards was adapted for a ballet, or '*azione mimica*,' as it was more properly called, which Antonio Monticini produced at the Scala, Milan, during the spring season of 1839.

Jules could not have seen either of these forerunners of his own work. He was in Vienna when poor Mlle Bertin's opera received its handful of performances at the Paris Opéra, and in Naples throughout the more respectable run of Monticini's ballet in Milan. An analysis of the scenario which Jules constructed with Lumley's help in 1843 and 1844 suggests that he had at his elbow not only Hugo's novel, but also his opera scenario. He might also have received first-hand impressions of Monticini's ballet from Fanny Cerrito, who had appeared in it – purely in a dancing rôle, for, as she would have explained, the action was entrusted entirely to mimes.

Both these earlier versions, even Hugo's own, were pale reflections beside the well constructed scenario – 'a model of ballet building,' as *The Times* described it[4] – that resulted from those nocturnal sessions in which Jules and Lumley struggled to reduce the novel to manageable proportions. For one thing, they had rescued from the pages of the novel the engaging character, excised from both the opera and the Italian ballet, of the poor poet Gringoire, an addition which not only provided a highly effective rôle for Jules himself but, much more importantly, intensified the psychological interaction between the principal characters. No less important was Jules' decision to use the

---

* The libretto was also used with greater success, by the Russian composer, Alexandre Dargomynsky, whose opera was produced in Moscow in 1847 and in St. Petersburg in 1851.

Jules Perrot

corps de ballet as an integral part of the drama, particularly to portray those ruffians of the Paris underworld, the truands, and the common people who sought their entertainment in the streets, whether taking part in a popular fête such as the Procession of the Fool's Pope, or witnessing the hanging of some unfortunate wretch.

In resuscitating Gringoire and giving prominence to the Parisian crowd, Jules was being wholly faithful to Hugo. But even where his plot did diverge, he could justly claim Hugo's authority on the strength of his opera libretto. It was Hugo, for example, who had whitewashed the character of Phoebus, transforming him from a callous profligate into a true lover who returns in the nick of time to save Esmeralda from being hanged for his murder. Esmeralda's deliverance, substituted for the novel's poignant climax, was the other significant change which Hugo had suggested, although he had contrived a tragic ending in his libretto by making Phoebus expire of his wound after saving Esmeralda from the gibbet. Jules recognised that Phoebus's death would be an artificial conclusion, diminishing the theatrical impact by diverting the audience's attention away from the heroine, but however much he may have wished to end the ballet with Esmeralda's death, he felt obliged to bow to public taste and close the ballet on a happy note. There were limits to the amount of realism that an audience of that time would take; while it was permissible to arouse pity by presenting the heroine in a series of awful predicaments from which she would eventually be extricated, good taste demanded that the horrors and miseries of real life should only be discreetly hinted at in the presence of ladies who had to be protected against such sordid impurities. 'Victor Hugo,' as the *Morning Post* observed, 'clearly relied for effect on loathsome images and repulsive horrors such as the unhallowed and unbridled love of the priest, the animal characteristics of the hunchback, the reckless villainy of the Bohemians, and on such scenes, for example, as that where Frollo is projected from the roof of the cathedral, and suspending himself for a time to a leaden gutter, which gradually [gives] way, . . . feels all the torturing gradations of despair and of the approach of inevitable death. In the ballet, instead of the exhibition of the rack and the torture of Esmeralda, a pleasing conclusion in accordance with poetic justice terminates the plot without the slightest loss of interest.'[5]

Adopting the structure he had used for *Ondine*, Jules arranged the action so that scenes using the full depth of the stage alternated with more intimate scenes played before a cloth much closer to the footlights, enabling the stage hands to prepare the set for the next scene without interrupting the action. Also, and again following the precedent of *Ondine*, he gave each scene a title, as if to emphasise his conception of the work as a selection of tableaux depicting some of the salient episodes of the novel.

As the title indicated, the scene that met the audience's eyes when the curtain rose after the overture was the terrible Cour des Miracles, the haunt of

An Essay in Dance Drama

Playbill of Her Majesty's Theatre, London, for April 13th, 1844 – the 11th performance of La Esmeralda *and the second of the polka. Theatre Museum, London.*

Jules Perrot

the thieves and beggars of the underworld, a place where honest men dared not penetrate. The sun is setting and the stage is filled with a wild and unruly throng of truands, in whom it was difficult to recognise the normally carefully regulated corps de ballet. The first impression was stunning. The 'loose, carefree revelries' of the truands, presided over by their 'king,' Clopin Trouillefou – a fifteenth-century gangster boss, played by Gouriet – had been skilfully planned, conveying 'an amusing bustle, which [was] not allowed to flag,' and developing into the dance, *Valse de vieux Paris*, performed by the *coryphées* of the corps de ballet. The choreographic construction of this dance was found 'new and striking,' as the dancers formed 'crosses ... which are bisected by moving lines at right angles very ingeniously'[6] – an effect that was particularly impressive when seen from the upper reaches of the theatre.

At the height of this revelry Jules made his first entrance, running in as Pierre Gringoire, the luckless poet, pursued by a band of truands intent on robbing him. He throws himself at Clopin's feet. Told to rise, he realises to his terror that he has stumbled into the infamous Cour des Miracles. He is set upon by the truands who find nothing on him but a poem. Disappointed, Clopin orders the unfortunate wretch to be hanged. Gringoire's pleas for mercy are greeted with laughter, and Clopin relents to invoke an ancient tradition that entitles him to a reprieve if he can find a woman who will take him as her husband. At Clopin's summons a number of women come out of the crowd to inspect him, but they contemptuously reject him. Crazed with fear, poor Gringoire throws himself imploringly at their feet. This was the moment for Carlotta's appearance as the street dancer Esmeralda, flitting gracefully through the ragged throng.* She passes before the poet, sizes up his plight, and in an impulse of pity consents to wed him. Gringoire's agony gives way to sudden joy, and there and then the marriage is celebrated, according to the custom of the truands, by the breaking of an earthenware pot. In this brief first meeting Esmeralda's changes of mood that led up to the extraordinary marriage were conveyed by Carlotta with 'wondrous piquancy,'[7] her initial repugnance and contempt finally dissolving into pity for the woebegone young man.

After receiving Clopin's blessing, the couple celebrate this unexpected turn of events by dancing a *pas caractéristique, La Truandaise*. This was no set-piece to display the ballerina's technical prowess, but a *pas de deux* that built up on the relationship between the artless Esmeralda and the besotted Gringoire, who can hardly believe his good fortune. 'Delicately imagined, novel and eccentric,'[8] the choreography hinted at Esmeralda's mysterious origin; 'the movement was,' as one observer noted, 'of the *Bolero* class, but no Spanish maid ever executed it with a thousandth part of the ease, the grace, the elegance and the precision' that Carlotta put into it.[9] Jules, who was still

---

* Carlotta Grisi was not accompanied, as other ballerinas later were, by a pet goat.

unable to dance full out, had been forced to limit his participation to supporting and displaying his ballerina, but what he sacrificed in virtuosity, he amply made up in the amusing by-play which he introduced into the dance to give it meaning in the context of the action. There was an extraordinary rapport between the two of them. The *Morning Post* admired his 'concealed support' of the ballerina, but appreciated even more the 'contrast of his assumed awkwardness' with Carlotta's 'infinite grace,' the enchanting interplay between Gringoire's 'joyful wonder' and the 'coquettish playfulness' of Esmeralda.[10] The *Morning Herald* went into greater detail, describing Carlotta's 'animated circling round the stage, tempting him to follow her, now dipping towards him, now avoiding him, now peeping at him archly under her arm, always within two paces of him, and yet eluding his touch, until he becomes almost tipsy with delight and fascination.' It was all 'exquisitely given, and . . . quite worthy of comparison with Elssler's *pas d'entraînement* in *La Gipsy*.'[11] In a later description the same critic wrote of 'the graceful dip of [Carlotta's] head, the animated circling among the dusky truands, and the good-natured humour with which [the *pas*] overflows.'[12] That movement of the head, a kind of 'tossing from side to side,' was a feature of her first entrance, designed as a key to her character, conveying, as *The Times* remarked, 'a playful heedlessness, a careless sense of enjoyment.'[13] But for all Carlotta's winning charms, it was the 'odd mixture of the grotesque and graceful'[14] in Jules' interpretation that held the dance together. 'How drolly does he follow his arch protectress, fascinated by her merry wiles! He is tipsy with delight. He tries to touch her, but she naively eludes him. Still he goes on, gaining fresh accessions of mad enthusiasm every moment, until in a whirl of excitement the simpleton falls prostrate at his tormenter's feet. How capitally all this is done by Perrot.'[15]

The truands and their womenfolk then join in a *bacchanale,* during which the cloaked figure of Claude Frollo, the ascetic archdeacon of the cathedral, makes his appearance. His eyes never leave Esmeralda, for whom he has contracted an obsessive passion. Every now and then she encounters his glance, and seems to shrink from him in repugnance.

At the sound of the curfew the crowd disperses, and only Frollo and Clopin are left on the stage. The priest confides his desire to the truand chief: he is determined to possess Esmeralda that very night. Learning that Esmeralda will shortly pass through the Cour des Miracles on her way to her lodging, Frollo summons his henchman, the hunchback Quasimodo, and the two men conceal themselves. Soon Esmeralda's footsteps are heard, and as she comes into view Frollo springs out at her. There is a brief struggle, but the attempted abduction is interrupted by the arrival of the archers of the guard on their nightly round. Frollo manages to escape, but Quasimodo is seized. Esmeralda is dazzled by the handsome appearance of her rescuer, the captain of the guard, Phoebus de Chateaupers. He is no less taken with her, and asks

Jules Perrot

her who she is. Coquettishly toying with the silk scarf he wears over his uniform, she tells him she is an orphan and alone in the world. At that moment she sees Quasimodo, struggling in the clutches of the archers. He is almost fainting with thirst, and filled with pity, she takes a gourd from her belt and offers it to him. She begs the guard to release him. Pheobus gives the order, and the hunchback limps away, casting a dog-like look of gratitude at Esmeralda. Phoebus now demands a kiss as his reward. Esmeralda modestly recoils, and hands back his scarf. He refuses to take it, but before he can press his attentions further, she has slipped from his arms and disappeared into the night. Phoebus orders his men to continue their round. Although disappointed at the girl's flight, his eyes are aglow, 'the joy of his past life . . . replaced with the troubled memory of the lovely vision on which he was gazing but a moment since.'[16]

Played on the front section of the stage, the second scene – '*La Nuit des Noces*' – was set in Esmeralda's humble lodging. She enters in a reflective and melancholy mood, holding Phoebus's scarf in her hands. Sitting at her rough table, she takes up some ivory letters, which she arranges to spell out the name PHOEBUS. She is lovingly gazing at them when Gringoire enters. For a few moments he stands in admiration before her, then assuming, in his simple innocence, that she loves him, moves forward with an air of timid triumph and slips his arm round her waist. Startled out of her reverie, Esmeralda pushes him away. He persists in his advances until she stops him short by pulling out her dagger from her belt and brandishing it before him. He starts back in fright. She makes it clear that she has married him only out of pity, and that he can hope for nothing more than to be her companion and to accompany her when she dances in the streets. Ruefully he accepts this arrangement, and Esmeralda begins to teach him to dance. Like the *Truandaise*, the *pas scénique* that followed, fitted naturally into the action by explaining the relationship that was developing between them. Gringoire watches the girl sweep through her dance, admiring her grace and her voluptuous movements, and then, made to accompany her, does his awkward best until, worn out by exertion and the day's excitements, he begs to be allowed to rest. Esmeralda shows him into the next room, and he leaves her with a look of disappointed resignation.

Esmeralda throws herself upon her couch. But scarcely has she done so than the door opens and Frollo and Quasimodo stand before her on the threshold. She rises in alarm and is about to call for Gringoire when Frollo falls to his knees, imploring her to listen to his declaration. She orders him to leave, and by showing him the letters spelling out the name of Phoebus, makes him understand that she loves another. Maddened with jealousy, Frollo rushes at the girl, who shrinks at his feet and implores him to have pity on her. Quasimodo makes no move to intervene, but his expression shows that he is torn between his duty to his master and gratitude to Esmeralda for rescuing him from the guard. When Frollo turns aside to make sure that the door of the adjoining room is fastened, Esmeralda manages to escape through a concealed door he has not noticed. Frollo is about to follow her when Gringoire, who has heard the disturbance, appears. Frollo threatens to strike him if he approaches. Quasimodo stays the arm of the priest, who swears that he will be revenged on Phoebus.

A change of mood heralded the third scene, for which William Grieve had painted one of his most effective sets, 'an exquisite Watteau picture on a large scale,'[17] depicting the garden of the Hôtel Gondelaurier, where preparations are in progress for the wedding of the daughter of the house. Jules entitled this scene – the centre-piece of the ballet – *'Fleur de Lys,'* after the high-born bride-to-be, who was played by a young ballerina from Florence making her first appearance in London, Adelaide Frassi. She made her entrance at the beginning of the scene, accompanied by two bridesmaids (played by Thérèse Ferdinand and Jenny Barville). The three girls begin weaving flowers into garlands, and when Madame de Gondelaurier enters, Fleur de Lys runs up to her and shows her her handiwork. This was the cue for a *pas des fleurs* for Fleur de Lys and her two companions, a conventional *pas de trois* in which Jules displayed the promising talent of Frassi, who danced with a suggestion of Cerrito's ebullience and showed a remarkable skill on her *pointes*. The opening of this scene presented a graceful contrast to the realism of the Cour des Miracles; the truands were a world away from the 'pretty combination of nymphs clad in white satin with silver embroideries, scarfs entwined with flowers, picturesque temples and foliage illuminated with lamps.'[18]

In this charming setting Phoebus – the man whom Fleur de Lys is to wed – makes a resplendent entrance. Of all Hugo's principal characters, it was he who had undergone the greatest transformation. Instead of the unattractive figure he cut in the novel, where he is depicted as an empty peacock of man, a coarse and unprincipled womaniser caring little for the girls who catch his roving eye, Saint-Léon presented him in a favourable light, although it was clear, from the manner in which he kisses Fleur de Lys' hand on his entrance, that he has grown indifferent to her. She senses this, and notices that he is no longer wearing the silk scarf she had embroidered for him. The guests are now arriving, and the festivities commence. Saint-Léon, exuding male allure, took a prominent part in a *pas de trois* with Elisa Scheffer and Adeline Plunkett, showing off his soaring elevation. 'Many of his steps are prodigiously difficult,' conceded the *Morning Post*, 'but in spite of the furious applause, we do not admire them, excepting in one extraordinary saltatory artifice, in which [he] looks as if he flew like the flying Mercury in the well-known picture of Pietro da Cortona.'[19]

Esmeralda then enters to dance before the guests, attended by the faithful Gringoire, who carries a guitar and her tambourine. Fleur de Lys is struck by the dancer's strange costume and wild beauty, and goes up to speak to her.

Jules Perrot

Esmeralda tells her she can read the future, and taking her hand, predicts happiness in her marriage. Enchanted, Fleur de Lys gives her a ring and invites her to dance. At that moment Esmeralda's eyes meet those of Phoebus, who, oblivious of the presence of his betrothed, takes her hand and begs her to dance with him. This led into the *pas de la Esmeralda*, in which Esmeralda's infatuation with Phoebus overcomes her prudence, and she seems to brim over with happiness. This moment of elation was Carlotta's '"crowning glory," in that she achieved, perhaps, one of the most perfect triumphs ever achieved in dancing.'[20] Meanwhile Fleur de Lys, hardly believing her eyes, reproaches her fiancé, who makes a cool protest in reply. Esmeralda then begins to dance with Gringoire, and wishing to give Phoebus a sign that she is thinking of him, displays the scarf. Fleur de Lys recognises it at once. Shattered by such a betrayal, she rushes forward to snatch it from the dancer's hands and, heaping bitter reproaches on Phoebus, falls fainting at his feet. After she has been led away, the scandalised guests turn on Esmeralda, but Gringoire shields her from their anger and leads her out of the garden. Phoebus, after a moment of hesitation, follows them.*

For the fourth scene, set in a cabaret overlooking the Seine, the action again moved to the front of the stage. Under the title of '*Amour et Jalousie*,' Esmeralda's assignation with Phoebus and its violent outcome was presented as a short but highly effective mime scene lasting only a few minutes. It was an important turning point of the drama, and Jules had followed Hugo's narrative as closely as contemporary taste would allow, refining it only so much as he felt necessary. In the novel Esmeralda restrains her passion only momentarily, and then not from modesty but because she would be breaking a vow she has made and endangering her chance of discovering her true parents (a motive excised in the ballet), and yields readily to Phoebus's advances. In the ballet Jules toned down Esmeralda's abandon with a show of modesty. The situation could so easily have caused offence, but where another choreographer might have timidly changed its whole purport, Jules retained as much of its original flavour as he dared and coached Carlotta to steer a middle course, playing down Esmeralda's passion for Phoebus, yet not altogether slurring over the significance of the scene. How well she fulfilled his purpose was illustrated by the comment of *The Times* that 'not only what she did, but what she did *not* do, stamped her as an artist of a high order.'[21]

---

* This scene was to be extensively reworked, with new music, for Fanny Elssler in Milan the following winter. The piano score published in London in the summer, while complete for Scenes 1, 2 and 5, omitted Scene 4 altogether and included only three dance numbers from Scene 3 – the *pas des fleurs* (later to be known as the *pas des corbeilles*), the *pas de la Esmeralda*, a *Tyrolienne* and a *Galop* ('as danced by Mlle Carlotta Grisi and M. Perrot'). The last three were to be replaced in Jules' later revision of this scene: see pp. 136 and 232.

An Essay in Dance Drama

The scene opened with the entrance of Clopin, bearing a torch. He is closely followed by Frollo, to whom he shows a dark corner where he can hide. Left alone, Frollo draws from his cloak Esmeralda's dagger, which he has somehow purloined, and then, hearing a sound on the stairs, withdraws into the shadows. He is clearly there with evil intent. Soon Phoebus and Esmeralda enter. The soldier passionately declares his love, but Esmeralda holds back, asking how he can love two women at the same time and in a momentary burst of jealousy throwing down the ring which Fleur de Lys has given her. Then, taking a feather from his plume, she breathes on it and allows it to float to the ground, telling him that such is the worth of his love. But the blandishments of the experienced seducer soon have their effect, and in a show of innocent coquetry, she falls to her knees before him. The sight of her gazing so lovingly into Phoebus's eyes is more than Frollo can bear. Unable to restrain his jealousy, he leaps from his hiding place with the dagger in his hand. He freezes, for he realises that the lovers are still unaware of his presence, and when Phoebus leads Esmeralda into the adjoining bedroom, he stealthily follows them. Offstage a blow and a groan are heard, then the fall of a body. Frollo rushes back and makes his escape through the window. He is followed by Esmeralda who, distraught with terror, falls fainting to the floor. A crowd of strangers, Clopin at their head, come running into the room. Clopin enters the bedroom and returns to announce that murder has been committed. He denounces Esmeralda, who is seized and carried away, weeping and protesting her inocence. Frollo's plan has succeeded all too well.

The full stage area was then revealed for the fifth scene, a reconstruction of old Paris, with the forbidding wall of a prison on the right and the twin towers of Notre Dame rising in the background. All the principal characters were to be featured in the action leading up to the final *dénouement*, but equally prominent was the rôle of the corps de ballet, again employed with impressive realism, this time as the people of Paris whose reactions added colour and excitement to the dramatic events that lead Esmeralda to within a hair's breadth of the hangman's noose. The title which Jules gave to this scene, the '*Fête des Fous*,' stressed the crowd's importance. This incident, in which Quasimodo is borne in procession through the streets as the Fool's Pope, was placed much earlier both in the novel and in the opera to establish the physical deformity of Quasimodo and his relationship with Frollo, but Jules used it to contrast the carefree enjoyment of the Paris crowd with the awful predicament of his heroine. Taking up the story from the drama that had ended the assignation in the cabaret, he opened the scene with Esmeralda being taken to prison under an escort of archers, preceded by the sinister figure of Frollo and followed by a crowd of curious onlookers. Gringoire then enters, and standing outside the prison gates, is horror-struck to hear the sentence of death being pronounced on Esmeralda. He protests passionately to those around him at

Jules Perrot

the brutality of hanging the dancer who has given everyone such pleasure, and is beginning to arouse their pity and anger when the procession of the Fool's Pope erupts on to the stage. The crowd turns away from Gringoire to join in the revelry, and the injustice to Esmeralda is forgotten in a moment. In a scene 'full of uproarious gaiety and licence,' Quasimodo is carried in by the truands 'on a tray and surrounded by tall candles.'[22] At that moment Frollo comes out of the prison, and seeing Quasimodo so sacrilegiously attired, tears the mock papal robes from his shoulders. This outburst brings on another change of mood. The prison doors open, and Esmeralda is led out to the scaffold. The procession pauses to allow her to bid farewell to Gringoire, to whom she confides her last wish – to be buried with Phoebus's scarf. Frollo then approaches and tells her he can save her if she will return his love. In her anguish she bitterly turns away and calls down the vengeance of God upon him. He signals the archers to continue on their way, but at that moment Phoebus, whose wound has not been fatal after all, appears among the crowd. Esmeralda swoons at the sight of him. Flinging himself on his knees before her, he declares her to be innocent and points an accusing finger at Frollo, who is immediately arrested. Gradually Esmeralda comes to her senses to see Phoebus at her feet, offering her his hand and heart. Her face lights up with joy. But the happiness of the lovers drives Frollo to his final act of madness. He rushes at Esmeralda with the dagger, but Quasimodo stops him and, seizing the weapon, plunges it into the archdeacon's heart. The ballet ended with the crowd rejoicing at Esmeralda's deliverance.

The applause that had punctuated the performance seemed hardly to cease at all when Carlotta was on the stage, and Lumley felt more than adequately compensated for the cool reception accorded to the opening opera. Less than eight weeks remained before Carlotta was due to return to Paris, and of the nineteen performances that were given during that time, *La Esmeralda* was included in fifteen, the first twelve in unbroken succession.

The care, not to say love, with which Jules had fashioned the rôle of Esmeralda shone through every nuance of Carlotta's performance. Her triumph in this new creation transcended the perfection of her dancing, resting on an insight into the character as much as on her natural charms. No one understood her artistic capabilities so thoroughly as Jules, for whom she remained a fountain of inspiration in spite of their separation, and with his profound awareness of her potential he moulded her interpretation into a portait glowing with the exquisite grace and delicate intricacy of her movements and her own personal enchantment, yet faithful to Hugo's novel, which he had certainly made her read and discussed with her. The result was 'a wild, lively girl, sensitive and affectionate, waggish and passionate – full of archness and amiability, waywardness and *espiéglerie*'[23] – 'a compound of merriment, sprightliness, love and benevolence,'[24] though with a gaiety that was touched by 'a certain pensiveness . . . which [was] individual and captivating.'²⁵ How perfectly she had woven her interpretation, under Jules' guidance, into the fabric of the drama was the subject of a thoughtful account in *The Times*.

Carlotta, wrote its critic, 'possesses the characteristics of all schools, and has blended them into a school of her own. In her representation of Esmeralda, there was something of the innocent playfulness of Cerrito, of the arch coquetry of Elssler, and of the quiet poetry of Taglioni. Yet all was so attuned as to produce a perfect representation of the graceful, the tender, the impassioned Esmeralda. The achievements she performs in her *pas* frequently astonish less, because she has acquired such a mastery over her art that she can perform them without effort. Difficulties, when executed by her, appear difficulties no longer. On Saturday, all the resources of her art were employed dramatically, all were illustrative of the character. The first bound on the stage with the tambourine was the rush of youthful spirits; her tantalising *pas de deux* with Gringoire was a compound of good humour, a mild sort of malice. She could not help pitying the poor wretch, and yet she was amused at his trouble. When alone with her lover Phoebus, nothing could be more exquisitely managed than her pantomime. The timidity with which she recoiled from him, and which gradually gave way to the overpowering effects of her love, the contest between two feelings, which gradually subsided, was most beautifully managed. Those who have read the novel itself, and know what the scene in the cabaret is in the original, can alone appreciate the delicacy with which a situation so critical was preserved without the slightest offence, while all the emotions were retained.'[26]

The injury that had effectively closed Jules' career as a virtuoso dancer had to a large extent dictated the nature of his own rôle in the ballet, and may even have led him to choose the character of Pierre Gringoire. Both Hugo in the opera libretto and the author of Monticini's ballet scenario had transformed the profligate Phoebus into a tender, loving hero and discarded Gringoire as superfluous. Jules had also felt obliged to give Phoebus the honour of saving and winning Esmeralda at the end, but realising how ill-suited this braggart was to his own nature, he sought another part for himself in the pages of the novel and discovered Gringoire. It proved a perfect choice. With an affecting combination of humour and pathos, he gave a sympathetic portrait of a common man possessing natural goodness – a striking contrast to the stock ballet hero to which audiences were then accustomed. Humour was the keynote of his performance, an impish humour stroked with touches of sadness in a mixture that only true comedians can achieve. The *Spectator* described his performance as 'an exquisite piece of serio-comic pantomime' in which 'the quaint simplicity and quiet earnestness which he throws into the character render it at once ludicrous and touching.'[27] 'Ruefully qaunt' was the impression he made on the *Athenæum*.[28] He acted with great energy, investing his movements with 'much character and meaning,'[29] while never exceeding the bounds set by the narrative. His presence always added emphasis to the course of the action. *The Times* cited two examples of this: Gringoire's 'highly comical' terror when the truands threaten to hang him in the first scene, and at the end, 'his grief when he saw Esmeralda led to execution,' expressed with 'a fine touch of pathos, heightened by the general drollery of the character.'[30]

If Jules had taken the part of Phoebus, he would certainly have made it into a more rounded character than did Saint-Léon, who appeared merely as 'an excellent representative of the military Adonis,'[31] earning his applause primarily by his spectacularly virile dancing. The character of Claude Frollo, on the other hand, was central to the plot and, while necessarily less developed than in the novel, came across strongly in the 'effective pantomime' of Louis Gosselin, while Coulon who, as Quasimodo, had little to do except to give Frollo his quietus at the end, 'artistically sketched off the rugged peculiarities of the hunchback.'[32]

Sharing, in a somewhat modest degree, in Jules' triumph was Cesare Pugni, who had written the accompanying music. It did not please every musical ear, reactions to it ranging from the 'very bad'[33] of the *Athenæum* to the 'pleasing'[34] of *The Times*. More specific was the *Morning Post*, which spoke of its 'musical imagery'[35] and – influenced surely by what Jules did with it – even saw it as posing a threat to opera. 'We feel the greater necessity of resisting the encroachments of the increasing enthusiasm for the ballet, and of assigning to it its rightful place,' explained its critic, 'since [it] possesses all the attractions that can militate against the supremacy of its lyrical rival. Signor Pugni is decidedly a traitor to Euterpe; he is clearly capable of writing far better operas than some we are doomed to endure. The music of the ballet is, from end to end, highly descriptive and characteristic; the air of the *truandaise*, the plaintive transition when "the curfew tolls the knell of parting day," the charming violoncello instrumentation in the third tableau, as well as the spirited chorus dances, are instances of infinite talent.'[36]

* * *

Meanwhile old Deshayes, who was now living in retirement in Paris, was following Jules' career from occasional letters which arrived for him from London. Jules himself was a very dilatory correspondent. When he did write, his letters were wittily expressed, but his correspondence tended to fall into arrear, particularly when he was working at the pressure demanded of him during the London season. It was, therefore, Coulon who gave the old man the news of Jules' new triumph. 'The ballet of *La Esmeralda*,' he wrote, 'has had a brilliant success which grows with every performance. Perrot has been completely successful with the corps de ballet numbers and in general with all his dances. Mlle Frazi (*sic*) is a young person whom the administration is anxious to boost. She is very pleasant, but in my opinion will not be up to the leading rôle if by ill chance they cannot get Carlotta's leave extended.'[37]

An Essay in Dance Drama

Happily, Lumley was able to persuade the Paris Opéra to allow Carlotta to remain in London until the beginning of May, which enabled him not only to make the most of *La Esmeralda*, but also to fit in four performances of *Giselle*. This was a much appreciated treat, for Carlotta had refined her rendering of Giselle to a point that emphasised more than ever Jules' use of dance in conveying the action. 'One peculiar feature of this beautiful ballet,' the *Morning Post* informed its readers, 'is that, like *La Esmeralda*, the dance forms the very essence of the character. The joyousness of the light-hearted Silesian maiden constantly expands itself in the dance, and the wili is essentially a dancing spirit. In the delineation of the character by Carlotta Grisi there is natural pensiveness of expression and an eloquent graceful abandon, and a daring, combined with elegance and poetry.'[38] In her last performance in the rôle before returning to France 'she exerted herself even more than her wont, displaying first with matchless grace the ingenuous enthusiasm of youth, headlong in the pursuit of innocent pleasure,' and then, in the mad scene, giving 'an exquisite piece of pantomime, portraying the wounded spirit of the young girl suddenly withering like a crushed flower.' It was still in the second act that she made the greater impression. 'Her performance after her resuscitation in the realms of the Queen of the Wilis is, however, what most remarkably displays her wonderfully light, graceful and agile style of dancing.'[39]

The extension of Carlotta's leave that Lumley managed to extort from the Opéra allowed Jules to prepare a farewell *bonne bouche*. In the past few weeks a new dance had become the rage in the London ballrooms. Everyone seemed to be dancing the polka, and Jules decided to exploit the new craze by arranging a version for the stage which he and Carlotta first danced on April 11th and repeated four times more during her last three weeks in London. The audiences adored it, and in no time the print shops were displaying Joseph Bouvier's new lithograph of the two dancers in a characteristic pose, he with his arms akimbo, wearing a scarlet knee-length tunic, spurred boots and a military cap of Polish style, and she in a matching scarlet bodice and plain white skirt, with the most elegant little boots just covering her ankles. Another souvenir for enthusiasts was the piano arrangement of Pugni's music, entitled 'The Opera House Polka,' which found its way into many a home, where the jogging little melody revived memories of the exhilarating dance. It was never intended to be more than an entertaining trifle, and if the critic of *The Times* doubted whether it was an authentic example of Bohemian folklore, he conceded that, thanks to Carlotta, 'the most attractive of coquettes,' it made an 'agreeable' and 'pretty spectacle.'[40] Another critic, in the *Spectator*, described it as 'one of those smart, jerking, military dances, in which the heels have full as much work to do as the ankles.' There was none of the rarified balletic elegance in the 'quaint, coquettish, playful' manner in which the two dancers performed 'the brisk, romping movements.'[41] As they

Jules Perrot

got into their stride, they 'stamp at one another, and smile at one another, and the lady looks a myriad of coquetries over her shoulder at the gentleman.'[42] Then, as the dance drew to its conclusion, Carlotta, 'holding with both hands the arm-akimbo of her partner,'[43] wheeled him around the stage with vertiginous speed, 'as if she thought the arm and the socket of the shoulders should be divorced.'[44]

Jules did not consider this trifle important enough to claim credit for its arrangement, but there can be little doubt that he was responsible for it. The polka craze had in fact burst upon Paris after his departure, but its reverberations spread quickly across the Channel and London's leading dancing masters were already teaching the new dance. The technical details of it would have been readily available to Jules, most probably through his friends, the Coulons, for Eugène, the brother of the *régisseur de la danse* at Her Majesty's, ran a successful dancing school in Great Marlborough Street and had been one of the first teachers to introduce the dance to London. The polka proved to be no passing fad; as well as acquiring a lasting place in ballroom dancing, it was to be eagerly taken up by choreographers as an addition to their vocabulary. Jules could claim an almost proprietary interest for having introduced it on the London stage, but he may have done even more to popularise it if he was the Perrot whose name appeared with that of Adrien Robert on the title-page of an amusing little booklet on the polka craze, *La Polka enseignée sans maître*, that came out in Paris later in the year.

Lumley had gone to extraordinary lengths to retain Carlotta in London until the very latest minute, hiring a special train – at a cost, it was reported, of £24 – to take her to Folkestone after her benefit performance. From the theatre she went straight to her lodging, where she ate a hurried supper before emerging to make her way through a crowd of cheering admirers to the carriage that was to take her to the South Eastern Railway terminus at London Bridge. She crossed the Channel to Boulogne on one of the fastest steamers, and from Boulogne continued her journey by carriage, arriving in Paris just nineteen hours after leaving London. The following morning she presented herself to the Director of the Opéra.

Meanwhile Cerrito had arrived to take her place at Her Majesty's, and *La Esmeralda* had to give place to her repertory. *Ondine,* with a new *pas de quatre*, and a reduced and revised version of *Alma* – the first scene being cut and the ballroom scene reset to include two new numbers, a polka for the corps de ballet and a new *pas de deux* for Frassi and Henri Montessu – were revived, and plans were laid for a new ballet.

On a more frivolous level, there was another distraction which gripped the dancers and all those who feasted on backstage gossip. A bitter contest, with no holds barred, was being fought between two of the young soloists, Adeline Plunkett and Elisa Scheffer, for the affections of Lord Pembroke. It was finally Scheffer who won the day – so decisively that she was to share the Earl's life

An Essay in Dance Drama

until the end of his days – and the slender, elegant Plunkett was seething with indignation at being worsted by her more fleshy rival. Their hostility reached its climax when, as a result of some confusion in the wardrobe department, they were given each other's costumes for a performance of *Ondine*. Plunkett's dresser managed with a few stitches to make the larger costume fit, but such an adjustment was not possible for Scheffer, who could not get into hers. There was a violent confrontation and their *pas de deux* had to be omitted. That was not the end of the matter. A few minutes later Plunkett seized an opportunity to aim a savage kick at her rival in the wings, and in the resulting fracas the lamp supplying the moonlight for Cerrito's *pas de l'ombre* was brought crashing to the ground.

Ominous murmurs began to be heard in the audience, and a black-suited official nervously came out from the wings to make an announcement. His voice could hardly be heard above the hubbub, and an ugly scene seemed to be brewing when, with great presence of mind, Jules stepped forward in his fisherman's costume. At his appearance the house fell silent, and his words could be heard by everyone. '*Mesdames et messieurs, un accident impossible à prévoir a dérangé la machine de la lune . . . C'est une éclipse complète.*'[45] This timely display of humour had an immediate effect. The audience dissolved into laughter, and waited patiently while the lamp was placed back into position and repaired.

Jules was then in the throes of preparing a new ballet for Cerrito, and the friendly critic of the *Morning Post* caught an illuminating glimpse of him in rehearsal. Having been deeply impressed by the dramatic sweep of *La Esmeralda*, this critic was curious to observe the ballet-master's method of using the dance to develop or heighten some aspect of the narrative. During a break in the rehearsal Jules explained what he wanted to achieve in a *pas d'action*. It was his aim to express the action entirely in terms of dance and to avoid 'the tedious gesticulations and mimicry between the *pas* which the public had formerly to endure, and . . . those sudden transitions that mar the illusion.' 'This portion of the ballet,' Jules explained, 'should bear the same relation to the grand feats of dancing which the *récitatifs* do to the *bravura* in an opera.' The journalist was much struck by the infinite pains to which the choreographer went to perfect these passages of danced action. 'As long as any member of the troupe is imperfect in his part,' he observed, 'he accompanies each step by an extempore dialogue of his own invention, explaining the feeling the performer is to express.'[46]

Unhappily, despite all the attention to detail and the lavish expenditure which Lumley had authorised for a creation for Cerrito, the new ballet, *Zélia, ou les Nymphes de Diane*, was a dismal failure. Drastically shortened after the first night on June 25th, its second performance was marred by an incident which dealt it a fatal blow. It was to be Jules' only complete failure. The causes were not hard to seek, for the pressures on the ballet department were apparent to everyone who followed the programmes at Her Majesty's. 'The management,' explained the Vicomtesse de Malleville in one of her weekly articles on the London scene, 'might require a new divertissement or ballet, not in three months, nor in one month, nor three weeks, but in ten or twelve days' time. Perrot sketches a scenario – mythological, historical, mediaeval or fairy-tale – in thirty-six hours, works out the scenes, casts the parts, rehearses them, and impressses upon the dancers the characters that each has to assume. Pugni writes the music with no less speed, and scene painters and machinists join forces to bring about the rapid birth of the work which is invariably produced on the day and hour appointed.'[47] The wonder was that Jules' inspiration did not fail him more often.

In the case of Zélia, however, he unwisely concocted a scenario of the anacreontic type that had long been out of fashion. With an interesting plot he might have overcome this disadvantage, but for some unaccountable reason the man who only a few weeks before had brought the stage dramatically alive with *La Esmeralda* turned to a story that was wholly devoid of interest. Lumley attributed the failure to the public's increasing reluctance to 'applying their mind and attention to the comprehension of a plot expressed in action,'[48] but the ballet was fundamentally flawed. It was 'too far-fetched to be easily intelligible,' and in spite of Jules' intentions, contained 'a good deal of superfluous pantomime.'[49]

The first scene, for which Grieve had painted 'a piece of water with some trees illuminated by warm sunny tints,' opened with Cupid – appropriately played by Adeline Plunkett – awakening to the sound of a horn that announces the approach of Diana (in the person of the mature Mme Copère) and her nymphs. The God of Love has a score to settle with Diana, who despises him for having once seduced one of her nymphs. From his hiding place he watches Diana instruct the nymphs in the use of the bow. This provided the theme for a *pas des flèches*, in which Cerrito, making her first entrance as Zélia in a fetching leopard-skin costume, carried all before her with 'her favourite *ronds de jambe*,' varying 'her step by a pretty action with her bow.'[50] She is awarded the prize, a rose, and is entrusted with the guardianship of this sacred spot. Cerrito then danced a *pas de la couronne* in which she gathered some flowers and forming them into a crown, placed them at the foot of Diana's statue. At that moment Amyntas, a young shepherd (Saint-Léon) who has fallen in love with Zélia, steals in and tries to snatch the crown to offer it instead to the statue of Cupid. The resulting struggle was depicted in a *pas de deux* that ended with Zélia's flight. Amyntas is in despair at being abandoned. Life seems hardly worth living, but Cupid comes to console him, promising that he will gain his heart's desire in the end.

The scene then changes to the moonlit temple of Diana. The goddess instructs Zélia to tend the sacred flame on her altar, but Cupid, bent on mischief, animates the statues who, at first imploringly and then with menaces, force Zélia to join them in worshipping the God of Love. At the sound of Diana's approach, Zélia realises the wrong she has committed and flees the sacred spot in shame.

In the third scene Zélia is discovered in the depths of a forest, where she has fallen asleep from fatigue, Diana's rose still firmly clasped in her hand. She stirs uneasily as if dreaming of her betrayal of the goddess. Pan – an impish rôle that Jules created for himself – then appears and steals the rose. Zélia wakes immediately and tries desperately to recover the flower in a *pas de la rose*, designed to express the conflict between prudence and passion. The struggle to gain possession of a desired object was a favourite motif in Jules' choreography, going back to the bouquet *pas de deux* in *Der Kobold*, and in *Zélia* being used both in the *pas de deux* in the first scene and now in the *pas de la rose*, which by general consent was the one redeeming feature of the entire ballet, being 'deliciously exhibitive of the floating style of Cerrito.'[51] Before Diana arrives in pursuit, Cupid sends a band of little amorets to carry Zélia away to the realms of love.

In the last scene Zélia is discovered bathing in a pool, fed by a waterfall and overlooked by a statue of Venus. At the outset there was some laughter at Cerrito's awkward simulation of swimming, her head bobbing up and down as she lay behind a ground-row painted to represent water. Zélia's attention is then caught by a butterfly, which she catches and presses to her bosom. Frightened by the violent effect it has on the beating of her heart, she throws it aside, but it is too late, for the butterfly is Cupid in another form and she is now hopelessly enslaved by love. Unfortunately the effect of this dance was ruined by the ridiculous aspect of the property butterfly, and the audience again broke into laughter as it flapped above Cerrito's head, looking like some 'emancipated cobweb.'[52] Cupid now comes to enjoy his triumph, bringing with him Amyntas, who has no difficulty in pressing his suit, and the ballet ended with a series of dances, a *ballabile*, a *pas de deux* for Scheffer and Montessu, and finally a *pas de deux* by Cerrito and Saint-Léon, supported by Mlles Ferdinand and Barville.

Next morning's newspapers left Jules in no doubt that the ballet had not been a success. While the choreography certainly had moments of real originality – 'we have rarely seen a ballet in which there was so much new in sculpturesque grouping and mazy figuring,' wrote one critic[53] – *The Times* damned it as a 'very sorry affair . . . dull in the highest degree,' with far too much 'uninteresting action,' and recommended that it should be reduced to a divertissement by condensing the first and last scenes and dividing them by the *pas de la rose*.[54] It had come at the end of a long programme, and the curtain had finally descended around one o'clock, by which hour many of the audience had already gone home. During the performance Cerrito had fallen, and Jules had badly sprained his foot. The doctors ordered him to rest for several weeks. His absence alone would have necessitated shortening the ballet,

Jules Perrot

but *The Times*' advice was heeded and it was very heavily cut for its second and last performance two days later, all that was retained being the archery scene and the dances that concluded the final scene.

At this second performance the *coup de grâce* was administered to this sorry ballet by an incident that brought it abruptly to a premature end. The cause was to be found, not in the shortcomings of the ballet itself, but in the attention that Saint-Léon was beginning to pay to Cerrito, who was to become his wife the following spring. Some of the men in the omnibus boxes were so offended that a mere dancer should presume to court their desirable favourite that they hissed and jeered at the poor man throughout the *pas de deux*. Saint-Léon finally could bear it no longer, and in a moment of exasperation, responded with an unmistakable gesture that aroused the fury of the young bloods. Saint-Léon's action, provoked though it was, was professionally unforgivable, and Lumley could only advise him to apologise, which he handsomely did in a letter to *The Times*. This, added to the reactions of the majority of the audience who objected very vocally to this baiting of the dancer, was the end of the matter and the incident was soon forgotten. So, too, was *Zélia*.

In fact, in the weeks leading up to *Zélia*, Jules' thoughts had been increasingly preoccupied with a far more absorbing and ambitious project. Fanny Elssler had arrived in London, and preparations had begun on the 'new grand ballet entitled *Jeanne d'Arc*' that had been announced as one of the season's important novelties, and in which it was confidently expected that Elssler would 'display her complete supremacy in the art of pantomime' in the rôle of Joan.[55] Alas, this exciting plan was upset when the doctors ordered Jules to rest his sprained foot, for it was now too late in the season to consider any postponement. This hitch proved fatal. If Elssler had been re-engaged the following year, it might have become the major creation of 1845, but that was not to be, and since *Jeanne d'Arc* was so specifically tailored to her exceptional dramatic skill, there could be no question of producing it for anyone else.

Fanny Elssler took her benefit on July 25th, by which time Jules had sufficiently recovered to arrange a divertissement, introduced by a modest narrative scene designed to bring out the lighter side of her talent. He was even able to take part himself, though only in a mime rôle, for he had not recovered enough strength to partner her in any of the dances. The title of the piece was *La Paysanne Grand Dame*, and its plot was admirably simple and easy to follow. The Count de Versai (Gosselin) has fallen in love with a village beauty Casida (Elssler), and by dazzling her mother (Mme Copère), he manages to entice the girl into his mansion. She is there received by his major domo Mognoz (Coulon), given fine clothes and instructed in the graces and manners of a lady. Her village lover Tonino (Perrot) gains access to the mansion and bitterly reproaches her for her inconstancy. Moved by his tears, Casida tears off her finery. At that moment the Count reappears. He begins by venting his indignation and anger, but his better feelings prevail and finally he gives the sweethearts his blessing.

This unpretentious trifle revealed Elssler's exquisite sense of comedy. She gave a hilarious performance, 'running round after her train like a kitten chasing its tail, coquetting with feathers in her headdress, and trying to see herself in a glass on every side,' then being taught 'to curtsy, to flirt with her fan, and ape the airs of a woman of quality,' and finally ordering the major domo out of the room in a display of mock authority. The support which Jules gave her in the rôle of her sweetheart did not go unnoticed. 'Earnestness [was] the secret of his success,' observed the *Spectator*. 'Whatever character he assumes, he never loses sight of dramatic propriety, nor steps out of his part, while his by-play is so quiet and significant that the eye follows him everywhere.'[56]

As a result of the disruption of *Jeanne d'Arc*, the season had to end, as it had begun, with *La Esmeralda*, which was revived on August 3rd, with Fanny Elssler in the title-rôle. Disappointed though he must have been, Jules coached the Viennese ballerina in the part of Hugo's heroine with the same care he would have devoted to moulding her into Joan of Arc. Presented with Elssler's unique sensitivity and histrionic power, the character of Esmeralda acquired an entirely new emphasis. The contrast between the interpretations of Carlotta and Elssler proved no less fascinating than the distinction between their two Giselles, and because their renderings were so different, and at the same time equally viable, the reputations of both of them were enhanced by the comparison.

Several critics maintained that Carlotta's reading of the character was more faithful to the original, but there was no disputing the tremendous dramatic force that Fanny Elssler brought to the part. In the words of one observer, she displayed 'a transcendent genius which, had her language been the poetry of words instead of the poetry of motion, would have made her one of the greatest actresses the world has ever seen.'[57] While Carlotta's Esmeralda had been 'far more native and unsophisticated,'[58] Elssler's was 'characterised by far higher intellectuality, and the shades of feeling and passion [were] deeper marked'[59]; it was 'more womanly and methodical,' with 'less exuberant joyousness, less of spontaneous mirthful spirit.'[60]

There were some moments in the ballet in which Carlotta was judged to be superior. One of these was the *Truandaise*, in which Elssler lacked Carlotta's 'playfulness,' but on the other hand Elssler had made a more impressive first entrance, conveying 'a dash of wantonness in her gaiety and of wilfulness in her generosity, and her smile [revealing] "the lurking devil in her eye."'[61] Another passage in which Carlotta had the edge was the cabaret scene. Here, it was remembered, she had given 'a more affectionate and languishing cast' to the assignation with Phoebus, yielding to him with the 'feebleness of a lovesick maiden,' simple and trusting. Elssler's rendering of this passage was very

Jules Perrot

different, 'grand and classical – effective, but not engaging,' yet mounting to a 'magnificent' peak at the moment when Esmeralda is accused of Phoebus's murder. 'At first she is overcome with terror, but presently she swells with pride and innocence, and indignantly confronts her denouncers, until, being sensible of her weak and forlorn condition, her courage forsakes her, and she droops into dejection and submissiveness.'[62]

Elssler's interpretation was perhaps a more conscious creation, highlighting the scenes that brought her great dramatic gifts into play. Her gesture of pity at Gringoire's predicament in the opening scene gave an indication of the great moments that were to follow. In Esmeralda's confrontation with Frollo in the second scene, she expressed the heroine's revulsion at the priest's declarations with great force, working this confrontation into 'an incident of terrific importance by the skill of the actress. The attitude she assumed, expressive of fear and horror, was startling; the cold shiver that seemed to pervade her frame, the fixed uplifting of her arms, and the apprehension depicted on her countenance presented altogether a picture of mental uneasiness and womanish timidity not often realised on the stage; and it may easily be imagined that the subsequent struggle with the infuriate ravisher was elaborated strongly and effectively.'[63] But the full flood of her powers was reserved for the last scene of all, with 'her prayer to heaven, her resignation to her fate, mingled with her remembrance of her lover, and her sorrow at parting with her friends . . . all expressed in a few seconds with marvellous truth.'[64]

To many it must have seemed that the art of mime could be carried no further, and reading these impressions, recorded by eye-witnesses still aglow with the memory, one is filled with a sense of loss that *Jeanne d'Arc* was to remain a choreographer's unfulfilled dream.

Before leaving London Jules spared a thought for his old friend Deshayes, to whom, as his conscience reminded him, a letter was long overdue. 'Dear Monsieur Deshayes,' he began in his neat sloping hand, 'My heart is too full of remorse on your account for me not to bare it a little before having the joy of embracing you in person. I feel an ungrateful fellow, a negligent wretch, for I have responded to your flattering interest in me by a culpable silence. I am angry with myself, I swear, and crave your indulgence to forgive me for wrongs for which I have only myself to blame. I was moreover looking forward to the pleasure of telling you about my works, and through long-winded descriptions enabling you, so to speak, to share in the happy successes I have obtained . . . In truth, my dear Monsieur Deshayes, if I did not have the right to call myself the laziest and most forgetful creature of all time, I would certainly consider myself the least deserving of the precious title of friend. Having said this, let me assure you that my heart is in the right place and that I still regard you with the warmest affection. My business with Mr. Lumley for next season was concluded several days ago. His behaviour to me has been noble and delicate, and thus I owe him my head, legs and more than that . . .

An Essay in Dance Drama

'A very slight indisposition has detained me here for much longer than I had planned, for I am impatient to see my dear little daughter and all my friends again. I leave tomorrow, and shall be in Paris on Friday or Saturday at the latest.'[65]

Unlike the last few winters, Jules had only two months in which to relax and prepare for his next engagement. Early in November he had to tear himself away from Paris and the enchanting company of his Julie, who was now a growing child of seven, and set out, by coach, for Milan. At the end of the fatiguing journey an exciting prospect awaited him, for his destination was the prestigious Teatro alla Scala, where he was to produce *La Esmeralda* with Fanny Elssler in the title-rôle.

He was able to start rehearsals soon after he arrived, beginning with the corps de ballet, who first had to accustom themselves to his occasional lapses into English.

'Now leddies,' he would cry, forgetting he was no longer at Her Majesty's, 'take your pleeces – again if you plees,' and they soon understood the meaning of his commands of 'Stoppe!' and 'Go on!'[66]

With the details of the choreography still fresh in his mind, he had no difficulty in teaching the company their parts with a minimum of delay. The Scala had a strong complement of specialised mimes who acted in a manner renowned for its forceful gestures, and with their participation *La Esmeralda* inevitably acquired an Italian accent. The principal rôles were undoubtedly more strongly shaded than they had been in London, Domenico Ronzani making an impressive Frollo, with Effisio Catte as a memorable Quasimodo in a skilfully padded costume, and Gaspare Pratesi presenting Phoebus as a 'cold and fatuous lover.'[67]

The production was ready in good time for the opening night of the Carnival season on December 26th. Its success was not for a moment in doubt. Jules' ingenuity in condensing Victor Hugo's novel into five scenes was fully appreciated by the Milanese, who could remember two earlier attempts to stage it – Antonio Monticini's ballet, and more recently, an opera by Mazzucato – and unanimously acclaimed the new ballet as infinitely superior. As in London, it was performed straight through without an interval, and even though the audience had sat through an opening ballet and a complete performance of Verdi's *I Lombardi* they were gripped from beginning to end by the mounting tension of the drama. The complexity and variety of the action and the situations made an immediate impact, and if the ballet seemed occasionally to flag when Jules and Elssler were not on stage, that was probably due more to the audience's fatigue than to any shortcoming in the ballet itself.

The various *pas de deux* in which the relationship between Esmeralda and Gringoire was established aroused great interest, the two dancers seeming to complement one another perfectly. Jules' acting – refreshingly free from

Jules Perrot

exaggeration with which, to northern eyes at least, Italian mimes tended to play comic rôles – was in no way overshadowed by the performance of Elssler. The *Truandaise* and the dancing lesson scene remained unchanged from the London production, but for the danced scene in the betrothal festivities Jules created an entirely new *pas d'action*, replacing the *pas de la Esmeralda*, the *Tyrolienne* and the *Galop* of Pugni's score to new music by Bajetti.* Prompted by Elssler's extraordinary power of dramatic projection, the motive behind this revision was to highlight the poignant situation where Esmeralda finds herself forced to entertain the guests after discovering that the object of her devotion is the intended bridegroom. By concentrating the attention still more on the plight of Esmeralda, this *pas* immeasurably increased the emotional intensity of the scene, and indeed of the whole ballet. It was to remain a feature of the ballet for as long as Jules was to be concerned with it, and for quarter of a century after that.

Jules had to leave Milan at the end of January in order to honour his contract with Lumley, and on the evening of his farewell, on the 26th, he was given an ovation 'two or even three times greater than a male dancer or a choreographer had received in a long while'[68] and presented with a triumphal crown. It was only a month since *La Esmeralda's* first performance at the Scala, and it had already been given there seventeen times. Before the season ended, eight more performances were to be added with his fellow-countryman, Hippolyte Monplaisir, taking the rôle of Gringoire.

This double triumph as choreographer and mime awakened old longings in Jules' heart. He began to hope that *La Esmeralda* might prove the key to the Paris Opéra, and later that year he approached the Director, Léon Pillet, with a proposal to revive it in Paris. But once again the Fates were against him. Now more than ever he must have appeared as a threat to the established *maîtres de ballet*, who protested no doubt as a matter of principle against the idea of presenting a ballet that had been previously performed elsewhere. To Jules' dismay their objections prevailed, and in November it was briefly announced that the Opéra's plans to stage *La Esmeralda* had fallen through. It was reported that a few snatches of his choreography for *La Esmeralda* were introduced by Carlotta Grisi in two of the *pas de deux* in *Le Diable à quatre*, which Mazilier created for her that summer, but if that was true, they could only have been the tiniest scraps from the great dramatic work on which London and Milan had feasted. Although the very nature of *La Esmeralda's* narrative and setting made it unquestionably appropriate for the

---

* In the violin rehearsal score now at the Bibliothèque Nationale, used for later productions in St. Petersburg, the music for this *pas de deux* is bound separately. Another manuscript rehearsal score of the *pas de deux*, which is obviously earlier in date, bears the pencil note: '*Milan, dans la Esmeralda, Ellssler (sic) Perrot* This *pas de deux* was attributed by Bajetti in the piano score published in Milan by Ricordi.

repertory in Paris, Jules was never to have the satisfaction of producing it there, and its only Paris production – at the Théâtre de la Porte-Saint-Martin in 1856 – was by another hand.

11

The Championing of Lucile Grahn

The ballet department of Her Majesty's was now running like a well-oiled machine, driven by men who had worked harmoniously together for several years under the paternal supervision of Benjamin Lumley and the inspiring direction of Jules Perrot. Sadly, however, the season of 1845 saw a change in the team. Death had claimed William Grieve, when still in his forties, and to take his place as chief scene painter Lumley had secured the services of Charles Marshall, a no less distinguished artist who had learnt his craft at Drury Lane from the vastly experienced Gaetano Marinari, who himself in his younger days had designed scenery for Noverre's last productions in London. A competent and experienced staff was becoming more and more essential to take full advantage of Lumley's increasingly ambitious engagement lists. The announcement of forthcoming attractions for 1845 reflected the growing prosperity of the theatre. For the ballet alone the subscribers were promised, in addition to the return of Cerrito and Carlotta, a young Danish ballerina, Lucile Grahn, who would be making her London début, a children's troupe, the Danseuses Viennoises, who had made a sensation in Paris, and the return of the great Taglioni who for the past two years had 'hesitated, wavered and finally rejected'[1] the offers Lumley had made her, but now, at the third time of asking, had agreed to give what was announced as her farewell season.

Since none of the more renowned ballerinas was available, Lucile Grahn was to bear the main burden of the first few weeks of the season – an exceptional opportunity, but, as events were to prove, a most gruelling test – and so it was for her that Jules planned the important ballet creation, *Eoline, ou la Dryade*, that was to follow Verdi's opera *Ernani* on the opening night of the season, Saturday, March 8th. Turning away from the strongly dramatic form which he had so effectively used in *La Esmeralda*, and which had tempted him to consider a ballet about Joan of Arc, Jules had gone to the rich store of Germanic legend and found his subject in the mildly satirical folk tales which Johann Musäus had written towards the end of the previous century. One of these, *Libussa*, which had recently been translated into English by John

Oxenford, had provided the idea he sought – the tale of a girl, part wood-nymph and part mortal, who assumes the form of a dryad when her human body is asleep. Also from Musäus Jules had discovered for himself the fantastic character of Rübezahl, prince of the gnomes.

In Musäus's story Libussa owed her supernatural nature to her dryad mother, who had vanished after the oak tree on which her existence depended was destroyed by lightning. Libussa's father was Duke of the Bohemians, and on his death Libussa was elected as his successor. Two powerful suitors contended for her hand, but she fell in love with a young man who had once come to her for advice. In time her people became dissatisfied with female rule, and demanded that she should choose a husband, but she outwitted the two suitors and, without causing offence to either of them, manipulated the magic signs so as to marry the man she loved. Rübezahl did not appear in this tale, but was featured in a number of other stories as the Spirit of the Giant Mountain, an unpredictable power, capricious and tempestuous, with alternating moods of good nature and malice, who could succour the unfortunate and then wreak vengeance on the luckless wayfarer who unwittingly insulted him by addressing him by his hated nickname of Rübezahl, the Turnip Counter, which recalled some unflattering episode he preferred to forget.

In the ballet scenario the character of Rübezahl remained close to Musäus's conception, but the tale of Libussa, which in the original was spread over a long period of time, gave place to a much simpler narrative which owed only the origin of its heroine to its literary source. Significantly, even her name had been changed. Libussa must have sounded harshly in Jules' ear, for he gave his heroine the more euphonious name of Eoline, suggested no doubt – and perhaps subconsciously – by a memory of *La Fille de l'air*, on which he had based *Der Kobold*. That piece had contained a minor character, the attendant of the heroine Azurine, called Eolin, and the name had registered in his mind like a musical phrase, which now surfaced to serve as the title for his new ballet. Following what had become his standard practice, Jules gave each scene a title of its own, and alternated scenes requiring the full stage with scenes that used only the front part of the stage, so as to eliminate intervals.

The curtain rose on a prologue, '*Le Palais du Gnome – La Vision.*' In the vast underground cavern where Rübezahl has his abode, attendant gnomes are performing mystic rites. To explain their master's preoccupation, a section of the cavern wall between two basalt columns dissolves into a tableau showing Rübezahl yearning amorously for a beautiful girl who is lying asleep on a bed. After the tableau has faded, Rübezahl makes his appearance from one of the columns which closes behind him. Obsessed with his passion, he must see the object of his desire once more, and another tableau is conjured before his eyes. The same girl is depicted, but she is now being wooed by a young lover, and Rübezahl, consumed by an uncontrollable rage, summons his myrmidons to make plans for seizing the girl.

Jules Perrot

The scenery of the cavern then rose into the flies to reveal a set of breathtaking beauty for the scene, '*Le Chêne et la Drayde – Les Jardins du Château.*' In the distance stands a castle surrounded by a lake whose surface is dappled by the reflections of the moon. Day has not yet broken, and a group of woodcutters, who have risen early, are awe-struck at the sight of dryads gambolling among the trees. Then, to add to their astonishment, a fairy-like creature comes gliding across the lake. It is Eoline, sister of the castle's owner, the Prince of Silesia. Being the Child of a mortal father and a dryad, she is fated, unknown to herself, to assume a dryad's form between midnight and cock crow. Slowly the moon fades, and the warm tints of the rising sun illumine the landscape and the distant castle. This scene was a masterly demonstration of the stage designer's art. Charles Marshall's use of the diorama to convey the transition from moonlight to dawn, and again the ingenious effect showing Eoline, a 'faint transparent figure,'[2] gliding across the lake created a hauntingly poetic illusion.

Eoline, having now resumed her human form, comes out to enjoy the sunshine. The reason for her happiness is revealed when her chosen bridegroom, Count Edgar, arrives, followed by her brother. A gaily costumed crowd from the castle and the village fill the stage to take part in the festivities. Four dances then follow in a sequence dictated not only by the need to achieve a gradual mounting of interest but also to separate the two *pas de deux* which were designed to display the new ballerina, Lucile Grahn, for whom the rôle of Eoline was created. First, the crowd parted to give space to the *coryphées* to perform a '*Valse Silésienne*.' Then came the first of the *pas de deux*, in which Grahn was partnered by Henri Toussaint, the young French dancer who was playing Edgar. Jules' aim in this *pas de fiancée* was to show off the ballerina's classical style and technique, with particular emphasis on her remarkable steadiness on *pointe*. The critic of the *Morning Post* was duly impressed. 'Supported by her partner,' he wrote, '[she] performed all the feats which have been deemed the greatest difficulties of the art of dancing. When she poised herself on the tip of her toe, raising the other admirably-shaped foot in mid-air, there was an ease and *aplomb* which we never saw surpassed, and we were much struck by the succession of beautiful curves her whole form presented. In these consist all the witchery of such steps; without this study of the line of beauty the most extraordinary appear more or less painful *tours de force* to the critical spectator.'[3] Next, to give the ballerina time to recover her breath, came a *pas de cinq*, danced with unaffected charm by Louise Weiss and Mlles Ferdinand, Demelisse, Cassan and Moncelet. Jules had delegated the arrangement of this one dance to his assistant, Gosselin, and there could hardly have been a more striking contrast when the last and most impressive dance in this divertissement followed.

At the end of the *pas de cinq* the mood of the scene suddenly changed as Rübezahl came rushing on to the stage in an eye-catching costume with a zigzag pattern in red and black that at once marked him as some sort of demon. Although instinctively repelled, Eoline is mesmerised by his personality and is unable to resist his will – a situation that provided the theme for the *mazurka d'extase*, a brilliantly original *pas d'action* which the Morning Post described as 'one of the most extraordinary creations of the genius of Perrot.'[4] The Times echoed this praise by calling it 'the best thing of the sort that has been done since the *valse de fascination* in *Alma*, and . . . marked by greater profundity of thought than that.'[5] Jules had perceived at once that Lucile Grahn possessed an unusual talent as a mime, and she responded by realising his conception in a 'truly wonderful'[6] manner, revealing herself to be 'a great pantomimic artist, manifesting an intelligence and aptitude, as well as a poetic feeling, likely to win the highest kind of repute. The composition of this *pas* is ingenious and characteristic. The fiend tempts the unwilling [Eoline] to dance. She is animated by an unnatural energy, which relaxes at each successive touch of the malicious Gnome, who catches her in his arms as she whirls "tipsily" before him; she recoils convulsively as his evil fingers compress and collapse her heart, until, bewildered and paralysed by his insidious power, she sinks down motionless at his feet. All this is described with consummate skill. Perrot's personation of the Gnome is a finished bit of demonianism; the glance of his eye is fiendish, and . . . poor [Eoline], all lightheartedness and innocence, seems to be benumbed as she comes under its withering influence.'[7] As she sinks exhausted to the ground at the end of this dance, her brother and Edgar hasten to her assistance, but when they turn to confront the demon, he vanishes from sight down a trap.

Eoline is carried, in a faint, to her room, where the third scene – '*La Chambre de la Fiancée – La Métamorphose*' – was played on the front portion of the stage while the scenery for the next scene was being set. Even there she is not safe from Rübezahl's influence. He appears to her again, and she seems powerless to resist his advances until the chimes of midnight are heard. Now is the moment when she assumes her dryad form, and to Rübezahl's amazement and dismay, she soars into the air and vanishes before his eyes.

The fourth scene – '*La Fôret des Dryades*' – was another scenic triumph for Charles Marshall, who carried out Jules' intentions not only with complete understanding but with an imagination that matched that of the choreographer. It was no ordinary forest scene that met the eye, but an array of 'huge oaks, spreading their knotted arms overhead, forming a dense mass of interlacing foliage.' By an ingeniously contrived lighting effect, the trees become transparent, and 'couching in the trunks and lying carelessly upon the branches are seen the figures of delicate wood-nymphs, whose gestures and draperies were brought into distinct form' by what was variously described as 'a flood of moonlight'[8] and 'a sort of flickering light.'[9] It was, wrote The Times, 'a charming idea – the best realisation of the spiritual we have seen. The doubtful point between existence and its contrary is exactly hit, and the

Jules Perrot

trees seem animated by a sort of indefinite life that fades if we would apprehend it.' From each tree a dryad emerges to join the slight form of Eoline in the *grand pas des dryades*, a dance scene in which Jules created a mood that was dreamily romantic. *The Times* found 'the grouping of the principal dryads, who occupy the front of the stage during this scene and form themselves into little knots, to break them again, in a *pas d'ensemble*,' to be 'admirable, and the entire picture . . . most complete.' Grahn herself was displayed most effectively as the central figure, dancing with 'innocent sportiveness' and 'a neatness without effort' that 'completely realised the notion of a fairy creature of the most amiable kind.'[10]

The drama reached its *dénouement* in the fifth scene, '*Les Noces Interrompues – La Vengeance du Gnome*,' in which Rübezahl sets fire to the forest in his anger at being spurned. As the tree that sprouted from her mother's oak is consumed by flames, Eoline's life-force leaves her, and in the final apotheosis – '*La Fôret embrasée*' – the dryads are seen flying away and Eoline bids a last farewell to the sorrowing Edgar.

The first performance, on March 8th, 1845, ended at an hour when all self-respecting Englishmen should have been in bed. The curtain had risen on *Ernani* – the first of Verdi's operas to be heard in England – long after the appointed time, and since the ballet did not start until midnight, it was half past one in the morning when the audience emerged into the sharp night air to go home. As one critic observed, it was asking for trouble to present two new works, with completely new scenery, at the beginning of the season. 'The stage of this immense theatre is so cramped for room as to render each manoeuvre a *tour de force* – whilst the various occupants of the stage are each speaking a different language and are constantly misunderstanding one another at the beginning of the season until they have established a sort of conventional jargon, or *lingua franca*, the most risible that can be imagined.'[11]

In such circumstances a mediocre ballet would have exasperated a weary public, but not so *Eoline*. It was an immediate success, and in the course of the next five months would be performed in its entirety no less than fourteen times. It was admired on several counts – for the continuity of the action, achieved as in Jules' earlier ballets by interposing the scenes so as to avoid intervals, for the absence of lengthy mime passages, and generally for the skill with which he had constructed his theme on Musäus's romantic conception. 'Rich and fertile as are the imaginations of the writers of Germany,' observed the *Morning Post*, 'and redolent with the wild and the beautiful as are every mountain and glen and forest of that spirit-haunted land, we doubt whether any of its innumerable legends possess a more fanciful thought than this legend. M. Perrot has seized the salient features of the story and has aptly given "a local habitation and a name" to its wild imaginings at Her Majesty's Theatre.'[12] Although considering the ballet to be a little too long, *The Times* thought it contained 'more novelty and originality . . . than . . . any work of the sort that has appeared for some time. The constructor has caught the spirit of the tale, and has been most fertile in his expedients for illustrating the position, half human half supernatural, of Eoline. His "effects" show poetical and original invention, and are complete departures from the beaten track.'[13]

The ballet had been set to a score by Pugni which, to the ears of those who took the trouble to listen to ballet music, sounded 'spirited and graphic,' and followed 'every contrast and transition of feeling'[14] in the action, with duly sinister passages to accompany Jules' own rôle of Rübezahl.

He had constructed this rôle with a double purpose. Dramatically it was fundamental to the theme, personifying the evil influence that had to be thwarted in traditional fashion at the end, when the heroine is spirited away from his clutches, not to live happily ever after, but, romantically, to find ultimate fulfilment in a sphere he can never enter. He threw himself whole-heartedly into the part, to which he brought his own brand of sardonic humour, his portrayal being 'filled . . . to the brim with amusing quaintness,'[15] 'meaning and busy self-importance.'[16]

But there was another aspect to the predominance of his rôle. By being on the stage during all the important dramatic passages, he could fulfil his responsibility towards Lucile Grahn, steering her towards the triumph Lumley expected her to obtain on her London début. Even so, it did not prove to be an easy evening for her. Whether or not the lateness of the hour had anything to do with it, she failed to arouse the audience's enthusiasm. Perceptive critics could see how unjust this was. For a dancer of her 'high degree of physical force and cultivation' and 'refined artistic feeling,' *The Times* considered her reception to be 'anything but adequate to her merits.'[17] Not that she did not enjoy a reasonable measure of success, however, for the critics were generally impressed with her technique and her miming. Her upbringing in Copenhagen's Royal Theatre, mixing there not only with dancers but also with the singers and actors who shared its stage, had developed her interpretative talent to an unusual degree, and Jules had fully exploited this in the *mazurka d'extase*. Her dance training she had received under Jules' friend, Bournonville, and although she had left Copenhagen to broaden her experience and had polished her style in Paris, her dancing was still refreshingly free of flamboyance. Her 'quiet air,' however, made it difficult to break through the public's reserve. 'The light easy gracefulness of her movements,' explained *The Times*, 'approaches an appearance of nonchalance, and as she does not take her spectators by storm, they are disposed to overlook her consummate skill.'[18]

Throughout the long run of *Eoline* Lucile Grahn 'toiled on without being cheered by anything like her need of applause.'[19] But gradually the public warmed to her, and later in the season she was given the accolade of one of the coloured lithographs in which London excelled. The artist, S.M. Joy, chose

Jules Perrot

the moment when Eoline, in dryad form, was seen skimming across the lake in the early morning light, and the finished lithograph, drawn on stone by Edward Morton, was one of the loveliest of ballet prints. It appeared on sale at the fashionable library of its publisher, John Mitchell of Old Bond Street, in July, only a few days before she finally sealed her triumph in the *Pas de Quatre*.

That was still many weeks ahead. Meanwhile, in the early performances of the season she had to struggle for the favour of the audiences at Her Majesty's, and the hitches that occasionally bedevilled the performances of *Eoline* did not make her task any easier. There was, for example, the occasion when the forest scene was halted by a mechanical mishap. From the wings the ballerina could only look on in dismay as 'several huge trees were torn up violently by the roots, disclosing certain ungainly pieces of carpenter's work evidently not intended for the eye of Her Majesty or her lieges. Windlasses were heard to groan, and hot interjections from the lips of infuriated stage managers flew from side to side. The little dryads peeped pitifully from their sanctuaries in the foliage overhead and wondered how the disruption of their paternal oaks would end, but the rebellious canvas, which was curiously cobbled up in mid-air, suddenly swung heavily down again, and the trees took to their roots again – to the intense satisfaction of everybody both on and off the stage.'[20]

* * *

Even at the end of April, with the season nearly two months old, Lucile Grahn was still 'working on her toilsome way in the favour of an indifferent public.'[21] This was in spite of all Jules' efforts to present her to best advantage and the absence of any other ballerina of comparable status. The only competition she had to face came from Josephine Weiss's troupe of Viennese children, who arrived early in April and enraptured the London public with their infantile charms and the unprecedented precision of their ensemble dancing. There were no stars among them, but a few of the children were featured in dances arranged for two, three or four girls, and one of them, Fanny Pragher, won the unstinted admiration of Lucile Grahn. Feeling that the repertoire of the Danseuses Viennoises gave this girl no opportunity to display her natural gift for expression, Grahn suggested to Jules that he should arrange a short ballet with a part for the talented child. This was the germ from which grew, in a few weeks, the one-act ballet of *Kaya, ou l'Amour voyageur*, which was presented on April 17th.

In several respects it was as much Grahn's ballet as Jules'. The choice of Norway for the setting was hers, but her contribution went further than that. She actively collaborated in working out the action, being responsible for the idea behind the principal *pas d'action* and also, no doubt, the last-minute change of the hero's name from Frédéric to the more characteristic Knud. Her help was even more indispensable in the arrangement of the music.

Norway, which was then joined in a not very happy union with Sweden, had a much closer affinity, both culturally and linguistically, with Denmark, and she had grown up knowing many of its national melodies by heart. Not surprisingly, Pugni, who had the task of providing a score at very short notice, knew little of these northern folk tunes, but once Grahn had sung them to him, he 'immediately made them his own, and linked and instrumented them for the purpose of the ballet.'[22]

For the setting Charles Marshall had imagined a fertile valley nestling between snow-covered mountains with a farmer's cottage and its garden in the foreground. From this neat dwelling, Lucile Grahn made her entrance as Kaya, the farmer's daughter, establishing the locality of the scene with a character dance, *La Norwégienne*, performed to an authentic folk melody. Jules probably played little part in the arrangement of this dance. It consisted of 'a series of rapid motions, broken by curtsies, circlings on one leg, after the manner of the Scottish lilt, and certain quick steps which suggested the double shuffle of the sailor's hornpipe. Its animal spirit was enlivening, but it lacked elegance.'[23] *The Times* called it 'an eccentric sort of dance, quite of the native school, requiring the limbs to be flung about in the most reckless fashion,' and was surprised that the audience failed to respond to it.[24] As the plot begins to unfold, it soon becomes apparent that Kaya is headstrong and spoilt, and that her suitor Knud – played by Jules himself – is exasperated at her aloofness, particularly since he enjoys the favour of her father. In an attempt to raise his spirits, Knud's companions have invited him to go hunting, but as he is about to leave he sees a little urchin boy lying exhausted at the side of the road. This was the rôle devised for little Fanny Pragher. Knud knocks on the door of Kaya's cottage, and she takes the boy in, but refuses to allow Knud to remain. Disappointed, he leaves to join his friends. Under the care of Kaya and her family the boy gradually revives and shyly expresses his gratitude. The peasant girls crowd round him, but he has eyes for Kaya alone. She sits at her spinning wheel with the boy at her feet, but his timidity soon disappears and he becomes so mischievous that she is forced to banish him to a corner of the garden.

This led into an unusual mime scene between the two characters, the *pas des cinq sens*, which was based on an idea of Grahn's. 'Grahn,' as the *Morning Post* informed its readers after the dress rehearsal, 'who . . . is a highly intellectual person, has imagined a new device – a psychological step!' and went on to describe its action in detail. 'The little fellow in his banishment employs his time of penitence in finding some strawberries, which he gathers and presents to his protectress. He begs so humbly and perseveringly that she finally accepts the strawberries, which please her *taste*. The little urchin then gathers a beautiful rose, which Kaya wishes to have, but he refuses to give it up, and the same time that he maliciously wafts it so near to her, the sweet *smell* gives her a still greater desire to possess it. At length, insisting on its possession, she snatches it from him; a thorn pierces her finger, she throws it away, but the *feeling* of pain remains; the sting has remained within. The boy endeavours to console Kaya, who weeps from pain. He brings her back the rose, which she will not accept. He tries to apply the rose leaves to her bleeding finger, but she snatches away her hand. At this moment the sound of the horn is heard in the distance, and the mountain echo reverberates the melody which, as it approaches, fixes the attention of Kaya, and singularly fascinates her *ear*. Steps are heard approaching; Knud enters, and Kaya is confused at his *sight*. She hears with less indifference than usual his ardent prayers, and at length takes refuge in flight.'[25] Alas, this conception, original though it was, proved 'too impracticable to be made out with sufficient clearness to be understood.'[26]

In an attempt to arouse Kaya's jealousy, Knud begins flirting with her companions, stirring up in the process a lover's quarrel between Kaya's sister and her sweetheart. Kaya's father is mortified at this development, and seeing the boy looking on with malicious amusement, accuses him of being the cause of the trouble. The boy runs off, but is soon discovered and drawn from his hiding place. To everyone's amazement a most extraordinary metamorphosis has taken place. Wings have sprouted from his shoulders, and he is recognised as none other than Cupid, the God of Love. Naturally his very presence is enough to transform Kaya's feelings for Knud, and the ballet moved into its final divertissement.

It was only at this point that the audience began to warm to the occasion. Jules had devised a brilliant *pas de six* for himself and Grahn, with Mlles Moncelet, Ferdinand, Demelisse and Cassan in support, a composition that had 'all the characteristic fire of Perrot's peculiar genius, his exquisite grouping, and his steeplechase rapidity of execution which conceals all the studied mechanism.' It included a stunning variation for Lucile Grahn which displayed her virtuosity to perfection. 'She flew from end to end of the stage, poised on the point of her toe, acquiring a marvellous power of locomotion by the most singular oscillations and swaying of her form – fraught, however, with all-pervading grace; next she revolved with a rapidity indescribable, executing steps so minute that it is impossible to define their character. The applause elicited was deafening – a moment's pause followed, and then a general cry of "encore" procured the repetition of the step, and the return of the general astonishment at this elegant feat of most graceful agility.'[27] It was in this dance, with its memorable 'revolution on the point of the foot,'[28] that the London public at last began to appreciate her true worth.

In the finale of the divertissement the whole company rushed forward to acknowledge Cupid's supremacy and then, just as quickly, separated to reveal a group of wheatsheaves, out of which emerged a veritable corps de ballet in miniature – the Viennese children – who proceeded to dance a *pas des moissonneurs* devised by their director, Frau Weiss. It was an irresistible

The Championing of Lucile Grahn

bonus, and when it ended with the children breaking into a romp and pelting one another with straw, the applause knew no bounds. The final divertissement had saved the day. In the words of *The Times*, the audience 'completely passed from the frigid to the torrid zone,'[29] and Lucile Grahn savoured a real triumph for the first time since her arrival in London.

The tempo of the season was now about to quicken, with both Cerrito and Carlotta coming in May, and Taglioni expected in June. Realising that Grahn's undivided claim on his services would then be ended, he revived for her one of his early successes, *Le Pêcheur napolitain*, a scene of summer jollity by the Mediterranean seashore, culminating in the rousing tarantella which he had originally set for himself and Carlotta. Grahn proved herself a worthy successor, capable of the impetuous speed the dance demanded and assuming a convincing southern temperament. This little divertissement was also appreciated for Jules' 'figured dances' for the corps de ballet which were 'uncommonly picturesque and pretty,'[30] but it was performed only once more after its revival on April 24th, for Jules was then in the throes of preparing another divertissement, designed to enable Grahn to hold her own when Cerrito made her reappearance on May 1st.

Something strikingly unusual was required if Grahn was to make an impression in the same programme as the buoyant Cerrito, and with this in mind he devised a brief divertissement, *La Bacchante*, to be inserted between the second and third acts of the opera *I Puritani*. Hastily produced though it was, it was an example of his uncanny ability to draw out a dancer's full potential. London's first view of Grahn was as a dancer of the romantic style associated with Taglioni, the 'ideal school' as the English critics called it, but Jules had also perceived a dramatic flair, which he had exploited in the *mazurka d'extase*, and had encouraged her to extend her range in national dances. Now he boldly uncovered another aspect of her talent by effectively presenting her as a voluptuous bacchante. He established the mood he desired in the opening group of bacchantes, looking, said a classically minded critic, just as Ovid must have imagined them, wearing mantles of panther skin, with ivy-bound brows and hair falling disshevelled on to their shoulders. In this unexpected guise appeared Grahn with her long blonde hair flowing loose and brandishing a goblet. 'An amorous youth is not wanting,' described the *Morning Herald*, 'and Perrot slips cautiously into the group. It is plain to see that he is smitten with the beautiful Maenad; he follows her here and follows her there, peeping under her arm and over her shoulder, and describes with all the emphasis of pantomime that his heart is irrevocably gone. He soon entices the fair enchantress into the complexities of a *pas de deux*,[31] in which, with her 'beautiful hair [streaming] like a meteor,'[32] she performed a sequence of 'rapid flying revolutions that could scarcely have been excelled by any dancer.' Her movements, 'free, broad and vigorous,'[33] had 'the indispensable wildness and revelling spirit characteristic of the priestess.' Then, suddenly,

147

Jules Perrot

the movement ceased, as she dropped, 'with an air of rapturous abandonment,' on the arm of her partner. 'Applause, which Perrot justly shared, an encore, and a call before the curtain, were the instant results.'[34]

As he stood at her side Jules would have felt a warm glow of satisfaction, for the ovation was not only his reward for many weeks of determined perseverance on Grahn's behalf, but also a tribute to his own compelling performance. So fervent was his desire for the bacchante that it was difficult to keep one's eyes off him, and to certain critics who had not yet yielded to Grahn's gentle charms, her new-found expressiveness paled into insignificance when he was on the stage. 'His very soul seems entranced by her beauty,' described the *Spectator*, 'and his limbs move with a flowing ease and angularity – a striking contrast to the rigid angularity of action and cold fixed smile of the form he hovers around.'[35]

The extraordinary efforts which Jules had devoted to convincing an indifferent public of Grahn's true merits had been whole-heartedly supported by Lumley, if not carried out on his express instructions. Lumley was very much taken with her. Indeed, for all the shy modesty of her stage presence, Grahn was fully aware of her sexual attraction and had been skilfully cultivating the manager. As the *Satirist*, the repository of London's social gossip, knowingly reported, she was 'believed to have the most *recherché* toilette of any *danseuse* of the Opera' and 'to achieve this grand object of female ambition she spared no labour either *night* or day.'[36]

In June, at the open air party which Lumley gave for his singers and dancers in the Vale of Health, in Hampstead, the 'undivided attentions'[37] he paid to Lucile Grahn did not pass unnoticed, and shrewd observers thought it significant that the ballerina was herself established in a furnished cottage nearby. Lumley's favours had also obtained other benefits for her, not the least being the services of the *claque*, which never 'failed to reserve [its] "power" for her appearance, in strict compliance with the instructions [it] had previously received.'[38]

Demands on Jules' time now multiplied rapidly as the great international stars began reporting for duty. There was *Ondine* to revive for Cerrito, and later *La Esmeralda* and the second act of *Giselle* to be restored for Carlotta. Jules was also resuming the rôles of Matteo, Gringoire and Albert. To his relief his weak leg gave no trouble, although he was careful to reduce the technical demands of these rôles and to concentrate on the task of supporting the ballerina.

There was another good reason for husbanding his strength. Marie Taglioni was to make her return to London after an absence of several years, and Jules was anxious to be fit enough to serve her, both as choreographer and, to the best of his abilities, as partner. He had not seen her since 1835, and ten years was a long time in a dancer's performing career, particularly when she has passed the age of forty. For her reappearance on June 26th, he reduced

La Sylphide to a single act and took his place at her side in the principal role of James, relegating young Toussaint to the part of Gurn, or Georges as the playbill renamed him. Taglioni wore her years wonderfully well, and there was nothing in her performance to suggest that age had in any way dimmed her glory. Her legendary elegance had lost none of its poetry, her steps were as exquisitely finished as ever, and the long aerial bounds for which she was famous conveyed 'the easy confidence of a mind perfectly sure that it can regulate every corporeal action.'[39]

* * *

Taglioni had arrived in time to grace Lumley's 'operatic fête champêtre' in Hampstead. It was an occasion for celebration, for the seemingly inextricable and interminable litigation over the affairs of the theatre had at last been brought to a final settlement, and the way was opened for Lumley to purchase the lease. When the day of his party dawned, all the intricate details seemed to be slotting into place. Under a clear blue sky Lumley beamed at his guests with the confident pride and expansive bonhomie of a man no longer troubled by care. He saw himself surrounded by the elite of society who had given him constant support and by such a galaxy of singers and dancers as had never been assembled in any one place before. Lovers of the dance were given the unprecedented treat of rubbing shoulders with four of the greatest stars of the ballet – Lucile Grahn, whom the host regarded as his own discovery and special favourite, Fanny Cerrito and her new husband, Arthur Saint-Léon, Carlotta Grisi escorted by the Baron de Vidil (the 'Baron des Gants,' as he was nicknamed behind his back on account of his family's trade connections), and Marie Taglioni on the arm of Prince Troubetskoi. And there, too, discreet and unassuming, was Jules, casting wry glances at Carlotta and already aware of Lumley's latest flight of fancy.

This was nothing less than to persuade all four of these proud ballerinas to combine in a single divertissement as a sort of 'house-warming' celebration. Lumley was fully aware of the difficulties he would encounter. Governing a great nation, he felt sure, would be child's play to exercising his dominion over subjects who considered themselves far above mortal control, for as he remainded himself, each of them saw herself as a queen in her own right – 'alone, absolute, supreme.' His achievement two years before in persuading Elssler and Cerrito to appear together in a *pas de deux* had been regarded as something of a miracle, but was it practicable even to contemplate the idea of combining four ballerinas of equal status in a single *pas*? These thoughts were passing through Lumley's mind as the project took shape, but he did not allow them to deter him, and recalling the old French proverb, '*Si c'est possible, c'est déjà fait; si c'est impossible, cela se fera,*' he resolved that the impossible should be done.[40]

The *Pas de Quatre* did not, however, spring from a last-minute flash of

Jules Perrot

inspiration, but evolved out of an ambitious proposal that was openly announced, without promise of realisation, before the season opened. It was realised that Taglioni, Grisi and Cerrito would be in London at the same time, and the idea of their appearing together must have been broached to them and not rejected out of hand, for the advance publicity in February had whimsically held out the hope that all three might 'appear in one single ballet – a collision that the most carelessly managed railroad could hardly hope to equal.'[41] The original idea might even have been more ambitious than the final realisation, for the *Morning Chronicle* disclosed that it was at first intended to produce a mythological ballet, and that Jules was advised by Nadaud, who conducted the band for the ballet, to reduce the framework to a simple *pas de quatre* without any introductory narrative.'[42] Even so it was a formidable task. It had required much coaxing, flattery and supplication on Lumley's part to obtain the ballerinas' cooperation, but this was only a preliminary step to the well-nigh superhuman task of devising the choreography. Of all the ballet-masters working in Europe at that time, probably Jules alone had the skill and tact to carry out Lumley's instructions. 'Every twinkle of each foot in every *pas* had to be nicely weighed in the balance, so as to give no preponderance. Each *danseuse* was to shine in her peculiar style and grace to the last stretch of perfection; but no one was to outshine the others – unless in their own individual belief.'[43] At the same time Pugni received similar instructions for composing the music.

Soon the participants were preparing for this historic occasion. Taglioni, Cerrito and Grahn were working several hours each day with Gosselin, while Carlotta was probably taking class with Jules. As the day of the first performance, July 12th, dawned, all seemed well, but during the morning a smouldering undercurrent of hostility between Cerrito and Carlotta erupted into a violent quarrel over precedence, and the very existence of the divertissement was in jeopardy. Neither ballerina questioned Taglioni's right to dance the final variation, but both claimed the penultimate dance. Taglioni said afterwards that it was Cerrito who started the quarrel, and that Carlotta flew into a great rage and called her colleague 'a little chit.' Jules fled from the stage to seek help from Lumley, whom he found in his office, in conference with his lawyers. Without regard for the weighty discussion that was in progress, Jules 'uttered frantic exclamations, tore his hair, and at last found breath to say that all was over – that the *Pas de Quatre* had fallen to the ground and never could be given!' With difficulty Lumley managed to calm him down so as to give a lucid explanation of the crisis.

'*Mon dieu*,' he exclaimed in despair, '*Cerrito ne veut pas commencer avant Carlotta – ni Carlotta avant Cerrito – et il n'y a pas moyen de les faire bouger, tout est fini!*'

Putting aside for a moment the business of buying the opera house, Lumley gave the matter thought and came up with a solution worthy of Solomon.

'The question of talent must be decided by the public,' he said. 'But in this dilemma, there is one point on which I am sure the ladies will be frank. Let the oldest take her unquestionable right to the envied position.'

The effect was miraculous. 'The ballet-master,' wrote Lumley in his memoirs, 'smote his forehead, smiled assent, and bounded from the room upon the stage. The judgment of the manager was announced. The ladies tittered, laughed, drew back, and were now as much disinclined to accept the right of position as they had been before eager to claim it.'[44]

Many of those who took their seats in Her Majesty's that evening were doubtful whether the curtain would really rise on the promised *Pas de Quatre*, for rumours of the morning's incident had percolated to the world outside. But rise it did – between the acts of Donizetti's *Anna Bolena* – to reveal a sunny landscape ('the well-known divertissement bower,'[45] as one critic reported) before which a number of figurantes, dressed in muslin and pink tights, were arranged in picturesque groups. Then, from the wings, the great four appeared, hand in hand, in a simple straight line, in costumes of the palest pink, adorned by a rose to two in the hair and on the bodice. Amid a tumult of cheering and clapping and stamping of feet, they advanced slowly, still in line, to the front of the stage and curtsied.

It was at this moment that a rain of coloured sheets of paper fluttered down from the gallery, released by admirers of Cerrito and containing an adulatory sonnet in Italian. For one moment the occupants of the pit thought the ceiling was falling on their heads, but a burst of good-humoured laughter soon followed. Not everyone was amused, however. To some such a display of partisanship was in bad taste, and it was also noted, to Cerrito's discredit, that she had singled herself out from the others by wearing a single rose in her hair instead of a flowered headband.

Then, as the musicians began to play, the house fell silent. The four dancers began with a series of exquisite groups, picturesque and elegant in design, and performed with perfect precision and with no apparent exertion or striving for effect. Taglioni was always at the centre of these groups, with the others positioned around and above her, their arms outstretched as if in homage. In the most striking of them she appeared in their midst, head thrown back, giving the impression that she was reclining in their arms. These groups were succeeded by a 'quick transverse movement,'[46] which led into a brilliant solo by Grahn, the youngest of the quartet. Then followed a *pas de deux* by Cerrito and Carlotta, which was in turn succeeded by a series of broad aerial *jetés* across the stage by Taglioni. Each display culminated in a storm of applause, a rain of bouquets, and a curtsy, and as time went on, the boards disappeared under a carpet of petals. More than once the venerable Duke of Wellington was seen to lean from his box to throw

Jules Perrot

flowers.* Next, to an allegro variation, Lucile Grahn appeared, revolving with 'dainty semi-circular hops'[47] on the *pointe*, as light as 'a feather in a current of wine'[48] yet vigorous and, in her poses, astonishingly firm. Then followed an andante movement for Carlotta, performing 'tip-toe flights' and 'lightning gyrations'[49] of 'equal dexterity and number, mingled, however, with a world of little sprightly steps, which multiplied her feet into thousands'[50] – a piquant, coquettish variation in which she brought her youthful grace and fascination into fullest play. A romantic note was now struck, as the tempo changed to a slow, expressive andantino movement danced by Taglioni and Grahn. But this mood was only momentary. Cerrito, who had been calmly contemplating her rivals from the back of the stage, burst into action with a rapid sequence of turns, taken diagonally across the stage, followed by some *jetés* so buoyant that, in the words of one spectator, 'you could see she would have striven to "put a girdle around the earth in forty minutes."' A shower of bouquets rewarded her for this amazing show of vigour, and flushed and exhilarated, she surveyed them lying in profusion at her feet with an expression of feigned astonishment, before picking them up 'with a sly humility' that was deliciously amusing.[51] There were more wreathes and nosegays than her arms could carry, and Taglioni came forward to help her, handing her a chaplet with a smile of congratulation.

It was now the turn of the supreme ballerina herself, and it was a tribute to her artistry that, in spite of the triumphs that had gone before, she could raise the enthusiasm to new heights. Hers was an allegro variation, gentle and languid in mood, in which she 'displayed all her commanding manner, relying much on that advancing step of which, we believe, she was the inventress, and astonishing by some of her bounds.'[52] In it she introduced 'steps with the knee bent forward' which were so completely her own that no other dancer had succeeded in imitating them, and it was observed that her 'line of dancing was always maintained nearer the perpendicular' than that of her companions.[53]

Then came the coda, in which all four vied with one another in performing 'steps of various and dazzling complexity,'[54] 'flying with a rapidity the eye could scarcely follow, mingled in beautiful evolutions and presenting a moving picture of which no description can give any idea,'[55] and finally coming together with precision to form a 'sculpturesque' group.[56] The final sustained chord from the orchestra was lost in the swelling roar that broke forth from the audience.

---

* The Iron Duke, who was exceptionally assiduous in his attendance at the Opera, saw the *Pas de Quatre* four times, missing only two of the 1845 performances. In 1846 he saw 10 out of the 12 performances of *Le Jugement de Pâris*, a score that was only exceeded, among those whose presence was reported in the press, by the Countess Brunnova, the wife of the Russian Minister, who missed only one performance.

The Championing of Lucile Grahn

The appearance of the four ballerinas before the curtain was the signal for redoubled enthusiasm, which mounted to fever-pitch as Cerrito placed a crown of white roses on Taglioni's head. There were shouts, too, for Jules, who had been seen working quite as hard as the dancers, conducting the proceedings from the wings, beating time, fuming and fidgeting in an agony of zeal and anxiety. But his worries were now over as he came forward to receive his due share of the ovation. He was called before the curtain after each of the three performances that followed before Carlotta's departure, and on the night of her benefit, the four ballerinas dragged him on to the stage. A special bouquet fell at his feet, and *The Times* described how 'the inventive genius gallantly parted the flowers and, having flung one to each of the ladies, bowed to the audience.'[57]

Jules was left in no doubt that he had produced a masterpiece. 'There are more than ten ballets of the calibre of *La Esmeralda* in this new effort of Perrot's,' wrote the Vicomtesse de Malleville.[58] 'Never was such a *pas* before,' added *The Times*. It was 'the greatest Terpischorean exhibition that ever was known in Europe.'[59] It 'shook one's soul to the very centre,'[60] wrote the *Era*, and the *Morning Herald* declared that it marked 'an era in the records of the ballet-maker's art, and those who saw it chuckle to this day with satisfaction, and talk boastingly to those who did not.'[61]

* * *

There was now just one more task for Jules to accomplish, a new divertissement for Taglioni to close the season with a flourish. Time was short, and the new piece, *Diane*, was produced in little more than a week, being presented to the public on July 24th, just twelve days after the *Pas de Quatre*. Emergencies such as this were taken in their stride by the team at Her Majesty's. Pugni could be relied upon to produce music to an early deadline, Marshall had no difficulty in painting an appropriately romantic backcloth, using the diorama to give the illusion of water sparkling in the moonlight, and Jules, exhausted though he must have been, was always inspired when working for Taglioni. *The Times* called it 'one of the prettiest and most elegant little pieces that can be conceived,'[62] and the *Era* described it as being full of 'calm and graceful beauty, and . . . a most felicitous medium for the unapproachable powers of Taglioni.'[63]

There were only two characters, Diana and Endymion, played by Taglioni and Jules. As the curtain rose, Taglioni made her entrance, her elegant figure picked out in a shaft of simulated moonlight. She discovers Endymion asleep, but he wakes at her approach and together they dance a *pas de deux*, which stirred treasured memories in those who had seen them in their prime at the Paris Opéra fifteen years ago. But if Taglioni appeared to be ageless, Jules' features had noticeably coarsened. The *Morning Post* was indulgent. 'Wags may cavil at Perrot appearing *sous les traits* of Endymion, but this is a new version of Diana's *faux pas*, and it is quite natural that Taglioni should fall in love with talent. Besides, the classical commentators pretend that Endymion was really an astronomer in love with the moon, and as its goddess was impersonated last night, Perrot had many persons near him as lunatic as himself. Need we say that Taglioni was treated to the last step with a *furore* of applause – Perrot himself having a sufficient share to gratify him, were not his laurels gained on the invention of the unrivalled *Pas de Quatre* too recent to require any present addition.'[64] Of plot there was very little, but the *pas de deux* that formed the centre-piece of the divertissement was devised as much to reveal the dancers' 'pantomimic elegance' as to display their 'choreographic skill.' At the end, after Endymion had departed, abandoned, the goddess was joined by her nymphs, clad in the familiar leopard-skin costumes which had been used several times before, for a finale.

A few weeks later this most brilliant of seasons reached its end, and Jules packed his bags to return to France. He was looking forward to a rare respite, a winter without engagements that he could spend in the company of his eight-year-old daughter. All the cares and demands of his profession slipped from his shoulders as one idle day followed another, and importunate letters from impresarios lay unanswered on his desk. Among these were requests from Carlo Balocchino, the director of the Vienna Opera, and Lanari of the Fenice theatre in Venice to revive *La Esmeralda* for Fanny Elssler, but neither of them received a reply. Consequently they both turned to Domenico Ronzani, who 'knew the ballet by heart'[65] and had already staged it in Bologna. It was thus by default that Ronzani began to revive Jules' ballets in Italy, Vienna and later in America, a task he was to perform with respect for the original choreography and also, one hopes, under some businesslike arrangement whereby Jules received a return for what a later age would recognise as his copyright.

12

The Season of the Golden Apple

What was a welcome winter of repose for his ballet-master was the busiest of times for Benjamin Lumley. The next season had to be planned, singers and dancers sought out, contracts negotiated, new productions planned and a thousand and one details to be attended to if the interest and financial support of the subscribers were to be maintained. Lumley was seldom at a loss for new ideas, and prompted perhaps by the debt which Gautier owed to Heine in the conception of *Giselle*, made a point of calling on the poet when he was passing through Paris in the hope of persuading him to write a ballet scenario. Heine happened to be in an obliging mood, and in a couple of hours roughed out a story of a Christian knight who falls under the spell of the goddess Diana, is killed and is then resurrected in the Venusberg, to dwell there with the goddess in eternal bliss. Lumley was at first so confident of its suitability that he allowed the *Morning Post* to hint that the opera season would open with a new ballet whose 'plot [was] written by one of the most imaginative poets of our time.'[1] This announcement, however, turned out to be premature, probably because Jules rejected Heine's scenario of *Die Göttin Diane* as soon as he first read it. His objections were not hard to understand, for Lumley had allowed himself to be blinded by Heine's reputation and had accepted a hastily written work that was devoid of originality and human interest. In any event Jules preferred to work out his own scenarios. Lumley eventually saw his ballet-master's point and agreed that the Heine project should be abandoned in favour of a more dramatic and realistic idea which Jules now put forward.

It was very much a last-minute substitution, and although Jules was used to working fast, the first version of *Catarina, ou la Fille du bandit*, which London saw when the season opened on March 3rd, 1846, was only a preliminary sketch of the definitive production he was to stage in Milan at the end of the year. In the six or seven weeks available between his arrival in London and the opening of the season, he found himself working under exceptional difficulties, for the new productions had to be prepared simultaneously with the extensive decoration of the theatre. The auditorium was a

Jules Perrot

HER MAJESTY'S THEATRE,
ITALIAN OPERA HOUSE.

THIS EVENING,
SATURDAY, March 14th, 1846,

When will be performed, **for the 4th time in this Country**, Verdi's celebrated Opera of '**NABUCO**,' under the Title of

NINO.

Nino,	Sig. FORNASARI,
Idaspe,	Sig. CORELLI,
Orotasphe,	Sig. BOTELLI,
Abdallo,	Sig. DAI FIORI,
Fenena,	Madlle CORBARI,
	Her 4th appearance in this Country.
Anna,	Madlle BELLINI,
Abigail,	Madlle SANCHIOLI.
	Her 4th appearance in this Country.

To conclude with an entirely **new grand Ballet**, in 5 Tableaux, by **M. Perrot**, called

CATARINA.

Catarina, (Chief of the Banditti)		**MADLLE L. GRAHN,**
Diavolino,		**M. PERROT.**
Salvator Rosa,		M. GOSSELIN.
Florida,		Made PETIT STEPHAN,
Innkeeper,	M. BERTRAND.	**Officer,** M. DIA MATTIA.
Chief Judge,	M. VENAFRA.	**Jailor,** M. GOURIET.
Principal Model of Salvator Rosa,		**Madlle L. TAGLIONI.**
		Her 1st appearance.

Models representing the Graces. Mesdlles MONCELET, DEMELISSE, CASSAN.
Other Models, Madlle LAMOUREUX, &c.

1st Tableau—Pas Strategique, by Madlle L. GRAHN, &c.
New and Original Valse a Cinq Temps, by Madlle L. GRAHN & M. PERROT.

2nd Tableau—La Romanesque, by **Made P. STEPHAN & M. PERROT.**
La Saltarelle, by Madlle L. GRAHN & M. PERROT.

3rd Tableau—Pas des Modeles, by **Madlle L. TAGLIONI,** &c.

5th Tableau—Pas du Masque, by Madlle L. GRAHN, &c.
La Folle du Carnaval, new and Original Grand Galop Final.

Application for Boxes, Pit Stalls, and Tickets to be made at the Box Office, Opera Colonnade.

Doors open at 7 o'clock: commence at half-past 7.

STUART, Printer, 38, Rupert Street) corner of Archer Street) Haymarket.

Playbill of Her Majesty's Theatre, London, for March 14th, 1846 – the sixth performance of Catarina. *Theatre Museum, London.*

maze of scaffolding, with painters and workmen swarming all over it, embellishing every square inch of wall and ceiling and filling the air with the noise of their activities, and in the midst of this pandemonium serious work was proceeding on the stage, with 'Terpsichorean bands in every imaginable attitude, Perrot, with his aides-de-camp, Gosselin and Petit, commanding the manoeuvres, and Lucile Grahn floating about with aerial steps in the centre . . . The scenery of the new ballet was taking up its position in the background – the arrival of each piece of canvas accompanied by observations, more positive than poetical, of the chief mechanist to his crew in the flies above.'[2]

Lumley planned to unveil the refurbished auditorium with an appropriately dramatic effect. The theatre was darkened when early comers made their way to their boxes and their seats. Then, all of a sudden, the lights were turned up. The splendour was stunning, and evoked a spontaneous burst of applause. It was difficult to believe it was the same theatre they had left only a few months before. In place of the familiar begrimed curtains were silk amber-coloured hangings specially woven in Spitalfields, new leather seats replaced the uncomfortable straw-filled chairs, the boxes were newly hung with chintz, the primitive gas lights in the corridors had been replaced by modern fitments, the ventilation had been improved to make life more tolerable for those in the upper reaches, and a new chandelier sparkled overhead. Everything was in excellent taste by the standards of early Victorian England; indeed, edifying in its conception, with copies of paintings by Guido Reni, Albano, Raphael and Giulio Romano, and no suspicion of the despised, decadent style of Louis Quinze 'with its pretty affectation, its pretty migniardise and gilded rococo.'[3]

Lumley had planned a full and varied programme for the opening, beginning with Verdi's opera, *Nabucco*, renamed *Nino* so as not to offend the English public by introducing a biblical subject into the theatre. After the opera, the National Anthem was sung by the assembled company, and there were curtain calls and shouts for Lumley, who, after enjoying his share of applause, brought on Balfe, who had conducted the opera. As a result of all this, the overture to the new ballet, *Catarina*, did not begin until well after midnight, and it was nearly two o'clock when the performance ended and Jules, Lucile Grahn, Joséphine Petit-Stéphan and Gosselin were called before the curtain.

The source of the dramatic plot for *Catarina* was no doubt Lady Morgan's life of the seventeenth-century Italian painter, Salvator Rosa, whose wild, picturesque landscapes had acquired a new relevance in the context of Romantic art with their dark overladen skies, their twisted trees and massive rocky crags, their ruined buildings and the mysterious banditti lying in wait for their victims. For Jules, who was essentially a man of the Romantic theatre, the story of Rosa's life must have had a double appeal, for apart from the influence of his paintings, the man himself had been a dashing rebel with ideas that would have struck echoing chords in Jules' own temperament and singled him out as an ideal stage hero. In the course of his eventful life Rosa had fought a nocturnal duel under the walls of the Vatican, and led a band of artists in the cause of liberty against foreign oppression in Naples, and had supported the insurrection of Massaniello against the Spanish conquerors.

The event in Rosa's life that was the touchstone for Jules' scenario was his supposed capture by banditti. According to Lady Morgan, he had lived for some time with the outlaws, whom he came to see, not as common cut-throats but as men driven by poverty and desperation to reject the established order, and leading lives of high adventure in the mountains. In the wild countryside Rosa found inspiration for many of his pictures, and the experience remained vividly etched in his mind for the rest of his life, finding vivid expression in an engraving which Lady Morgan graphically described in her biography. 'In the midst of rocky scenery appears a group of banditti, armed at all points, and with all sorts of arms. They are lying, in careless attitudes but with fierce watchfulness, round a youthful prisoner, who forms the foreground figure, and is seated on a rock, with languid limbs hanging over the precipice, which may be supposed to yawn beneath. It is impossible to describe the despair depicted in this figure; it is marked in his position, in the droop of his head, which his nerveless arms seem with difficulty to support, and in the little that may be seen of his face, over which, from his incumbent attitude, his hair falls in luxuriant profusion (and the singular head and tresses of Salvator are never to be mistaken). All is alike destitute of energy and of hope, which the fierce beings grouped around the captive seem, in some sentence recently pronounced, to have banished for ever. Yet one there is who watches over the fate of the young victim: a woman stands immediately behind him. Her hand stretched out, its forefinger resting on his head, marks him the subject of a discourse which she addresses to the listening bandits. Her figure, which is erect, is composed of those bold straight lines, which in art and nature constitute the *grand*. Even the fantastic cap or turban, from which her long disshevelled hair has escaped, has no curve of grace; and her drapery partakes of the same rigid forms. Her countenance is full of stern melancholy – the natural character of one whose feelings and habits are at variance, whose strong passions may have flung her out of the pale of society, but whose feminine sympathies still remain unchanged. She is artfully pleading for the life of the youth, by contemptuously noting his insignificance. But she commands while she soothes. She is evidently the mistress, or the wife of the Chief, in whose absence an act of vulgar violence may be meditated. The youth's life is saved: for that cause rarely fails to which a woman brings the omnipotence of her feelings'[4]. It was surely from these pages that came the inspiration for Catarina, the bandit's daughter, and not, as some commentators suggested, from Scribe's libretto for Auber's opera, *Les Diamants de la couronne*, which happened, perhaps by mere coincidence, to introduce a character of the same name and calling.*

The painter Léopold Robert, whose pictures directly inspired Jules on more than one occasion, may have also provided one of the sources for *Catarina*. In the 1820s several of his studies of Italian bandits had been exhibited in the Salon, where Jules could have seen them. One in particular, *Brigand on the Watch*, might almost be a sketch of Diavolino, the rôle which Jules designed for himself, for the main figure bears an uncanny resemblance in detail of costume – the cut of the open-necked shirt, the conical hat, the locket hanging from the neck, and the cross-lacing of the stockings – to the lithograph that John Brandard drew of Jules dancing with Grahn in the first act of the ballet.**

To an English audience of the 1840s the Italian banditti suggested another analogy. Italian liberty was a very live issue, and Jules' own sympathies lay squarely with the patriots who were gathering their strength to throw off the rule of the Austrians in the north, the temporal depotism of the Papal government, and the effete Bourbon dynasty that ruled in Naples. In the Papal States the oppression was particularly intolerable, and the struggle of the patriots, waged with great ferocity, gained much sympathy in the tolerant lands of England and France. Jules' banditti in *Catarina*, therefore, while not presented as fighting in a specific political cause, would nonetheless have a sympathetic appeal to a largely Protestant London audience.

The rise of the curtain revealed a wild and picturesque mountainscape in the Abruzzi, with a stream coursing through a steep channel overhung on both sides by massive rocks. It is the lair of bandits who have seized a passing traveller. They are in the process of dividing his possessions, but the victim, who is none other than the artist Salvator Rosa (convincingly played by Gosselin), is strangely unconcerned. He has taken out pencil and paper to sketch the more interesting types among his captors, scattering the results of his labours around him. To his astonishment a girl appears among these rough brigands. It is Catarina, the daughter of the former bandit leader, who has been killed in a skirmish and whose power has devolved on her. For this moment Jules devised a highly effective first entrance for Lucile Grahn, who appeared high up among the rocks, musket in hand, in an attitude of commanding authority. Her costume could not have been more striking nor more

---

* Nor could the unsuccessful and shortlived vaudeville, *Salvator Rosa*, presented at the Ambigu-Comique in Paris at the end of 1836, have been an influence, for Jules had been in Vienna at that time.
** The painting, *Brigand on the Watch*, is now in the Wallace Collection, London. It is tempting to conjecture whether Jules and Robert ever met, for Robert's correspondence contains several references to a friend by the name of Perrot, who may have been the Louis Perrot of the Department of Fine Arts, and the name of Coulon also appears in his letters. However, Robert was working almost exclusively in Italy from 1818 until his death, by his own hand, in March 1835.

Jules Perrot

flattering. Her trim figure was set off by a black bolero jacket embroidered with gold, cunningly cut to emphasise the slimness of her waist. From her belt, in which two pistols were thrust ready for use, hung a horn, and loosely tied round the blue skirt was a scarf of black, red and yellow panels. On her head she wore a coquettish pointed hat decorated with a flowing red ribbon. After holding her opening pose for a few seconds, she burst into movement, bounding across the stage to loud applause, with her musket on her shoulder. Noticing the artist, she is so taken by his sketches that she spontaneously offers him his freedom and orders his belongings to be returned. Fascinated, Salvator asks her to tell him her story. He then begs her to abandon her life as an outlaw and share a more tranquil existence with him. But Catarina will not forsake her companions. At this point Jules made his own entrance in the part of Diavolino, Catarina's devoted lieutenant, a young bandit of passionate temperament who is secretly in love with her. He has captured an officer who, on being interrogated by Catarina, offers an amnesty if the bandits will surrender their arms and disperse. Catarina defiantly rejects such a suggestion, and exhorts her followers to continue the struggle.

Lost in admiration, Salvator sketches a portrait of the spirited girl, who for her part finds herself greatly attracted to him. She sounds her horn, and a bevy of amazons appear dramatically among the rocks and clamber down to perform a *pas stratégique*, a brilliant ensemble dance designed to convey their military prowess and their deft handling of weapons. Catarina herself directs their movements as the troop of red-jacketed warriors march and countermarch and perform their military evolutions. Lucile Grahn's interpretative talent was effectively displayed in this dance. Particularly noticeable was the way she never stepped out of character as she demonstrated the drill sequences with her musket, loading it in a pose on one leg that was imitated by the troop with military precision, going through a series of poses that were always beautiful to the eye and, for those to whom Rosa's pictures were familiar, evoking images of bandit life for which that artist was renowned. The vigour of her dancing was softened by a captivating grace, and one critic found it fascinating 'to watch her countenance as she falls into the successive poses' of this dance. 'There is a quite confident intelligence in her face which shows that she not only executes them as a *danseuse* but understands the situation as an actress.'[5] In an astonishing climax, the bandits scale the rocks, pose momentarily among the crags, and then rush down again in fierce array towards the audience, coming simultaneously to a halt with their muskets pointed at M. Nadaud, who was conducting the orchestra.

This exciting moment was followed by a dance of great originality in which Jules came forward to join Lucile Grahn. Described as a *valse à cinq temps*, it was an 'eccentric dance' in 5/4 time with 'steps and attitudes' performed with 'the most extraordinary velocity of motion.'[6] Because its rhythm was so unusual and its character not strictly classical, it was not fully appreciated.

The Season of the Golden Apple

However, it had been devised with an eye to the ballroom, Pugni's music – arranged for piano and bell! – being published under the title of *La Perrotiana* and dedicated to Mme Michau of Brighton, 'the only Authorised Teacher of this NEW DANCE.'* Pugni followed it with a *Perrotiana No.2*, which was dedicated to the great Parisian ballroom dance teacher, Henri Cellarius, who, in his book, *Fashionable Dancing*, credited 'his illustrious friend Perrot' with the invention of this curious new dance. He was clearly doubtful whether it would catch on, for having described how it should be performed,** he was careful to note that it had not yet 'received the sanction of the public.'[7]

Salvator looks on fascinated, but no sooner has the dance ended than the bandits discover they are surrounded by soldiers. Shots are heard, and in a sharp engagement the bandits are overpowered. Only Catarina and Diavolino escape.

In the second scene the two fugitives take refuge in an inn at the gates of Rome. Day has not yet broken, and the sound of their pursuers can be heard outside. The innkeeper asks them what they want, and catching sight of the weapons in Catarina's belt, is about to call for help when Diavolino pulls out his pistol and restrains him. Catarina explains their requirements – shelter, clothing and silence, on pain of death. She hands him a purse in exchange for some servant's clothes. After she and Diavolino have left the room, a squad of soldiers enter. The innkeeper is about to disclose their presence when Diavolino reappears, now disguised too as a servant. Shown the dagger

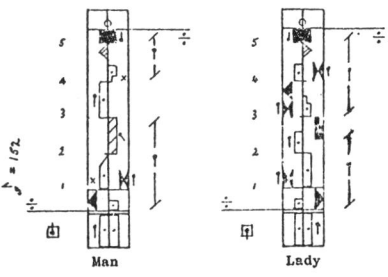

* There were a number of Michaus teaching dancing in Brighton, of whom Mme Sophie Michau, to whom *La Perrotiana* was dedicated, was the most celebrated. In her younger days 'her academy [was] the resort of all those who [had] any intimacy with the Graces' and she had 'the privilege of the entrée at the Pavilion, where her fascinating evolutions [were] highly admired.' In the 1840s she was living at No.11 Cannon Place. Another branch of the Michau family was connected by marriage to the D'Egvilles, a distinguished dynasty in the social dance world.

** Cellarius explained that in its theatrical form the *valse à cinq temps* was 'executed *en sautant*, and was composed of several figures and steps which have been suppressed to transplant it into society.' He went on to say that, 'putting aside the attraction it gained in my eyes from the marvellous execution of its author . . . [it appeared] to unite every condition of attraction and grace,' and that 'there [would] be found in its execution an originality, which [owed] to the piquant and clashing character of the rhythm.' The basic steps for the ballroom version, so far as they can be understood from Cellarius's verbal description, are shown above in Labanotation.

161

Jules Perrot

concealed under his shirt, the innkeeper understands the threat and denies knowledge of the fugitives.

With the coming of day the inn begins to fill with customers. It is carnival time, but Diavolino cannot share in the gaiety, casting anxious glances towards the room where Catarina is concealed and deploring the fate that has condemned him to the life of a fugitive. Then in bursts a band of revellers, headed by Salvator and his fiancée Florida (played by Joséphine Petit-Stéphan), who are celebrating the artist's safe return. Salvator recognises Diavolino, and tries in vain to raise his spirits. At Florida's request Diavolino reluctantly agrees to join her in a dance, *La Romanesca*, full of 'pert and stately'[8] steps, in the course of which he skilfully dispossesses her of a medallion of Salvator.

No sooner have Salvator and his friends retired than the soldiers return, now bringing their prisoners, whom Catarina immediately recognises as Diavolino's companions. She has reappeared disguised as a servant, looking very fetching in a 'saucy village cap,' and now proceeds to ply the soldiers with drink. Then, to distract the attention of their officers, she takes up a mandoline and, strumming out the rhythm of a *Saltarella*, works herself up into 'a coquettish whirl of vivacity and excitement,'[9] performing 'rapid evolutions and threatening advances, with one foot forward,'[10] towards Jules as Diavolino, whom she inveigles to accompany her. The use of the saltarella for this dance scene was particularly appropriate, for aside from its sexual connotation as a courtship dance, it was geographically associated with the Abruzzi, the mountainous region where these bandits had taken refuge. Pugni was not very specific about the category of this dance, which he entitled '*Saltarella* or *Tarantella*,' but whatever its derivation, its combination of 'naiveness and activity [presented] a round of smart, piquant groupings,' while Grahn's performance of it was distinguished by 'an executive tact which Elssler herself could not outdo.'[11]

Meanwhile, the soldiers have been so engrossed by her dancing that they have not noticed Diavolino slip away to release the prisoners, who have all quietly made their escape. Another squad of soldiers then arrives, commanded by the very officer whom Diavolino had earlier captured. The clothes that Catarina has discarded are now discovered and recognised, but happily Salvator comes to the aid of the two fugitives, and by providing them with carnival costumes, enables them to give the soldiers the slip.

The third scene opens with Salvator recalling nostalgically in his studio the beauty of the mountains where he had been held prisoner. When Catarina and Diavolino arrive to seek refuge, he willingly conceals them. He is then joined by Florida and several other beauties who act as models for the large mythological painting on which he is working. The artist explains what he wants of them, and they pose before him in a *pas des modèles*. Louise Taglioni, a first cousin to the eminent Marie, and making her London début on this occasion, was a delightful Venus,. her 'grace, distinction and modesty of manner' and 'her poetry of motion'[12] earning her an encore. In the course of this display of feminine beauty Florida discovers Catarina, and observing that she is wearing a portrait miniature of the artist, realises that she is her rival for his affections. The soldiers then arrive. Salvator once again intervenes to save his friends, but this time without success. Catarina is seized and taken off to prison.

The fourth scene, set in the prison, was played entirely in mime. The Chief Judge comes to tell Catarina that she has been condemned to death. Her only regret now is that she has found love too late. Startled out of her reverie by a sound, she sees Diavolino climbing through the window to rescue her. Her hopes reawakened, she shows him Salvator's miniature. Diavolino is shattered, for he too is passionately in love with her. In a bitter outburst he swears that he will kill his rival. Catarina refuses to follow him. But when he calms down into a more reasonable mood, she relents. They then make their escape through the window, just as footsteps are heard in the passage and the clank of the lock announces the arrival of the gaolers.

The fifth and last scene plunged the audience into the hurly-burly of the Roman Carnival, a scene blazing with colour and variety. Diavolino and Catarina are discovered jostling their way through the masked revellers. Diavolino's one idea is to lead his beloved out of the city to safety, and to remove her once and for all from Salvator, whom he has recognised in the crowd. But Catarina, who has seen him too, gives him the slip. Suddenly there is a cry to make way for a fortune teller, and a young girl darts forward. The crowd falls back to give her room to dance a *pas de masque* with three girls dressed in pink (Mlles Moncelet, Demelisse and Cassan). In this dance Lucile Grahn – for the gypsy girl is none other than Catarina – performed 'prodigies of vigour.'[13] Her entrance was extraordinarily brilliant. She bounded 'along the stage as though she would compass its whole breadth with a single spring,'[14] displaying, in her 'bold, aerial flying steps,'[15] a force that was truly 'wonderful, and the more so, as it was never obtained at the expense of gracefulness.'[16] When the dance is over, the fortune teller warns Salvator that his life is in danger. He follows her, and Diavolino, as if suspecting that the girl is Catarina, goes in pursuit. Reunited, the lovers decide to flee, but they are again discovered, this time by Diavolino and Florida. Then Catarina is swept away in the confusion of the galop, *La Folie du Carnaval*, and it seems that the lovers have eluded their pursuers. But suddenly, by a brilliant dioramic effect, the whole city is illuminated, St. Peter's shining out with a thousand lights and scores of torches bursting into flame on every side. The crowd dramatically separates to reveal Salvator and Diavolino facing one another, their swords drawn. In the duel that ensues, Diavolino profits from a momentary lapse by his opponent and lunges forward furiously. At that very moment Catarina darts between the two men and receives the fatal blow in her breast.

Jules Perrot

As she falls, the bells of the city chime out the hour of midnight. From the Castel Sant'Angelo a cannon shot announces the end of the Carnival, the Tiber is plunged into darkness, and the curtain falls.

After a first viewing at the dress rehearsal the *Morning Post* found the ballet 'deeply picturesque,' like Rosa's own paintings, possessing 'a dreamy distance, affording full scope to the imagination, and ample latitude for any appropriate suppositious addition.'[17] Reactions from the press were favourable without exception, and if its impact appeared weaker than that of *Ondine* and *La Esmeralda*, that was perhaps to be expected now that the public had those two classics as yardsticks for their judgment. Lumley himself called *Catarina* 'one of the best constructed of Perrot's choreographic compositions.'[18] Once again Jules had skilfully interwoven passages of dance into the narrative, first expressing Catarina's allure and authority over the bandits in the *pas stratégique*, then revealing her easy relationship with Diavolino in the *valse à cinq temps*, and in the last scene evoking the heady atmosphere of the Roman carnival with the *pas de masque* and the concluding galop which provided the background for the hunt that ends in the final tragedy. Taken as a whole, wrote the Vicomtesse de Malleville, these dances 'would be enough for three or four choreographic reputations.' In Lucile Grahn, she added, Jules had found 'the most intelligent and the cleverest interpreter of his work. Never, so far as we are aware, had the young dancer excelled herself more. We do not believe that anyone else could have rendered the spirit, feeling and colouring of her rôle as she did. Her miming could not have been more true to life; it was impossible to imagine poses more charming, or dancing that was lighter or more graceful.'[19]

Once again Jules benefited greatly from the collaboration of Cesare Pugni. His score contained 'much graceful music,' catching the 'martial character'[20] of the opening scene, adding *couleur locale* by the injection of Italian dance rhythms, and concluding on an exciting note with the hectic gaiety of the carnival dances. The *Morning Post* devoted considerable space to praising his contribution. 'There is more melody, thought and inspiration in such ballets as *Ondine* and *Esmeralda* than in many operas,' wrote its critic after hearing the score two or three times, 'and it must be remembered that ballet music is in one respect more difficult than any other to compose – it must obtain its triumphs despite its subserviency to the feet of the dancers and the fancies of the ballet-master, and it must always be descriptive to such a degree that we can make an approximate guess of the nature of the action when we have not the performance before our eyes.'[21]

The same critic reverted to *Catarina* two weeks later. 'To appreciate a new composition like *Catarina*,' he wrote, 'we must remember how many elements are necessary to constitute a ballet. If dancing be the natural expression of the most unsophisticated feelings, choreography is certainly the most artificial of all inventions – one that can only acquire perfection from the intimate combination of many arts in their most intimate relation. So artificial is stage dancing that no artist can transfer any "counterfeit presentments" of any *pas* to paper or to canvas without the figures betraying that effort which it is the sole object of the study of dancing to conceal. This is effected only so long as the movements are rapid, but no sooner does a pause occur than the effort, or at least the immense exertion of muscular power necessary to produce the lightest steps, are revealed. Even *la danse noble* . . . such as it was in the reign of Deshayes* at the Opera, despite its favour with the older amateurs, was a most absurd infraction of all natural rules, and never more so than when the *danseuse* slowly raised her foot to the level of her head, and when there, made it gesticulate as if it were a hand. In all respects, we repeat, no performance more taxes the power of illusion in the audience, or at least those spectators who have reached mature age. Great obligation is due to those who invent good ballets at the present day, [for] not only is this taste improved, but the public are saved from being misled by *tours de force* and exhibitions purely physical. It is to descriptive music, to picturesque scenery, to pictorial grouping, and solo dancing of a refined and graceful character that we must resort to prevent this evil. These are the characteristics of the ballet of *Catarina*.'[22]

* * *

Although his rôle in *Catarina* had made no exhausting demands, Jules now felt he had sufficiently recovered from his injury to test his strength, and with this in mind he arranged a new *pas de trois* for himself, Louise Taglioni and Joséphine Petit-Stéphan which was offered to the public on April 2nd. It was a somewhat tentative effort, to be sure, the *Morning Post* recording that he 'displayed all his consummate mastery of the art in the very few feats he undertook,' but it helped restore his confidence. Nor had he neglected the two ladies dancing with him; with his usual flair he had displayed young Taglioni's 'grace and intellectuality' and had given Petit-Stéphan 'one step totally new in its conception, and of the most finished elegance.'[23]

Early in May Fanny Cerrito and her husband, Arthur Saint-Léon, arrived in town, and at once the energies of the ballet department were directed to their needs. *Catarina* gave way to *Alma* and *Ondine*, and plans for a new ballet quickly began to take shape. The power of Cerrito's hold over the public was forcefully demonstrated one evening when an indisposition of the ballerina forced a last-minute change of programme. Audiences did not take kindly in those days to managerial decisions depriving them of their just due, and when the curtain rose to show Jules and Grahn, a storm of shouting and stamping

---

* The Deshayes referred to was the ballet-master who had helped Jules stage *Giselle* in London in 1842. As a young man he had been a brilliant dancer in the noble style, and as such had delighted the London public, first in 1800, and a little later, in eight successive seasons between 1804 and 1811.

drowned the orchestra. In an attempt to calm the outburst Jules walked to the footlights and above the hubbub declared his readiness to withdraw if this displeasure was directed against him. He then left the stage. After some minutes the storm blew itself out, and when the cause of the substitution was explained, the ballet was resumed.

It was to exploit Cerrito's extraordinary popularity that Jules was now putting together an ambitious new ballet – 'the great *ballet d'action* of the season,' as Lumley saw it[24] – for which a quite exceptional expenditure had been authorised. For his theme Jules had gone to the poem, *Lalla Rookh*, written some thirty years before by the Irish poet, Thomas Moore, and despite, or perhaps because of, its florid flavour, still immensely popular. Lalla Rookh was an Indian princess who is to be given in marriage to the King of Bucharia,* and the poem describes her journey to Cashmere and her wooing, en route, by the king himself, disguised as a poet. Jules had never been to the East, nor can he have seen any genuine Indian dancing.** His research for this ballet must therefore have depended largely on his reading and such pictures as he was able to find, but he did have one first-hand source in the person of an Indian friend of Lumley's, Dwarkanath Tagore.

Tagore was one of the most remarkable Indians of his time. A member of an enormously wealthy Brahmin family,*** he commanded great respect among the English by his active opposition to some of the more barbaric Hindu customs. He mixed easily in London society, becoming a popular and highly picturesque social lion. He even acquired a taste for opera and ballet, and was a conspicuous figure in the audiences at Her Majesty's that season. Lumley found him particularly sympathetic, and spoke to him freely of the difficulties he had with his temperamental stars. One day, when he had been particularly nettled by some capricious prima donna or *danseuse*, the manager commented that the transgression of Eve was the origin of all the world's tumults, and was met with the gentle reply, 'Ah, that's your doctrine,' which suggested that Dwarkanath's theological convictions were less ungallant. This enlightened Indian willingly found time to give Jules advice for his new ballet, which must have been one of his last pleasures, for he died, suddenly and rather mysteriously, in his London hotel at the beginning of August.

An important feature of the ballet – indeed, virtually the whole of the middle section – was to be a series of moving tableaux and scenes arranged to Félicien David's symphonic ode, *Le Désert*. Although not intended for the stage, this work, scored for a large orchestra, chorus and solo voices, was a

---

* The spelling of the names follows that of Thomas Moore. Bucharia is Bokhara.
** He had been in Vienna and Milan when the small group of Indian dancers known as the Bayadères had appeared in Paris towards the end of 1838.
*** He was the father of Debendranath Tagore, the Maharishi, and the grandfather of Rabindranath Tagore.

musical description of a caravan making its way across the desert, passing through a sandstorm, and finally disappearing into the distance as silence returned again to the empty land. Lumley had presented the work in concert form in March 1845, and its reception had encouraged him to revive it with visual effects on the stage. In the belief that one desert is like another, the transposition from Arabia to India posed no problem, and no one was at all concerned that the inspiration for David's score was very specifically Middle-Eastern.

Moore's poem, written at the instigation of Byron, was strongly Romantic in its exotic appeal, presenting an idealised vision of India in its days of Mogul glory before the arrival of the British. The action of the ballet was placed in the same period, Venafra being cast as its only historical character, the Mogul emperor Aurungzebe, a contemporary of Louis XIV, but for the London public in the summer of 1846, the setting of the country between Lahore and the Vale of Cashmere had a topical interest, for only a few weeks before it had been the scene of a stirring exploit of British arms – the battle of Sobraon, which had ended a brief and bitterly fought war against the Sikhs in the Punjab.

Thomas Moore viewed the adaptation of his poem into a ballet with amused detachment. He was in London at the time, and cheerfully gave his consent. But when Lumley invited him to dinner and offered him a seat in his box for the first night the elderly poet seemed to treat the matter very lightly and did not trouble to accept.

With a vast quantity of music at his disposal, Jules found himself working on an enormous canvas. Most of David's symphony was to be used for the central scenes, for which a veritable regiment of supers had been specially engaged. To Pugni was allotted the task of writing the music for the opening and concluding scenes, which would contain most of the dances, and also of interpolating a certain amount of dance music into David's score itself, including Cerrito's principal variation, the *pas de chibouck*, which he adapted from one of David's songs. The two composers were of very different calibre, and their contributions did not mix very happily. Of the two it was Pugni who suffered, his tunes sounding thin alongside David's powerful orchestral colouring, although they provided a sprightly accompaniment to the dances.

In a remarkably short time this extraordinary ballet was conceived, planned and set upon the stage with a cast of more than two hundred and an exceptionally complex sequence of spectacular scenery and stage effects. It was offered to the public on June 11th, little more than a month after Cerrito had arrived in London, and although it suffered from numerous imperfections, not all of which were removed with repetition and excision, the work was generally recognised to be a very considerable achievement.

The audience had already sat through Cimarosa's *Il Matrimonio Segreto*

Jules Perrot

when the curtain rose again, after an interval, for the first performance of the ballet. They were transported to the Hall of the Durbah in Aurungzebe's palace in Lahore – a scene of 'the most gorgeous magnificence'[25] – the Emperor himself being seated on a peacock-tail throne to receive the ambassadors of the King of Bucharia, who have come to ask for the hand of his daughter, Lalla Rookh, the 'tulip cheek' princess, a vision of loveliness in the form of Fanny Cerrito in a dazzling white costume, trimmed with roses, her features concealed by a spangled veil. It is agreed that the wedding will take place in Cashmere, where the king will set eyes on his bride for the first time, and that the couple will remain for a while in the Vale of Cashmere before crossing the mountains to Bucharia. In the suite that has been sent to accompany Lalla Rookh on her journey there are a bevy of Tartar and Kashmirian maids of honour and a young poet, Feramorz – the rôle designed for Cerrito's husband, Saint-Léon – who has been given the privilege of entering the pavilion of the princess to entertain her with his songs. The bard, carrying his kitar, is presented to Lalla Rookh, who is much taken with his graceful bearing and pleasing manners. He is immediately entranced by the princess's beauty. But there is one person in Lalla Rookh's entourage who stands aloof, glowering at the poet with unconcealed suspicion – her Grand Nazir or Chamberlain, Fadladeen, 'a personage in his own opinion of infinite importance, . . . who looks with the keenest jealousy on all whose talents or attractions bring them into notice.'[26] While the poet is entertaining the princess, Fadladeen is continually interjecting offensive remarks aimed at ridiculing the young man, but they have no effect and he retires, almost bursting with enraged impotence. This unlikeable personality introduced Jules in one of his most amusing character studies, in which he conveyed 'the critical discontent of the supercilious chamberlain with much comicality.'[27]

A more serious note is then struck, as the most beautiful women of Lahore enter bearing pink scarfs to extol the beauty of the princess. Scarf dances were a not uncommon feature in ballets at that time, but this one was different. Apart from being 'one of the most elegant scarf dances ever yet contrived,' it contained 'a series of artifices highly agreeable to look at, and here and there disclosed features of ingenious and unexpected novelty.'[28] It was called a *pas symbolique* – symbolic, it was explained, of Lalla Rookh's perfections – and was built around a sequence of imaginative and elaborate groups, in which Cerrito always formed the central figure, designed to represent the following motifs: Hermes, The Shell, The Kiosks, The Cage, The Mirrors, The Harps, The Famed Picture of the Morning Breeze, The Stars, The Pine-Apples, The Car of the Rising Sun, The Butterflies, The Sun's Rays, and The Living Statue and its Pedestal. Each of the *coryphées* who headed the corps de ballet (Mlles Demelisse, Cassan, James and Honoré) was given a variation, but the eye always came back to Cerrito, and the culminating group, in which she represented the Statue and the corps de ballet, with their scarfs, arranged themselves to suggest a flight of steps, underlined the originality that had distinguished the whole dance. Since Jules could have had little, if any, direct experience of Indian dancing, the regional colouring must have been superficial, and in an appreciative comment the *Morning Post* related these groups to the works of French and Italian painters. 'In every movement there was poetry,' this critic proclaimed, 'every group was pictorial, as if it had stepped forth from the canvas of Boucher, or the still greater Guido.'[29] However, to judge from another review, Jules did manage to convey a flavour of India to a willing European imagination. The Vicomtesse de Malleville found that it contained all 'the variety, the abundance of motifs, the multiplicity of line and curve, and the wealth of colour of one of those Indian cloths that the skill of the European workman has not yet succeeded in copying. Nothing could have been more novel, graceful, or methodical in its seeming disorder than the evolutions with the pink scarfs, evolutions that in other contexts are so banal, but here are so unexpected and striking in the original way in which they are activated.'[30]

After this brilliant opening there followed 'a species of drama in which painting and music conjoined to produce their combined effects.'[31] In a series of scenes, accompanied largely by David's symphony, Charles Marshall depicted the desert through which the caravan passed on its journey to Cashmere. Marshall was usually more successful with architectural scenes than with landscapes, and his desert backcloths were criticised as being 'somewhat monotonous,' with 'a surface uniformly brown, with a heavy sky (sky is not Mr. Marshall's forte) overarching them.'[32] The caravan was seen first as 'a point on the horizon,' with the city of Lahore in the distance – a panorama that might have been recognised by readers of the *Illustrated London News*, which had published an engraving of the site a few weeks before. The illusion of the caravan gradually approaching was obtained by the use of cut-out figures of increasing size 'until, at last, living things took the place of the painted ones, and the cortège filled the stage with a splendour . . . seldom . . . approached, much less equalled, on any stage. Besides dromaderies, palankeens, etc. there was the mixture of characteristic costumes of the different castes and occupations of India, with the Asiatic elegance of Lalla Rookh and her fair attendants, and the gorgeous dresses of the leaders'[33] (Scene II). This was the scene that gave trouble. The horde of supers – according to the *Morning Post*, as many as two hundred in number – caused such a congestion in the wings that it was a miracle that the scene ever proceeded to its end. The oaths of the stage hands could be heard in the house as they coped with their complicated tasks as best they could after an unfortunate start when the sliding cut-out of the distant caravan failed to run smoothly. Then, when the supers began to troop across the stage, led by a circus-like character strutting along in red boots, some of the audience could not restrain their laughter.

Jules Perrot

This scene was graphically accompanied by David's movement entitled 'March of the Caravan.' 'A low monotonous sound, consisting of one note, held on without break or interruption by the violas, and blended with a succession of vague, uncertain harmonies, excite the idea of that void and dreary aspect which the wilderness presents,' described a music critic after hearing it in concert. 'The distant murmur of the approaching caravan, swelling by degrees as it comes nearer and nearer, has a wonderful effect. We imagine we hear the tramp of many feet, mingled with the gay chorus of the travellers. The music is a march, of a very marked rhythm and animated character, which gradually, by the intervention of minor chords and dissonances, becomes dark and gloomy.'[34]

This change of mood accompanied a change of scene, showing the caravan approaching a desolate wasteland, covered with low bushy jungle relieved only by an occasional white flag fluttering from a bamboo staff, marking a spot where a tiger has claimed a human victim (Scene III).

The sky has become dark and lurid 'with sundry dioramic changes,'[35] and to the music of 'The Storm in the Desert,' a choking storm sweeps across the sand. Marshall's backcloth for this scene mystified some of the spectators, for his attempt to reproduce the impressionistic effects of Turner and John Martin was not successful. Meanwhile, from the orchestra pit 'the howling of the storm, the confusion of the multitude, and their cries of terror and despair [formed] a musical picture of the most striking kind,'[36] the effect being reinforced by some inspired groupings of the large cast. 'The fall at the approach of the sandstorm'[37] was a particularly impressive effect.

The caravan is thrown into disarray, and the travellers flee in every direction, abandoning the princess to battle alone with the full fury of the simmoon. At length, overcome by terror and exhaustion, she sinks to the ground senseless. At that very moment Feramorz comes running in and catches her in his arms. Desperately he looks around for water, and finding none, goes off in search. Meanwhile stragglers are making their way back, and among them is Fadladeen, still shaking with fright at his experience. Lalla Rookh remains motionless on the ground, but soon Feramorz reappears, bearing some precious water in a leaf. As he presses it to her lips, she regains consciousness and, to his delight, gazes tenderly into his eyes. Fadladeen can hardly contain his rage, and he angrily separates them (Scene IV).

Gradually the storm abates, and a profound calm spreads over the desert. This was expressed in the music by 'soft and melodious sounds of the wind instruments,'[38] reminiscent of a passage in Beethoven's Pastorale Symphony. While the travellers are giving thanks to Allah for preserving them from disaster, night begins to fall. The caravan sets up camp, the princess's attendants erect her pavilion, and the travellers forget the alarms of the day in a display of exuberant dancing, for which Pugni may have arranged David's 'Dance of the Almées.' The mood of the music then changed again – to David's 'Hymn to

Night' – as Venus, the evening star, rises above the horizon and the desert is shown bathed in the light of the moon (Scene V).

The next scene (Scene VI) was set in Lalla Rookh's pavilion, where she implores Fadladeen to send for Feramorz. The chamberlain tells her she ought to rest rather than listen to the minstrel's frivolous nonsense, but Lalla Rookh's Persian slave has slipped out to convey her mistress's wish to Feramorz. In no time at all he enters, and Lalla Rookh asks him for a song to soothe her after the excitement of the storm. To the melody of one of David's loveliest songs, *Les Hirondelles*, he complies, while Fadladeen can only grumble disapprovingly and take to his pipe, the sweet-smelling chibouck.

Observing that the fumes have sent Fadladeen to sleep, Feramorz takes up a more seductive melody, and Lalla Rookh rises from her couch and begins to dance before him with 'quaint Moorish steps,'[39] and making sinuous patterns in the air with her scarf. The music which Pugni had borrowed from another of David's songs, *Le Chibouque*, had a 'peculiar broken rhythm' that provided a haunting accompaniment to the dance of love in which the princess and the minstrel declare their feelings for one another. Cerrito seemed to have no difficulty in coping with the Arab inflections, strange though they appeared to the ears and eyes of the audience. To 'this most spirited, but most difficult music,' explained the *Morning Post*, 'Cerrito dances such a variety of steps and baffles all description – now executing exquisitely small twinkling steps, at the next moment bounding like an antelope. There was in this dance the characteristic movement, as well as measure, of the dances of the East – of that Eastern world, which through the Moors conveyed the premature form of the bolero, cachucha, guaracha, &c. to Spain.'[40]

Following this dance, David's *Le Désert* was resumed with the movements entitled 'Sunrise' and 'The Departure of the Caravan.' As the sun rises and lights up the sandy waste, the volume of sound swelled from a gentle *tremolo* from the violins to the full power of the orchestra. The arrangement of the sleeping travellers was very artistic – 'worthy of the genius of Perrot,' as *The Times* put it.[41] Then, to a repeat of 'The March of the Caravan,' the travellers awake and the caravan moves on (Scene VII).

With this the selections from David's symphony came to an end, and the last two scenes were performed to music entirely composed by Pugni. In the eighth scene, Lalla Rookh has arrived in Cashmere. Her heart filled with what she believes to be an unrequitable love for Feramorz, she resigns herself despairingly to her fate and allows the bridal veil to be placed on her head. As she prepares for the nuptial ceremony, her glance falls on Feramorz and for a moment she contemplates refusing the hand of the king. But Fadladeen expostulates with her and warns her of the consequences of withdrawing. She yields, and is led from her kiosk like a victim to the sacrifice.

As the dropcloth of the kiosk scene rises – unfortunately becoming stuck in mid-air on the first night – a scene of incredible splendour met the eye. Lit by 'a

Jules Perrot

mother-of-pearl moon,'[42] the Vale of Cashmere stretched away into the distance, a set that achieved a fine effect of perspective within the limitations of the shallow stage at Her Majesty's, although the clouds were criticised as being 'badly painted.'[43] From a jetty a carpet of cloth of gold led to two stately thrones, on one of which is seated the king, attended by his brilliantly attired courtiers. Lalla Rookh steps out of her barge, and escorted by Fadladeen and surrounded by her ladies, moves forward with faltering steps and eyes downcast. The king comes forward to meet her, and at the touch of his hand she looks up and, with a cry of surprise, falls fainting at his feet. For the king is none other than her beloved Feramorz, whose modest guise he assumed to win her heart. Fadladeen's consternation at this *dénouement* is pitiable. He makes the humblest of obeisances, and protests that never has there been so great a poet than His Majesty.

The happy ending was then traditionally celebrated with a divertissement, 'The Feast of the Roses,' which made full amends for the tedium of the preceding scenes, for 'the house rang with applause, mixed with outbursts of bravos and encores and showers of flowers.'[44] In the opening number, a *pas des corbeilles*, danced by Mlles Lamoureux and Julien with the full corps de ballet, Jules introduced some discreetly lascivious gestures as if to remind the audience that these were nautch girls from some Indian temple, but it was all in the best of taste according to Victorian standards.[45] Every now and then the dancers formed themselves into arresting groups with their baskets of flowers, and one of the most charming features of the choreography was the way in which these groups were 'so prettily broken'[46] to lead into the next passage.

The most extraordinary dance of all was kept to the end – the *pas de neuf*, featuring Cerrito and Saint-Léon, Louise Taglioni and Mlles Demelisse, Cassan, James, Lamoureux, Julien and Honoré – extraordinary because until then no choreographer had arranged a *pas* for so many individual dancers, each having a specially arranged part. 'Never,' wrote the *Morning Post*, 'had such a number of dancers been employed in one *pas*, in such a variety of groups, each dancer in each group being as essential in his place as if he were a part of a picture or of a *basso relievo*.'[47] It was acclaimed as 'one of the best dances of the grand style ever invented'[48] and 'perhaps one of the most artistic and classical *pas* ever produced.'[49] A rare 'intellectuality'[50] was discerned in the design of the 'irregular groups,'[51] in which the six supporting *danseuses*, some carrying mirrors and others feather screens, clustered about Cerrito. 'We are at a loss to imagine,' commented the *Morning Post*, 'what could suggest to Perrot the employment of [the] odd number [of nine], and the bold attempt to form from them a varied succession of groups. But its result is a novel and surpassing triumph of choreographic art. Even the two beautiful children, Julien and Lamoureux, did wonders; as to Cerrito, Louise Taglioni and Saint-Léon, they were repeatedly and vehemently encored.'[52] In arranging Cerrito's part Jules exploited both her voluptuous appeal and her remarkable speed. In the slow movement she melted into a series of languid poses, while in the faster passages of her variation, she produced a sequence of turns so rapid that they seemed 'to spring from the suggestion of the moment.'[53] One step – not, alas, described in technical detail – was 'the most daring saltatory flight we ever witnessed. It brought down at once three successive peals of most vehement applause, followed by cheers and a general cry of encore.'[54] At her side Saint-Léon appeared as her 'ruling spirit,' complementing her femininity and exuberance with a brilliant display of virtuosity, including some 'wonderful saltatory feats.'[55]

When the curtain fell after the last scene there were loud calls for the two principals, who dragged Pugni with them to receive his share of the applause. In spite of the lateness of the hour, the public would not go home without giving Jules his due also, 'and [blushing] like Garrick through his mask of pigment, he was drawn on perforce to receive the hearty acknowledgments of the audience.'[56]

It was obvious that the ballet would have to be compressed, for with all the hitches that bedevilled the first performance, it lasted nearly three hours and the audience had begun to thin out well before the end. At the second performance the sliding cut-out was omitted, and by bringing a semblance of order to the desert scenes, the intervals were reduced and 'all the brilliant parts, scenic and choreographic, were applauded to the utmost.'[57] At the third performance the problems had been overcome still further and the ballet 'proceeded ... in the most satisfactory manner,'[58] and after the fourth performance it could be reported that it had 'established itself permanently in public favour.'[59] It was certainly not the 'failure' that the disgruntled *Morning Chronicle* stated it to be,[60] even if, as *The Times* put it in its summing up of the season, the public had not been converted to the new principle Jules seemed to be advancing of relying 'more upon the effect of an ensemble than on that of individual dancing.'[61] Its boldness of conception, with the exotic romance of Moore's poem juxtaposed with David's musical impressions of the desert, proved to be the ingredients of success, and with a judicious application of the pruning knife, the ballet enjoyed the very respectable number of fifteen complete performances and four more of single scenes or selections in the last two months of the season.

* * *

One figure was conspicuously absent from Her Majesty's that summer, for Alfred Bunn had succeeded in tempting Carlotta Grisi to Drury Lane, where she appeared with Lucien Petipa in her latest Paris creation, *Paquita*. Jules may have been too busy with *Lalla Rookh* to have seen very much of her, but she brought in her wake the devoted Théophile Gautier, who remained in London long enough to pay a visit to Her Majesty's. He was specially curious

Jules Perrot

to see Cerrito, who had not yet danced in Paris, and he came away impressed both with her and with the ballet. *Lalla Rookh* was just the sort of ballet to appeal to his taste for the exotic, but when he saw it the production had been considerably tightened up, and his only comment on the desert passages was an amused description of the dromedaries, each of which was impersonated by two men in an animal skin – 'two very worthy camels,' he conceded, 'whose front legs could have quarrelled, in the best English manner, with the hind legs if they had been out of temper with one another.'

Also included in that evening's programme was a revival of *La Bacchante*. Having accustomed himself to the small area of the stage at Her Majesty's and, to his Parisian eyes, the negligent brushwork of English scene designers, who seemed to conceive their backcloths as if they were painting water colours, he was not particularly shocked by the scenery – 'a set,' he described, 'completely festooned with vine branches and crazy garlands twining round white marble columns whose flutings were displayed against a sky saffroned with autumnal tints.' His attention, however, was soon distracted by the entrance of Jules, who came bounding on the stage in a panther-skin costume in pursuit of Lucile Grahn as a coquettish bacchante. In typical balletic fashion she did not seem to be making any great effort to escape, and predictably, 'after a few *glissades* and *coulés*,' the faun seized her by the waist. Gautier now had the opportunity of observing the progress which 'the lovely and expressive' young Danish ballerina had made since he had last seen her at the Opéra some years before, and he was at once conquered by 'the nobility of her poses, her modestly voluptuous grace, her elevation, and her soft arm movements,' all of which classified her as belonging to 'the elegant and poetic school of Taglioni.' 'In vain the male dancer declares his love with *flic-flacs, jetés battus* and *ronds de jambe*,' he continued. 'The bacchante is unmoved, and finishes her *écho* with an air of disdain. The poor devil then realises that instead of getting out of breath in his efforts to please, he must resort to ingenuity. So he picks a bunch of grapes, and squeezes it over the bacchante's upturned head. A stream of ruby-red juice flows into her rosy mouth, and the girl, so intractable a few moments before, now blushingly and tearfully falters, to lean on the shoulder of the man she has but recently repulsed. All these varying shades of feeling could not have been conveyed more intelligently or more movingly than they were by Lucile Grahn. A pretty woman's frenzy must always be tempered by modesty.

'Am I mistaken,' wondered Gautier in a whimsical mood, 'or do I detect some subtlety in all this and search for a profound truth in an interlude lasting only a few minutes? Is not the faun telling us, as he crushes the grapes into the mouth of the rebellious bacchante, that wine is a more potent seducer than love, and that it is good to precede a declaration of love with a few bottles of Bordeaux or Champagne, or a few flasks of Anisette or Kirsch?'[62]

* * *

The Season of the Golden Apple

Perrot teaching the Gods and Goddesses how to dance.

A MONO-RHYME.

Minerva, as she did appear at the Italian Opera.

Minerva, as she ought to have appeared at the Italian Opera.

Neptune, as he probably will appear at the Italian Opera.

OH, Monsieur Perrot! oh, Monsieur Perrot!
Whatever on earth could have made you do so?
Put the Judgment of Paris all into dumb-show!
Bring the Gods and the Goddesses down from *en haut!*
Paris—Mercury—Venus—Minerva—Juno—
To trip "on the light fantastic toe!"
For who ever heard of a Fandango—
A Gavotte—a Cotillion—a Bolero—
Balancez—avancez—chaine des dames—dos-à-dos,
Or indeed any *pas* (excepting a "*faux*")
Perform'd by a Goddess, I'd like to know?
   Whate'er in the name, too, of Lemprière and Co.,
Could have made it come into your head to bestow
On the Goddess of Wisdom, so *comme il faut,*
And who Keightley informs us was "chaste as snow,"
A petticoat scarcely, Sir, reaching below
The knees of the lady—and looking as though
'Twas a kilt of book-muslin or calico!
Whereas every classical cameo
Assures us she usen't her legs to show—
Perhaps they were bandy and form'd like a bow—
Or her ankles were gummy—but whether or no
Sure the Goddess half-naked objected to go.
   Now it wouldn't have been such a dreadful blow,
And to Mamselle Minerva much more *à propos,*
Had you comb'd back the hair of the Virago—
Dress'd it *à la Chinoise* 'stead of *en Bandeau*—
While a pair of "blue specs" would have served to throw
Round the Goddess of Wisdom a learned halo!
But short Petticoats surely are rather *de trop*
For the Sapient Minerva and Stately Juno!!
   Then Oh. Mister Lumley! Oh, Monsieur Perrot!
And Oh, Lucille Grahn! and Oh, Cerito!
Whatever on earth could have made you do so?

The Gods and Goddesses behind the scenes at the Italian Opera.

'*Oh, Monsieur Perrot!*' A *caricaturist's view of* Le Jugement de Pâris. (The Comic Almanach for 1847)

Jules Perrot

For Jules there was no respite as the season advanced, for the interest of the subscribers had to be maintained by a carefully spaced sequence of novelties. The second half of July was to prove particularly exciting and satisfying. On the 16th Marie Taglioni made her reappearance, and Lumley found himself with three ballerinas of the first magnitude under his roof. Of the great quartet who had come together in the *Pas de Quatre* only Carlotta was absent. For want of a worthy replacement, any idea of reviving that historic divertissement had to be abandoned, and Lumley instructed Jules to prepare an even more ambitious multi-stellar ballet, generously offering to give the first performance on his benefit night. Although only three ballerinas were to be involved, the project was conceived on a much more ambitious scale than the *Pas de Quatre*. Originally it was to consist of three tableaux, the culminating divertissement – the *Pas des Déesses* – being preceded by an introduction humorously portraying the difficulties confronting a ballet-master who has to satisfy three star ballerinas. In this form Jules was considering a title such as *Les Tribulations d'un maître de ballet* or *Un Maître de ballet dans l'embarras*. However, as the rehearsals proceeded, it soon became clear that such buffoonery would be an extremely inappropriate prelude to the exquisite dancing of the three ballerinas, and wisely, after much expenditure of time, labour and money, it was scrapped.

Even in the truncated form in which it was presented to the public, as *Le Jugement de Pâris*, on July 23rd, it was considerably longer than the *Pas de Quatre*. The *Morning Herald* called it 'a vastly complicated affair,' adding that 'the combinations are unquestionably of a more attractive character than any Perrot has yet invented, the multiplicity of individuals concerned in it giving both breadth and originality to the groups.'[63]

The overture caught the fancy of the audience at once. 'There was not an old *habitué* of the Opera,' wrote the *Morning Post*, 'but smiled and felt greatly amused as the first measures of the overture were struck. Pugni has hit off an excellent and pleasing imitation of that old style of music to which the *grand monarque* himself danced ballets, and of the ancient mythological ballets of Noverre, Gardel, and their colleagues, considered the master-minds of the ballet until Perrot and his compeers appeared to adapt dancing to the wonderful improvements of choreography.'[64]

At the conclusion of the overture, this rococo pastiche was followed by a march in a grander strain, and the curtain rose. The set that came into view was 'simple, but of very good taste,'[65] showing the gods of Olympus, with their symbolic attributes, seated in the clouds. Little time was wasted in preliminaries; the audience was presumed to be familiar with the legend. To the strains of the march, the three goddesses entered – Taglioni, Cerrito and Grahn – to contest for the golden apple which Saint-Léon, as Paris, held in his hand. The divertissement began, as had the *Pas de Quatre*, with a series of 'the most elegant and elaborate groups,'[66] 'the disposition of some ten or a

Ondine, *Scene 4: Ondine dancing with her shadow.*

Ondine, *Scene 5: Ondine, holding the withering rose, feels the creeping burden of mortality. Engraving by F.M. Wall from a drawing by E. Courbould.*

Above *Silk programme for the Command Performance at Her Majesty's Theatre, July 20th, 1843. Theatre Museum, London.*
Top right *Fanny Cerrito and Fanny Elssler dancing the* pas de deux *arranged for them by Jules Perrot for the Command Performance of July 20th, 1843. (*Illustrated London News, *August 5th, 1843).*
Bottom right *Jules Perrot and Fanny Elssler in* Le Délire d'un peintre. (Illustrated London News, *August 12th, 1843).*

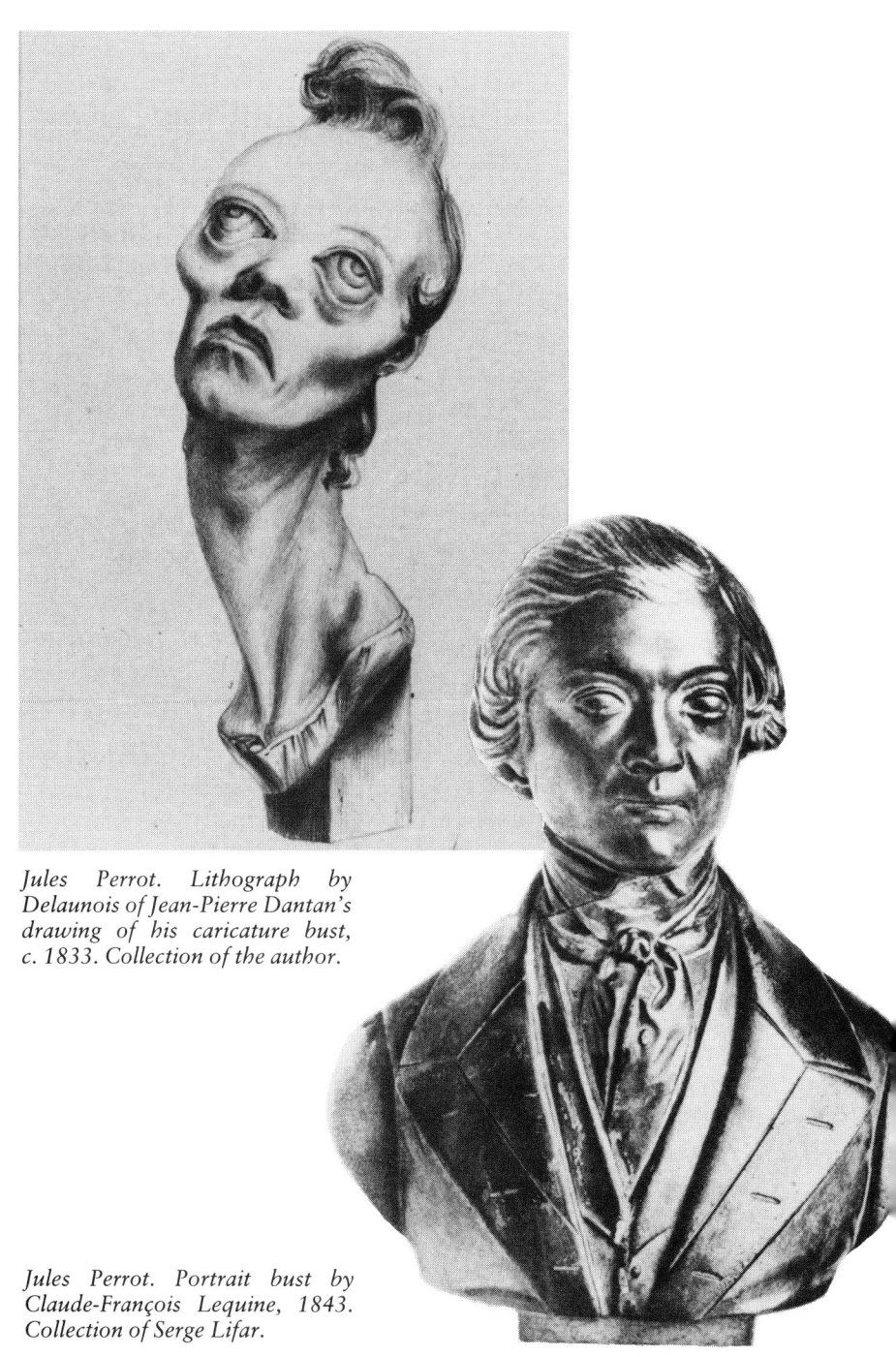

Jules Perrot. Lithograph by Delaunois of Jean-Pierre Dantan's drawing of his caricature bust, c. 1833. Collection of the author.

Jules Perrot. Portrait bust by Claude-François Lequine, 1843. Collection of Serge Lifar.

Adèle Dumilâtre in the pas de Diane chasseresse. *Lithograph by Joseph Bouvier. Theatre Museum, London.*

Jules Perrot and Fanny Elssler in La Castilliana Bolero *in* Le Délire d'un peintre. *Lithograph by Joseph Bouvier. Theatre Museum, London.*

Left *Jules Perrot and Carlotta Grisi in the* truandaise *in* La Esmeralda. *Lithograph by Joseph Bouvier. Theatre Museum, London.*

Below *Arthur Saint-Léon in Scene 3 of* La Esmeralda, *with Adelaide Frassi, left, as Fleur de Lys, and in the background, Jules Perrot as Gringoire and Carlotta Grisi as Esmeralda. Lithograph by John Brandard. Theatre Museum, London.*

Right *Jules Perrot and Carlotta Grisi in the dance lesson scene in* La Esmeralda. *(Pictorial Times, March 16th, 1844).*

Below right *The Festival of Fools, with Quasimodo as the Fools' Pope, in the last scene of* La Esmeralda. *(Illustrated London News, March 16th, 1844).*

Above *Jules Perrot and Carlotta Grisi in* The Polka. *(Illustrated London News, April 27th, 1844)*

Bottom left *Jules Perrot and Carlotta Grisi in* The Polka. *Lithograph by J.H. Lynch. Collection of the author.*

Bottom right *Carlotta Grisi in* The Polka. *Lithograph by John Brandard. Theatre Museum, London.*

Above Eoline, *Scene 4: Count Edgar among the dryads.* (Pictorial Times, *March 15th, 1845*).

Bottom left *Lucile Grahn's first appearance in* Eoline, *skimming over the lake. Lithograph by Edward Morton from a drawing by S.M. Joy. Theatre Museum, London.*

Bottom right *Jules Perrot and Lucile Grahn in the* mazurka d'extase *in* Eoline. *Lithograph by John Brandard. Theatre Museum, London.*

Left *The first page of Cesare Pugni's manuscript score of the* Pas de Quatre. *Bibliothèque Nationale, Paris.*

Right *The* Pas de Quatre, *with, left to right, Carlotta Grisi, Marie Taglioni, Lucile Grahn and Fanny Cerrito. Lithograph by T.H. Maguire from a drawing by A.E. Chalon. Collection of Parmenia Migel Ekstrom.*

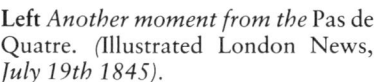

Left *Another moment from the* Pas de Quatre. *(Illustrated London News, July 19th 1845).*

Right *Cesare Pugni. Lithograph by Victor. Bibliothèque de l'Opéra, Paris.*

Right *Lucile Grahn dancing the* pas stratégique *in* Catarina. *Teaterhistoriske Museum, Copenhagen.*

Bottom left *Lucile Grahn and Jules Perrot in the* valse à cinq temps *in* Catarina.

Bottom right *Léopold Robert*, Brigand on the Watch. *Wallace Collection.*

Above Catarina, *Scene 2: Catarina fascinating the soldiers while Diavolino releases the bandits.* (Illustrated London News, March 14th, 1846).

Below Catarina, *Scene 5: Catarina receiving Diavolino's sword-thrust intended for Salvator Rosa.* British Library.

Right *Dwarkanath Tagore.* (Illustrated London News, *August 8th, 1846*)

Far right *The eight danseuses in a group from the* pas de neuf *in* Lalla Rookh. (Illustrated London News, *June 13th, 1846*)

Right *Fanny Cerrito and Arthur Saint-Léon in the* pas de chibouk *in* Lalla Rookh. *Lithograph by John Brandard. Theatre Museum, London.*

Far right *Six of the danseuses in a group from the* pas de neuf *in* Lalla Rookh. *Water colour by A.E. Chalon. Collection of Derek and Silvie Cooke.*

Above *Arthur Saint-Léon with, left to right, Fanny Cerrito, Marie Taglioni and Lucile Grahn in* Le Jugement de Pâris. *(Illustrated London News, August 1st, 1846)*

Left *The final pose of the* pas des déesses *in* Le Jugement de Pâris, *with, left to right, Fanny Cerrito, Arthur Saint-Léon, Marie Taglioni and Lucile Grahn. Lithograph by Joseph Bouvier. Collection of Keith Lester.*

dozen figures being varied with great artistical taste, forming exquisite tableaux of irregular composition, sometimes scattered and sometimes compressed.'[67] Then the three goddesses came forward to dance before the Olympians.

Jules' uncanny understanding of his ballerinas' potential enabled him to exploit and contrast their individual styles so effectively that not one of them would complain of being shown to disadvantage or outshone by the others. Interspersed with passages in which first Cerrito and Grahn, and later Grahn and Jules danced together and a section for all three ballerinas, gliding forward before Saint-Léon, that was 'too graceful not to be encored,'[68] each was provided with a variation that was both novel and perfectly suited to her resources, and this comparison of their personal characteristics, added to the alternation of the *noble* and *demi-caractère* styles in the choreography, gave the work a piquancy that riveted the audience's attention.

To begin her variation, Grahn, the youngest of the three, darted forward 'with all that audacity and vigour for which she is famous, ever spirited and ever thoroughly in earnest.'[69] Her variation contained 'a set of sharp circlings and a coda to match,'[70] and introduced 'a step entirely new and exquisitely graceful; and though it must be of a most difficult achievement, she executes it with an ease and lightness which gives her the appearance of flying. It is a species of *valse renversée* on a grand scale.'[71] 'Alternately she flew in the air, she revolved on the points of her feet, and she vaulted with a grace which no exertion could disturb.'[72]

Cerrito, whose turn came next, displayed no less vigour in her variation, but in contrast to Grahn's 'intense ardour,' went through her steps with 'a playfulness and . . . a heedlessness of manner that [were] perfectly charming.' Many of her distinctive *tours de force* were skilfully inserted. Her 'favourite rotatory movement,'[73] for instance, was not forgotten, and one of the most effective moments in the whole divertissement came when she entered, accompanied by Saint-Léon, 'executing *jetés battus* in the air and at the same moment turning her head suddenly to catch a sight of the much-desired apple.'[74]

Taglioni's ultimate triumph seemed only just. 'She had scarce traversed the stage with her flowing, gliding, exquisite steps, than the audience acknowledged there was but one Taglioni in the world.'[75] One *pas* of particular elegance and rapidity, in which she flitted across the stage with a succession of steps executed with 'inconceivable lightness' and 'enchanting grace,'[76] was greeted with an enthusiastic demand for an encore which allowed of no refusal. Her supremacy was never in doubt. Cerrito and Grahn, observed the *Morning Post*, 'have had the advantage of starting from the eminence to which Taglioni, by her sole inspiration, carried the art. Their style possesses the greatest modern novelty, of which unlimited daring in their graceful feats is a striking feature. Taglioni has had the wisdom to adhere to her own

Jules Perrot

peculiarly intellectual style, and the regret would be universal if any violent gyration should deprive her admirers of the sight of her countenance, and of her poses, each fraught with a grace nothing can surpass. Always distinguished by her tasteful costume, in this divertissement she affords the most exquisite picture, to which the star on her forehead and the other splendid gifts of the great sovereigns, mixed with her tresses, impart more than wonted light and effulgence.'[77]

The three goddesses and Paris were not the only characters in the divertissement; room was also found for the three Graces (Louise Taglioni, 'decidedly the pet of the ballet,'[78] and Mlles James and Honoré), Cupid (Mlle Lamoureux), Hymen (Mlle Julien), two nymphs (Mlles Cassan and Demelisse) and Mercury, this last part being played by the choreographer himself, of whom it was written: 'Nothing was more novel than the dancing of Perrot... All his pristine vigour for this occasion returned, and with the addition of that peculiar grace which conceals muscular exertion and which is peculiarly his own.'[79] To another critic Jules' 'whirling' was quite as impressive as Saint-Léon's 'leaping.'[80] Perched on their seats in the clouds, the Olympian gods were not indifferent to the contest, for they were seen to enjoy the proceedings with a 'love of mischief,'[81] clearly intended by the choreographer.

Finally the goddesses came to rest in a 'statuesque group, with Saint-Léon in the centre, still holding the apple high in the air,'[82] 'taking especial care that the respective right to beauty should still remain one of discord'[83] – a group that was preserved for posterity by Joseph Bouvier in one of the loveliest of souvenir lithographs.

It had been judged advisable that the identity of the goddesses whom the ballerinas represented should not be too clearly specified, and the announcement merely listed them as 'the goddesses.' In a report in the *Morning Post* on the day of the first performance it was explained that Jules, 'as an experienced and accomplished diplomatist of the Green Room ... [had] eluded the difficulty of assigning to each of the three goddesses their distinctive titles, leading the spectator to select the Venus to his own liking.'[84] A rival newspaper, the *Morning Chronicle*, purported to reveal the secret, identifying Grahn as Juno, Cerrito as Venus, and Taglioni as Minerva, but Pugni confused the issue when extracts from his music were published for the piano, by dedicating the Venus Quadrille to Taglioni, the Minerva Grande Valse to Grahn, and the Hebe Grand Galop to Cerrito. In Bouvier's print, however, the attributes of the goddesses – Venus's girdle, Hebe's flowers, Minerva's shield and spear – were unmistakable, as were the likenesses of the ballerinas portrayed, and assuming that the artist had drawn what he saw, there could be no doubt that Cerrito was Venus, Grahn was Minerva, and Taglioni, wearing the star on her forehead, was Hebe.

It was a master stroke to end the divertissement with the apple still unawarded, for even to the dancers themselves the actual identity of the rôles seemed of minor importance. When Lucile Grahn recounted her triumph in a letter to Deshayes, she was confused about which goddesses were portrayed by Taglioni and Cerrito, although she knew that she herself had been Minerva. 'I have to tell you of a magnificent success,' she wrote. 'It is *Le Jugement de Pâris*, which we have just given for the first time at Perrot's benefit a week ago. It was Taglioni and I who shared the honours, Cerrito was also quite good, but she always does the same thing. Perrot also danced in it, and very well, but he had to cut his variation. You will understand the immense impression this work produced when I tell you who played the rôles – Taglioni as Venus, Grahn as Minerva, Cerrito as Juno, Saint-Léon as Paris, Perrot as Mercury. I did the music of my variation myself.'[85]

The extraordinary storm of applause that broke out at the fall of the curtain had been gathering throughout the performance. From beginning to end bouquets had rained upon the stage, and the three ballerinas had gathered them up and presented them to each other 'with affectionate politeness.'[86] The *Morning Chronicle* referred ironically to the 'affecting scenes... between the rivals,' finding it 'quite touching to see the *danseuses* exchange complimentary wreaths and laurels, for the sincerity of such stage friendships must be undeniable.'[87] Some of the bouquets had been tossed by exalted hands. The Duchess of Sutherland had been seen to lean out of her box and deftly cast her offering at Taglioni's feet, while occupants of the centre boxes, not wishing to be deprived of the opportunity of demonstrating their delight, begged to be admitted into boxes close to the stage to throw bouquets at the end. Finally all the dancers appeared before the curtain. The audience was determined that the choreographer should receive the honours due to him. Cries of 'Perrot' rent the air, and the three ballerinas endeavoured to drag him into the view of the public. At first he modestly resisted, but he was finally persuaded and thrust forward. Cerrito then had to force him to his knees, and placed a large wreath of flowers on his head amid renewed cheering and laughter.

It was as if the golden apple were being bestowed upon him by popular acclaim. If the *Pas de Quatre* had been seen as the apotheosis of Taglioni, *Le Jugement de Pâris* was acclaimed as the ultimate triumph of the choreographer. 'The grouping, so pictorial and so highly artistic, which was so new a trait in the *pas de neuf* in *Lalla Rookh*,' wrote the *Morning Post*, 'is here advanced one step further towards a perfection unforeseen.'[88] 'A greater success is not on record,' added the same paper a day later. 'It was universally agreed that the *Pas des Déesses* is superior to the *Pas de Quatre*, the former possessing the advantage of a well-known and intelligible subject, and one which affords scope for an endless variety of groupings, full of the most graceful and poetical artistic touches, and the latter being the mere combination of great talents.'[89] Only the *Morning Chronicle*, which was waging an open campaign against Lumley and was clearly biassed, resisted the general

Jules Perrot

euphoria, finding the new divertissement inferior to the *Pas de Quatre*, and criticising Pugni's music as 'very commonplace, all cornet, piccolo, clarionet, cymbals and drums.'[90]

Le Jugement de Pâris was the sensation of the season. Night after night it took its place between two acts of the opera, being preceded by a little ceremony when the prompter's box was removed, a man came on to water the stage with a watering can, and M. Nadaud took Mr. Balfe's place to conduct the orchestra. 'There as yet appears to be no limits to the success of the *Pas des Déesses*,' wrote the *Morning Post* after the fourth performance. 'As the first measure of its music is struck, all the *habitués* rush in from parties and balls, and no less from the two Houses of Parliament, and then commences a scene totally unparalleled.'[91] A murmur of applause rolled on unceasingly throughout the performance, every now and then breaking into a thunderous burst, and at the end 'the tremulous and blushing modesty of M. Perrot in the nightly coronation and apotheosis bestowed upon him by the *déesses*'[92] never failed to send the audience home in good humour.

Many subscribers must have seen it several times. The Queen and Prince Albert took the King and Queen of the Belgians to see it twice, and the Duke of Wellington missed only two of the twelve performances. One evening – it was the fifth performance – the Iron Duke invited Lady Westmorland to share his box, and she sent a detailed account to her husband, who was then ambassador in Berlin. 'Taglioni danced much better than the first time I saw her,' she wrote, 'and we all think her immensely superior – as she is – to anything else, though Cerrito exerts herself to the utmost; but she has not the soul and dignity which makes the other so enchanting. The applause was ten times greater for Taglioni in the *Pas de Trois*, but all the bouquets for Cerrito. It is not so good as the famous *Pas de Quatre*, but it is very pretty.'[93] The Duke seemed to have his preference, for a week later he was reported as having thrown a bouquet on to the stage, and 'the fair dancer at whose feet it was cast stopped for an instant, overcome by her emotion, whilst a thunder of cheers and plaudits confirmed the judgment displayed.'[94]

On the last night of the season, the divertissement stirred the audience into a frenzy of enthusiasm. 'The spectators rose *en masse* with waving of hats and hankerchiefs, amidst constant peals of cheers and bravos, whilst dozens of bouquets, thrown by the great personages in the house, descended at each *pas* on the stage, strewing the whole proscenium with leaves. When we left,' concluded the *Morning Post*, 'the dancers had twice been recalled before the curtain and the entire audience, still rooted to the spot, were shouting for the lessee.'[95]

News of Jules' latest achievement spread quickly to the other European capitals where ballet was cultivated, and his predecessor as ballet-master at Her Majesty's, Deshayes, came specially from Paris to see it for himself. During the old dancer's stay in London he was wined and dined by many of his younger colleagues. He spent an intimate evening with Coulon, Nadaud and Jules, and a few days later was invited to a formal dinner organised by Taglioni and Cerrito, at which he regaled the company with an unending stream of reminiscences until the early hours of morning. There were toasts galore, the champagne flowed, but no one thought of escorting the old man home and, when everyone dispersed, he was still so stimulated that he wandered into the fields instead of going home to bed and nearly broke his neck falling into a ditch. The shock to his system was probably greater than it appeared at the time, and may well have hastened his death a few months later in Paris. His disappearance removed one of the last links with the ballet of the early years of the century, but Jules mourned him not merely as a historical figure and an influence in his development as a choreographer, but as a friend whose generous advice, good nature and old-world courtesy he would never forget.

13

The Unfinished Masterpiece

Few choreographers can ever have worked at greater pressure than Jules during his summers at Her Majesty's. For those who crossed his path at this time, it might not always have been easy to discern the man within the human dynamo from whom grand ballets, divertissements and *pas* flowed in such unremitting profusion, but Jules was by nature approachable, and with an eye on his forthcoming return to Milan, he found time to talk about himself to Giuseppe Crippa, who was preparing an article for an Italian periodical. Crippa was lucky to catch him in an expansive mood, and his curiosity was whetted when Jules remarked that his head had been measured by a phrenologist. Crippa pressed him to tell more. Jules showed no reluctance, and revealed that what the phrenologist called his 'affective faculties,' and in particular the sentiments, or feelings that were surcharged with emotion, were more highly developed than his 'intellectual faculties.' One of the sentiments that phrenologists imagined could be detected from the contours of the skull was that of imitation, which no doubt Jules, like several great actors who had been examined, possessed to an exceptional degree, but what was particularly remarkable in his case was the development of the areas connected with benevolence and self-esteem, evidencing a sociability and a need for other people's company on the one hand, and – to a lesser degree – ambition on the other.

From his own understanding of Jules' character Crippa found this assessment to be very accurate. 'His heart speaks more strongly than his head,' he observed, 'which is why he seldom applies himself completely to the study of a subject of which he wishes to treat, and rarely makes full use of his faculties. But Nature has been lavish with her gifts and has provided him with such a talent for imitation that when the moment arrives, he ponders, conceives and creates with a really wonderful facility and rapidity. Often, when talking or joking with friends, a word or phrase has suggested an idea, and he has said to me, "I have found my subject," and described it as vividly as if it were happening before his very eyes. He would only have four or five days to stage it, but that was all he needed.'[1]

The Unfinished Masterpiece

Crippa saw Jules as a natural genius who, if circumstances had not led him to choreography, could have become equally eminent as a musician, sculptor or painter. Yet in spite of this exceptional gift, he was attractively free of pride and pretension. His friends loved him for his cheerful companionship and wit, and it was revealing of his natural modesty and good nature that few of them were aware of the help he generously gave to those less fortunate than himself.

Crippa was a connoisseur of the ballet, with opinions that were naturally coloured by his experience in his native Italy. Sylphides, wilis, naiads and the like who populated so many ballets in those Romantic times seemed a foreign infusion to one of his Italian outlook, a product of the mists of Northern Europe rather than the sunny south, and knowing that Jules was expected in Milan for the Carnival season, he advised him to 'devote himself to a grander type of composition more worthy of his talent, and revive the historical and philosophical ballet of Viganò.'[2] In fact, in spite of the success of *Ondine*, Jules' own inclinations lay in the same direction, as he would shortly show in his choice of themes for the ballets he was to produce at the Scala.

He was increasingly becoming aware of his spreading reputation, and it was now a comforting thought that if the doors of the Paris Opéra remained closed, there were other equally prestigious theatres that would be glad of his services. Vienna, London and Milan already knew his worth at first hand, and he now discovered that his progress was being followed by the authorities in St. Petersburg, who were desperate to find a talented ballet-master. By an unfortunate mischance, though, a letter which the Director of the Imperial Theatres there, Count Alexandre Guedeonov, addressed to him in Milan when he was producing *La Esmeralda*, never reached him, but towards the end of May 1846, when he was up to his ears in preparing *Lalla Rookh*, another approach was made, enquiring whether he would be free for the season of 1846–47. By then he had already committed himself to the Scala for the following Carnival season, but there was a gap of about three months between the close of the London season and the day he was expected in Milan. So he replied to his Paris agent, through whom the offer had been transmitted, proposing that he should arrive in St. Petersburg early in September, be given a month or five weeks in which to stage a ballet – *La Esmeralda*, for example – and appear in twelve to fifteen performances before his departure. And, in case this would not be acceptable, he added that if the Imperial Theatres were only interested in a full season's engagement, the earliest date he could consider was September 1847.

As for money – 'that awful metal for which people do such beautiful and dreadful things' – he made his requirements very clear. 'I will not base my demands,' he wrote, 'on the rate of the fabulous salaries which, I have heard it said, have been so generously granted to the Princes of Opera and laid at the

183

Jules Perrot

divine feet of the Goddess of the Dance,* and with which our French actors are crowned, for being by nature a doubting Thomas and not having actually seen those fabulous contracts, I would be fearful of passing in St. Petersburg for a cunning fellow or a fool because I too can claim to be a Prince in my profession. I will merely say that in Milan I earn 1,500 gold napoleons** for the Carnival, which is three months, as you know. In London I am paid on the same footing. And in Rome I have refused 12,000 francs to stage a ballet for eight evenings. So, taking into account the difference in the cost of living from one country to another, and bearing in mind that I am everywhere paid more than anyone comparable in the dance field for more than sixteen years, I will close with the following proposals: an engagement of six months each year, from September 15th to March 15th of our calendar, 10,000 roubles a month, that is to say 60,000 roubles for six months, a full benefit free of all expenses, and my travelling expenses paid on the basis of 1,000 roubles per journey.'[3]

A curse seemed to have been laid on this correspondence, for this letter too failed to reach its destination. By the time Jules realised this, it was too late to consider a short engagement in 1846. 'It must be Fate that is frustrating my plans with regard to the Imperial Theatres of St. Petersburg, like a sort of interfering devil,' he moaned.[4] However, it was probably not so much postal difficulties as the scale of his demands that put an end to these negotiations, for two years later, when he eventually succeeded in concluding a contract for St. Petersburg, the salary he accepted was only a fraction of the astronomical demands he made in 1846.

Meanwhile he was increasingly feeling the strain of the London season, and had in fact made up his mind to break the exhausting pattern of the past few years. The offer he had received from the Scala, Milan, was made doubly tempting by the thought that he would be working there with Fanny Elssler, and commiting himself for the whole of the Carnival season of 1846–47 meant that he was effectively reducing his availability for the 1847 season in London from seven months to four. A further attraction was that in Milan there would be no question of his being called upon to produce ballets and divertissements to order at short notice, his responsibilities being strictly limited to reviving *Catarina**** and producing a new ballet.

The Scala might not have appreciated the extent to which he planned to revise *Catarina*, which was no doubt intended for the opening performance of

---

* For each of her four seasons in St. Petersburg between 1838–39 and 1841–42 Marie Taglioni received a salary of 40,000 roubles in addition to bonuses (*feux*) of 1,000 roubles for each appearance and two benefits, each with a guarantee of 6,000 roubles. The rate of exchange was 4 francs to the rouble.
** A gold napoleon was a 20 franc piece.
*** The Italians made a slight change in the spelling of the title, *Catarina* becoming *Caterina*. The former spelling is used throughout this book for consistency.

the season on December 26th. But all the preparations that were required, coupled with a back injury he sustained during rehearsals, played havoc with the schedule and the ballet was not ready to be shown until January 9th, 1847.

By all accounts the final result was well worth waiting for. As one critic put it, its impact on the public was like an electric shock.[5] By comparison with this definitive version, the hastily prepared London production of the previous spring was little more than a preliminary sketch. The activity of the London season was so hectic that there had been no question of Jules reworking it once it had been put on, but he had been able to note which passages needed to be extended and which characters filled out to make the work dramatically more effective, and generally how the production itself could be improved. And the opportunity of revising it on a stage provided with advanced scenic resources, and with a cast that included not only experienced Italian mimes but the greatest dramatic ballerina of the age, was not to be resisted.

The detailed scenario which the Scala, Milan, published for its patrons revealed most clearly how much the action had been elaborated, for although only a brief synopsis had been issued in London, the critics there had described the action in considerable detail in their notices. Such an extensive reworking had demanded revisions and additions to the score, and since Pugni had not accompanied Jules to Milan, this task had devolved on one of the *maestri al cembalo*,* Giovanni Bajetti, who had performed a similar operation on *Giselle* some years before to expand it into five acts. As revised for Milan, the score of *Catarina* was published by Ricordi in a piano reduction, in which Bajetti's contributions were meticulously identified.

This definitive version of Catarina opened with Salvator Rosa – effectively played by the mime, Effisio Catte – standing on a rock marvelling at the beauty of the mountain landscape, a scene set to entirely new music by Bajetti. A group of bandits are then seen stealthily approaching. They set upon the artist and rob him. Other bandits come leaping over the rocks and discover the artist's carriage, a property for which there could have been no room in the cramped surroundings of Her Majesty's. After the meeting of Salvator and Catarina there followed a number entitled *L'Abruzzese*, presumably an ensemble dance, for which Bajetti had revised a section of Pugni's score. Later in the scene Jules made his appearance as Diavolino, bringing on the officer he has captured. He lays the booty he has stolen on his foray at Catarina's feet, after which, to music added by Bajetti, the captured officer hands Catarina a note informing her that a full pardon awaits whoever delivers the bandits into the hands of justice. The *pas stratégique* that follows – probably little changed, if at all, from the original – had the purpose, as the scenario

---

* A *maestro al cembalo* directed the orchestra from the harpsichord or piano. The term was in use at the Scala until 1853.

explained, of conveying the bandits' defiance and readiness for battle. During this dance Diavolino observes that Salvator and Catarina are mutually attracted to one another, and being secretly in love with her himself, becomes consumed with jealousy. He persuades Catarina to dance with him, and they perform, first, the *Romanesca* – in the Milan production shifted from the second scene – and then the *valse à cinq temps*. At the end of these dances Catarina is informed that soldiers have been seen in the vicinity, and the remainder of the scene was devoted to the battle. Except for an opening march movement taken from Pugni's score, the music for the finale of this scene was added by Bajetti. The bandits retire to their side of the mountain stream. Catarina has told Salvator to escape while he can, but he has preferred to remain and defend her. The soldiers advance across the bridge, and are soon engaged in hand-to-hand fighting with the bandits. Salvator begs Catarina to flee with him to safety, but she insists on sharing the fate of her companions. He then declares his love, and she is so taken aback that she hesitates. Profiting by her momentary indecision, he hustles her across the bridge, destroying it behind them. A burst of fire is heard, and Salvator is wounded. Catarina is about to tend him when Diavolino, with soldiers at his heels, comes running up to her and forcibly carries her away. As the curtain falls the rest of the bandits are overwhelmed and taken prisoner.

The second scene, in the inn, was considerably expanded with the addition of a new character, the Duke of Colle Albino, Salvator's patron. After Catarina has left the stage to change into servant's clothing, Diavolino was given a mime scene with the innkeeper in which the play of his hands amusingly reveals his character as a compulsive thief. For this additional piece of action Bajetti had composed some pages of new music entitled *Il Borsaiulo*, the pick-pocket. This was followed by the entrance of the Duke's page, who has come to order a meal for his master and his friends. Seeing that the page is the same size as himself, Diavolino engages him in conversation and slyly persuades him to enter the inn for a drink. As day breaks, a masked lady seeks refuge in the inn, pursued by the Duke and his friends, who have been pestering her to unmask. At the same moment Salvator enters, and the lady gives a start of joy and begs him to protect her. Recognising the Duke, Salvator tells him of his recent adventure in the mountains. The mysterious lady appears greatly agitated, for reasons that become clear when she raises her mask and reveals herself as Salvator's fiancée, Florida. The whole of this section had been heavily revised, and Bajetti had been called upon to make many additions to Pugni's score. Salvator then recognises Diavolino, who has reappeared wearing the page's clothes, and is still more astonished to recognise Catarina performing the duties of a servant. He is unable to speak to her, but they exchange significant glances as Catarina shows the Duke and his friends into the adjoining room for their meal. The innkeeper sends Catarina on some errand, so she is not present when a troop of soldiers arrive with their prisoners. When Catarina returns to serve beer to the soldiers, Diavolino tells her what has happened. One of the men begins to strum a tune on a lute. Catarina takes it from him and plucks a melody that brings Salvator from the other room. Diavolino's features darken at the sight of him, and he chides Catarina for not thinking of their unfortunate companions. But there is a hidden motive behind Catarina's action, for this is the prelude to the *Saltarella* which she dances with such fire that the soldiers who have been detailed to guard the prisoners are drawn in to watch her. After a while Diavolino, who has quietly slipped out, returns to tell her that he has freed the captives. The music for this dramatic dance passage was written by Bajetti and was entitled a *Tarantella* in the printed score, although both the scenario and the rehearsal score specify a *Saltarella*. The soldiers soon discover what has happened. Diavolino urges Catarina to make her escape, and is about to drag her away when the captain, the very officer whom Diavolino had captured, appears in the doorway. Diavolino hastily disappears, while Catarina grasps Salvator's arm for protection. Salvator asks the Duke to escort her out of the inn, and holding Florida's mask before her face, she leaves without being recognised. Diavolino is not so fortunate, but he slips from his captors' grasp and leaps through a window with the soldiers in pursuit.

Judging from the lack of detail in the descriptions of the London critics, the action of the third scene had then been only briefly sketched out, but Jules now elaborated it very extensively with a considerable amount of new music by Bajetti. As the scene opens, some students are making preparations in the artist's studio. The Duke and his friends then arrive. Salvator is summoned to receive their compliments, and asks the Duke what became of the girl he confided to his care. The Duke tells him that as soon as they were outside the inn, she slipped away and disappeared. Florida then enters, still doubting that Salvator loves her. With reassuring gestures, he takes her and the others into an adjoining room to inspect one of his pictures. Catarina then comes running into the empty studio in a state of exhaustion. A servant goes to announce her arrival, but is intercepted by Florida who, suspecting that this must be the girl who has made such an impression on her lover, feigns an interest in her and hides her in a closet. When the others return, Salvator begins work on a new canvas. The Duke flirts idly with Florida and, piqued at being rebuffed, mischievously shows her a portrait that Salvator has painted of Catarina. When Florida reproaches Salvator, he placates her by giving her a miniature of himself. The *pas des modèles* then follows, showing Salvator arranging the groups he requires for his new composition. This dance culminates with Florida introducing Catarina among the models. Salvator is momentarily stupefied by Catarina's unexpected appearance, and Florida sees this as proof that he has deceived her. She dashes the miniature to the floor. Catarina quickly picks it up. At that moment a squad of soldiers enters, and Florida denounces Catarina. Salvator shows his contempt for Florida's action. Before being led away, Catarina begs to be allowed to keep the miniature, and asks Florida to love Salvator with the same constancy that she herself would have shown. In the hands of Fanny Elssler, this display of resignation and forgiveness in the face of an act of betrayal acquired an extraordinary emotional intensity. It was a supreme example of her power of projection as a mime, matching her great moment at the end of *La Esmeralda*, when Esmeralda warns Frollo of the divine retribution that awaits him. The whole of this scene had been virtually created afresh. Bajetti had been required to write new music for the whole of the opening section down to Catarina's entrance, and to add to and adapt Pugni's music for the rest of the scene. The only part of the original score that remained untouched was the *pas des modèles*.

By contrast Pugni's score was left intact for the fourth scene, which opened, as it had in London, with the death sentence being pronounced on Catarina by the judges. Then a mysterious cloaked stranger is admitted to her cell. He asks if she has any final wishes, and when she begins to tell him of her love for Salvator, he throws back his cowl and reveals himself as the artist himself. They are interrupted by a sound at the window, and as Salvator moves into the shadows, Diavolino climbs into the room. He tells Catarina that he has come to rescue her, and that below the window is a boat in which they can make their escape. Catarina is overjoyed at the prospect of being united with the man she loves. Diavolino, thinking that he must be the object of this rapture, is so overcome that he confesses that he has long loved her in secret. But at the sight of the miniature the truth dawns upon him that it is not him but Salvator that she loves. Reacting with characteristic passion, he swears to kill his rival, but time is short and he produces a rope ladder. From his hiding place Salvator signals to Catarina to escape while she can. Footsteps are heard. Diavolino hides, and the gaoler enters to fetch the stranger. When the lock clanks back into place, Diavolino comes out of hiding and helps Catarina climb through the window.

The final scene had undergone only minor adjustments, and Bajetti had made only slight alterations in the *pas de masque* – in the Ricordi score described as the '*grand pas mimo-dansant*' – and the death scene at the end. The ensemble dance, *La Follia del Carnevale*, had been moved to an earlier place in the scene, coming now after the passage when Diavolino, having lost Catarina in the crush, has provoked Salvator but has withdrawn at the approach of soldiers searching for the fugitives. Following this general dance, Catarina enters disguised as a fortune teller and, after dancing the *pas de masque*, manages to warn Salvator that his life is in danger. He is not deceived by her disguise and begs her to flee with him. This led to the final *dénouement*. Burning with a desire for vengeance, Diavolino hurls himself in the path of the lovers at the very moment that the piazza and the distant dome of St. Peter's are illuminated. All is confusion. The soldiers reappear, still searching. Diavolino attacks Salvator, who draws his sword in defence and severely wounds the bandit. Diavolino's weapon is struck from his hand, but he pulls out a stiletto and with his dying force lunges at his rival. As he does so, Catarina darts forward and receives the fatal blow. The ballet closes as she places Salvator's hand in Florida's and dies in his arms.

The opportunity of revising the scenario and reworking the production in the light of experience in actual performance enabled Jules not only to add polish to the work but to heighten the emotional effect of the drama. The critic of the theatrical paper, *Il Pirata*, praised him unstintingly for his achievement. 'Every idea,' he wrote, 'is expressed with great simplicity, with unusual clarity, with masterly brush strokes and touches of the most exquisite verisimilitude. Every scene has been thought out and presented with great good sense and good taste, and with tremendous effect. One's interest is held throughout, there is always something new to see, and the ballet ends all too soon, for there is not a moment of boredom. Not for a long time have we seen such a beautiful, polished, entertaining and delightful ballet at the Scala. It is full of original arrangements and groups and novel combinations, and the miming is so closely linked with the dancing that it is often difficult to say where the one finishes and the other begins ... This ballet speaks to the imagination, the senses, the heart, the soul, and you leave the theatre feeling uplifted ... And there is another reason for praise. The music is well suited to the subject, following the author's intentions and indications, and fulfilling the philosophical and aesthetic requirements of the situations. Whoever the music is by, Pugni or another, it is stimulating, electrifying, entertaining. "Entertaining" – a blessed quality, which is met all too rarely in our theatres, as witness our powerful yawns!'[6]

However, the production did not escape criticism entirely. The *Corriere delle Dame* had reservations, feeling it missed being 'a great ballet' because it lacked 'originality and tautness in the action' and offered neither 'great situations' nor 'proper development of passions or characters,' but nevertheless recognising 'a certain grandeur and imagination, a variety in the dances and groups, splendid scenery, and occasionally a really successful moment ... One could have wished for a more appropriate and less precipitate development of the plot,' this critic concluded, 'but Elssler made one forget such quibbles.'[7]

Fanny Elssler's interpretation of Catarina was central to the ballet's triumph, for the entire action revolved around the fate of the heroine. Her miming was miraculously expressive and powerful, communicating a vast range of moods from a light gentleness of manner to the most ardent passion. 'It would be no exaggeration,' wrote *Il Pirata*, 'to say that her arms and hands possess the gift of speech. And when she danced she never became the conventional ballerina, but remained a truly inspired and creative artist moving with lightness, ease, elegance and delicacy that concealed all the mechanics of her technique.'[8] An admirer who saw the *valse à cinq temps* as

Jules Perrot

something of an anachronism and found the musket drill of the *pas stratégique* somewhat awkward, could still appreciate her marvellous qualities. 'Elssler's manner of moving is made for great passions,' he wrote. 'Her mobile features, a certain slow solemnity in her movements, a placid sobriety in her actions that recalls the simple forms of ancient art, are staggeringly effective when employed to express sublime resignation, deep love and unconquerable repugnance.'[9] She was called back several times during the first performance. Nor was Jules himself overlooked. If he was no longer able to perform feats of virtuosity, 'the way he moved was so intelligent and graceful that the public was beside itself with astonishment.'[10] But it was his character study of the headstrong Diavolino that lingered in the memory. The young bandit's violent, single-minded devotion to Catarina was conveyed 'with the same almost facile naivety and ingenuity'[11] that had coloured Jules' rendering of Gringoire in *La Esmeralda*, and the extraordinary display of emotion and passion in the prison scene, ranging from an unrestrained, almost hysterical joy to the deepest despair, was a *tour de force* of miming. It was a worthy portrait to be set beside Elssler's Catarina.

* * *

With *Catarina* so successfully launched – it was to be performed twenty-five times during the season – Jules was able to concentrate on his next important task, the creation of a new ballet for Fanny Elssler. He had found her to be a near-perfect interpreter of Giselle, Esmeralda and Catarina, but not until now had he had the opportunity to design a work expressly to exploit her genius as an actress-dancer. Clearly the essential ingredient had to be a rôle that would enable her to pull out every stop of her great dramatic range. Perhaps, just for a moment, his thoughts turned to an old idea, and he imagined her as Joan of Arc, but his eventual choice was to fall on a more obscure figure from French history, Odette de Champdivers, the *'petite reine'* whose gentle ministrations brought comfort to King Charles VI in his madness.

The fifteenth century exerted a strong fascination on Jules' imagination. Brought up in the heady atmosphere of Romantic drama, he shared the preoccupation with the late Middle Ages that had inspired other creative artists of his time, not least among them Victor Hugo, whose vivid picture of Paris in *Notre Dame de Paris* had provided the inspiration for *La Esmeralda*. For his new ballet Jules had been drawn back to old Paris, but to a period nearly a hundred years earlier than that of Hugo's novel.

The sources for his scenario of *Odetta, o La Demenza di Carlo VI re di Francia* may conceivably have included experiences in the theatre, for in his younger days he could have seen one or more of the plays about Charles VI that had appeared on the Paris stage in the 1820s and 1830s. In one of them, produced by the Comédie Française in 1826, the great tragedian Talma had played the king. However, none of these pieces bore any real resemblance to Jules' ballet scenario, and such influence as they may have had must have been limited to drawing his attention to the poor demented king as a figure of tragedy. As for Odette, she had featured as a major character in only one of these pieces, a vaudeville given at the Ambigu-Comique in 1832, called *Odette, ou la Petite Reine*, in which she was presented as a young girl of ten. A more recent production, of which Jules may have retained a vivid memory, was Halévy's opera, *Charles VI*, produced at the Opéra in 1843, in which Odette, the principal soprano rôle, was presented as a sort of precursor of Joan of Arc, taking part in the struggle against the English and dying gloriously in the last act, rallying the supporters of the Dauphin behind the royal standard.*

A more likely and historically more reliable source, however, was Michelet's great *Histoire de France*, which had been coming out, a volume or two at a time, over the past thirteen years. The fourth volume, covering the reign of Charles VI, had appeared in the bookshops in 1840, and Jules, in common with countless other readers, must have been thrilled by the historian's imaginative evocation of the past. Significantly, many of the elements which Jules moulded into the narrative of the ballet were to be found in Michelet's pages, with the surprising exception of the character of Odette herself, whom the historian never mentioned.

Jules set the action of the ballet before the battle of Agincourt, at the time of the onset of the king's madness, frankly confessing, in the preface to the scenario, that he had intentionally tampered with history to make the story more interesting. Central to the theme, and presented as a suffering personification of good, was the King, whose insanity resulted in a disastrous period of factional strife. A bitter and unrelenting power struggle had ensued, which Jules featured in his narrative through the characters of the Queen, Isabella of Bavaria, and the King's younger brother, the Duc d'Orléans, who were presented as being joined in an uneasy and mistrustful alliance. Savoisy, who in real life had been one of the leading supporters of the Queen and the Duke, made his appearance in the ballet as the King's chamberlain and companion. Odette herself, a shadowy figure in the pages of history, was presented by Jules as a girl of humble origin, whose father was given the name, and a little of the character, of Caboche, the leader of a popular revolt that had forced through a celebrated but short-lived programme of reform. Finally there was Jules' own rôle, the only principal character in the ballet who had no

---

* These productions were *La Démence de Charles VI*, a tragedy by N.L. Lemercier (Théâtre de l'Odéon, September 25th, 1820), *Charles VI*, a tragedy by De Laville de Mirmont (Théâtre Français, March 6th, 1826), *Odette, ou la Petite Reine*, a 'chronique-vaudeville' by Octo, V. Ratier and Saint-Yves (Ambigu-Comique, April 24th, 1832), and *Charles VI*, an opera by Halévy to a libretto by Casimir and Germain Delavigne (Opéra, March 15th, 1843).

Jules Perrot

counterpart in history – Joan Villon, the King's jester, so named no doubt as to suggest he might have been an ancestor of François Villon, whose poetic genius and escapades against authority must have struck a responsive chord in the choreographer's romantic imagination.

From his choice of characters the threads of Jules' story took shape: the distress of the stricken King and his neglect by the Queen, the power struggle in which she and his brother play leading parts, the treasonable dealings with the English aimed at placing the young Duke of Lancaster on the French throne, and the growing power of the populace. The audience was supposed to view the action as contained within a short space of time, somewhere in the early part of the King's reign, but in constructing his plot Jules had exercised his dramatist's licence and telescoped events that had actually taken place over a much longer period. No one quibbled over this, and the work no doubt gained theatrically from the time-condensing process. In fact, Isabella married Charles VI in 1385 and her official entry into Paris took place four years later. Charles's first attack of madness followed in 1392. The Duc d'Orléans became the Queen's constant companion until he was assassinated in 1407, and it was only after that that Odette was introduced to the King's side with the consent of the Queen. The reversion to the French crown was not offered to Henry V of England until 1420, two years before the death of the poor demented King.

The production of Jules' ballet on this stirring historical theme was unluckily delayed first by his back injury, and then by a bout of jaundice which he suffered in the cold days of January. When the ballet could be postponed no longer if it was to be given at all, Jules reluctantly had to agree to its being presented in an unfinished state, taking the precaution, however, of explaining the circumstances in the preface to the scenario and craving the public's indulgence.

So long had *Odetta* been awaited that the audience that filled the theatre for the first performance on March 16th, 1847, was in a high state of expectation. Such fears as Jules may have had were soon dispelled by the applause with which the ballet was received and the favourable reactions of the critics. 'We must not blame him,' wrote one, 'if instead of giving us a perfect ballet, he has only presented us with a fine ballet in which dancing, acting and décor all combine to beguile the eye and the mind and leave us still wanting more.'[12] Lambertini, the critic of the *Gazzetta di Milano*, acclaimed it as a brilliant vehicle for the acting prowess of Elssler, whose portrayal of Odette was most effectively supported by the choreographer himself and Effisio Catte in the rôles of the jester and the King. Unfinished it might have been, but its power was such as to haunt the memory long after the curtain had fallen. Indeed, one spectator still remembered it after nearly thirty years as 'a masterpiece superior not only to *La Esmeralda*, but also to *Faust*,' which followed *Odetta* a year later.[13] The *Corriere delle Dame* thought *Odetta* was 'one of the finest ballets we have ever seen on our stage,' expressing the opinion that 'if time and the choreographer's health had allowed him to finish it completely, it would certainly have equalled . . . *La Esmeralda*. We will even say it would have surpassed [it] in its combination of historical interest, dramatic invention, and the excellent correlation between dancing and action, because *Odetta*, while presenting an authentically historical picture of the life of the unhappy Charles VI, also presents us with the most beautiful dance groups and *ballabili* imaginable without in any way detracting from the action, which seems almost to gain a new means of communication from the dances. The use of the dance not merely as an excuse for graceful movements, but to add significance to the human relationships and dramatic situations is a happy innovation of modern choreography, due, we believe, to Perrot himself.'[14] As a final accolade Jules found himself described, in a theatre annual, as 'a composer of great finesse and astonishing power who, with his great skill and long experience, has consoled Italy for the loss of Viganò and Gioja.'[15]

No doubt both choreographer and ballerina sensed how formidable a combination they made, and no less fully appreciated the opportunity of working with one another. Writing in a biographical compilation entitled *Pleiade Artistica* that was published in Milan that spring, Benedetto Bermani called Elssler 'the first among ballerinas just as she is the most prodigious of mimes. Give her the smallest of parts in the most mediocre of ballets, and she will clothe it with such riches of taste and intelligence as to make it almost great. Give her a choreographer such as Perrot, and you will see what marvels will result from the association of two artists who alone can understand one another in all their greatness. It is a matter for regret, however, that while they each wish to work with one another, Fate has always frustrated this and made it impossible for Perrot's major works to appear under the aegis of this sublime artist. With the exception of *Le Délire d'un peintre*, Perrot has had to entrust all his important ballets to artists who, however eminent, are greatly inferior to Elssler. It is only in Milan that the wishes of these two great figures have at last been fulfilled with the magnificent creation of *Odetta*.'

Bermani went on to speak of Jules as a creative artist. 'Perrot's exuberant intelligence,' he explained, 'has brought his art to such a pitch of perfection as to transform it into something entirely new . . . As a composer he displays wit, ingenuity and a delicate sensitivity . . . Clarity, grace, a wealth of invention, taste and elegance are the hallmarks of his fertile imagination. An accomplished erudite artist, and endowed with the broad understanding of a remarkable intellect, Perrot lavishes treasures of artistic beauty on every scene of his ballets, and particularly on the group scenes and dances. Such prolific invention, and a variety of composition such that there is never a hint of repeating himself, would be the envy of the most distinguished sculptor.'[16]

For the production of *Odetta* Jules was particularly well served by the scene designer, Carlo Fontana, who painted a series of evocative backcloths, and by the costumier, Raviglia. For once Cesare Pugni could not be at Jules' elbow – perhaps the circumstances of his departure from Milan a dozen years before were still held against him – and since no one could be found to compose so rapidly as he, the task of providing the score had to be divided among three musicians. Most of it was the work of the Scala's two *maestri al cembalo*, Giacomo Panizza and Giovanni Bajetti, Panizza being responsible for the action music and Bajetti composing the divertissement of the Elements in the prologue and the *pas d'action* in Act III, which was partly an adaptation of existing music, possibly taken from Halévy's opera. The third composer was Giovanni Battista Croff, who wrote the *pas de bouquet* in Act II and, jointly with Bajetti, the *pas des corbeilles* in Act IV.

The opening prologue evoked the splendid entry into Paris of Isabella, for which, as Michelet described, the fountains spouted wine, bands of musicians played at the gates of the city, and by the Pont Notre Dame a man holding a torch in each hand was lowered by a rope from the heights of the cathedral. The curtain rose to show the square before the Pont au Change, the bridge decorated with banners bearing the arms of France and framed by a triumphal arch. At one side was a pavilion, and at the back, dominating the roofs of Paris, rose the twin towers of Notre Dame. A colourful crowd is awaiting the arrival of the Bavarian princess who is to marry Charles VI. A court official announces that largesse will be distributed, and wine suddenly flows forth from the fountains. Surging round them to fill their cups, the people throw themselves into a frenzy of rejoicing, every now and then breaking into quarrels, but always returning to good humour in the bacchanalian spirit of the occasion. It was a brilliant opening, 'a really grandiose and enchanting scene,' as one observer put it, in which 'Perrot's imagination [was] displayed in its entirety.'[17]

During this tumult the official has been choosing some of the prettiest young girls to present gifts to the princess. Then the square momentarily empties, and in runs Odette, pursued by the mischievous Joan Villon, the King's jester. This was the entrance of Fanny Elssler and Jules, who played a brief mime scene together. Odette, who has become separated from her father in the crowd, is anxious and scared, and her indignant efforts to repulse the jester's advances serve only to encourage him further. Her plight is only ended when two well-dressed men appear, one of whom orders the jester to desist and begs the girl's pardon. Villon grudgingly obeys, for he recognises one of the two men to be the King, who has put on a disguise to catch an early glimpse of the princess he is to marry – another touch of Michelet, who had described how Charles mixed with the crowd to see Isabella pass by and was even buffeted by constables for attempting to approach too close. Odette's father, Caboche, then arrives and is delighted to find his daughter. Hearing the story of her adventure, he thanks the King profusely. Meanwhile, the official returns with the girls he has selected, and the King's companion, Savoisy, points to Odette who, with her father's ready consent, is added to their number. A distant fanfare is heard, and the royal procession appears. Isabella (played by Carolina Bagnoli-Quattri), accompanied by the Duc d'Orléans (Gaspare Pratesi) and the court, is escorted to the pavilion to receive tributes and gifts. A divertissement is then performed in her honour to the theme of the elements, with gallant allusions to her surpassing beauty. Gnomes, ondines, salamanders and the spirit of the air all take part in 'one of the loveliest passages of dancing that has ever been imagined – graceful, aerial, and with such elegantly arranged groups and entrancing movements as to arouse the audience to the highest pitch of enthusiasm.'[18] Odette took the part of the spirit of the air in the final section, and the King, watching the proceedings, unrecognised, from among the people, is enraptured by her grace. Her father Caboche (played by Francesco Razzani) overhears his words of admiration and proudly declares to all and sundry that the beautiful young dancer is his daughter. The princess is just as impressed, and rewards the girl with a bracelet before continuing her progress through the city.

Some time has elapsed when Act I opens. Odette's father has been appointed a royal forester by the grace and favour of the Queen, and the scene is set in his cottage, with the forest seen through the windows and the door. Here the royal hunting party pauses to partake of refreshment, and it is only then, after offering fruit and milk to the Queen, that Odette realises that the man who came to her rescue in the crowd was the King. The King is once more fascinated by her, but suddenly he is overcome with melancholy; he stares into space, then casts his eyes about him with a look of anxiety and fear. For the moment no one is disturbed by his behaviour, and Odette prepares to present a bouquet to the Queen. Before she can do so, however, Villon snatches it from her. This incident was the pretext for a graceful *pas de deux*, constructed to a formula which Jules had used several times before. Odette 'tries to take it back. The jester will not let her. He eludes her grasp, backs away from her, then approaches her pretending to offer it back, only to slip away once again. Odette's flirtatious impatience and the jester's teasing then melt into more graceful movements and dancing of a more delicate and difficult kind. Here the art of [Perrot and Elssler] comes out in all its splendour.'[19] The Queen is greatly taken with Odette, and presses her to come to the court, a wish to which her father accedes with reluctance. The sound of a horn announces the resumption of the hunt, but the King stays behind, watched over by Villon, who hovers solicitously in the background. The King's melancholy seems to have passed. He begs Odette for a few words, and gradually her shyness vanishes before his kind and gentle manner, as he tells her of his unhappy marriage and the inordinate vanity and pride of the Queen. Not knowing how to respond to these intimate confidences, Odette is trying to bring the conversation to an end when the King's thoughts take another turn. Once again he seems overwhelmed by some dread, and he is about to go into the

Jules Perrot

forest when he is confronted by an old man who – as Michelet again recorded – restrains him with the cry, 'Stop, noble King, go no further, you are betrayed.' The King is terrified by this apparition, and his mind gives way in a fit of uncontrollable violence. The hunting party returns. The poor King is overpowered, bound, and taken back to Paris. The act then closed with a mime scene for Odette to which only an artist with Elssler's unusual command and ability to project could have done justice. Odette, whose presence has been forgotten in the general consternation, wishes to follow the King. Her father tries to restrain her, but she is so filled with pity that she resolves to devote herself to taking care of the King and alleviating his anguish. At that moment she notices Villon seated at the table, miserably finishing off the remains of the repast. With tears in her eyes she begs him to take her to Paris. Before leaving her humble home, she surveys it as if to imprint every familiar object on her memory, bids a tearful farewell to her father, and after kneeling at the threshold to offer up a prayer, grasps Villon's arm and vanishes with him into the forest.

For Act II, the scene moves to the Pré aux Clercs with the castle of the Louvre dominating the background across the Seine. It is a feast day, and a crowd of Parisians from all walks of life is making merry. The opening *ballabile* in this scene was accounted one of the finest moments in the whole ballet – 'really original, thanks to the artistic architectural arrangement of the groups ... The variety and matching of the colours are in wonderful harmony with the graceful movements and poses of the dancers. It is a most beautiful sight – a moving crowd of well-dressed people, separating, combining, dividing and coming together again, and dancing beautifully all the time.'[20] The multiplicity of patterns in the arrangement of this *ballabile* for a hundred or more dancers was astonishing. They all seemed to move 'as though operated by a single spring, forming a homogeneous unit without giving the slightest appearance of confusion or disorder, so that one could say, as of a Flemish painting, that there is not a moment of uncertainty or faulty precision.'[21]

The Duc d'Orléans then enters with Salvoisy. Now that the King's illness seems to be permanent, he covets the throne for himself. To win over the people, he liberally scatters largesse. At this point Odette and Villon appear. The Duke recognises them and asks what has brought Odette to Paris. Naively she tells him of her desire to comfort the King. The Duke offers to take her to him, but aware of his licentious reputation, she declines. Determined to reach the palace, Odette implores a ferryman to row her across the river. But she has no money, and Villon is as broke as she. They find themselves surrounded by a group of drunken soldiers, who clamour for a dance. Odette is frightened, but Villon advises her to humour them, and joins her in a dance. The crowd is so enchanted by her that no one notices a decree being posted up announcing a new tax imposed by order of the Queen. The ferryman becomes more amenable after seeing her dance, and agrees to row her to the palace. Meanwhile the Duke, who has been observing this scene, wagers Salvoisy that he will add Odette to his list of conquests and hires another boat to follow her. When Caboche appears shortly afterwards, he sees the two boats crossing the river and concludes that his daughter has been abducted by the Duke. His fury knows no bounds. Tearing down the decree, he swears to be avenged.

The mood changed as a cloth descended for Act III, representing a small room in one of the towers of the Louvre, adjoining the bedroom of the King. Villon presents Odette to the Queen, who receives her with kindness and, touched by the girl's mission to alleviate the King's distress, gives orders for her to be dressed appropriately for the banquet that is to be given that evening.

Following this short mime scene, the cloth rose to reveal the set for Act IV – a magnificent ballroom in the Hôtel St. Paul, filled with a brilliant assembly who have come to honour Lord Bedfort (*sic*), the representative of the young Duke of Lancaster, who is about to be appointed King of France. In a *pas de deux* Odette enchants everyone with 'her exquisite and elegant dancing, full of coquetry and grace – a model of artistic perfection,'[22] and in the *ballabile* that followed the corps de ballet came forward with baskets of flowers which they lay at her feet as they proclaim her queen of the ball. But suddenly this charming scene is brutally interrupted as Caboche bursts into the ballroom with a band of followers, intent on assaulting the Duc d'Orléans. The unexpected sight of Odette seems to strike Caboche with horror. He hesitates, and she looks on helplessly as he is quickly overpowered and taken away.

Act V, another mime scene was set in the King's bedroom. The Queen and the Duke enter, supporting the mad King, who rejects their ministrations. Believing that there is no hope of his recovery, Isabella takes pleasure in the thought of ruling the kingdom in his name, but the Duke, equally ambitious for his own account, proposes that she puts herself under his protection so that they can share the supreme power. Isabella pretends to agree, and the two of them leave the King asleep. Odette then enters to beg the King to pardon her father. She is followed by the Duke, who offers to save her father if she will consent to be his mistress. In a furious outburst of indignation, she raises her arm as if to strike him, but a sound from the King's room restrains her. The Duke leaves, uttering dark threats. Villon then takes her to the King, who is overcome by a fit of madness at the very moment she begins to speak to him. Desperately she employs all her wiles and charm to bring him back to reason. At last the King seems on the point of understanding and granting her wish, when a commotion is heard in the street below. Odette rushes to the window, and looking out, sees her father being led to the scaffold. Turning back to the King, she finds that he has relapsed into apathy, the pen has fallen from his hand, and Villon has taken possession of the paper. Odette implores

Jules Perrot

Villon to give it to her, but he treats the matter as a joke until, weary of teasing her, he asks why it is so important to her. When she explains, he ruefully shows her that it has not been signed. She returns to the King's side, but realising that his wits have left him, she runs out of the room in despair. But soon after she has gone, the King comes back to his senses and asks for her. When Villon tells him that she has gone to the place of execution, the King remembers her request and signs the pardon. Villon takes it, and the two men leave, the King in a state of great agitation, as if suddenly consumed by some all-absorbing purpose.

This scene was considered by the critic of the *Corriere delle Dame* to be 'one of the most dramatic and powerful in the whole ballet.'[23] This was also the opinion of *Il Pirata*, which called it 'worthy of a sublime poet and the most celebrated painter. In this act Elssler appears as an actress, a mime, who by means of gestures makes you almost imagine she is speaking. With a movement, a glance or a sigh she conveys as much as an ordinary actress can in an hour. She explores every by-way of the heart, and covers the whole spectrum of the emotions, probes all the secrets of the soul, passing wonderfully from a simple request to desperate imploring, from calm to indignation, from quiet reason to anger, and from anger to fury. In this act Jules Perrot makes a highly dramatic point, and is fortunate to have found an interpreter who, through her extraordinary talent, is able to do full and brilliant justice to his ideas. To create an effect out of something commonplace is not difficult, but to enhance something already sublime is an achievement of which only Elssler is capable.'[24]

For the last scene, Act VI, the audience was transported to the Place de Grève, which is filled with a vast crowd that has gathered to watch the execution. To the sound of a funeral march, Caboche is about to mount the scaffold when Odette thrusts her way through the throng and breathlessly throws herself into his arms. Their touching farewell is interrupted by the arrival of Villon bearing the royal pardon, which he triumphantly hands to Odette. She at once passes it on to the judges, whose first reaction is to ignore it. But at the last minute the King himself arrives and imperiously confirms that he has pardoned Caboche. The ballet then ended with the people rejoicing at the King's clemency and recovery and hurling abuse at Isabella and her adherents.

Several critics commented on the absence of dancing in this last scene, which suffered more than any other from being under-rehearsed. 'It could have been more polished,' observed the *Corriere delle Dame*, 'and the action could have ended on a less cold note, particularly when one remembered the splendid and imaginative staging of the opening.'[25] *Il Pirata* defended Jules' decision not to end the ballet with dancing, posing the question, 'How could a *ballabile* be introduced after such a powerful and wide-ranging display of emotion, after such tremendous agonising? Who could dance it? Odette, who has been at her wits' end with her father's life in danger, and has even followed him to the scaffold? Any sort of dancing would have weakened Perrot's magnificent production, and altered its beautiful and grandiose character.'[26]

It had, however, been Jules' original intention, as his violin rehearsal score reveals, to end the ballet with a seventh act, constructed around a long *pas de deux* in which both he and Elssler would have danced variations before coming together again in a final coda, but there was no time for him to work on this scene – perhaps, as it turned out, to the ballet's advantage.

Seven performances of this remarkable work had been given by the time Easter brought the Carnival and Quadragesima season to a close. Jules might have hoped for the opportunity to perfect it in a later season, as he had been able to do with *Catarina*, but this was not to be. *Odetta* was to be restaged by several Italian choreographers in Italy in the 1850s, and by Domenico Ronzani in Vienna in 1852, with Amalia Ferraris and Gustave Carey as Odette and Villon, but Jules himself never had the courage to pick up the threads again, unable perhaps to contemplate any other ballerina following in the footsteps of Fanny Elssler.

* * *

At the end of the Carnival season both Jules and Fanny Elssler set out for London, where, to their mutual disappointment, they were to appear at rival theatres. While they were dancing together in Milan a great schism had riven the London operatic world asunder. Led by Giulia Grisi and Mario, a strong group of singers had defected from Her Majesty's to support a break-away venture at Covent Garden, and the opera-going public and the press had been caught up in the resulting feud. Feelings ran high as London society, on which both theatres counted for support, split into two factions. Operatic politics provided an inexhaustible fund of gossip, and many witty epigrams at the expense of one faction or the other enlivened the dinner-table conversation at the London houses of the *haut ton*. One such exchange came to the ears of a contributor to the *Morning Post* and must have caused great glee among the supporters of Her Majesty's Theatre.

To demonstrate the great strength of that theatre's ballet department, a certain Viscount cited the *Pas de Quatre* and the *Pas des Déesses*. 'And now,' he went on to predict, 'we are to be astonished with a *pas de sept*, an exhibition quite impossible at Covent Garden.'

His companion, a Countess, concurred. 'At all events,' she remarked with a gleam in her eye, '*they* are sure to give a *pas du tout*.'[27]

Jules was, of course, returning to Her Majesty's, the scene of so many of his triumphs, but Elssler, who owed no such loyalty to Lumley, had been captured by Covent Garden. So their ways parted when they arrived in London. Jules himself arrived on April 14th to find the season already in full swing. Her Majesty's had opened earlier than usual, in February, and because of his commitments to the Scala, another ballet-master – Paul Taglioni from Berlin

Jules Perrot

– had been engaged to produce the new ballets required to open the season. These ballets had introduced the London public to two young ballerinas – the choreographer's own daughter, named Marie after her celebrated aunt, and a promising young Italian star, Carolina Rosati, who mimed very expressively and possessed a gentleness of manner that reminded connoisseurs of Carlotta Grisi. Jules was set to work at once, and made his first appearance on April 20th in a new *pas de deux* which he had arranged for himself and Rosati.

It must have been very frustrating for him to think of Fanny Elssler appearing in a mediocre divertissement only half a mile away. On May 1st he went to Covent Garden to support her in what must have been a very trying ordeal, for a rumour had been started – perhaps not unconnected with the feud between the rival theatres – that her powers were on the wane. Elssler found herself facing a cold public. She desperately needed a spark of encouragement, and seeking some friendly face on which to focus her performance, she 'spied out little Perrot, who sat in one of the boxes, gazing at her with a look of mingled sympathy and astonishment – sympathy for the great creature who stood before him unacknowledged, astonished at the pig-like stupidity of the mob. She spied out little Perrot, and she said within herself, "Perrot is my audience – he is the greatest artist in the world – he alone understands me – and to Perrot alone will I dance." And with wonderful respect for Perrot, wonderful contempt for the audience, and wonderful unconcern for herself, this creature of a thousand triumphs . . . moved leisurely to the back of the scene, and made herself ready, in a pose, to accomplish her first step in the *pas de trois*. She danced! . . . The whole crowd . . . as some gigantic animal roared and shouted with an ecstasy of delight. *Encore! Encore!! Encore!!!* was the unanimous cry. But no, Fanny was not such a butterfly. There must be time for her heaving bosom to subside . . . For a while she stood moveless and resolute, hardly deigning to acknowledge, by the slightest inclination of her charming head, the clamorous acclamations of the multitude. Fanny's soul thirsted for revenge, and she drank of the overflowing cup until she had emptied it to the very dregs. Then . . . by degrees composure came over her like a soft vision . . . At first a pout of pretty irony – then a smile of sweet complacency – then a little frown that curled itself up in a corner of her brow like one of the good-natured devils of the German mythos – then a look that flashed the full consciousness of victory – and then she condescended to repeat the dance. A more complete and astounding triumph we never witnessed. And . . . if you could have heard little Perrot applaud, and seen the content that sat upon his face, it would have done your heart good.'[28]

A few minutes later, when she returned to perform the *pas de masque* from the last act of *Catarina*, Jules must have felt doubly frustrated at the thought that London was not to see the finished version of the ballet, on which he had lavished so much thought and energy.

If he had not managed to secure Fanny Elssler, Lumley had engaged most of the other great ballerinas of the day, who arrived in London one after the other when the season reached its height, and for whom it was Jules' duty to supervise a constant succession of revivals. Lucile Grahn had made her reappearance some days before his own arrival in town, and Cerrito had disembarked on English soil only the day before. Carlotta followed him by a few days, having recently recovered from an indisposition which the *Morning Post* euphemistically identified as measles. However, the weekly retailer of the town's gossip, the *Satirist*, apparently knew better and had no scruples about publishing a different diagnosis – citing Jules as informant, although surely he must have given the information in an unguarded moment and without realising he was speaking to a journalist. 'Carlotta Grisi,' revealed this paper 'has lost much of her youthful appearance, which Perrot attributes to her mishap in losing a *young danseuse* just prior to her leaving the French capital. Perrot is confident of soon being able to repair this loss.'[29]

Influenza and injury added to Lumley's difficulties that season. Cerrito was absent for a few days, and Grahn was reported to have fallen seriously ill in May and did not reappear that summer, although she was observed, looking very flirtatious, at the Ascot races in June. Jules himself, however, was spared, and was never busier. There were revivals of *Lalla Rookh, Ondine* and *Alma* to prepare for Cerrito, and of *La Esmeralda* and *Giselle* for Carlotta, but with the sensational vogue for the opera, created by the appearance of Jenny Lind, there was to be no opportunity to produce a new grand ballet. His only creation was another multi-stellar divertissement – now a seasonal requirement – in the form of a ballet of the elements, using the music which Bajetti had written for the divertissement in the prologue of *Odetta*. On the evidence of the scenario and contemporary descriptions, added to the fact that Jules included it as a separate item in his list of works, the choreography was new, as was the basic concept of featuring three ballerinas instead of only one.

Les Eléments was given its first peformance on June 26th. The curtain rose on an empty stage, with a backcloth representing an ornamental garden. Then, one by one, the elements made their appearance. First, a bush at the back parted, and four dancers in yellow (Mlles Honoré, Cassan, James and Thévenot), the spirits of the earth, rose from the ground behind it, being joined by their attendants. Then, as the bush sank beneath the stage, it disclosed a waterfall through which Carolina Rosati made her appearance as Water, seated in an aquatic car decorated with dolphins, and attended by naiads, all dressed in light blue. Next, a mountain slowly rose, from which a number of dancers in red emerged. Its summit began to emit flame and smoke – 'a mean and disparaging squib,' commented the disappointed *Morning Herald* – and when the air cleared, there was Carlotta Grisi in 'a robe of flame-coloured gauze' personifying Fire. The mountain disappeared in its turn, and the stage was invaded by some rather substantial-looking clouds, which opened to reveal Fanny Cerrito as Air, dressed in white, 'with a pair of

Jules Perrot

gossamer wings' attached to her shoulders, and surrounded by a train of white-clad spirits of the air.[30] 'Thus,' as *The Times* concluded, 'we have a Rosicrucian congress to which water, fire and air each sends a first-rate *danseuse* as a representative, while earth sends four members in the persons of as many *coryphées*.'[31]

The *adage* which followed, danced by the whole cast, was somewhat similar in conception to the opening passages of the *Pas de Quatre* and *Le Jugement de Pâris*, consisting mainly of a series of groups, the effect of which was enhanced by the contrasting colours of the costumes. Into this passage Jules had injected a slight theme. 'Some inscrutable gestures now take place,' explained the *Morning Herald*, 'intended, we doubtfully surmise, to denote natural repugnance of Fire and Water, healed, it seems, by the civil intervention of Air, who contrives, with marvellous felicity of pacification, to make Carlotta Grisi and Rosati shake hands.'[32]

'A splendid series of quick variations'[33] then stirred the enthusiasm of the audience. Each dancer seemed determined to exert herself to the utmost to win the public's favour, and, whether by Jules' design or not, there were 'numerous small incidents and accidents which created in the spectators most amusing ideas of rivalry.' First came Cerrito and Carlotta Grisi, dancing in unison 'with the fidelity of a looking-glass' – a reminiscence of the *pas de deux* which Jules had created for Elssler and Cerrito four years before. Then followed Rosati, 'with certain quaint and sharp poses, and a coda of twinkling velocities, after the manner of Fanny Elssler.' Next, Carlotta Grisi, who had been 'smiling all the while in the corner in her own arch and piquant manner,' covered the stage with boldly executed turns, their difficulty artfully concealed by the grace of her movement and her air of gentle unconcern, while Cerrito, being the oldest of the three, had the pride of place and danced the last variation, astounding the audience with 'the abundance of her power, the scope of her revolutions, and the dexterity of her "cuts" in the air.'[34]

'At the end,' as *The Times* recorded, 'in answer to repeated acclamations, [the three ballerinas] all crossed the stage, accompanied by Perrot, who, although he had not danced in this beautiful little divertissement, well deserved, as its inventor, to participate in its glories.'[35]

Although creating less of a stir than either the *Pas de Quatre* or *Le Jugement de Pâris, Les Eléments* aroused extraordinary enthusiasm and was considered by Carlotta Grisi to be 'one of the best works that Perrot has devised.' Describing it in a letter to the critic, Pier Angelo Fiorentino, she explained : 'Cerrito represents Air, Rosati Water, and I myself Fire. We each have a separate entrance, after which there is a scene, short but very pretty, in which Water attempts to extinguish Fire. Then follow the *pas*. For my entrance I emerge from flames, which is very effective because it all happens so quickly that no one can perceive how I arrive on the stage. Then I have a very brilliant variation which gives me a magnificent success at the outset. As to the *pas*, if I am not mistaken and from what I hear, it is I who had the greatest success of us three. I dance a great deal with Cerrito, which is not very much to her liking, though I enjoy it. We have a variation together in the *allegro* movement of the piece, which we always have to repeat. This variation has contributed much to the success of the divertissement, for even without Lind we have had two magnificent houses, and the Queen has honoured us with her presence.'[36]

The season's offerings culminated in the arrival of Marie Taglioni, whom Lumley had coaxed to return to the stage for what this time were really to be the final performances of her career. Her father having retired several years before, she could not have wished for a more understanding ballet-master than Jules, who not only had danced at her side in her heyday, but had conceived the two apotheoses that had crowned her career. The first of these, the *Pas de Quatre*, was revived for her reappearance, with Rosati taking the place of the absent Grahn, and was given two performances. Taglioni's variation was vehemently encored, and when the four ballerinas, in company with the choreographer, took their call before the curtain at the end, she plucked a flower from one of her bouquets and presented it to the young Rosati, as if to seal her admission to the ranks of the elect.

The revival of *Le Jugement de Pâris* a week later was a greater triumph still, both for the ballerina and for the choreographer. The critic of the *Morning Post* spoke of it as 'the most remarkable of all specimens of choreography ever produced,' but pointed out what he believed to be a fundamental flaw in divertissements of this kind. 'The audience,' he observed, 'look upon the rivalry of the dancers as they do on a race; each spectator looks on as a judge, or is a partisan backing his favourite; and the charm of the performance in the eyes of all is the struggle for superiority by racers nearly on a par of strength – so that, to borrow a term from the turf, the race is "neck and neck," but with this immense difference in its favour, that the contest is for the superiority of agility and grace.'[37]

The same analogy occurred also to the dancers themselves, whose exertions were made doubly exhausting by the competitive spirit provoked by the vocal support of their partisans. Cerrito's husband, Saint-Léon, did not view them with much approval, as he made clear in a letter referring to them as 'steeplechases which Lumley makes these ladies dance in the name of ballet.'[38]

One final task, and one no doubt of great sentimental meaning, now remained for Jules to perform before the season ended. Taglioni appeared, on two evenings, in the second act of *La Sylphide*, and it was Jules, himself now a veteran too, whom she chose to support her as her last partner. On August 21st, the final night of the season, she appeared in public for the last time in *Le Jugement de Pâris*, accompanied, appropriately, by such a gathering of celebrities as would never again in that century be assembled on stage together – Jules himself and Saint-Léon, Fanny Cerrito, Carlotta Grisi and, representing the younger generation, Carolina Rosati. It was a moment of supreme glory,

Jules Perrot

Playbill of Her Majesty's Theatre, London, for August 7th, 1847 – Marie Taglioni's last performance as the Sylphide, partnered by Jules Perrot. Theatre Museum, London.

although one at least of her colleagues viewed it with less enthusiastic detachment. 'Taglioni,' remarked Cerrito tartly, 'is not only the most famous ballerina in the world, but also the most courteous. She takes so long to say goodbye.'[39]

Once again the London season had provided Jules with gratifying triumphs, but he cannot have failed to notice an ominous shift in public taste, a growing disinterest in ballets with strong dramatic themes. It was a shift that had undoubtedly been accelerated by the sudden rise in popularity of opera resulting from the success of Jenny Lind. Lumley, whose ear was always finely tuned to the foibles of the small segment of society on whose financial support he depended, took due note of this and Jules too was no doubt shrewd enough to sense which way the wind was blowing. The narrative ballets on which he had built his reputation had found acceptance in London because of the close integration of the dance with the action, but the vogue for the divertissement – ironically enough, stimulated by his 'steeplechases' – had reached such proportions as to make him wonder whether London was the best field for the development of his ideas. 'The old historical ballet of action seems to have for ever departed,' remarked the *Morning Post* that summer. 'The *pas nobles*, like the wearisome *tirades* of French tragedy, are rather considered as bores than as ministering to the delights of modern opera-goers. We look more for the romantic than the classical or the didactic. Perrot triumphs over Gardel, and detail gives place to generalities. In lieu of the fabled gods of the Pantheon we have the imaginings of Victor Hugo and Henri Heine choreographed; where strode stalwart zephyrs, we now have the elements symbolised, if not etherealised. *Pas* usurp the place of story, and picturesque groupings that of prosy plots. The divertissement has pushed the old ballet from its time-honoured throne. The aged deem this rebellion; the youthful, revolution.'[40]

With much of this Jules would not have quarrelled, but the conclusion seemed to exclude the dramatic framework that he had used to such brilliant effect in *La Esmeralda*, *Catarina* and *Odetta*, and it was precisely a ballet of this type that he was contemplating as he packed his belongings to return to Paris.

14

The Year of 'Faust'

Although the thought of producing a ballet on the theme of *Faust* might well have crossed his mind before, it was only after another project on the same subject had been abandoned that Jules consciously began to plan his own version This other project had been envisaged as the major attraction of the London season that had just ended. In spite of the rejection of Heine's synopsis for *Die Göttin Diane*, Lumley had persisted in his efforts to coax a ballet scenario out of the German poet, and early in 1847 had felt sufficiently confident of success to slip the word to the *Morning Post* that one of the three new ballets to be presented during the season would be the brain-child of 'that great and original genius, Henri Heine' and 'selected from the old black letter legends of Germany.'[1] At that time Heine had not delivered his manuscript, but Lumley knew, from a discussion he had with him some weeks before, that he was intending to treat the theme of *Faust* in a highly original manner. What he had heard was enough to make him nervous, and he had urged Heine to add an explanatory note about his sources to prepare the public for what they were to see. For Heine had no intention of producing a balletic version of Gœthe's poem. Instead he was purporting to revive 'the original Faust of old German legendary lore,' and in the process had dredged up a hodgepodge of erotic and satanic scenes from old chapbooks, obscure puppet plays and his own memories of performances by strolling players. His theme was frankly sensual, even morbid, with none of Gœthe's religious and philosophical overtones. It was to be presented as a kind of nightmare in which the devil assumed the form of a beautiful woman, Mephistophela, and took Faust on a fantastic journey which embraced a witches' sabbath, a vision of classical Greece shattered by a massive cataclysm, and finally a Brueghel-inspired fairground scene that led to the climax in which Faust was to be mercilessly consigned to the fires of Hell. Heine's Faust was to be vouchsafed no final redemption such as awaited the Faust of Gœthe's poem. The emphasis throughout Heine's scenario was placed on Faust's craving for physical passion.

In his memoirs Lumley recalled that 'preparations were already in progress for the production of this work'[2] when the scenario reached him in

March. Presumably he had been given sufficient information in advance to set Charles Marshall to work on designing the scenery. Pugni may have been alerted too, and Lumley must surely have involved the ballet-master in these early preparations. Had all this taken place a year earlier, Jules would have been at hand, but this year he was still in Milan during the opening weeks of the season and Paul Taglioni was in charge of the ballet department. If the plan had been to present the ballet early in the season – and Heine was expecting it to be given before the end of April – the task of producing it must have been allotted to Taglioni. Serious thought also must have been given to casting the rôle of Mephistophela, the most likely choice being Carolina Rosati, who was engaged for the whole season, and whose unusual potential for dramatic characterisation was already evident.

The arrival of the scenario, however, threw Lumley and his staff into confusion. The preparations ground to a halt, even though no immediate decision was made to abandon the project. Meanwhile, in Paris, Heine was in daily expectation of hearing that his ballet had been presented, and writing to Lumley whenever a new idea occurred to him. 'Please explain to the ballet-master what I have written on the subject of the witches' sabbath,' he requested in one letter, 'and ask if it would not be possible to allow the Countess to dance a frightfully grotesque *pas de deux*.'[3] He was confident of success. 'You will find,' he wrote early in May, 'that my ballet will excite a furore beyond all expectations.'[4] By then it was clear that Paul Taglioni would have no time to produce it, and on Jules' arrival in London in the middle of April, Lumley must have turned to him.

In spite of the rôle of Mephistophela being offered to Carlotta Grisi, Jules objected in principle to being saddled with a ready-made scenario. Heine, who was made aware of Jules' views, attributed the failure to stage his *Faust* to 'the resident ballet-master [who] considered my work to be a dangerous novelty.' That he was blaming not Paul Taglioni but Jules, whose childhood exploits in a monkey-skin at the Théâtre de la Gaîté were common knowledge, was clear from the phrase he used to vent his scorn for the men of ballet. He had been thwarted, he alleged, by the choreographer's attitude that 'the prestige of his art would be much endangered if a poet were allowed to write the story, thus displacing ballet-monkeys writing with the collaboration of some starving hack!'[5]

Heine's other explanation for the abandonment of his ballet was that the extraordinary success of Jenny Lind, the Swedish Nightingale, had postponed all other productions indefinitely. There was some truth in this, for Lumley would have been foolhardy not to exploit the sensation Lind had created. Depending so much on the support of his subscribers, he could not ignore box-office considerations, and apart from *Les Eléments*, no new ballets were produced during the summer, the novelties – *Coralia*, *Théa* and *Orithia* – all having been staged by Paul Taglioni before Jenny Lind's début.

Jules Perrot

There was, however, another, more fundamental objection, which again was advanced by Jules. If Heine's scenario was to be scrupulously followed, the nature of the dances and the mime scenes would be certain to scandalise the subscribers, and in the context of the struggle with the rival house at Covent Garden, this could have disastrous results. Nor could it be overlooked that the list of subscribers was headed by Queen Victoria. Lumley did not find it easy to abandon his pet project, but the risk of losing royal patronage was the deciding factor. Slowly he came round to his ballet-master's point of view, and the production was shelved on the pretext that there was no longer time to stage it. Lumley was to put it somewhat circumspectly in his memoirs. 'It was found, unfortunately, impracticable in respect of its "situations" and scenic effects for stage purposes,' he explained. 'True, it was the work of a poet; but of a poet unacquainted with the necessities of stage representation, especially in England – of a man of powerful imagination, who presupposed that a public would see the effects as *he* saw them, and feel with *his* feelings. In short, the execution of the ballet was an impossibility. In spite of the expenses already lavished on this work of a poet by the manager, it was found necessary to lay the ballet aside.'[6]

There was never any suggestion that Jules' objections were motivated by a desire to produce his own version of the Faust legend, but the incident certainly set him thinking seriously along these lines. By the end of the summer his plans were no longer secret, and the *Coureur des Spectacles*, reporting in August that he was in negotiation with the new Directors of the Paris Opéra, hinted that he might be engaged to produce his *Faust*.[7] However, there were more pressing calls on his services, and it was the Scala, Milan, that was to have the privilege of mounting this new work.

Jules arrived in Milan towards the end of 1847 with his imagination fired with ideas for this new creation, on which he could concentrate his entire attention, since no other ballet was required of him. His scenario, which was probably completed, at least in outline, before his arrival, owed nothing to the wild imaginings of Heine. In basing his narrative on Gœthe's poem, he was not treading new ground. In the 1830s a number of choreographers had been drawn to the theme, but most of their works had lain outside Jules' direct experience. He could only have heard about the 'romantic ballet' which Bournonville had staged in Copenhagen in 1832 and Salvatore Taglioni's version for the San Carlo in Naples in 1838. A third ballet on the subject, which Carlo Blasis had planned for the Scala, he could not have seen either, for, though fully rehearsed, it had been abandoned when the Emperor Franz I died on the eve of the first performance in 1835. In fact Jules' only experience of another choreographer's conception had been that of his old master, Deshayes, in whose version he had danced during his visit to London in 1833.

Memories of this no doubt surfaced when he was working out his scenario,

The Year of 'Faust'

but his main source of inspiration lay in an earlier experience still – the drama of *Faust*, produced at the Porte-Saint-Martin when he was dancing there in his 'teens. The great Frédérick Lemaître's swaggering performance as Mephistopheles, with its echoing bursts of diabolical laughter, had been the sensation of Paris, and few could have been more deeply impressed than the eighteen-year-old youngster who was privileged to observe it, at close hand, night after night. The text of the drama had been published at the time, and Jules undoubtedly possessed a copy. Although one of its authors was the novelist Charles Nodier, it possessed no real literary merit and in fact reduced Gœthe's masterpiece to the more prosaic dimensions of a popular entertainment. For Jules, however, its significance lay in its effectiveness as a theatrical spectacle. He revealed his indebtedness to it by using the name of Berthe for Marguerite's mother, whom Gœthe left unnamed, and borrowing a minor character among the villagers called Peters. But Jules' research certainly had not stopped there, for his enquiring mind must have led him to Gœthe's poem itself, which was accessible in several French translations. Two of these had come out in the same year as the drama, 1828. One, by Albert Stapfer, was a luxurious edition with illustrations by Eugène Delacroix that may have contributed to Jules' conception of the background and, more particularly, of the lissom, mocking character of Mephistopheles that he fashioned for himself. The other was by Gérard de Nerval, a member of Théophile Gautier's circle of friends. Yet a third translation had come out very recently, in 1847, with drawings by Tony Johannot.

While Gœthe's poem was the principal source, an English friend may have directed Jules' attention to the *Doctor Faustus* of Christopher Marlowe, from which the idea of introducing the Seven Deadly Sins could have come, although Jules was to introduce them to ensnare Marguerite and not, as Marlowe had done, to tempt Faust himself with their forbidden delights.

From these sources Jules constructed his scenario. He divided the action into seven scenes, skilfully designed so as to introduce a varied succession of dances and dance scenes, and accompanied by some startling stage effects that he was assured would present few problems to the resourceful machinists of the Scala under their chief, Giuseppe Ronchi. Since *Faust* was to be the only new ballet of the season, no expense was spared to make it as splendid a production as the designer, Carlo Fontana, and the costumier Raviglia could achieve. At the same time Giacomo Panizza was hard at work on the score, which was to contain two interpolations by other hands: the *pas de fascination* in the second scene, which was to be danced to music by Michael Costa – probably a borrowing of the dance of the same name in *Alma* – and the *pas de sept* in the fourth scene, the music for which was provided by Giovanni Bajetti.

A work on such a grand scale demanded more time than usual to prepare, but there was to be an added distraction that Jules could hardly have taken into account – the growing spirit of restiveness and excitement that was taking hold of the Italian population, as if they subconsciously knew that the hour was at hand to rise against their Austrian overlords. But more serious still, as it then seemed, was the foot injury sustained by Fanny Elssler, his chosen Marguerite. It soon became apparent that *Faust* could not possibly be ready by the opening of the season, and to fill the gap an old ballet by Louis Henry had to be revived, *Edoardo III o l'Assedio di Calais*. For a while it must have seemed that Jules' *Faust* was doomed to the same fate as that of Blasis, but early in February – responding, perhaps, to a politically motivated pressure aimed at distracting attention from the growing unrest in the city – Elssler agreed to appear even though her injured foot had not fully recovered its strength, and the management announced 'with certainty' that the long-promised 'grandiose spectacle' of *Faust* would be presented in a week's time, on February 12th, 1848.

It may have been against Jules' better judgment that the curtain rose on his ballet when still in an imperfect state, but rise it did on a performance that was to be chiefly remembered as a portent of the revolution that was to break out a few weeks later.

The first scene introduced Faust – in the person of Effisio Catte – in his laboratory, an old man finishing a lesson and dismissing his pupils with advice that they should moderate their passions (an echo of Faust's opening lines in the 1828 drama). As they leave, his eyes follow them with a look that belies his words and hints at the insatiable desires that still burn within him. An old book falls from the shelf, and picking it up, he sees that it contains incantations for conjuring up infernal spirits. Without further thought he begins to experiment. Suddenly there is a burst of coloured fire and Mephistopheles springs out of the floor. Terrified, Faust bids him to be gone. Mephistopheles refuses, and after consulting the book again, Faust pronounces the words that send him back through the boards with a burst of demoniac laughter. This short scene introduced Jules in his long and complex rôle of Mephistopheles, modelled no doubt on his memories of Lemaître and including a mimed impression of the great actor's famous laugh. Faust's assistant Wolger then comes running into the room. He has heard the commotion. With a gesture of annoyance Faust explains that he has only been carrying out an experiment, but Wolger hangs back, as though to satisfy himself that all is well. His hesitation is fatal, for he suddenly vanishes, and by means of a skilfully managed substitution, Mephistopheles reappears in his place, now dressed as a student. Again Faust bids the devil to be gone, but Mephistopheles has divined his secret desires and offers to serve Faust for the rest of his life in exchange for his services thereafter. Faust indignantly refuses to sign such an infamous contract, but Mephistopheles transfixes him with a glance and the old man falls into a drowsy stupor.

The room fills with a mist which, in the first of a series of transformations, clears to reveal Marguerite in her bedchamber. Making his appearance just as she is about to say her prayers, Mephistopheles is forced to withdraw before the power of her piety. Another scene then materialises – a graveyard, where at Mephistopheles' command a creature resembling Marguerite emerges from one of the tombs. Once again the scene changes – this time to an enchanted garden, where the creature, now in the form of a beautiful peasant girl, inflames Faust's passions as she dances with her companions in a *ballabile della seduzione*. Elssler's first appearance at this point aroused expectations of wonders to come. 'This masterful dancer has only to appear to give you a feeling of elation, as if you were seeing some heavenly vision,' wrote P.A. Curti in *La Fama*. 'I can find no words adequate to describe the grace, precision and charm of her poses and movements, which are all models of artistry and classical purity. Think of a gentle swaying of arms and hands, a soft inclination of the head, and an ease of adapting the body to the forms required of it . . . But do not ask whether she revealed any new feats of difficult footwork or other marvels of dancing, for alas, her recent foot injury forced her to eschew such delights.'[8] This number was effectively woven into the narrative by the active participation of Jules and Catte who mimed the reactions of Mephistopheles and Faust to the wiles of the enchantress. Noticing Faust's resistance weakening, Mephistopheles again produces the contract. Again Faust refuses to sign, and Mephistopheles summons his creature from the bowels of the earth, bearing a cup filled with a magic liquid. After a moment's hesitation Faust quaffs it down, and is thrilled to feel a strength that he has not experienced for many a long year. Mephistopheles makes a sign to his creature that the moment of signing is now at hand. While the dancing continues, the transformation of Faust into a virile young man is completed. Desiring only to possess her, he puts his signature to the contract. But the vision then fades, and Faust turns reproachfully to Mephistopheles. The devil bids him to be patient, and – another direct borrowing from the 1828 drama – Faust and Mephistopheles make a flying exit, borne aloft on the latter's cloak.

The backcloth for this opening scene had been placed so as to use only the front portion of the stage for the action. To represent the mist a gauze must have been lowered, concealing the backcloth while it was raised to reveal the cloths for the various visions – the bedchamber, the graveyard and the garden – which were set further back to give room for the dances. Then, for the end of the scene, the original backcloth would have been lowered into place again to allow the stage hands to prepare the set for the second scene behind it. Making full use of the deep stage, this next scene represented a village square swarming with a crowd that has gathered for the annual election of the *rosière*, the most virtuous maiden. A young soldier who has been making enquiries about some of the villagers is joyfully recognised as Valentine, a lad who had left some years before to serve in the army. He is looking for

Marguerite, his childhood sweetheart. At that moment she appears with her mother, and the two are reunited. A flourish of music in the distance then announces the approach of Mephistopheles, who has assumed the guise of a charlatan. He is accompanied by Faust and a troupe of gypsies. Faust points to Marguerite as the object of his passion, and is annoyed that Mephistopheles does not at once grant his desire but proposes instead to try out his powers on her virtuous character. While Faust shyly approaches Marguerite, Mephistopheles sizes up her companion, Martha, as a vain girl whom he can use to his own ends. The Burgomaster is suspicious of the newcomers, but Mephistopheles explains that they have only come to entertain. He orders his gypsies to perform 'a most beautifully devised *pas de caractère*.'[9] Then, to carry out his intention of tempting Marguerite, he assumes the character of an elegant gentleman with smooth, self-confident manners – a transformation that Jules amusingly spiced with a touch of grotesque comedy. Thus disguised, he induces Marguerite to dance with him. She herself is fascinated; she loses her apprehension and fear, and carried away by a strange feeling of ecstasy, she surrenders to his power. She seems like a marionette in his hands, one moment standing frozen in a pose, at another rushing forward in a sudden burst of passionate energy, and then stopping short suddenly, her chest heaving with elation, by the side of Faust, who has been looking on with trembling expectation. Mephistopheles then places his hand on Faust's chest, as if to draw out the ardent passion that consumes him, and lays it against Marguerite's heart. Overcome by an emotion she cannot comprehend, she falters, but Mephistopheles catches her and whirls her into a frenzied galop. This extraordinary dance scene was the *pas de fascination* – adapted from the dance of that name in *Alma* – in which Jules and Elssler were supported by three young pupils of Blasis (Angela Negri, Carolina Citerio and Angela Tommasini) as village girls. At the end of it Marguerite is exhausted, and Faust is irretrievably enslaved.

The time for the election of the *rosière* has now come, and the choice falls on Marguerite. All the young men are overjoyed, but the other girls are disappointed and Martha cannot conceal her jealousy. The scene ended with more stage magic. Seeing that the crowd is about to disperse, Mephistopheles fills a glass with wine and proposes a toast to Marguerite. The villagers find their glasses are empty, but the sinister stranger has only to plunge his dagger into the table for wine to spout from the holes. Suddenly the wine turns to fire, and the villagers recoil in fright. Mephistopheles' mocking laugh is heard again, as he and Faust vanish and the crowd disperses in terror.

A cloth representing Marguerite's bedroom was then lowered for the third scene, a bed bearing the sleeping heroine being pushed in from the wings. Mephistopheles and Faust seem to appear out of nowhere. Faust moves over to the bed to contemplate the object of his desire, while Mephistopheles places a casket of jewels in her cupboard. Marguerite begins to stir. Faust is on the point of throwing himself at her feet and avowing his love, but Mephistopheles restrains him. As they leave, Faust picks Marguerite's handkerchief from a chair and thrusts it into his jacket as a keepsake. They have no sooner left when Marguerite awakes, leaping from her bed as if to escape the memory of a nightmare. The melody of the *pas de fascination* still echoes in her brain, and she seems to be struggling to free herself from the clutch of some invisible partner. Gradually, as she recognises the familiar surroundings of her own room, her fears subside. She remembers Mephistopheles' elegant young companion, then modestly tries to banish the thought from her mind by thinking of Valentine, to whom she is betrothed. As she kneels down to pray, a knock is heard at the door. Searching for her handkerchief, she goes to the cupboard where, to her amazement, she discovers the casket. The knock is repeated. It is Martha, who is proudly wearing a ring that Mephistopheles has given her. Marguerite then shows her the casket. Martha, whom Mephistopheles has made his accomplice, feigns surprise and urges her to try on some of the jewels.

Marguerite is reluctant, and goes to her spinning wheel. At this point Mephistopheles appears, and at a sign from him, Martha takes her leave. There now followed a *pas d'action* more complex than any Jules had attempted before, narrating the temptation of Marguerite by the seven deadly sins. Mephistopheles, who has conjured them up, hovers in the background as a sort of directing force in the ensnaring of the innocent girl. First Sloth appears to induce her to stop spinning. Then Pride and Envy tempt her to try on the jewels. Observing how their sparkle makes her humble costume appear tawdry, she yields to the blandishments of Wrath, angrily flinging the jewels to the floor. But Pride and Avarice then persuade her to pick them up and conceal them in her dress. Mephistopheles is overjoyed to see her yielding so easily to temptation, and gives the signal for a transformation. The backcloth becomes translucent and the bedroom turns into a fantastic garden. Gluttony inveigles her to pluck the fruit from the trees. Finally Lust comes forward to whisper in Marguerite's ear, and she is filled with a strange yearning as a vision of Faust appears before her eyes. Then, suddenly, her natural virtue warns her of danger, and she recoils from these unnatural thoughts and prays for guidance. The spell is broken. The evil spirits vanish, and the scene ends with Marguerite falling into the arms of her mother.

At this juncture the curtain fell for the interval between the ballet's two parts, the first three scenes having been played straight through without interruption. In the second half, however, a technical difficulty had presented itself. The set designed for the fifth scene was extremely elaborate, and the stage staff pointed out that they did not have enough room to dismantle it and set up the stage for the sixth scene and the apotheosis if there was to be no break in the second half. Jules was, therefore, forced to change the order so as

Jules Perrot

to separate these two scenes, even though the scene that was interposed must have needed a considerable area of the stage.

What then became the opening scene of the second part – the fifth scene according to the scenario – required a double set, one side of which showed Marguerite's room, and the other the garden. It began with Mephistopheles and Faust surreptitiously entering the garden. Faust is becoming increasingly impatient, and Mephistopheles has to calm him by explaining that they must first send Marguerite's mother to sleep. For this purpose he has procured a powerful sleeping draught, which he hands to Faust, assuring him that it is harmless. Footsteps are heard, and the two men hide. Marguerite and her mother then enter the garden, followed by Valentine and Martha. Marguerite is downcast and pensive, but Valentine is in high spirits at the thought of his forthcoming marriage. But the hour is late and he cannot linger. The old lady escorts him to the gate, followed by Marguerite and Martha. At this moment Mephistopheles comes out of hiding and whispers sweet blandishments in Martha's ear. Seeing Faust on his knees before her, Marguerite is so agitated that she runs back into the house. Faust follows, begging her to let him stay. When she explains that this is impossible because of her mother's presence, he gives her the draught. At that moment Martha comes running back to tell Marguerite that her Mother and Valentine are returning, having noticed her absence. Faust refuses to leave unless Marguerite consents to see him again. She is forced to comply, and he and Mephistopheles vanish just before the others enter the room. Martha makes the excuse that Marguerite felt unwell. Ashamed at being implicated in a lie, Marguerite averts her gaze, but her mother is taken in and presses Martha to stay. Valentine senses that something is afoot, and leaves with a presentiment of foreboding.

Marguerite is left in the room with her mother, who seems to have no desire to go to bed and asks for a book. Ashamed at the thought of deceiving her, Marguerite is about to tell her everything when she senses Mephistopheles' burning gaze upon her. Her mother asks for a cup of water, and Marguerite, as if in a trance, pours the draught into it. The effect is instantaneous. Placing his hand on the old lady's heart, Mephistopheles rejoices that Marguerite is now in his power. He leads her into the garden, where Faust is waiting. Coming to her senses, she finds herself on Faust's arm. She tries to break free, but Faust restrains her, and his ardent declaration moves her to confess that she is in love with him. Observing Mephistopheles in the garden, she begs Faust to break off his relationship with his sinister companion, but he will not hear of it, explaining that it was through him that they found one another. At this point Martha warns them that Valentine has returned. Marguerite runs back to the house in a state of alarm. Valentine enters with his sword drawn, and attacks Faust. Martha, having failed to calm him, goes in search of help. Urged by Mephistopheles, Faust draws his own sword and Valentine falls mortally wounded. Mephistopheles and Faust disappear. Villagers quickly arrive on the scene and discover the dying soldier. Meanwhile Marguerite has been trying to revive her mother, who she realises to her horror is dead. The door into the garden then swings ajar, and she sees Valentine lying prostrate on the ground. As she kneels at his side, he curses her with his dying breath. The villagers shrink from her in disgust. She rises and, uttering a horrifying burst of laughter, disappears through the trees. The bodies of the old lady and Valentine are found to have vanished, and the scene closes in confusion.

The transposition of this scene and the next, though it may have been expedient for technical reasons, made no sense dramatically. As Jules conceived it, this next scene – set in a rich hall in an enchanted palace – was intended to follow the bedroom scene and show another vision conjured up by Mephistopheles. Faust is seated at a banquet, disconsolate. To dispel his melancholy, Mephistopheles produces a vision of Marguerite coming to receive her prize as the *rosière*. Faust's eyes light up with joy, and together they watch some dances which precede the ceremony. But the rose crown is passed through the hands of Vice, and the flowers blacken and wither. The onlookers are aghast at this ominous transformation. However, all this action must have been omitted, for Marguerite's appearance could not have been justified after the deaths of her mother and Valentine. Presumably, therefore, the scene was reduced to an interpolated divertissement, containing a waltz charmingly danced by Carolina Vendt, but even so it seemed irrelevant and broke the dramatic thread of the narrative.

The sixth scene was set in a bleak wasteland in the Harz Mountains. Mephistopheles assures Faust that he will soon find Marguerite again. As the stage fills with weird and fantastic creatures, Mephistopheles leads him away so that he does not see Marguerite come running in, her mind deranged. She seems to be reliving a dreadful tragedy. She falls to her knees, rocking her arms as if nursing a baby, which she holds out, pleadingly offering it, as it were, to an invisible lover. Tears flowing, she caresses the imaginary child, covers it with her dress, and then seems to throw it into a stream. She appears to be about to drown herself too, when her strength fails and she falls to the ground in a faint. At that moment Faust, who has been revolted at the sight of the witches' sabbath, reappears and, seeing the prostrate figure of his beloved, takes her into his arms. Opening her eyes, Marguerite recognises him and tells him of her sufferings and the death of their child. He wants to take her away, but she shrinks from him. Mephistopheles now urges them to escape while they can, for the soldiers are coming in search of her. But she breaks from his grasp, determined to give herself up. Shrugging his shoulders, Mephistopheles tells Faust that Marguerite is now lost, and they vanish as she is taken into custody.

The backcloth then rose to reveal the impressive set for the seventh and final scene, representing another part of the Harz Mountains, where a witches' sabbath – '*La Tregenda*' – is in progress. Amid a growing tumult the stage fills with fantastic creatures of all sorts, some awesome, others alluring. As the dancing gathers intensity, the noise becomes more and more strident and discordant until suddenly this *rondo infernale* is interrupted by the appearance of Mephistopheles descending from the sky with Faust, asleep, in his arms. Placing Faust on a rock, he conjures up the beautiful apparition that had first fascinated Faust in his laboratory. Bewildered, Faust follows her, but soon returns, pale and disgusted. A mighty roar is then heard. The mist at the foot of the mountain then disperses, revealing a vision of Marguerite being led to the scaffold. She falls to her knees in a final prayer and the executioner raises his axe, but before it falls the mist closes in again and the infernal dance is resumed. Then, out of the mist, there appears a flame, which Faust knows instinctively is the soul of Marguerite. Realising that she is dead, he draws his sword in fury and lunges at Mephistopheles, but the blade shatters in his hand. As Faust falls to his knees in despair, Mephistopheles brandishes the contract and claims his part of the bargain. But the wandering flame flutters down on to the parchment and sets it alight. Faust is released from his bond, and as the flame rises into the sky, it seems to beckon him to follow. Mephistopheles, enraged at being deprived of his prey, calls all the infernal spirits to his aid in a desperate struggle to regain his control over Faust. In a final cataclysm, the earth splits open and flames burst out of the mountains, which collapse with a terrible roar. All the infernal creatures are swallowed up in the abyss. The evil vapours at length clear and the sky brightens, showing Marguerite surrounded by angels and extending her arms to Faust, who is being borne heavenward towards her, while down below Mephistopheles impotently gives vent to his fury.

When the curtain fell at last, after three long hours, it was abundantly clear that the ballet was not the success that had been hoped for. Even if the performance had proceeded in a normal atmosphere of calm, its faults would have been apparent. To begin with, it was at least double the normally acceptable length. Jules would have done well to have had at his elbow an adviser performing the same function that Lumley had in preparing *La Esmeralda*. Struggling with 'a subject too vast and too profound to be circumscribed within the limited confines of a mimed performance,'[10] he seemed to have been 'carried away by the profusion of his ideas, by his desire to expand them and explain them over and over again, by the very fecundity of his genius'.[11] Lambertini in the *Gazzetta Priviligiata di Milano* criticised him for overburdening the ballet with fantastic effects that followed one another without respite – spirits of the underworld, witches, angels, visions appearing out of the mist, disappearances, flights, magic fire, and finally the flickering flame with a mind of its own that played a significant part in the *dénouement*.[12]

The attention of the public began to waver in the first scene, but it was not until the third scene that its patience seriously wore thin. During the dance of the Seven Deadly Sins a few murmurs of discontent were heard, but after the interval the audience became increasingly restive, particularly during Faust's seduction of Marguerite in the garden and in the scene of Marguerite reliving the drowning of her baby. The sheer spectacle of the last scene, with the collapse of the mountain and the brilliant apotheosis of a sun emitting its rays, was stunningly impressive, but came too late to restore the good humour of an audience that had been fidgeting in their seats for far too long.

A degree of relief was afforded by the dances that were interspersed in the lengthy narrative, the *ballabili* being particularly appreciated for their originality and graceful arrangement, and the logical manner in which they fitted into the action. The main cause for dissatisfaction, however, lay in the disappointing performance of Fanny Elssler, who was to receive no thanks for courageously appearing when not fully fit. 'The ballet would certainly have been much more successful,' commented a critic who was counted among her admirers, 'if Elssler could have matched the choreographer's inspiration by the powerful expressiveness of her dancing, but she was unwell and had to tailor her very charming steps to the unsteady strength of her foot.'[13] Her incapacity deprived the ballet of much of its effect, for the rôle of Marguerite was developed as much in the dances that Jules had created for her as in the mimed part of the action.

It must have been almost impossible that evening to separate the disapproval of the ballet on artistic grounds from the politically motivated demonstrations that punctuated the performance. Because of its prestigious position in the social and musical life of the city, the Scala was frequented by many high-ranking Austrian officers and officials connected with the government of the province, and the sight of such an array of white uniforms was an obvious affront to Italians who were thirsting more than ever before for their independence. Most of the wealthy Italians who rented boxes and would have had to rub shoulders with Austrians stayed away in sympathy with the patriotic cause, and a boycott of the theatre was effectively enforced by agents who recorded the names of all those who entered. In the upper parts of the house, however, where Austrians hardly penetrated, no such rule applied, and it was mainly from there that the resentment against Elssler found its voice. Being herself an Austrian, she found herself virtually on enemy soil, where political passions had become so enflamed that even artists were embroiled in the struggle. Conceivably, allowances might have been made if the ballet itself and her own performance had been more acceptable, but an incident occurred that aroused such fury among the vocal elements in the gallery as to make disaster inevitable.

The corps de ballet, not to be outdone in championing the Italian cause, decided to appear wearing medals showing the Pope blessing a united Italy. Regarding this as a provocation directed against herself, Elssler refused to continue unless the medals were removed. Their absence was noticed at once, and news of Elssler's demand spread like wildfire through the audience. A storm of whistling rose in protest, and from that moment on her efforts met with sepulchral silence from the few boxes that were occupied and abusive shouts from the upper reaches.

After this disastrous evening *Faust* was withdrawn. The ballet needed to be drastically shortened, and so long as the revolutionary atmosphere prevailed, it was out of the question for Elssler to reappear. She did not leave Milan at once, however. Her departure was not reported until March 11th, and she may well have remained in the turbulent city to help Jules coach the ballerina who was to replace her as Marguerite. This new dancer, Augusta Maywood, had also come from Vienna, where she had established her reputation, but she was an American citizen and therefore untarnished with the mark of her oppressor. When she appeared at the Scala in *La Sylphide* she was received sympathetically by the meagre audience. Her style was very different from Elssler's. She danced with 'immense vigour and lightness,' but was found lacking in elegance, caused, it was thought, by striving too much to impress the public with *tours de force*. 'Perhaps,' surmised *The Times*, 'she laboured to please Italian taste, which is not the finest as far as the ballet is concerned.'[14]

To revise his *Faust* Jules had to work with great haste, for there were only a few weeks of the season left. He reduced the number of scenes to six and made ruthless cuts so that the whole ballet could be played through without a break. The first scene he left untouched. In the second, he tightened the ending by omitting the passage where Mephistopheles proposes Marguerite's toast and makes wine flow from the table. The third scene was heavily cut, the dance of the Seven Deadly Sins being replaced by a brief mime scene in which Marguerite's mother surprises her daughter as she is trying on the jewels and insists that she hands them to the Burgomaster. At the end of this scene Mephistopheles arrives, in disguise, to summon everyone to the crowning of the *rosière*. The fourth scene was restored to its original position, taking its place more naturally in the narrative as a celebration of the *rosière* festivity, and with a new *pas*, in which Valentine, joined by Mephistopheles and Faust, rejoices at Marguerite's triumph. Since the sixth scene was cut altogether, the fifth scene had to close with the scene of Marguerite surrendering to the soldiers. The final scene and the apotheosis remained as originally conceived.

These changes were a decided improvement, although some critics still considered the ballet to be too long. A larger audience than usual that season gathered to see the second performance on March 7th, which passed without any untoward incident. In its revised form, its qualities became more apparent. *Il Pirata* said that it was 'certainly not one of those ballets that lose their impact on being seen a second time. Its beauties are real and positive, and stand out more prominently at a second viewing.'[15] Fanny Elssler's withdrawal must have come as a disheartening blow to Jules, but it did reduce the tension. 'We are dancing on a volcano,' wrote an Austrian diplomat in his diary that evening. 'The ballet *Faust* was performed with Maywood, who was much applauded. She is like a grasshopper, but a grasshopper with a poetic charm that defies description.'[16] Although the young American could not approach Elssler as an actress, her colt-like vigour pleased the public and, in its abbreviated form, *Faust* was given five more performances, making six in all for the season.

In spite of the small audiences, the Scala was sufficiently impressed to approach Jules about including it in the programme for the next Carnival season. As events were to work out, he was to be in Russia at that time, but he presumably raised no objection to its being revived by Domenico Ronzani, who had already proved his abilities by reproducing *La Esmeralda* and *Catarina* in Vienna and elsewhere in Italy.* For the revival of *Faust* in the Carnival season of 1848–49, it was truncated still further by the omission of the third scene, in Marguerite's room, and generally curtailed. In this form, with Maywood again playing Marguerite and Ronzani taking over Jules' rôle as Mephistopheles, it was to attain the impressive tally of forty-seven performances.

Meanwhile Fanny Elssler had arrived back in Vienna to find that revolution had broken out there and that Metternich, the Chancellor who had dominated the Imperial government for more than quarter of a century, had resigned and fled into exile. When this momentous news reached Milan, the people rose in open revolt and drove the Austrians from the city. These stirring events in the streets were drama enough for the Milanese, and the Scala closed its doors, even though several weeks of the season remained. Jules, whose sympathies were wholly on the side of the Italians, could not resist taking an active part in the excitement, and saw that news of his exploits filtered through to London in time to herald his return with a useful piece of publicity. 'M. Perrot, or *il famoso* ballerino Perrot,' reported the *Satirist*, 'has in Milan become a *maître de bataille* as well as a *maître de ballet*, for, calling together the waiters of the hotel in which he found himself, he reviewed them with great stage tact, and then led them forth against the Austrians, vowing he would not return till he had made these garçons men; which vow this old theatrical religiously performed.'[17]

*   *   *

* Ronzani revived *Faust* in Vienna in 1851 and 1854. Fanny Elssler made her last stage appearance in the 1851 production, which was divided into three acts and seven scenes, the dance of the Seven Deadly Sins being restored, and the rôles of Faust and Mephistopheles being played by Ronzani and Gustave Carey. In 1854, when Maywood played Marguerite and Pasquale Borri Mephistopheles, one of the soloists was Katti Lanner who, over forty years later, in 1895, produced her own version of *Faust* at the Empire Theatre, London, which may have owed something to her memories of Jules' ballet.

Jules Perrot

London had not been without its own troubles in the spring of 1848, but the 'monster meeting' of the Chartists that had assembled on Kennington Common a fortnight or so before Jules returned had been contained and the manace of revolution was receding. The opera season at Her Majesty's had not been interrupted, and all seemed normal when Jules was seen in the audience on the night of Cerrito's return on April 27th.

As had happened the year before, the ballet department had been directed in the early weeks of the season by Paul Taglioni, whose daughter Marie had accompanied him, being engaged for the whole season as one of the ballerinas. As usual the company was strong in stars. Carolina Rosati was also engaged for the whole season, and when Carlotta arrived a few weeks later, Jules had a full complement of ballerinas not only to revive *Les Eléments*, but to produce his fourth multi-stellar divertissement, *Les Quatre Saisons*, for which Pugni provided the music, some of which he abstracted from the score of *Faust*.

First given on June 13th, this new work was to be Jules' only major contribution to the season's offerings. Even in rehearsal, lacking the advantage of full stage lighting, and with scenery and costumes still only half finished, it emerged as an impressive work – 'a *pas monstre*,' the *Morning Post* called it, recording that it lasted fifty minutes without pauses or encores.[18]

The seed of its theme may have been James Thomson's poem which had served Haydn for his oratorio, *The Seasons*. It opened very elegantly with a prologue in which four ladies assemble in the conservatory of 'some princely palace . . . like that of Chatsworth,'[19] as the scenario explained, to plan an allegorical masque of the seasons. Charles Marshall had designed a brilliantly lush setting. Dominating his conservatory was a 'globular fountain,'[20] surrounded by statues, and behind its jet of real water was arranged a luxuriant profusion of flowers. The ladies then retire, to reappear shortly afterwards, having exchanged their long dresses for ballet costumes appropriate to the seasons they were portraying, and each accompanied by eight attendants. The dancing now began with a prelude in which the seasonal changes were graphically depicted in a series of effective groups. The year then unrolls, each season having its own section, which was divided into two parts, first a sort of danced recitative showing the season establishing her dominion, and then a classically conceived *pas*, complete with variation for the ballerina and ensemble dances for her attendants. Interestingly, there was no dispute over preference, and the dancers appeared in order of age, but this time with the oldest appearing first. Up to quite a late stage in the rehearsals Jules had planned to open the ballet with Winter, but in performance it began with the arrival of Spring, represented by Cerrito, who bounded about the stage, plucking flowers from the baskets of her attendants and scattering them 'with the most joyous abandon.' In due time she has to be driven away by Summer, in the person of Carlotta Grisi, bearing a sickle as her symbol, and 'looking more lovely and dancing with greater eloquence – for every attitude speaks for itself – than ever.'[21] Summer's hour of glory proves no less transitory, being brought to an end in its turn by the appearance of Carolina Rosati, cap in hand, as Autumn, with a train of bacchantes. Reluctant to depart, Summer circles round the newcomer, striving to 'elude and dispute her sovereignty, now rising, now crouching to the earth.' Finally, the whistling of the wind announces the approach of Winter, played by the younger Marie Taglioni 'wrapped in a snowy mantle, covered with snowdrops,'[22] whose attendants represent the season's greatest charm – fire. Autumn vainly attempts to linger and strengthen her courage with the juice of the grape, but her appointed hour has passed.

In time Spring makes her appearance once again, followed closely by Summer and Autumn. 'Then, as occurs but all too often in our real English atmosphere, the seasons quarrel for supremacy.' Spring offers flowers, Summer her harvest wealth, Autumn the joys of the vintage, and Winter shows 'how she gives peace to the soil, covering the earth and protecting the seed by snow, whilst fire warms the domestic hearth.'[23] None of the four ladies can establish a permanent supremacy, and as if realising that they form part of a larger pattern imposed by nature, they join in a *pas de l'union des saisons*.

With this finale the delight of the audience reached its climax, the applause at the end 'coming like a thunder-storm upon the festival.'[24] The personal ovation, which Jules received with his usual modesty, as if he had never expected such a tribute, was fully deserved. Notwithstanding that the sight of four internationally famous ballerinas dancing together was now an expected culmination of the London season, *Les Quatre Saisons* was acclaimed as the most remarkable of Jules' productions in this genre. It was both the longest and the most complex. A fifty-minute composition consisting almost entirely of dancing was, for that time, a unique achievement. 'We had never dreamt,' declared the *Morning Post*, 'that choreography could attempt such things, still less succeed, as it did last night.'[25] 'Unquestionably,' wrote the same critic two days later, 'the art of choreography never attained such perfection as in the hands of Perrot; and he has here produced the result of a naturally imaginative mind, improved by the constant study of the best resources of pictorial art, and inspiration derived from the poets.'[26] A measure of its quality was that it enabled ballet to hold its own when Jenny Lind was turning the heads of the public in *Lucia, La Sonnambula* and *La Figlia del Reggimento*. Such a feast of *bel canto* could only have been counterbalanced by an outstanding display of *bella danza*, and this was most successfully achieved by choreography that contained 'classical thought in every group and attitude without the coldness of the more classical form. There was a poetical spirit and an imagination throughout the composition which does not beg, but commands, the loud applause it so justly receives.'[27] The final

Jules Perrot

judgment was that it was 'the most remarkable piece of choreography ever brought out on any stage,'[28] marking 'the utmost limit of perfection'[29] to which the art had ever attained.

In no way blinded by this fulsome praise, Jules was well able to perceive the significant shift away from the long narrative ballet that had taken place in public taste – or, to be more accurate perhaps, in Lumley's assessment of the desires of the subscribers who funded his enterprise. In the last two months of the season the multi-stellar divertissements were completely predominant. *Le Jugement de Pâris* was revived on July 25th, with Cerrito, Rosati and the younger Taglioni, and only the *Pas de Quatre* was not resurrected. From the revival of *Les Eléments* in May to Taglioni's departure in August one or other of these divertissements was included in thirty-one performances out of thirty-three.

A few performances of *Alma* and *Ondine* which Cerrito gave that season were abbreviated, and the only dramatic work which Jules revived personally was *La Esmeralda*, which was only given twice in its complete form. It was nonetheless welcomed by a sizeable section of the public. The *Morning Chronicle* found it 'quite "refreshing" also, after the brief divertissements, all done by petticoats, which have recently been given, to have a full ballet performed, and to see a pair of – what we may not mention – upon the stage, when they belong to such a pleasant little fellow as Perrot.'[30]

It was in this revival of *La Esmeralda* that Jules interpolated what was to be his last creation for London – a *grand quintette dansante* for Carolina Rosati, supported by Louis Dor, Joséphine Petit-Stéphan and Mlles Julien and Lamoureux, 'an elaborate work, consisting of an introduction, an adagio, an allegro, followed by variations, and a coda, with solos, groups, attitudes innumerable, but succeeding each other with as much rapidity as variety, and the whole of moderate duration.'[31]

It was another striking example of Jules' choreographic invention and taste, leading his admirer on the *Morning Post* to reflect on the very remarkable contribution he had made to his art during his seven seasons in London. 'Whilst witnessing the execution of these works of M. Perrot – some descriptive, some characteristic, some of classical attitude – we could not help reflecting that of all classes of society, the denizens of the stage – in whatsoever department – are those who have most palpably made the greatest strides in the vaunted march of intellect. It is but a short time since that actors were deemed vagrants, although not so long back there had been such actors as Shakespeare and Molière. The followers of the operatic stage were, perhaps, those who laboured the longest under such misconstruction. So little was the profession of a musician thought to be compatible with intellect that Voltaire, hearing Grétry speak like a man of sense, in his astonishment exclaimed, "How, you are a musician and you a man of sense?" But of all performers dancers were thought, up to the present time, the most brainless. M. Perrot would alone suffice as a triumphant instance of dancers possessing remarkable acumen. What he has effected requires not only musical efficiency and the most perfect knowledge of every graceful movement that a dancer can execute, but he has likewise observed and then applied to his art all that sculpture and painting can supply; and these suggestions he has embodied in purely imaginative compositions, with new designs and modifications of his own, like the new *pas* of last night.'[32]

His departure at the close of the season was to be a great loss for London. Lumley may have urged him to return, but the trend against the narrative ballet that was his true forte must have weakened his desire to remain bound to Her Majesty's. There seemed little for him to contribute in London beyond reworking the formula of the multi-stellar divertissement. Also, opportunities were beckoning him elsewhere.

15

The Lure of Russia

The life of a wandering ballet-master entailed a bewildering amount of organisation. In addition to negotiating engagements to fill as much of the year as possible with profitable employment and haggling to obtain the best terms, journeys had to be planned, sometimes across half Europe, by stage coach or, more and more frequently now, by the infinitely more rapid and comfortable railways, lodgings had to be found in foreign cities, passport formalities attended to, clothes purchased for different climates, and a hundred and one other distracting details to be attended to that had the habit of arising at most inopportune moments. In Jules' case some of this may have been handled by agents such as Collignon in Paris, but much of the burden could not be delegated and it was he who had to make the decisions. He was, however, a shrewd and practical man who knew the true worth of his services and was quite capable of striking a hard bargain, but nevertheless it must have been extremely tiresome, particularly when in the throes of a frantic London season, to have to turn aside from his work in the theatre to cope with the accumulation of business problems.

He found himself singularly beset with such matters during 1848, when, ironically, a contract he had signed with the Paris Opéra became an obstacle in his ambitions. There had been a time when it had been his most cherished desire to return to the Opéra, and when Roqueplan and Duponchel took over the direction in 1847 with the avowed intention of injecting new life into the ballet, he discovered to his delight that he featured in their plans. Being then free of commitments for the autumn and the winter, he signed a contract with them from September 1st, 1848, to March 31st, 1849, and similar periods in each of the following two years, the first period being regarded as probationary, since power was reserved for either party to terminate the engagement by giving notice before January 1st, 1849. For each of these seven-month periods he was to receive a salary of 19,000 francs.

So far so good, but suddenly the opportunity arose, too tempting to resist, to accompany Fanny Elssler to Russia. Elssler had long yearned to emulate Taglioni and crown her career with a Russian triumph, and was no doubt planning her approach to the authorities in St. Petersburg when Jules and she were together in Milan. It was hardly surprising that her friend and colleague, in whose ballets she had established herself as the supreme dramatic ballerina of her time, should be involved in these plans. Why, she must have asked, could he not accompany her to Russia to stage his masterpieces there? And indeed, little more than a week after she had written to Count Guedeonov, the Director of the Imperial Theatres, to enquire about the possibility of visiting Russia during the season of 1848–49, he made known his own wish for a Russian engagement.

He channeled his approach through the Russian Minister in London, Count Brunnov, who was not only a leading subscriber and an assiduous visitor to Her Majesty's Theatre and closely in touch with the world of opera and ballet, but acted as a confidential adviser and agent to Guedeonov. This was not a service offered to a friend, but part of his official duties as representative of his sovereign, for the Imperial Theatres were an appanage of the Tsar's household and controlled by the Minister of the Court.

'I have learnt that Perrot wishes to go to Russia as *maître de ballet*,' Brunnov wrote to Guedeonov on June 4th. 'I have no doubt about his merit. But without a *première danseuse* of great talent he will produce nothing remarkable. I thought of Fanny Elssler, but, take it from me, she is completely in decline. The one you want is Carlotta Grisi. Since her contract has come to an end, there is nothing she would like better than to go to Russia. She has told me so herself, but without your authority I have not wanted to become involved in useless negotiations. Moreover I need to know precisely whether it would be convenient for the Direction to make an offer to Carlotta Grisi and on what terms. For the moment I shall do nothing more than tell you that such an engagement can be concluded if you wish. I think I can promise you that the success of this affair will be complete, and the receipts it will produce will probably cover your expenses. It has occurred to me, further, that on the occasion of the marriage celebrations of the Grand Duke Constantine, you might be interested in giving a festive atmosphere to the Imperial Theatres. If that is your intention, Carlotta Grisi would be the best present I could give you. Please let me have a reply without much delay to enter into negotiations before C. Grisi signs another engagement.'[1]

However, Carlotta proved to be unavailable, and some weeks later, on June 27th, Brunnov wrote again to Guedeonov. His advice was motivated by an awareness of the enormous financial burden that maintaining the Italian opera and the ballet in St. Petersburg placed on the Tsar. 'Bearing this in mind,' he wrote, 'I think you would do best to keep the Petersburg ballet on its present footing. With such a good ballet school you can obtain a satisfactory ensemble. For that you have no need of a ballet-master of Perrot's talent. That, I think, would be too expensive for you. In Paris and London he has been used to having talents of the first order at his disposal. This year he has just mounted the ballet of Les Quatre Saisons in London, with Carlotta Grisi, Cerrito, Rosati and the young Taglioni. I am sure he would be continually worrying you to bring over first-class artists, and would not be content with staging his own ballets with what he could get from our ballet school, however satisfactory that might be. Perrot's pride would aim at producing more brilliant results. That would lead to unpleasant arguments that I would like to spare you. Moreover, I have no reason to believe that he would accept an engagement on moderate terms. Success, and above all your administration's reputation for generosity, would make him less modest in his demands. I have no doubt you would find it easy to engage Fanny Elssler, and probably on easy terms, for the very simple reason that she will have difficulty in obtaining better terms anywhere else than from us. Twenty years ago she was a delightful dancer, but I regard her now as finished.'[2]

The very day after Brunnov wrote this letter in London, Fanny Elssler wrote to Guedeonov from Hamburg requesting that Jules should be engaged with her to stage some of his ballets in St. Petersburg. She also wrote to Jules, telling him what she had done, and adding the flattering remark, 'Your genius is as great as ever, there is no one else who comes near you.'[3]

While these negotiations were proceeding, the Paris Opéra found itself in grave financial difficulties. The revolution that had toppled Louis-Philippe from his throne in February, and had started the wave of revolutions in Europe, had been followed, in June, by an uprising in the streets of Paris that was quelled at a cost of several thousand lives. Nervously the citizens of Paris kept to their homes, and the effect on theatre box-offices was disastrous. At the Opéra salaries were cut across the board, and an approach was made to Jules with a view to reducing the theatre's obligations to him that year. In August it was agreed that the first period of his engagement should be cut down from seven months to five by deferring the commencement date to November 1st, the two months deducted to be carried forward to a later period to be fixed by mutual agreement. Jules had also indicated to the Opéra's agent that he had entered into negotiations which might allow him to meet the Opéra's wishes immediately by not coming to Paris at all that winter, adding that the matter was still 'only in the project stage.'[4] At that moment Fanny Elssler was expecting to be engaged in St. Petersburg from September 15th, but Guedeonov, who had taken offence because she had appealed over his head to the Tsar, was insisting that she should sign a formal contract. He was also being difficult over her request that Jules should be engaged with her, pointing out that there were ballet-masters in Russia who could stage the new productions with her assistance.

Fanny Elssler eventually forced the issue by turning up, unannounced, in St. Petersburg, and by an order of the Tsar Guedeonov was forced to instruct the Russian Consul-General in Paris, M. de Spies, to negotiate a formal contract with Jules.

The Lure of Russia

'We have with us, for the season, until the end of February (new style),' he wrote in his letter of instructions of September 28th, 'Mlle Fanny Elssler, who, having established her reputation mainly in ballets composed by Jules Perrot, wishes this choreographer to come here to stage them and play the rôles he himself created. I am therefore writing to ask you to be so good as to invite this choreographer to come and discuss with you the conclusion of an engagement which I can offer him. The present situation in Europe,' he went on, referring to the outbreak of revolutions in 1848 from which Russia had been spared, 'means that artists can only be thinking of our theatres, particularly for the autumn and winter season. Consequently their demands must be less excessive than in the past, and Mlle Elssler has said that M. Perrot, who has told her of his wish to come here, would be reasonable over his terms. This is the only reason why I have decided to negotiate with this choreographer, for in spite of his talent, I would not otherwise have given him a thought after the excessive demands he made when there was question earlier of securing his services for Russia. These are my thoughts on how to deal with this matter. M. Perrot should lose no time in coming here by steamer from Le Havre or from Lubeck. For each of his grand ballets which he stages here I will give him 4 to 5,000 francs, for a short ballet in one or two acts 2,500 francs and for a divertissement 1,000 francs, provided that he supplies the music and remains here until February 1st, by which time his last work must be staged. I cannot specify the number of works he is to stage, for that will depend on the time he needs to stage them, but I am thinking that two grand ballets, two short ones and several divertissements could easily be produced. What I have indicated is the maximum, and the more you can reduce the cost, the more grateful I shall be, but the number of works he is to produce must not be specified in the contract. Also, if it is absolutely necessary to prevent the matter falling through, he can be given a benefit performance net of the usual expenses. If you reach agreement with him, please make him leave at once and endorse his passport. It would be desirable for him to come by sea, both to accelerate his arrival and to avoid difficulties in crossing the land frontier, for as you know a special order is needed, and when I hear that he is at Cronstadt, an order will be made out allowing him to come to St. Petersburg.'[5]

Finding, perhaps, all this to be rather a bitter pill to swallow, Guedeonov delayed two days before writing to Jules himself about this development. 'Mlle Fanny Elssler, whom I discover is in St. Petersburg,' he began, knowing full well that she had been in the city for more than a week, 'and who is engaged for the season that has just opened, has told me that you would not be averse to coming to stage some of your choreographic works here. A few years ago my correspondent Collignon informed me of the terms you required, but those terms not being acceptable, the negotiations lapsed. Now that circumstances have changed, and first-class artists are all offering their

Jules Perrot

services to Russia on much lower terms than hitherto, I think you will be able to accept the proposals which M. de Spies . . . is authorised to offer on my behalf. If you sign the contract that is in M. de Spies' hands, I beg you to leave without delay so that you can benefit from a sea journey, and you will be here in time to stage several works.'[6]

Jules duly called on M. de Spies and was told of Guedeonov's terms. Having learnt, perhaps, of the derisory fee that Elssler had been forced to accept, he was determined not to sell his services cheaply, and explained to de Spies that his contract with the Opéra contained a penalty clause that would come into operation if he did not take up his duties in Paris by November 1st. This was, of course, strictly true, although he probably knew that the Opéra would be only too happy to release him for the winter. De Spies was left under the impression that Guedeonov's proposals were wholly unacceptable, and on October 20th reported back to St. Petersburg to this effect.

Jules, however, had no intention of allowing the negotiations to lapse, and in anticipation had already released the Opéra from its commitment to him that winter. On November 8th he wrote direct to Guedeonov expressing his readiness to come to Russia immediately if he were offered terms that were a little more favourable, and explaining that if his engagement did not materialise, he would lose three months employment since he had cancelled his engagement with the Opéra. Guedeonov now tried to dissuade him from his intention, pointing out that, with the season due to close on February 25th, there woud barely be enough time to mount a single ballet, for he could hardly arrive before December 19th and a new work could not be performed earlier than the end of January or the beginning of February. The Director appeared torn between his duty to secure Jules' services as desired by his Imperial master and his personal antipathy to the Elssler visit. But, as he admitted to de Spies, he had been forced to agree to let Jules come at this late stage 'in order to avoid his complaints,' and was applying for the Tsar's permission to conclude the contract.[7]

Swallowing his pride, Guedeonov hastened to reassure Jules that all was not lost and put forward a formula to resolve the difficulty. 'If you had given M. de Spies the explanation you have now given me,' he wrote on November 20th, 'I would have lost no time in fixing a salary for your services as a performer, for no mention was made in the engagement proposals of your dancing or playing rôles . . . because I thought you devoted yourself entirely to choreography and only took rôles to improve the ensemble of your works. I am particularly sorry about this because, even if you set out at once, you could not stage more than one work, for assuming that this letter, like yours, will take eleven days to arrive, it will not be in your hands until December 1st. Allowing at least three or four days for you to make preparations for the journey and have your passport endorsed by our Chargé d'Affaires or M. de Spies (which is indispensable to cross the Russian frontier), you will not be able to start before December 5th or 6th. The railway will get you to Berlin in 3 or 4 days, and you will not be able to leave there until the 10th or 11th, after which you will need 6 to 8 days to reach St. Petersburg. So it will be between the 16th and the 19th that you can be here. Assuming you arrive on the 20th, you will need 5 to 6 weeks to stage a grand ballet, which means it cannot be performed until towards the end of January or in the first days of February, even assuming that the work does not require great preparations on the part of the scene painters and the machinists. After that, only 20 to 25 days will be left before the end of the season, for this year our season ends on February 27th of your calendar and not on March 11th, as you thought. If you are agreeable to coming in spite of these remarks, I am ready to receive you and to give you 6,000 francs for a grand ballet in several acts, 2,000 francs for a short one in two acts, 500 francs for a divertissement, but I repeat that only one or two can be staged, and your services as a performer will be paid for at the rate of 2,000 francs a month, as you wish, from the date of your arrival until the end of our season, and on top of all that, a performance for your benefit.

'Had you written to me at the same time as M. de Spies told me of your response, we would have 20 more days at our disposal. Your delay in writing to me was very unfortunate, but nevertheless, if you are agreeable to come, this letter will serve as the basis of a contract that will be prepared on your arrival, and I shall be very pleased to see you arrive. But should the shortage of time before the end of the season make you give up the journey this time, please let me know if you intend coming in 1849, and at what time and on what terms. Your London engagement cannot be an obstacle, as their season finishes in August while ours begins on October 1st and finishes on March 15th, 1850. But you can leave us on March 1st, after staging the last work for the 1849–50 season, if you wish to be in London earlier.

'As the winter here is very extreme, you must equip yourself in Berlin with a good pelisse and warm boots so as not to catch cold.'[8]

Guedeonov still hoped that Jules would decide, of his own accord, not to come for the tag-end of the season. In a letter to de Spies of November 24th, asking him to warn Jules not to start his journey until the special authorisation to cross the Russian frontier had been received, he added hopefully: 'Well, I suppose he will give up the engagement now that so little time remains before the end of the season.'[9] In this he was mistaken, for the authorisation was issued the next day and Jules was quickly on his way.

When he arrived in St. Petersburg in the middle of December, Elssler had already been performing at the Bolshoi Theatre for two months. She had chosen to make her first appearance in *Giselle*, and the intensity of her interpretation had made an immediate impact in what was otherwise an insensitive imitation of the Paris production, staged originally by the elderly ballet-master, Titus. For her next rôle she had herself mounted *Le Délire d'un peintre*, in which she inserted her *Cachucha*, and these two works, together

Jules Perrot

with *La Fille mal gardée*, had kept the Russian audiences content in the weeks before Jules arrived to put the finishing touches to *Esmeralda*.*

To ensure that it would be ready in time for her benefit on January 2nd, rehearsals had already started under Elssler's direction and with the assistance of a promising young French dancer, not long engaged in St. Petersburg, Marius Petipa. The rôles had also been allotted, but Jules could have had no reservations on this score. The most important part after those of Esmeralda and Gringoire, which Elssler and he were to play, was Claude Frollo, and this had been given to Nicolai Goltz. Goltz, who was approaching fifty, had been a *protégé* of Didelot, and from being a splendid dancer in his prime, had become, in middle age, a mime of extraordinary power. He gave the rôle of Frollo a new importance, and old Titus, seeing him perform it by the side of Elssler and Jules, exclaimed that he had never seen such a glorious trio on the stage. Goltz's contemporary, Pierre Didier, supported him with a sensitive portrayal of the hunchback Quasimodo, for which he was so skilfully disguised in a padded costume that 'Hugo himself, the monster's creator, would have been delighted.'[10] The rôle of Phoebus was allotted to another Frenchman, Frédéric Malovergne, professionally known only by his forename, while that of Fleur de Lys was given to Tatiana Smirnova, who at that time was one of the very few Russian ballerinas to have visited Western Europe, where she had danced briefly in Paris and Brussels in the summer of 1844.

The rehearsals were held in the Theatre School, where the pupils had the privilege of watching – a treat they looked forward to for a variety of reasons, not all of them artistic. For not only were they petted by the dancers, who used their dormitories as dressing rooms, but when the company broke for tea, they would be offered some of the smoked fish that they brought with them for refreshment. Jules' impending arrival was another source of excitement, for his reputation had preceded him and the early rehearsals of *Esmeralda*, which Elssler had taken, had given an exciting glimpse of his extraordinary choreography, which made the work of old Titus seem flat and fusty in comparison. The rehearsal at which Jules first appeared was not to be forgotten on account of the fuss he made when the corps de ballet turned up in long dresses.

'I do not see their legs,' he cried out. 'Why are they not wearing ballet costume?'

'The corps de ballet is not required to take daily dance classes,' explained Marcel, the régisseur. 'They do not possess ballet costumes.'

'Then I insist that they have them.'

'That is rather difficult, for the corps de ballet are paid so little.'

---

* The ballet had been entitled *La Esmeralda* when it was produced in London and Milan in 1844, but it became *Esmeralda* when Jules produced it in Russia, and as such it has been known ever since.

'Maybe, but surely they have tutus? Let them come in tutus if they do not have short dresses.'[11]

The result was instantaneous, and at the very next rehearsal, Jules was pleased to see that every one of them was wearing a short skirt. The cost, which they had found from their modest salaries, was money well spent, for they quickly found that they were to be allotted an important part in the new production.

For the St. Petersburg stage, where a ballet was expected to occupy a full evening's performance, *Esmeralda* was divided into three acts, the first consisting of the scene in the Cour des Miracles, the second containing the scene in Esmeralda's room and the betrothal festivities, and the third, the scene in the cabaret and that before Notre Dame. The scene painters worked wonders to reproduce old Paris on the stage. For the betrothal scene the designer Wagner had conceived an arcaded gallery giving on to a garden aglow with summer colours and freshened by a fountain spouting real water, a particularly welcome sight in mid-winter when, outside, the city was gripped by twenty degrees of frost. Equally impressive was the final scene – designed by the academician Roller, whom the audience honoured with a call to himself – depicting Notre Dame and the Tour de Nesle against the night sky, towering over the roofs of the city, and the Seine in the background with lights reflected in the water.

There was little that Jules needed, or had time, to change in what Elssler had supervised, and the ballet was ready in time for her benefit performance on January 2nd, 1849, barely a fortnight after his arrival. While it was naturally Elssler's portrayal of Esmeralda that absorbed the audience's attention, the novel qualities of the choreography did not pass unnoticed. The unprecedented prominence of the corps de ballet was most apparent in the first two numbers. The design of the groups in the opening *Valse Bohémienne*, and the *Pas des Truands* that followed Gringoire's reprieve when Esmeralda agrees to marry him, made an instant impression. The *Truandaise* that followed was no less appreciated for its originality and the meaning that Elssler and Jules put into it. From the very beginning the unfolding of the plot was marvellously clear. Esmeralda's first meeting with Phoebus was so delicately done that one critic placed it alongside such great love scenes in literature as those of Amy Robsart and Leicester in Scott's *Kenilworth*, and Gœthe's Egmont and Clärchen.[12] The extraordinary rapport between Elssler and Jules was also appreciated in the scene in Esmeralda's room. In the middle act the betrothal festivities opened with a long divertissement. The *pas des corbeilles* had been considerably reworked to accommodate a greater number of dancers than in London, Smirnova, as Fleur de Lys, being given a variation in which she was supported by three soloists and twenty-four *danseuses* of the corps de ballet. The opening of this scene apparently lost none of its effect by being revised in this way, and one critic praised it as 'real poetry.'[13] The remainder of this scene had also been expanded. In place of the *pas de trois* which had given Saint-Léon the opportunity to display his dancing prowess in the original London production, Jules had substituted a new *pas de quatre*, unconnected with the action, for Eugène Huguet, Anastasia Yakovleva, Elizaveta Nikitina and Varvara Volkova. For this some new music had been composed which, in the score, was headed, for a reason now obscure, 'Charles Millot.'

Finally there came the dramatic *pas d'action* that followed the arrival of Esmeralda and Gringoire to dance before the guests. The narrative was resumed, dissolving into a *pas de deux* 'full of frightening technical difficulties but performed with inimitable artistry'[14] by Elssler and Johansson, who was introduced to partner her. In relinquishing his rôle as partner in this central *pas d'action*, Jules seemed to be accepting the decline in his powers as a dancer, but no doubt he made sure that the *pas*' dramatic point of showing Esmeralda made brutally aware that Phoebus loves another and having to dance as if nothing had happened, was not lost on the audience.*

The last act relied largely for its effect on Elssler's powerful miming, but here, as in the first scene, the corps de ballet came into prominence to create the turbulent atmosphere of the Paris streets, the background against which Hugo had set his poignant story.

There was no doubt that *Esmeralda* was a resounding triumph for the choreographer. 'Our excellent ballet company had lacked a master choreographer,' wrote one critic, 'but Perrot's arrival has filled the gap.' The fact that his performance, though admired, created no great stir among a cast so strong in dramatic talent only served to emphasise that 'his real usefulness would be as a choreographer, for,' as was observed, 'we have personnel enough for rôles such as Gringoire.'[15]

Jules was determined to stage *Catarina* for his own benefit, but considerable pressure was needed to make Guedeonov proceed with a production that could only be given a limited number of performances before the end of the season. Authorisation was eventually given, and in a burst of activity Jules had the ballet ready in time for the benefit performance on February 16th. Although the season had little more than a week to run, the ballet was repeated at matinée performances throughout Butter Week, and had already been given ten times by the time the theatre closed for Easter.

It provided another dramatic triumph for Fanny Elssler, who was supported by Jules in his original rôle of Diavolino, and by the elegant Johansson as Salvator Rosa. Jules probably altered little from the definitive version he had staged in Milan. The ballet made an immense impression on the Petersburg public. 'The plot,' wrote Rafail Zotov in *Severnaya Pchela*, 'has

---

* The music used was basically that which Bajetti had written for the Milan production of December 1844 (see p. 136), with the addition of a new variation for Johansson and the shortening of the coda.

many absurdities, as is always the case in ballet, but the interest is sustained until the end, the dances are wonderful and the groups enchanting. Everything seethes with life and gaiety. It is splendidly zestful and excellently performed, and from beginning to end all eyes are on Fanny Elssler, whose dancing is incomparably novel and original. It is not the movements of her legs, nor the curve of her body, nor the lightness and fascination of her feet that holds the attention, but her miming, her silent dialogue, her acting, which makes you forget the charm and artistry of her dancing.'[16]

Perceptive connoisseurs of the ballet saw beyond Elssler's dominating performance to the merits of the choreography. *Catarina*, like *Esmeralda* before it, had marked a new development in ballet as a narrative art, most notably in its much greater reliance on the corps de ballet, as the critic of the *Sanktpeterburgskiye Vedomosti* observed in his review. 'It is in the arrangement of the groups that the most marked feature of Perrot's talent lies,' he observed. 'After Didelot's day the ballet generated into a jumble of jumps and pirouettes. The soloists had much to do, but the corps de ballet was kept in the background. Neither the ballet-master nor the public was interested in it, and indeed who would want to go on watching monotonous poses and movements performed by all alike at the same time! Then Perrot appeared among us, and the gifted band of *coryphées* and *figurantes* came to life and began to stir, timidly at first, but gradually becoming more animated and dashing up to the forestage, throwing themselves into groups and elegant measures such as they had never been asked to perform before, to the astonishment of the public. Perrot has not spared the corps de ballet. He is continually giving them work to do. Dramatic situations lead into balletic and, if I may use the word, transcendental *pas* by the soloists, general evolutions by the corps de ballet, and character dances by the principals. Go to the ballet this winter, and see what I mean.'[17]

On the strength of these two productions, the St. Petersburg authorities were fully convinced of Jules' worth, and negotiations were opened to secure his services for the whole of the following season as ballet-master, dancer and mime. He made an attempt to extract an increase in his salary over and above the rate he was already receiving, but a flat refusal by Tsar Nicholas, delivered as protocol required through the Minister of the Court and the Director of the Imperial Theatres, put an end to any bargaining and on March 10th Jules put his signature to a formal contract. This bound him to arrive in St. Petersburg not later than October 15th, and to give his services until the end of the season on March 17th, 1850. In addition to his duties as choreographer and performer, he was required to undertake a certain amount of teaching, but he was not to be obliged to take more than six pupils. He would supply, without extra charge, the music for any of his existing ballets he might revive, but the cost of a specially composed score for a new ballet was to be borne by the Direction. His salary was agreed at

Jules Perrot

8,000 silver roubles for the season, and in addition he was to be given a benefit.

* * *

Jules' first task on returning to Paris in the spring was to discuss the variation of his contract with the Opéra. This bound him for three seven-month periods, from September to March, spaced over three years, the first of which had been postponed to allow him to go to Russia. It was apparently already understood that the first seven-month period would commence immediately on his return from Russia, for he had made no arrangements to go to London that summer. The political situation in Paris, which had been the reason for deferring his contract the year before, must have been raised at his meeting with the Directors, for it directly affected the prosperity of the theatres. There were encouraging signs that the unrest of 1848 was beginning to die down, and the Opéra had boldly embarked on a major operatic production, Meyerbeer's long-awaited *Le Prophète*. The election of Louis Napoleon as President seemed to presage a return to stability, but it was too early to be certain, and the Directors were still anxious. Nevertheless, it was agreed that Jules' engagement should go ahead as planned and that the first seven-month period of his contract should begin on April 1st.

His immediate task was to prepare a new ballet for Carlotta, and almost at once he ran into a difficulty over the choice of subject. Having so triumphantly staged *Esmeralda* in London, Milan and St. Petersburg, he may well have been expecting to revive this masterpiece in Paris. The Opéra, however, had other ideas, and insisted on an entirely new work, for which – apparently without Jules being consulted – Saint-Georges had been commissioned to write a scenario. Since Carlotta's engagement at the Opéra had only been extended until the end of the year, it was vital that there should be no delay. Realising this, Jules apparently tried to assert his views by making difficulties. Finally, when he failed to turn up at a meeting on stage that had been arranged with Saint-Georges, the exasperated Directors next day, May 8th, sent him a strongly worded letter reminding him of his contractual obligations.

'This further delay,' they pointed out, 'added to the already numerous delays you have caused, place us . . . in an embarrassing position and compel us to take steps to enforce our contract. We must therefore require you to begin rehearsing the ballet with which we have entrusted you.'[18]

The practice of accepting a ballet scenario on its own merits and then imposing it on the choreographer had long been established at the Opéra, and Jules, who had been accustomed in London and Milan to devise his own plots, no doubt expected a hassle on this issue. The Directors would not yield. They were convinced that their decisions on the form of the new ballet were in the interests of both Jules and Carlotta, and maintained, as a matter of principle, that it was for them, not him, to decide what their money should be spent on.

The Lure of Russia

Saint-Georges was no stranger to Jules, for he had been a member of the team that had produced *Giselle* eight years before. Sensing that the public would be in no mood for realism at this time, he had produced a variant on the theme of the Sleeping Beauty, full of situations that called for spectacular scenic effects.* It was undoubtedly deliberate that it was much more complex in its structure than *Giselle*, for while the earlier ballet had been designed to present a young débutante, this new work had to be commensurate with the prestige of the unchallenged prima ballerina that Carlotta had now become. If Jules had been unhappy about the involvement of Saint-Georges, he could have had no reservations on the choice of composer, for Adolphe Adam was unquestionably the finest musician then writing for the ballet. Understandably, he was also a very busy man, and he fulfilled his task with the assistance of a talented pupil, Alfred de Saint-Julien, who was to be given credit as his collaborator. Also at work on the new ballet were the designers, Despléchin and the partnership of Cambon and Thierry, and the costumier, Paul Lormier, all of whom could be relied upon to uphold the Opéra's reputation for impressive spectacle, while Victor Sacré, the chief machinist, had been given a list of effects that would tax his ingenuity to the hilt. Having made these dispositions, the Directors of the Opéra considered that the specification for the new ballet was not open to further discussion, and Jules grudgingly submitted.

The dispute had upset the Opéra's original plan of presenting the ballet for Carlotta's return from London in the summer, and on May 23rd it was reported that it was not yet ready and that she would make her reappearance in an old work.[20]

For Carlotta this was to be an unhappy summer. Although she was only thirty, she was already showing signs of strain. An American who had seen her driving in the Champs Elysées the year before, had been struck by her tired expression and her 'pale and wan' complexion. She seemed 'worn with excitement.'[21] Her physical resistance was low, and when cholera broke out in Paris in June, she caught the dreaded disease, but mercifully only mildly, and was ordered to rest for several weeks.

Then another blow fell. In the middle of July the Directors of the Opéra, finding their treasury exhausted by the enormous expense of *Le Prophète*, decided to close the theatre, ostensibly for redecoration, while they sought means to reduce their overheads. It had proved another disastrous summer for the theatres of Paris. There was still a very real threat of civil war, for it was too early to see that General Changarnier's dispersal of a Socialist

---

* Saint-Georges' preoccupation with fairy stories at this time was also revealed in the libretto which he and Scribe wrote for the comic opera, *La Fée aux roses*, produced at the Opéra Comique exactly one week before *La Filleule des fées*, on October 1st, 1849. 'At the present time fairies are victorious all along the line,' observed Paul Scudo in his review of the ballet (*Revue et Gazette Musicale de Paris*, October 14th, 1849).

demonstration on June 13th had sealed the triumph of the forces of order for some time to come. Added to this, a sweltering heatwave settled on Paris in June and July and the cholera epidemic kept the people off the streets and the theatres empty.

This was the background against which Jules belatedly set to work on the new ballet. Much valuable time had been lost, and the Directors' patience had worn very thin. Faced with the need to cut expenses, they were coming to the view that a guest choreographer, particularly one who had shown himself to be difficult, was an unwarranted luxury, and on July 25th they served another notice on Jules – this time exercising their power to terminate his contract. Feeling very aggrieved at this unexpected development, he testily acknowledged the notice the next day.

'Gentlemen,' he wrote, 'I have the honour to acknowledge your letter of the 25th instant in which, in exercise of the power given to each of us under Clause 8 of our contract, you notify me that I shall cease to be in your employment as from November 1st. While accepting this decision, I must express my disappointment at the somewhat premature step you have taken with regard to me. You have chosen the most inopportune moment to inform me of your decision. I can only bow before your sense of economy.'[22]

When the Opéra reopened its doors early in September, the new ballet was still far from ready and Carlotta, now fully recovered, had to make her reappearance in *Giselle*. Rehearsals were already in full swing, however, and the corps de ballet was patiently absorbing the unusually complex groups that Jules was devising for them. The dancers found themselves participating in the act of creation to a much greater degree than they were accustomed to, for Jules was in his element when composing for the corps de ballet. His method was to use them much as a sculptor works with his clay, and the dancers soon became used to his habit of communing with his muse. 'He had a method of composing all his own,' described the omniscient Charles de Boigne. 'As soon as the spirit moved him, he would squat down on the stage with his head in his hands, just like a china monkey. When the corps de ballet saw him sitting on the floor like a tailor, they knew he would be there for a long time and occupied themselves in their own ways, some working at their embroidery, others eating their lunch or reading, while the soloists sent out for refreshments. After some time a noise was heard. It was Perrot snoring. He was woken up; the *ballabile* was finished – it had come with the snoring.'[23]

While these preparations were in progress Jules lost one of his closest colleagues. Antoine Coulon, who had supported him so staunchly during his years in London, and had been his first Quasimodo, was one of the last victims of the cholera epidemic. Jules sadly accepted the task of delivering the oration at the graveside, where on a mild September day he paid his last tribute to a dear friend and valued adviser, whom he remembered above all for his gentle, self-effacing nature. Movingly, he told how both his private life and his professional life had been illuminated by this friendship. 'You were always too modest,' he said. 'You cared too little for personal renown, wearing yourself out by serving other men's reputations with greater zeal than you would have needed to acquire one for yourself. Devotion and self-denial were the keynotes of your character. I myself owe a great deal to your inestimable advice. Your words, always tolerant and kind, taught me to love truth, which is often unwelcome to the young. I listened to you, and corrected myself. This tribute to your memory is a sacred debt that I could not have paid during your lifetime, for your excessive modesty would have prevented you from listening to me. Farewell, honest and faithful friend. Your memory will live always in my heart, and in the hearts of all who are now gathered round your grave, for no one could know you and not love you.'[23]

This sad duty performed, Jules returned to the final preparations for *La Filleule des fées,* which a month later, on October 8th, was presented for the judgment of the first-night public, among whom were the most eminent critics of Paris, Théophile Gautier of *La Presse,* Jules Janin of the *Débats,* and Pier Angelo Fiorentino of *Le Moniteur.* It was a work that demanded serious attention, not only on account of its scale – the whole performance, which included a single act from an opera, lasted three and a half hours – but also for its intrinsic merits, and all three of those critics wrote measured reviews, finding much to praise in the choreography, the music and the spectacle, even if certain passages were found to be absurd or obscure.

Adolphe Adam's overture led into a prologue recounting the incident that gave rise to the strange happenings that were to follow. The scene, representing a farmhouse in Provence, had been so skilfully adapted from the set for the first act of *La Sylphide* that no one seems to have recognised its provenance. The prosperous farmer Guillaume has invited his friends to celebrate the baptism of his daughter Ysaure. At first it seems as if the festivities will never begin, for three times one of the guests, a little merry with wine, is interrupted with his leg in the air just as he is about to lead the company in a saraband. Each time a knock is heard at the door, and one after another three old women beg to be admitted. The first two are gladly welcomed, but the third is turned away because her presence would bring the number up to thirteen. As the festivities draw to a close, the two old women – played by Célestine Emarot and Louise Taglioni – reveal themselves as the White and Rose Fairies, the child's fairy godmothers, who bring gifts of beauty. This transformation was impressively managed, the old women's long cloaks of brown 'glazed perculine' being pulled off in a twinkling of an eye to reveal the magnificent fairy costumes they wore underneath. Simultaneously sixteen old women who had entered in their train – and had not been counted as guests! – were similarly transformed, their crutches changing into fairy wands.[24] Suddenly a peal of thunder shatters the calm, and the rejected beggar-woman emerges from the fire-place. Flinging off her cloak, she shows herself to be the

Playbill of the Paris Opéra for October 8th, 1849 – the first performance of La Filleule des fées. *Bibliothèque de l'Opéra, Paris.*

The Lure of Russia

La Filleule des fées, *Act I. Alain (Jules Perrot), the unwanted lover, in a conversation with Father Guillaume (Louis Lenfant), with Ysaure (Carlotta Grisi) making known her feelings behind them. Caricature by Lorentz (Journal pour rire, October 20th, 1849)*

Black Fairy – a majestic portrayal by Louise Marquet – and at a wave of her wand a black cloud descends from the flies bearing the message: 'I shall withhold my gifts until her fifteenth birthday.' At this point Gautier winced at what he considered a serious breach of the rules of ballet-making.

Fifteen years have gone by when the first act begins. In a fresh country landscape villagers are making preparations for the spring festival. This was the moment for Carlotta's entrance as Ysaure, who is followed by her foster-brother Alain, whose love she is unable to return. When he is alone, Alain

Jules Perrot

gives way to 'a comical despair,'[25] an emotion so expressively rendered by Jules that those who knew him might have seen it as a reflection of the unhappiness he had felt in real life when he had lost Carlotta. Suddenly, in Alain's path, there appears an old woman who promises to help him in exchange for a kiss. At the touch of his lips she turns into the Black Fairy and leads him away. A young huntsman – Lucien Petipa – then arrives on the scene, weary from the chase. He is approached by two other old women – the good fairies, of course – who, in return for alms, tell him that he is about to fall in love. As

La Filleule des fées, *Act I. Count Hugues (Lucien Petipa), the preferred lover, with, behind him, Alain, Ysaure and, probably, Ysaure's nurse (Aline). Caricature by Lorentz.* (Journal pour rire, *October 20th, 1849*)

they point to Farmer Guillaume's cottage, its walls become transparent and Ysaure is seen in her room. The young man is immediately enamoured, but the vision fades when the Black Fairy returns in a fury. All attempts by the young huntsman and his companions to enter the cottage come to nought, and while they have gone to fetch a log to batter down the door, the Black Fairy causes the cottage to vanish and reappear at the top of the hill. Notwithstanding these extraordinary happenings, the festivities begin. Alain has such faith in the Black Fairy's support that he adopts a confidently possessive attitude towards Ysaure that amuses her enormously. But when the moment arrives for her to be crowned Queen of the Spring, the official deputed to perform the task mysteriously vanishes and his place is taken by the young huntsman – a substitution effected by a double trap – who is now recognised as Prince Hugues of Provence. At this point Jules inserted a long divertissement, beginning with a *ballabile* and culminating with a *pas de cinq* for Ysaure, her two suitors and two supporting dancers (Mlles Robert and Caroline). This contained an important variation for Carlotta, as well as a solo passage for Lucien Petipa who, as a contemporary caricature disclosed, had first to remove his hunting boots, revealing dance slippers that he was already wearing inside them.* At last, as the gaslight dimmed for the effect of nightfall, the festivities are brought to a close and the Prince prepares to leave for his castle. He begs Ysaure for another meeting. When Alain steps between them and takes Ysaure's arm, the fairy godmothers intervene, making the Prince vanish and reappear in Ysaure's chamber. The scene closes with the Prince's bewildered companions searching for their master, while Ysaure ascends the hill to her cottage.

A dropcloth descended for the scene change to Ysaure's chamber. The Prince, who has been magically transported there, hides as Ysaure, her mother and Alain enter. Alain offers Ysaure a bouquet, and is upset when she refuses it. Noticing his distress, Ysaure agrees to accept it, but it is now too late. Wryly, Alain shows her that he has crumpled the flowers in his misery, and he runs off to gather another bouquet. Ysaure is left alone, and Hugues seizes the opportunity to emerge from his hiding place. He kneels at her feet and declares his love. She can hardly contain her delight, but after he

---

* The manuscript score at the Paris Opéra includes at this point a number entitled 'Variation de Perrot,' but the reviewers made no specific mention of this and probably it was no more than a technically uncomplicated passage designed to contrast Alain's awkwardness with the elegance of the Prince. Gautier wrote in his account that Jules 'allowed himself only a few little unimportant scraps of waltz and mazurka' (*La Presse*, October 15th, 1849), and Scudo clearly stated that 'Perrot, whom we used to know as the most agile and aerial of dancers, is now reduced to skimming the ground and miming the rôle of Alain with a talent of the first order. Who would have thought that Perrot's physiognomy would become so expressive and eloquent?' (*Revue et Gazette Musicale de Paris*, October 14th, 1849).

has gone, she becomes embarrassingly conscious of her humble circumstances. Then, by magic skilfully simulated by the machinist, her modest looking glass turns into a magnificent full-length mirror, the rustic chairs and cupboards become pieces of elegant furniture, the little room itself expands into a palatial chamber, and Ysaure finds herself wearing a splendid gown of white brocade. A fanfare sounds, and Ysaure excitedly opens the door, expecting to find her Prince outside. But on the threshold is the Black Fairy, who has come to announce her birthday gift. The fairy godmothers, who have appeared to protect the girl, have made her so beautiful, she tells them, that no man will now look on her without losing his reason. Fearful of harming her beloved, Ysaure tries to escape, but the Prince's companions restrain her. She covers her face with her hands. As the Prince draws her hands away, she turns sharply to find herself looking into the eyes of Alain, who at that moment has returned with a fresh bouquet. Deprived of his senses, he tries to prevent the Prince from following Ysaure. The Prince pushes him aside and clasps her in his arms, but she breaks free and leaps through the window. The fairy godmothers wave their wands, and instead of falling, she is, as a satirist described, 'borne away by four thick iron wires supporting a wooden glory that carries 200 to 300 kilos of fairies, as the curtain falls with a precision that does honour to the machinists.'[26]

The second act, designed by Despléchin, was a miracle of the scene designer's art, a moonlit glade containing an ornamental pool, surrounded by statues, and with a fountain in the centre, throwing a jet of water high into the air. The moonlight that shone through the trees was simulatd by the latest innovation in stage lighting, electricity, first used only a few months before for the sun in Le Prophète. In the flies above the stage on the O.P. side, carbon-arc lamps had been installed, angled obliquely so as to flood the stage with an intense cool light that took the breath away by its novelty. In this mysterious setting the fairy godmothers are waiting for their godchild Ysaure, and as she is borne towards them in a boat fashioned in the form of a swan, the statues stir and form graceful groups about her. After warning Ysaure that she must on no account show her face to the Prince, the fairies cause Alain to appear. He pursues her, but she eludes him. The fairy godmothers then admit Ysaure to their sisterhood, and wielding her new wand, she joins the nymphs as they skim across the water on to the grass. The *pas des fées* that Jules arranged for this scene was one of the highlights of the ballet, praised by Janin as 'very well constructed, and Good Heavens, how charming, with eight dancers striving to shine like brilliant stars around a meteor – or, we should say, Carlotta.'[27] It included short solos for the two fairies and another important variation for Carlotta that preceded the entrance of the leading soloists and the corps de ballet. When day breaks, Ysaure cannot resist testing her newly-bestowed powers to see her beloved once more. She causes him to appear, and is dancing around his sleeping form when Alain returns. Snatch-

The Lure of Russia

ing the wand from her hand, he awakens the Prince. Ysaure flees from him, but Alain follows and touching her with the wand, renders her immobile. She is rescued by one of the fairy godmothers, who seizes her by the hand and spirits her into the grotto, which closes behind her. Maddened with fury, Alain drags the Prince towards the grotto and waving the wand again, causes the rocks to open before them.

In the third act the fairy godmothers have brought Ysaure to an underground cavern, the dwelling of the spirits of the springs that feed the pool. The spirits welcome her, and as each retires to her niche in the rock, a spring of water gushes out in which Ysaure sees her own reflection. Here Alain finds her again, dragging the hapless Prince towards her. To protect the Prince, the fairies strike him blind, and when Ysaure endeavours to use her powers to restore his sight, they cause her wand to break in her hand. At that moment the Black Fairy appears. She is beside herself with fury at being thwarted, but is finally persuaded to relent and agrees to permit the Prince to recover his sight with impunity on condition that he recognises Ysaure among the naiads. Clouds envelop the scene as this trial takes place. The naiads lavish their caresses on the Prince as he moves among them, but whenever he approaches Ysaure, Alain tries to hold him back. But eventually the paths of the two lovers meet, and the Prince recognises his beloved by the beating of her heart. The test is successfully passed, and the clouds disperse to reveal an apotheosis of extraordinary brilliance, the Fairies' Paradise, with golden clouds leading to 'a crystal temple, encrusted with carbuncles, sapphires, rubies and topazes, like a heavenly Jerusalem, seen against a dazzling sun spinning like the wheel of a burning chariot.'[28] – another effect produced by the miraculous new carbon-arc lamp, outshining even the memorable electric sun of *Le Prophète*.* In this glorious setting nearly ninety fairies, nymphs and statues appear from every side to celebrate the union of the happy couple, while Alain, his reason now restored, deplores his follies and is forgiven.

The critics dwelt at unusual length on the choreography, awarding special praise for Jules' skill in handling masses and composing groups. 'Choreography,' theorised Fiorentino, 'consists not only in inventing steps, designing attitudes and poses, and determining the number of variations. Above all it is the art of disposing large numbers of dancers and presenting them to the audience in a way that is both pleasing and varied, of not breaching the rules of perspective and line by bizarre combinations or by movements that are ungraceful or clash, of skilfully resolving the confusion of arms and legs that may occasionally fill the stage, and of manoeuvring with precision and unison a large and undisciplined army of supers and machinery for effects, the latter

---

* The scenery inventory described it as 'a spherical sun mounted with 85 iron slats.' It undoubtedly closely resembed the electric sun illustrated in M.J. Moynet's *L'Envers du théâtre* (Paris, 1873). (Archives Nationales, AJ[13] 233)

being neither the more obstinate nor the least intelligent. Perrot, who is no tyro, has overcome difficulties of this sort, before which ordinary choreographers would quail. The dances, if not notable for originality, are mostly pretty to watch, and the groups are arranged with artistry and taste.'[29]

Gautier was more enthusiastic. 'The ensemble dances are arranged with unusual intelligence and care,' he wrote. 'It is quite obvious that the eye of a master has peered into every corner and left no detail to chance. Nobody can manipulate large numbers of dancers with more facility than Perrot. The whole crowd, from footlights to backcloth, is dancing, and each dancer is performing something pretty and well designed.'[30]

Jules' own performance seemed to bind the work together. As Gautier put it, 'no one else could have better combined the talents of actor and dancer, even though he did not dance, for the *pas* in a ballet belong to the favoured lover, and in *La Filleule des fées* Perrot, who does not win his bride at the end, is reduced to the state of a comic opera bass.'[31] Nevertheless he succeeded in imparting an extraordinary pathos to the luckless Alain. Playing the part with a light humorous touch, he reminded one critic of his old colleague, Bouffé. His performance, this observer wrote, 'is truth itself, nature caught in the act. Here are simple yet profound feelings, drawn with the finest and most delicate shades, conveying a nature of gentle melancholy that gradually takes fire to the point of insanity. It could not have been better balanced in its restraint, its emotional effect, or its dramatic impact. Never has the art of pantomime been brought to such a pitch.'[32] In the words of another critic, 'he marked every situation with a meaning so delicate, natural and affecting that the features of the character became detached from everything else, etching themselves in extraordinary relief on the spectator's imagination.'[33]

Inspiration had also come through the presence of Carlotta, for whom he found himself creating with all the ardour and skill of earlier, happier years. No one understood the secrets of her art better than he, and Gautier, who was specially sensitive where she was concerned, was in raptures. 'Never perhaps has the charming ballerina appeared more correct, more graceful, stronger and lighter than in *La Filleule des fées*,' he wrote. 'She seemed to be flying, as if held in the air by some invisible hand, the tip of her white satin slipper alighting with no more sound than a snowflake. Her poses have such charm, and she appears so demure and naive in her enjoyment; she invests her entire rôle, played on the *pointe* virtually from one end to the other, with poetic simplicity. What abandon she puts into her *tours de force*! What grace she brings to her strength! And how easily she achieves the impossible! A *pas* by Perrot danced by Carlotta – nothing more wonderful can be imagined!'[34]

Not every critic, however, was carried away by Carlotta's technique. Escudier had noticed that 'wrinkles were already furrowing her cheeks and her smile,' and sadly realised that she was entering the autumn of her career.[35] For Jules, too, it was a moment of disillusionment. The achievement of a long-held ambition to return to the Opéra had been soured beyond recall first by the dispute with the Direction and then by the abrupt termination of his contract in a manner that could hardly have been more hurtful to an artist of his standing. It must have been a bitter and scarring experience, but it resolved, with finality, the question of where he would settle for the remainder of his career. Within a few weeks of dancing the rôle of Alain for the last time in Paris, he was on his way to Russia.

* * *

He arrived in St. Petersburg towards the end of November, somewhat later than the date stipulated in his contract. The delay had been unavoidable because of the terms of his engagement with the Opéra, and the Direction of the Imperial Theatres apparently raised no objection, knowing that the ending of his connection with Paris left him free to work exclusively for them. In the early weeks of the St. Petersburg season his presence had been greatly missed, for the enthusiasm for the ballet seemed to have suddenly waned. This had come about as a result of a sudden vogue for the Italian opera, stimulated by the Russian débuts of Mario and Giulia Grisi. St. Petersburg society had flocked to see and hear these two great singers, and the ballet, even with Elssler as its star, had found itself overshadowed and neglected. To those who remained loyal, Jules' return offered a hope that a new production might redress the balance of public favour, and on his reappearance in *Catarina* on December 6th he was greeted as 'the long-awaited Perrot'[36] and given several ovations.

Marius Petipa had a special interest in his return, for he was hoping to enlist his assistance for his benefit, which was to take place on the 16th. Elssler had agreed to take part, and Marius's father, Jean Petipa – aided, it seems, by his son, who was already harbouring ambitions to become a choreographer – was preparing a two-act ballet under the title of *Lida, ou la Laitière suisse*, in which Jules was asked to play the rôle of the country boy Fritz and to arrange two important *pas*.

Lida was no more than a version of an old ballet that had given Elssler one of her early triumphs in Vienna twenty years before. Old Petipa's revival – produced hurriedly and perhaps with few enough rehearsals – turned out to be quite unremarkable, only coming to life, in fact, in the two *pas* that Jules contributed. Working to a favourite formula of his, he devised a *scène dansante* between the milkmaid and the infatuated Fritz which opens with the boy begging for a kiss and being refused. To gain his end he then teasingly entices her with a basket of cherries, which she tries to snatch away without giving the desired reward. In the hands of two such experienced performers as Jules and Elssler, it was an enchanting little scene. This was followed by a *pas de trois* in which they were joined by Christian Johansson. This too was constructed on a slight theme, Fritz now trying to snatch a garland that the milkmaid was intending to give to the lady of the manor.

245

Jules Perrot

Having to compete with *Esmeralda* and *Catarina* in the repertory, *Lida* was not surprisingly dropped after two performances. A revival of *La Tarentule* on January 1st, 1850, in which Jules took the comic part of the Doctor, fared little better, being given only four times.

As the New Year progressed, Jules' time was becoming increasingly taken up with the preparation of *La Filleule des fées*, in which he was coaching Elssler in the part he had created for Carlotta. No serious objection had been made when the scenario was presented to the Imperial censor, but Guedeonov had raised a curious point which perhaps aroused a smile of disbelief when Jules heard of it. 'It might seem odd,' the Director had observed in all seriousness, 'that fairies are able to be godmothers,' and as a result the title, which was given in Russian, had to be changed to 'The Foster-child of the Fairies.'[37]

Jules had brought with him from Paris a first violin reduction of Adam's score, and this was newly orchestrated by Konstantin Lyadov, who took heed of the criticisms that had been voiced of the original orchestration and carefully avoided the excessive use of bells and triangles that had jarred on Parisian ears. Roller and Wagner were brought in to design the scenery and devise the manifestations of stage magic that the scenario called for, and electric light was to be used for the first time on the Russian stage to repeat the effects that had made the Paris production so remarkable. The use of inscriptions to convey the Black Fairy's pronouncements were unhappily repeated – in St. Petersburg they had to be in 'fiery Russian characters'[38] – and again drew unfavourable criticism. However, this was only a small blemish in a ballet of such length and splendour as *La Filleule des fées*. For sheer spectacle, nothing like it had been seen before in St. Petersburg. Wagner's set for the second act, with fountains playing and the electric light flooding the stage, caused a sensation, and Roller triumphed with his multi-coloured temple for the apotheosis and the extraordinary illuminations at the end of the ballet, when 'a sea of fire invades the stage, and from its depths there shines forth a great light so brilliant that it can barely be endured by the naked eye.'[39] For some tastes the liberal addition of red fire rather spoilt the effect of the electric light, but generally the production was considered to have surpassed the splendour of the original in spite of the obstinacy of some of the effects to function at the first performance.

The casting of the ballet presented few problems. The rôle of Ysaure was taken, of course, by Elssler, and Jules himself played his original part of Alain. Johansson was cast as Hugues, and Elena Andreyanova was an imposing Black Fairy, with Tatiana Smirnova and Anastasia Yakovleva as the Rose and White Faries. Among the lesser rôles, Didier played Ysaure's father. With such experienced artists the mime scenes were quickly assimilated, but in arranging the dances Jules was presented with a real problem in the time available. It was impossible to reproduce the ballet exactly as it had been

The Lure of Russia

given in Paris because he had there used a number of passages from *Esmeralda* and *Catrrina*, borrowings that had gone unperceived in Paris, where neither of those ballets had been seen. But since they were both in the St. Petersburg repertory, these passages had to be excised and replaced. It is no longer possible to specify the extent of this reworking, but it was probably substantial, for the critic Tan, in recording this fact, said that the St. Petersburg production only resembled the original version in its general development.[40]

This ballet was presented at Jules' benefit on February 24th, which was late in the season for a ballet creation and allowed time for only nine performances before the theatre closed.* Its choreography and spectacular production, however, were arresting enough to distract the public from its infatuation with the Italian opera, and the critics paid it serious attention in their columns.

These Russian critics were much more interested in the dramatic content than were the French. Saint-Georges' scenario had imposed a framework that demanded a compound of rustic comedy and faery ballet, and while in principle this was not objected to – for the mixture had worked well before in *La Sylphide, Giselle* and *Ondine* – the passages dealing with the real world were found lacking in human interest, and this, it was felt, had led Jules to heighten their effect with comedy. This was the explanation of Rafail Zotov's observation that 'some people were of the opinion that the content was too commonplace and farcical,' a view that he himself considered to be mistaken. 'They have failed to understand,' he went on, 'that this subject is ancient, mysterious, profound and filled with philosophy. It is a prehistoric legend, a myth about dualism, about the struggle between good and evil, about the gigantic wars of Ormazd and Ahriman which are recounted in the Zendavest. Underneath the fairy's golden tulle you seem to perceive the wings of a hawk. Throughout the whole fairy-tale course of the ballet, you have a cosmogonical sense of ancient philosophy. You realise that all the misfortunes of the heroine stem from her father's failure to observe the priestly laws of hospitality. The profound lesson of the legend is applicable to all ages and to all peoples.' Passing to an analysis of the plot, he considered that 'the power of evil was conveyed too strongly. The evil fairy forced the good fairies to tremble and obey her, and finally to seek her help. This is contrary to the thought in the ancient myth and to the true teaching of philosophy. Let evil exist as an inevitable sign of human weakness, but it must always be weaker than good and order. Let evil do harm, let it even triumph momentarily, but

---

* It was retained in the repertory the following season, 1850–51, achieving another 7 performances, but then was dropped. Jules never produced it elsewhere, but Salvatore Taglioni and Gustave Carey jointly produced a version, entitled *Isaura*, with different music by Giaquinto, in Naples in 1856.

this must be by means of mysterious machinations and not through the prevailing of a greater power. Good should be clearly victorious without having recourse to a humiliating appeasement to evil. The choreographer ought to have created his *dénouement* so that the evil fairy is finally defeated by the good fairies and compelled to slink away in shame.'[41]

The dances met with complete approval. The *valse de la coquetterie* between Elssler and Jules in the first act – probably created for the St. Petersburg production – was beautifully designed and performed to perfection. The *pas de cinq* that followed, in which Elssler, Jules and Johansson were joined by Zina Richard and Anna Prikhunova, consisted 'not of mere dances, but of whole scenes of love, coquetry, seduction and jealousy.'[42] The highlight of the second act, as in the original version, was the *pas des fées*, danced in the cool light of electricity to soft strains of violins. As St. Peterburg saw it, it contained a memorable *tour de force* in which Elssler performed a *glissé* sequence, traversing the stage obliquely, first in one direction and then in the other.* Finally, in the last act, there was the *grand pas plastique*, a display of pure poetical dancing that accompanied the blind groping of Hugues in his search for Ysaure among the nymphs and Alain's mad attempt to thwart his efforts.

This was one of the two scenes of Alain's madness which Fyodor Koni described as 'the summit of artistry.' As a mime, he wrote, Jules was 'unsurpassed, especially in comic rôles, and in this respect we have met with only one other like him in the whole of Europe, Louis Schneider of the Berlin ballet. Perrot's features are expressive to the highest degree, his gestures natural, his movements agile. And he is so eloquent and convincing in everything he does that, watching him, you can really write that he speaks. This came across not only in passages of uproarious comedy, but on occasion in moments of pathos.'[43]

Fanny Elssler gave a very different reading to the rôle of Ysaure from that of Carlotta, who, as Jules already knew, would be joining him in St. Petersburg in the autumn. She had signed a contract in January at a salary of 30,000 francs for the season – only three-quarters of what Elssler was receiving.** The question had arisen whether both ballerinas could be afforded, but with only three or occasionally four ballet performances a week, the Direction considered that the expenditure involved would be quite out of proportion, and

---

* The text on which this description is based reads as follows: 'A glissade on one leg, taken obliquely across the whole stage, and back on the other leg, is one of those wonderful *tours de force* of the art of dancing in which Fanny Elssler seems to have no rivals on this earth.' (*Severnaya Pchela*, March 5th, 1850)

** Towards the end of the season, in February 1851, Carlotta was granted a gratuity of 2,500 roubles (10,000 francs) to equate her remuneration with what Elssler had received.

furthermore there would be problems over allotting rôles – Giselle, for example. In these difficult negotiations Jules was inevitably involved. To help, he offered to produce four new ballets, two for each ballerina, but as Guedeonov reported to his Minister, 'the production of four ballets would cost 50,000 to 60,000 silver roubles, whereas only 12,000 francs* is allotted for two productions, and there would be no end to the quarrels and inconvenience.'[44] In the end it was decided that Elssler would not be re-engaged, and – whether to save her from embarrassment or to avoid the bother of protests from her admirers – the Tsar gave orders that this should not be officially announced until the season had ended.

Jules' decision not to return to Paris that summer enabled him to accompany Fanny Elssler on a visit to Moscow in May. Each of the three ballets in which she appeared there – *Le Délire d'un peintre, Giselle* and *Catarina* – had been reproduced in Moscow at one time or another,** but under his personal touch they took on the appearance of new works. *Catarina*, for example, which Frédéric, the Phoebus of the St. Petersburg production, had staged there only a few months before, was transformed almost out of recognition, and with the leading rôles played by Elssler, Johansson and Jules himself, aroused the most fervent enthusiasm that was not at all dampened by the sweltering heatwave. Before they all returned to St. Petersburg, Jules was given his reward in the form of a half-benefit.

His own commitments in St. Petersburg were to prevent him from sharing in the extraordinary triumph that was to crown Fanny Elssler's career in Moscow during the following winter. Her retirement was now imminent, and he must have known, when he returned to St. Petersburg, that their association, which had enriched each of them beyond measure as artists, had come to an end. But with many a loss there comes a compensating gain, and certainly Jules could feel no sadness that summer. He had yielded willingly to the lure of Russia. He had formed a deep and satisfying attachment with a young Russian girl, Capitolina Samovskaya – a native of St. Petersburg, not yet twenty-one, and apparently unconnected with the world of the theatre – and he probably married her some time that summer, for the elder of their two daughters was to be born the following May. For him it was a happy and settling event, for it enabled him to enjoy at last, and perhaps almost for the first time, the security of family roots and a happy home.

---

* The exchange rate was 4 francs to the rouble.
**ardin *Le Délire d'un peintre* by Sankovskaya in 1849, *Giselle* by Didier in 1843, and *Catarina* by Frédéric in January 1850.

16

Carlotta's Indian Summer

On the strength of the ballets he had produced for Elssler, the Imperial Theatres had been eager to secure Jules' services for the 1850–51 season, when Carlotta Grisi would be making her Russian début, and terms had been agreed for his engagement as *maître de ballet*, dancer and mime for one year from March 21st, 1850. In addition to his duties as choreographer and performer, he was to give classes to such members of the company and pupils as the Direction confided to his care, and for all this he was to receive a salary of 10,000 silver roubles, together with the proceeds of a benefit, at which a new grand ballet was to be given its first performance. The contract further provided that he could take six weeks' leave of absence during the summer 'if he finds it necessary,' but he certainly did not leave Russia at all that year, for after his return from Moscow in June, he was commanded to produce a divertissement for an Imperial fête at Peterhof on July 15th.

These fêtes were the choicest of summer pleasures not only for those who lived in the vicinity of Peterhof, but also for the city dwellers who had not departed to their country estates. Everyone seemed to know when they were being held, and all day long the steamers – one of them being appropriately named 'The Sylphide' – plied to and fro across the bay, carrying their complements of tightly-packed passengers, all in a state of great excitement and anticipation and the best of humour. At the journey's end the lovely white and pink palace of the Tsar seemed to materialise like a vision through the haze, set high upon its terraces amid the rich verdure of its gardens and park. The climax of the day, for which everyone was waiting, did not come until nightfall, at about half past ten, when the illuminations – devised on this occasion by the stage designer Roller – were turned on. It was an incredible sight. The surrounding countryside seemed to blaze into view, its salient features picked out, as if by magic, as a veritable regiment of lamp-lighters lit nearly half a million lamps of all colours in a breath-taking crescendo of light.

As a complement to this magical display, groups of dancers fom the Imperial ballet had been brought from St. Petersburg to give an open-air performance on a specially built stage in front of the Ozerka pavilion. With the lake providing the scenery, and the surrounding trees ablaze with a multitude of lamps, it was the ideal setting for the sporting of naiads, and Jules had put together a short divertissement, inspired by *Ondine*, but in fact a fragment of a radical reworking of that ballet which he was preparing for future production at the Bolshoi.

The divertissement opened with the arrival of a young fisherman – called, as in *Ondine*, Matteo, and played by the choreographer himself – rowing his boat to the stage and disturbing the naiads who are sporting themselves there. They hide at his approach. As he steps ashore, the song of a nightingale reminds him of his fiancée Giannina, whom he is to marry in the morning. After casting his net, he leaves to gather flowers for a bouquet to take back to her. The naiads then appear from the bushes at the sides. One of them, Azurina – played by Anna Prikhunova, one of the most promising of the younger Russian dancers – has fallen in love with Matteo. Determined to practice her charms on him, she persuades her companions to fill his net with silver and golden fishes. On his return, Matteo is astonished by such a catch. He casts his net again, but when he draws it in, it contains, not more fish, but Azurina herself. This was the introduction that led to a scene, probably adapted from the *scène dansante* in *Lida*, in which the naiad demands his bouquet in return for her gift of fishes, and becomes angry when Matteo refuses. He then begins to tease her, extending the bouquet towards her in exchange for a kiss. Azurina manages to seize it, and Matteo demands and receives his reward before she slips from his grasp and disappears.

The mood of the music then changed, and a jaunty melody announced the approach of a noisy crowd of villagers. Among them is Giannina, played by Zina Richard, another up-and-coming young ballerina who was half French, her father being the French dancer, Joseph Richard. The naiad is forgotten, and Matteo joins in the boisterous tarantella. The dancing is interrupted by the sound of a distant bell. Along with the villagers, the young couple kneel and pray for their happiness. As the villagers leave, the naiads re-emerge, but Azurina, realising the hopelessness of her passion, is filled with melancholy. The divertissement ended with Matteo continuing on his way, and Azurina disconsolately letting the bouquet fall from her hands.[1]

The summer months passed quickly, and as the days began to shorten, the preparations for the season's opening in October intensified. Jules must have been relishing the prospect of working with Carlotta again, and this time, unlike the earlier years in London, with no other ballerinas to be satisfied at the same time, *Giselle*, *Esmeralda* and *La Filleule des fées* were to be revived for her, and it was to be for her, of course, that he would be producing his new grand ballet. And to make life even more congenial, another old friend had appeared to lend a hand – Cesare Pugni.

It was no doubt at Jules' request that Pugni had been engaged as composer of ballet music. Guedeonov had agreed terms with him in London in July,

Jules Perrot

offering him a salary of 12,000 francs for just the one season of 1850–51. Pugni, who was never able to make ends meet, managed to insist on being paid an advance of 4,000 francs by the Russian Minister in London, Baron Brunnov, a few days before his departure, no doubt to provide for the family he was to leave behind. He was also given 600 francs for his travelling expenses.

His first tasks were minor ones – several small jobs of patching while Jules prepared the productions of *Giselle* and *Esmeralda* for Carlotta. Rehearsals usually took place in the Theatre School, and sometimes the pupils were allowed to watch. One of them was to retain a vivid memory of Jules at work, with Pugni sitting at his side and showing him the music he had composed for some additional number. As the old lady remembered the scene half a century later, Pugni would write a tune at the top of a sheet of manuscript which, if Jules did not care for it, was turned upside down to become another tune. This piece of musical legerdemain highly amused the pupils who were watching. They were also fascinated by the two violinists in attendance – Alexandre Lyadov and Sokolov, who when his services were not required, would put down his violin and quietly knit socks.

Jules was a popular figure with the children of the School, no doubt appearing much more approachable and *sympathique* than his predecessor, old Antoine Titus. They called him 'Handsome Jules Ivanovich,' having discovered his father's Christian name and given him the customary patronymic. Nor was the adjective entirely ironical, for although Jules was short of stature and, with his thick nose, certainly not good-looking in the ordinary sense, they thought he had fine eyes and an attractive mouth.

When the rehearsal began, so the old lady remembered, Jules and the régisseur Marcel might select a number of couples from the *coryphées* and the corps de ballet, and the choreographer would give the word for the violinists to begin. 'Then, as the music played, Perrot would sit, cross-legged, on the floor in the middle of the studio, pull out his snuff-box, take a sniff and listen to the music. No one makes a noise. Perrot listens to the passage, and already the idea is complete in his mind. Placing the chosen couples in position, he tells them to watch and demonstrates what he wants them to do. "First the *pas* on its own, and then all the others join in, this side beginning with the right foot, and that side with the left. Now begin." And the corps de ballet would perform the steps that have been demonstrated, and when everything is right, Perrot thanks them.'[2]

Carlotta had arrived in St. Petersburg in September, and after a month of rehearsals, she made her Russian début in her best-known rôle, Giselle. The Petersburg production of this ballet had in the first place been staged by Titus, who had based it on notes he had taken of the original production during a visit to Paris. In 1848, before Jules' arrival in St. Petersburg, Fanny Elssler had retouched this version and given it a personal gloss, inserting a *pas de trois* in the first act that may have been her own invention, and cutting the entrance of the peasants in the second act. Elssler's Russian appearances in the ballet were all given before Jules' arrival, so that it was only now, in 1850, when Carlotta joined him in St. Petersburg, that he had his first opportunity to revise the production. From then until he ceased his activity in Russia at the end of 1858, the preservation of Giselle was to be in his hands, but apparently he did not give it much attention and it was not performed often during those years.

After Carlotta's Russian début the ballet was reviewed by Rafail Zotov in the *Severnaya Pchela* as if only minor adjustments had been made to the choreography. Zotov directed his attention mainly to Carlotta's technique and style – to her wonderfully clean *entrechats,* her firmly executed pirouettes, and her graceful poses – and gave few details of the revisions Jules had made to the production. The most notable of these was the insertion of a new *pas de cinq* in the first act for Giselle and Albert with three supporting soloists (Anna Prikhunova, Anastasia Amosova and Maria Sokolova), which was remarkable for a sequence of picturesque groups and for its conclusion when Carlotta, resting on Johansson's knee, leant back in a bewitching pose. While assessing Carlotta, Zotov was careful to do justice to the ballerina, Elena Andreyanova, who had created the rôle of Giselle in Russia and now enjoyed the favour of the Director, Guedeonov. Thus he noted that in the second act, after Giselle has risen from her grave and wings have sprouted from her shoulders, Carlotta lacked the speed and attack that Andreyanova used to bring to the celebrated pirouettes. Carlotta's triumph, however, was not for a moment in doubt. The dances in which Giselle exerted her charms on Albert were ravishing, and it was only with regard to her miming that Zotov expressed reservations, wishing that she had conveyed 'more veiled sadness and compassion for her beloved, whom she is compelled, against her will, to exhaust unto death.'[3]

Before the year was out Carlotta appeared in three more rôles she had created – first Ysaure in *La Filleule des fées,* then Esmeralda, and finally the basket-maker's wife in *Le Diable à quatre.* Her success grew with each interpretation. Her Ysaure made a greater impression than her Giselle; her Esmeralda was seen as virtually a new creation, standing on its own merits for its natural simplicity and the absence of the heroic quality that had marked Elssler's interpretation; and then, in a lighter vein, came her Mazourka in *Le Diable à quatre.* This last work was produced for Carlotta's benefit on November 26th, presumably at her own request. The ballet had been created for her by Joseph Mazilier at the Paris Opéra in 1845, and Jules never considered it as an original work of his own, even though he apparently composed a considerable quantity of new choreography and Pugni made additions to Adolphe Adam's score. Among the scenes and dances that were produced or choreographed anew were the dancing lesson in Act I and the *pas de deux* in Act III, both performed by Jules and Carlotta, the *pas des nymphes,* and a final *galop-krakoviak,* again performed by Jules and Carlotta.

In the scene of the dancing lesson Jules took great pleasure in caricaturing the part he had himself played in Carlotta's artistic development. With his experience of broad comedy acquired on the popular stages of Paris, he gave a hilarious sketch of the dancing master. For the passage where he is teaching the basket-maker's wife to become a grand lady, he needed a violin. 'And whose violin? That of Vieuxtemps!' added an observer, leading one to imagine a piece of comic business in which the distinguished violinist, who was then playing in the Bolshoi orchestra, may have handed up an instrument from the orchestra pit – though surely not his own! – amid a burst of laughter.[4]

Jules' contract entitled him to present a new ballet at his benefit, which this year was fixed for February 11th, 1851. Knowledgeable balletomanes were already aware that he was working on a project that was being intriguingly referred to as *La Guerre des femmes* or *La Guerre des servantes*, but when the bills were posted up, they announced an entirely different title, *The Naiad and the Fisherman*. 'The balletomanes were bewildered,' reported an observer. 'Allowing for the freest translation, it was quite impossible to translate *La Guerre des servantes* as *The Naiad and the Fisherman*! Does this then mean some other ballet, and is the war not to take place? Did the balletmaster fail to show sufficient *casus belli*, and are we to see an idyll instead of a battle? Never mind, for in spite of the dashed hopes, the public besieged the box-office of the Bolshoi Theatre until it was closed and the "Sold Out" sign went up.'[5]

The mystery was only cleared up when the performance began, with Pugni himself conducting the orchestra. The projected *Guerre des servantes* had had to be temporarily put aside, and in its place Jules had hastily substituted the work based on *Ondine* of which fragments had been shown at Peterhof the previous summer. While it contained elements from the original London version, these were so few – only about one sixth of the total – and the narrative had been so much changed that it was virtually a new work. It even had a new title, *The Naiad and the Fisherman*. That Jules had seen fit to undertake such a drastic revision of a work that had been highly successful in its original form was surprising in itself. Perhaps he felt that *Ondine* belonged in a sense to Cerrito as much as to himself, since she had herself arranged several passages and might still wish to dance in it again – and even in St. Petersburg, if ever she were to be engaged there. Or perhaps it was done to satisfy Carlotta, who may have been reluctant to dance another ballerina's speciality, and who may also have insisted on the ballet ending with Ondine being united to Matteo instead of sacrificing herself for the happiness of Matteo and Giannina. The new ending was no less 'Romantic' in that it preserved the underlying idea of the quest for the infinite and the unattainable, expressed by a mortal-spirit relationship that must inevitably culminate in sacrifice. But by being drawn out into three acts, with intervals in between, the cohesion that had distinguished the original *Ondine*, which had been played through without a break, was lost. The conditions in St. Petersburg, where a grand ballet had to fill a complete evening, were not wholly beneficial to Jules, who had a natural tendency to be profuse, and this reworking of *Ondine* was very much a case in point. While containing some interesting and effective innovations, the flow of the narrative and its dramatic impact had certainly been substantially weakened in the process.

The ballet opened in much the same way as *Ondine*, with the naiad rising out of the sea on a shell and confessing her love to Matteo, who is only prevented from leaping into the water after her by the fortuitous arrival of some of his friends. When the fisherfolk reassemble, Matteo seems to forget his strange adventure. From this point on the scene was completely reworked. After a *Furlana* by the soloists and the corps de ballet, Jules and Andreyanova, who played Giannina, danced a *barcarolle*. This was followed by a *grand pas scénique*, an impressively complex dance scene – 'the height of sculptural beauty.'[6] as one critic described it – that brought the act to a close. It opened with two couples competing for an oar garlanded with flowers and wreaths. Each of the young fishermen, played by Johansson and Marius Petipa, was given a variation, that of the latter being performed to a cornet solo by Bœhm. They were partnered with Maria Sokolova and Anastasia Amosova. Suddenly another dancer appears in their midst 'like Schiller's "girl from an unknown land,"'[7] a young peasant girl carrying a coral basket of flowers. Each of the men pay court to her, but her attention has fixed on Matteo, who to Giannina's annoyance cannot keep his eyes off her.

This dance was remarkable both for the way in which it appeared to fit naturally into the unfolding of the action, and also for the ingenious use of a prop – the oar – in the choreography. Some ten years later Fyodor Dostoyevsky called it to mind when reviewing the annual exhibition of the Imperial Academy of Arts. Observing how stage-like was the arrangement of the figures in a certain painting, he reflected on the skill with which a choreographer could produce an illusion of naturalness by means that were overtly artificial. 'Nature is distorted,' he wrote, 'but the public is so bedazzled by the stage effect that it accepts it without question. For an example of this attitude, consider the patience of the audience and its refusal to hiss even an ordinary oar when it makes an appearance in a ballet. It is true, this oar is not quite an ordinary one: it is considerably heavier than those used for rowing and it has, in its centre, a sort of projection or notch. A dancer playing the part of a fisherman appears a few times with the oar so as to give this familiar object a degree of conventional stage naturalness. So far the public does not know the purpose of the notch and why the poor dancer has been burdened with an oar that is neither graceful nor ordinary. Later this is made clear. A series of general dances follows, with the usual sort of groupings, and the

Jules Perrot

male dancer, after making various turns and expressing his feelings with his legs, places himself in the centre of the stage, with one end of the oar on the ground and the other resting on his shoulder. This could not be done more smoothly, gently or gracefully. The principal ballerina, the prima donna, then appears, and after performing various graceful turns and bends with the support of another male dancer, places one leg in the wretched notch in the oar and stretches the other as if it were the out-stretched hand of a statue of a falconer. Then she slowly rotates her leg. The stalwart male dancer keeps the oar steady, trying to show that it is no effort, and that it even gives him great pleasure. To keep her balance, the ballerina supports herself with one hand on his shoulder and the fingers of the other touching the fingers of the other male dancer, who helped her climb on to the notch in the oar and perform this feat. Then the ballerina springs down to the ground with the lightness of thistledown blown by "the breath of Aeolus" and continues to express her feelings with her legs. The public is not at all put out; on the contrary, it is delighted and clamours for this feat to be repeated. So once again the male dancer burdens his shoulder with a hundred pounds or so of thistledown-light ballerina, and the leg that reminded us of a falconer's hand once again solemnly and slowly makes its circle to the strains of some quite charming music. Clearly, stage naturalness is not natural. And it follows that what is beautiful on the stage is not the same as what is beautiful in nature and in other arts, such as literature.'[8]

Finally, as if realising that she has Matteo in her power, the peasant girl, who is none other than Ondine in human form, runs off and leaps into the water. Believing she is a mortal like everyone else, the fisherfolk are aghast. As they rush towards the shore, she reappears, visible now only to Matteo, in her naiad form.

The mime scene that followed, when Ondine appears in the hut to torment Giannina and Matteo's mother with her mischievous pranks, was little changed, being played, as in London, in the front of the stage while, behind the cloth, scene-shifters were preparing the set for the vision scene. Here the unrivalled resources of the Bolshoi Theatre came into their own to produce the illusion of water flooding into the hut and gently rocking the bed as Ondine and her companions dance seductively around the fisherman and lull him to sleep. The walls of the hut disappear, and the bed turns into Matteo's boat, seen drifting towards an island shore, guided by Ondine and her companions, who are seen swimming in the water beneath it.

The island is the playground of the naiads, who display their fascinating attractions in an ensemble dance, the *pas des naiades*. Still bemused, Matteo wakes and prepares his net to make his catch of fish. There followed the scene Jules had devised for the Peterhof gala, beginning with the song of the nightingale that reminds him of Giannina, then continuing with Ondine's appearance, caught in his net, and the scene in which Matteo teases her with the bouquet. Carlotta was here in her element, getting 'very prettily angry' and 'making fascinating pouts.'[9] In the final moments of this scene Jules wove into Ondine's dances numerous effects to emphasise the visionary effect on Matteo's mind of her supernatural condition, presenting her in various forms, 'flitting through the rushes, swinging on the boughs of trees, floating about him like a shadow, and appearing like a playful fish sporting in the water. He pursues her and strives to seize her, but light as a feather, she runs into the water, and he is left alone with his yearning.'[10] He comes to his senses, remembers Giannina, and pulling in his net, discovers that the naiads have filled it with an extraordinary catch of fish.*

The fourth scene was based on the scene that had originally preceded the famous shadow dance, which was replaced by an equally striking highlight, a dance scene whose underlying theme, as well as Carlotta's opening pose, had been suggested to Jules by Léopold Robert's painting of a ragged guitarist entertaining a group of fishermen by the sea shore.** The curtain had risen to show the fisherfolk celebrating the wedding of Matteo and Giannina. The happy couple are completely absorbed with one another when, suddenly, the naiad rises out of a well and appears to Matteo. He turns away, and in an attempt to banish the vision from his mind, joins a group of his friends who are drinking outside a tavern. Giannina is on the point of following him when her attention is caught by the sound of a mandolin. She glances back to discover the source of this haunting serenade and sees a handsome young fisherman sitting on the edge of the well. His song – for which Pugni had written a delightful *barcarolle* for two clarinets with pizzicato accompaniment – draws her irresistibly to his side. She is completely captivated, and when he declares his love, she lets him take her ring and kiss her hand. Wonderfully played by

---

* The earliest printed scenario of *The Naiad and the Fisherman* appears to be that published in Moscow in 1861 for Théodore's reproduction of the ballet, originally staged there in 1857. In the absence of an earlier scenario, it has been necessary to rely on the descriptions which the critics wrote in 1851 to reconstruct the action as it was given at the première that year. Some of these descriptions, particularly that published in the magazine *Panteon*, were quite detailed, and it is clear that in the 1850s Jules reworked parts of the action. Assuming that the action in Théodore's revival followed that of Jules' definitive version, Jules added a new ending to the scene – a mime passage between Ondine and the naiad queen, Hydrola, in which Ondine is left distraught at Matteo's departure and determines to follow him in spite of Hydrola's warning that if she persists in her passion, she will wither and die like a rose.

** Jules had no doubt seen this painting, entitled *L'Improvisateur*, when it was hanging in the Louvre. When the 1848 Revolution broke out, it was in the Château de Neuilly, where it was largely destroyed by fire. The centre fragment, showing the musician sitting on a rock with a boy listening to him at his side, was saved and is now in the Musée de Neuchâtel.

Jules Perrot

Carlotta and Andreyanova, this dance scene was 'such a beautiful combination of mime, grace, feeling and joy that it was difficult to take one's eyes off it.'[11] Glancing towards them, Matteo cannot believe his eyes. In a fury of jealousy he throws himself at the stranger, only to discover, just before he vanishes, that it is the naiad in another form. Realising that Giannina, like himself, has succumbed to a supernatural force, he gently chides her for flirting, while she in turn reproves him for frivolity. They are soon reconciled, and the dancing continues with a *pas de cinq*, containing a beautiful adagio and an effective solo for Prikhunova.

The fifth scene was similar to the second half of the Peterhof fragment, opening with the entrance of the revelling pilgrims that echoed Léopold Robert's painting, *Le Retour du pèlerinage à la Madonne de l'Arc*, featuring the tarantella with the interruption for the evening prayers, when Ondine reappears to Matteo. But in place of the earlier conclusion, in which Ondine realised the hopelessness of her passion, Jules arranged a more dramatic *dénouement*. In desperation Ondine upbraids Matteo for his cruel indifference and rushes into the water. Horrified, and unable to resist, he follows her and drowns.

The apotheosis, splendidly conceived by Roller in a colour scheme of blue and silver, depicted the underwater court of the Queen of the Naiads. The lovelorn naiad and the drowned fisherman kneel before the Queen, who blesses their union, while poor Giannina is seen vainly striving to reach her lover, prevented by a wall of water that rises out of the fountains.

At the time he was preparing *The Naiad and the Fisherman* for Carlotta, Jules was also dutifully putting together a novelty for the benefit of Elena Andreyanova on February 18th. It appeared in the programme under the title of *Les Tribulations d'un maître de ballet*, a two-scene divertissement whose title suggests that it might have been akin to his original conception of what emerged in London six years before as *Le Jugement de Pâris*, although the content of the dances was quite different. Performed only twice, it was a hurriedly arranged *pièce de circonstance* that the choreographer was happy to allow to be forgotten. It was 'no more than an after-piece, in the style of Italian *lazzi*,' and 'did not please the public.'[12] The first scene was 'a sort of improvised farce in which a number of back-stage pranks are represented – funny enough to make you laugh when you see it the second time.' Then, between the two scenes, Jules, as the exasperated ballet-master, had a scene to himself, presumably in front of the curtain, conducting the orchestra and delivering himself of some voluble Italian! Then the curtain rose again for the second scene which, far from being a revival of the *Pas des Déesses* from *Le Jugement de Pâris*, was 'nothing more than a divertissement of old dances.'[13]

The season ended a few weeks later, leaving the public and the authorities well pleased with *The Naiad and the Fisherman*. In the summer Jules was commanded to produce fragments from it at Peterhof to celebrate the nameday of the Queen of Württemburg, formerly the Grand Duchess Olga, on

July 23rd. Without doubt, this was to be the most fantastic of all the fêtes staged at Peterhof in Imperial times. In addition to the illuminations there were military choruses and gypsy choirs. The ballet was given, as in the previous year, on a special stage almost level with the water in front of the Ozerka pavilion. The naiads made their appearance sailing across the lake in small shell-shaped boats. A full moon shone down upon the scene, reflecting in the water and sparkling on the spangles and jewels sewn on the ballet skirts of the naiads. Beyond the lake, in the distance, the village of Babigon was illuminated so that the outline of every cottage could be seen. When the ballet was over, the Tsar, the Imperial family and their guests drove in open carriages to the sea-front villa of Monplaisir for supper, while the great crowd of visitors from the city and the surrounding countryside lingered to savour the illuminations before making their way home. For many it would be a very long day; the steamers were still arriving back in St. Petersburg, completely full, well into the following afternoon.

The occasion was to be marked by the publication of a lithograph, drawn from a painting by A. Charlemagne, showing the scene where Matteo has discovered his net to be filled with fishes and is kneeling in amazement before Ondine, who is dancing before him. His boat is moored in the background, and behind a group of naiads is a grotto that presumably served as an entrance to the stage. The fisherman is certainly Jules himself, but whether Ondine was danced on this occasion by Carlotta or by one of the Russian ballerinas, history does not record.*

Imperfect though it was, *The Naiad and the Fisherman* drew from the critic, Fyodor Koni, a remarkable analysis of the qualities of the master choreographer that were so clearly evident in Jules Perrot. 'Ever since that magician Perrot has been with us,' he wrote, 'ballet has seen the return of the golden age of the poetic Didelot . . . It is only by examining such artists as this that we can fully understand what it is that goes to make up a ballet-master, or rather a choreographer, for Perrot is not merely a ballet-master who produces dances, but a choreographer in the sense of a creator and interpreter of marvellous images that spring forth, one after the other, like shadowy pictures from his imagination. First of all, such a man must be a poet, a true-born poet, not a versifier or a story-teller pouring out rhymes and jumbled events, but a man in whose mind a poetic idea is born aesthetically fully formed, like

---

* The original lithograph gives the date incorrectly as July 4th, 1851 (July 16th in the new style), but a cruder engraving published in A.F. Geyrot's *Pictures of Peterhof* corrects this, as can be verified by the fact that it was the Grand Duchess Olga's name-day. It is intriguing to note that the artist has based the two principal figures in the picture on a French lithograph showing Jules and Carlotta in Act II of *La Filleule des fées*. In the engraving in Geyrot's book the poses of the central figures are slightly different, and there is one more naiad – twelve instead of eleven – in the background.

Jules Perrot

Minerva rising out of the stormy sea in all his beauty and strength. Secondly, he must be a painter – of living pictures full of movement and naturalness, not always in sharp focus, but changing with the first breath of passion or at the first whim of fantasy, yet always remaining faithful to the underlying idea and the original intention. He must also be a sculptor, enhancing the human figure with a plastic charm, devising curving forms and beautiful poses, correctly placed. And last of all, he must also be a ballet-master, a man who can animate painting and sculpture, design and plastic relief with the vitality of thought, passion, mimetic expression and dance – in short, who can invest the images of his fantasy with living human forms. He presents his characters and scenes, not through the medium of verbal expression, but through the expression of harmony, for everything moves to the measure and beat of the music – and for that he must also be a musician. So a good choreographer is fundamentally an artist endowed by nature not with one talent but with five, combining every natural quality as well as being fully receptive to inspiration and fantasy. That is why the best choreographers appear only once in every century, and why there have been no more than five or six since ballet began. Perrot most certainly belongs to their number.

'Perrot's new ballet is distinguished by these qualities, as have been all the earlier works he has composed. Like them, it is an elegant work containing a wealth of fantasy, interwoven with scenes of everyday life, and an abundance of local colour, and it is given a graceful performance. And as in his other ballets, the dances are neither commonplace nor lacking in purpose, but possess a mimetic meaning that combines the expression of feelings with grace of movement.'[14]

* * *

Jules' marriage had of course given his life a new orientation. Far from wishing to take his young wife and baby daughter Marie, who was born that summer on May 13th, back to France, he decided to settle in St. Petersburg. This gave him a longer perspective in his negotiations for a new contract with the Imperial Theatres, but for some reason these negotiations were delayed and did not culminate in agreement until the 1851–52 season was well under way.

The new contract was for the residue of that season and for the three succeeding seasons, or more precisely from December 13th, 1851, to March 13th, 1855. The terms were not significantly different from those of his previous contract: a salary of 10,000 silver roubles a year, but now with the addition of a '*feu*' or bonus of 25 roubles for every performance in which he took part, and three benefits during the course of the engagement, at each of which a première of a grand ballet was to be given.[15]

Although, as before, he was engaged in the multiple capacity of dancer, mime and *maître de ballet*, it was clear from the special conditions that his usefulness was now primarily as a choreographer. He was obliged to submit two ballet scenarios for approval every year, one by March 27th and the other by

July 27th. Subject to making any changes the Direction might require, he was to produce these ballets so that the first would be ready by the end of October and the second not later than January 13th. A penalty of 50 roubles a day was to be witheld from his salary in the event of delay due to his default, illness being excepted if certified by one of the theatre doctors. The Direction also had the right to require him to revive old ballets, and to produce short ballets, divertissements and *pas* either for ordinary occasions or for benefits, so long as this did not interfere with the production of the season's two main ballets. It was also expressly provided that he was to be entitled to leave of absence after the end of the season, but he was to be back in St. Petersburg on June 27th under pain of a penalty.

Whatever it was that caused the delay in concluding the contract — whether Jules had been ill or injured, or whether difficulties had arisen in the course of the negotiations — the Direction must have eventually realised that he might not be available for the 1851–52 season. The consequent engagement of Joseph Mazilier as choreographer would have been a wise precautionary measure, but it may also have been a warning to Jules, if he had been to blame for the delay, that he was not regarded as indispensable. It certainly seems to have been a last-minute decision, for Mazilier left unfinished an important ballet he was preparing for the Paris Opéra, *Vert-Vert*, which Saint-Léon was to complete for its première there in November, and by the time he arrived in St. Petersburg, it was too late for him to create anything wholly new. The season had in fact opened with *The Naiad and the Fisherman*, and it was not until three weeks later, on the occasion of Carlotta's benefit early in November, that his first work was ready, a new version of the nine-year-old *La Jolie Fille de Gand*. This was followed, for his own benefit in January, by *Vert-Vert*. Neither production was particularly successful. It required no great perception to realise that he was not in the same class as Jules, who resumed his duties towards the end of the season, for the time being, however, as a performer only, but content in the knowledge that the following season he would be in full charge.

With Carlotta, his muse of old, once again engaged as star ballerina for the 1852–53 season — at a considerably increased salary of 12,500 silver roubles — and Pugni re-engaged too, after a year's interval, Jules had an added incentive in planning the two new ballets that were required of him under his new contract. The first of these, for which he had managed to obtain approval after a protracted wrangle with the censorship department, was a remarkable work on any count. The scenario had been submitted some two years before under the title *Wlastha, ou la Guerre des servantes*, but had finally emerged, apparently considerably altered, with a Russian title translatable as *The War of the Women, or the Amazons of the Ninth Century*. As the change in title indicated, there were certain aspects of the plot that had touched some sensitive spots in the security apparatus of Nicholas I's Russia. Revealingly, the copy of the final version of the scenario that was left in the censor's files was endorsed with a note in the hand of Dubbelt, the notorious Chief of Police who was also personally responsible for the political section known as the Third Department: 'If this had been a play, it would not have been passed.'[16]

Those responsible for the security of the state were always watchful for signs of revolt against authority. Russia had escaped the wave of revolution that had swept across Europe in 1848, but the dangers to authoritarian rule and the existing structure of society were still very real a few years later. Dealing as it did so explicitly with the theme of revolt, Jules' original scenario invited rejection. This first version was summarised by the censors as follows: 'A young duke who owns a large castle and estate and spends his time philandering with his companions, abducts a young servant-girl from her family and her fiancé. The sorceress Vlasta plans vengeance against him and all men who abuse womenfolk, and to that end assembles an army of beautiful women with which she besieges the duke's castle, defeats him and, furthermore, strips him of his ducal dignity, replacing him by the fiancé who has merited it by freeing his sweetheart.'[17]

The censorship could hardly fail to have been disturbed by the underlying theme of rebellion, and to overcome this a formula was devised by which the duke was presented as a usurper and the girl's fiancé as the dispossessed heir. Jules may have made no secret of his liberal views, but he was in no sense an opponent of the régime, and in his official position with the Imperial Theatres, which he had struggled to obtain and preserve, he can hardly have intended his scenario to be taken as a political statement. Like any self-respecting author, he may, of course, have resented being required to make changes for reasons that were not artistic, and the time it took for the ballet to be approved suggests that he resisted these demands. But eventually the changes were made, and the villain of the piece was transformed into a usurper and the hero was acclaimed at the end as the ruler by right of birth, instead of being placed on the throne by the victorious, but nonetheless rebellious, amazons, which in the prevailing ideology of hereditary autocracy would have presented him as the usurper.

There was another original feature in the story, which passed unnoticed at the time; it presented women as a discontented class in a male-dominated society. Such an attitude had hardly yet impinged itself on the social consciousness, although the legend of the amazons of Greek mythology and the exploits of such historical figures as Joan of Arc had stirred imaginations down the centuries. The amazon theme had even inspired a number of ballets, in one of which, Filippo Taglioni's *La Révolte au sérail*, Jules had enjoyed a sensational success as the partner of Marie Taglioni. But compared with all amazon ballets that had gone before, his new ballet, even after the censor had put his heavy hands on it, contained one most significant difference – his amazons not only went into battle, but they emerged victorious.

Almost certainly, the seed from which the ballet grew was implanted, as so often with Jules' works, by a theatrical experience. In the summer of 1837, when he was in Paris with time on his hands, the Porte-Saint-Martin presented a melodrama entitled *La Guerre des servantes*, about a women's uprising led by a serving woman who had been betrayed in love by the King of Bohemia.* The part of the heroine, Vasla, had been played by Mlle George. Although the detail of the plot was pure invention, the revolt itself was an historical fact. Its leader had been a woman by the name of Vlaska, who commanded the female bodyguard of Libussa, the consort of the first Prince of Bohemia, Přemysl. After Libussa's death Vlaska led her warriors into the mountains and established a régime in which men were reduced to cultivating the land and menial duties, and were forbidden to ride or bear arms. Vlaska's rebellion lasted for eight years before she was killed in a decisive battle with the army of Přemysl.**

It proved impossible to have the ballet ready by the time stipulated in Jules' new contract, and once again Carlotta made her first appearance of the season in *The Naiad and the Fisherman*. However, the public only had to wait a few weeks, for *The War of the Women* was announced on November 23rd, 1852. It proved to be well worth waiting for, and was to be given no less than twenty-one times before the season ended in March.

The curtain rose, after the overture, to show a village in the countryside of Bohemia, with the roofs and spires of Prague seen in the distance. Anyone familiar with Spanish literature might have recognised that Jules had based his first act closely on the first act of Lope de Vega's drama, *Fuente Ovejuna*.*** Skilfully he introduced all his leading characters in the first few minutes of the action. A crowd of servant-girls assemble by a village well, and among them is Vlaida, immediately recognisable as the heroine, being played by Carlotta. In a charactistic *pas d'action*, she is trying to shake off the persistent attentions of Kolo, the duke's jester, a character that Jules assumed for himself. Then, out of one of the houses there appears Ulrich, a personable young man who, being recognised as Johansson, was clearly marked out as the hero. He is deep in thought, absorbed by dim memories of being snatched from his home as a child, but the villagers dispel his pensive mood by bearing him off to take part in a marksmanship contest. A fanfare of hunting horns announce the arrival, with his attendants, of Mitsislas, who has seized the dukedom of Bohemia by force – a rôle that Jules entrusted to Marius Petipa. Discovering

---

* By Théaulon, Alboize and Harel, first performed on August 24th, 1837.
** In the course of his reading, Jules may have had his attention drawn to V. Hanka's edition of Dalimil's *Chronika Česká*, published in Prague in 1851, in which the story of Vlaska's revolt was told, but the original idea must have come to him in 1850, if not earlier.
*** *The Sheep Well, c. 1614.*

from Vlaida the reason for her displeasure, he casts an angry look at Kolo, who falls to his knees to beg forgiveness. But the Duke too has taken a fancy to Vlaida, and he tries to win her favour by offering her a ring. She manages to slip away, and the Duke, left alone with his companions, brags that in one way or another she will be his. Ulrich then returns with the men of the village, being acclaimed by them as the champion of the archery contest, and soon everyone is dancing a rousing *pas d'ensemble, La Slavone*, to celebrate his forthcoming marriage to Vlaida. Kolo, having slipped away from his master, returns to flirt with the girls, and the festivities culminate in a *pas de deux* in waltz time by Carlotta and Johansson.

But suddenly the convivial atmosphere is broken by the appearance of the sorceress Vlasta, authoritatively played by Elena Andreyanova. When Vlaida timidly enquires the reason for her arrival, Vlasta announces that she has come to protect her against the evil schemings of Mitsislas. Ulrich swears that no one will part him from his beloved Vlaida, to which Vlasta replies with a hollow laugh. Once upon a time Mitsislas swore everlasting love to her, she tells them, but he abandoned her and she has sworn to have her revenge. The wedding guests are embarrassed when she calls on them to join her. Turning to the girls, she tells them to take up the bows that the men have piled on the ground. All of them – save Vlaida, who is laughing at such apparent frivolity – obey her, and in a *pas des arcs* begin practising with these weapons. Vlaida continues to resist Vlasta's appeal, saying that the only weapon she knows is the spindle, and that a woman's rôle is to love and be loved, not to instil fear. With an imperious gesture Vlasta foretells that she will join her in the end.

The men, whose first reaction was one of amused surprise, decide that this comedy has gone on long enough and take back their weapons, forcing the girls to resume dancing. Vlaida helps them disarm her companions, as does Kolo, who has been mischievously enjoying the scene. At this point Jules inserted a *pas de deux* for Carlotta and Johansson. Vlasta stands sternly aloof from the resumed gaiety.

But once again the light-hearted mood of the villagers is interrupted. The duke's guards burst upon the scene and order Vlaida to accompany them to the castle. Ulrich and her father call on the menfolk to protect Vlaida, but they faint-heartedly sidle off, and the two men are seized and taken away. Only the women remain, shattered by this brutal display of force. Vlasta curses the cowardly menfolk. 'Forget those craven peasants who cannot defend us,' she cries, and the young women willingly place themselves under her command.

Roller's set for the second act, a splendid hall in the duke's castle, earned him an ovation before the action could begin. When the applause had died down, Vlasta appears, stealthily looking about her. Familiar objects awaken memories of her lost happiness, but her thirst for vengeance is unquenched. A servant helps to admit her amazons, and at Vlasta's request brings them rich clothing. There is to be a banquet that evening, and the amazons hide as the duke and his guests approach. The festivities begin. Kolo is in specially high spirits, amusing everyone by his pranks. Mitsislas cynically proposes a toast to the lake duke, whose statue stands at the side. Jestingly, Kolo offers a goblet to the statue, which to his amazement takes it and drains it. Kolo scurries away in fright, much to the amusement of the guests, none of whom have seen the statue move. At this moment Vlaida is brought in. The duke has arranged the banquet in her honour, but her only thought is to return to her home and her sweetheart. The duke does not conceal his annoyance. Reduced to tears, Vlaida is forced to take part in the festivities, a situation which Jules skilfully developed in a *pas scénique*, expressing her inner misery and the malicious glee with which Kolo, who has now recovered from his fright, echoes his master and amuses the company at the girl's expense.

The stage then darkens, and Vlasta appears, her features concealed by a veil. She announces that she has come to join in the festivities, and that at a sign from her a thousand lights will blaze and a bevy of beautiful girls will come flying to the duke's arms. She is as good as her word. By an ingenious use of Schönbein gun-cotton, the light blazed up with extraordinary brilliance, and the amazons, now dressed in ravishing costumes, are discerned arranged in a group where before there had been no one. Roller was given another call, although the credit for this effect was really due to the fire master, Shisko. Vlasta now tells Vlaida to do as she bids if she wishes to be rescued. After a *grand pas de séduction* by the disguised amazon girls, the scene moves to its finale. The dancing becomes more and more animated, developing into a *grande bacchanale* featuring all the solists of the company – 'the best part of the ballet' in the judgment of one critic.[18] Vlaida recovers her spirits, and the beauty of her movements and her unsophisticated graces stir the duke's passion more than ever. He turns to Vlasta in delight. She asks him to give her his hand to receive the reward for his hospitality. Unsuspectingly he does so, whereupon Vlasta fiercely accuses him and tells him she has come to free his innocent victim. She throws back her veil. The male guests realise that the girls have been relieving them of their arms. The duke springs at Vlasta with a dagger, but the statue moves again, restraining him in its stony grip and snatching the weapon from his hand.

The third act opens with a scene in a forest, where Mitsislas is discovered in a pensive mood. Unobserved, Vlasta pours a sleeping draught into his glass, and both he and Kolo, who has taken a surreptitious sip, fall into a deep sleep. Mitsislas dreams that Ulrich has come to assert his claim to the dukedom, and realises that he is the rightful heir. His first thoughts, on waking, are to send Kolo to the prison with an order to murder his prisoner, and to exhort his soldiers to exterminate the amazons.

The scene changes to the amazon camp, with Mitsislas's castle seen perched on a rocky summit in the background. It is night, sentries stand guard, and the silence is broken only by an occasional trumpet call. Vlasta emerges from her tent, expressing hatred for the usurper. At daybreak the amazon warriors parade before her. All are present except Vlaida, who eventually arrives, late and troubled by a dream that her father and her sweetheart had been put to death. Vlasta tells her to remain calm. The amazons, no less than eighty of them, perform a *grande danse pyrrhique* with their weapons, and Vlaida takes her place at their head, brandishing her sword and shield as if warding off a swarm of arrows. At that moment Kolo is brought on, having been taken prisoner. The amazons taunt him for being a coward, and he begs for mercy. They discover that he is carrying an authority from Mitsislas to be admitted to the prison to murder Ulrich. Vlasta orders him to continue on his way to the prison in the charge of Vlaida, and when there, to drug the guards and liberate the two prisoners. No sooner have they left on this mission than the battle begins. Victory seems in the amazons' grasp when a small enemy detachment infiltrates their lines and captures Vlasta.

The fourth and last act opens in the prison. Kolo and Vlaida, now disguised as a young soldier, arrive. Vlaida produces the duke's order, and while the slow-witted gaoler tries to decipher it, manages to alert Ulrich of their presence. Kolo laughs at the gaoler's ignorance, and reads out the order himself, adding that his companion has been charged with carrying out the murder. The gaoler and the other guards treat Vlaida as one of themselves, slapping her roughly on the shoulder and inviting her to join them in a game of dice. They begin to carouse, and while Vlaida distracts them with some lively character dances, Kolo mixes the sleeping draught in their wine. Satisfying herself that they are sound asleep, Vlaida takes their keys and frees Ulrich. She gives expression to her joy in a *pas seul, La Délivrance*, before they make their escape – only just in time, for the captain of the guard then arrives to discover that his prisoner has gone.

This scene of 'Liberation,' played in the front of the stage, leads into the final scene, 'The Assault of the Fortress.' The cloth representing the prison interior rises to reveal the full stage. Mitsislas, who is now besieged in his castle, has Vlasta brought before him. He offers to spare her if she will order her amazons to lay down their arms and return to their tasks in the home. She scornfully refuses. She is prepared to die, she tells him; the hour of vengeance is at hand, and her soul will give life to the statue of the rightful duke. Mitsislas is shaken by this prophesy, but his spirits revive when Kolo appears. The jester tells Mitsislas that he has fulfilled his mission, while at the same time conveying to Vlasta that Ulrich is alive and safe. Mitsislas orders Vlasta to be taken back to her cell. The assault begins, and the amazons breach the walls with their battering rams and pour into the castle. Mitsislas fights desperately, but suddenly the statue comes to life and grasps him once more. A trap opens in the stage, and the usurper is swallowed up in the earth. The women are victorious. Vlasta and her amazons hail Ulrich as their rightful ruler, and the ballet ends with scenes of general rejoicing.

The scale of the production was magnificent almost beyond belief, even by St. Petersburg standards, and the choreography and the performance matched it for brilliance. In working for Carlotta, Jules seemed doubly inspired, and he gave her a rôle that must have stretched her powers to the furthest limit. Rafail Zotov in the *Severnaya Pchela* awarded her 'the palm of perfection . . . She was amazingly good . . . To perform eight fatiguing dances without hardly leaving the stage in the course of four hours might have seemed more than human strength could bear, but in all that time Carlotta Grisi gave not the slightest hint of fatigue.'[19]

The critics dealt with the choreography and the manner in which Jules translated the narrative into action on the stage with disappointing brevity, but his scenario was full of pretexts for the type of dance scene at which he was so adept, illustrating and advancing the story. It also required an unusual degree of participation from the corps de ballet, particularly in the first act. Apart from the *pas des arcs* with the bows, which was probably a set dance, there were passages of action in which the villagers were presented, not as an aimless crowd decorating the background, but as a group of individuals playing an essential and integral part in the drama. The ballet opened with servant-girls coming in from every side to assemble by the well. A happy, carefree mood was thus established at the start, but this was brutally broken when the duke's men seize the heroine's father and fiancé. At this point a conflict erupted between the sexes that was central to the theme, the menfolk being unwilling to make an active protest, and the women seething with indignation at such weakness to the point of revolt. All this was dramatically enacted by the corps de ballet in a scene that was intended to be crucial to an understanding of the motive for the women's revolt. Apart from the very novelty of the idea behind this scene, such prominent use of the corps de ballet in the development of the plot was a bold and imaginative stroke for which there were no precedents outside Jules' own ballets.

However, a number of inconsistencies in the action were noticed which may have resulted from the tinkering with the scenario to comply with the censor's requirements. Fyodor Koni thought that Vlasta's magic powers were superfluous, since they were employed only once, to effect the sudden illumination of the banquet hall, and were apparently of no avail to save her from capture in battle. He also found the dream scene, inserted to stress the point that Mitsislas is a usurper, and the intervention of the statue to be unnecessary.[20]

These, however, were minor blemishes that did not detract from the overall effect of the production, which Zotov hailed as Jules' 'finest ballet.'[21] 'The dances,' added Koni, 'were so good that it was impossible to take one's eyes off them. Each group, taken individually, was a work of art. The martial evolutions of the women were graphically and very skilfully composed, particularly since it was not easy to make them interesting when we have seen

Jules Perrot

such evolutions before in *La Révolte au sérail* and *Catarina*.'[22] But the overriding impression was of Jules' mastery in 'disposing masses of dancers,' the 'picturesque' quality of his groups and scenes, and his use of Bohemian dance forms, particularly the mazurka, to give an idea of the location of the action.[23]

Pugni had been no less inspired by the powerful and original drama, and had produced an excellently orchestrated score that was 'full of felicitous melodies and rich in motifs.'[24]

*   *   *

Jules was obliged under his contract to produce another grand ballet that season, with the right for the first performance to be given at his benefit. This duly took place on February 24th, 1853, when the curtain rose on *Gazelda, or the Gypsies*, a grand ballet in two acts and four scenes, preceded by a prologue.

This time he had given the censor no problems,* presenting an unobjectionable scenario based on a formula frequently used at that time – that of a stolen child who is identified and restored to its rightful station. Themes of this sort generally enabled a hero of an apparently modest station to marry a high-born heroine, or vice versa, a union that otherwise would have been unacceptable to the class-structured society of that time, and particularly to the aristocratic or fashionable nucleus of an opera house audience. For his new work Jules had chosen a gypsy background, casting himself as a member of the tribe, not born into it but adopted after being stolen as a child, who – unlike Gringoire in *Esmeralda* and Kolo in *The War of the Women* – wins his girl at the end. It was unusual for him, with his undistinguished features, to assume a character belonging to the aristocratic class, but since the disclosure of his identity came in the last act, he was able to feel comfortable in the part and even to add a touch of comedy at the point when he had to begin taking on the manners of a high-born young man.

The clue to the source of the narrative lay in the hero's name of Zingaro, which a Parisian audience would have instantly recognised as having strayed from the opera-ballet, *Zingaro*, in which Jules had presented Carlotta for her Paris début in 1840. Common to both works, too, was the underlying theme of a child stolen by gypsies during the sack of a castle and brought up by them in ignorance of her origin. The idea of a brutal abduction of an innocent child may have been sown, subconsciously, in Jules' mind by tales he had heard from his parents of the excesses of the French Revolution. To the audience such an idea could also have had a more topical relevance, suggesting dangers against which society was still fearfully watchful after the scares of

---

* The printed scenario contains a note to the effect that the censor's approval was given on October 26th (old style), 1862, but this is clearly a misprint for 1852.

Carlotta's Indian Summer

1848. But such sinister associations were no doubt far from the thoughts of the first-night audience, who looked forward only to being entertained and transported into a world of make-believe, and who would have seen the gypsies not as a menace but as an evocation of Romantic *couleur locale*.

When the curtain rose, the gypsies were on stage in full force, encamped in a forest and awaiting their evening meal at the end of the day. Their leader is Narda, a woman of feeling and honour, imperiously played by Andreyanova, but among them are some who are disaffected and follow the rascally Hayraddin. The whole tribe seems to burst into joy at the arrival of Zingaro and Gazelda – Jules and Carlotta – who have been brought up by the gypsies since childhood and are held in special affection. A short *pas seul* for Carlotta established the happy carefree nature of Gazelda's character. She and Zingaro have spent the day in the nearby town, where her beauty attracted the attention of a young man who gave her a medallion. Innocently she now offers this to Narda, who questions her and seems relieved to learn that she did not respond to the young man's words of love. The sound of a hunting horn is then heard through the trees, and the gypsies disperse. Soon Zingaro reappears, carrying a young woman (Alexandra Ryukhina) whom he has just saved after her horse had run wild with fright. She is Emma, daughter of the Baroness Rosenthal, and when she revives, she offers him a purse. He refuses to accept it, saying that his reward lies in his heart. This tender scene is interrupted by Hayraddin and his cronies, who are intent on robbing the girl. Zingaro springs to her defence, and is only saved from being overpowered by the appearance of Narda. Zingaro has been injured in the struggle, and Narda's refusal to allow Gazelda to tend his wounds betrays the depth of her own feelings towards him. While Gazelda calms Emma's fears, Narda demands to know the cause of the fight. Zingaro remains silent, but Emma accuses the gypsies who have tried to rob her. Narda orders them to be punished, but Zingaro intercedes in their favour. Two other members of the hunt then arrive, Emma's cousin Rodolf and her fiancé, Karl, played by Johansson and Marius Petipa respectively. Gazelda recognises Rodolf as the admirer who gave her the medallion, and Narda is pleased to see how they are attracted to one another, for she cannot help being jealous of Gazelda for her relationship with Zingaro. Gazelda insists on returning the medallion, but Rodolf gives it to Emma, from whom Gazelda cannot refuse it as a thank offering for her rescue by Zingaro. Meanwhile, Karl's roving eye has settled on Gazelda, whose indifference merely intensifies his passion for her. The rest of the hunting party, which now includes Emma's mother, the Baroness, who has arrived in a sedan chair, then gathers. The gypsies serve them a repast and entertain them with dancing.

These dances were skilfully woven into the action that brought this scene to an end. They began with a *pas caractéristique* for the whole company, led by Jules and Carlotta. This was followed by a character dance, *La Fantasia*, performed by Andreyanova with Jules as her partner. The choreographic climax was then reached in the final number of this divertissement, a *pas scénique* entitled *La Bonnaventura*, in which Gazelda presumably displayed her fortune-telling powers to the hunting party. In this expressive dance Carlotta was accompanied by four soloists (Anna Prikhunova, Nadezhda Amosova, Alexandra Makarova and Maria Snetkova), and was joined by Johansson and Petipa in their rôles of Rodolf and Karl, who no doubt competed for her favour in seeking to have their fortunes told. When the dancing is over, the Baroness announces her wish to take Zingaro into her household in gratitude for rescuing her daughter. When he refuses to be separated from Gazelda, Emma asks that Gazelda should be engaged too, as her companion. Narda, however, will not allow Zingaro to leave, and the two young people are separated. Their leave-taking is heart-rending, and Zingaro is inconsolable. With a great outburst of emotion, he falls senseless at Narda's feet, and the curtain fell with her looking down at him with a mixture of tenderness and pity.

The scene changes to the Baroness's castle, where Gazelda has become Emma's inseparable companion. The opening action was recorded in detail by Jules himself, writing his notes in pencil above the music of his violin rehearsal score.

> Emma is sitting pensively in the armchair, Gazelda on a little stool at her feet. After two bars Gazelda asks her friend why she is so pensive. Emma says she is thinking of nothing. 'Ah, you are hiding something, give me your hand.' Emma does so. 'I see in your hand,' says Gazelda, 'that your thoughts are far away.' Emma rises, troubled. Gazelda goes to pick up the woollen shawl that the mother has let fall. Now it is Gazelda's turn to be pensive. She is very happy in this household, but alas, she misses her former companions and her liberty. Emma is quick to bring her back to earth, saying that she has caught her at it too. 'Yes,' says Gazelda. 'I was thinking of my friend Zingaro, your rescuer.' Emma is deeply moved. 'Come, let us not think of that and begin our lesson.' At the end of these little *lazzi* of Gazelda, she sits down. Deportment lesson. Emma demonstrates how to walk and curtsy. Gazelda gets up to imitate her, but does so only with a graceful awkwardness. Emma repeats it. The gypsy girl does better the second time. Emma and the fan. She hands the fan to Gazelda, who has difficulty in opening it. She succeeds. The young lady then explains its purpose. 'When a handsome young man comes up to pay you a compliment,' she says, 'you conceal your face. Sit down and try.' Emma pretends to be a young man approaching Gazelda and complimenting her on her beauty. She thanks him with a curtsy instead of appearing demure. Her teacher takes back the fan and starts again.[25]

The lesson develops into a dancing class, as Emma shows Gazelda how to play a guitar and dance the bolero. Rodolf then enters. He has fallen in love with Gazelda, and asks his aunt, the Baroness, for permission to marry her. The Baroness indignantly refuses. Gazelda feels humiliated, and being plagued by Karl's unwelcome advances, determines to leave the castle. When she is alone with her misery, she suddenly sees Zingaro appear at the window. His presence revives her spirits, and she leaves to put on her gypsy costume. While she is out of the room, Emma chances to enter. She recognises Zingaro, and finds him a sympathetic listener to her tale of unhappiness at being about to marry a man she does not love. A servant comes to remind her that it is time to prepare for the marriage contract ceremony. She leaves, and when Gazelda rejoins Zingaro, the two of them prepare to escape through the window. They are interrupted, however, by the appearance of Karl. Gazelda runs into an adjoining room to avoid his advances, and Zingaro angrily bars his way. The tempers of the two men only cool when the family and their guests are heard approaching for the signing ceremony. Zingaro withdraws into the other room, but bursts out, with Gazelda, at the moment when Karl is taking up his pen. Faced with their accusations, Karl storms out. The Baroness restrains Rodolf from challenging him to a duel, and orders Gazelda to leave the castle.

The second act opened to show the gypsies encamped in the courtyard of a ruined castle, near a wayside inn. Hayraddin enters with a casket, which he hides in a corner. Then Narda appears, worried because she cannot find Zingaro. Hayraddin takes this opportunity of declaring that he loves her, adding that he possesses a secret that will make it impossible for the love of Zingaro and Gazelda to be fulfilled. He then describes how, many years before, when the castle was burnt by the gypsies, he carried away a casket full of treasure which he buried under an oak tree. This he now offers to share with her, but she refuses and threatens to hand him over to justice. She is on the point of pressing him to reveal his secret when Zingaro returns with Gazelda. Everyone rejoices at the girl's return except Narda, who reproaches Zingaro for abducting Gazelda from her benefactress. Zingaro tells Narda what has happened, and that he and Gazelda are going to leave the tribe. At this point Jules inserted another character dance for Andreyanova, *La Zinganka*, in which 'he skilfully introduced steps from Russian folk dances.'[26] Once again he served as her partner, and backing them were the same soloists who had appeared earlier in *La Bonnaventura*, with the addition of Maria Surovshchikova. Then, finally, Carlotta appeared with eight soloists to perform a long and complex number, *La Cosmopolitana*, which was intended to convey the nomadic nature of gypsy life by introducing a succession of national dances – Moorish, Tyrolese, Spanish and English.

The gypsies are then joined by a group of young men who pay court to them and show particular interest in Gazelda. Among them, shrouded in a cloak, is Karl, who tries unsuccessfully to bribe Narda to assist him in abducting the girl. Hayraddin, on the other hand, has no scruples about accepting his money. Karl's men invite the gypsies into the inn. In the deserted courtyard Karl plans the abduction, unaware that he is being observed by Rodolf, who has followed his beloved Gazelda. Gazelda is lured out of the inn by Hayraddin and seized. In an attempt to save her, Rodolf attacks Karl, mortally wounds him, and dashes off in pursuit. At that moment Zingaro comes out of the inn, stumbles over Karl's body, and is discovered sprawled on the ground. He is assumed to be the assailant, and is arrested in spite of his protestations of innocence. Narda begs Hayraddin to reveal his secret, and under threat of exposure, he reveals that neither Zingaro nor Gazelda are children of the tribe. The gypsies prepare to depart, and Hayraddin goes to recover his casket.

Gazelda is carried off to Karl's castle, where the story reached its *dénouement* in a scene that unfolded rapidly. The old servant who has been put in charge of her is puzzled by her likeness to a portrait of a child hanging on the wall. The sound of a gunshot is heard. The old man runs out to see what has happened, and Zingaro climbs in through the window. Telling Gazelda how he has escaped from his guards, he hides in a closet. The guards then arrive in pursuit, but finding no one but Gazelda, leave to continue their search elsewhere. Zingaro comes out of hiding, but catching sight of a portrait of a little boy, falls to the floor in a faint. The guards return and find him, and he is arrested. Following them come Narda, Karl, who is carried in on a stretcher, and Rodolf. Narda protests that Zingaro is innocent, but no one believes her until Hayraddin is brought in under arrest, and the mystery is solved. The villainous gypsy had been caught in the act of digging up the casket, which bears the arms of the former owner of the castle. The old servant recognises it. Narda then discloses that not only had Hayraddin stolen it, but that he had also abducted the two children. Zingaro and Gazelda are recognised as the long-lost pair, whose portraits hang on the wall. Rodolf joyfully welcomes Zingaro as his childhood friend, and unhesitatingly gives consent to his marrying Emma. The two men seem to relive their early memories as they leap around each other in delight, but Zingaro suddenly stops short, realising his newly discovered rank, and with a comically assumed dignity orders Hayraddin to be taken away. The announcement of Karl's death casts a shadow over this joyful *dénouement*, but Zingaro wants everyone to be happy. Only one person stands aloof from the general rejoicing – Narda, who knowing that life has nothing left for her now that she has lost Zingaro, leaves with a broken heart.

The backcloth of the room then rose to reveal one of Roller's happiest creations, a lushly foliaged 'garden, illuminated by a multitude of green lamps, with a fountain playing in the centre.'[26] In this setting a divertissement was performed in celebration of the two approaching marriages. It contained, of course, a *grand pas de deux* for Carlotta and Johansson, with variations for them both, and concluded with a *grand pas des fleurs* by the *danseuses* of the corps de ballet, headed by the principal soloists.

Pugni had, as usual, contributed to the success. His score was richly orches-

The influence of Léopold Robert on Jules Perrot.

Above Le Retour du pèlerinage à la Madonne de l'Arc. *Musée du Louvre, Paris.*

Right *Fragment from* L'Improvisateur napolitain. *Musée d'art et d'histoire, Neuchâtel.*

Mephistopheles, as seen by three nineteenth-century artists.

Above *Moritz Retzsch (1828), Mephistopheles in the garden, observing Faust's wooing of Marguerite.*

Bottom left *Eugène Delacroix (1828), Mephistopheles and Faust fleeing after Valentine's death.*

Bottom right *Tony Johannot (1847), Mephistopheles gloating over Marguerite's final rejection of Faust.*

Above Les Eléments, *with, left to right, Carolina Rosati, Carlotta Grisi and Fanny Cerrito* (Illustrated London News, *July 10th, 1847*)

Below Les Quatre Saisons, *with Fanny Cerrito on the pedestal, as Spring, and Carlotta Grisi appearing, sickle in hand, as Summer to contest her supremacy.* (Illustrated London News, *June 24th, 1848*)

Above The Dance of the Seven Deadly Sins in Faust (Ronzani's revival, Vienna 1851), with Fanny Elssler as Marguerite and Gustave Carey as Mephistopheles. Lithograph by J. Sürch from a drawing by Cajetan. (Bild zur Wiener allgemeinen Theaterzeitung, No. 28) Theatersammlung, Öst. Nationalbibliotek, Vienna.

Left Amalia Ferraris as Odette in Odetta (Ronzani's revival, Vienna 1852). Lithograph by Eduard Kaiser. Raccolta di Stampe, Castello Sforzesco, Milan.

Esmeralda *in St. Petersburg*. **Above** *Scene 1: Esmeralda giving water to Quasimodo, with Phoebus and the watch looking on. Drawing by D. Timmo.*

Below *Fanny Elssler and Christian Johansson in the* pas de deux *in Scene 3, with Jules Perrot, as Gringoire, looking on at the right. Drawing by Adolphe Charlemagne. Bakhrushin Museum, Moscow.*

Esmeralda *in St. Petersburg.* **Above left** *Claude Frollo surprising Esmeralda and Phoebus in the cabaret.* **Above right** *Quasimodo as the Fools' Pope.*

Below *Esmeralda spurning Frollo's offer to save her, as Gringoire covers his face in despair. Drawings by Adolphe Charlemagne. Bakhrushin Museum, Moscow.*

Left *Carlotta Grisi in her first costume for Act I of* La Filleule des fées. *Lithograph by Alexandre Lacauchie. Bibliothèque de l'Opéra, Paris.*

Bottom left *Carlotta Grisi in her fairy costume for Act II of* La Filleule des fées. *Lithograph by Auguste Lagrange. Collection of Gilberte Cournand.*

Bottom right *Jules Perrot as Alain in* La Filleule des fées. *(Galerie Dramatique, No. 476) Bibliothèque de l'Opéra, Paris.*

La Filleule des fées, *Act II.* **Above**: *Ysaure, newly admitted into the fairy band, dancing before the entranced Alain. Bibliothèque de l'Opéra, Paris.*

Below *The* pas des fées. *Lithograph by Victor Coindre. Bibliothèque Nationale, Paris.*

Above Carlotta Grisi and Jules Perrot in La Filleule des fées, Act II. Bibliothèque de l'Opéra, Paris.

Below Jules Perrot in rehearsal, with Cesare Pugni sitting at his side. Drawing by Adolphe Charlemagne. Leningrad Theatre Museum.

Left *Carlotta Grisi as the naiad disguised as a fisherman in* The Naiad and the Fisherman. *Leningrad Theatre Museum.*

Below *An open-air performance of fragments from* The Naiad and the Fisherman *at Peterhof in 1851, with Carlotta Grisi and Jules Perrot. Lithograph by Borell from a drawing by Adolphe Charlemagne. Collection of Edwin Binney 3rd.*

Right Nadezhda Bogdanova in Esmeralda. Lithograph by Louis Veit from a photograph by R. Marovsky. (Eduard Bloch, Album der Bühnen-Costüme, vol. I, plate 18).

Bottom left Katrine Friedberg in Catarina. Lithograph by Louis Veit from a photograph by R. Marovsky. (Eduard Bloch, Album der Bühnen-Costüme, vol. II, plate 42) Collection of Stanislav Buzek and Otto Zajik.

Bottom right Jules Perrot in his first years in Russia. Leningrad Theatre Museum.

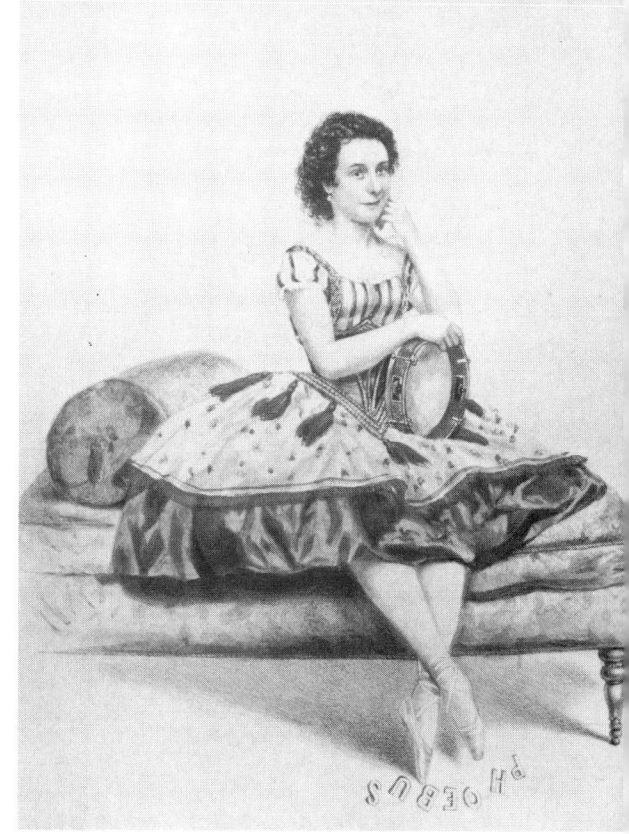

Top left *Praskovia Lebedeva as Marguerite in* Faust, *a rôle she played after Jules Perrot's retirement.*

Top right *Gabriele Yella. Photograph by Pesme. Theatre Museum, London.*

Bottom left *Louis and Zina Mérante. Photograph by Disdéri. Collection of the author.*

Bottom right *Martha Muravieva in Giselle. Photograph by Disdéri. Bibliothèque de l'Opéra, Paris.*

Above *Jules Perrot in rehearsal attire during his years in St. Petersburg.*

Right *Jules Perrot in morning dress, 1856. Bibliothèque de l'Opéra, Paris.*

Left *A page from Jules Perrot's annotated copy of Noverre's Letters. Bibliothèque de l'Opéra, Paris.*

Left *Carlotta Grisi in her Esmeralda costume during her last season, in Warsaw 1853, with her partner, Aleksander Tarnowski. Muzeum Teatralnego, Warsaw.*

Right *Edgar Degas*, La Classe de danse de M. Perrot. *Musée du Louvre, Paris.*

Above *Edgar Degas,* La Classe de danse, adage. *Glasgow Art Gallery.*

Left *Edgar Degas,* Le Danseur Perrot, assis. *University of California, Berkeley Foundation.*

trated, and contained solos for many of the distinguished instrumentalists who played in the orchestra. The music for *La Cosmopolitana*, however, may have been interpolated for in the manuscript full score, it bears the signature 'Dietsch,' suggesting that Jules had it arranged by the principal chorus master of the Paris Opéra.

Seeing the repertory enriched by two successful new ballets and the company adorned by Carlotta Grisi, who seemed to have lost none of her stamina and artistry, the balletomanes might have been excused for believing that their future enjoyment was secure for some years to come. But clouds were beginning to gather. The public had been distracted that season by the magnetic appeal of those stars of opera, Mario and Giulia Grisi, and the decline in the box-office receipts of ballet performances indicated that the popularity of ballet was waning. Rafail Zotov perceived the same forces at work in St. Petersburg that had much more dramatically affected ballet in London. 'Is it possible,' he asked, 'that poetry has no place in our materialistic and speculative century? In former times the public seemed to consist only of young people aged from seventeen to seventy, but today they seem to be all old men from seventy to seventeen. They now look on the most beautiful dancing as if they were listening to a lecture on philosophy, and only clap or shout out of courtesy or habit. It is strange but true! At first, being cast in an ancient mould, I was about to put it down to the fact that the public were conversant with the ballets of Didelot and wanted historical, dramatic and aesthetic subjects, but no! I am convinced that the public has not the slightest interest in the content of a ballet, and only wants dances, groups and spectacle.'[27]

These observations must have been disappointing enough to Jules, but more shattering still must have been Carlotta's decision not to return to St. Petersburg for the following season. It was generally known that she had been disappointed by the cooling of the public's enthusiasm for her.[28] To leave the St. Petersburg balletomanes with a final memory, she gave her services for Andreyanova's benefit on March 6th, appearing first in a *pas de deux* with Jules in an extract from Didelot's *Hungarian Hut*, and then taking the rôle of Cupid in a reconstruction of an even older ballet, *Cupid and Psyche*, which in its original form had been produced sixty years before, in the reign of Catherine the Great.* No doubt Andreyanova, whose evening it was, played the part of Psyche. By her side Carlotta must have appeared as enchanting as always, and when, little more than a week later, on March 15th, she appeared

---

* It is possible that some of the choreography of *The Hungarian Hut* was remembered, for this ballet, created in 1817, had been performed as recently as 1836–37, but Le Picq's *Cupid and Psyche* must have been long forgotten. It had originally been produced at the Hermitage Theatre, with music by Vincente Martin y Soler, on the occasion of the wedding of the Grand Duke Alexander (later Alexander I) in 1793, and had not been performed since 1798.

Jules Perrot

before the curtain in her dazzling costume for the last scene of *Gazelda*, it must have still seemed inconceivable that she was really making her final bow before the St. Petersburg public.

She had not quite reached the end of her road, for later that year she was to dance in Warsaw, ending her career there by portraying three of Jules' immortal heroines – Giselle, Esmeralda and, for her a new rôle, Catarina. With her retirement, at the age of only thirty-four, a flame must have died in Jules' heart. He had lost his muse, and no doubt he knew, deep down, that he would never find another.

17

The Emergence of Russian Talent

The question had to be faced: how was one to survive the St. Petersburg winter without a ballerina of exotic origin and international renown to stir one's enthusiasm on ballet nights? As the summer of 1853 drew to a close this appalling thought obsessed the minds of the balletomanes, who had been so spoilt in recent years that they could hardly imagine living without a Fanny Elssler or a Carlotta Grisi to enchant them. For Jules the decision of the Direction not to engage a successor of similar status must have come as a disappointment too, for throughout his career he had been accustomed to creating for the greatest dancers of his day, and the two ballerinas from Paris who had been engaged—on the strength, it appeared, of inexpert advice—for the opening of the 1853–54 season, Louise Fleury and Rosa Guiraud, were hardly likely to stretch his imagination. It was not surprising, therefore, that though his contract obliged him to produce a new ballet early in the season it was decided to allow them to try their wings in ballets that were already in the repertory.

Physically these two dancers were of very different types. Louise Fleury, to whom the honour fell of opening the season in *Catarina*, was strikingly tall and slender, with an aura of calm beauty that had undoubtedly impressed Jules ten years before, when she played the Queen of the Wilis in *Giselle* in London. The other new dancer, Rosa Guiraud, a lady of stockier build, was presented to the Petersburg public a week later in *Esmeralda*. Some unfortunately effusive publicity comparing her with Taglioni and Elssler deceived neither critics nor public, and her début passed almost unnoticed. A week after that, the two ladies were presented together in *Le Diable à quatre*, Guiraud of the unrefined figure in the rôle of the basket-makers's wife and Fleury well cast as the Countess. Jules did his best to arouse the public's interest in them. Just a week later, in the same programme, Fleury appeared in Elssler's rôle in *Le Délire d'un peintre*, and Guiraud in *La Fille mal gardée*, and later still, in November, Fleury took over the rôle of the naiad in *The Naiad and the Fisherman*, but the public could not be roused out of its indifference.

Fortunately for the balletomanes the Direction was to redeem this sorry

Jules Perrot

state of affairs by producing another ballerina whose reputation was no less obscure, but in whom Jules was to discover promising qualities. The newcomer came from Vienna, and her name was Gabriele Yella. Her origin was unusual for a dancer, for – as was no secret – she was a member of the aristocratic family of von Schliemann, though for stage purposes she had discreetly shed that name for that of Yella. Her upbringing and education had been very different from that of the ordinary professional dancer. Exceptionally intelligent, she possessed a remarkable aptitude for languages, which she displayed by mastering Russian during the three seasons she was to spend in St. Petersburg.

Her arrival in Russia was not attended by any flourish of publicity, for until then her career had been undistinguished. Her only previous engagement of note had been in Paris in the previous autumn, when she had appeared at the Théâtre Lyrique in Saint-Léon's opera-ballet, *Le Danseur du roi*. Now to be the object of an offer from the Imperial Theatres was like a dream come true; for the first time in her career, she was to be rewarded with an adequate remuneration.

Grateful for this opportunity, she set to work with exemplary zeal. Jules perceived at once the keen intelligence at work behind her somewhat plain exterior. For her début on January 19th, 1854, he coached her in Carlotta's rôle in *Gazelda*, in which she made a favourable impression, revealing an unusual fund of energy on which she drew to the full in the multiple *pas de caractère, La Cosmopolitana*, and especially in its final section, the English dance, which she was made to repeat. Jules also permitted her to insert, at the end of the ballet, the striking dance which Saint-Léon had arranged for her in *Le Danseur du roi, La Tauromachie*, but this 'mime portrayal of a bull fight'[1] did not create the impression that the advance publicity had led the public to expect.

Not surprisingly, it was Yella whom Jules selected for the leading rôle in his only new production of the season, a revision of his *Faust* which he had originally conceived six years before in Milan as a vehicle for the many-faceted talent of Fanny Elssler. Elssler had played the rôle of Marguerite only once before the 1848 Revolution caused the Scala to shut its doors, and when performances were resumed a few weeks later, Jules had to cut it drastically for Augusta Maywood, who took over the part. Three years later, in Vienna, Elssler had played the rôle again, but that production had been staged, not by Jules but by his 'reproducer,' Domenico Ronzani. Yella, who was Viennese, may have seen Elssler's Marguerite, and may even have danced in the corps de ballet, but it was from Jules that she learnt and studied the rôle in depth.

Without doubt the rôle of Marguerite, the pivot on which the ballet turned, was dramatically the most taxing that Jules was ever to conceive, comprising two sharply contrasting aspects. First, there was the Marguerite of real life, the innocent girl who finds herself buffeted by strange forces she can neither comprehend nor withstand, and is faced with irresistible temptation which brings in its wake so much horror, from the deaths of Valentine and her mother to the drowning of her own child. Interwoven with this complex character study was her fiendish double that Mephistopheles conjures up to bend Faust to his will. The interchanging of these two Marguerites was a far more intricate conception than the double rôle of Odette/Odile in *Swan Lake* was to be, in that it demanded contrasts of mood in close juxtaposition to one another throughout the ballet. For dramatic possibilities the rôle had no equal in ballet, and it said much for Yella's natural aptitude and quick intelligence that she accepted the challenge of following in Elssler's footsteps and gave such a poetic and convincing portrayal. The critic D. Zhiltsov singled her out for special praise in a long article devoted to Russian-born ballerinas, declaring that her 'wonderful miming as Marguerite attained the highest degree of dramatic perfection.'[2]

During the six years that had passed since the original production Jules' thoughts must have often strayed back to *Faust*, for the subject had obsessed him ever since he had seen Lemaître's Mephistopheles, and the time must now have seemed ripe to produce a definitive version with all the resources of the Imperial Theatres at his command. Interestingly he made no material change in his original scenario, and indeed restored it to the form he originally intended. It was probably expanded here and there, and Panizza's score adjusted and extended by Pugni, whose name was coupled with his on the playbill. Furthermore, since it was to occupy a full evening's programme, it could be presented in three acts, which enabled Jules to restore the scene of Faust's banquet to its proper position. The first act now consisted of the opening scene in the laboratory, the sequence of visions (Marguerite in her room, the graveyard, and the transformation to the grounds of an enchanted castle), and the scene in the town square; the second act opened with the banquet, or as it was now called, the ball scene; and the third act contained the double scene of Marguerite's room and the garden, the vision of Marguerite in prison, and a dazzling scene that began in the mountains, developed into the Underworld for the witches' sabbath, and closed with the apotheosis. In all, no less than thirteen new sets were painted and constructed. Roller designed the graveyard and the magic castle of the first act, and the ball scene, and was responsible for the mechanical effects, and the other scenes were credited to no less than five artists – Isakov, Serkov, Wagner, Bastide and Shanguine.

Thus restored to accord with the choreographer's original intentions, and produced with great attention to detail, it was to remain in the St. Petersburg repertory for more than twenty years and to achieve what was then the very rare distinction of a hundred performances. The celebrated critic A.N. Serov was to compare it advantageously with Gounod's well-known opera, stating unequivocally that Perrot displayed a greater understanding of Gœthe's poem than did Gounod's librettists, and that his work was therefore a truer

Jules Perrot

interpretation.[3] The extent of Jules' achievement was fully recognised, and an article in the magazine *Panteon* declared that the ballet had 'emerged victorious from the difficult struggle' of doing justice to Gœthe's masterpiece, and was 'the finest creation of the unquenchable Perrot.'[4] Certainly, as a ballet it was immeasurably superior to anything that Jules' successor Saint-Léon was to produce, and in 1863 a Petersburg critic cited it in support of a theory that a ballet scenario, like any other theatrical piece, must be based on an underlying idea which is never lost from view and must be developed faithfully within prescribed limits. Looking back on Jules' ten years' work in St. Petersburg, this critic too declared *Faust* to be his finest ballet, 'indeed a model, because the idea permeating the whole work is expressed to a greater or lesser degree in every dance, and also because miming is given its proper place, without any fear of boring some of the eternally young old-timers of the pit.'[5]

Yella responded intelligently to Jules' coaching and gave a touching portrayal of Marguerite. Her miming was 'expressive and very dramatic, particularly in the prison scene,' and her dancing remarkable for its 'lightness, intrepidity and facility.'[6] She must have derived added inspiration from having the choreographer on the stage by her side. The rôle of Mephistopheles appealed particularly to Jules' imagination, and brought into play 'the full brilliance of his superior miming.'[7] His interpretation was subtle and so unexaggerated that one critic did not think he was 'very much like the Devil, although it was impossible not to admire his dexterity, even if he did not inspire terror.'[8]

What more than anything else distinguished the St. Petersburg revival of *Faust* from the original Milan production was the strength of the company. The Italians, of course, were natural mimes, but in St. Petersburg Jules found equally impressive interpreters who acted with force, elegance and a sure understanding of character. For the rôle of Faust he turned to Marius Petipa, whose impassioned rendering added greatly to the overall effect of the drama, while Christian Johansson imparted his noble bearing to the smaller part of Valentine. In the sphere of pure dancing the Russian company was at that time revealing exceptional strength in the young talent that was coming to the fore, and Jules was inspired to revise the choreography to give opportunities to two of the younger ballerinas, Maria Surovshchikova, who was singled out from the pupils of the Ballet School to play the rôle of Marguerite's friend Martha, and whose provocative beauty seemed to attract every opera glass in the house, and Anna Prikhunova.

The drama of Faust's passion and its fateful consequences was played out in a skilfully and judiciously interlocked combination of dance and mime, every *pas* being motivated in some way by the course of the narrative, in some instances illustrating or stressing a situation, and in others actually carrying the action along a stage further. The first dance number, the *grand pas ballabile d'action* in the first act, presented the ballerina with an immediate opportunity to display both her technique and her power of interpretation. It came at the moment when Mephistopheles must overcome Faust's reluctance to sign away his soul. He sends Faust into a drowsy slumber, and conjures up from his evil domain a creature in Marguerite's form. Accompanied by a bevy of beautiful girls, this seductive siren appears to Faust in an enchanted garden. At this point one critic was shocked to see Faust himself joining in the dancing, but this made good theatrical sense as he was swept into the dance to be tempted by the false Marguerite into drinking an infernal potion. Far from being a conventional number for the corps de ballet, this dance was designed with movements that expressively suggested the evil behind their seductive appeal. Zotov described it as 'true Gœthe poetry. Behind every pose and group one is unfailingly conscious of something infernal, corrupt, and yet fascinating.'[9]

The *pas de fascination* in the scene in the town square, where Faust provokes Mephistopheles into displaying his infernal powers, and Marguerite, Martha and four of their friends (played by the graceful Prikhunova, Anastasia Amosova, Alexandra Makarova and Maria Snetkova) are subjected to his demonic influence, was fully appreciated for its skilful arrangement and dramatic impact. In the words of one critic, 'it displayed the wonderful imagination and the vast talent' of the choreographer,[10] and Zotov saw it as another perceptive transposition of Gœthe's thought into dance. Mephistopheles was the central figure, the pivot, of this *pas*, as he forced his dominant will on the girls. His commands were conveyed by movements that were echoed at his bidding. The motivation of this *pas* was never lost to view. 'The whole of this charming and artistic scene,' concluded Zotov, 'seemed to be animated by an evil purpose. The resistance of the girls to the last ounce of their strength in the face of an inexorable will was wonderfully thought out and composed.'[11] This was followed by the *grande valse*, a more conventional number danced by four couples and fourteen girls.

Considered from the viewpoints of pure choreographic invention and the ballerina's rôle, the highlight of the ballet was incontestably the dance of the Seven Deadly Sins that came at the end of the scene in Marguerite's bedroom. Although it was a device of the choreographer, it fitted quite naturally into the main scheme of the ballet. Zotov considered it 'a profound and beautiful conception based on an understanding of the human heart and the implacable principles of morality.'[12] It enabled the choreographer to disclose a weakness in Marguerite's character, as her simple innocence was tested by the temptation of material wealth at the discovery of the casket of jewels left in her bedroom. Yielding to a human impulse, she allows her imagination to wander and is soon carried away into a daydream in which she finds herself beset by one deadly sin after another. The effect of this extraordinary dance scene, in which 'all the expressions of inner passion and fantasy were realised on the stage,'[13] was greatly enhanced by the participation, as the sins, of seven of

Jules Perrot

the most promising young soloists: Maria Snetkova (Sloth), Anastasia Amosova (Envy), Alexandra Makarova (Pride), Ekaterina Parkacheva (Wrath), Alexandra Ryukhina (Avarice), Nadezhda Amosova (Gluttony) and Anna Prikhunova (Luxury). Jules served each of them according to her individual style and personality, and it was hard to see how anyone could resist them. By common consent the most alluring was Prikhunova, who made a memorable entrance as Luxury, wearing a splendid costume and bearing a dove in her hands. Her miming was remarkable for its variety of expression and its elegant finish, while in her dancing she displayed 'extraordinary delicacy, fluency of movement and lightness'[14] and performed movements of technical complexity as if difficulties did not exist for her.

The ball scene, which to some seemed over-long, contained a wealth of dancing, including a *danse de caractère d'ensemble*, a gypsy number which one critic described as 'a sort of krakoviak mazurka,' danced by thirty-six *danseuses* of the corps de ballet, half of them in male costume, and culminating with 'a remarkable *pas d'action*' which involved Faust and Mephistopheles. This was studded with a sequence of six brilliant variations in which Jules took advantage once again of the talent within the company and did not overlook the men. Nadezhda Amosova came forward to dance the first variation; then came Marius Petipa; next was Surovshchikova to dance a mazurka; after her, Prikhunova, 'ethereally light and with a flowing graceful passion, was carried away in a whirlwind of magical dancing'[15] in a dazzling *valse de la folie*; next, Johansson was given the male dancer's place of honour; and the final variation was awarded to Yella.*

With all these stunningly inventive dances, each fitting so naturally into the general framework, *Faust* bore the stamp of its creator more deeply than any of his other works. It was the boldest of conceptions. Jules had 'done all he could not to depart from the supreme work [of Gœthe], and went some way to achieving this.'[16] 'Anyone who can read knows, of course, the great work of Gœthe's genius,' observed Zotov. 'This dark fantasy is entirely suitable for ballet, and M. Perrot, supreme artist that he is, has been successful in adapting it. Many dramas have been made from it, but they have all been involuntarily diminished by the narrow framework of dramatic convention. People come into the theatre with a preconceived idea of Gœthe's work, and are not going to be satisfied with feeble, cold and colourless fragments from his poem, adapted for the stage. German mysticism can be understood through reading, but appears monstrous when presented in the theatre. It is really only in ballet that magic, fascination and forces of mystery are made bearable. In this sort of work there is no dialogue, but instead scenes set to movement, and

---

* Jules' violin rehearsal score includes, at the beginning of this scene, a *pas de deux* for Zina Richard and Eugène Huguet, but this was probably added subsequently, since it is not listed among the dances in the bill for the first performance.

thus it has been possible to reproduce all the poetry of Gœthe's work in pictorial fashion ... Perrot ... has devised magnificent choreographic scenes from *Faust*, he has reproduced all the beauties of the work, and as a result of a profound study of the mind of the German poet, he has fully understood his highly moral side ... M. Perrot has preserved Gœthe's basic plot perfectly and in its entirety. The ballet even possesses a certain individual quality of its own; it is a work of genius imbued with the spirit of Gœthe.'[17]

* * *

By now Jules had settled comfortably into Russian life, his family being increased in 1853 by a second daughter, who was given the name Alexandrine. He was a long way from his native land, but he no doubt found St. Petersburg less alien than its distance from Paris might have suggested, for the Imperial court and the aristocracy spoke French as their second language. Furthermore, there were several of his countrymen already ensconced in the ranks of the Imperial ballet — Frédéric, the Petipas, Eugène Huguet, Marcel the régisseur — while the young ballerina, Zina Richard, possessed a French father, whom Jules had probably known when a young man in Paris.

With his interest in history, which had revealed itself so tellingly in some of his most effective ballets, Jules must have been a keen follower of international affairs, which he could not help viewing, so to speak, through a Russian lens, as he discussed them with his family and their Petersburg friends and read, as one assumes he did, the French-language newspaper, the *Journal de Saint-Pétersbourg*. In his position as ballet-master, and as an employee of the Imperial household, he was much closer to the political fulcrum than he had ever been in Paris, London, Vienna or Milan, and his blood must have quickened at the thought of the extraordinary concentration of power that lay in the hands of the autocratic Tsar. But affairs were now moving in a direction that was to strain his loyalties as a Frenchman, and for nearly two years he was to find himself a captive of circumstances that must have produced stresses both in his domestic and his professional life. The Crimean War was to affect him hardly less intimately than if he had been a participant on the battlefield.

The dispute that had caused the conflict in the first place had been building up for a long time before war was declared. On the surface it seemed to be about the protection of Christian holy places, but the real causes went much deeper and were rooted in the shifting balance of power and the vacuum that was appearing in the Middle East as the influence of the Turkish Empire, which abutted on Russia's southern frontier, waned. Tsar Nicholas, his imagination gripped by the glittering prize of Constantinople, had sent an army to occupy the principalities of Moldavia and Wallachia on the west coast of the Black Sea. The Turks had not weakly submitted, as he had expected, and Britain and France, taking alarm at Russia's expansionist

Jules Perrot

policy, had reacted vigorously. The situation reached a point where neither side would give way, and towards the end of March 1854, a few weeks after the St. Petersburg theatre season had ended, Britain and France declared war on Russia.

There was no question of Jules visiting Paris that summer, which he must have spent agonising over how the situation might develop. The war cast a shadow over the new season, which opened in September 1854, for the British and French armies had landed in the Crimea and won their first victory on Russian soil at the River Alma. It was to be a disappointing season. Gabriele Yella was the only foreign ballerina, and the only novelty was to be an insignificant little ballet called *Marcobomba*. But there were compensations too. At a time when public opinion, stirred by patriot sentiment generated by the war, was particularly favourable to the encouragement of anything Russian, a clutch of promising young ballerinas, home-born and home-trained, were given the opportunity to spread their wings. For some time the Russian public had been aware of the exceptional quality of its corps de ballet, and now, at a time of national peril, it was heartened by the discovery that if its generals could not dislodge the enemy armies, its ballet was producing dancers who could stand comparison with Europe's best.

Yella was naturally given the honour of opening the season, appearing successively in *Catarina*, *Gazelda* and *Faust*, but in October these young Russian ballerinas began to take over the stage. First Zina Richard assumed the rôle of Vlaida in *The War of the Women*, following this with another of Carlotta's rôles, the naiad in *The Naiad and the Fisherman*. Equally well served was Anna Prikhunova, whose artless, mischievous Lise in *La Fille mal gardée* distracted the public from the grave news of the Battle of Balaclava, and who later, at Jules' side, played the Countess in *Le Diable à quatre* and made a sensitive Giannina in *The Naiad and the Fisherman*. No less encouraging was the progress of Maria Surovshchikova, now married to Marius Petipa, who was tested in the dramatic rôle of Esmeralda. While these fledgling ballerinas were trying out their wings, a favourite from an earlier generation, Tatiana Smirnova, now concealed on the playbills under her married name of Mme Nevakhovitch, returned to give a few performances of the first act of *La Sylphide*. Thus, thanks not only to the circumstances of war but equally to the strong repertory of ballets that Jules had built up over the past few seasons, the message that Russia's ballet could be self-sufficient was forcefully brought home to the public and Direction alike. In a period of military and political disappointment, the ballet had provided a welcome modicum of self-respect and hope.

Jules did not neglect the claims of Yella, who to all outward purposes was the star of the season. While no important new ballet was to be produced for her, she chose to appear in the first act of *Giselle* at her benefit on January 30th, 1855, coached no doubt by the ballet-master himself. In the light of its

The Emergence of Russian Talent

later acceptance as a classic, *Giselle* was surprisingly ignored by Jules during his years in Russia. Not only did Yella appear in only half of it, but she gave only the one performance, and at one moment it seemed that even that might be cut short. For at the very beginning she suddenly faltered and fell. A few members of the audience, who were vaguely aware that Giselle dies in the piece, thought it was just part of the action until she was lifted up and carried into the wings. One of the French actors who was taking part in the benefit came on to the stage and explained that she had injured her knee at rehearsal that morning and was appearing against her doctor's advice so as not to disappoint the public. When she reappeared a few minutes later, she was encouraged by a prolonged ovation, but after only a few more steps she collapsed again. There was another delay, and she emerged from the wings for the third time. This time all was well, and having aroused everyone's sympathy, she went on to gain a definite triumph in what could hardly be called an unadulterated version of the ballet, for Jules had made an appearance to accompany her in an inserted *polka comique*, 'a clumsy dance full of piquant and gentle touches.' This interpolation apart, however, her portrayal of Giselle, learnt hurriedly for this single occasion and unpolished by the experience of repetition, was impressive enough to draw from the critic Charles de Saint-Julien the remark that 'few other dancers have developed the art of mime as much as Mlle Yella, who quite simply is a great actress in the ballet.'[18]

The season's only novelty was *Marcobomba*, a one-act comic ballet which Jules produced for the benefit performance of Marius Petipa on December 5th, 1854. The scenario was taken from an old ballet that was probably known to both Jules and Petipa. It had originally been produced by Jean Ragaine at the Théâtre de la Renaissance in Paris on August 23rd, 1839, when Jules and Carlotta could well have seen it. So too, no doubt, did Marius Petipa and his father, who were about to sail for America, for the latter produced a version of it at the Bowery Theatre, New York, on November 23rd of that same year with Marius in a leading rôle.

The action of the ballet was simple and slight. It took place in Spain, where a happy band of peasants learn that all the able-bodied young men are to be called to the colours, and determine to do all they can to avoid military service. So when the recruiting sergeant arrives with his squad, the villagers put on every type of infirmity. One feigns blindness, another pretends to be a cripple, and so on. The sergeant retires, apparently baffled, and no sooner are the soldiers out of sight than the villagers resume their boisterous by-play. But the cunning sergeant is not so easily deceived. He returns surreptitiously and surprises them. A burlesque fight ensues, with the soldiers chasing the peasants and eventually rounding them up, and the ballet ended with a divertissement.

Jules enjoyed himself immensely in the rôle of Sergeant Marcobomba, which suited his penchant for burlesque comedy. Marius Petipa and Christian Johansson were the leading peasants, and Zina Richard and Anna

283

Jules Perrot

Prikhunova were prominently featured as the daughters of the Mayor. The programme listed only two dances: a *pas d'action* by Jules, Zina Richard and Prikhunova, and a *pas de cinq* by Johansson, Petipa, Richard, Prikhunova and Nadezhda Amosova. A good time was had by dancers and public alike, and if the ballet was no more than an unpretentious trifle, it turned out to be a useful addition to the repertory, being performed on and off at the Bolshoi Theatre for several years.

* * *

Few of those who laughed whole-heartedly at Jules' antics as Sergeant Marcobomba could have realised what an effort it must have been for him to present such a jovial front. For throughout the season he had been growing increasingly embittered by what he considered was a deliberate attempt by the Direction to frustrate his creative activities. His contract obliged him to submit two scenarios for new ballets, one of which it was his right to have performed for the first time at his benefit. He had duly submitted an ambitious project for a four-act ballet entitled *Armida*, based on Tasso's epic of *Jerusalem Delivered*, which he conceived as a pendant to *Faust*, with no doubt Yella in mind for the title-rôle. But what with one thing and another, it was utterly impossible for him to complete it.* Apart from being constantly called upon to undertake tasks that ought to have been left to a répétiteur and to rehearse new dancers in old ballets, he was required to stage no less than four divertissements for Italian opera productions – for Donizetti's *Poliuto* and *La Favorita*, Rossini's *L'Assedio di Corinto*, and Verdi's *Sivardo il Sassone* (as *Macbeth* was renamed in St. Petersburg). Furthermore, to his ill-disguised fury, he often found himself denied access to the stage because it had been allotted for an opera rehearsal, and was consequently forced to work on some of the ensemble numbers that required large crowds of dancers in halls that were much too small for the purpose.

His complaints to Guedeonov went unheeded, and eventually, on February 1st, 1855, he addressed an exasperated appeal to the Tsar, complaining bitterly that the conditions under which he was forced to work were damaging his creative inspiration. 'A thousand incidents and personal disappointments' were paralysing his ardour and depriving him of energy, and he was afraid that this could lead to his engagement being terminated. 'I cast myself at Your Majesty's feet to beg his supreme favour,' he concluded. 'Pass judgment on me. I shall submit to your verdict, whatever it may be, always blessing Your Majesty's name, and I shall be exceedingly happy if this verdict does not dash my cherished hope to place at Your Majesty's service, for so long as God

---

* The delay cost Yella the opportunity of an important creation, for she was not re-engaged after this season. She died in Vienna on January 9th, 1857, after a protracted illness.

allows, the skill and strength which has been bestowed on me by divine providence.'[19]

As a result of these frustrations, Jules not only found it impossible to complete *Armida*, but he was deprived of the benefit performance that was his due, incurring thereby an unascertainable but very substantial financial loss. All this rankled deeply, and his relations with Guedeonov became strained. But graver events ensued that made it politic that he should bear this injustice patiently and in the hope of righting it at a later date. For as the season had progressed, grim news had come from the seat of war in the Crimea, and the theatres had been half empty, as if people were reluctant to be seen indulging in frivolous entertainment at a time of national peril. Also, it was no secret in court circles that the Tsar was sick with worry, grieving for his soldiers who were giving up their lives, and personally shattered by the defeats that his beloved army was suffering. His face was ashen and haggard from loss of sleep, and though in the closing weeks of the season he tried to carry out his duties as if nothing were amiss, his spirit at last broke under the strain and he resigned himself to the care of his doctors. On March 2nd he died on his simple camp bed in the Winter Palace. As his life had ebbed away, one of his last thoughts was for his beloved Peterhof, with its sparkling cascades, the illuminations, and the open-air ballets by the lakeside which his ballet-master had staged at his command.

Jules' contract was due to expire at the end of this season, and much as he resented being treated as a court official by Guedeonov, he was prepared to sign a new three-year engagement. In January 1855 the draft of a new contract had been submitted for the Tsar's approval. This had lain, unattended to, in the office of the Minister of the Household, who was probably reluctant to burden his sick sovereign with more work than was essential. The Direction had sent a reminder on the very day of the Tsar's death, and it was the new monarch, Alexander II, who finally, after a second reminder, approved the engagement. The new contract was little different from the previous one. It bound Jules to the Imperial Theatres for another three years, until March 1858, at the same salary as before of 10,000 silver roubles a year, together with an annual benefit and a doubled performance bonus of 50 roubles.

Shortly before the new season opened, in the summer of 1855, Jean Petipa, the father of Lucien and Marius, died in the fullness of his years and it fell to Jules, both in his official capacity of ballet-master and as a friend and fellow expatriate in a time of war, to deliver the funeral oration by the graveside.

The burden of the war now seemed to have no effect on the budget for the Imperial Theatres. A generous expenditure was authorised for *Armida*, and as if to mark the first season of the new reign, a celebrity of international renown was engaged to head the company – none other than Jules' comrade of old, Fanny Cerrito, who was now the only one of the original participants in his *Pas de Quatre* to be still dancing. Like Elssler before her, Cerrito was

Jules Perrot

coming to Russia in the sunset of her career, but Jules appreciated the value of experience as a counter-weight to youth and, loath to delay *Armida* any longer, resolved to stage it for her début. The production, much of which had been prepared during the previous season, was virtually ready by the time she arrived in St. Petersburg, and only a few weeks' delay was needed to give her time to learn the title-rôle.

To fashion a ballet out of the epic poem of Torquato Tasso was a bold undertaking. Written towards the end of the sixteenth century, the stirring tale of the capture of Jerusalem by the Crusaders might have seemed almost too vast a theme for a ballet, and perhaps only Jules among his contemporaries would have been capable of doing it justice and distilling its essence into a ballet, as he had done so successfully with Gœthe's *Faust*. Tasso's poem offered a subject that was familiar to a public brought up in the French culture, and Jules, who was an avid reader, no doubt knew the work from his youth in one of the excellent French translations available, possibly that of Lebrun which, in some editions, was published with engraved illustrations. But apart from the interest of the plot, the personality of Tasso himself had acquired a special significance for Jules' generation, who saw him as an archetype of the poet as artist, consumed by melancholia and buffeted by fortune, an image that accorded very much with the Romantic conception of the artist as a man isolated from society.

In working on this ballet Jules had another important source on his library shelves. In the third volume of the 1803–04 St. Petersburg edition of Noverre's *Lettres sur la danse, sur les ballets et les arts* was to be found the scenario for one of Noverre's early ballets, *Renaud et Armide*, first produced nearly a century before. Although conceived on a more modest scale, it contained several ideas that Jules was to incorporate. In Noverre's ballet, Rinaldo is enticed to Armida's island, where naiads appear out of rose bushes and trees in flower to entwine him with garlands. He falls asleep and is discovered by Armida, whose desire for revenge turns to love at first sight. The two express their love in a *pas de deux*, which was followed by a *pas de six*, in which the lovers are joined by the Graces and Cupid. Ubaldo and a Danish knight them come in search of Rinaldo, and after struggling against Armida's wiles, manage to lead Rinaldo out of the enchanted spot. The thwarted Armida vents her despair by invoking Hatred, Anger and Revenge, and abandons her palace, which is destroyed in a final conflagration.

In his own scenario Jules adopted Noverre's use of flowers to represent the bonds with which Armida enmeshes Rinaldo; he too brought Armida on to the stage with the intent to kill Rinaldo; the spirits of Hatred, Anger and Revenge again make their appearance to personify Armida's feelings, and Cupid and Ubaldo are also featured among the cast. However, Jules' conception was based much more substantially on Tasso's poem than was Noverre's, or indeed that of any of the other choreographers who had based ballets on it.

Playbill of the Bolshoi Theatre, St. Petersburg, for November 8th/20th, 1856 – the first performance of Armida. *Leningrad Theatre Museum.*

Jules Perrot

Jules had even taken part in one of these earlier productions – the modest ballet by Therese Elssler, in which he had first danced with her sister Fanny in 1834 – but apart from perhaps making him aware of the story, it can hardly have influenced him to any substantial extent more than twenty years later. In Jules' early years at the Porte-Saint-Martin Jean Coralli may have spoken to him about the ballet which he had staged on the subject in Marseilles in 1822, but this would have been a very remote memory.

Jules' ballet, which was divided into a prologue and four acts, and performed to a score by Pugni, occupied a very long evening, and was first presented on November 22nd, 1855, which was the occasion not only of his own benefit, but also of Cerrito's Russian début. Unlike Noverre, he had chosen to present a contrast between the historical basis of the story and the fantasy that Tasso added, and since the plot was somewhat involved, the audience was offered, for 30 kopecks, a printed scenario to help them follow the action, which even so did not become entirely clear.

After a musical introduction, the ballet opened with a short prologue, in which the magician Idreo is discovered in a cavern, poring over an ancient manuscript to learn the future fate of Palestine. Shocked by what he reads, he summons up a monster and commands it to create havoc among the Crusaders who have invaded the land. The situation is then illustrated by a series of tableaux, showing first the Crusaders' camp, where their commander, Godfrey of Bouillon, has banished Rinaldo for killing a fellow knight in a duel, and next a battlefield strewn with the corpses of Moslems slaughtered by the Christian forces. To avert such a calamity, the magician has already formulated a plan in which his niece, the enchantress Armida, is to play a part, and the scene ends with a final tableau showing her appearing before the Sultan.

When the first act opens, Rinaldo has already fallen under Armida's power by wandering into her enchanted garden, where he has been overcome by sleep. Armida enters, brandishing a dagger, intent on destroying the enemy in her clutches. But she is unexpectedly restrained by Cupid, in whose hand the dagger becomes an arrow. Cupid touches her heart with it, and at once her desire for vengeance is transformed into love. When he wakes, Rinaldo is no less enamoured of Armida than she of him. Nymphs and sylphs then come to entwine them with chains of flowers, and two little cupids bring in a mirror in which Armida recognises the extent of her feelings. In this *grand pas scénique*, entitled *La Captivité, ou les chaînes d'amour*, the two protagonists – Fanny Cerrito and Marius Petipa as Armida and Rinaldo – were joined by an enchanting seventeen-year-old pupil from the Theatre School, Martha Muravieva, as Cupid, and a bevy of *danseuses*, among whom, as one of the nymphs, was another white hope, Lyubov Radina. The idea of Rinaldo succumbing to a voluptuous force was delightfully expressed in the sinuously graceful movements that Jules had conceived for the attendant nymphs, and was repeated in the variation he arranged to introduce Cerrito to the St. Petersburg public, a variation 'adorably danced and most picturesque in its construction.'[20]

At the conclusion of this *pas* the lovers are led to a secluded arbour. The stage empties and the eye is drawn to the stretch of water in the background. Here Roller displayed his unrivalled understanding of stage illusion and lighting. 'The horizon shimmers with golden light. The sea is phosphorescent, flowing lazily along with drops of silver and mother-of-pearl making sparkling reflections, and beneath the clear water nymphs are seen swimming with divinely voluptuous poses, criss-crossing through the luminous waves.'[21] A boat now appears, drawn magically across the water by a stately old man. In it are seated the knight Ubaldo and the minstrel Gianneo, who are searching for Rinaldo. The old man gives Ubaldo a gleaming shield and a golden staff that have the power to counter the magic that will be pitted against him, and then vanishes.

No sooner have the two men stepped ashore than they are surrounded by the nymphs, in the form of sirens. Gianneo cannot resist their wiles, and Ubaldo disperses them with his magic staff. He seizes a young sylph, demanding to be led to Rinaldo, but is directed the wrong way. Gianneo then returns, pursued by the nymphs, one of whom assumes the form of his sweetheart, Clorinda. Gianneo is left defenceless, and in a *scène dansante, La Fontaine du rire*, falls victim to the nymphs. The audience easily saw through Gianneo's make-up to recognise the choreographer himself, who extracted every comic and dramatic possibility from the situation. In this dance with Maria Petipa as the leading nymph, whom he takes to be Clorinda, and twelve attendant nymphs, Gianneo is tempted to drink from the spring of Laughter. Helplessly he begins to laugh, passing from hearty chuckles to a painful, convulsive hysteria, and ending with a cacophonous shriek as he falls senseless to the ground. The nymphs vanish. Rinaldo then appears with Armida, and at the sight of his favourite minstrel, begs her to revive him. Opening his eyes, Gianneo implores Rinaldo to return to the camp, but the knight refuses to abandon Armida. At that moment Ubaldo returns, and holding up the shield, manages to make Rinaldo see the error of his ways. Rinaldo tears off the garlands hanging round his neck, and putting on a suit of armour that Ubaldo has brought, begs to be led away from this perilous place. Unable to deflect Rinaldo by her tears, the thwarted Armida collapses in a faint. After a moment of hesitation, Rinaldo leaves his two companions. Recovering her senses, Armida summons up the fiends of Hatred, Anger and Revenge, but Cupid drives them away and reawakens her passion, assuring her that he will restore her to her lover. The act ends with Armida and Cupid flying away in a chariot drawn by two winged dragons.

That the second act was constructed entirely of mime and contained no dancing disappointed some members of the audience, but to more serious

Jules Perrot

observers afforded 'repose for the eyes and emotion for the heart.'[22] By a combination of the skills of the choreographer and the designer Roller, it presented one of the most striking episodes of the poem. When the curtain rose, a barren desert met the eye. Here the Crusaders have pitched their camp. The heat of the sun is merciless. Water is short, the men are becoming disaffected, and some are ready to abandon the crusade. But Peter the Hermit leads them in prayer, and suddenly and miraculously storm clouds gather and rain — in the form of real water, used in this way for the first time — cascades down on them.

How the stage was dried after this deluge, contemporary accounts did not reveal. Conceivably the corps de ballet moved forward in a mass to conceal this necessary task, and the noise of brooms and swabs may have been further deadened by the chanting of a prayer, the words of which were written beneath the music in Pugni's orchestral score. And no doubt the stage was still too wet to permit any dancing until a more effective drying operation could be undertaken after the scene had ended.

Their thirst satisfied, the Christian warriors come to their senses and beg Godfrey to forgive them. Armida then appears in their midst, wearing a long silk dress. She lays the insignia of her power at Godfrey's feet, imploring him to come to her aid against her rebellious subjects. The sight of a lady in distress blinds the knights to her deceit. All of them offer their services, but she chooses only ten and leaves with them. Rinaldo then returns with Ubaldo and Gianneo. After Peter the Hermit has prophesied that only Rinaldo can triumph over the magic that lies in the wood, Godfrey entrusts Rinaldo with the sword of the Danish hero, Sweyn, whose death he commands Rinaldo to avenge. All the knights rally to Rinado's call, and the bravest of them are selected to accompany him to the enchanted forest.

The scene changes to the edge of the forest, where Rinaldo is attacked by a gigantic serpent. He is saved by the appearance of Cupid, now dressed as a young boy, who tames the monster with caresses. Rinaldo's companions, seeing him enter the forest, prepare to follow him, but the young boy then turns into a monster, attended by fire-eating snakes, to bar their way and force them to retreat.

The third act opened with Armida walking disconsolately in the forest, for which Wagner had recreated 'a marvellous Salvator Rosa landscape'[23] of rocky promontories crowned by greenery, with richly foliated trees and limpid streams. Through the trees at the back enters Rinaldo, bearing the Sword of Sweyn. As if by some invisible agency, bridges miraculously appear across the chasms and torrents that bar his way. At his approach Armida runs towards him. This was the introduction to the ravishing *pas de deux* that was unanimously declared to be the highlight of the ballet, *La Naissance des fleurs*. At a wave of her wand, flowers sprout from the earth beneath Rinaldo's feet, and she weaves her way through them, appearing to glide on their stalks. Rinaldo tries to grasp her, but she evades him and lures him deeper and deeper into the wood, only to vanish into a myrtle tree. This led into the *grand pas des fleurs animées*, in which nymphs appear out of the oak trees and lead Rinaldo to Armida's tree, from which a gentle sound is issuing. It was an ensemble dance on a vast scale; the bill listed by name no less than thirty-five *danseuses* from soloists to pupils, and there were many more besides, concealed in anonymity under the words 'and other *danseuses* and pupils.' There were opportunities for the leading soloists to shine, particularly Zina Richard, whose variation was specially well received, while the graceful little Muravieva flitted among the nymphs in the form of a genie. Armida reappears, and tries in vain to reawaken Rinaldo's love. Realising his intention, her first thought is to protect her tree, and as he smites it, she becomes a monstrous giant and the nymphs turn into demons. Undeterred, Rinaldo continues to hack at the tree, which emits a painful wail at every stroke. At last the tree is felled, and the magic of the wood is destroyed.

Joined by his companions, Rinaldo continues on his way. Armida is left alone with her misery. Cupid tries to comfort her, and promises his help. The act then moved into its closing scene, *Les Amours forgerons*, 'a masterpiece of invention . . . piquant, charming, original beyond anything that can be imagined, and . . . wholly the product of the fertile imagination of M. Perrot.' From the bowels of the earth there rises a forge, peopled by a workforce of little amorets with wings of swan's feathers – sixty pupils from the Imperial Theatre School – and a number of sylphides with butterfly wings. While the sylphides operate the bellows, the amorets, wielding hammers that seem almost impossibly big for them, begin to make arms for Armida, who now thirsts for revenge. The audience was enchanted by 'the evolutions, exercises and movements, so cleverly combined, of this army of ravishing little amorets with their diaphanous wings, their coquettish Phrygian bonnets and their heavy hammers, who manoeuvre, form figures and strike the anvils with charming mathematical precision. Not an error, not a false movement, not a single uncertain hammer stroke disrupts the unbelievable perfection of this scene, which is performed almost entirely by children.' While all this work was proceeding, Cupid, now in the form of a Sylph, darts to and fro among them, but his attempts to dampen these warlike preparations are of no avail. 'Out of the great labour of the blacksmith amorets comes a lance, then spears, a helmet and a gold breastplate, and Armida, who is equally beautiful with her lovely dark hair sparkling with diamonds or hidden in a splendid helmet, resolves to place herself at the head of a troop of amazons to fight the army of the knight.'[24]

For the last act Roller recreated the Valley of Josaphat, with Jerusalem, 'very faithfully depicted,'[25] overlooking the scene from a hilltop. The Mohammedan army, assembled to defend the city against the Crusaders, parades before the Soudan of Jerusalem. Armida arrives at the head of her amazons, whom she places at the Soudan's service, promising to bestow her riches on whoever brings her Rinaldo's head. A quarrel breaks out between two of the Moslem leaders, each of whom wishes to be her champion, but she pacifies them. Indeed, everyone is charmed, and a feeling of joy pervades the scene as a divertissement of dances, alternating with martial evolutions, begins. Here, as elsewhere, the dances had a purpose. It is necessary to arouse the courage of the African warriors, and in her final variation, inserted in a *pas des voiles* which was otherwise considered the least original part of the ballet, Armida coquettishly 'deploys the most diabolical aerial grace.'[26] Suddenly the dancing stops, for the Christian army, with Godfrey and Rinaldo at its head, has come into sight. Within a few minutes the battle has been joined. The Christians are victorious, one of Armida's champions being killed in the battle and the other slain by Rinaldo himself. Armida unlooses her arrows at Rinaldo, but the Sylph sees that he is unharmed. Unable to face the shame of defeat, Armida thinks of killing herself, but she falls exhausted to the ground. Once again, the Sylph, who is now revealed as Cupid, intervenes, and Armida revives to find herself in Rinaldo's arms. As the lovers are borne away in a traditional apotheosis, Godfrey of Bouillon and the Crusaders give thanks to God for their victory over the infidels.

Reactions to this long and ambitious ballet were mixed. To begin with, there was some surprise that Fanny Cerrito should have consented to appear under conditions in which she was outshone by a mere pupil, Martha Muravieva, whose precocious style and childlike grace were displayed to perfection in the rôle of Cupid. But considered on its merits, *Armida* was not an easy work to judge after a single viewing. Not only was it a very long ballet – the first performance lasted four and a half hours – but it was exceptionally complex in its construction and most observers found the action somewhat obscure and the proliferation of effects distracting.

Nevertheless it was received, if not with universal enthusiasm, at least with respect. One critic, Charles de Saint-Julien, devoted two unusually lengthy articles to it in the *Journal de Saint-Pétersbourg*, describing it as 'a vast drama, a gigantic and marvellous epic of chivalry . . . a poem bestrewn with miracles and fantasies, all glittering, sparkling and shimmering' . . . a succession of 'splendid mirages, visions, poet's dreams conjured up by the magic wand of the powerful wizard named Jules Perrot.'[27] However, complaints that it contained insufficient dancing were no doubt partly justified, even allowing for the growing public distaste for complex narrative ballets, a trend that had not escaped the notice of the critics. Zotov, who thought that the ballet could be advantageously shortened by about an hour, was beginning to wonder whether the public had been spoilt by all the extravagant magnificence of the spectacle.

This reaction against serious dramatic content in ballet, which was to grow in strength under Jules' successors, Saint-Léon and Marius Petipa, ran completely counter to Jules' choreographic credo. For him a ballet was much more than a glorified divertissement designed mainly to dazzle the audience with the dancers' skill, and in 1855 there was still a strong body of opinion that appreciated his efforts to subordinate technique to a ballet's dramatic requirements, whether by establishing a mood or intensifying the relationship between the characters. His dances were never ends in themselves. Their purpose was to convey an aesthetic expression, while at the same time adding to the underlying conception of the choreographer seen as a dramatist working not in words but in movement. 'No one, I suppose, will deny the progress that choreographic art has made in recent times,' commented Saint-Julien. 'This progress is evidenced in a more intelligent economy shown in ballet composition ... and in the rejection of *tours de force*, which have nothing to do with the art of Elssler, Taglioni and Cerrito, and turn dancing into a sport of jumping jacks. They had to be replaced by something more rational, more artistic, more charming, and it was found that a simpler, more natural grace would work wonders, and so, by the injection of *plastique* and characterisation, choreography attained a new perfection. Today a *pas* must trace supple, elegant and clearly designed lines in space.

'The idea also arose that the various elements of a ballet should be consistent with its principal idea, and that this idea should motivate the *pas*, the ensemble numbers, the evolutions and the cadenced movements. From that moment ballet became a drama, a work that had a serious side to its fantasy, a poetic creation that may be bizarre in appearance but had a *raison d'être*, a logic and an infinite charm of its own. In order to grasp and understand all this, it is essential to put oneself in the right frame of mind, to subject one's imagination to the conception of the author, and to stop expecting a choreographic work to be a continuous succession of capers, pirouettes and eye-catching jumps.'

Turning his attention specifically to *Armida*, Saint-Julien unequivocally declared that the choreography was as successful in its general harmony as in each of its separate parts. 'Not only does it correspond to the subject of the drama, but it is subordinated, with a perfect understanding, to the nature of the action as it unfolds, to the episodes that spring from it, and to the poetic ideas to which they give expression. All the aesthetic elements that can possibly be found in a ballet are present. The dances are appropriate, and the scenes, evolutions and ensemble numbers all contribute to the harmony I have mentioned.'[28]

Armida was to retain its place as the major production of the season with a total of fourteen performances, more than was given of any other work, but since it lacked the human interest that was so evident in *Faust*, it never became really popular. It was dropped after Jules' retirement in 1859, having by then been performed thirty-one times. Nor did it prove a particularly interesting work for the ballerina playing Armida. Cerrito, finding herself outshone

Jules Perrot

by Muravieva, could hardly have considered it suitable to her own talents, even though these were on the wane. The part did, however, give one dancer an unexpected triumph. On the eve of the performance announced for January 10th, 1856, Cerrito sent word that she was indisposed, and the rôle was taken over at the shortest of notice by Lyubov Radina, who had only recently graduated from the Theatre School and was still in the corps de ballet.

* * *

Jules found himself under almost as much pressure as during the previous season, for in addition to serving Cerrito, he had to accommodate Yella and the young Russian ballerinas who were coming to the fore. Cerrito's requirements were his first priority, but here his task was simplified by her desire to appear in two ballets from her own repertory. For these his responsibility was limited to setting them on the stage, no doubt in close consultation with her. He must have been familiar with both works, too, for they had been frequently given in London when he was ballet-master there, and he had certainly seen the versions which Saint-Léon had staged at the Paris Opéra. When *La Vivandière* was produced for Petipa's benefit on December 25th, 1855, the playbill credited it as 'a ballet by M. Saint-Léon, staged by M. Perrot,' but Jules claimed no part in its authorship and could hardly be held responsible for the surfeit of 'tedious miming'[29] of which one critic complained. More substantial was his contribution in the other ballet, *La Fille de marbre*, given for Cerrito's benefit on March 2nd, 1856, and this he did count among the works of his own composition. It was a ballet that needed no intellectual effort to follow the action, and Jules was required to do little more than to compose some new dances. This task he performed with his accustomed skill, as well as appearing as the demon figure Periphite, which he had played fourteen years before in London in the original version of the ballet, when it was called *Alma*. No one held him responsible for the poverty of the plot, and the dances he created were praised on their own merits: an effective *pas de tambourin* in the first act, danced by Cerrito, Johansson and himself, with Nadezhda Amosova and Alexandra Ryukhina in support; two *pas de deux* in the second act, one for himself and Ryukhina, and the other for Cerrito and Johansson; and a fine *pas d'ensemble* in the last act. The Spanish *pas de caractère* which Cerrito introduced at the end, *L'Aldeana*, was interpolated from her own repertory.

The cool reception which the Russian public gave to Cerrito was embarrassingly noticeable during the course of *La Fille de marbre*, and the reason was not far to seek. During the last few weeks of the season a new star, a Russian star, had appeared above the horizon to dazzle the public – Nadezhda Bogdanova. This young ballerina had arrived in St. Petersburg with the aura of a national heroine, a victim of war. When the Crimean War had broken out, she had found herself trapped in Paris with an unexpired contract to dance at the Opéra, and for many months she had endured the humiliations of an expatriate on enemy soil. Amid the celebrations of French victories, she had suffered deeply for her country's misfortunes. All this had been well publicised when she finally returned to her motherland in the dark days of defeat, and she was greeted with an outburst of emotional affection – a reaction she could never have produced in normal times, for she was quite unknown to the greater part of the ballet-going public of St. Petersburg.

For her début Jules turned his attention to an earlier ballet which, for all its recognised merits, he had neglected since the departure of Carlotta – *Giselle*. In recent years only separate acts had been given at very infrequent intervals – the first act with Yella, the second with Zina Richard – but now the complete work was to be revived for Bogdanova. Probably the choice was hers, not his, for she had been dancing in it in many European cities on her journey back to Russia. No doubt Jules carefully rehearsed the production, but he apparently made no substantial alterations. Bogdanova had arrived with an already formed interpretation of the title-rôle, although that is not to say that she did not listen to the advice that Jules must have given her. The testing nature of *Giselle* was well understood in St. Petersburg, and Rafail Zotov was to judge her from the experience of seeing a succession of distinguished interpreters; Carlotta Grisi, the original Giselle, Elssler, who had been unrivalled in the first act but less effective in the second, Grahn and Richard who had shone more in the second act, and Andreyanova, who in his opinion stood alone in being equally excellent in both acts. Bogdanova, who was only twenty, was still maturing as an artist, and Zotov made allowances for the fact that her experience in Paris could have offered her little awareness of the dramatic potential of ballet. This was an aspect in which Russian ballet was exceptionally strong, not only because ballets were longer and there was more scope for developing the narrative, but more specifically because of the quality of the repertory which Jules had built up. In *Giselle* Bogdanova's inexperience was particularly noticeable in the dramatic passages of the first act, but in the second she enraptured the audience by her finished technique, even if it was marred here and there by touches of French style that offended St. Petersburg taste – 'Parisian innovations,'[30] as Zotov scornfully called them, such as a certain jump which ended with a rise on to one foot, probably the *pointe*, that may have been sensationally novel, but appeared lacking in grace.[31]

Her reception was in large measure an emotional demonstration in favour of a young Russian dancer. This was clear from the 'deafening roar of applause and shouting'[32] and the bouquets of camellias that greeted her on her first entrance. After that, every opera glass was focussed on her, and the ovations grew in fervour. There seemed no end to the flowers, which in February were extremely expensive, and the public's affection, so unexpected in its warmth, moved her to tears in the second act and forced her to withdraw into the wings to recover her equanimity. In the last few weeks of the season a section of the public was giving her the treatment that was normally reserved for the great international stars.

While this was hard on Cerrito, it could not be denied that the stir Bogdanova created was giving a much-needed boost to the ballet. Thanks largely to her, the season which had opened in the gloom of Sevastopol's fall had ended on a stirring note of hope. Never had the ballet company seemed stronger, and with the emergence of so many brilliant young Russian dancers and the promise of peace, the balletomanes could take a euphoric view of the delights to come.

Jules, who no longer had the energy that used to carry him through a hectic London season and was finding conditions of working for the Imperial Theatres increasingly irksome, could hardly share these sanguine expectations. That summer the restoration of normal relations between Russia and France following the Treaty of Paris gave him the opportunity to escape from St. Petersburg and spend the summer in France for the first time in four years. The Baltic crossing and the railway journey from Lubeck provided ample time for reflection. Had it been wise to sign a new engagement? Had he been excessively swayed by the security that his post in St. Petersburg offered? Would there be any improvement in his conditions of work when he returned? Was his creative impulse on the decline? How would the public's growing aversion to the dramatic ballet that was his forte affect him? These were questions which only the future could answer.

18

Last Years in Russia

The contrast between the moods of Paris and St. Petersburg could not fail to strike a traveller from one city to the other that summer. Jules had left the Russian capital immersed in the gloom of its wounded pride and resigned acceptance of the peace terms that had ended the fighting in the Crimea. Paris, on the other hand, was jubilant, not only at the victories of French arms and the successful peace conference, but also at the birth of an heir to the throne, all of which seemed to symbolise the stability which Napoleon III had brought to France and its often turbulent capital. Though as a Frenchman, Jules must have shared in the general rejoicing, even if his political leanings may have been republican rather than Bonapartist, his visit was clouded by domestic anxiety, for he found his father much changed in health, and not long after his arrival he was to be given another reminder of the impermanence of human existence when his old friend and collaborator, Adolphe Adam, died suddenly in his sleep at the age of fifty-two. Perhaps he was not altogether sorry when the time came for him to return to St. Petersburg. He arrived there punctually in accordance with the terms of his leave, on June 27th, looking forward to what, for him, would be the unique experience of assisting in the festivities accompanying the coronation of the new Tsar.

Five days after his arrival, Jules set off for Moscow, where the coronation was to take place, at the head of an important contingent from the St. Petersburg ballet, including the régisseur Ivan Marcel and his assistant and many of the leading dancers, among them Johansson, Frédéric, Goltz, Marius Petipa, Lev Ivanov, Bogdanova and Prikhunova. They were able to travel comfortably by train, for the two cities had been linked by railway for several years. This also made it possible for Jules and some of the dancers to return briefly to St. Petersburg a few weeks later to present a short ballet, *La Débutante*, at Peterhof before the Tsar and the court.

Jules' work was not unknown at the Bolshoi Theatre in Moscow, for although he had not visited that city since accompanying Fanny Elssler in 1850, several of his ballets had been reproduced there by Frédéric and Théodore. His task in the coronation festivities was to produce *La Vivandière*

Jules Perrot

for the gala performance, but he also had time to correct the production, originally staged by Théodore in 1854, of *Gazelda*, improving it out of all recognition and discovering, for the title rôle, a dramatic dancer after his own heart in the young Moscow ballerina, Praskovia Lebedeva. He may also have turned his attention to *Giselle*, in which Lebedeva enjoyed another triumph.

The choice of Cerrito as the ballerina for the gala in preference to one of the brilliant young Russians was dictated by the desire to have an illustrious name adorning the programme, and the reasons for selecting *La Vivandière* as the ballet were obviously practical: first, the ballet was to follow an opera, and a more substantial work would make the performance much too long, and secondly, the time available for rehearsals was limited. The preparations at the Bolshoi Theatre were only a part of the frenzied activity that seemed to be occupying every moment of everybody's time. At last the long-awaited day of the Tsar's entry arrived, and the fabulous procession, appearing to all eyes that saw it like a fairy tale come to life, of the new Emperor escorted by his family, his courtiers and his guards, wended its way through the crowds. On September 5th, in the Cathedral of the Assumption of the Kremlin, Alexander II was crowned Emperor of all the Russias, and for several weeks Moscow indulged in a brilliant round of social activities. Since Petersburg society had come *en masse* to Moscow, there was entertainment in plenty at the theatres, but for sheer splendour nothing could compare with the coronation gala of September 9th. In the glorious blaze of illumination devised specially for the occasion by the theatre architect Alberto Cavos, the enamelled stars and the coloured silk ribbons of countless orders gleamed on uniforms of every cut and hue, and jewels sparkled in profusion in the coiffures and toilettes of elegantly groomed ladies. Punctually at eight o'clock the Tsar and the Imperial family appeared in the state box. The applause that greeted them dissolved into the solemn strains of the Imperial anthem, and the audience turned, almost in anti-climax, to take their seats for the performance. It was an easily digestible programme, opening with Donizetti's entertaining opera, *L'Elisir d'Amore*, and concluding with *La Vivandière*, in which Cerrito was joined by Jules himself, Frédéric and Johansson. The Tsar was in the best of moods, and as a mark of his pleasure, presented Jules with a gold snuff box bearing a miniature by Boucher and the inscription, '*Au grand petit Perrot.*'

Before leaving Moscow, Jules mounted on the company *La Fille de marbre*, in which Cerrito played the rôle she had originally created, but the performances of it were interrupted by an accident which might have had fearful consequences. At the end of the ballet one evening Cerrito was knocked to the ground by a falling piece of scenery. Her costume caught fire from a gas burner, but mercifully help was at hand, the flames were quickly extinguished and she escaped with no more than a painfuly bruised shoulder and shock.

* * *

Last Years in Russia

It was probably this injury that delayed Cerrito's reappearance in St. Petersburg when the new season opened a few weeks later. In the event the public was to be in no way disappointed, for her absence enabled the young Russian ballerinas to rise splendidly to the occasion. Jules had no need to create anything new for them, for the impressive repertory he had built up over the past few years provided them with ample opportunities. The main burden was borne by Bogdanova who to the rôle of Giselle now added no less than four dramatic portrayals, Gazelda, Esmeralda, Marguerite in *Faust* and Catarina. The gifted Anna Prikhunova also had occasion to shine, not only in supporting rôles such as Fleur de Lys in *Esmeralda* and the Queen of the Wilis in *Giselle*, but in leading parts in *Le Diable à quatre* and Marius Petipa's *Paquita*. She also played her original rôle in *Marcobomba*, and made a charming Lise in *La Fille mal gardée*, encouraged by hilarious performances by Jules himself as Marcelline and Timofei Stukolkin as Nicaise.* Another young ballerina now rapidly coming to the fore was Muravieva, whose success in *Armida* earned her the title-rôles in *La Péri* and *Satanilla*.

Serving these three ballerinas by presenting them in such an extensive repertory must have taken up a great deal of time, but Jules' contract bound him to stage two new ballets each year, an obligation which, this season, he fulfilled with only a bare minimum of effort. The main novelty he presented, *La Débutante*, featured all three of the young Russian stars, but it was not strictly a creation, since it had been put together some months earlier for a command performance at the Court Theatre at Peterhof on August 3rd. It was a very slight piece, comprising just two scenes, which he had hurriedly assembled to music that Pugni had partly cobbled out of the scores of two ballets that had been dropped from the repertory, Adolphe Adam's *La Filleule des fées*, and *Vert-Vert* by Deldevez and Tolbecque.

The occasion for its entry into the repertory was Bogdanova's benefit on January 29th, 1857, after which it was to be given only three more times before being quietly interred. Very little imaginative effort could have been expended in devising the plot. The curtain rose to reveal the Foyer de la Danse of the Paris Opéra in the days of Louis XV. The dancers have assembled to await the arrival of the ballet-master who is to rehearse them in his new ballet, 'The Abduction of Proserpine.' His quirks and mannerisms are a continual source of amusement to them, and before his arrival, the ebullient Zephirina (Anna Prikhunova) mimics him to everyone's delight. After Jules' entrance as the ballet-master, their high spirits continue and, while the old man becomes lost in thought as he devises steps for them to dance, they pick his handkerchief and snuff box from his pocket. They sample the snuff, and a thunderous sneeze jolts him out of his meditation. Meanwhile, in a scene between Marius

---

* In other productions of *La Fille mal gardée*, these characters are known as Simone and Alain.

Jules Perrot

Petipa and his young wife, a dashing Marquis enters to pay court to the prima ballerina, Guimard, and when the others turn round and discover they have eloped, the ballet-master is inconsolable, for not only is he partial to her charms himself, but he has designed the leading rôle in his ballet specially for her. Happily a solution is at hand when a young débutante, Clorinda (Nadezhda Bogdanova), offers to learn the rôle.

The second scene, which was devoted to Clorinda's triumph in the new ballet, was little more than a divertissement, beginning with a lively galop and concluding with a Spanish dance, *La Gallegada*, which Bogdanova and the choreographer danced with characteristic Hispanic fire.

Jules' benefit, on February 12th, customarily the occasion for the first performance of a new grand ballet, this year contained only a very modest novelty, an interlude, composed for Muravieva and entitled *La Petite Marchande de bouquets*. Short and slight though it was, it was another demonstration of Jules' uncanny ability to exploit a dancer's individual qualities. Muravieva's miming was full of wit and the joy of life. In a few minutes she enchanted everyone as a simple flower seller who teasingly refuses to give flowers to a succession of admirers until the young man she loves comes along.

Meanwhile, poor Fanny Cerrito had been quite overshadowed by the emergence of the Russian ballerinas. Her repertory remained unchanged from that of the year before – *Armida*, *La Vivandière* and *La Fille de marbre* – and it was only towards the end of the season that she appeared in anything new. For her benefit on February 19th the French actors from the Mikhailovsky Theatre gave their services, and an inconsequential little piece was put together. Entitled *L'Ile des muets*,* it was a curious mixture of light comedy and divertissement, which Jules produced to a scenario by Eugène Deligny and music by Théodore Labarre, possibly taken from some earlier ballet.

The story was based on the idea of an island whose inhabitants communicate with one another only by mime and dancing. The idyllic peace of the place is broken by the arrival of a balloon. Out of its basket clambers Count Hercule de la Tuberose, followed by his servant. The islanders welcome them with wine, and the two travellers fall into a heavy sleep. The scene then changes to an exquisite landscape, dominated by an enormous bee-hive standing on a hill-top. Out of this hive emerge the corps de ballet dressed to represent a swarm of bees. They flutter charmingly about their Queen (played by Cerrito), some of them flying in and out with the aid of wires as if to gather

---

* It may have been only a coincidence that *Polichinel Vampire*, in which Mazurier made his name in Paris in the 1820s, and was aped so successfully by Jules himself (see Chapter 2), was set on the 'Île des muets.' There seems to be no recognisable similarity, however, between the two plots.

honey from a neighbouring mound. At the end of this ballet of bees, the travellers awake. Flora, the queen of the island, played by the actress, Alice Théric, then makes her appearance. The Count falls in love with her, but is tormented by a series of inexplicable illusions, such as a magic table that revolves on itself without any human agency. In the end Flora agrees to marry him, and the ballet concluded with more dancing, including a Spanish dance, *La Maja*, which Cerrito performed with Marius Petipa.

L'Ile des muets was even more ephemeral than *La Débutante*; it was given only once more.

* * *

Jules left St. Petersburg much earlier than usual that season. Word reached him that his father's health was failing, and he was given leave from March 8th until June 13th to go to his bedside.

He passed through Paris just a few weeks too late to catch a performance of *Esmeralda*, which had been presented at the Porte-Saint-Martin at the end of December 1856. He had not been directly concerned in its preparation, being in Russia at the time, but whoever was responsible modestly withheld his name,* the ballet being presented as the work of Jules himself. Indeed this was the main point of interest to the Paris critics, most of whom had heard of the ballet but never seen it. Saint-Victor called Jules 'the greatest choreographer to have appeared since Viganò,'[1] while Théophile Gautier remembered him as 'the last man to have danced . . . who now designs *pas* as well as he used to perform them.' To Gautier the main disappointment was Maria Scotti's Esmeralda. It was, he acknowledged, 'a terrible and dangerous rôle for a *danseuse*, just as Célimène is for an actress. Furthermore, Carlotta Grisi danced it, and no one who saw her, all white, pink and blonde, with her violet eyes and her mouth in full bloom, remembered that the poet's Esmeralda was wild and bronzed like a child of Egypt with glints of blue in her jet-black hair. She danced it as no one else ever will, with the grace of flight, a charm that was irresistible, and such precision and suppleness. Mme Scotti,' whose hair, incidentally, was black, 'is a well-trained dancer. She knows the secrets of her profession, a rarer quality than you would suppose, and mimes the dramatic passages intelligently. She was deservedly applauded in the *Truandaise*, but she is not the poet's Esmeralda, nor Perrot's. The movements composed for Carlotta require too much elevation for her. However, she was liked. Rosita Comba [as Fleur de Lys] reminds me a little of Cerrito with her rounded arms, the grace of her poses and her provocative manner. The male dancer,

---

* Possibly Domenico Ronzani, who had already reproduced several of Jules' ballets in Italy and Vienna, including *Esmeralda*. He was ballet-master at Her Majesty's Theatre in London in the summers of 1856 and 1857, and paid a rapid visit to the Eastern states of the U.S.A. in the spring of 1857.

Jules Perrot

M. Paul, has much elevation; he springs up towards the flies and stays there, but today the public no longer takes any notice of men in ballet.'[2] Jules found the memory of this production still fresh in the minds of those who had seen it, and while he may have regretted not having produced the work himself at the Opéra, he must have been gratified that his name had been brought to the notice of the French public again and that his Parisian friends had been given some idea of what he had accomplished.*

It was several years since he had seen his friends in Paris, and no doubt he quickly brought himself up-to-date with Mazilier's recent productions at the Opéra, *Le Corsaire, Les Elfes*, and the most recent, *Marco Spada*, which was given its first performance on April 1st. He must also have been delighted to find Zina Richard, newly engaged, making such a favourable impression on the Paris public, and another pleasant occasion came at the end of April, when he attended the wedding breakfast of Francisque Berthier, the popular régisseur and comic dancer, at the celebrated restaurant, Les Trois Frères Provençaux, and took the floor in a quadrille with Lucien Petipa, Louis Mérante, Adeline Plunkett, and the teacher, Mme Dominique.

When the time arrived for Jules to return to Russia, his father was dying. The end came on June 18th, and there was much distressing business for Jules to attend to before he could think of leaving. He found himself in a worrying dilemma, for under his contract with the Imperial Theatres, a penalty of 4,000 roubles could be imposed if he did not return to St. Petersburg on time. But family business had to take priority, and it was not until August 18th, more than two months late, that he reported for duty. Fortunately, the authorities were understanding, and the Tsar, to whom the question was referred, ordered that the penalty clause was to be waived in this instance and his salary paid in full for all the time he had been away.

The opening of the 1857–58 season was too imminent for a new ballet to be mounted, but Jules had returned to find the young Moscow ballerina, Praskovia Lebedeva, who had impressed him so much at the time of the Coronation, preparing for her St. Petersburg début. During her brief visit to the northern capital, Lebedeva was to appear in *Gazelda* and *Esmeralda*, and Jules was soon hard at work coaching her in the two rôles. To his delight she was not only intelligent and surprisingly gifted for one so young – she was only eighteen – but seemed ideally suitable to follow Carlotta in these two rôles. There was indeed a strong similarity with Jules' former muse. Lebedeva's playful naivety in the opening scene of *Esmeralda* was enchanting, and if the heavier drama that came later seemed a little beyond her means, that was probably due to memories of the more histrionic interpretation of

* The production was first given for the benefit of the chief machinist Caron on December 24th, 1856. Marie Taglioni, Mazilier, Mérante, Louis Marquet, Célestine Emarot and Marie Guy-Stéphan were among the audience. It was given nineteen performances, the last being on January 15th, 1857.

Fanny Elssler. That she was faithfully carrying out the choreographer's intentions was confirmed by a critic's judgment that she '[belonged] to the serious classical school and [reminded] us of Grisi in many things.'[3]

Lebedeva was at the same time a child of the modern generation, schooled in a technique that had subtly developed in response to the taste of the 1850s. This emerged in the *pas de deux*, when she strove to achieve a spectacular effect by exaggerating some of the movements that Jules had taught her. Older critics such as Zotov disapproved, for example, of the lift in which her partner held her high above his head with her legs spread wide in a *grand écart*, and again of an *arabesque* she performed with her back leg so much out of the horizontal as to be pointing skywards and her head lowered towards the ground. 'We may be mistaken,' Zotov commented, 'but Taglioni did not perform such tricks, and the school of Didelot was more miserly still so far as eccentricity in dancing was concerned. But we live in another age, with other tastes.'[4]

Lebedeva's visit to St. Petersburg was all too brief, and in October she came to bid Jules goodbye before returning to Moscow. Their paths would not cross again, and both of them may have looked back later, with nostalgic regret, to those few short weeks of happy cooperation. For in the years ahead neither was to achieve real fulfilment. Though he did not then know it, Jules' career was approaching its unhappy end, while Lebedeva's fate was to work under a choreographer, Saint-Léon, for whom she had little respect and to retire prematurely in a spirit of frustration.

Meanwhile the season continued with Bogdanova now firmly in possession as the principal ballerina, holding *Giselle, Esmeralda, Catarina* and *Faust* in her fief, while Cerrito's rôles were passed on to Prikhunova, who took over *La Vivandière*, and Muravieva, who inherited *La Fille de marbre*. It was a strong repertory, and for the moment these new interpretations served to compensate the public for the absence of anything new, for the trifle that Jules staged for the benefit of the régisseur Marcel on October 20th, *The Rose, the Violet and the Butterfly*, was hardly worthy of serious attention. No doubt Jules put it together in response to a request that could not be refused, for the music was composed by the Tsar's cousin, the Grand Duke of Oldenburg. At its one and only performance at the Bolshoi, the leading rôles were danced by Muravieva (as the Butterfly), Radina and one of the Amosova sisters. Jules did not list it among his works, and some of the choreography may have been by Marius Petipa, who had produced it a few months earlier at the Grand Duke's summer residence, with Muravieva, Maria Petipa and Matilda Madayeva.

In spite of Bogdanova's success, the Direction persisted in its quest for outside talent, and soon there arrived in St. Petersburg an eighteen-year-old ballerina who had made something of a reputation in London during the preceding two seasons. Ekaterina Friedberg was only partly Russian, but she might

Jules Perrot

have been a regular member of the St. Petersburg ballet had she not been weeded out of the Theatre School as unsuitable, no doubt partly on account of her height. She was fortunate in that her father, who owned a tobacco factory in St. Petersburg, could afford to take her abroad, where she had completed her training and eventually obtained an engagement at Her Majesty's Theatre in London under the name of Mlle Katrine. Her 'tall, handsome' figure and her 'broad sweeping style, perhaps rather cold and stately than graceful,'[5] made a favourable impression on the manager, Lumley, and the critic of *The Times* had described her as 'proudly floating through the air' with 'marvellous bounds' and conveying an impression of seriousness and grandeur.[6]

When this tall, fair-haired girl presented herself before him in St. Petersburg, Jules may have seen her as an acceptable successor to Cerrito in *Armida*, but her début in that ballet on November 17th was only modestly successful, and her appearance shortly afterwards in a revival of *Le Délire d'un peintre* passed almost unnoticed.

It was on the full-length ballet that Jules was preparing for his benefit on January 21st, 1858 – a new version of the Parisian success, *Le Corsaire* – that the young ballerina's hopes were pinned. She seemed undaunted by the task of following in the footsteps of Carolina Rosati, recognised as the most dramatic ballerina then dancing, who had created the rôle of Medora in Paris and played it also in London, but Jules must have felt deprived at being saddled with a ballerina of such inexperience. There can be little doubt that she was the Direction's choice, and the scenario may likewise have been imposed, probably in the absence of any synposis presented by him. That he accepted the situation apparently without seriously pressing an objection may have been due to his preoccupation with family affairs following his father's death. Certainly new ideas were not coming to him as freely as formerly. Also, he may have seen the task as a sort of tribute to his friend, Adolphe Adam, whose music for *Le Corsaire* had been his last work for the ballet, completed only a few months before his death.

The scenario of *Le Corsaire* had been written by another old friend, Saint-Georges. As the title revealed, Saint-Georges had based it, if superficially, on Byron's celebrated poem and, being highly experienced in theatrical matters, had blatantly pandered to the public's taste for exotic *couleur locale* and stage spectacle. The most important element in the story was the amazing climax when the ship bearing the corsairs and their women breaks apart in a storm and sinks with all aboard, only the two lovers being saved, picked out by a spotlight as the waters subside to reveal them embracing on a rock. Both Paris and London had been overwhelmed by this scene, and in Guedeonov's eyes one of the attractions of the scenario must have been the opportunity it offered to surpass the splendour of the staging at the Paris Opéra and Her Majesty's Theatre with the enormous resources of the Bolshoi stage. The scenic spectacle was placed in the hands of a team of experienced specialists under the overall supervision of Roller. Working with him were two other designers, Wagner and Petrov. The famous shipwreck scene at the end was to be a product of collaboration, Wagner being responsible for painting the scenery, Roller designing the complicated machinery for the shipwreck, and the fire master Shishko setting up the new electro-galvanic lighting to produce the lightning flashes of the storm.

When Jules listed his works at the end of his career, he did not include *Le Corsaire*. This could hardly have been an oversight, for it was one of his last productions, and the inference must be that he did not consider it wholly a work of his own. He had doubtless seen Mazilier's original production at the Paris Opéra in 1856, and his own staging perhaps incorporated too many ideas and passages from his colleague's choreography for him in all honesty to claim authorship for his own version, even if the programme for the Petersburg production stated that it was 'arranged and staged with the dances expressly composed' by him.

Saint-Georges' narrative and Adolphe Adam's score formed the foundation of the St. Petersburg production. Cesare Pugni added music for a few new dances, but the action followed the Paris scenario to the letter. For the opening scene in a square in Adrianople where the slave market is held, Roller successfully caught the effect of sunshine brightening the colours of the costumes. The love of the corsair chief Conrad and Medora, the ward of the bazaar keeper, was quickly established by Marius Petipa and Ekaterina Friedberg, and in a striking solo Medora expresses her love by plucking flowers from her hair and her dress and forming them into a bouquet, which she lays at Conrad's feet. Conrad is determined to rescue Medora from the clutches of her unscrupulous guardian, but before he can act, Seyd, a lecherous old pasha comically portrayed by Jules himself, arrives to inspect the slave-girls. None of them takes his fancy, and his leering eyes alight on Medora. Her guardian is tempted to sell her. A sequence of dances then begins: first, a Spanish character dance, *L'Aragonaise*, featuring Wiktoria Kozlovska, a guest from the Warsaw Opera, with five other dancers in support, and finally a stirring *ballabile d'action,* the *danse des pirates*, in which twenty-four female soloists, half of them *en travesti*, were supported by an unspecified number of other *danseuses*. While this dance is still in progress, Conrad and his men draw their weapons and carry off Medora and the slave-girls.

In the next scene, designed by Wagner, Medora finds herself in the pirates' lair, a vast cavern overflowing with the booty which Conrad and his men have amassed. In an impassioned mime scene Medora implores her lover to give up his life of piracy. The other corsairs then appear with their captives, whom they force to dance for them. This formed the introduction to one of the choreographic highlights, the *pas des éventails*, in which one beautifully

Jules Perrot

arranged group succeeds another, all with Medora as the central figure. Prompted by the delight it has aroused, Medora begs Conrad to free the slave-girls, which he does impulsively, after a moment of indecision, to the fury of his men. He manages to quieten them with a terrible glance, but Birbanto, one of his henchmen, plans revenge. He tells the bazaar keeper, who has also been captured, that for a suitable ransom he will free both him and his ward, cynically suggesting that he will be able to recover the ransom by selling Medora to Seyd Pasha. He explains that he will carry out his plan with the aid of a drugged bouquet of lotus flowers. The concluding minutes of the act were largely taken up with a *scène dansante* between Conrad and Medora, one of those dramatic passages at which Jules excelled. When the pirates sit down to their evening meal, Medora insists on serving Conrad herself. A young girl slips the bouquet into Medora's hands, and unsuspectingly Medora offers it to her lover, who is soon overcome by the drug. Medora is gazing tenderly at his sleeping figure when the dissatisfied corsairs rush forward and seize her. She puts up a spirited defence, wounding Birbanto in the arm with her dagger. As she is dragged away, Conrad is left bemusedly pressing the bouquet to his lips.

The scene for the second act, Seyd's palace on the island of Cos, was designed by Roller. Here the pasha makes his appearance, still fuming at the abduction of Medora, and now given added annoyance by the squabbles between his favourite Sultana Zulma (Nadezhda Troitskaya) and the irrepressible Gulnara (Lyubov Radina). The opening minutes were enlivened by an effective *pas des odalisques*, featuring Anna Prikhunova and the two Amosova sisters, and this was followed by an amusing *scène de séduction* between Seyd and Gulnara, in which Jules skilfully brought out Radina's coquettish charms. The animosity between the two girls surfaces again, but their quarrel is interrupted by the arrival of the bazaar keeper, accompanied by Medora. Infuriated by her guardian's intention, Medora seizes the pasha's dagger, but is quickly disarmed. The sale is concluded, and Seyd is settling down to enjoy his new acquisition when there is another interruption. A caravan of pilgrims, bound for Mecca, has entered the garden. Their leader, a pious old dervish, approaches to seek hospitality. The pasha takes a malicious pleasure in shocking the saintly old man by the lascivious dancing of his women. Medora refuses to take part in this exhibition until the dervish approaches her and discloses that he is Conrad in disguise. She then joins in the dancing, performing a variation expressing her delight at finding her lover again. As daylight fades, Seyd's eunuchs come forward to lead Medora away. At a signal from Conrad, the corsairs throw off their heavy cloaks. Medora flies into Conrad's arms. At that moment Gulnara runs in, pursued by Birbanto, and implores Conrad's protection. Recognising Birbanto as the corsair who tricked her and sold her back to the bazaar keeper, Medora denounces him to Conrad, and it is only when Birbanto raises his arm to swear

Last Years in Russia

his innocence and uncovers the scar from the wound made by Medora's dagger that he is made to confess his guilt. The two women restrain Conrad from shooting him on the spot, and Birbanto takes advantage of his hesitation to escape. A few minutes later the pasha's guards, who have been alerted by the treacherous Birbanto, surround the corsairs, and Conrad is seized.

The last act opens in the pasha's apartment, a scene designed by a third artist, Petrov. Seyd is prepared to spare Conrad if Medora will yield to his desires and become his wife. When Conrad learns of this from Medora he indignantly refuses to be released on such terms, insisting on being put to death. But meanwhile Gulnara has slipped into the kiosk and overheard the lovers' conversation. She offers to help them, and in a whisper explains her plan. So on Seyd's return, Medora tells him she will accept his terms. Conrad is then freed and leaves, giving Medora a secret sign that he will soon be back. Preparations now begin for the marriage. Unknown to Seyd, Gulnara, her face concealed by her veil, takes Medora's place at the wedding. The act ended with another of Jules' *scènes dansantes*, performed by himself and Friedberg. The ceremony over, Medora, who has now put on the bridal veil, arouses the passions of the pasha to such a pitch that he willingly hands her his dagger and pistols and allows her to tie his wrists with her scarf. At that moment Conrad appears at the window. Seyd is powerless to prevent Medora's escape, and the act ended with him seething with frustrated rage at being tricked.

The kiosk set then rose to reveal the entire depth of the stage utilised in an astonishingly realistic representation of the open sea, with the pirate ship in full sail rolling gently on the water. On board the corsairs are celebrating the return of their chief. But soon the sky darkens, and a furious storm breaks. Battered by waves and struck by lightning, the vessel sinks. The storm gradually passes, and in the final moments a shaft of light picks out the lovers, clasped in one another's arms on a rock, miraculously saved by the purity of their love.

This was the great scene that had astonished Paris, London and Warsaw, but in St. Petersburg it brought the ballet to a close with a display of the machinist's skill that far outshone the efforts of the earlier productions. 'The battling of the ship with the waves, the rending of the sails, the collapse of the masts with sailors on the rigging, and finally the sinking of the ship beneath the stormy waters, inspired real fear among the audience,' recorded a contemporary critic. 'The ballet must be seen for this scene alone. Roller surpassed himself, and everyone who had seen the ballet in Paris awarded him the palm over the machinists of the Opéra. Extraordinarily effective also in this scene was the lightning that flashed through the clouds, blazing up and illuminating the whole stage.'[7]

Unfortunately not even such a spectacular climax could efface the indifference with which the public had received the earlier scenes. The ballet lacked

Jules Perrot

cohesion, a shortcoming that was partly explained no doubt by the imposition on Jules of another choreographer's scenario. Ekaterina Friedberg had a disappointing reception, although she danced very gracefully and performed the mime scenes competently enough, particularly the *scènes dansantes* which ended the first and second acts. The only dancer to be awarded the honour of a second call that evening was Anna Prikhunova, for her variation in the *pas des odalisques*. Marius Petipa expended much energy in presenting Conrad as a Byronic hero, casting the terrible looks that the scenario called for at appropriate moments. One critic complained that he had no dancing to do in the ballet, and indeed, very unusually for a Perrot ballet, there was no conventional *pas de deux* containing a variation for the male dancer,* although Petipa was featured in one of the *scènes dansantes*.

Jules' own part of Seyd seems to have made little impression, and his reception at the end of the evening was so half-hearted that the critic of the *Sanktpeterburgskiye Vedomosti* chided the public for its want of feeling. 'Bearing in mind that he was working to someone else's idea, he performed his task conscientiously, and we were sorry that the public gave him a cool reception, forgetting all that he has done in the past and that it was the occasion of his benefit. We hope that when they take a closer look at the dances he has arranged, they will make amends for their coldness and remember that the Perrot who has staged this ballet . . . is also the Perrot who gave us *Catarina, Esmeralda, Faust, The War of the Women, Armida* and *Gazelda*. In the new ballet he plays a thankless part, but let us not forget that he is the motivating force behind everything that is done on the stage.'[8]

Jules must have been disheartened by this reception, although thanks largely to the spectacular climax, the ballet continued to draw full houses and was given fourteen times before the end of the season. In the course of these performances, a new *pas* was inserted for Muravieva in the first scene. In years to come *Le Corsaire* was to retain its place in the repertory, being revived from time to time by Marius Petipa. Its popularity seemed immune to the passing of time, and with elements of the original choreography remaining, it would still be arousing enthusiasm a century and more later.

* * *

Meanwhile the term of Jules' contract with the Imperial Theatres was running out. It was in fact due to expire on March 13th, but a request for its renewal had already been made, and on February 26th the Minister of the Imperial Court, Count Vladimir Adlerberg, officially notified Guedeonov of the Emperor's approval to an extension, on the same terms as before, for a further three years. The new contract was not drawn up then and there be-

---

* The celebrated *pas de deux* from *Le Corsaire* that is frequently performed as a separate number, was added, to music by Drigo, by Marius Petipa in 1899.

cause by that time, it seems, Jules had left St. Petersburg for France, permission to this effect having been granted a week earlier. Consequently he missed the last performances of the season, which were given in April that year, and the rôle of Seyd Pasha in *Le Corsaire* was taken over by Nicolai Goltz.

By the terms of the permission, he was obliged to return to Russia on June 27th, but he did not reappear in St. Petersburg until July 13th, returning with a dancer of the corps de ballet, Vodobievskaya. Two weeks' overstaying of leave was not taken very seriously, however; his excuse that he had been detained by family affairs connected with his father's estate was accepted, and no deduction was made from his salary.

He returned to find a new occupant in the Director's office. In May Guedeonov had been replaced by Andrei Ivanovitch Saburov, a boorish official whose twenty years at the Ministry of Finance seemed to have taught him little administrative acumen. His short tenure of the post – he was to leave under a cloud of scandal in 1862 – was to be remembered only for his financial irresponsibility and his unacceptable philandering among the girls at the Theatre School. All this lay in the future, but if Jules was a good judge of character, he cannot have viewed his future at the Bolshoi Theatre with much confidence.

The new contract arrived at the office of the Imperial Theatres shortly after his return, but he was reluctant to sign it. At this stage this was certainly not out of contempt for the new Director. The cause was more fundamental, stemming from a growing anxiety over his physical condition and its effect on his work. His right leg had been giving trouble for some time, and on several occasions he had had to interrupt his duties and rest at home until the pain disappeared and he could walk on it again. For the opening performance of the ballet season on October 5th, he was billed to partner Prikhunova in *La Vivandière*, but he was in such agony that he had to be replaced. The theatre doctor, Dr. Heidenreich, diagnosed him to be 'suffering from rheumatism in the three-headed muscle of the right leg, which also affects the lower ankle joint of the same leg. As a result, M. Perrot can neither walk nor stand on his right leg.'[9] Two days later Goltz took over his part in *Le Corsaire*, but massage and rest brought an improvement, and a week later Jules was able to appear in his rôle in *Armida* and on the 26th was well enough to play Nicaise in *La Fille mal gardée* at Goltz's benefit.

The new Director was anxious to impress the public, and more specifically to gain the favour of the influential balletomanes, and to inaugurate his new management, he had the good fortune to secure a celebrity of the first order. Friedberg's talents having proved all too modest and the native ballerinas being considered lacking in exotic appeal, an engagement had been concluded with Amalia Ferraris, the star of the Paris Opéra, a pupil of Carlo Blasis and an exceptionally accomplished virtuoso. Jules was delighted to learn that she was to make her Russian début at his benefit on November 16th,

Jules Perrot

and to receive approval for the production of a new version, greatly expanded from the original, of *Eoline, ou la Dryade*, which he had devised for Lucile Grahn in London thirteen years before.

It had not been revived since the year of its creation, 1845, and much of the choreography had to be created afresh, particularly now that it was to be expanded to fill a whole evening's programme. So he and Pugni set to work to transform it from a ballet designed to be played straight through without an interval into a full-length work in four acts. The scenario was elaborated, some subsidiary characters being given greater prominence and even names – notably a young couple, Frantz and Berta, to be played by Stukolkin and Maria Petipa, and Berta's wise old father, Hermann – and Pugni filled many pages of manuscript with additional action music and new dances, adding solos to be played by some of the distinguished instrumentalists in the orchestra: Ludwig Minkus the violinist, Ciardi the flautist, Cavalini on the cornet, Oscka Böhme on the cornet à piston, Montarini the trumpeter, and Schultz the harpist.

All the resources of the theatre were at his disposal. Roller was, as usual, in charge of the scenic spectacle and the machinery for the effects, having at his command Wagner, Shishkov, Chushkin and Egorov to help with the scene painting, Calvert and Stolyarov to produce the costumes, Gavrilov to manufacture the properties, and the fire master Shishko to handle the lighting effects. All these were highly skilled professionals, and everything was ready by the time the curtain was rung up for the first performance on November 16th, 1858.

Among the audience on that evening was an old friend from Jules' Paris days. Théophile Gautier had arrived in St. Petersburg on a tour of Russia, and had lingered there specially to see the ballet. He was curious to see how Ferraris would fare before a Russian audience, for he had not only watched her performances at the Opéra as a critic, but had written the scenario for her most recent triumph there, *Sacountala*. Now, under the chandelier of the Bolshoi, he was a focus of attention with his imposingly stout figure and leonine head, deriving obvious enjoyment from the occasion. He was revelling in the attention paid him as a celebrity, and played his part as a connoisseur and the ballerina's champion with great panache, applauding her with ostentatious enthusiasm. Brandishing the playbill, he declared himself fascinated by the strange names of the Russian *danseuses*, names that caressed him 'like unfamiliar bird songs.'[10] After the performance he was to write a long article on Ferraris's début for the French-language newspaper, the *Journal de Saint-Pétersbourg*.

The expansion of the ballet had turned it into virtually a new work, the greatest change being apparent in the first act. Gautier was overwhelmed from the very first rise of the curtain, revealing a vast underground mine, with a great stairway leading to an aperture far above, where a patch of open sky was to be seen. The arrival of the miners' wives and children, tripping faultlessly down the steps, gave him an enchanting introduction to the St. Petersburg corps de ballet. This was the signal for the miners to break off their work to celebrate the approaching marriage of their lord, Count Edgar, unaware that their mine is the domain of a more powerful master, Rübezahl, the King of the Gnomes. This was the rôle Jules had created in London, and he again reserved it for himself in St. Petersburg. Gautier described his entrance at this point of the ballet. 'An enormous block of liquified slag suddenly splits apart, and out darts a supernatural creature – half god, half demon – wearing a short white cloak on his shoulders, a breast plate and spangled greaves that were no doubt forged by Vulcan, his mythical forbear. This is Rübezahl. At first irritated by all this noise, he quickly recovers his spirits at the sight of the dancing, and comes down from his rock to join in. Making himself invisible, as if he were wearing the ring of Gyges, he circulates among the groups, playing pranks and upsetting them all.'[11] This was the dramatic thread that ran through the *danse des mineurs*, a *ballabile* to march-like music for twenty *danseuses* and an unspecified number of other dancers of both sexes, which introduced incidents involving Rübezahl and the young couple, Frantz and Bertha.

Count Edgar himself, played by Christian Johansson, then arrives, followed shortly by his fiancée Eoline – a moment interrupted by a burst of applause to greet Ferraris on her first appearance. An interesting effect had been thought up to convey the dual nature of Eoline, mortal by day and dryad by night. Again in Gautier's words, 'behind her beauty you admire that of another being, shining through the first like a flame in an alabaster globe. The impression is given, by sudden phosphorescences,' – produced by the imaginative skill of Shishko – 'that Eoline is only the envelope, the transparent veil of a superior being, a goddess condemned by some fate to live among men.'[12] The noble party are entertained by the miners, who perform a local dance, *La Silésienne*, in which they are joined by both Edgar and Eoline. Rübezahl then reappears, and it is clear from his ecstatic pose with hands outstretched that he is infatuated with Eoline. In a flash he turns into a miner, to approach her in so awkward a manner that everybody bursts out laughing. He vanishes in confusion, only to reappear with bars of gold and silver and jewels, which he lays at her feet. Turning to Edgar, he accuses him of stealing minerals from his domain and declares himself a contender for Eoline's hand. Edgar draws his sword, but strikes empty air, for Rübezahl has already vanished into the earth. Edgar and Eoline and the miners leave the cave in confusion.

When they have gone, the gnomes – represented by forty-four pupils of the Imperial Theatre School – emerge from their caves, followed by four sprites. In a *danse des gnomes*, Rübezahl's page Trilby (a travesty rôle for Vera Lyadova) and the gnomes and sprites try in vain to arouse their master's spirits. To explain the cause of his sombre mood, he produces a vision of Eoline reclining on a couch as Edgar whispers words of love at her feet. The very sight of this sends Rübezahl into a frenzy. A second vision depicts a wood inhabited by drayds, who point to the oak tree to which Eoline's fate is linked. To emphasise the point, Eoline's everyday costume suddenly vanishes and she appears as a dryad. The vision then fades. Rübezahl swears that the girl will be his, and as he flies off to attain his end, his subjects bow in submission.

The second act bore a much greater similarity to the original version. Day is breaking over the castle. At one side is a ruined tower, with the remains of an old oak tree, blackened by fire, alongside. A group of miners and their wives are preparing for the wedding ceremony. One of them suggests cutting down the old tree, but an old man restrains him and mimes the legend attached to it. Long ago, it appears, the tree was the refuge of a spirit who inhabited the wood at night. It was also the favourite haunt of Eoline's mother, then the owner of the castle. But one day lightning killed both her and the tree, and the spirit was seen no more. While the miners are inspecting the mysterious tree, Rübezahl appears briefly 'amid a crackle of sparks'[13] from a fissure in the tower wall. A spirit, recognisably in the form of Eoline, is then seen gliding across the river, hovering sadly at the tree before flying away at the approach of a stranger. This is Trilby, whose interest has been aroused by the arrival of some women who have come to pick flowers. He watches them as they dance a *pas des fleurs*, arranged for fifteen *danseuses* led by Muravieva, who was given a variation. He then enjoys himself at Berta's expense, and finally chases them all away with his pranks. Rübezahl, who has more important work to do, puts a stop to this frivolity and leads him away.

The wedding festivities begin, and are in full swing when Rübezahl, 'dressed in bizarre magnificence'[14] as a nobleman, reappears among the guests. Eoline, who has just danced a charming *andante* variation to a harp solo, trembles with fear at this strange apparition. When Rübezahl asks her to dance, she is filled with revulsion, but finds herself unwillingly following his steps as if impelled by some unseen force. This was the prelude to the *mazurka d'extase*, the *pas d'action* that had caused such a sensation in London many years before. In Gautier's review of the St. Petersburg production, he went to some length to record his impressions of Ferraris in this dance. 'You can sense the supernatural force that dominates the will, overcomes resistance, fascinates like a snake, and draws its victim to the abyss,' he wrote. 'Hypnotised by his glance, Eoline rises to her feet and begins to dance with him. She is like a dove flying down, from branch to branch, towards the reptile that lies in wait at the foot of the tree – feathers ruffled, wings aquiver, terrified yet fascinated. It is obvious that Eoline has no love for Rübezahl, yet this magical dance benumbs and intoxicates her. An insidious languor softens her movements, her head droops, her eyes become misty, and her lips part in a smile as her breathing quickens. Half fainting, she falls into Rübezahl's arms.'[15]

Obtaining its effect by dance movements rather than mime, this *pas* was so masterfully conceived that it concealed Ferraris's shortcomings as an actress. One critic, M. Rappaport, claimed it was 'almost entirely a repetition of the mazurka in the ball scene of *Faust*,'[16] but he could only have been referring to the part played by the corps de ballet, who were undoubtedly given the conventional mazurka step to perform.

The third act opened with a mime scene set in Eoline's chamber. Eoline wakes from a troubled sleep, and while trying on her wedding dress, is startled to see in her mirror the reflection of Rübezahl. Filled with panic, she looks again to find that it has vanished . . . but so too has her own reflection. Rübezahl then flies in through the window to complete his conquest. Declaring his love, he seizes her as she tries to escape and takes her into his arms. She is about to submit when a distant clock strikes midnight, and a ray of moonlight shines into the room. It is the hour of her metamorphosis, and the dryad liberates itself from Eoline's mortal shell, disappearing into the night. Edgar, alerted by Eoline's cries, rushes into the chamber and finds Rübezahl there. The gnome tells him that Eoline is dead. Edgar draws his sword, but as the weapons clash, blue sparks fly from Rübezahl's sword and Edgar's arm falls useless to his side. Before he can recover, Rübezahl has vanished.

The scene changes to the wood. The emergence of the dryads from their trees to welcome Eoline leads into the *grand pas des dryades*, in which Ferraris and three soloists – Anna Kosheva, Elizaveta Nikitina and Maria Efremova – were supported by sixty-four *danseuses* of the corps de ballet. Some thought that this dance was too long-drawn-out, distracting attention from Eoline herself, whose participation added nothing to the development of her character or to the understanding of her predicament. The dryads are interrupted by Rübezahl, now in the form of a woodcutter. In his search for Eoline he draws the dryads out of their trees by threatening to hack them down. Finally he comes to Eoline's oak. She appears, imploring him to spare her tree. Her 'graceful entreaties and chaste blandishments calm the demon's anger, and he is then surrounded by her companions, who form groups that conceal her as she makes her escape.'[17] Edgar is then discovered in the dryads' midst. He cannot believe his eyes when he sees Eoline, whose lifeless body he had discovered in her room. But in her dryad form she has no recollection of her earthly existence. Confused, Edgar joins in the dryads' dance, and Eoline gives him a twig from her tree. Danger, however, is lurking in the shadows; a burst of flame announces the return of Rübezahl, and the dryads disappear into their trees. Surrounded by gnomes, Edgar finds his sword arm paralysed, and Rübezahl stands before him, laughing in triumph as the curtain falls.

The last act opened in a gallery of the castle. It is the day of the wedding. Eoline has resumed her mortal form, and her stepfather reveals the secret of her birth. Edgar, believing that Eoline is lost to him, thinks he is suffering from a hallucination when he sees her. He tells her of his meeting with the

Jules Perrot

dryads and shows her the twig, but she looks at him in utter incomprehension. After the wedding procession has moved into the chapel, Rübezahl appears. Thwarted by the sanctity of the chapel, he resolves in desperation to destroy the oak tree, and departs, making menacing gestures.

The bridal couple emerge from the chapel, and the final divertissement begins with a *grand pas de cinq*, containing four variations, and moves on to the crowning set-piece, a *pas de deux* for Ferraris and Johansson. In it Jules had summoned all his insight and skill to display Ferraris's extraordinary talent. Gautier called it a 'supreme *pas*,' in which the ballerina expressed 'the chaste intoxication and heavenly joy of lawful love,'[18] but in a more down-to-earth analysis, it was a technical display of staggering brilliance in which she never lost the precision and polish that were the hallmarks of her style. A triple pirouette on *pointe* drew gasps of amazement from the audience for the speed with which she spun, her waist held lightly in the safe hands of Johansson. More sensational still were turns performed with the working leg stretched horizontally in *arabesque*. Her feats on her *pointes* were no less extraordinary. She not only stepped on her *pointes*, but she jumped on them, no mean feat in days when the blocked shoe had not been developed. At one moment 'she stands on the *pointe* of one foot, supporting herself on the shoulder of Johansson, who then slips away from under her hand to perform a slow pirouette, leaving her on *pointe*, occasionally giving a little quiver to maintain her balance . . . And then she turns gently on one foot so smoothly that her whole body seems to remain still, as if she were being revolved by an unseen force. The best ballerinas hop slightly when performing a turn like this.'[19]*

Nor did Jules neglect Johansson, who was presented with a fine opportunity to show off the classical precision of his style. In his variation he was loudly applauded for a *double tour en l'air*, performed with his whole body impeccably stretched and without seeming to deviate by a single inch from the perpendicular.

When the applause had died down, the action of the ballet was resumed. Eoline is filled with a presentiment of disaster. Suddenly the gallery is lit by a fiery glow. With a loud crack, the windows fall in and the dryads' wood is seen to be on fire. As the flames take hold – a spectacular effect brilliantly managed by the fire master, Shishko – Eoline's oak tree is consumed with the others. After a touching farewell to her husband Eoline dies. Rübezahl appears to savour his triumph, laughing diabolically, while in an apotheosis the dryads, with Eoline in their midst, are seen rising into the sky amid swirling clouds of smoke and flame.

It was nearly midnight when the audience emerged into the cold square outside the theatre. They had received good value for their money – being a benefit performance, the higher Italian opera prices had been charged – but

---

*From the description this would seem to be a *promenade* on the flat foot.

five hours had been a long time to sit through a single ballet. However, they still had energy left to give the dancers a prolonged ovation at the end, and Jules took several calls with Ferraris. After the disappointing reception of *Le Corsaire*, he could feel satisfied that his creative powers had not deserted him. The only pity, as the *Sanktpeterburgskiye Vedomosti* pointed out, was 'that Perrot was unwilling or perhaps unable to make it shorter. The ballet world is subject to numerous pressures, of which the public is unaware, and which are traps for the ballet-master, binding him hand and foot, fettering his imagination, and forcing him to do things he would not have done if he had been a completely free agent. It is very difficult and sometimes impossible to contend with these pressures. During the preparation of a ballet "influences" in tutus and tights are continually pestering the unfortunate ballet-master. "I want to dance a solo." "I too." "And I." "Give me the pride of place." "And me." "And me." "I have not had a variation for a long time." "Why have you given a solo to her, and not to me?" This cacophonous chorus, rising to a crescendo at each rehearsal, becomes a deafening *tutti*. The ballet-master's head spins, he loses his concentration, and fantasy begins to distort the inventiveness which, in the original conception, had a pristine beauty. This lady and that must be placated, everyone must be placated. That is why we do not blame Perrot for the length of the ballet, but merely record it with regret.'[20]

In response to such criticism the ballet was shortened at the second performance, and continued to draw good houses during the remainder of the season. By any standard it was a creditable addition to Jules' repertoire. Its subject had an obvious appeal to St. Petersburg society, with its strong German element, the spectacular effects were perfectly managed, and last but not least, the choreography was as inventive as anything Jules had created.

* * *

At the end of November, while dancing in *Eoline*, Jules' leg failed him again. He was at the time coaching Ferraris to play Marguerite in *Faust*, and this task may have had to devolve on someone else. She was not an ideal choice for the part, which she first played on December 21st; as a virtuoso she was inimitable – and Jules had added 'some felicitous novelites'[21] specially for her – but the passages that relied on dramatic interpretation, such as the Dance of the Seven Deadly Sins and the mad scene, were beyond her.

Jules was unable to play his old rôle of Mephistopheles, as he had planned, for three days before, in another performance of *Eoline*, he had collapsed in excruciating pain, far worse than anything he had experienced before. His doctor told him that his ankle was inflamed as a result of overwork. To add to his troubles, the theatre began to press him to return to work. He fully understood the Direction's concern, and was 'embarrassed and annoyed' that he could not tell them when he would be well enough to resume his duties. He

Jules Perrot

was faced with an agonising problem.

'I can only assure you of my zeal and my goodwill,' he wrote to the Head of Repertoire, Pavel Fyodorov, on January 11th, 'but reflecting on the series of relapses I have had, I am wondering whether I ought to take on the responsibility for the end of the season. This is a very serious question, which I cannot resolve from my sickbed. Time is pressing, and uninterrupted attention is needed to complete the work I had begun to compose for Mme Ferraris's benefit. But can I be certain that when I have recovered, I shall not be struck down again, for the sixth time, and even more seriously, at the most critical moment? Alas, I cannot. You see the quandary I am in. The Direction and the doctors must make the decision, for it scares me to think that my previous accident in *La Dryade* was only a month ago and was much less serious.'[22]

The state of the ballet-master's health soon became general knowledge. 'Perrot is unwell and is confined to his bed,' it was reported. 'Who then will stage the new ballet, and will there even be a new ballet?'[23] New ballet there was not, and for her benefit on February 12th, 1859, Ferraris had to be content with a programme cobbled out of the first acts of *The Naiad and the Fisherman* and *Giselle*, with the addition of a reproduction of *Le Carnaval de Venise*, hastily arranged by Marius Petipa.

Jules was so shattered by the deterioration of his health that he could not bring himself to sign the new contract. His reluctance had been reinforced by a disturbing incident in his apartment on the Perspectiv Nevsky. One evening when he and his family were entertaining some friends, a large mirror suddenly fell from the wall of the salon for no apparent reason and shattered into pieces. Jules, who was very superstitious, took this as a sign that he should leave Russia.

Meanwhile he was becoming increasingly out of favour. The new Director, Saburov, was hostile to him from the start, and even in November was proposing to the Minister that he should be retained for one year and that two months of his salary should be withheld for absences. Count Adlerberg, however, was more understanding, and Jules continued to receive his basic salary.

In the summer of 1859 he was granted leave to go to France for three months for treatment, but as a precaution he was made to sign an undertaking that he would be back in St. Petersburg by August 1st to produce a new ballet for the opening of the season. Saburov had little confidence that he would comply and accordingly made contingency plans. He was authorised to conclude a contract with Arthur Saint-Léon for the forthcoming season, ostensibly as ballet-master in Moscow, but with a provision that, if needed, he would stage the ballet *Jovita* in St. Petersburg. Since Jules was still in receipt of his salary, the Ministry made it clear that the salary of 6,000 roubles to be paid to Saint-Léon was to come out of the funds allotted to the Direction, and that Saburov could only look to the Court in the event of Jules being dismissed.

In the event this proved a wise precaution, for Jules wrote from Paris saying that he was still ill and that it would be some time before he would be well enough to return. He was thereupon notified that his salary would not be paid during any period of absence without leave, and Saint-Léon obligingly arrived in St. Petersburg to produce *Jovita*.

When Jules eventually returned to St. Petersburg in November, he may have expected a cool reception from Saburov, but he was certainly not prepared for the extraordinary scene that was enacted when he called to discuss the renewal of his contract. On entering Saburov's office, he began to state the object of his visit.

'I have the honour to present myself to you, Monsieur l'impresario, in order . . .'

At this point Saburov abruptly interrupted. 'Monsieur Perrot,' he spluttered, 'you should know that I am not an impresario, but a high dignitary . . .'

'Your Excellency,' Jules interposed, 'a theatre director is also called an impresario.'

'No, Monsieur Perrot! For the second time I must tell you that I am an important dignitary in the Emperor's service.'

Without more ado Saburov stood up and left the room. Jules waited for a while in case the Director cooled down and returned, but after a few minutes, realising that the interview was at an end, he departed too, being heard to mutter on his way out: 'And an important fool too!'[24]

Although he did not resume his duties, the Imperial Theatres continued to pay his salary, but insisted on making a deduction for the three and a half months' unauthorised absence. In spite of feeling increasingly aggrieved at the financial loss which was accruing from his illness, Jules still clutched at the hope of returning to work, and early in 1860 he submitted a new scenario for approval.

This was given a formal reading in May 1860, and afterwards Jules took the opportunity of speaking to Count Adlerberg about his financial worries. Saburov had expressed willingness to cancel the deduction from his salary, but explained that this could only be done if the Minister authorised it. Jules then raised the question of the period of his service to be counted towards a pension. He had first arrived in St. Petersburg in December 1848, but it was only towards the end of 1849, when his contract with the Paris Opéra ended, that he had been exclusively engaged by the Imperial Theatres. Consequently, under the pension regulations, the entitlement period could not begin earlier than on March 1st, 1850. But then his service had been interrupted in March 1851, with the result that the commencement date had been advanced to March 1852. He felt it was very unfair that this interruption should be counted against him when during the course of it, he had been commanded to organise the famous gala performance at Peterhof in July 1851, and he suggested that this should entitle him to be treated as a special case.

Jules Perrot

A few days after this interview, before leaving for his summer visit to Paris, he took up the Minister's suggestion to put his case in writing. The financial consequences of his illness had been considerable, he explained. He had lost 2,000 roubles in 1858–59 and 3,000 roubles in 1859–60 in performance fees, and another 3,000 roubles through forgoing his benefit in 1859–60. Then there were the 2,888.89 roubles deducted from his salary because he had overstayed his leave in 1859. Casting his mind back to earlier years, he cited a loss of 3,000 roubles resulting from the postponement of his benefit in 1854–55 because he could not finish *Armida* in time, and the interruption of his service in 1851–52, which had cost him 7,500 roubles in salary and the loss of another benefit. In all, these losses added up to 24,388.89 roubles, 'almost a fortune for a dancer.' It was all most unfair considering the zeal with which he had not only served the Imperial Theatres, but also performed the duties of court choreographer at Peterhof, Tsarskoe Selo, the Hermitage, and the palace of the Duke of Edinburgh, Queen Victoria's second son who had married the Tsar's daughter Marie. Nor should it be overlooked, he added, that 'my injury was received in the course of my duties, and that it was in resuming my duties that it was aggravated to the point of paralysing my career as a dancer.'[25]

On May 21st, 1860, Jules left St. Petersburg, having done nothing in the theatre during the season that had just ended. He returned early in September accompanied by two other dancers who had been given foreign leave at the same time, Evdokia Apollonskaya, a *coryphée*, and Vodobievskaya, a dancer of the corps de ballet.

Saburov felt that the situation could no longer be tolerated, and wrote to Adlerberg on November 27th: 'The ballet-master Perrot has not fulfilled the terms of his contract with the theatre, in spite of the indulgence we have shown him and his high salary. Last year he did not perform a single one of his duties; he did not produce a single ballet, and did not appear in a single performance. Consequently he was completely useless, and the high salary he received was completely wasted. During the present season, despite all the encouragement we have given him and his promises, he has not so far done anything, and I do not expect him to carry out any of the obligations for which he has been engaged at a high salary. Saint-Léon is performing all his duties, as he did last year, for half his salary. Consequently I consider that to retain M. Perrot any longer would set a bad example to the company, and that he should be dismissed from his post. This seems all the more justified because, as Your Excellency already knows, M. Perrot refused to sign the contract when Acting Privy Councillor Pusenov offered to extend it, and since then has continued without any contract at all. Because of this he is free to leave St. Petersburg at any time he wishes, and the Direction is equally at liberty to dismiss him.'[26]

The Minister agreed that enough was enough, and with the Tsar's approval, Jules was notified that he was dismissed and that his salary would cease to be paid from the date of the Tsar's decision, December 5th, 1860. Mercifully the blow was softened. To assure him that he was not being dismissed with ignominy and assuage his injured feelings, the Tsar gave him a farewell gift which he would treasure to the end of his days – a snuff box in blue enamel, decorated with the Emperor's portrait surrounded by as many diamonds as the years he had spent in the Imperial service.

19

Frustrations of Retirement

Very depressed, and still smarting from a feeling of injustice at his treatment by the Imperial Theatres, Jules arrived in Paris in the summer of 1861. He settled first of all in a bachelor flat in the Boulevard Saint-Martin until he was joined by his family, for whom he found a pleasant and commodious apartment in the Rue des Martyrs that was to be their home for the next seventeen years. Soon he was accustoming himself to being a Parisian, surrounded by his wife, his two growing daughters – Marie, now ten years old, and Alexandrine, who was eight – and a first cousin of his wife, Maria Samovskaya, who was known to the children as Tante Marie.

He was feeling very vulnerable. At the age of fifty-one, he found it hard to accept that he no longer possessed the stamina and the creative energy of his prime, his pride had been deeply wounded by the ignominy of his dismissal by the Imperial Theatres, and he could not understand why the Paris Opéra did not avail itself of his services. This bitterness bit more deeply into his soul when he learnt that Marius Petipa and his wife had arrived in Paris and were being received with open arms by Alphonse Royer, the Director of the Opéra. Enjoying the protection of the Duchesse de Morny, wife of the Emperor's half brother and President of the Chamber, and the support of his brother Lucien, who was now chief ballet-master, Marius Petipa had been honoured with an invitation from the Opéra to stage a short ballet in which Maria Petipa was to make her Paris début. *Le Marché des Innocents* was only a trifle, a revival of a minor work he had produced in St. Petersburg two years before, but it provided Maria Petipa with a brilliant triumph when it was presented to the Parisians at the end of May 1861, and as a token of appreciation, since no fee had been arranged, Royer had granted her the exceptional favour of a benefit.

This was to take place on August 6th, and wishing to present his wife in a striking novelty appropriate to the occasion, Marius Petipa conceived the idea of interpolating into his ballet the set of national dances, *La Cosmopolitana*, from Jules' ballet *Gazelda*. Very conveniently he had brought the orchestral parts with him in his luggage, and all that was needed was the apparent formality of obtaining Jules' permission.

Frustrations of Retirement

It must have seemed that a more propitious setting for a request could hardly be chosen than a wedding reception, and by a happy chance just such an event was at hand. Zina Richard, who had left the St. Petersburg ballet some years previously to accept an engagement at the Opéra, had fallen in love with the young *premier danseur*, Louis Mérante. They made an attractive pair, she pert and petite in her white dress and he youthfully slender and handsome in his new black suit, as they stood before the altar in the Church of Notre Dame de Lorette. Behind them stood their bridesmaid, a thin slip of a girl whose plain features would have attracted little attention in any other gathering, but whose name, Emma Livry, was on everyone's lips in the church that day. The favourite pupil of Marie Taglioni and the white hope of the Opéra ballet, she had made a sensational début in *La Sylphide* not three years before, and in the winter just past had had her first important creation in Marie Taglioni's new ballet, *Le Papillon*. The dance community was well represented in the congregation, and as Jules looked about him during the service, he recognised many familiar faces, including his fellow choreographer, Joseph Mazilier, and also the Petipa family – Lucien, Marius and Maria.

Confident that he had chosen his moment cunningly well, Marius Petipa took his opportunity to broach the matter of *La Cosmopolitana*. To his surprise the response was negative.

'No, my friend, I cannot consent.'

'But why?'

'Because the Director of the Opéra here, and everybody else, have quite disgracefully turned against me.'

'But it is not the Director who is asking a favour, but me, your friend,' Petipa pleaded.

Jules remained adamant. 'No,' he said flatly, in a tone that made it clear that the matter was closed.

Clearly Petipa had not expected such a rebuff, which seemed to him quite unreasonable, but he was equally determined not to change his plans.

'As you wish, old friend,' he replied angrily, 'but my wife will dance the *pas* all the same, in spite of your refusal. Good day!'[1]

Although Marius Petipa made a few changes in the choreography and altered the title to *La Cosmopolite*, it was virtually the same *pas* that Jules had arranged in *Gazelda*. There was no question of Petipa holding it out as his own choreography, for he gave Jules full credit in the programme,[2] but that was small comfort for Jules when he reflected on how much the benefit must have brought Maria Petipa. If the sum, virtually earned in a single evening, was as high as 18,000 francs, as Petipa stated in his memoirs, Jules must have contrasted this gain bitterly with the losses he had suffered over the years through injury.

Not only was no notice taken of his demand that the Opéra withdraw the *pas*, but it was quite deliberately flouted, for the *pas* was repeated three times

Jules Perrot

after the benefit. Incensed at being treated in such an off-hand fashion, Jules consulted his lawyer and instituted proceedings against Marius Petipa.

The case came up for hearing in the First Chamber of the Tribunal Civil de la Seine the following summer, on July 11th, 1862, and broke new ground by being the first action in the French courts for breach of copyright in a choreographic work. Jules was represented by a brilliant young lawyer, Maître Etienne Carraby, who opened his case with a quotation from a friend of his client who had described Petipa's behaviour as 'choreographic larceny.' Asserting that choreography was as much a fine art as sculpture, he argued that the groups and plastic arrangements that composed it could equally be the product of creative genius. It was not merely poetry expressed in movement, but being an imitative art, it was more vivid in its impact than ever *basso relievo* could be. A *maître de ballet* was, therefore, just as much entitled to the product of his creation as a composer was to an aria he had written. Petipa had no right to pirate Perrot's works on the boards of the Opéra. Nevertheless, he had to concede that 'from the outset the case presented perhaps some difficulty, and it was no doubt on this,' he continued, 'that the defendant has relied. For how can it be established, as a fact, that a *pas* danced in St. Petersburg is the same as a *pas* danced in Paris? Some choreographers commit their *pas* to writing, others memorise them ... But unfortunately Perrot creates his works on the dancers and does not write them down.'

As evidence in support of his case, Me Carraby put in a declaration by Arthur Saint-Léon, who had seen both works and attested them to be one and the same, and who, somewhat gratuitously, posed the question why Perrot, the author of so many works, should go to so much trouble in establishing his rights in a single *pas* if it was not incontravertibly his own work in law.

Petipa's defence was conducted by one of the most distinguished advocates of the Paris bar, Louis-Adolphe Chaix d'Est'Ange, a man whose experience and forensic skill was no doubt matched by his fee. He based his defence on the copyright treaty between France and Russia, which did not extend to dramatic works. He conceded that copyright could exist in a printed ballet scenario, but argued that the steps themselves were quite a different matter, for 'it is the dancer herself who is everything, it is her grace, her strength, her expression, all the skill of her body, and her features that achieve the success.' Many ballets, he pointed out, had included *pas* such as the one in dispute, and he cited two which had been produced at the Opéra, *La Péri* and *Le Corsaire*. And as for the contention that there was plagiarism because the same music had been used, the composer in this case, Pugni, had expressly given Marius Petipa permission to use any of his music he wished. Finally he made the observation that Jules himself was not wholly innocent of the sort of plagiarism he was alleging, for in St. Petersburg he had staged works by other choreographers which had been presented as being by him, such as *La Fille de marbre*.[3]

The judge, M. Benoit-Champy, found in favour of Jules, but clearly viewed the dispute as being of minor importance, for he did not award him the damages he claimed – 10,000 francs – but put his loss at the modest figure of 300 francs. In his judgment he held that 'a *pas* from a ballet composed of national dances from different countries, but combined in such a way as to form a particular and distinct composition, constitutes an intellectual work that is protected by the law of literary and artistic property.'[4] He also rejected M[e] Chaix d'Est'Ange's plea about the Franco-Russian treaty because although the *pas* was created in Russia, it was composed by a Frenchman and the court therefore had jurisdiction.

* * *

At the time this law suit was pending, Jules was re-reading one of the great classics of dance literature – Noverre's *Lettres sur la danse, sur les ballets et les arts*, which he had bought, in the four-volume edition published in St. Petersburg in 1803–04, when he was in Russia. Many of the principles first laid down by his celebrated predecessor, who had done so much to establish the *ballet d'action* as a theatre form in its own right, still seemed very valid in the context of the Romantic ballet a century after they had been written, but Jules did not accept all of them without question. One passage in particular bore a special relevance for him. In his Thirteenth Letter, Noverre had dismissed as of little value the system of notation, known as *Chorégraphie*, that was still studied and used in his day. Here Jules knew from experience that Noverre had been wrong, for the absence of a written record of his own works had been mentioned specifically by his counsel in his action against Petipa, and he was painfully aware of how fragile still were the laws protecting a choreographer's copyright. 'It is a matter of regret,' he wrote in pencil in the margin alongside this passage, 'that *Chorégraphie* has not kept abreast of progress in dancing. The creative ballet-master would not then have been exposed to being robbed by base rogues.'

Apart from this one passage, which touched a very sensitive nerve, Jules found it a fascinating exercise to consider Noverre's theories in the light of his own work, marking the passages that seemed particularly apt and, here and there, adding brief comments in the margin. These pencillings offer a unique, if disappointingly inadequate, insight into his artistic philosophy, for he lived in the days before newspaper interviews, and being almost congenitally reluctant to put pen to paper, never recorded his own thoughts in the way that his articulate colleague Bournonville did. That he did not do so was posterity's loss, for he was the most innovative ballet-master of his time and had he been able to follow Noverre's example and set down his own doctrine of choreography, he would have illuminated so many corners of the Romantic ballet that are now lost in darkness. As it is, his lightly annotated volumes of Noverre's Letters open a thin but valuable chink in the curtain, revealing

Jules Perrot

some of his reactions to the principles of his predecessor, many of which he developed to a degree which their originator had never been able to attain in the conditions of his own period.

In his First Letter Noverre set out his basic principle for constructing a *ballet d'action* – that the dance element should be combined with the action to give the work meaning and purpose – and with this Jules was wholly in agreement. 'To the best of my ability I have followed what the author says,' he noted alongside this passage, 'and I believe I have succeeded in several of my works.' It was this intimate interlocking of dance and pantomime that entitled ballet, in Noverre's eyes, to be regarded as an imitative art. Noverre went on to draw an analogy with painting. A close study of the old masters could teach a choreographer many useful lessons, such as how to break the rules of strict symmetry to obtain greater realism and a more expressive effect. In arranging the action in a general scene, for example, it was essential to vary the attitudes and shades of expression of the performers. This seemed an obvious truth to Jules, who had demonstrated it so clearly in many of his ballets – most notably in *Esmeralda, Catarina* and *Odetta* – but he had to admit that even in his day most choreographers practised their craft in blissful ignorance of it. 'Why is this advice so seldom followed?' he asked. The answer revealed his contempt for the majority of his colleagues. 'It is because talent and imagination are needed to do so.'

Since a narrative was, by definition, an essential element in a *ballet d'action*, much depended on the use of pantomime, and Noverre, never losing sight of the importance of moving the audience, underlined the danger of slavishly following the formal rules at the expense of allowing the performers to feel their parts through their gestures. Again he returned to the analogy with painting. The choreographer must look on his work as if it were a painting, for both arts were representations or imitations of nature, and he should exclude anything from his stage picture that a painter would reject from his canvas. The action must all be part of the general picture. In a ballet about Telemachus on the Island of Calypso, for example, Mentor should be introduced as a dancing character with steps appropriate to his age and calling, if he was not to appear out of place and his powers of expression wanting in grace. On this point Jules was not convinced. 'Noverre, this is going too far!' he exclaimed. 'In our time a dancing Mentor would cause the audience to split its sides with laughter.'

Constantly Noverre stressed the need to arouse the audience's emotions. He was sure that once this was achieved, dancing would receive the same level of praise and respect that was accorded to poetry or painting. In his day the *ballet d'action* was still a novel and experimental form, but he saw its potential very clearly, even if he himself was never to put his ideas into practice to his complete satisfaction. Jules found that these Letters were still extraordi-

Frustrations of Retirement

narily relevent and, having developed the *ballet d'action* further than any other choreographer of his time, he could derive much satisfaction from judging his own works against the yardstick of his predecessor. One passage which he marked was obviously directly applicable to such ballets as *Esmeralda*, *Catarina*, *Odetta* and *Faust*, in which he had succeeded in gripping the audience by the intensity of the drama so that they identified themselves with the fate and the feelings of the characters:

> If our art is able to fascinate and enthral the spectator in its present imperfect state, and dancing can at times stir our emotions and create a pleasing flutter in our hearts without the added charm of expression, how strongly could it dominate our senses if its movements were directed with wit and its tableaux drawn with feeling! Ballet would undoubtedly vie with painting if the performers were not such automatons, and the choreographers were better trained.
>
> A beautiful painting is only a copy of nature, while a beautiful ballet is nature itself, embellished with all the charms of art. If simple images can create illusion, if I can be carried away by the magic of painting, imagine how deeply I would be moved by a performance that was even truer to life and played by my fellow creatures, and how much my imagination would be fired by living and varied tableaux. Nothing interests man more than man himself.[5]

Jules shared Noverre's exasperation at the bad taste and bad habits that had been prevalent among dancers and ballet-masters in his time, and had not been eradicated a hundred years later. Noverre's solution was for a reformer, like himself, who would abolish mincing manners and make the dancers express themselves simply and naturally. His ideal choreographer would not only compose his dances with wit and meaning, but be able to impose his will so that everything was in good taste. If this could be achieved, Noverre remarked in a rare flash of humour, many bad dancers and choreographers would be freed for more useful work in factories and workshops! Jules marked this whole passage, wishing perhaps that some of his own colleagues could have been directed into more gainful employment.

As his pencillings reveal, Jules paid particular attention to the intellectual accomplishments which Noverre sought in his ideal *maître de ballet*. Genius, imagination and taste were, of course, essential prerequisites that could never be acquired by study, and these Jules must have confidently and in all modesty felt he possessed in good measure. But did his own education, fragmented by the exigencies of his career, match up to the other requirements? Noverre insisted on a very solid background of knowledge: history, legend, ancient poetry and modern science; music, of course, anatomy and stage machinery; geometry to bring clarity, order and precision to the choreography, and the ability to combine the vision of the poet with that of the painter, the one to conceive and the other to execute. Jules agreed fully about the importance of music. 'Yes,' he wrote, 'it is essential to be a musician, and well organised.' But he may have felt somewhat deficient in some of the other subjects, for he

325

added: 'Noverre demands too much knowledge from a *maître de ballet*. It is possible to design felicitous groups without being a painter. Taste and yet more taste.'

Tastes had changed enormously since Noverre's time, and nineteenth-century audiences were drawn from a much wider section of the public. The tragic style of pantomime which Noverre favoured as being so forceful and distinct would have appeared unacceptably exaggerated to the public of Jules' day. The old ballet-master's warning against mixing styles, however, was still very relevant, and Jules, on the strength of his own experience, endorsed Noverre's comment that Paris audiences were over-indulgent in this respect. He himself had introduced an element of comedy into his serious ballets only very occasionally and when dramatically justified, and he had been careful to take the comic rôles himself so that it was always kept under control. Gringoire's comic scenes in *Esmeralda* were designed to show the awkwardness of his devotion to the heroine; Villon in *Odetta* was a professional jester with his heart in the right place; Gianneo in *Armida* was a foil to the more serious characters; while Seyd Pasha in *Le Corsaire*, a much less rewarding rôle, became more than a stock villain thanks to the judicious touches of comedy that Jules injected into his performance.

Jules' comments and markings become rarer after the Fifth Letter, not that he got no further in his reading, but no doubt because of his natural disinclination to take up his pencil. He had annotated the book purely for his own interest, but in doing so he left a striking example of the continuing tradition of his art, and proof that he saw himself as an artist working, not in isolation, but fed by the experience, the ideas and the discoveries of his predecessors. Just as he looked back gratefully and appreciatively to Noverre, so later choreographers – and particularly Marius Petipa, even if he was not in Jules' good books just then – were to regard him as a master and a model.

* * *

Jules' hot-headed recourse to the courts was not likely to improve his chances of being employed at the Opéra, and early in the following year, 1863, his sense of grievance at being passed over was aggravated by the news that plans were afoot to revive *Giselle*, and that Lucien Petipa was to be in charge of the production. Perhaps he felt a further twist of the dagger when he recollected that because his contribution to the choreography, however significant, had been anonymous, he would have no right to any royalties. The decision to revive *Giselle* had stemmed from the engagement of Martha Muravieva as guest ballerina during the summer months separating the St. Petersburg seasons. It was planned to produce a new ballet for her, but because of the limited term of her engagement the Opéra was anxious to present her to the public as soon as possible after her arrival. *Giselle* seemed a very appropriate choice, being in the St. Petersburg repertory, and although it had not been given in Paris for some years, being remembered sufficiently well there to be produced quickly.

Happily Muravieva had been well advised before leaving Russia, and she lost little time, after her arrival in Paris in seeking out Jules and asking him to coach her in the rôle. This approach must have given him some much-needed satisfaction. Once again he could feel wanted as the sprightly, dark-haired ballerina paid regular visits to his apartment in the Rue des Martyrs to check the choreography and discuss her interpretation.

Muravieva had also hoped that he would produce the new ballet that had been promised her. It had been he of whom she had thought first of all when she had spoken to her teacher, Eugène Huguet, shortly before her departure, and Huguet had passed on her wishes to the new Director of the Opéra, Emile Perrin. 'She is very anxious,' he explained, 'that you should choose Perrot or Saint-Léon. They have already composed for her in St. Petersburg. And she could see herself working under Lucien Petipa.'[6] In the end the choice was not to be made by her, for Saint-Léon, who was coming to France at the same time, skilfully engineered an invitation for himself.

The French critics seemed completely unaware of the part Jules had played in preparing Muravieva for the rôle of Giselle, which she first played at the Opéra on May 8th. Indeed, that this significant fact was revealed at all was due to a solitary review in a Petersburg journal, undoubtedly written by someone with inside knowledge and from a source close to the ballerina, if not from herself direct.[7] Jules' advice gave an authoritative polish to a rôle which, in Russia, she had learnt only at second hand – probably from Saint-Léon – and added numerous little details of performance as well as imparting a more profound understanding of the ballet itself. At the close of the *pas de deux* with Mérante, who played Albert, she produced an exciting effect by changing the tempo, '[breaking] measure with a *rallentando* such as singers use at the end of an aria.'[8] The mad scene at the end of the first act, the *danse de folie* as it was then called, being perhaps presented with a greater dance content than later became the rule, was very skilfully handled, considering that her dramatic ability was not specially developed. The way in which she conveyed the heroine's anguish and vulnerability was moving without being histrionic. Jules Janin, the doyen of the Paris critics, thought she suffered 'in the true Taglioni manner,' but it was of course the tradition of Carlotta – not of Taglioni, who had never danced the rôle – that she had absorbed in the hours she had spent in Jules' apartment. Like Carlotta, her talents were more naturally suited to the second act, where her part depended on the meaning she gave to her dancing. In the pure white costume of a wili, she revealed 'a perfect understanding of fantasy and fascination,' and appeared, in the words of Janin, 'a shadow, a mist, like a dream come forth from the ivory gates.'[9]

Later in the summer, after Muravieva had returned to Russia, her compatriot Zina Mérante took over the rôle. She and her husband were close friends

Jules Perrot

of Jules and his family, and knowing how much Muravieva had benefited from his coaching, Zina must surely have availed herself of his experience to prepare for a rôle she had never played before.

That summer a pall of sadness descended upon the dance world. The previous winter, Emma Livry had been grievously burned when her costume caught fire from a gas jet during a rehearsal. After months of suffering, she seemed on the road to recovery and, in July, well enough to stand a carriage journey to Neuilly, but only two days afterwards her condition took a sudden turn for the worse. The news of her death was a shattering blow to the dancers who loved her and, in a wider sense, to the future prospects of French ballet, and Jules was probably among the band of mourners who paid their last respects as her coffin was lowered into the grave in the Monmartre Cemetry.

* * *

If he still felt that the Paris Opéra seemed to be studiously ignoring him, Jules could comfort himself with the thought that there were other theatres which would be honoured to employ him should he wish to resume his career. London, which he might have considered out of nostalgia for the past, had ceased to be a serious centre of ballet, but no such trend affected Milan. The Scala still maintained its celebrated ballet school, and still presented ballets with strong dramatic themes. As he knew from the theatrical press, the new generation of Italian choreographers was headed by Pasquale Borri and Giuseppe Rota, who both worked in this idiom, and two of his own ballets had been successfully revived at the Scala not many years before – *Catarina* by Palladini in 1853 and *Esmeralda* by Ronzani in 1854.

Luck seemed to be moving his way at last when the management of the Scala approached him with an unsolicited offer to stage a ballet during the Carnival season of 1863–64. It was to be an ambitious season, comprising three operas by Verdi, including the first Italian production of *I Vespri Siciliani*, and ballets by two choreographers, Jules being given the honour of precedence over his colleague, Rota.

The first rumours to reach the ears of the press were that he was to revive his *Faust*, which he had created there for Fanny Elssler more than a quarter of a century before,[10] but by the end of the year the choice had shifted to a more recent work, *Gazelda*. It may have been a result of this change of plan that Rota's *La Contessa d'Egmont* was revived by a minor ballet-master, Giuseppe Bini, for the opening night of the season. It was not a success, and the theatrical weekly, *La Fama*, had to allay the public's concern by announcing the imminent production of *Gazelda*, the rehearsals of which were 'progressing rapidly to meet present needs.'[11]

Jules had decided to elaborate some of the action of *Gazelda*, and since Pugni was in Russia, the consequent adaptation of the score was entrusted to Paolo Giorza, an experienced and prolific composer of ballet music, who con-

Paolo Giorza, an experienced and prolific composer of ballet music, who contributed an introductory march and a *ballabile* to the last scene. These changes* revolved mainly around the introduction of a new character, Barrabone, as the villain of the piece, and the transformation of Hayraddin into a senile former chief whose authority has been taken over by Narda. The history of the theft of the casket and the adoption of the two children by the tribe was explained in greater detail. Jules now presented Hayraddin in the early moments of the ballet as being obsessed with a remote memory that is somehow associated with a cross. In a new scene tagged on to the end of the prologue, Hayraddin was to be shown rediscovering the oak tree, marked with a cross, where long ago he had burried the casket. Those early memories were further stimulated when Barrabone, who has dug the casket out of the ground after Hayraddin's strength has failed him, offers to share the treasure with Narda. The old man then remembers with horror how he had killed a woman he was trying to abduct after the sack of the castle, a mother with two children clinging to her skirt, but his identification of Zingaro and Gazelda as those children was not to be made until the final *dénouement* of the ballet.

Having, as he thought, made the narrative clearer, Jules confidently awaited the judgment of the Milanese public, but alas, it was to be bitterly disillusioned on the evening of the first performance, on January 27th, 1864. Neither the magnificent scenery by Filippo Peroni, nor Luigi Zamperone's sumptuous costumes, nor the combined talents of the skilled mimes and the Scala's corps de ballet could stave off disaster. Older opera-goers, whose memories went back to the days of *Esmeralda, Catarina, Odetta* and *Faust*, were at a loss to comprehend the choice of such a tedious work as *Gazelda*, and why no one seemed to have advised the choreographer that a ballet lasting two and a quarter hours would never be tolerated in Milan. Wrote one critic: 'We are used to the powerful and compact conceptions of Rota, and the elegant, graceful works of Borri, men who understand the current requirements of the art and the tastes of today's public. To appreciate a ballet such as *Gazelda*, which may be more suited to the costumes and tastes of foreigners, one would have to turn the clock back twenty years.'[12]

It did not take long for the rowdy elements to protest. The brunt of their displeasure was directed at the mimes Baratti and Magri, who played the rôles of Hayraddin and Karl. In the course of the opening scene a furious storm of whistling broke over their heads, interspersed with insistent shouts of '*Basta! basta!*' With remarkable courage the performers carried on, wondering whether the curtain would be rung down in mid-scene. But a saviour was at hand in the person of Claudina Cucchi, the ballerina whom the Scala had engaged to play the rôle of Gazelda. Already a favourite with the Milanese as a fine product of their own school, she had added an elegant polish to her style

---

* For the scenario of the original production, see Chapter 16, pp. 269–272.

Jules Perrot

from a year at the Paris Opéra, and had since gathered fresh laurels in Berlin and Vienna. She was feeling exceptionally nervous as she made her entrance. The house had fallen silent, but not for long, for the whistling broke out again as the supporting dancers moved into the introduction to her *pas*. Coldly, she inclined her head and walked into the wings. There she was stopped by Jules and the Director of the theatre, the Marchese Calcagnini, who begged her to return to the stage and, adding force to their persuasion, gave her a hearty shove. Her unexpected exit had momentarily disconcerted the audience, and all was quiet again when she suddenly made her reappearance. As she began to dance, the ugly murmurs became transformed into a growing roar of applause. Her personal triumph was complete, but it took place in a curious atmosphere. 'She only had to appear,' described Paolo Cominazzi, 'for the derisive tumult to change into a roaring ovation just for her, and then to change back again into the most rabid disapproval. Several times it seemed that the gale must surely blow itself out, but it would die down suddenly while she made a brief reappearance or performed a short *pas*, only to recommence afterwards with redoubled fury.'[13]

If he had not been feeling so excessively upset, Jules might have taken heart from the thought that the enthusiasm that greeted Cucchi reflected on his own work in arranging her *pas*. She possessed a strong technique and great musicality, which conveyed the impression of complete control in everything she did. He had been quick to recognise this quality, and capitalised it by showing her how to vary the speed of her turns, now slowing them down in a gentle *rallentando*, now whipping up their speed and making her stop suddenly, rock-steady, on the final note. Her partner, Aniello Amaturo, shared much of her applause, playing the rôle of Zingaro that Jules had originally designed for himself. When he played it, Jules' days as a virtuoso were long past, and it had been Johansson who had come forward to partner Carlotta in the final *pas de deux*. Amaturo, on the other hand, was a powerful young dancer, and Jules had rearranged Zingaro's rôle so as to incorporate the responsibilities of the *premier danseur* that he had been unable to assume.

Apart from the dances for Gazelda and Zingaro, the choreography appeared very sketchy in the eyes of the Milanese critics. Jules' well-known aptitude for arranging *ballabile* seemed to have eluded him, for the corps de ballet was given little to do. Perhaps the rehearsal period had been too short. It was only in the general dance preceding the final *pas de deux* that the corps de ballet came into its own, wearing costumes of many different colours and weaving in and out, with great precision, in a 'ring dance of the kind more in vogue in earlier times.'[14]

The very length of the ballet condemned it, but Jules' offence was compounded by the insipidity of the story and the music, 'the most vacuous, monotonous and somniferous to have been heard at the Scala within human memory.'[15] The Italians were accustomed to ballets with strong plots and had

Frustrations of Retirement

The revival of Gazelda *at the Scala, Milan, in 1864, as seen by a caricaturist. Jules Perrot and the Marchese Calcagnini, Director of the Scala, are depicted in the middle of the bottom row. (*Il Trovatore, *January 30th, 1864)*

a taste for historical themes as well as fantasy, but they expected the action to be varied and to develop smartly, and they liked their music to be lively and strongly rhythmed. On every count *Gazelda* was found lacking. In a nutshell, Cucchi's performance apart, it was one long bore.

In the aftermath of this disaster Jules surveyed the damage and, with the grit of a true professional, set about salvaging what he could. *La Contessa d'Egmont* was substituted at the next performance while *Gazelda* was hurriedly reduced to a more manageable length. Jules succeeded in cutting down the playing time to an hour and a half, which was still very long by Italian standards. The storm of the première did not recur, but as reported in *La Fama*, whose critic reviewed the scene as if the dancers were a beleaguered army with Jules as their general, 'little squalls growled insistently, drowning the halting, flabby harmonies produced by the musicians . . . There was only one moment when disaster threatened, but the Herculean strength and the proven artistry of Claudina Cucchi . . . averted the imminent storm and the ballet continued, not without glory for the general and the combattants.'[16]

To continue the military analogy, Jules had met his Waterloo. Even in its shortened form *Gazelda* did not please. It struggled on for ten performances only because Rota, who arrived in Milan early in February, needed several weeks to stage a new ballet for Cucchi. Jules must have been shattered by the experience, and his stay in Milan was further soured by a dispute with the management over his fee. There was a rumour that litigation was to ensue, but the matter was eventually settled without recourse to the courts.

* * *

Sadly chastened, Jules returned to Paris and his family, and retreated once more into private life. Never again would he produce a ballet, nor even revive one of his tried successes. But if he seldom emerged from the privacy of his home, he did not turn his back on the world of the dance, for it was the world to which he had always belonged, which he still loved, and in which he had formed many friendships, not only in Paris but throughout Europe. Also, the slights which had wounded his pride, and the awful failure of *Gazelda* soon receded into the past and could be viewed in a more distant perspective. With each year that passed he found himself readier to accept retirement and to enjoy being an elder statesman in his profession, whose lifework was behind him but who could still usefully give advice to those who sought it. At first, no doubt, he secretly wished for a call from the Opéra, but the Director, Emile Perrin, refused to consider engaging him, saying he was 'old . . . rusty . . . worn out.'[17] Jules' aspirations were now weakening, and it did not trouble him that his successor in St. Petersburg, Saint-Léon, was welcomed back to Paris each summer as guest choreographer at the Opéra. Perhaps there were times when he felt passed over and ignored, but there were also moments of compensation, as when a telegram was delivered early in 1869, conveying the congratulations of the St. Petersburg dancers on the hundredth performance of his *Faust*.

He no doubt attended the Opéra to see the new productions, gathering round him, in the intervals, a circle of friends seeking his opinion on a new ballet or a new dancer. Like most old professionals, he no doubt remained highly critical, and perhaps also intolerant at times, particularly on the subject of choreography, but his views were based on a long and unrivalled experience and must have been specially prized and respected by those who heard them. Alas, he never found himself a Boswell, and as he always admitted, he was incurably lazy with the pen. One can only, therefore, imagine him in the distance, animatedly discoursing on the merits of Saint-Léon's later ballets – *Néméa, La Source,* and the evergreen *Coppélia* – and the charms of the younger generation of dancers who were spreading their wings. In the second half of the 1860s Adèle Grantzow, a *protégée* of Saint-Léon, won acceptence as the leading star of the ballet, visiting Paris between Russian seasons. She took over the rôle of Giselle, and perhaps she too made the pilgrimage to Jules' apartment in the footsteps of Muravieva and Zina.

Like nearly every Parisian at that time, Jules was a fascinated observer of the massive construction works for the new Opéra. He had returned from Russia to find that the familiar theatre in the Rue Le Peletier was under sentence of demolition and was to be replaced by a grandiose new building, more spacious than any other opera house in the world, that was to occupy an island site fronted by a vast new square and beyond it, a wide avenue that was to be known as the Avenue Napoléon III.* The foundation stone was laid in an impressive ceremony in the summer of 1862, and over the next few years the great building took shape behind a high wooden wall. In 1867 the scaffolding was removed, and the exterior walls of the new Opéra were revealed in all their dazzling, pristine splendour of stone and marble.

Jules was privileged to be shown the progress of the works, and one day in 1869, when he was on the site, he noticed standing near him, a graceful child and her father. It was to be a historic encounter, particularly for the little girl who, as Rosita Mauri, was to make her début ten years later on the boards of that very theatre and become its star ballerina for many years. Long afterwards, learning of Jules' death, she recorded her recollections of this meeting.

In 1869 I had come to Paris with my father to study ballet under Mme Dominique, who taught the children at the Conservatoire in the Rue Richer. Paris was a marvellous place for a child coming from the mountains of Catalonia, and I had eyes for only one thing, M. Garnier's new Opéra which was then in the course of construction. One day, with my father, I was looking over the fence that surrounded the site – we were in

---

* For only a short time, alas. After the fall of the Second Empire, and ever since, it has been known as the Avenue de l'Opéra.

Jules Perrot

the Rue Halévy, where Carpeaux' statue now stands – watching a group standing around some carriages that had brought some important people to inspect the works.

A man of about fifty approached us and said to me: 'Do you want to go in too, my child? Would you like me to get you a pass?' Very confused, I declined the offer. But when my father asked this unknown gentleman who it was that we had the honour of addressing, he answered with a smile, 'I am a small part of the building.' 'You must be the architect?' 'No, a dancer, a *maître de ballet*. My name is Perrot.' 'You are M. Perrot, the M. Perrot who produced *La Filleule des fées* with Carlotta Grisi, the first Giselle!' 'Just so.'

'Well, well,' said my father, 'my daughter is studying dance with Mme Dominique.' At that moment I pulled myself up with a certain pride. 'Aha,' said M. Perrot, 'I can see such a look of determination in your eyes that it would not surprise me if you enter this building one day by the grand entrance.' Please God, hear his prayer, said I in Spanish.

A short time afterwards the war came, and we left Paris. I went to Milan, and later, when I made my début at the Opéra in Gounod's *Polyceute*, one of the callboys brought me a tiny bouquet of violets in which I found an envelope. This little bouquet made such a contrast with the baskets of flowers cluttering up my dressing room that I eagerly slit open the envelope. These were the words that I read: 'Jules Joseph Perrot greets the star whom he met ten years ago.'

Of all the tributes that were paid me, this one gave me the greatest pleasure.

M. Perrot was then very old, but every time I had a rôle to create, he gave me advice, which I valued very highly.[18]

The 1860s had their moments of sadness. As happens inevitably in middle age, Jules found his friends and colleagues beginning to disappear. In 1868 Joseph Mazilier died, as did another contemporary, Jean-Baptiste Barrez, well-known as a teacher, and two years later Saint-Léon, Jules' junior by more than ten years, collapsed and died in the afterglow of the triumph of *Coppélia*. Jules was among the mourners at his funeral on a September day in 1870.

The leaves of the trees were still luxuriant in their summer colours, but a sense of foreboding pervaded the city. Since July France had been at war with Prussia, a war begun with confidence and enthusiasm, which had evaporated with humiliating suddenness as the German armies quickly asserted their superiority. Instead of the glorious strike towards Berlin that many had expected, it was the Germans who were menacing Paris, and already many Parisians were leaving the capital with their families for safer havens in the country. Within a few days of Saint-Léon's funeral, Jules and Capitolina, Tante Marie and the girls took a train to Lyon, leaving the governess behind to look after the apartment and the two dogs.

Before they even descended from the train, they became aware that refugees were not welcome in Lyon. Hearing people exclaim, 'Ah, here come all the *bourgeois* from Paris, scuttling from danger; they'll soon see what sort of life they are going to lead,' Jules made an instant decision. The stories his father had told him as a child must have flashed through his mind, and realising the inflammatory and unpredictable temperament of Lyon's working class, he told his family to stay on the train.

They continued their journey to Geneva, where they found a quiet corner to spend the winter. They had no servants, and the work was shared between the three ladies, Marie doing the housework, Alexandrine being in charge of the shopping and cooking, and Tante Marie helping as best she could. Nearby lived Carlotta Grisi in her property at Saint-Jean, who in the warmth of her heart may have brought comfort to the poor refugees, just as she had to Théophile Gautier's daughter Estelle, whom she was looking after under her own roof. When the war ended, the Perrots returned to Paris, happily finding their apartment and possessions – including the dogs, who had miraculously escaped being eaten during the Siege – intact and unharmed.

Paris was still stunned by the calamity. The Siege, with the German bombardment and the appalling shortages of food and fuel, had been followed by civil insurrection, and the establishment of the Commune and its ruthless repression by the army. Peace only came in the summer of 1871, and the charred ruins of the Tuileries were a brutal reminder of the disaster and the fall of the Imperial régime.

The Opéra, which had closed when the Germans were about to encircle Paris, reopened in July 1871. There was a new Director, and in the ballet so many faces were missing that virtually a new start had to be made. Saint-Léon was dead, and the new ballet-master, Mérante, had not yet tried his hand at choreography. Marie Taglioni, who had been in charge of the perfection class, had retired to London. And there were other painful gaps, for a number of dancers had died during the intervening months. By some, Mérante's inexperience was seen as a serious disadvantage, and a rumour spread among the dancers in October that Jules was to take his place.[19]

Such a resumption of activity was far from his mind, although, thanks to his friendship with the Mérantes, he frequently gave classes at the Opéra. His presence was to be vividly recorded by an artist who seemed never to get in anyone's way as he quietly sat sketching the dancers in class. Edgar Degas, for such was his name, had discovered the Opéra before the war, but it was only in its aftermath that he became obsessed with the forms and movements of the dancers and began to haunt the Foyer de la Danse and the rehearsal studios. In April 1874, at the First Exhibition of the Impressionists, he exhibited an oil painting showing Jules taking a class, a stocky white-haired figure in a loose white blouse, leaning on his heavy cane with his left hand thrust forward as though explaining some point to the dancers.*

---

* The original painting, *La Classe de danse de M. Perrot*, is in the Louvre (Jeu de Paume). In 1875 Degas painted another version with a modified background and the dancers differently placed.

Jules Perrot

Degas worked Jules into another important study of a dance class, painted in 1873 and recorded by Edmond de Goncourt in unmistakable detail in his journal entry for February 13th, 1874. 'Yesterday I spent the afternoon in the studio of a painter named Degas,' he recorded before going on to describe the canvas. 'We see the Foyer de la Danse at the Opéra,* with dancers coming down a little staircase, their legs fantastically silhouetted against the light from a window, a bright red splash of tartan amidst all those puffed-out clouds, with the vulgar figure of an absurd ballet-master to serve as a foil. And there before us, caught to the life, we have the graceful, sinuous movements and gestures of these little monkey-girls.'[20] There is certainly nothing absurd, by any standards except perhaps a prejudice that considers dancing to be an absurd calling for a man, about the distinguished figure of the teacher who is giving a class. Easily recognisable as Jules, it is, if anything, a flattering portrait.

These two paintings were among the last pictures of the historic opera house in the Rue Le Peletier, which was burnt to the ground in a furious conflagration in October 1873. Painted, not on the spot but in Degas' studio from sketches made at the Opéra, they vividly evoke the atmosphere of the theatre that enshrined so many memories for Jules and his contemporaries.

The familiar building with its graceful ghosts was now no more, but the Opéra continued, housed for the time being in temporary quarters, for the new theatre was not yet ready. In 1872 Rita Sangalli, a young ballerina trained in the Milan school, had successfully made her Paris début in a revival of *La Source*, and the question of a new ballet was being discussed behind closed doors. In the spring of 1874 a rumour reached *Le Figaro* that Jules was to be asked to produce *Esmeralda* for her, but this was quickly denied, although the way the item was worded in the theatrical column – that the story was 'unfounded, or at least premature'[21] – suggested that the idea had been considered.

Esmeralda would have given Sangalli an exciting challenge to develop a character and display her dramatic ability, but there was a variety of reasons why the ballet might have been rejected. After so many years of retirement, Jules may have been reluctant to return to the fray, fearing perhaps that he might lack the physical stamina to undertake such a task, and not wishing to risk a repetition of the ordeal he had suffered in Milan. Equally the task might have appeared too daunting to Sangalli. However, apart from these personal considerations, there would have been a basic objection to the proposal. *Esmeralda* was, as everyone knew, an old ballet, and for the first ballet crea-

---

* Here Goncourt is mistaken. The room may be a rehearsal studio in the Opéra, or a studio in the Conservatoire de Danse in the Rue Richer. It is not the Foyer de la Danse, which Degas painted as the background for another of his paintings, *La Classe de danse de M. Mérante*, now in the Louvre.

tion at the new opera house, it would have been unthinkable to present anything other than a complete novelty. The fact that *Esmeralda* had been given in Paris before, and at the Porte-Saint-Martin too, might have added weight to any argument that it was unsuitable. But there was also a very valid musical reason. Pugni's score, acceptable though it may have been twenty or even ten years before, would now sound too thin and inconsequential. The musical content of a ballet was given much greater importance in Paris than elsewhere, and the choice of *Sylvia* as the first new ballet to be presented at the new Opéra was dictated mainly by the opportunity it gave of commissioning a new score from Léo Delibes.

Jules probably had few regrets at this decision, and was even pleased that it would give Louis Mérante the chance of trying his hand at a major composition. The Perrots and the Mérantes had become very close friends, and on many an evening, at the home of one or the other, the new ballet must have been discussed at great length across the dining table. Jules would also have been a welcome guest at the rehearsals, and may have played a valuable part in the ballet's preparation by counselling the younger choreographer from the accumulated wealth of his experience. In later years other ballets – *Yedda, La Korrigane, La Farandole, Les Deux Pigeons* – took *Sylvia*'s place as the all-absorbing topic of conversation at these reunions.

On occasion there must also have been other guests, specially invited: the composer, perhaps, of the ballet in preparation, and the ballerina for whom it was intended – first Sangalli, who created the rôles of Sylvia and Yedda, and after her, Rosita Mauri, who was to be the first Gourouli in *Les Deux Pigeons*, and was unfailingly to seek Jules' advice whenever she had a new rôle to perform.

As Jules celebrated his seventieth birthday in 1880, the years were beginning to take their toll, but he continued to take a close interest in the ballet classes at the Opéra. In 1882 Zina took over the perfection class, and through her Jules began to take an interest in her most gifted pupil, Julia Subra, who became a welcome visitor to the Perrots' home. He also kept in touch with the training of the children and the corps de ballet through the Théodores, whom he had known from his years in Russia. Mme Thérèse Théodore was the widow of Théodore Chion, professionally known just as Théodore, who had reproduced several of Jules' ballets in Moscow, and she and her daughter Adeline were always happy to put their young charges through their paces before the critical gaze of Jules Perrot.

In the same year that the Théodores were engaged, 1879, Jules and his family moved into a new and more spacious apartment at No. 52 Boulevard Magenta, where they settled down comfortably among the possessions they had accumulated over the years, including an impressive collection of icons. Here Jules continued to preside over the gatherings of 'La Timbale,' a select circle of friends, all well-known in their respective fields, and representative of the younger generations as well as his own. Many, though not all, came from the world of the theatre, and among them, no doubt, was his close friend, Victor Jacques Vernet, who had been an actor of the French Theatre in St. Petersburg throughout Jules' stay in Russia and had returned to Paris after his retirement in 1869.

In his capacity of chief *'timbalier,'* Jules was an impressive figure, and the painter, Edgar Degas, taking a day off from sketching the toiling dancers, painted him in his black frock-coat, bending forward on the sofa, grasping his stick, as if on the point of rising to greet a visitor. Like Degas' other portraits, it is a picture of profound psychological insight. By stressing the immobility of the heavy body and the none too secure legs, the artist seemed to be stressing the contrast with his subject's former agility, and in the old man's expression caught the disabling pain of his rheumatism and a character prone to frustration and not slow to take offence. There was also something infinitely sad in the disintegrating change that was coming over his face. The left side still possessed an alertness, the eye wide open and bright, but the right side presented a different aspect, in which old age had taken the upper hand and dimmed and dulled the look.

Much as Degas was affected by the struggle within the ageing body, an astonishing transformation could still come about when the youthful spirits came to the fore, as they did when memories were stirred of his dancing days and colleagues of his youth. Around New Year's Day the blood would surge through his veins again as he dictated his annual greeting to his most celebrated ballerina, Marie Taglioni, who was then living in London. Typical of these was the letter he wrote on the last day of 1879, before the family settled down to their first New Year celebration in the new apartment in the Boulevard Magenta:

Dear Friend,
    According to our old custom in the Rue des Martyrs, those of our friends who survive will join the family to celebrate, at midnight, the coming of the New Year. If by some magic a telephone line could be laid from the Boulevard Magenta to Connaught Square, you would hear, at the first clink of the champagne glasses, your own dear name ringing in your ears with New Year wishes of health, happiness and prosperity.
    Thank you for remembering us, dear Countess. My wife could not have been more deeply touched, and asks me to thank you from the bottom of her heart. To reinforce my own contribution, allow me to add to these lines a vision of your zephyr of half a century ago; he will remind you what good comrades and sincere friends we were, and he will tell you that if he still remains 'handsome,' he cannot boast of remaining young. But what does that matter, for beneath his snowy hair the memories and feelings have been kept alive and youthful.
    In repeating our sincere wishes for your happiness and that of your family, allow me to send you kisses from our two babies, as well as embraces for everyone. Mmes Vellard and Alexandrine particularly wish to be remembered to you.
                        Your very affectionate
                             Jules Perrot[22]

Frustrations of Retirement

A year later, on January 4th, 1881, another of these affectionate missives was carried from the Boulevard Magenta across the Channel to Taglioni's London mansion in Connaught Square:

My dear Countess,

Just because we have known one another for more than half a century, there is no reason to treat a friend as an 'old' comrade. Take care! If I were to take the thing seriously, I might really believe it. But, like you, I do not accept the word 'old,' which my youthful mind rejects. I come, therefore, with a heart which I feel to be almost adolescent, and with happy memories of our past, to send you the loving thoughts of my family.

What can I wish you to add to the happiness you already have? Nothing but to pray that it will continue unchanged.

With that, a kiss on each of your cheeks. Believe me, my dear friend, as in the past, in thought at least,

Your young and passionate Zephyr of 1830,
Jules Perrot[23]

Hardly a year now passed without a colleague from the past disappearing. At the end of 1879 Jules read of the death of his old friend, August Bournonville, whom he had known since they were pupils of Vestris together in the 1820s. Although their paths had seldom crossed since, they had followed one another's careers and kept in touch, even if their correspondence tended to be somewhat one-sided, for Jules was an unconscionably idle letter-writer, while Bournonville's pen was never still. Earlier in the year of his friend's death, Jules had received a visit from his grandson, August Tuxen, who was visiting Paris for the first time. Young Lieutenant Tuxen was a favourite of his grandfather, whose letters to him were full of wise information and advice, and frequently mentioned his old friend Perrot. 'I do not know how good your Russian is,' he wrote in one of them, 'but a few well turned phrases will be all the rage in the family circle of M. Perrot, from whom I have already received the most enthusiastic reply about you. This old comrade, whose ugliness disappears in the light of his wit, his great talent and his frank good humour, will, I am sure, be an agreeable person for you to visit.' 'Many good wishes to my excellent comrade Perrot and his wife.' 'Cultivate the Perrots and do not talk too much about my own compositions. On the contrary, you should dwell on the memories I have of his perfect talent.' 'I beg you to cultivate those persons who have received you with such friendly warmth. For example, it was wrong of you to allow two weeks to pass without paying a visit to the Perrot family, who love seeing you.'[24]

Bournonville died quite suddenly in November, and Jules lost no time in dictating a warm letter of sympathy to August Tuxen:

Jules Perrot

My dear Monsieur Tuxen,

I was very much grieved this morning when reading my paper, *Le Figaro*. Can it be true that my worthy colleague, my dear good friend Bournonville, my modest and indulgent comrade of my young days, has passed away, struck down with an unrelenting seizure in a street of his native city? What a shock this must have been, what sorrow must have descended at the news of this sudden death, and how grief-stricken your family must be! Be assured, my dear M. Tuxen, that I share your sorrow and mourn deeply the loss of this good man and eminent artist. All our past relationship has been passing vividly through my mind, and I am so distressed by the thought of the culpable silence with which I responded to his witty and friendly letters of recent times. My poor friend! He must have thought me indifferent, when it was only the insuperable indolence of an incurable and hateful laziness.

Believe me, I am truly saddened today. Such memories fill me with remorse and add to my sorrow, in which my family shares, making me very conscious of the cruel loss you have suffered. And to think that I cannot be present in person at the honours that will be paid him.

Instead of my presence, allow me to give you, as a tribute to his memory, the enclosed photograph which has just been taken specially for him, and which I was keeping back to send him as a New Year's gift. It will enable you to remember the features of a very sincere friend of him whom your whole family is now mourning. And please convey to your grandmama, the worthy companion of his life, the sincere thoughts I express in this letter.

Always remember that I am interested in your future, and accept, my dear M. Tuxen, with the good wishes and condolences of all my family, a warm and friendly handshake.

Jules Perrot.[25]

In his last years Jules exchanged letters with the young Danish officer at the beginning of each year. Those from Jules were always carefully written out for him, probably by Alexandrine, for as his signature revealed, his hand was becoming increasingly crippled by rheumatism and he could only grasp a pen with difficulty. Generally, however, his health remained good. 'You will be pleased to know,' he wrote in January 1881, 'that all goes well in my house, beginning with myself whom the year 1881 finds quite steady and in a condition, God willing, to see it through like the past seventy years which I have put up with quite cheerfully.' Five years later, his signature had become painfully shaky, and he excused his delay in writing as being due to 'an indisposition (back trouble) which kept me in bed for several days.' Apart from increasing immobility, he kept well, and two years later, on the occasion of Tuxen's marriage, he reported: 'Thank God, my health is good . . .'[26]

His later years were clouded by the loss of two of his dearest friends, Louis and Zina Mérante. Louis was not yet sixty when he died in the summer of 1887. He and Zina had been looking forward to many happy years together in their newly-built home in Courbevoie. As an expression of his love for her, he had romantically named it the Villa Zina and installed stained-glass windows depicting two of her favourite ballets, *Esmeralda* and *Giselle*. He was widely mourned, for he had been a popular leader, and the ballet company felt his death all the more keenly for losing him so unexpectedly, for he had been dancing with them only a few weeks before. Rosita Mauri and Julia Subra were seen weeping openly at his funeral. For a while afterwards Zina continued teaching the perfection class, but by the summer of 1890 she became too ill to continue. She withdrew to the Villa Zina, suffering from cancer, and her death was announced that very September.

Nor did death claim only those who had fulfilled their life's work. Jules had by then long since given up teaching, but there were still occasions when his advice was sought, not only by the dancers of the Opéra, but at least once by a visitor from distant St. Petersburg. In the summer of 1888 a talented young dancer, Alexandra Vinogradova, arrived in Paris specially to study the rôle of Esmeralda under its creator. Tragically, not long after she returned to Russia, she contracted Addison's disease, and she died the following year, carrying all the advice he had given her to her grave.

* * *

The Perrots were a close-knit and happy family, and when his wife's mother died Jules purchased a burial plot in the Père Lachaise cemetery, where they could all rest together when the time came for them to be gathered. As the 1880s ran their course, and into the 1890s, life went on peacefully. Servants aside, just the four of them lived in the Boulevard Magenta apartment – Jules, the devoted Capitolina, who had long ago lost the slender figure of her youth and had become very stout, Tante Marie, and the younger daughter, Alexandrine. Jules' elder daughter, Marie, had married Alfred Auguste Vellard, an employee of the Post Office, shortly after the Franco-German War, but she and her husband and their two sons, Jules, named after his grandfather, and Georges, born in 1874 and 1877 respectively, were regular visitors. Alexandrine had chosen to remain unmarried to help her mother look after her father who, suffering from gout, became increasingly house-bound and needed more and more assistance. At the end this involved considerable sacrifice for her, since she had fallen in love with a young widower, Edouard Charles Dumont, who had been left with three infant children. The Dumonts soon became intimate friends of the whole family, and to everyone's joy the eldest child, Louise, was to marry Jules Mérante, the son of Louis and Zina. It was not until after Jules died that Alexandrine felt free to accept M. Dumont's proposal.

Seen through the eyes of the children, the aged Jules Perrot was rather a frightening figure, quick to take anger and extremely impatient, wanting everything to be done at once. He was never separated from his walking stick, which was so disproportionately large for his diminishing stature that it seemed to the children that it was almost as long as he was tall when he

Jules Perrot

stamped the floor with it in his rages. Jules loved talking about his old days in the ballet, and almost visibly swelled with pride when he spoke of the two Tsars he had served. Dinner time, when he had his family captive round the table, was his great moment, and often while carving the meat he became so carried away that everyone else had to resign themselves to a long wait as he brandished the carving knife to illustrate his flow of reminiscence.

The family spent their summer holidays on the Brittany coast, at first at Saint-Enogat near Dinard, and later, just across the estuary of the Rance, at Paramé, in a modern three-storeyed villa with a flight of steps leading up to an imposing colonnaded porch, and the name 'Les Sapins' emblazoned in gilt letters on a marble slab above the first floor balcony. It was a gentleman's villa, an appropriate retreat for a retired ballet-master of the Tsar. It was here, while on holiday with his family in the summer of 1892, that he was taken ill and died at 12.25 p.m. in the afternoon of his eighty-second birthday, August 18th.

His remains were brought to Paris and, after a funeral service at the Eglise Saint-Martin in the Rue des Marais, attended by many dancers and actors, were interred in the family plot at Père Lachaise. There, beneath a high and narrow mausoleum of undistinguished design, surmounted by a cross and bearing the proprietary inscription 'Famille Jules Perrot,' he was to be joined, first by Tante Marie, who died in 1900, then by Capitolina who died in 1909, and finally by Alexandrine, who survived until the German occupation of World War II and died in the centenary year of *Giselle*, 1941. There, too, is Alexandrine's husband, Edouard Dumont, who had predeceased her by twenty-nine years, and her stepson Albert. There is no poetic epitaph to record the fame and genius of the head of the family; only a simple inscription that spoke all that was needed:

> ex-artiste of the Opéra
> ex-maître de ballet of the Imperial
> Theatres of St. Petersburg

His true memorial was to be in his work, ephemeral though it was, in one sense, in an art that owed its survival almost entirely to human memory. At the time of his death several of his ballets still survived in St. Petersburg in productions revised by Marius Petipa, who had then become the dominant figure in the Imperial ballet, and although it was more than thirty years since he had retired, he was remembered and revered by dancers and balletomanes alike as no other ballet-master before him, not even Didelot, whose ballets were discarded almost as soon as he was no longer there to revive them. Two of Jules' ballets were to survive into the twentieth century, *Giselle* and *Esmeralda*, the first of them to achieve immortality as the supreme classic of the Romantic ballet – the glorious flowering of his art which he had done so much to foster.

Giselle was the creative product of a great artist and his muse, whose union

Frustrations of Retirement

M

Vous êtes prié d'assister aux Service, Convoi et Enterrement de

Monsieur Jules-Joseph PERROT

EX-ARTISTE DE L'OPÉRA
EX-MAITRE DE BALLET DES THÉATRES IMPÉRIAUX DE SAINT-PÉTERSBOURG

décédé, muni des Sacrements de l'Eglise, le 19 Août 1892, à PARAMÉ, à l'âge de 82 ans, qui se feront à PARIS, le Vendredi 26 courant, à *midi très précis,* en l'Eglise Saint-Martin (rue des Marais).

On se réunira à l'Eglise

De la part de Madame PERROT, sa veuve; de Monsieur et Madame A. VELLARD, de Mademoiselle A. PERROT, ses filles et gendre; de Messieurs JULES et GEORGES VELLARD, de Monsieur et Madame JANIN, de Monsieur et Madame VERNET et leurs enfants, de Monsieur et Madame BOSS, ses petits-enfants et arrière-petits-enfants; de Monsieur et Madame GAUDUCHON, ses neveu et nièce; de Mademoiselle MARIE SAMOWSKY, sa cousine, et de toute sa famille.

L'Inhumation aura lieu au Cimetière du Père-Lachaise

PARIS, boulevard de Magenta, n° 52.

Règlement des Convois, ROBLOT place du Louvre, rue de la Pompe-Passy, 80, rue Drouot 7, rue de Bretagne, 57 et rue Saint-Marc, 22

Invitation to the funeral of Jules Perrot. Bibliothèque de l'Opéra, Paris.

Jules Perrot

had also borne fruit in the physical sense. Somewhere in the background of Jules' life – probably brought up by his parents – had lived Marie-Julie, the daughter that Carlotta had given him in the flush of their young love. Her shadowy existence is evidenced only by a single reference in one of her father's letters, and a dedication of one piece in a selection from *La Filleule des fées*, arranged for the piano. From the time Jules went to Russia and married, she seems to disappear into obscurity. However, she survived her father, from whom she apparently inherited a fierce determination to fight for her due. Being illegitimate, she had no legal right to any part of his estate, but when her mother died in 1899, she came forward to claim a share of her property. Carlotta's only other child, Léontine, born about fifteen years later – her father was Prince Leon Radzivill – and brought up by her mother, was also illegitimate. She had, it seems, been kept in complete ignorance of her elder half-sister's existence, and the latter's appearance, to claim half of Carlotta's estate, came as a complete shock. Julie did not long survive her mother. She died, unmarried, in 1901, and was buried with Jules' parents in the family tomb in the Loyasse cemetery in Lyon. Hers must have been a sad, deprived existence. She was apparently never received by her father's Russian family, for when, towards the end of her long life, Alexandrine's stepdaughter Yvonne was asked whether Jules had a daughter by Carlotta, all she would say was: 'No one ever knew.'

Appendices

The Survival of Jules Perrot's ballets after his retirement

A considerable proportion of Jules Perrot's work remained in the repertory of the Imperial Theatres after his retirement in 1859, but the scraps that now survive are generally so diluted and corrupted that, with the exception of *Giselle*, none of his ballets could be revived today in a form even remotely approaching the original. Ballets from the past survive in one of two ways – if regularly performed, through human memory, which is fallible, and in a few cases through being recorded in some method of notation or word descriptions. Perrot's work has benefited very little from notation, for no notation system was in use in any of the theatres where he worked, and apparently he himself never attempted to record his choreography, even in words. It was not until some thirty years after his departure from Russia that the Stepanov system of notation was invented and introduced into the Imperial Theatres. *Giselle, Esmeralda* and *Le Corsaire*, being still in the repertory in the early 1900s, were then notated in rough form for rehearsal purposes. These notes were among those brought out of Russia by the régisseur Nicolai Sergueyev during the turmoil following the Revolution, and can be consulted today in the Harvard Theatre Collection. It is also known that *Le Délire d'un peintre* was notated by Stepanov himself from Christian Johansson's recollection of the work and produced for an examination performance by pupils of the ballet school at the Maryinsky Theatre in 1893, but this record was not among Sergueyev's papers. How useful these records would be in reconstructing a long-forgotten ballet still has to be put to the test, but in the case of Perrot's work there is the additional drawback that they were made more than forty years after he had left St. Petersburg, and in the meantime the ballets had been revised, modernised, and here and there completely renewed where passages had been forgotten or something more spectacular was required to show off the virtuosity of a particular dancer.

Perrot's most popular ballets were preserved in the repertory by Marius Petipa, who became principal ballet-master after Saint-Léon's death in 1870 and was the virtual dictator of the St. Petersburg ballet until his retirement in 1903. Petipa was already in the company when Perrot first came to Russia in

Jules Perrot

1848, and being entrusted with leading rôles in most of Perrot's productions, was exceptionally placed to observe his choreographic methods. A budding choreographer could not have had a better grounding, and when Perrot's employment in Russia came to an end, Petipa took it upon himself to preserve his master's most impressive ballets, which no doubt he regarded as models. Consequently six of these works – *Faust, Catarina, The Naiad and the Fisherman, Le Corsaire, Esmeralda* and *Giselle* – remained in the repertory for many years, kept fresh by Petipa with a conscientious regard throughout for the original conception but without exaggerated reverence. They were not old enough to be regarded as inviolable classics, and Petipa felt no constraint in adjusting the choreography where he felt it necessary, particularly to take account of the greater technical virtuosity of his dancers, but this retouching was always done with discretion. He never deviated from the structure and intention of the narrative, and the greater part of the choreography was preserved intact.

FAUST

Faust was the first of these ballets to be dropped from the repertory, its strong dramatic structure having little appeal to later audiences. Petipa revived it on two occasions – in 1867 for the visiting Italian ballerina, Guglielmina Salvioni, and in 1875 for Evgenia Sololova. Its last performance at the Imperial Theatres, the 121st, took place during the 1882–83 season, although excerpts were still being given ten years later.

CATARINA

Catarina, another ballet with a complicated plot, survived a little longer. Petipa revised it only once, in 1870 for Adèle Grantzow. Its second and last revival in St. Petersburg in 1888 for Luigia Algisi, was entrusted to Enrico Cecchetti, who worked from notes made by his father many years before from an Italian 'reproduction' of Perrot's original. Cecchetti added several new dances to music supplied by Riccardo Drigo. The ballet was last performed in St. Petersburg in 1894, when it had been given 98 times.

Perrot's St. Petersburg version was reproduced in Moscow by Frédéric (Malovergne) in 1850 for Irka Mathias. It was revived by José Mendez in 1890, and last given in 1898.

THE NAIAD AND THE FISHERMAN

The Naiad and the Fisherman survived in St. Petersburg until 1905 with 92 performances to its credit. Petipa periodically brought it up to date as a vehicle for a distinguished succession of ballerinas. In 1867, for Ekaterina Vazem, he composed two new variations and elaborated the *pas de l'ombre* to include double turns and additional *pointe* work. He revised the entire production in 1874, when Evgenia Sokolova took over the rôle, and again in 1892 for Varvara Nikitina. His assistant, Alexandre Shiryayev revived the ballet for Anna Pavlova in 1903, and Shiryayev's pupil, Piotr Gusev, claims to remember the choreography and to be able to distinguish which passages derive from Perrot's original version. If his memory is really so good, it would be an exciting project for a Soviet researcher to make a record of what he remembers before another precious piece of tradition vanishes for ever.

The Naiad and the Fisherman was produced in Moscow by Théodore (Chion) for Thérèse Théodore in 1857, revived in 1879, and last danced there in 1900.

LE CORSAIRE

Le Corsaire, which Perrot never really considered his own, is still occasionally given in its complete form in the Soviet Union, although elsewhere it is known only for the spectacular *pas de deux* which was added to the ballet more than forty years after the original production. Petipa revised this ballet on four occasions, in 1863, 1868, 1880 and 1899, making two very substantial additions: the divertissement, *Le Jardin animé*, to music by Delibes, which was added in 1868, and the well-known *pas de deux* to music by Drigo which was added for Pierina Legnani in 1899. Petipa's last revision remained in the repertory until 1928. By then it had been performed more than 200 times in St. Petersburg. Since then Vaganova (1931), Gusev (1955) and Konstantin Sergueyev (1973) have produced the ballet afresh, retaining some elements from Petipa's version and presumably from Perrot's original production too.

Le Corsaire also survived in Moscow, where Perrot's production was reproduced by Frédéric (Malovergne) in 1858 for Praskovia Lebedeva. Gorsky revised it in 1912, preserving many elements of the traditional choreography, and in that version the ballet retained its place at the Bolshoi Theatre for many years.

The ballet is today to be found in the repertory of eighteen Soviet theatres, the productions being by different choreographers and having very little in common with the original version.

ESMERALDA

Esmeralda has fared even better, and judging from the credits used in the programme in early Soviet times, remained reasonably faithfully to its original conception. From time to time Petipa grafted on to it passages of his own invention. He revised it first for Claudina Cucchi in 1866, when he added a new *pas de deux* of such originality that it was long remembered as the 'pas Cucchi'. For Evgenia Sokolova, in the early 1870s, he arranged a *pas de dix* to music by Gerber, and a new *pas de cinq* was inserted when Adèle Grantzow first danced in it in 1872. Petipa's definitive revision was produced in 1886 for Virginia Zucchi, for whom he replaced Perrot's *pas d'action* in the third act with a dramatic *pas de six* to music by Drigo. This version was revived in 1899 for Mathilda Kshesinskaya. With this constant refurbishing, *Esmeralda*

Jules Perrot

retained enough of its dramatic power to be regularly performed until well into the Soviet era. By 1935, when it had been performed over 250 times, it had lost much of its original power. Agrippina Vaganova then revised the production, preserving some of the traditional choreography, including the *pas de deux* for Esmeralda and Gringoire in the Cour des Miracles (the *Truandaise*) and the dancing lesson, both of which derived from Perrot's production, and the *pas de six* which Petipa had inserted for Zucchi. In this version *Esmeralda* became a popular favourite during the Second World War. In 1981 Piotr Gusev and Nicolai Boyarchikov ventured to revive the Perrot-Petipa *Esmeralda* at the Maly Theatre, Leningrad, assisted considerably in reconstructing the rôle of Esmeralda by Tatiana Vecheslova, who had danced at the Kirov before and after Vaganova's revival, but much had been forgotten and had to be created afresh.

In Moscow *Esmeralda* was originally staged by Perrot himself in 1850 for Fanny Elssler. In 1890 José Mendez based a new production on Petipa's revision, for Lydia Geiten. In 1902 Gorsky produced a completely new version of the story, *Gudule's Daughter*, to music by Antone Simone. In 1926 Vasily Tikhomirov revised the earlier version for Ekaterina Geltser, and in that version it remained in the Bolshoi Theatre repertory for many years.

In Soviet times *Esmeralda* has been produced by over thirty choreographers in various theatres in the Soviet Union, and some of these productions are still in the repertory.

GISELLE

The apportionment of the choreography of the first production of *Giselle* in Paris between Perrot and Coralli has been the subject of weighty consideration by Slonimsky, Lifar and Beaumont in their studies of the ballet, and they all concur that Perrot was responsible for the passages for the two principals, Giselle and Albert. In St. Petersburg Perrot was in sole charge of the ballet until 1859, and no doubt felt free to revise Coralli's contribution as and where he felt it necessary. The responsibility then passed into other hands. In the 1860s Giselle was given a new variation towards the end of Act II which was arranged, in all probability by Saint-Léon, for Grantzow. Later *Giselle* underwent a series of revisions by Petipa – in 1884, 1887 and 1899 – and today's productions are based on Petipa's editing of the original. It seems no longer possible to be specific about the extent of these revisions, but they would appear to have given new life to the ballet and saved it from extinction, for tastes being what they then were, critics and balletomanes generally found it an intolerably old-fashioned piece. Petipa's first revision in 1884 was apparently somewhat tentative, but three years later he reworked the ballet much more thoroughly. By then the invasion of Italian virtuoso ballerinas had begun, and it was necessary to adjust the rôle of Giselle to display the technique of Emma Bessone. It was probably then that Perrot's original variation for Giselle in Act I was discarded, never to be restored again.

It was only in the early years of the twentieth century, when the Romantic period had become sufficiently remote, that dancers and public began to appreciate *Giselle*. In 1903, not long before he retired, Petipa prepared Anna Pavlova for the title-rôle and had the satisfaction of knowing he had produced a worthy successor to Carlotta Grisi. By then *Giselle* had assumed its definitive form, from which all of today's productions stem.

* * *

It is ironic that in London, where Perrot produced some of his greatest work, his ballets did not long survive the end of his engagement as ballet-master at Her Majesty's Theatre in 1848. This came about principally because that theatre was operated on a seasonal basis, being opened only for five months in the spring and summer. Perrot's successor, Paul Taglioni, produced a new repertory of his own works, and such of Perrot's ballets that survived did so, for a few seasons, only because they were enshrined in the repertories of the ballerinas for whom they were created. Hence Carlotta Grisi continued to dance in *Giselle* until 1850 and *Esmeralda* until 1851, and Cerrito was seen in *Ondine* until 1851. The last Perrot ballet to be seen on the London stage was *Esmeralda*, which Domenico Ronzani revived in 1857 for Carolina Pochini.

Ronzani was one of several choreographers who reproduced Perrot's ballets. He had first staged *Esmeralda* for Fanny Elssler in Bologna in 1845 and Vienna in 1846; later he produced it for Pochini at the Scala, Milan, in 1854 and in London in 1857; and in the U.S.A. in 1858. The Viennese production was so successful that it was performed for nearly half a century, receiving its last performance in 1892, the year of Perrot's death. Ronzani's reproduction of *Catarina* survived in Vienna for ten years, from 1847 to 1857. He also revived *Faust* in Milan for Augusta Maywood in 1848 and later in Vienna where it was given from 1851 to 1854, and *Odetta* in Vienna in 1852.

Other 'reproducers' were Fanny Elssler, whose staging of *Le Délire d'un peintre* survived at the Vienna Opera from 1844 to 1853; Hippolyte Monplaisir, who produced *Esmeralda* in New York in 1848; Frédéric (Malovergne) who produced *Catarina* in Moscow in 1850, *Gazelda* in Vienna in 1853 and *Le Corsaire* in Moscow in 1858; Théodore (Chion), who was responsible for the Moscow productions of *Gazelda* in 1854 and *The Naiad and the Fisherman* in 1857; and Andrea Palladini, who produced *Catarina* in Milan in 1853.

The Choreographic Works of Jules Perrot

1832
October 13th, Paris Opéra. *Pas de deux* in Rossini's opera *Moïse*. Danced by Perrot and P. Montessu.

1835
February, Grand Th., Bordeaux. *Pas de deux* inserted in the ballet, *La Tempête*.

1836
July 7th, King's Th., London. 'The original Tarantella, as imported from Naples.' Danced by Perrot and Grisi. Possibly performed earlier at the Teatro di San Carlo, Naples, between December 1835 and March 1836.

August 30th, Th. Français, Paris. *Pas de deux*. Danced by Perrot and Grisi.

September 29th, Hofoper, Vienna. *Die Nymphe und der Schmetterling*, anacreontic ballet in 2 scenes. *Pas de deux* and principal rôles (performed by Perrot and Grisi) arranged by Perrot, corps de ballet sections by Campilli. Attributed to Perrot alone when revived in Munich on June 19th, 1838.

November 23rd, Hofoper, Vienna. *Das Stelldichein*, rustic ballet in 2 scenes, music by Aigner. Danced by Perrot and Grisi. Revived in Munich, June 26th, 1838, and at the Teatro Fondo, Naples, as *L'Appuntamento*, on December 10th, 1838.

1837
September 5th, Opéra Comique, Paris. *Pas de deux*. Danced by Perrot and Grisi.

1838
January 10th, Hofoper, Vienna. *Die neapolitanischen Fischer*, a character study. Principal rôles by Perrot and Grisi. Revived at Her Majesty's Th., London, April 28th, 1842, music reported to be largely from Auber's opera, *La Muette de Portici*. Revived there again on April 24th, 1845, rôles being played by Perrot and Grahn.

March 2nd, Hofoper, Vienna. *Der Kobold*, faery ballet in 2 acts and 5 scenes, music by Reuling. Principal rôles by Perrot and Grisi.

August, Scala, Milan. *Pas de deux* inserted in Cortesi's ballet, *I Figli di Edoardo*. Danced by Perrot and Grisi.

1839
January 12th, Teatro di San Carlo, Naples. *Pas de deux* inserted in S. Taglioni's ballet, *Il Rajah di Benares*. Danced by Perrot and Grisi.

1840
February 1st, Th. de la Renaissance, Paris. Dances inserted in, and possibly also production of, the opera, *Zingaro*, libretto by Sauvage, music by Fortuna. Principal characters by Perrot (Zingaro) and Grisi (Gianina).

1841
February 12th, Paris Opéra. *Pas de deux* inserted in Donizetti's opera, *La Favorite*. Danced by Grisi and L. Petipa. Revived at Her Majesty's Th., London, April 26th, 1842.

April 4th, Paris Opéra. *Pas de deux* inserted in Mozart's opera, *Don Juan*. Danced by Grisi and L. Petipa.

June 28th, Paris Opéra. *Giselle*, ballet-pantomime in 2 acts, scenario by Gautier and Saint-Georges, music by Adam. Choreography attiributed to Coralli, but dances and scenes for Grisi (as Giselle) arranged anonymously by Perrot. Revived by Perrot at Her Majesty's Th., London, March 12th, 1842 (with Grisi) and March 30th, 1843 (with Elssler); also revived by him in St. Petersburg.

1842
July 14th, Her Majesty's Th., London. *Une Soirée du carnaval*, divertissement, introducing dances by other choreographers as well as by Perrot. Among Perrot's dances, a Double Cachucha, based on Elssler's dance.

June 23rd, Her Majesty's Th., London. *Alma, ou La Fille du feu*, ballet in 4 scenes by Deshayes, with *pas* by Perrot and Cerrito. Music by Costa. Cast included Perrot and Cerrito.

1843
March 11th, Her Majesty's Th., London. *L'Aurore*, divertissement. Music by Pugni. Cast at first performance included Perrot and A. Dumilâtre.

April 6th, Her Majesty's Th., London. *Un Bal sous Louis Quatorze*, divertissement. Music composed and arranged by Nadaud. A framework for a number of *pas*, including the Menuet de la Reine and Gavotte (danced first by Elssler and A. Dumilâtre, later by Elssler and Cerrito).

April 27th, Her Majesty's Th., London. *Pas de Diane chasseresse* inserted in *Un Bal sous Louis Quatorze*. Danced by A. Dumilâtre.

June 22nd, Her Majesty's Th., London. *Ondine, ou la Nayade*, ballet in 6 scenes. Music by Pugni. Principal characters by Cerrito (Ondine), Perrot (Matteo), Guy-Stéphan (Giannina).

July 20th, Her Majesty's Th., London. *Pas de deux* for Elssler and Cerrito.

August 3rd, Her Majesty's Th., London. *Le Délire d'un peintre*, divertissement. Music by Pugni. Principal rôles by Elssler (Blanche d'Oviedo) and Perrot (Stephano).

1844

March 9th, Her Majesty's Th., London. *La Esmeralda*, ballet in 5 scenes. Scenario by Perrot, assisted by Lumley, based on Hugo's *Notre Dame de Paris*. Music by Pugni. Principal characters by Grisi (Esmeralda), Perrot (Gringoire), Saint-Léon (Phoebus), Gosselin (Frollo), Frassi (Fleur de Lys), Coulon (Quasimodo). Revived by Perrot at Scala, Milan, December 26th, 1844, with Elssler (Esmeralda), Perrot (Gringoire), Pratesi (Phoebus), Ronzani (Frollo), Wuthier (Fleur de Lys), Catte (Quasimodo). Revived by Perrot at Bolshoi Th., St. Petersburg, January 2nd, 1849, with Elssler (Esmeralda), Perrot (Gringoire), Frédéric (Phoebus), Goltz (Frollo), Smirnova (Fleur de Lys), Didier (Quasimodo), Johansson.

April 11th, Her Majesty's Th., London. *Polka*. Music by Pugni. Danced by Perrot and Grisi.

June 25th, Her Majesty's Th., London. *Zélia, ou la Nymphe de Diane*, ballet in 4 scenes. Music by Pugni. Principal rôles by Cerrito, Perrot, Saint-Léon, Plunkett.

July 25th, Her Majesty's Th., London. *La Paysanne Grande Dame*, divertissement. Principal characters by Elssler, Perrot, Gosselin, Coulon. One dance (*pas de deux* for Plunkett and Scheffer) arranged by Gosselin to music by Nadaud.

1845

March 8th, Her Majesty's Th., London. *Eoline, ou la Dryade*, ballet in 6 scenes. Music by Pugni. Principal characters by Grahn (Eoline), Perrot (Rübezahl), Toussaint (Count Edgar). One pas, a *pas de cinq*, was by Gosselin. Expanded version produced in St. Petersburg, 1858 (q.v.).

April 17th, Her Majesty's Th., London. *Kaya, ou l'Amour voyageur*, ballet in one scene. Music by Pugni, comprising themes from Norwegian folk melodies. Principal characters by Grahn, Pragher, Perrot and Di Mattia.

May 1st, Her Majesty's Th., London. *La Bacchante*, divertissement. Music by Pugni. Principal dancers: Grahn, Perrot.

July 12th, Her Majesty's Th., London. *Pas de Quatre*. Music by Pugni. Danced by M. Taglioni, Cerrito, Grisi, Grahn.

July 24th, Her Majesty's Th., London. *Diane*, ballet divertissement. Music by Pugni. Principal characters by M. Taglioni (Diana), Perrot (Endymion).

1846

March 3rd, Her Majesty's Th., London. *Catarina, ou la Fille du bandit*, ballet in 5 scenes. Music by Pugni. Principal characters by Grahn (Catarina), Perrot (Diavolino), Gosselin (Salvator Rosa), Petit-Stéphan (Florida). Revived by Perrot at the Scala, Milan, January 9th, 1847, in an expanded form with additional music by Bajetti, with Elssler (Catarina), Perrot (Diavolino), Catte (Salvator Rosa), Bagnoli-Quattri (Florida). Revived by Perrot at the Bolshoi Th., St. Petersburg, February 16th, 1849, with Elssler (Catarina), Perrot (Diavolino), Johansson (Salvator Rosa).

April 2nd, Her Majesty's Th., London. *Pas de trois*. Danced by L. Taglioni, Petit-Stéphan, Perrot.

June 11th, Her Majesty's Th., London. *Lalla Rookh, or The Rose of Lahore*, grand oriental ballet in 10 scenes, based on Thomas Moore's poem. Music by Pugni, introducing selections from F. David's symphonic ode, *Le Désert*. Principal characters by Cerrito (Lalla Rookh), Perrot (Fadladeen), Saint-Léon (Feramorz).

July 23rd, Her Majesty's Th., London. *Le Jugement de Pâris*, divertissement comprising the *grand pas*, *Le Pas de Déesses*. Music by Pugni. Principal characters by M. Taglioni (Hebe), Cerrito (Venus), Grahn (Minerva), Perrot (Mercury), Saint-Léon (Paris).

1847

March 16th, Scala, Milan. *Odetta, ou la demenza di Carlo VI re di Francia*, historical ballet in a prologue and 6 parts. Music by Panizza (for the action), Bajetti and Croff (for the dances). Principal characters by Elssler (Odetta), Perrot (Villon), Catte (Charles VI), Pratesi (Duc d'Orléans), Bagnoli-Quattri (Isabella).

April 20th, Her Majesty's Th., London. *Pas de deux*. Danced by Perrot and Rosati.

June 26th, Her Majesty's Th., London. *Les Eléments*, ballet divertissement. Music by Bajetti, arranged and augmented by Nadaud. Principal characters by Grisi (Fire), Cerrito (Air), Rosati (Water).

1848

February 12th, Scala, Milan. *Faust*, grand fantastic ballet in 2 parts and 7 scenes. Music by Panizza, with additions by Costa (*pas de fascination* in Scene 2, probably from *Alma*) and Bajetti (*pas de sept* in Scene 4). Principal characters by Elssler (Marguerite), Catte (Faust), Perrot (Mephistopheles). Shortened to 6 scenes after the first performance, Elssler being replaced by Maywood. Revived at the Bolshoi Th., St. Petersburg, February 14th, 1854, with additional music by Pugni. Principal characters by Yella (Marguerite), M. Petipa (Faust), Perrot (Mephistopheles).

June 13th, Her Majesty's Th., London. *Les Quatre Saisons*, ballet divertissement. Music arranged and composed by Pugni, much of it taken from Panizza's music for *Faust*. Principal dancers: Cerrito (Spring), Grisi (Summer), Rosati (Autumn) and M. Taglioni the younger (Winter.)

July 18th, Her Majesty's Th., London. *Grand Quintette Dansante*, pas de cinq interpolated into *La Esmeralda*. Dancers: Rosati, Petit-Stéphan, Julien, Lamoureaux, L. Dor.

1849

October 8th, Paris Opéra. *La Filleule des fées*, ballet fantastique in a prologue, 3 acts and 6 scenes. Scenario by Saint-Georges. Music by Adam and

A. de Saint-Julien. Principal characters by Grisi (Ysaure), L. Petipa (Hugues), Perrot (Alain), Marquet (Black Fairy), L. Taglioni (Rose Fairy), Emarot (White Fairy). Revived by Perrot at the Bolshoi Th., St. Petersburg, with music reorchestrated by K. Lyadov, with Elssler (Ysaure), Johansson (Hugues), Perrot (Alain), Andreyanova (Black Fairy), Smirnova (Rose Fairy), Yakovleva (White Fairy).

December 16th, Bolshoi Th., St. Petersburg. Two *pas* inserted in J. and M. Petipa's ballet, *Lida*: a *scène dansante* and a *pas de trois*. Danced by Elssler, Perrot, Johansson.

1850

July 15th, Peterhof. *L'Ile des Naiades*, a reworked scene based on *Ondine*. Principal characters by Perrot (Matteo), Nikitina (Hydrola), Prikhunova (Azurina), Richard (Giannina).

1851

February 6th, Bolshoi Th., St. Petersburg. *The Naiad and the Fisherman*, fantastic ballet in 3 acts and 5 scenes. Music by Pugni. Principal characters by Grisi (the naiad), Perrot (Matteo), Andreyanova (Giannina).

February 18th, Bolshoi Th., St. Petersburg. *Les Tribulations d'un maître de ballet*, divertissement in 2 scenes. Music by Pugni. Principal characters by Perrot and Andreyanova.

1852

November 23rd, Bolshoi Th., St. Petersburg. *The War of the Women, or the Amazons of the Ninth Century*, grand ballet in 4 acts and 6 scenes. Music by Pugni. Principal characters by Grisi (Vlaida), Perrot (Kolo), Andreyanova (Vlasta), Johansson (Ulrich), M. Petipa (Mitsislas).

1853

February 24th, Bolshoi Th., St. Petersburg. *Gazelda, or The Tsiganes*, grand ballet in a prologue, 2 acts and 4 scenes. Music by Pugni. Principal characters by Grisi (Gazelda), Perrot (Zingaro), Andreyanova (Narda), Johansson (Rodolf), M. Petipa (Karl), Ryukhina (Emma). Revived by Perrot at the Scala, Milan, January 27th, 1864, with additional music by Giorza. Principal characters by Cucchi (Gazelda), Amaturo (Zingaro), Carmine (Narda), Vismara (Rodolf), Magri (Karl), G. Pratesi (Emma).

1854

December 5th, Bolshoi Th., St. Petersburg. *Marcobomba*, ballet in 1 act. Music arranged by Pugni. Principal characters by Perrot (Marcobomba), M. Petipa, Johansson, Richard, Prikhunova.

1855
November 20th, Bolshoi Th., St. Petersburg. *Armida,* grand ballet heroi-fantastique in 4 acts and 5 scenes, preceded by a prologue. Music by Pugni. Principal characters by Cerrito (Armida), M. Petipa (Rinaldo), Perrot (Gianneo), Goltz (Godfrey), Frédéric (Ubaldo), Muravieva (Cupid).

1856
March 2nd, Bolshoi Th., St. Petersburg. *La Fille de marbre,* ballet in 3 scenes. Music by Pugni. New dances by Perrot added to production by Saint-Léon. Principal characters by Cerrito (Alma), Perrot (Periphète).

August 3rd, Peterhof. *La Débutante,* ballet divertissement in 2 scenes. Music arranged and composed by Pugni, much of it taken from scores by Adam for *La Filleule des fées* and Deldevez for *Vert-Vert.* Revived by Perrot at Bolshoi Th., St. Petersburg, January 29th, 1857. Principal characters by Bogdanova (Clorinda), Maria Petipa (Guimard), Prikhunova (Zépherine), Perrot (the ballet-master), M. Petipa (the Marquis).

1857
February 12th, Bolshoi Th., St. Petersburg. *La Petite Marchande de bouquets,* choreographic interlude. Danced by Muravieva.

February 19th, Bolshoi Th., St. Petersburg. *L'Ile des muets,* comedy by Deligny. Music by Labarre and Pugni. Principal characters by Cerrito and Théric, Vernet and Leménil of the French drama company.

October 20th, Bolshoi Th., St. Petersburg. *The Rose, the Violet and the Butterfly,* choreographic interlude. Music by Peter II, Grand Duke of Oldenburg. Principal characters by Muravieva (Butterfly), Radina and Amosova. Previously staged by M. Petipa at the Grand Duke's summer residence.

1858
January 21st, Bolshoi Th., St. Petersburg. *Le Corsaire,* grand ballet pantomime in 3 acts and 5 scenes. Scenario by Saint-Georges and Mazilier, after the poem by Byron. Arranged and staged with new dances specially composed by Perrot. Music by Adam and Pugni. Principal characters by M. Petipa (Conrad), Friedberg (Medora), Perrot (Seyd Pasha), Frédéric (Birbanto), Radina (Gulnara).

November 16th Bolshoi Th., St. Petersburg. *Eoline, ou la Dryade,* grand ballet fantastique in 4 acts and 5 scenes. Music by Pugni, much of it added for this production. Principal characters by Ferraris (Eoline), Perrot (Rübezahl), Johansson (Count Edgar), Goltz (Ratibor), Lyadova 2 (Trilby), Marie Petipa (Berta), Stukolkin (Frantz). New and expanded version of the ballet of the same name produced in London in 1843 (q.v.).

(The above list excludes divertissements for operas which Perrot arranged during his engagement in St. Petersburg.)

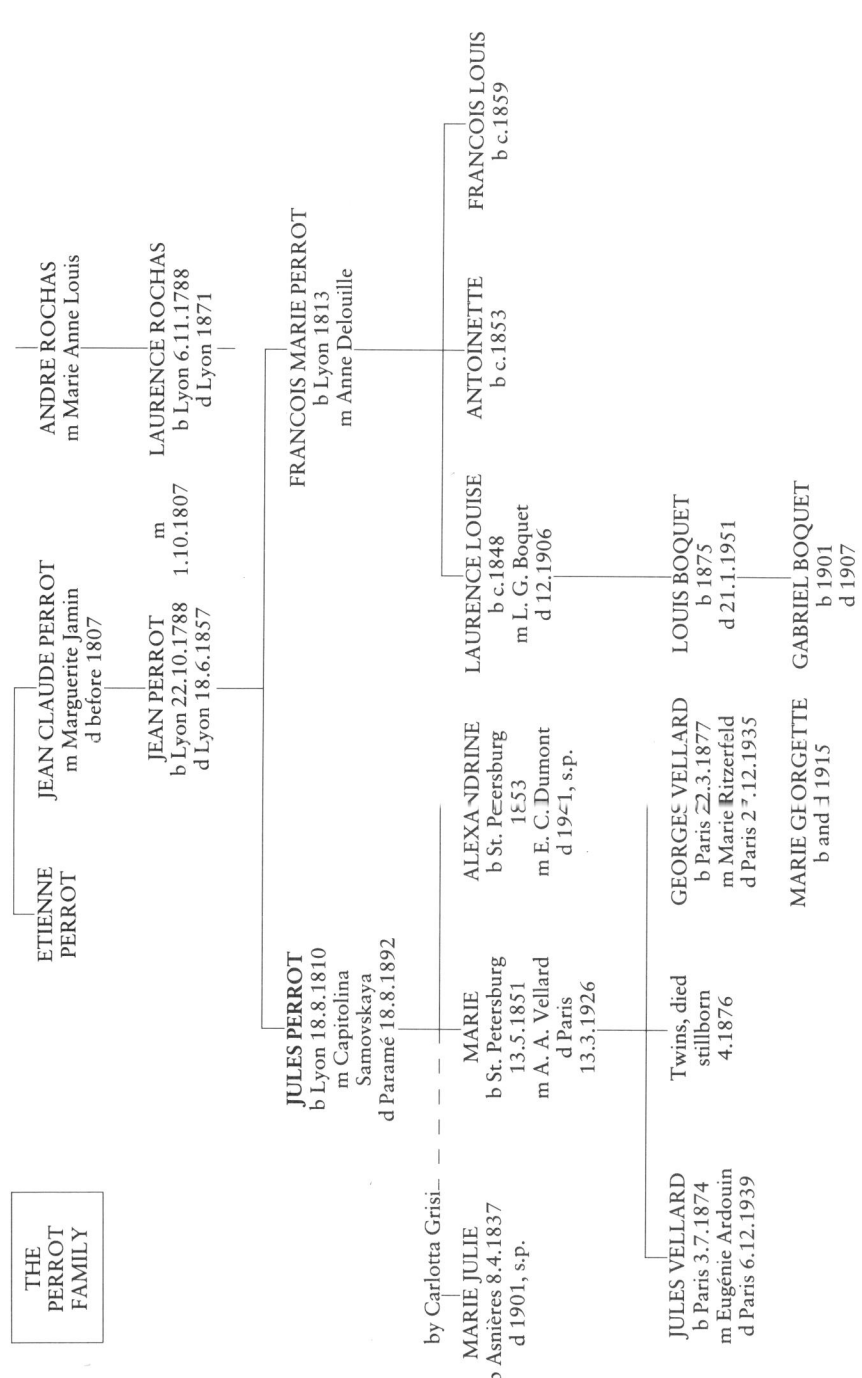

THE
SAMOVSKY
FAMILY

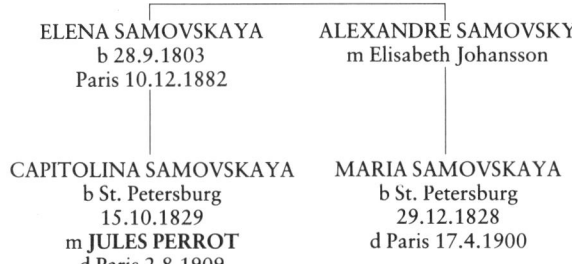

ELENA SAMOVSKAYA
b 28.9.1803
Paris 10.12.1882

ALEXANDRE SAMOVSKY
m Elisabeth Johansson

CAPITOLINA SAMOVSKAYA
b St. Petersburg
15.10.1829
m **JULES PERROT**
d Paris 2.8.1909

MARIA SAMOVSKAYA
b St. Petersburg
29.12.1828
d Paris 17.4.1900

THE
DUMONT
FAMILY

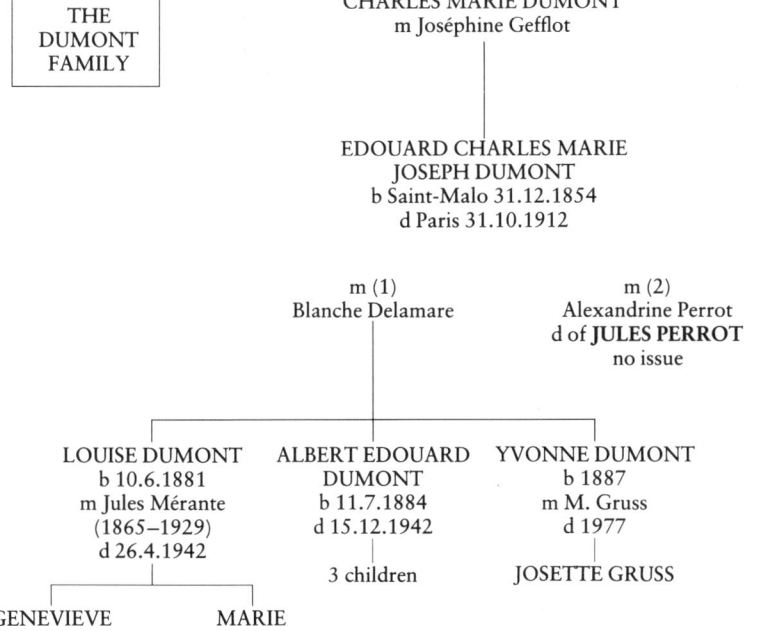

CHARLES MARIE DUMONT
m Joséphine Gefflot

EDOUARD CHARLES MARIE
JOSEPH DUMONT
b Saint-Malo 31.12.1854
d Paris 31.10.1912

m (1)
Blanche Delamare

m (2)
Alexandrine Perrot
d of **JULES PERROT**
no issue

LOUISE DUMONT
b 10.6.1881
m Jules Mérante
(1865–1929)
d 26.4.1942

ALBERT EDOUARD
DUMONT
b 11.7.1884
d 15.12.1942

3 children

YVONNE DUMONT
b 1887
m M. Gruss
d 1977

JOSETTE GRUSS

GENEVIEVE   MARIE

Bibliography

ADICE, G. Léopold *Théorie de la gymnastique théâtrale* (Paris, 1859)
ANON. *Almanach de plaisirs de Paris et des communes environnantes* (Paris, 1815)
ANON. *Cesare Pugni* (Gazzetta Musicale di Milano, August 9th, 1885, p. 274)
ANON. *Jules Perrot* (Galerie Théâtrale, Paris, 1872)
ARAGO, Jacques *Mémoires d'un petit banc de l'Opéra* (Paris, 1844)
ARRIGONI, Paolo and BERTARELLI, Achille *Ritratti di musicisti ed artisti di teatro conservati nella Raccolta delle stempe e dei disegni* (Milan, 1934)
AU, Susan *The Bandit Ballerina: some sources of Jules Perrot's Catarina* (Dance Research Journal, vol. 10, no. 2, pp. 2–5, New York 1978)
AU, Susan *The Shadow of Herself: some sources of Jules Perrot's Ondine* (Dance Chronicle, vol. 2, pp. 159–171, New York, 1978)

BARBIERA, Raffaello *Figure et figurine del secolo che muore* (Milan, 1899)
BEALL, Chandler B. *La Fortune du Tasse en France* (Eugene, Or., 1942)
BEAUMONT, Cyril W. *The Ballet Called Giselle* (London, 1944)
BÉRAUD, A and MERLE, J.-T. and NODIER, Charles *Faust* (Paris, 1828)
BERMANI, Benedetto *Pleiade artistica* (Milan, 1847)
BERTHOUD, Dorette *Vie du peintre Léopold Robert* (Neuchâtel, 1935)
BINNEY, Edwin, the 3rd *Les Ballets de Théophile Gautier* (Paris, 1965)
BOGGS, Jean Sutherland *Portraits by Degas* (Berkeley and Los Angeles, 1962)
BOIGNE, Charles de *Petits Mémoires de l'Opéra* (Paris, 1857)
BÖRNE, Ludwig *Briefe aus Paris 1830–1831* (Hamburg, 1832)
BOUFFÉ *Mes Souvenirs, 1800–1880* (Paris, 1880)
BOURNONVILLE, August *Lettres à la maison de son enfance* (Copenhagen, 1969–78)
BOURNONVILLE, August *Mit Theaterliv* (Copenhagen, 1848–77)
BOURNONVILLE, August *Nytaarsgabe for Danse-Andere* (Copenhagen, 1829)

BOURNONVILLE, August *Reiseminder, Reflexioner og biographiske Skizzer* (Copenhagen, 1878)
BRIFFAULT, Eugène *Jules Perrot (Galerie des Artistes-Dramatiques*, Paris, n.d.)

CAMBIASI, Pompeo *La Scala, 1778–1889* (Milan, 1889)
CASTIL-BLAZE *L'Académie Impériale de Musique* (Paris, 1855)
CASTIL-BLAZE *La Danse et les ballets depuis Bacchus à Mademoiselle Taglioni* (Paris, 1832)
CELLARIUS *Fashionable Dancing* (London, 1847)
CHASLES, Philarète *Ondine (Beautés de l'Opéra*, Paris, 1845: English edition edited by Charles Heath, *Beauties of the Opera and Ballet*, London, 1845)
CHORLEY, H.F. *Thirty Years' Musical Recollections* (London, 1862)
CHOUET, Dominique *Carlotta Grisi, la bonne dame de Saint-Jean (Tribune de Genève*, December 23rd–26th, 1978)
CHRISTOUT, Marie-Françoise *Jules Perrot (Enciclopedia dello Spettacolo*, Rome, 1954–62, vol. VIII, cols. 15–18)
CHRISTOUT, Marie-Françoise *Le Merveilleux et le théâtre du silence* (Paris, 1965)
CRIPPA, Giuseppe *Giulio Perrot (Strenne Europea Teatrale*, vol. X, pp. 99–112, Turin, 1847)
CRUIKSHANK, George, and others *The Comic Almanach for 1847* (London, 1846)
CUCCHI, Claudina *Venti anni di palcoscenico* (Rome, 1904)

DASH, Comtesse *Portraits contemporains* (Paris, 1859–61)
DESHAYES, A.J.J. *Faust* (London, 1833)
DUPREZ, Gilbert *Souvenirs d'un chanteur* (Paris, 1880)

ESCUDIER, Léon *Mes Souvenirs* (Paris, 1863)

FRIDERICIA, Allan *August Bournonville* (Copenhagen, 1979)

GAUTIER, Théophile *Carlotta Grisi (Galerie des Artistes Dramatiques*, Paris, 1841)
GAUTIER, Théophile *Giselle (Beautés de l'Opéra*. Paris, 1845: English edition edited by Charles Heath, *Beauties of the Opera and Ballet*, London, 1845)
GAUTIER, Théophile *Une Journée à Londres (Revue des Deux Mondes*, vol. XXX, pp. 270–296, Paris, 1842)
GÉRÉON, Léonard de *La Rampe et les coulisses* (Paris, 1832)
GINISTY, Paul *Le Mélodrame* (Paris, 1910)

Bibliography

GONCOURT, Edmond and Jules de *Journal: mémoires de la vie littéraire* (Paris, 1956)
GUEST, Ivor *Cesare Pugni (Dance Gazette,* no. 170, pp. 22–24, London, 1979)
GUEST, Ivor *Fanny Cerrito* (London, 1956)
GUEST, Ivor *Fanny Elssler* (London, 1970)
GUEST, Ivor *Letters from a Ballet-master* (London, 1981)
GUEST, Ivor *The Miracles of Jules Perrot (Opera Ballet Music-hall,* Paris, Winter 1952, no. 2, pp. 51–60)
GUEST, Ivor *The Pas de Quatre* (London, 1970)
GUEST, Ivor *The Romantic Ballet in England* (London, 1954)
GUEST, Ivor *The Romantic Ballet in Paris* (London, 1966)

HADAMOWSKY, Franz *Die Wiener Hoftheater (Stattstheater)*, vol 2 (Vienna, 1975)
HEINE, Heinrich *Doktor Faust* Translated and edited by Basil Ashmore (London, 1952)
HEINE, Heinrich *Méphistophéla et la légende de Faust (Revue des Deux Mondes,* Paris, 1852, vol. XIII, pp. 635–663)
HEINE, Heinrich *Works* Translated by C.G. Leland (London, 1893)
HERVEY, Charles *The Theatres of Paris* (Paris, 1846)
HÜBNER, Alexander Count von *Ein Jahr meines Lebens 1848–1849* (Leipzig, 1891)

LARTIGUE, Pierre *Magie blanche (Ballet/Danse,* Paris, January–March 1980, no. 1, pp. 11–17)
LECOMTE, L.-Henry *Un Comédien au XIXe siècle: Frédérick Lemaître* (Paris, 1888)
LECOMTE, L.-Henry *La Renaissance* (Paris, 1905)
LIFAR, Serge *Carlotta Grisi* (Paris, 1941)
LIFAR, Serge *La Danse* (Paris, 1938)
LIFAR, Serge *Giselle: apothéose du ballet romantique* (Paris, 1942)
LILLIESTAM, Åke *Christian Johansson och hans brev till August Bournonville (Särtryck ur Personhistorisk tidskrift,* Stockholm, 1973, vol. 69, pp. 75–103)
LOUIS, Maurice A.-L. *Danses populaires et ballets d'opéra* (Paris, 1965)
LUMLEY, Benjamin *Reminiscences of the Opera* (London, 1864)
LYONNET, Henry *Dictionnaire des comédiens français* (Paris, 1904)

MAUTNER, Franz H. *Nestroy* (Heidelberg, 1974)
MIGEL, Parmenia *The Ballerinas* (New York, 1972)
MONTMORENCY, Duc de *Lettres sur l'Opéra (1840–42)* (Paris, 1922)
MOORE, Lillian *Artists of the Dance* (New York, 1938)

MOORE, Lillian *The Origin of Adagio in Ballet (Dancing Times*, London, April 1936, pp. 16–19)
MOORE, Thomas *Memoirs, Journal and Correspondence* (London, 1853–56)
MORGAN, Lady Sydney *The Life and Times of Salvator Rosa* (London, 1824)

NALBACH, Daniel *The King's Theatre 1704–1867* (London, 1972)
NEIIENDAM, Robert *Lucile Grahn: en skaebne i Dansen* (Copenhagen, 1963)
NIEHAUS, Max *Himmel Hölle und Trikot: Heinrich Heine und das Ballet* (Munich, 1959)
NOVERRE, Jean-Georges *Lettres sur la danse, sur les ballets et les arts* (St. Petersburg, 1803–04)
NOZIÈRE, F. *Madame Dorval* (Paris, 1930)

PAZDIREK, François *Manuel universel de la littérature musicale* (Vienna, 1905)
PENZEL, Frederick *Theatre Lighting before Electricity* (Middletown, Conn., 1978)
PLUNKETT, J. de *Fantômes et souvenirs de la Porte-Saint-Martin* (Paris, 1946)
POUGIN, A *Adolphe Adam, sa vie, sa carrière, ses mémoires artistiques* (Paris, 1877)
POUILLET, Eugène *Traité théorique et pratique de la propriété littéraire et artistique et du droit de représentation* (Paris, 1879)
PUDEŁEK, Janina *Warszawski Balet Romantyczny 1802–1866* (Warsaw, 1968)

Q [Charles G. Rosenberg] *You Have Heard of Them* (New York, 1854)

REES, Terence *Theatre Lighting in the Age of Gas* (London, 1978)
REGLI, Francesco *Dizionario biografico dei più celebri poeti ed artisti ... che fioririno in Italia dal 1800 al 1860* (Turin, 1860)
RICHARDSON, Joanna *Théophile Gautier, His Life and Times* (London, 1958)
RIES, Frank W.D. *Giselle: Travels with a Chameleon Romantic (Dance Magazine*, New York, August 1979, pp. 61–73)
ROBERT, Adrien and PERROT *La Polka enseignée sans maître* (Paris, 1844)
ROSLAVLEVA, Natalia *Era of the Russian Ballet* (London, 1966)
SAINT-LÉON, Arthur *La Sténochorégraphie* (Paris, 1852)
SORLEY-WALKER, Kathrine *Perrot and his Lost Choreography (Ballet*, London, April 1946, pp. 29–36)

Bibliography

STREHLY, G. *L'Acrobatie et les acrobats* (Paris, 1904)
STUMME, Gerhard *Faust als Pantomime und Ballet* (Leipzig, 1942)

TANI, Gino *Carlotta Grisi (Enciclopedia dello Spettacolo*, Rome, 1954–62, vol. V, cols. 1790–95)
THOMPSON, Edward *Rabindranath Tagore* (London, 1948)
TILD, Jean *Théophile Gautier et ses amis* (Paris, 1951)
TOUCHARD-LAFOSSE, G. *Chroniques secrètes et galantes de l'Opéra* (Paris, 1846)

VAILLAT, Léandre *La Taglioni, ou la Vie d'une danseuse* (Paris, 1942)
VERNIÈRES, Jules *Les Coulisses de l'Opéra (Revue de Paris*, Paris 1936, vol. XXXI, pp. 303–322)

WADEPUHL. Walter *Heinrich Heine, sein Leben und sein Werke* (Vienna, 1974)
WARNER, Mary-Jane Evans *Gavottes and Bouquets: a comparative study of changes in dance style between 1700 and 1850* (Doctoral thesis, Ohio State University, 1974)
WESTMORLAND, Priscilla, Countess of *Correspondence* (London, 1909)
WINTER, Marian Hannah *The Pre-Romantic Ballet* (London, 1974)
WINTER, Marian Hannah *Le Théâtre du merveilleux* (Paris, 1962)

Published Scenarios of Ballets produced by Jules Perrot

In view of the scarcity of some of these scenarios, a library where a copy exists has been indicated. This does not infer that copies are not to be found elsewhere. Scenarios were often republished for reproductions by other ballet-masters: these have not been listed.

Der Kobold (Le Lutin) Paris, [1840]. Bibl. de l'Op., Paris.
Giselle Paris, 1841. Bibl. de l'Op., Paris.
Ondine London, [1843]. Indiana University.
La Esmeralda London, 1844. British Library.
La Esmeralda Milan, 1844. Museo Teatrale alla Scala, Milan.
Eoline London, [1845]. Theater-Museum, Munich.
Eolina St. Petersburg, 1858. Lunacharsky Th. Library, Leningrad.
Catarina Milan, 1847. Bibl. Braidense, Milan.
Lalla Rookh London, [1846]. Indiana University.
Odetta Milan, 1847. Bibl. de l'Op., Paris.
Les Eléments London, [1847). Indiana University.
Faust Milan, 1848. Two versions: in seven scenes for Elssler, in six for Maywood. Bibl. Braidense, Milan.
Les Quatre Saisons London, [1848]. Indiana University.

La Filleule des fées Paris, 1849. Bibl. de l'Op., Paris.
The War of the Women St. Petersburg, 1852. Lunacharsky Th. Library, Leningrad.
Gazelda St. Petersburg, 1852. Lunacharsky Th. Library, Leningrad.
Gazelda Milan, 1864. Bibl. Braidense, Milan.
Armida St. Petersburg, 1855. Lunacharsky Th. Library, Leningrad.

БОРИСОГЛЕБСКИЙ, М. *Материалы по история русского балета* Ленинград, 1938
ВОЛЬФ, А. *Хроника петербургских театров с конца 1826 до начала 1855 года* СПБ, 1877
ГЕЙРОТ, А. Ф. *Описание Петергофа* СПБ, 1868
ДОСТОЕВСКИЙ, Ф. В. *Полное Собрание Сочинений* Москва & Ленинград, 1930
ДРИЗЕН, Барон Н. В. *Драматическая ценцура двух епох 1825-1881* СПБ, 1917
КАРАТЫГИН, П. А. *Записки* Ленинград, 1929
КРАСОВСКАЯ, В. М. *Русский балетный театр от возникновения до середины XIX века* Ленинград, 1958
КРАСОВСКАЯ, В. М. *Танцовщица Надежда Богданова* (*Ученые записки*, т. 1, стр. 295-322, Ленинград, 1958)
ЛЕШКОВ, Д. *Мариус Петипа 1822-1910* Петроград, 1922
ЛИФАРЬ, С. *История русскаго балета* Париж, 1945
ЛОПУХОВ, Ф. В. *Хореографические откровенности* Москва, 1972
НАТАРОВА, А. П. *Из воспоминаний артистки А. П. Натаровой* (*Исторический вестник*, СПВ, 1903, стр. 25-41, 421-442)
НЕХЕНДЗИ, А. сост. *Мариус Петипа: материалы, воспоминания, статья* Ленинград, 1971
ПЕТИПА, М. *Мемуары Мариуса Петипа, солиста его величества и балетмейстера имп. театров* СПБ, 1906
ПЕТРОВ, О. *Русская балетная критика конца XVIII – первой половины XIX века* Москва, 1982
ПЛЕЩЕЕВ, А. А. *Наш балет, 1673-1899* СПБ, 1899
СЕРОВ, А. Н. *Избранные стати* Ленинград, 1950
СИЛЬВО, Л. Г. *Опыт алфавитнаго указателя балетам, пантомимам, дивертиссементам ... 1672-1900* СПБ, 1900
СЛОНИМСКИЙ, Ю. И. *Драматургия балетного театра XIX века* Москва, 1977
СЛОНИМСКИЙ, Ю. И. *Жизель: этюди* Ленинград, 1969
СЛОНИМСКИЙ, Ю. И. *Мастера балета* Ленинград, 1937
СЛОНИМСКИЙ, Ю. И. *Эсмеральда* (Р. А. Шапиро ред., *Эсмеральда*, Ленинград, 1935, стр. 29-41)

Periodicals

Ежегодник императорских театров:
  1891-92, стр. 484-486
  1899-1900, приложение 3е, стр. 53-108
  1900-01, приложение 2е, стр. 66-162

Periodicals

BOLOGNA
  Teatri, Arti, e Letteratura
BORDEAUX
  L'Indicateur
LONDON
  Athenæum
  Courrier de l'Europe
  Court Journal
  Era
  Examiner
  Illustrated London News
  Maestro
  Morning Chronicle
  Morning Herald
  Morning Post
  Musical Examiner
  Musical World
  Pictorial Times
  Punch
  Satirist
  Spectator
  Sunday Times
  The Times
LYON
  La Gazette universelle
  Le Journal de Lyon
  La Semaine lyonnaise
  Le Spectateur lyonnais
MILAN
  Corriere delle Dame
  La Fama
  Gazzetta dei Teatri
  Gazzetta Musicale di Milano
  Gazzetta Privilegiata di Milano
  Il Pirata
  Il Trovatore
MOSCOW
  Московские ведомости
NAPLES
  Giornale del Regno delle Due Sicilie
PARIS
  Le Corsaire
  Coureur des Spectacles
  Courrier des Théâtres
  Le Constitutionel
  L'Entr'acte
  La France Musicale
  Le Figaro
  Gazette des Tribunaux
  Journal des Débats
  Journal des Théâtres
  Journal pour rire
  Le Ménestrel
  Le Monde dramatique
  Le Moniteur
  Moniteur des théâtres
  Le Musée Philippon
  La Musique
  Le National
  La Presse
  Revue des Deux Mondes
  Revue et Gazette Musicale
ST PETERSBURG
  Библиотека для чтения
  Пантеон
  Санктпетербургские ведомости
  Северная пчела
  Современник
  Современное слово
  Якор

TURIN
  Strenna Europea Teatrale
VIENNA
  Allgemeine Theaterzeitung
  Der Humorist
  Der Sammler
  Wiener Zeitschrift für Kunst, Literatur, Theater und Mode

Notes

Titles of works cited, abbreviated in these notes, are to be found in full in the Bibliography. Dates relate to the nineteenth century, unless otherwise indicated. Dates of Russian periodicals are given in both styles, the New Style which was in general use in Western Europe being given second.

CHAPTER 1 (pp.1–6)

1 Briffault, p. 1.
2 Dossier d'artiste, J. Perrot. Bibl. de l'Op., Paris.
3 *Fama*, 13.3.39.
4 *Jnl. de Lyon*, 1.6.20.
5 *Gaz. Univ. de Lyon*, 8.6.20.
6 Briffault, p.2.

CHAPTER 2 (pp. 7–16)

1 *Cour. des Ths.*, 20.8.23.
2 *Jnl. de Paris*, 30.12.23.
3 *Jnl. de Paris*, 30.1.24.
4 *Mng. Post*, 25.5.46. This anecdote was related about Perrot, but the title of the piece was, presumably erroneously, given as *Polichinelle Vampire*.
5 *Cour. des Ths.*, 10.5.24.
6 Bournonville, *Lettres à la maison*, I, p. 70.
7 *Sapajou* libretto, pp. 18–19.
8 Bournonville, *Nytaarsgabe*, p. 18.
9 Bournonville, *Mit Theaterliv*, I, pp. 74–75
10 Royal Library, Copenhagen.
11 *Cour. des Ths.*, 27.4.27.
12 *Alm. des plaisirs*, pp.22–23
13 *Alm. des plaisirs*, pp. 22–23.
14 Saint-Léon, *Notice sur Jean Coralli*.
15 *Cour. des Ths.*, 10.6.28.
16 Béraud, *Faust*, p. 21.

CHAPTER 3 (pp. 17–29)

1 *Mng. Post*, 22.2.30
2 *Mng. Post*, 8.3.30.
3 *Cour. des Ths.*, 10.4.30.
4 Arch. Nat., Paris AJ[13] 118.
5 *Cour. des Ths.*, 11.6.30.
6 *Cour. des Ths.*, 17.6.30.
7 *Cour. des Ths.*, 24.6.30.
8 *Cour. des Ths.*, 7.7.30.
9 Heine, *Works*, IV, pp. 266–67.
10 Castil-Blaze, *L'Académie Impériale*, II, p. 221.
11 *Jnl. des Débats*, 20.3.31.
12 *Jnl. des Débats*, 11.4.31.
13 Dash, III, pp. 128–129.
14 *Cour. des Ths.*, 16.3.31.
15 *Cour. des Ths.*, 17.3.31.
16 *Cour. des Ths.*, 26.4.31.
17 *Jnl. des Débats*, 12.9.32.
18 Text accompanying woodcut of bust.
19 *Court Jnl.*, 9.3.33.
20 *Court Jnl.*, 23.2.33.
21 *Court Jnl.*, 16.3.33.
22 Letter dated 23.4.29. Dossier d'artiste: Deshayes. Bibl. de l'Op., Paris.
23 *Cour. des Ths.*, 28.8.33.
24 *Constitutionnel*, 6.12.33.
25 *Jnl. des Débats*, 6.12.33.
26 *Ménestrel*, 2.2.34.
27 *Mng. Herald*, 7.4.34.
28 *Mng. Post*, 12.5.34.
29 Géréon, p. 41.
30 *Cour. des Ths.*, 21.1.35.

CHAPTER 4 (pp. 30–37)

1 *Indicateur*, 10.2.35.
2 *Cour. des Ths.*, 16.2.35.
3 *Mng. Post*, 23.3.35.
4 *Cour. des Ths.*, 31.3.35.
5 *Court. Jnl.*, 2.5.35.
6 *Times*, 29.5.35.

7 *Mng. Herald*, 30.6.35
8 Letter dated 15.9.33. Museo Storico Civico, Milan.
9 De Boigne, p. 249.
10 Gautier, *C. Grisi*.
11 *Cour. des Ths.*, 18.3.36.
12 *Mng. Herald*, 13.4.36.
13 *Mng. Post,* 13.4.36.
14 *Mng. Herald*, 13.4.36.
15 *Mng. Herald*, 30.7.36.
16 *Cour. des Ths.*, 17.8.36.
17 De Boigne, p. 249.
18 Derra de Moroda Dance Archives, Salzburg.
19 *Jnl. des Débats*, 5.9.36.

CHAPTER 5 (pp. 38–49)

1 *Sovremennik*, 1850, vol. 24, p. VI, p. 44.
2 *All. Thztg.*, 1.10.36.
3 *All. Thztg.*, 29.10.36.
4 *Sammler*, 19.12.37.
5 *All. Thztg.*, 7.1.37.
6 *All. Thztg.*, 20.3.37.
7 *All. Thztg.*, 13.1.38.
8 Lithographed scenario. Bibl. de l'Op., Paris.
9 *All. Thztg.*, 5.3.38.
10 *Wiener Zeitschrift*, 10.3.38.
11 *Sammler*, 31.3.38.
12 *Humorist*, 9.3.38.
13 *All. Thztg.*, 5.3.38.
14 *Sammler*, 31.3.38.
15 *Humorist*, 9.3.38.
16 *Humorist*, 9.3.38.
17 *Cour. des Ths.*, 2 and 12.2.41.
18 *Teatri Arte e Letteratura*, 4.10.38.
19 De Boigne, p. 250.
20 *Daily Telegraph*, 24.5.99.

CHAPTER 6 (pp. 50–59)

1 Duprez, pp. 161–163.
2 Arago, p. 116.
3 Dossier d'artiste: J. Perrot. Bibl. de l'Op., Paris.
4 *Presse*, 2.3.40.
5 *Zingaro* libretto, p. 12.
6 *Zingaro* libretto, pp. 19–20.
7 *Zingaro* libretto, p. 22.
8 *Jnl. des Débats*, 2.3.40.
9 *Cour. des Ths.*, 6.3.40.
10 *Presse*, 2.3.40.
11 *Cour. des Ths.*, 1.3.40.
12 *Cour. des Ths.*, 2.3.40.
13 *Cour. des Ths.*, 4.3.40.
14 *Cour. des Ths.*, 2.9.40.

CHAPTER 7 (pp. 60–77)

1 *France Musicale*, 1840, p. 105.
2 Arch. Nat., Paris, AJ^{13} 194.
3 Letter written in April 1841. Royal Library, Copenhagen.
4 De Boigne, p. 248.
5 *Jnl. des Débats*, 15.2.41.
6 *Moniteur des Ths.*, 20.2.41.
7 Pougin, p. 162.
8 *Presse*, 5.7.41.
9 *Moniteur*, 25.2.56; article reproduced as preface to *Tableaux de voyage* (Paris, 1858).
10 Heine, VI, pp.138–140.
11 Heine, I, pp.59–60, 69–71.
12 *Presse,* 5.7.41.
13 Pougin, p. 162.
14 Pougin, p. 162.
15 Bibl. Nat. (Musique), Paris, MS 2644.
16 De Boigne, p. 252.
17 *Cour. des Ths.*, 27.4.41.
18 De Boigne, p. 255.
19 Montmorency, p. 144.
20 Letter written in May 1841. Royal Library, Copenhagen.
21 Bournonville, *Journal à Paris et Naples 1841* MS. Royal Library, Copenhagen.
22 Bournonville, *Mit Theaterliv*, I, pp. 30–31.
23 Letter dated 29.6.41. Lifar, *La Danse*, pp. 282–284.
24 *France Musicale*, 4.7.41.
25 *Monde Dramatique*, 1.7.41.
26 *Cour. des Ths.*, 19.6.41.
27 Gautier, *Giselle*, p.23.
28 *Augsburgische Allgemeine Zeitung*, 7.2.42.
29 *Moniteur des Ths.*, 30.6.41.
30 *Moniteur des Ths.*, 3.7.41.
31 *Sylphide*, 4.7.41.
32 Crippa, p. 105.
33 *Cour. des Ths.*, 28.10.41.

CHAPTER 8 (pp. 78–89)

1 Dossier d'artiste: Deshayes. Bibl. de l'Op., Paris.
2 Letter dated 6.3.42. Chantilly, C 472.
3 *Times*, 14.3.42.
4 *Mng. Herald*, 21.3.42.
5 *Times*, 14.3.42.
6 *Times*, 14.3.42.
7 *Era*, 17.4.42.
8 Chorley, p. 219.
9 Letter dated 17.3.42. Chantilly, C.472.
10 *Times*, 24.6.42.
11 *Times*, 4.7.42.
12 *Times*, 15.8.42.
13 *Times*, 4.7.42.
14 Lumley, p. 53.
15 *Times*, 15.7.42.
16 *Mng. Post*, 18.7.42.
17 *Sunday Times*, 24.7.42.
18 *Corsaire*, 14.9.42.
19 *Moniteur des Ths.*, 15.6.42.
20 *Moniteur des Ths.*, 24.6.42.
21 *Moniteur des Ths.*, 2.7.42.
22 *Cour. des Sp.*, 8.12.42.
23 Adice, p. 11.
24 *Era*, 18,12,42,

369

Notes

CHAPTER 9 (pp. 90–111)

1 *Cour. des Sp.*, 31.1.43.
2 *Dancing Times*, Dec. 1936.
3 Lumley, p. 85.
4 *Times*, 13.3.43.
5 *Era*, 19.3.43.
6 *Times*, 31.3.43.
7 *Mng. Post*, 30.3.43.
8 *Times*, 31.3.43.
9 *Mng. Post*, 3.4.43.
10 *Times*, 28.4.43.
11 *Times*, 20.5.43.
12 *Spectator*, 27.5.43.
13 Letter, Coulon to Deshayes, dated 19.5.43. Dossier d'artiste: Deshayes. Bibl. de l'Op., Paris.
14 *Examiner*, 24.6.43.
15 *Mng. Herald*, 14.8.43.
16 *Beauties of the Opera and Ballet*, p. 70.
17 *Spectator*, 24.6.43.
18 *Times*, 26.6.43.
19 *Mng. Post*, 14.8.43.
20 *Mng. Post*, 23.6.43.
21 *Times*, 23.6.43.
22 *Mng. Post*, 14.8.43.
23 *Times*, 23.6.43.
24 *Observer*, 26.6.43.
25 *Mng. Herald*, 14.8.43.
26 *Mng. Post*, 26.6.43.
27 *Mng. Post*, 23.6.43.
28 *Mng. Post*, 23.6.43.
29 *Mng. Post*, 14.7.43.
30 *Examiner*, 24.6.43.
31 *Mng. Post*, 23.6.43.
32 *Mng. Post*, 26.6.43.
33 *Mng. Post*, 23.6.43.
34 *Mng. Herald*, 26.6.43.
35 *Mng. Post*, 23.6.43.
36 *Mng. Herald*, 23.6.43.
37 *Athenæum*, 24.6.43.
38 *Mng. Post*, 26.6.43.
39 *Beauties of the Opera and Ballet*, p. 80.
40 *Mng. Post*, 6.5.44.
41 *Spectator*, 24.6.43.
42 *Athenæum*, 24.6.43.
43 *Sunday Times*, 23.7.43.
44 *Mng. Post*, 21.7.43.
45 Lumley, p. 76.
46 *Times*, 4.8.43.
47 *Mng. Herald*, 4.8.43.
48 *Spectator*, 22.6.44.

CHAPTER 10 (pp. 112–137)

1 *Mng. Post*, 11.3.44.
2 *Mng. Herald*, 11.3.44.
3 *Mng. Post*, 13.3.44.
4 *Times*, 11.3.44.
5 *Mng. Post*, 13.3.44.
6 *Mng. Herald*, 11.3.44.
7 *Mng. Herald*, 11.3.44.
8 *Mng. Post*, 11.3.44.
9 *Court Jnl.*, 16.3.44.
10 *Mng. Post*, 11.3.44.
11 *Mng. Herald*, 11.3.44.
12 *Mng. Herald*, 5.8.44.
13 *Times*, 5.8.44.
14 *Spectator* 16.3.44.
15 *Mng. Herald*, 5.8.44.
16 *La Esmeralda*, scenario.
17 *Mng. Post*, 11.3.44.
18 *Mng. Herald*, 11.3.44.
19 *Mng. Post*, 11.3.44.
20 *Court Jnl.*, 16.3.44.
21 *Times*, 6.5.44.
22 *Mng. Herald*, 11.3.44.
23 *Mng. Herald*, 5.8.44.
24 *Mng. Herald*, 11.3.44.
25 *Athenæum*, 16.3.44.
26 *Times*, 11.3.44.
27 *Spectator*, 16.3.44.
28 *Athenæum*, 16.3.44.
29 *Mng. Chronicle*, 11.3.44.
30 *Times*, 11.3.44.
31 *Mng. Chronicle*, 11.3.44.
32 *Times*, 11.3.44.
33 *Athenæum*, 16.3.44.
34 *Times*, 11.3.44.
35 *Mng. Post*, 3.8.44.
36 *Mng. Post*, 11.3.44.
37 Letter dated 25.3.44. Dossier d'artiste: Deshayes. Bibl. de l'Op., Paris.
38 *Mng. Post*, 21.4.44.
39 *Mng. Post*, 1.5.44.
40 *Times*, 12.4.44.
41 *Spectator*, 13.4.44.
42 *Times*, 12.4.44.
43 *Spectator*, 20.4.44.
44 *Times*, 12.4.44.
45 *Cour. de l'Europe*, 18.5.44.
46 *Mng. Post*, 25.6.44.
47 *Cour. de l'Europe*, 29.6.44.
48 Lumley, p. 92.
49 *Maestro*, 29.6.44.
50 *Times*, 26.6.44.
51 *Maestro*, 29.6.44.
52 *Times*, 26.6.44.
53 *Maestro*, 29.6.44.
54 *Times*, 26.6.44.
55 *Teatri, Arte e Litteratura*, 18.7.44.
56 *Spectator*, 27.7.44.
57 *Mng. Chronicle*, 5.8.44.
58 *Times*, 5.8.44.
59 *Mng. Post*, 3.8.44.
60 *Mng. Herald*, 5.8.44.
61 *Spectator*, 10.8.44.
62 *Mng. Herald*, 5.8.44.
63 *Mng. Herald*, 5.8.44.
64 *Mng. Post*, 5.8.44.

65 Letter undated. Dossier d'artiste: Deshayes. Bibl. de l'Op., Paris.
66 *Mng. Post*, 7.12.44.
67 *Corriere delle Dame*, 28.12.44.
68 *Gaz. priv. di Milano*, 29.1.45.

CHAPTER 11 (pp. 138–154)

1 Lumley, p. 102
2 *Times*, 10.3.45.
3 *Mng. Post*, 10.3.45.
4 *Mng. Post*, 10.3.45.
5 *Times*, 10.3.45.
6 *Mng. Post*, 10.3.45.
7 *Mng. Herald*, 17.3.45.
8 *Mng. Herald*, 10.3.45.
9 *Times*, 10.3.45.
10 *Times*, 10.3.45.
11 *Mng. Post*, 10.3.45.
12 *Mng. Post*, 10.3.45.
13 *Times*, 10.3.45.
14 *Mng. Post*, 10.3.45.
15 *Mng. Herald*, 10.3.45.
16 *Athenæum*, 15.3.45.
17 *Times*, 22.8.45.
18 *Times*, 10.3.45.
19 *Times*, 9.5.45.
20 *Mng. Post*, 17.3.45.
21 *Athenæum*, 20.4.45.
22 *Mng. Post*, 17.4.45.
23 *Mng. Herald*, 18.4.45.
24 *Times*, 18.4.45.
25 *Mng. Post*, 17.4.45.
26 *Mng. Post*, 18.4.45.
27 *Mng. Post*, 18.4.45.
28 *Times*, 16.5.45.
29 *Times*, 18.4.45.
30 *Mng. Chronicle*, 25.4.45.
31 *Mng. Herald*, 2.5.45.
32 *Mng. Post*, 2.5.45.
33 *Times*, 9.5.45.
34 *Mng. Post*, 2.5.45.
35 *Spectator*, 3.5.45.
36 *Satirist*, 17.8.45.
37 *Satirist*, 29.6.45.
38 *Satirist*, 24.8.45.
39 *Times*, 27.6.45.
40 *Times*, 19.2.45.
41 *Mng. Chronicle*, 24.7.45.
42 Lumley, pp.115–116.
43 Lumley, pp.116–117.
44 *Mng. Herald*, 14.7.45.
45 *Mng. Herald*, 14.7.45.
46 *Mng. Herald*, 14.7.45.
47 *Mng. Post*, 16.7.45.
48 *Court Jnl.*, 19.7.45.
49 *Mng. Herald*, 14.7.45.
50 *Mng. Herald*, 14.7.45.
51 *Times*, 14.7.45.
52 *Mng. Post*, 16.7.45.
53 *Mng. Herald*, 14.7.45.
54 *Mng. Chronicle*, 14.7.45.
55 *Mng. Herald*, 14.7.45.
56 *Times*, 18.7.45.
57 *Cour. de l'Europe*, 19.7.45.
58 *Times*, 14.7.45.
59 *Era*, 24.8.45.
60 *Mng. Herald*, 20.8.45.
61 *Times*, 25.7.45.
62 *Era*, 27.7.45.
63 *Mng. Post*, 25.7.45.
64 Letters from Carlo Balocchino to Fanny Elssler dated 17.11.45 and 7.12.45. Weiner Stadtbibliothek.

CHAPTER 12 (pp. 155–181)

1 *Mng. Post*, 28.1.46.
2 *Mng. Post*, 16.2.46.
3 *Mng. Post*, 28.2.46.
4 Lady Morgan, pp. 117–119.
5 *Times*, 9.3.46.
6 *Mng. Post*, 4.3.46.
7 Cellarius, pp.48–52.
8 *Mng. Herald*, 5.3.46.
9 *Mng. Post*, 5.3.46.
10 *Times*, 9.3.46.
11 *Mng. Herald*, 5.3.46.
12 *Mng. Post*, 9.3.46.
13 *Mng. Herald*, 9.3.46.
14 *Times*, 1.5.46.
15 *Mng. Post*, 9.3.46.
16 *Times*, 9.3.46.
17 *Mng. Post*, 3.3.46.
18 Lumley, p. 146.
19 *Cour. de l'Europe*, 14.3.46.
20 *Mng. Post*, 4.3.46.
21 *Mng. Post*, 9.3.46.
22 *Mng. Post*, 25.3.46.
23 *Mng. Post*, 3.4.46.
24 Lumley, p. 150.
25 *Times*, 12.6.46.
26 *Lalla Rookh* scenario, p.4.
27 *Mng. Post*, 12.6.46.
28 *Mng. Herald*, 19.8.46.
29 *Mng. Post*, 12.6.46.
30 *Cour. de l'Europe*, 13.6.46.
31 *Mng. Post*, 12.6.46.
32 *Times*, 12.6.46.
33 *Mng. Post*, 12.6.46.
34 *Mng. Chronicle*, 28.3.45.
35 *Times*, 12.6.46.
36 *Mng. Chronicle*, 28.3.45.
37 *Times*, 12.6.46.
38 *Mng. Chronicle*, 28.3.45.
39 *Mng. Herald*, 12.6.46.
40 *Mng. Post*, 11.6.46.
41 *Times*, 12.6.46.
42 *Mng. Herald*, 12.6.46.
43 *Mng. Chronicle*, 12.6.46.
44 *Mng. Post*, 12.6.46.
45 *Cour. de l'Europe*, 13.6.46.

46 *Times*, 12.6.46.
47 *Mng. Post*, 15.8.46.
48 *Times*, 12.6.46.
49 *Mng. Post*, 17.6.46.
50 *Mng. Post*, 19.6.46.
51 *Mng. Herald*, 19.8.46.
52 *Mng. Post*, 12.6.46.
53 *Times*, 12.6.46.
54 *Mng. Post*, 12.6.46.
55 *Mng. Post*, 17.6.46.
56 *Mng. Post*, 12.6.46.
57 *Times*, 15.6.46.
58 *Mng. Post*, 17.6.46.
59 *Mng. Post*, 19.6.46.
60 *Mng. Chronicle*, 21.8.46.
61 *Times*, 19.8.46.
62 *Presse*, 30.7.46.
63 *Mng. Herald*, 24.7.46.
64 *Mng. Post*, 10.8.46.
65 *Cour. de l'Europe*, 25.7.46.
66 *Times*, 24.7.46.
67 *Mng. Herald*, 24.7.46.
68 *Mng. Post*, 24.7.46.
69 *Times*, 24.7.46.
70 *Mng. Herald*, 24.7.46.
71 *Ill. London News*, 1.8.46.
72 *Mng. Post*, 24.7.46.
73 *Times*, 24.7.46.
74 *Ill. London News*, 1.8.46.
75 *Mng. Post*, 24.7.46.
76 *Ill. London News*, 1.8.46.
77 *Mng. Post*, 27.7.46.
78 *Mng. Post*, 24.7.46.
79 *Mng. Post*, 24.7.46.
80 *Mng. Herald*, 24.7.46.
81 *Mng. Post*, 23.7.46.
82 *Mng. Herald*, 24.7.46.
83 *Mng. Chronicle*, 24.7.46.
84 *Mng. Post*, 23.7.46.
85 Dossier d'artiste: Deshayes. Bibl. de l'Op., Paris.
86 *Mng. Herald*, 24.7.46.
87 *Mng. Chronicle*, 24.7.46.
88 *Mng. Post*, 23.7.46.
89 *Mng. Post*, 24.7.46.
90 *Mng. Chronicle*, 24.7.46.
91 *Mng. Post*, 31.7.46.
92 *Mng. Post*, 27.7.46.
93 Lady Westmorland, p. 94.
94 *Mng. Post*, 10.8.46.
95 *Mng. Post*, 21.8.46.

CHAPTER 13 (pp. 182–205)

1 Crippa, p. 111.
2 Crippa, p. 112.
3 Letter written from London, end of May 1846. Soviet Hist. Arch., 497/1/11926.
4 Letter written from Paris, 12.9.46. Soviet Hist. Arch., 497/1/11926.

5 *Gaz. priv. di Milano*, 10.1.47.
6 *Pirata*, 12.1.47.
7 *Corriere della Dame*, 13.1.47.
8 *Pirata*, 12.1.47.
9 Barbiere, p. 293.
10 *Pirata*, 12.1.47.
11 *Corriere delle Dame*, 13.1.47.
12 *Corriere delle Dame*, 18.3.47.
13 *Fama*, 4.4.76.
14 *Corriere delle Dame*, 18.3.47.
15 *Strenna Teatrale Europea*, 1848, p. 290.
16 Quoted in *Gaz. priv. di Milano*, 29.3.47.
17 *Corriere delle Dame*, 18.3.47.
18 *Corriere delle Dame*, 18.3.47.
19 *Corriere delle Dame*, 18.3.47.
20 *Corriere delle Dame*, 18.3.47.
21 *Pirata*, 19.3.47.
22 *Corriere delle Dame*, 18.3.47.
23 *Corriere delle Dame*, 18.3.47.
24 *Pirata*, 19.3.47.
25 *Corriere delle Dame*, 18.3.47.
26 *Pirata*, 19.3.47.
27 *Mng. Post*, 4.4.47.
28 *Musical World*, 8.5.47.
29 *Satirist*, 6.6.47.
30 *Mng. Herald*, 28.6.47.
31 *Times*, 28.6.47.
32 *Mng. Herald*, 28.6.47.
33 *Times*, 28.6.47.
34 *Mng. Herald*, 28.6.47.
35 *Times*, 28.6.47.
36 Letter dated 1.7.47. Theatre Museum, London.
37 *Mng. Post*, 26.7.47.
38 Letter to Deligny, written August or September 1847. Arch. Nat., Paris, AJ^{13}486.
39 *Sovremennik*, 1850, vol. 24, book VI, p. 46.
40 *Mng. Post*, 30.6.47.

CHAPTER 14 (pp. 206–233)

1 *Mng. Post*, 21.1.47.
2 Lumley, p. 199.
3 Wadepuhl. p. 384.
4 Lumley, p.201.
5 Heine, *Doktor Faust*, p. 9.
6 Lumley, p. 199.
7 *Cour. des Sp.*, 11.8.47.
8 *Fama*, 14.2.48.
9 *Fama*, 14.2.48.
10 *Corriere delle Dame*, 18.2.48.
11 *Pirata*, 14.2.48.
12 *Gaz. di Milano*, 13.2.48.
13 *Corriere delle Dame*, 18.2.48.
14 *Times*, 14.3.48.
15 *Pirata*, 8.3.48.
16 Hübner, p. 18.
17 *Satirist*, 23.4.48.
18 *Mng. Post*, 13.6.48.
19 *Les Quatre Saisons*, scenario, p. 1.

Notes

20 *Les Quatre Saisons*, scenario, p. 1.
21 *Ill. London News*, 24.6.48.
22 *Les Quatre Saisons*, scenario, p. 2.
23 *Les Quatre Saisons*, scenario, p. 2.
24 *Ill. London News*, 24.6.48.
25 *Mng. Post*, 14.6.48.
26 *Mng. Post*, 16.6.48.
27 *Mng. Post*, 28.6.48.
28 *Mng. Post*, 8.8.48.
29 *Mng. Post*, 10.7.48.
30 *Mng. Chronicle*, 19.7.48.
31 *Mng. Post*, 18.6.48.
32 *Mng. Post*, 19.6.48.

CHAPTER 15 (pp. 224–249)

1 Soviet Hist. Arch., 497/1/11926.
2 Soviet Hist. Arch., 497/1/11926.
3 Lifar, *Istoria Russkogo Baleta*, p.135.
4 Arch. Nat., Paris, AJ[13] 195.
5 Soviet Hist. Arch., 497/1/11926.
6 Soviet Hist. Arch., 497/1/11926.
7 Soviet Hist. Arch., 497/1/11926.
8 Soviet Hist. Arch., 497/1/11926.
9 Soviet Hist. Arch., 497/1/11926.
10 *Sovremennik*, 1849, vol. 13, book V, p. 64.
11 Natarova, p. 431
12 *Sovremennik*, 1849, vol. 13, book V, p. 64.
13 *Sev. Pchela*, 30.12.48/11.1.49.
14 *Sovremennik*, 1849, vol. 13, book V, p. 66.
15 *Sev. Pchela*, 30.12.48/11.1.49.
16 *Sev. Pchela*, 27.2/11.3.49.
17 *SPB Vedomosti*, 17.2/1.3.49.
18 Arch. Nat., Paris, AJ[13] 195.
19 *Jnl. des Ths.*, 23.5.49.
20 Q, p. 148.
21 Arch. Nat., Paris, AJ[13] 195.
22 De Boigne, pp. 340–341.
23 *Musique*, 9.9.49.
24 Arch. Nat., Paris, AJ[13] 1040.
25 *Corsaire*, 11.10.49.
26 *Jnl. pour rire*, 20.10.49.
27 *Jnl. des Débats*, 20.10.49.
28 *Presse*, 15.10.49.
29 *Constitutionnel*, 16.10.49.
30 *Presse*, 15.10.49.
31 *Presse*, 15.10.49.
32 *Corsaire*, 11.10.49.
33 *Jnl. des Ths.*, 13.10.49.
34 *Presse*, 15.10.49.
35 *Musique*, 14.10.49.
36 *Sev. Pchela*, 9/21.12.49.
37 Drizen, p. 99.
38 *Sev. Pchela*, 21.2/5.3.50.
39 *Sovremennik*, 1850, vol. 20, book VII, pp. 119–120.
40 *SPB Vedomosti*, 22.2/6.3.50.
41 *Sev. Pchela*, 21.2/5.3.50.
42 *Sev. Pchela*, 21.2/5.3.50.
43 *Panteon*, 1850, vol. 2, part 3.
44 Soviet Hist. Arch., 497/102–939/126.

CHAPTER 16 (pp. 250–274)

1 *Sev. Pchela*, 18/30.7.50.
2 Natarova, p. 431.
3 *Sev. Pchela*, 20.10/1.11.50.
4 *Sovremennik*, 1851, vol. 24, book VI, p. 275
5 *Sovremennik*, 1851, vol. 26, book VI, p. 69.
6 *Panteon*, 1851, vol. 1, part 11, pp. 9–16.
7 *Panteon*, 1851, vol. 1, part 11, pp. 9–16.
8 Dostoyevsky, vol. 13, pp. 529–547.
9 *Sovremennik*, 1851, vol. 26, book VI, p. 70.
10 *Panteon*, 1851, vol. 1, part 11, pp. 9–16.
11 *Panteon*, 1851, vol. 1, part 11, pp. 9–16.
12 *Sev. Pchela*, 16/28.3.51.
13 *Sovremennik*, 1851, vol. 26, book VI, p. 71.
14 *Panteon*, 1851, vol. 1, part 11, pp. 9–16.
15 Soviet. Hist. Arch., 497/2/13172.
16 Drizen, p. 109.
17 Soviet. Hist. Arch., 780/29/1/472, quoted in Slonimsky, *Dramaturgiya*, pp. 205–206.
18 *SPB Venomosti*, 6/18.12.52.
19 *Sev. Pchela*, 24.11/6.12.52.
20 *Sev. Pchela*, 24.11/6.12.52.
21 *Panteon*, 1852, vol. 6, part 12, pp. 1–8.
22 *SPB Vedomosti*, 6/12.12.52.
23 *Panteon*, 1852, vol. 6, part 12, pp. 1–8.
24 Bibl. Nat. (Musique), Paris. MS. L.2709.
25 *SPB Vedomosti*, 26.2/10.3.53.
26 *SPB Vedomosti*, 26.2/10.3.53.
27 *Sev. Pchela*, 24.2/8.3.53.
28 *Sev. Pchela*, 3/17.5.54.

CHAPTER 17 (pp. 275–296)

1 *SPB Vedomosti*, 15/27.1.54.
2 *Sev. Pchela*, 6/18.3.56.
3 Serov, I, p. 454.
4 *Panteon*, March 1854, vol. 14, pp.44–52.
5 *Yakor*, 28.9/11.10.63.
6 *Panteon*, March 1854, vol. 14, pp.44–52.
7 Pleshcheyev, p. 164.
8 *Panteon*, March 1854, vol. 14, pp. 44–52.
9 *Sev. Pchela*, 19.2/3.3.54.
10 *Panteon*, March 1854, vol. 14, pp. 44–52.
11 *Sev. Pchela*, 19.2/3.3.54.
12 *Sev. Pchela*, 19.2/3.3.54.
13 *Sev. Pchela*, 19.2/3.3.54.
14 Pleshcheyev, p. 164.
15 *Panteon*, March 1854, vol. 14, pp. 44–52.
16 Pleshcheyev, p. 164.
17 *Sev. Pchela*, 19.2/3.3.54.
18 *Jnl. de St. Pétersbourg*, 23.1/4.2.55.
19 Lifar, *Istoria Russkogo Baleta*, p. 152.
20 *Jnl. de St. Pétersbourg*, 1/13.12.55.
21 *Jnl. de St. Pétersbourg*, 13/25.11.55.
22 *Jnl. de St. Pétersbourg*, 1/13.12.55.
23 *Jnl. de St. Pétersbourg*, 13/25.11.55.
24 *Jnl. de St. Pétersbourg*, 13/25.11.55.
25 *Jnl. de St. Pétersbourg*, 13/25.11.55.
26 *Jnl. de St. Pétersbourg*, 1/13.12.55.
27 *Jnl. de St. Pétersbourg*, 13/25.11.55.

Notes

28 *Jnl. de St. Pétersbourg*, 1/13.12.55.
29 *Sovremennik*, 1856, vol. 56, book V, p. 68.
30 *Sev. Pchela*, 9/21.3.56.
31 Pleshcheyev, p. 176.
32 *Sovremennik*, 1856, vol. 56, book V, p. 65.

CHAPTER 18 (pp. 296–319)

1 *Presse*, 28.12.56.
2 *Moniteur*, 29.12.56.
3 *Teatralny i Musikalny Vestnik*, 15/27.9.57.
4 *Sev. Pchela*, 27.9/9.10.57.
5 Lumley, p. 374.
6 *Times*, 12 and 24.5.56.
7 *SPB Vedomosti*, 12/24.1.58.
8 *SPB Vedomosti*, 12/24.1.58.
9 Certificate dated 23.9/5.10.58. Soviet Hist. Arch., 497/2/13172.
10 *Jnl. de St. Pétersbourg*, 11/23.11.58.
11 *Jnl. de St. Pétersbourg*, 11/23.11.58.
12 *Jnl. de St. Pétersbourg*, 11/23.11.58.
13 *Jnl. de St. Pétersbourg*, 11/23.11.58.
14 *Jnl. de St. Pétersbourg*, 11/23.11.58.
15 *Jnl. de St. Pétersbourg*, 11/23.11.58.
16 *Teatralny i Musikalny Vestnik*, 9/21.11.58.
17 *Jnl. de St. Pétersbourg*, 11/23.11.58.
18 *Jnl. de St. Pétersbourg*, 11/23.11.58.
19 *SPB Vedomosti*, 9/21.11.58.
20 *Teatralny i Musikalny Vestnik*, 14/26.12.58.
21 *Teatralny i Musikalny Vestnik*, 14/26.12.58.
22 Letter to P.S. Fyodorov, *chef du repertoire*, dated 30.12.58/11.1.59.
Bakhrushin Museum, Moscow. Ms. 247994.
23 *Teatralny i Musikalny Vestnik*, 11/23.1.59.
24 Nekhendzi, p. 49.
25 Letter dated 9/21.5.60. Soviet Hist. Arch., 497/2/13172.
26 Soviet Hist. Arch., 497/2/13172.

CHAPTER 19 (pp. 320–344)

1 Nekhendzi, pp. 46–47.
2 *Cour. des Ths.*, 6.8.61.
3 *Gaz. des Tribunaux*, 27.7.62.
4 Trib. Civ. Seine, 11.7.62, aff. Petipa. Pataille 73,234.
5 Noverre, I, p. 27.
6 Letter dated 3.3.63. Arch. Nat., AJ[13] 477
7 *Sovr. Slovo*, 4/16.5.63.
8 *Figaro*, 21.5.63.
9 *Jnl. des Débats*, 11.5.63.
10 *Fama*, 8.12.63.
11 *Fama*, 5.1.64.
12 *Trovatore*, 30.1.64.
13 *Fama*, 2.2.64.
14 *Fama*, 2.2.64.
15 *Fama*, 2.2.64.
16 *Fama*, 2.2.64.
17 Adice, *Notes sur la direction E. Perrin* MS. Bibl. de l'Op., Paris.

18 Ms. in author's collection. Printed in *Figaro*, 18.7.94.
19 *Figaro*, 21.10.71.
20 Goncourt, II, p. 968.
21 *Figaro*, 14.4.74.
22 Vaillat, p. 537.
23 Vaillat, p. 538.
24 Letters dated 11 and 22.1.79, 6 and 28.2.79. Royal Library, Copenhagen.
25 Letter dated 4.12.79. Royal Library, Copenhagen.
26 Letter and cards dated 9.1.81, 17.1.87 and 4.1.88. Royal Library, Copenhagen.

Index

Adam, Adolphe 24, 26, 70–75, 81, 82, 107, 235, 237, 246, 253, 297, 299, 304, 305, 353, 355, 357
Adami, Heinrich 40, 41, 45
Adice, G. Léopold 89
Adlerberg, Count Vladimir 308, 316–318
Adolphe, Mme 41
Aguado, Marquis 72
Aigner, Engelbert 39, 352
Albano (Albani), Francisco 157
Albert (François Decombe) 12, 21, 22, 26, 39, 62, 63, 72, 73
Albert, Prince 180
Alexander I, Tsar 273n
Alexander II, Tsar 285, 297, 298, 302, 308, 319, 342
Alboize de Pujol, J.E. 263n
Algisi, Luigia 346
Amaturo, Aniello 330, 356
Amosova, Anastasia 253, 255, 279, 280, 303, 306, 357
Amosova, Nadezhda 270, 280, 284, 294, 303, 306, 357
Anatole [Petit] 16
Ancellin, Mlle 30
Andreyanova, Elena 246, 253, 255, 258, 264, 269–271, 273, 295, 356
Aniel, Pierre 43, 46, 47
Apollonskaya, Evdokia 318
Auber, Daniel 35, 58, 83, 158, 352
Aurungseb 167
Aumer, Jean 19, 21, 75

Bagnoli-Quattri, Carolina 195, 354, 355
Bajetti, Giovanni 185–188, 194, 201, 209, 232n, 354, 355
Balfe, Michael 157, 180

BALLETS AND DIVERTISSEMENTS
 Alma (Deshayes, Perrot, Cerrito) 83–87, 96, 128, 141, 165, 201, 209, 212, 222, 294, 353, 355
 Appuntamento, L' see *Stelldichein, Das*
 Armida (Perrot) 285–294, 299, 300, 304, 308, 309, 318, 326, 357
 Armide (Coralli) 288
 Armide (T. Elssler) 28, 288
 Artistes, Les (Coralli) 16
 Atalante (Perrot) 96
 Aurore, L' (Perrot) 92, 93, 353
 Bacchante, La (Perrot) 147, 148, 174, 354
 Bal sous Louis XIV, Un (Perrot) 95, 96, 353
 Bazar d'Ispahan, Le (Roger) 4
 Belle au bois dormant, La (Aumer) 75
 Beniowsky (Deshayes) 87
 Brézila (F. Taglioni) 31
 Carnaval de Venise, Le (Milon) 5, 18, 30, 40, 316
 Catarina (Perrot) ii, 155–165, 184–190, 199, 200, 205, 219, 232, 233, 245–247, 249, 268, 274, 275, 282, 299, 303, 308, 324, 325, 328, 329, 346, 349, 354
 Chasse des nymphes, La (F. Taglioni) 31
 Contessa d'Egmont, La (Rota) 328, 332
 Coppélia (Saint-Léon) 333, 334
 Coralia (P. Taglioni) 207
 Corsaire, Le (Mazilier) 302, 322
 Corsaire, Le (Perrot) 304–309, 315, 326, 345–347, 349, 357
 Cupid and Psyche (Le Picq) 273
 Danina (F. Taglioni) 45n
 Danseur du roi, Le (Saint-Léon) 276
 Dansomanie, La (P. Gardel) 4
 Débutante, La (Perrot) 297, 299–301, 357
 Délire d'un peintre, Le (Perrot) 110, 193, 229, 249, 275, 304, 345, 349, 353
 Déserteur, Le (Dauberval) 11
 Deux Pigeons, Les (Mérante) 337
 Diable à quatre, Le (Mazilier) 136, 253, 275, 282, 299
 Diable boiteux, Le (Coralli) 45
 Diane (Perrot) 153–154, 354
 Edoardo III (Henry) 210
 Eléments, Les (Perrot) 201–203, 207, 220, 355
 Elève d'amour, L' (Cerrito) 83
 Elfes, Les (Mazilier) 302
 Eoline (Perrot) 46, 138–144, 310–316, 354, 357
 Epreuve villageoise, L' (Milon) 4
 Esmeralda (Monticini) 135, 355
 Esmeralda (Perrot) ii, iii, 92, 93, 111–130, 133–138, 148, 153, 154, 164, 183, 188, 190, 192, 193, 201, 205, 216, 219, 222, 230–234, 246, 247, 251–253, 268, 274, 275, 282, 299–303, 308, 324–326, 328, 329, 336, 337, 341, 342, 345–349, 354
 Farandole, La (Mérante) 337
 Faust (Blasis) 208, 210
 Faust (Bournonville) 208
 Faust (Deshayes) 24, 26, 71, 208
 Faust (Lanner) 219n
 Faust (Perrot) 192, 206–220, 276–282, 284, 293, 299, 303, 308, 314, 315, 325, 328, 329, 332, 346, 349, 355

375

Index

Faust (S. Taglioni) 208
Fee und der Ritter, Die (Arm. Vestris) 45n
Fête des nymphes, La (Deshayes) 83
Fiancée, La (Deshayes) 83
Figli di Edoardo, I (Cortesi) 352
Fille de marbre, La (Saint-Léon, Perrot) 294, 298, 300, 303, 322, 357
Fille du Danube, La (F. Taglioni) 74, 76
Fille mal gardée, La (Dauberval) 3, 4, 11, 30, 230, 275, 282, 299, 309
Filleule des fées, La (Perrot) 235–249, 251, 253, 299, 334, 342, 355–357
Flore et Zéphire (Didelot) 18, 21, 22, 75, 76
Follet, Le (Aniel) 47
Gazelda (Perrot) 268–274, 276, 282, 298, 299, 302, 308, 320, 321, 328, 349, 356
Gipsy, La (Mazilier) 119
Giselle (Coralli, Perrot) ii, iii, 64–76, 78–83, 88, 90, 91, 94, 95, 105, 107, 114, 127, 133, 148, 165n, 190, 201, 229, 235, 236, 247, 249, 251–253, 274, 275, 282, 295, 298, 299, 303, 316, 326, 333, 341, 342, 345, 346, 348, 349, 353
Gudule's Daughter (Gorsky) 348
Guillaume Tell (Léon) 18
Hamlet (Perrot, unperformed) 111
Houris, Les (Perrot) 96, 97
Hungarian Hut, The (Didelot) 273
Ile des muets, L' (Perrot) 300, 301, 357
Ile des naiades, L' (Perrot) 251, 356
Isaura (S. Taglioni, G. Carey) 247n
Jeanne d'Arc (Perrot, unperformed) 132–134, 138, 190
Jolie Fille de Gand, La (Albert) 63, 70, 71, 88, 261
Jovita (Saint-Léon) 316, 317
Jugement de Pâris, Le (Perrot) 152n, 175–180, 199, 202, 203, 222, 258, 355
Kaya (Perrot, Grahn) 144–147, 354
Kobold, Der (Perrot) 43–47, 50, 59, 65, 131, 139, 352
Korrigane, La (Mérante) 337

Lac des fées, Le (Guerra) 83
Lalla Rookh (Perrot) ii, 166–174, 179, 183, 201, 355
Léocadie (Coralli) 15
Lida (J. and M. Petipa) 245, 251, 356
Liebe, stärker als Zaubermacht (Campilli) 40
Lutin, Le see *Kobold, Der*
Manon Lescaut (Aumer) 19
Marché des Innocents, Le M. and L. Petipa) 320
Marcobomba (Perrot) 282–284, 299, 356
Marco Spada (Mazilier) 302
Maskerade im Theater, Die (Henry) 45n
Mazila (F. Taglioni) 31
Meuniers, Les (J.B. Blache) 3
Naiad and the Fisherman, The (Perrot) ii, iii, 43, 254–259, 261, 263, 275, 282, 316, 346, 347, 349, 356
Neapolitanischen Fischer, Die (Perrot) 43, 83, 147, 352
Néméa (Saint-Léon) 333
Nina (Milon) 30
Ninette à la cour (M. Gardel) 96
Nymphe und der Schmetterling, Die (Perrot) 38, 43, 47, 352
Oberon (Aniel) 43
Odetta (Perrot) ii, 190–199, 201, 205, 324–326, 329, 349, 355
Ondine (Perrot) ii, 46, 91, 98–108, 116, 128, 129, 148, 164, 165, 183, 201, 222, 247, 251, 254, 255, 349, 353, 355, 356
Ondines, Les (Henry) 98
Orgie, L' (Coralli) 23, 30
Orithia (P. Taglioni) 207
Ottavio Pinelli (Samengo) 45n
Papillon, Le (M. Taglioni) 321
Paquita (Mazilier) 173
Paquita (M. Petipa) 299
Pas de deux for Elssler and Cerrito (Perrot) 108–110, 149, 202, 353
Pas de Diane chasseresse (Perrot) 96, 353
Pas de Quatre (Perrot) iii, 144, 149–154, 176, 179, 180, 199, 202, 203, 222, 285, 354
Pas des Déesses see *Jugement de Pâris, Le*
Paul et Virginie (Deshayes) 31
Paysanne Grande Dame, La (Perrot) 132, 133, 354
Pécheur napolitain, Le see *Neapolitanischen Fischer, Die*

Péri, La (Coralli) 90, 91, 299, 322
Petite marchande de bouquets, La (Perrot) 300, 357
Psyché (P. Gardel) 4
Quatre Saisons, Les (Perrot) 220–222, 226, 355
Rajah di Benares, Il (S. Taglioni) 48, 353
Renaud et Armide (Noverre) 286
Révolte au sérail, La (F. Taglioni) 27, 262, 268
Ritorno di Ulisse, Il (S. Taglioni) 32
Rose, the Violet and the Butterfly, The (Perrot) 303, 357
Rossignol, Le (Deshayes) 36
Sacountala (L. Petipa) 310
Satanilla (M. Petipa) 299
Six Ingénues, Les (J. Petipa) 7
Soirée de carnaval, Une (Perrot) 87, 353
Somnambule, La (Aumer) 19, 31, 40
Source, La (Saint-Léon) 333, 336
Stelldichein, Das (Perrot) 39–41, 45, 47, 48, 74, 352
Swan Lake (M. Petipa, Ivanov) 277
Sylphide, La (F. Taglioni) 23, 24, 28, 29, 31, 40, 45, 63, 75, 76, 149, 203, 218, 237, 247, 282, 321
Sylvia (Mérante) 337
Tarantule, La (Coralli) 76
Tempête, La (Coralli) 30, 352
Théa (P. Taglioni) 207
Tonnelier, Le (Lefebvre) 8
Tribulations d'un maître de ballet, Les (Perrot) 258, 356
Undine (Henry) 98
Vert-Vert (Mazilier) 261, 299, 357
Vivandière, La (Saint-Léon) 294, 297, 298, 300, 303, 309
Volage fixé, Le (Duport) 4
War of the Women, The (Perrot) 254, 261–268, 282, 308, 356
Yedda (Mérante) 337
Zeffiro (after Didelot) 32
Zélia (Perrot) 129–132, 354
Zémire et Azor (Deshayes) 24
Zéphir Berger (Deshayes) 31

Balocchino, Carlo 38, 154
Baratti, Francesco 329
Barbaja, Domenico 32
Barrez, Jean-Baptiste 334
Barroilhet, Paul 50

Index

Barville, Jenny 121, 131
Bastide 277
Bayadères, The 166
Beaumont, Cyril W. 348
Beethoven, Ludwig van 75, 170
Bellini, Vincenzo 33
Bellon, Elisa 88
Benard, Adèle 97, 99n, 101
Benoit-Champy, B.G. 322
Bennett, Sterndale 107
Béraud, Antony 15
Bermani, Benedetto 193
Bernstein, Ferdinand 45
Berthier, Francisque 302
Bertin, Armand 115
Bertin, Louise 115
Bessone, Emma 348
Bias, Fanny 4
Bini, Giuseppe 328
Blache, Frédéric-Auguste 7
Blache, Jean-Baptiste 3
Blasis, Carlo 208, 210, 309
Bochsa, Nicholas 35
Bogdanova, Nadezhda 294–297, 299, 300, 303, 357
Boehm 255
Böhme, Oscka 310
Boïeldieu, François-Adrien 3
Boigne, Charles de 48, 71, 72, 236
Borri, Pasquale 219n, 328, 329
Boucher, François 169, 298
Bouffé, Hugues 11, 244
Bourguignon, Mme 7
Bournonville, August 10, 12, 62, 72, 73, 143, 208, 323, 339, 340
Bouvier, Joseph 96, 127, 178
Boyarchikov, Nicolai 348
Bradley, Miss 84, 112
Brandard, John 159
Brétin, Louis 47
Briffault, Eugène 3
Brueghel, Pieter, the younger 206
Brugnoli, Amalia 32, 33
Brunnov, Count 152n, 225, 226, 252
Brunnova, Countess 152n
Bunn, Alfred 50, 173
Burgmüller, Frédéric 75
Byron, Lord 167, 304, 357

Caboche 191
Calcagnini, Marchese 330
Calvert 310
Cambon, Charles-Antoine 235
Cambridge, Duchess of 106
Camille, Mlle 92, 97, 99n, 101, 102
Campilli, Pietro 38, 40, 352
Carey, Edouard 29, 73
Carey, Gustave 199, 219n, 247n
Carmine, Emilia 256
Caroline, Mlle see Dominique, Mme

Caron 302n
Carpeaux, Jean-Baptiste 334
Carraby, Etienne 322
Casati, Giovanni 18
Cassan, Mlle 140, 146, 163, 168, 172, 178, 201
Castil-Blaze, F.H.J. 21
Catte, Effisio 135, 185, 192, 210, 211, 354, 355
Cavalini 310
Cavos, Alberto 298
Cecchetti, Enrico 346
Cellarius, Henri 161
Cerrito, Fanny 33, 34, 83, 84, 88, 91, 97, 98, 100–103, 106–109, 111, 115, 121, 125, 128–132, 138, 147–153, 165–168, 171–174, 176–181, 201–203, 205, 220, 226, 254, 285, 286, 288, 289, 292–294, 296, 298–301, 303, 304, 349, 353–355, 357
Chaix d'Est'Ange, Louis-Adolphe 322
Champdivers, Odette de 190, 192
Changarnier, General 235
Charlemagne, A. 259
Charles VI, King of France 190–194
Charles X, King of France 15
Chassériau, Théodore 64
Chaudes-Aigues, J. 60
Chevalier, Mlle 99n
Chorley, H.F. 82
Chushkin 310
Ciardi, Cesare 310
Ciceri, Pierre 10, 14, 74, 82
Cimarosa, Domenico 167
Citerio, Carolina 212
Clara, Mlle 31
Claudet, Antoine 86
Cogniard brothers 43, 45
Collignon, F.J. 224, 227
Comba, Rosa, 301
Cominazzi, Paolo 330
Compan, Charles 6
Constantine, Grand Duke 225
Copère, Mme 81, 111, 112, 130, 132
Coralli, Jean iii, 14, 16, 21, 23, 30, 45, 62, 71–73, 75–77, 79, 288, 348, 353
Cortesi, Antonio 352
Cortona, Pietro da 121
Costa, Michael 18, 84, 209, 353, 355
Coulon, Antoine 22, 26, 27, 30, 31, 35, 81, 97, 111, 112, 126, 132, 181, 236, 237, 354
Coulon, Eugène 128
Coulon, Jean-François 15, 18
Crippa, Giuseppe 182, 183
Croff, Giovanni Battista 194, 355
Crombé, Mme 43

Crosnier, François-Louis 17
Cucchi, Claudina 329, 330, 332, 347, 356
Curti, P.A. 211

Dalimil 263
DANCES AND PAS
 Abruzzese, L' (Catarina) 185
 Aldeana, L' 294
 Amours forgerons, Les (Armida) 291
 Aragonaise, L' (Le Corsaire) 305
 Arcs, pas des (War of the Women) 264, 267
 Bacchanale, grande (War of the Women) 265
 Barcarolle (The Naiad and the Fisherman) 255
 Bohémischka, La (Zingaro) 54, 58
 Boleras de Cadiz, Las 83
 Bonnaventura, La (Gazelda) 270, 271
 Borsaiulo, Il (Catarina) 186
 Bouquet, pas de (Odetta) 194
 Cachucha 229
 Captivité, La (Armida) 288
 Castilliana, La (Le Délire d'un peintre) 110
 Chibouck, pas de (Lalla Rookh) 167
 Cinq sens, pas des (Kaya) 145
 Coquetterie, pas de la (La Filleule des fées) 248
 Corbeilles, pas des (Esmeralda) 122n, 231
 Corbeilles, pas des (Lalla Rookh) 172
 Corbeilles, pas des (Odetta) 195
 Cosmopolitana, La (Gazelda) 271, 276, 320, 321
 Couronne, pas de la (Zélia) 130
 Cracovienne, La 87
 Délivrance, La (War of the Women) 266
 Double Cachucha (Une Soirée de carnaval) 87, 353
 Dryades, grand pas des (Eoline) 142, 313
 Esmeralda, pas de l' (Esmeralda) 122, 136
 Eventails, pas des (Le Corsaire) 305
 Fantasia, La (Gazelda) 269
 Fascination, pas de (Faust) 213, 279
 Fascination, valse de la (Alma) 84, 85, 97, 141, 212
 Feast of the Roses, The, (Lalla Rookh) 172
 Fées, pas des (La Filleule des fées) 242, 248

377

Index

Fiancée, pas de (Eoline) 140
Flèches, pas des (Zélia) 130
Folie du carnaval, La
  (Catarina) 163, 188
Fontaine du rire, La (Armida)
  289
Forlana (Zingaro) 56
Furlana, La (The Naiad and
  the Fisherman) 255
Gallegada, La (La Débutante)
  300
Gavotte de Vestris (Un Bal
  sous Louis XIV) 95, 96, 111,
  353
Grande Quintette dansante
  (Esmeralda) 222, 355
Jardin animé, Le (Le Corsaire)
  347
Maja, La (L'Ile des muets) 301
Masque, pas de (Catarina) 163,
  164, 188
Mazurka d'extase (Eoline) 46,
  141, 143, 312, 313
Menuet de la reine, Le (Un Bal
  sous Louis XIV) 95, 96, 111,
  353
Modèles, pas des (Catarina)
  188
Moissonneurs, pas des 146
Naiades, pas des (The Naiad
  and the Fisherman) 256
Naissance des fleurs, La
  (Armida) 290
Norvégienne, La (Kaya) 145
Odalisques, pas des (Le
  Corsaire) 306
Ombre, pas de l' (Ondine) 103,
  104, 129
Ondes, pas des (Ondine) 101
Pas de neuf (Lalla Rookh) 172,
  179
Pas stratégique (Catarina) 160,
  164, 185, 190
Pas symbolique (Lalla Rookh)
  168, 169
Perrotiana, La Nos. 1 and 2
  161
Polka 127, 128, 354
Polka comique (inserted in
  Giselle) 283
Pyrrhique, grande danse (War
  of the Women) 266
Romanesca, La (Catarina) 162,
  186
Rose, pas de la (Zélia) 131
Rose flétrie, pas de la (Ondine)
  104, 105
Saltarella (Catarina) 164, 187
Séduction, grand pas de (War
  of the Women) 265
Seven Deadly Sins, The (Faust)
  213, 216, 218, 219n, 279,
  315
Slavone, La (War of the
  Women) 264
Tambourin, pas de (Armida)
  294
Tarantella 35–37, 83, 87, 147,
  352
Tarantella (Ondine) 102, 105,
  106, 108, 251
Tauromachie, La 276
Truandaise, La (Esmeralda)
  119, 126, 133, 136, 231,
  301, 348
Truands, pas des (Esmeralda)
  231
Tyrolienne (Esmeralda) 122n,
  136
Valse à cinq temps (Catarina)
  160, 164, 186, 189
Valse bohémienne (Esmeralda)
  231
Valse saxonne, La (Zingaro)
  54, 58
Valse silésienne (Eoline) 204,
  311
Voiles, pas des (Armida) 292
Zapateado, El 47
Ziguerrerina (Zingaro) 56
Zinganka, La (Gazelda) 271
Danseuses Viennoises 138, 144
Dantan, Jean-Pierre 23
Dargomynsky, Alexandre 115n
Darondeau, Henri 10
Dash, Countess 22, 23
Dauberval, Jean 4, 11, 30, 114
David, Félicien 166, 167, 169–
  171, 173, 355
Degas, Edgar 335, 336, 338
D'Egville family 161
Delacroix, Eugène ii, 209
Delavigne, Casimir 16, 191
Delavigne, Germain 191
Deldevez, Ernest 299, 357
Delibes, Léo 337, 347
Deligny, Eugène 300, 337, 357
Delorge, Joseph 1
Demelisse, Octavie 140, 146,
  163, 168, 172, 278
Deshayes, André-Jean-Jacques iii,
  24, 26, 27, 30, 31, 35, 71, 78–
  81, 83, 86, 87, 97, 134, 165,
  179–181, 208, 353
Desplaces, Henri 82n, 83, 87
Despléchin, E.D.J. 235, 242
Devéria brothers 64
Didelot, Charles 21, 32, 230,
  233, 259, 273, 303, 342
Didier, Pierre 230, 246, 249n,
  354
Dietsch, Pierre 272
Di Mattia, Girolamo 354
Dominique, Mme 241, 302, 333
Donizetti, Gaetano 32, 33, 63,
  73, 81, 92, 113, 151, 284, 298,
  353
Dor, Louis 222, 355

Dorval, Marie 13, 15
Dostoyevsky, Fyodor 255
Drigo, Riccardo 308n, 346, 349
Dubbelt, Leonty 262
Dubourg 98
Ducie, Mlle 99n
Dufour, Florentine 15, 16
Dumas, Alexandre, père 48, 64
Dumilâtre, Adèle 63, 91–93, 95,
  96, 353
Dumont, Albert 342
Dumont, Edouard-Charles 341,
  342
Dumont, Louise 341
Dupetit-Méré, Frédéric 10
Duponchel, Henri 28, 41, 224
Duport, Louis 4, 22, 39
Duprez, Gilbert 33, 34, 50, 73
Dupuis, Mimi 15
Duvernay, Pauline 22, 23, 28, 87

Edinburgh, Duke of 318
Efremova, Maria 313
Egorov 310
Elssler, Fanny 27, 28, 34, 45, 60,
  64, 72, 87, 91–96, 103, 108–
  111, 119, 122n, 125, 132–
  136, 149, 154, 162, 184, 188–
  190, 192–196, 198–200, 202,
  210, 211, 217–219, 224–233,
  245, 246, 248–250, 252, 253,
  275, 276, 285, 288, 293, 295,
  297, 303, 328, 348, 349, 353–
  356
Ellsler, Therese 27, 28, 288
Emarot, Célestine 237, 302n, 356
Emile 28
Escudier 244

Ferdinand (J. Le B. de Médicis)
  22
Ferdinand, Thérèse 121, 131,
  140, 146
Ferraris, Amalia 199, 309–316,
  357
Fiorentino, Pier Angelo 202, 237,
  243
Fitzball, Edward 99
Flexman, John 106
Fleury, Louise 81, 86, 87, 275
Florentine, Mlle see Dufour,
  Florentine
Fontana, Carlo 193, 209
Fortuna, Uranio 51, 57, 353
Franz I, Emperor of Austria 32,
  208
Frassi, Adelaide 121, 126, 128,
  354
Frédéric [Malovergne] 230, 249,
  281, 297, 298, 346, 347, 349,
  354, 357
Friedberg, Ekaterina 303–305,
  307–309, 357
Fyodorov, Pavel 316

378

Index

Galby, Clara 97, 99n, 101
Gardel, Maximilien 96
Gardel, Pierre 4, 176, 205
Garnier, Charles 333
Garrick, David 173
Gascoin, John S. 93
Gauthier, Aimée 16, 40
Gautier, Estelle 335
Gautier, Théophile ii, 34, 56, 64, 65, 67–69, 72, 73, 76, 80, 88, 90, 91, 114, 155, 173, 209, 237, 239, 241, 244, 301, 310–312, 314, 335, 353
Gavarni, Paul 57
Gavilov 310
Gay, Delphine 64
Geiten, Lydia 348
Geltser, Ekaterina 348
George, Mlle 263
Gerber, Y. 347
Geyrot, A.F. 259n
Giaquinto, Giuseppe 247n
Gide, Casimir 26
Gioja, Gaetano 91, 114, 193
Giorza, Paolo 329, 356
Glover, Miss 84
Gluck, Christoph Willibald von 14
Gœthe, Johann Wolfgang von ii, 15, 26, 84, 206, 208, 209, 231, 277–281, 286
Goltz, Nicolai 230, 297, 309, 354, 357
Goncourt, Edmond de 336
Gorsky, Alexandre 347, 348
Gosselin, Geneviève 81
Gosselin, Louis 81, 110, 112, 126, 132, 150, 157, 159, 354
Gottlieb 9
Gounod, Charles 277, 334
Gouriet 118
Grahn, Lucile 138, 140–152, 157, 159, 160, 162–165, 174, 176–179, 201, 203, 295, 310, 352, 354, 355
Grantzow, Adèle 333, 346–348
Grétry, André-Modeste 222
Grieve, William 82, 84, 92, 99, 100, 102, 104, 105, 112, 121, 130, 138
Grisi, Carlotta iii, 32–44, 46–51, 56–65, 70–78, 80, 81, 83, 87–91, 94, 111, 112, 118, 119, 122, 124–128, 133, 136, 138, 147–152, 173, 176, 200–203, 207, 220, 225, 226, 234–236, 239–242, 244, 246, 248, 250, 252–254, 257–259, 261, 263, 264, 265–271, 273, 275, 276, 282, 295, 301, 303, 327, 330, 334, 335, 337, 349, 352–356
Grisi, Ernesta 32, 33, 80, 83
Grisi, Giuditta 32, 33, 60
Grisi, Giulia 32, 33, 50, 60, 61,
108, 199, 245, 273
Grisi, Léontine 342
Grisi, Maria 342
Gruneisen, C.L. 95, 106, 107
Gruss, Yvonne 342
Guedeonov, Count Alexandre 183, 225–229, 232, 246, 249, 251, 253, 284, 285, 304, 308, 309
Guerra, Antonio 42
Guillet, Claude 32, 35
Giuraud Rosa 275
Gusev, Pyotr 347
Guy-Stéphan, Marie 85–87, 99n, 302n, 353

Habeneck, François 36, 75
Halévy, Fromental 26, 191, 194
Hall, Mr. 84
Hanka, Václav 263n
Harel, F.A. 263n
Haydn, Franz Josef 220
Hebenstreit, M. 45n
Heberle, Therese 26, 33
Heidenreich, Dr. 309
Heine, Heinrich 21, 64–67, 73, 76, 155, 205–208
Henry V, King of England 192
Henry, Louis 91, 98, 114, 210
Herold, Ferdinand 113
Hogarth, William 95
Honoré, Mlle 168, 172, 178, 201
Houssaye, Arsène 64
Hugo, Victor ii, 51, 56, 64, 67, 68, 92, 111, 112, 114–116, 121, 122, 124, 125, 133, 135, 190, 205, 230, 232, 354
Huguet, Eugène 232, 280n, 281, 327
Hullin, Joséphine 18

Isabella of Bavaria 191, 192, 194
Isakov 277
Ivanov, Lev 297

Jacotin, Henri 4
James, Elizabeth 168, 172, 178, 201
Janin, Jules 22, 23, 28, 36, 56, 63, 68, 237, 242, 327
Johannot, Tony 209
Johansson, Christian 232, 245, 246, 248, 249, 255, 263, 264, 269, 270, 272, 278, 280, 283, 284, 294, 298, 311, 314, 330, 345, 356, 357
Joly, Anténor 51, 57
Joy, S.M. 143
Julia [de Varennes] 18
Julien, Mlle 172, 178, 222, 355

Katrine, Mlle see Friedberg, Ekaterina
Koni, Fyodor 248, 259, 267

Kosheva, Anna 313
Kozlovska, Wiktoria 305
Kshesinskaya, Matilda 347

Labarre, Théodore 300, 357
Lablache, Luigi 35, 108
Lambertini, Angelo 192, 216
La Motte Fouqué, Friedrich de ii, 98, 99
Lamoureux, Louise 172, 222, 355
Lanari, Alessandro 33, 154
Lanner, Katti 219n
Laporte, Pierre 24, 80, 82
Laurençon 16
Laville de Mirmont, Alexandre de 191n
Lebedeva, Praskovia 298, 302, 303, 347
Lebrun, C.F. 286
Le Brun, Louis-Sébastien 19
Lefebvre, Auguste 7, 8, 11, 32
Legnani, Pierina, 347
Lemaître, Frédérick 13, 15, 16, 51, 73, 84, 209, 210, 277
Leménil 357
Lemercier, N.L. 191n
Léon, Arnaud 18
Leopold I, King of the Belgians 180
Lepaulle, Guillaume 73
Le Picq, Charles 273n
Lequine, Charles-François 111
Leroux, Pauline 60
Le Sage, Alain-René 97
Libussa 263
Lifar, Serge 348
Lind, Jenny 201, 203, 205, 207, 331
Liszt, Franz 108
LITERARY WORKS
Chronika Česka (Dalimil) 263n
Corsair, The (Byron) 304
De l'Allemagne (Heine) 64, 65
Egmont (Gœthe) 231
Fantômes (Hugo) 67
Faust (Gœthe) ii, 15, 84, 206, 209, 277, 278, 280, 281, 286
Faust (Heine) 206–208
Göttin Diane, Die (Heine) 155, 206
Histoire de France (Michelet) 191
Jerusalem Delivered (Tasso) 284, 286
Kenilworth (Scott) 231
Lalla Rookh (Moore) ii, 166, 167, 173
Libussa (Musäus) 138
Notre Dame de Paris (Hugo) ii, 92, 114, 115, 190
Nuits florentines, Les (Heine) 66

379

Index

Orientales, Les (Hugo) 67
Undine (La Motte Fouqué) ii, 98
Livry, Emma 321
Lorentz 64
Lormier, Paul 235
Louis XIV, King of France 167
Louis XVI, King of France 24
Louis-Philippe, King of the French 20, 226
Louise, Mlle 30
Lumley, Benjamin 78, 79, 82, 86, 88, 90–93, 98, 105, 108, 109, 112, 113, 115, 124, 127, 130, 132, 136, 138, 143, 148–151, 155, 157, 164, 166, 167, 176, 179, 199, 201, 203, 205–208, 216, 222, 223, 304, 354
Lyadov, Alexandre 252
Lyadov, Konstantin 246, 356
Lyadova, Vera 31, 357

Mabille, Auguste 57, 73
Madayeva, Matilda 303
Magri, Francesco 329, 356
Makarova, Alexandra 270, 279, 280
Malleville, Vicomtesse de 130, 153, 164, 169
Marcel, Ivan 230, 252, 281, 297, 303
Marie-Antoinette, Queen of France 24
Marinari, Giovanni 138
Mario, Giuseppe 108, 199, 245, 273
Marlowe, Christopher 209
Marquet, Louise 239, 302n, 356
Marshall, Charles 138, 140, 141, 145, 153, 169, 170, 207, 220
Martin, John 170
Martin, Mlle 30
Martin y Soler, Vincente 273n
Masaniello (T. Aniello) 158
Mathias, Irka 346
Mauri, Rosita 333, 337, 341
Maurice, Charles 18, 19, 20, 22, 29, 41, 47, 59, 72, 77, 89, 90
Mayer, Félix 5
Mayseder, Josef 40, 43
Maywood, Augusta 218, 219, 276, 349, 355
Mazilier, Joseph 4, 15, 16, 22, 23, 47, 62, 63, 72, 136, 253, 261, 302n, 305, 321, 334
Mazurier, Charles 5–11, 13
Mazzucato, Alberto 135
Mendez, José 346, 348
Mérante, Jules 302n, 327, 341
Mérante, Louis 302, 321, 327, 335–337, 340–342
Mérante, Zina see Richard, Zina
Merle, J.T. 15
Metternich, Prince 219

Meyerbeer, Giacomo 23, 234
Michau, Sophie 161
Michelet, Jules ii, 191, 194, 196
Milon, Louis 4, 5, 18, 30
Minkus, Ludwig 310
Mitchell, John 144
Molière 222
Moncelet, Mlle 140, 146, 163
Monnais, Edouard 60
Monplaisir, Hippolyte 136, 349
Montarini 310
Montessu, Henri 128, 131
Montessu, Pauline 4, 18, 19, 23, 24, 26, 352
Monticini, Antonio 115, 125, 135
Moore, Lillian 41n
Moore, Thomas ii, 166, 167, 173, 355
Morgan, Lady 157, 158
Morny, Duchesse de 320
Morton, Edward 144
Mozart, Wolfgang Amadeus 40, 353
Müller, Adolf 45n
Muravieva, Martha 288, 291, 292, 294, 299, 300, 303, 308, 326, 327, 333, 357
Musäus, Johann 138, 139, 142

MUSICAL WORKS
Désert, Le (David) 166, 355
Hirondelles, Les (David) 171
Seasons, The (Haydn) 220
Symphony No. 6 (Beethoven) 170

Nadaud, Jean-Baptiste 18, 81, 150, 160, 180, 181, 353–355
Nanteuil, Célestin 64
Napoleon III, Emperor of the French 234, 297
Negri, Angela 212
Nerval, Gérard de 64, 209
Nestroy, Johann 45
Nevakhovitch, Mme see Smirnova, Tatiana
Nicholas I, Tsar 226, 233, 249, 259, 261, 281, 284, 285, 342
Nikitina, Elizaveta 232, 313, 356
Nikitina, Varvara 346
Nodier, Charles 15, 209
Noverre, Jean-Georges 114, 138, 176, 286, 288, 323–26

Octo (J.F. Dupuis-Delcourt) 191n
Oldenburg, Peter III, Grand Duke of 303, 357
Olga, Queen of Württemberg 258
Ollivier, Charles 106

OPERAS
Adelia (Donizetti) 92, 113
Anna Bolena (Donizetti) 151

Assedio di Corinto (Rossini) 108
Barbiere di Siviglia, Il (Rossini) 108
Charles VI (Halévy) 191
Diamants de la couronne, Les (Auber) 158
Don Giovanni (Mozart) 40, 63, 73, 353
Elisir d'amore, L' (Donizetti) 298
Ernani (Verdi) 138, 142
Esmeralda (Bertin) 115
Esmeralda (Dargomynsky) 115n
Esmeralda (Mazzucato) 135
Faust (Gounod) 277
Favorite, La (Donizetti) 63, 73, 83, 284, 353
Fée aux roses, La (Halévy) 235n
Fernand Cortez (Spontini) 23
Figlia del Reggimento, La (Donizetti) 221
Gemma di Vergy (Donizetti) 81
Guillaume Tell (Rossini) 18, 31
Gustave (Auber) 35
Huguenots, Les (Meyerbeer) 65
Juive, La (Halévy) 63, 73
Lombardi, I (Verdi) 135
Lucia di Lammermoor (Donizetti) 34, 35, 221
Macbeth (Verdi) see Sivardo il Sassone
Matrimonio Segreto, Il (Cimarosa) 167
Moïse (Rossini) 23, 352
Muette de Portici, La (Auber) 58, 352
Nabucco (Verdi) see Nino
Nino (Verdi) 157
Norma (Bellini) 33
Petit Chaperon rouge, Le (Boïeldieu) 3
Pharamond (Boïeldieu) 75
Poliuto (Donizetti) 284
Polyceute (Gounod) 334
Prophète, Le (Meyerbeer) 234, 242, 243
Puritani, I (Bellini) 147
Robert le Diable (Meyerbeer) 23
Rossignol, Le (Le Brun) 19
Sivardo il Sassone (Verdi) 284
Sonnambula, La (Bellini) 221
Tentation, La (Halévy) 26
Vespri Siciliani, I (Verdi) 328
Zampa (Herold) 113
Zingaro (Fortuna) 49, 51–60, 64, 268, 353

Oxenford, John 139
Ozy, Caroline 58

Index

Palladini, Andrea 328, 349
Palmer, Mr. 112
Panizza, Giovanni 194, 209, 277, 355
Paradol, Mme 36
Parkacheva, Ekaterina 280
Pasta, Giuditta 33
Paul, Alexandre 302
Paul, Antoine 4, 12, 22
Paul, Pauline see Montessu, Pauline
Paul, Zélie 15
Pavlova, Anna 347, 349
Pembroke, Earl of 93, 128
Peroni, Filippo 329
Perrin, Emile 327, 332
Perrot, Alexandrine 281, 320, 334, 335, 338, 340–342
Perrot, Benoît 2
Perrot, Capitolina 249, 260, 320, 334, 341, 342
Perrot, François-Marie 3, 61
Perrot, Jean 1, 3, 41, 61, 302, 304, 309
Perrot, Jean-Baptiste 3
Perrot, Jean-Claude 1
Perrot, Jean-Marie 3
Perrot, Jules
  Birth in Lyon, 1; first stage experience, 3; early career in Lyon, 3–6; at the Gaîté in Paris, 7–11; studies under Auguste Vestris, 11–13; moves to the Porte-Saint-Martin, 13–16; influence of Frédérick Lemaître, 13; first season in London (1830), 17–18; début and engagement at the Paris Opéra, 18–20; partners Taglioni, 21–22; his ugliness, 12, 22–24, 50, 51, 57; his salary increased fourfold, 22; London engagement (1833), 24–27; London engagement (1834), 28; break with the Opéra, 28–29; London engagement (1835), 30–31; goes to Naples, 32; meets Carlotta Grisi, 32–34, their joint engagement in London (1836), 35–36; hitches in wedding plans, 36; presents Carlotta in Paris, 36–37; engagement in Vienna (1837–38), 42–43; produces Der Kobold, 43–46; dispute with Aniel, 46–47; domestic life with Carlotta, 48–49; produces Zingaro in Paris, 51–59; deceived by the Grisi family, 60–62; prepares Carlotta for her début at the Opéra, 63; collaborates in Giselle, 71–76; influence on the Paris Opéra ballet company, 77; engaged as ballet-master in London, 78; revives Giselle there, 79–83; collaborates in Alma, 83–87; final break with Carlotta, 88–89; delivers oration at Vestris's funeral, 89; consulted by Gautier for La Péri, 90–91; first meeting with Pugni, 91; injured on stage, 93–94; coaches Elssler in Giselle, 94–95; returns to the stage, 97; produces Ondine, 98–108; produces pas de deux for Elssler and Cerrito, 108–110; produces Esmeralda, 112–126; arranges stage version of the polka, 127–128; produces Zélia, his one failure, 129–132; plans to produce Jeanne d'Arc, 132; produces Esmeralda in Milan, 135–137; produces Eoline in London, 138–144; collaborates with Grahn in Kaya, 144–147; produces the Pas de Quatre, 149–153; produces Catarina, 155–165; produces Lalla Rookh, 166–173; produces Le Jugement de Pâris, 176–180; his character diagnosed by phrenology, 182; approached by the St. Petersburg Imperial Theatres, 183–184; produces definitive version of Catarina in Milan, 184–190; produces Odetta, 190–199; produces Les Eléments, 201–203; his part in the rejection of Heine's Faust; produces Faust, 206–217; sympathies in the 1848 revolution in Milan, 219; produces Les Quatre Saisons, 220–222; engaged by the Paris Opéra, 224; invited to accompany Elssler to Russia, 224–229; supervises revival of Esmeralda, 230–232; requires the corps de ballet to rehearse in tutus, 230–231; offered a new engagement in Russia and varies his contract with the Paris Opéra, 233–234; produces La Filleule des fées, 236–245; in rehearsal, 236, 252; delivers oration at Coulon's funeral, 236–237; revives La Filleule des fées in St. Petersburg, 246–248; marries, 249; produces naiad scene at Peterhof, 251; popularity with St. Petersburg dancers, 252; his gift for comedy, 254; produces The Naiad and the Fisherman, 254–260; his contract renewed for three years, 260; produces The War of the Women, 261–268; produces Gazelda, 268–273; revives Faust in St. Petersburg, 276–281; strains during the Crimean War, 281; difficulties with the Imperial Theatres, 284–285; his contract renewed for another three years, 285; produces Armida, 286–294; participates in the coronation festivities in Moscow, 297–298; death of his father, 302; works with Lebedeva, 302–303; produces Le Corsaire, 304–308; incapacitated, 309; produces Eoline, 310–315; continued inactivity, 311–316; contretemps with Saburov, 317; complains about his treatment by the Imperial Theatres, 317–318; is dismissed, 318–319; returns to Paris, 320; copyright dispute with Petipa, 320–323; annotates Noverre's Letters, 323–326; coaches Muravieva in Giselle, 327; revives Gazelda in Milan, 328–332; meeting with Rosita Mauri, 333–334; takes family to Geneva during Franco-German War, 334–335; painted by Degas, 335–336, 338; friendship with Mérante and Théodore families, 337; his new year's greetings to Taglioni, 338–339; keeps in touch with Bournonville, 339–340; recollections of his old age, 341–342; death, 342
Perrot, Laurence 1, 3
Perrot, Louis 60, 159n
Perrot, Marie 249, 260, 320, 334, 335, 338, 341
Perrot, Marie-Julie 41, 72, 135, 154, 344
Persiani, Fanny 34
Petipa, Jean 7, 245, 281, 283, 285, 297, 356
Petipa, Lucien 50, 51, 57, 63, 69, 73, 75, 76, 88, 91, 174, 240, 241, 285, 302, 320, 321, 326, 327, 353
Petipa, Maria S. 271, 278, 281, 289, 300, 303, 310, 320, 321, 357
Petipa, Marius i, iii, 230, 245, 255, 263, 269, 270, 278, 281–285, 288, 292, 294, 300, 301, 303, 305, 308, 316, 320–323,

381

Index

326, 342, 345–349, 355–357
Petit, Emile 157
Petit-Stéphan, Joséphine 157, 162, 165, 222, 354, 355
Petrov 305, 307
Piccinni, Alexandre 10, 14
Pillet, Léon 60, 63, 71, 136
Pius IX, Pope 217
Pixerécourt, Guilbert de 98
PLAYS
   Charles VI (Laville de Mirmont) 191n
   Démence de Charles VI, La (Lemercier) 191n
   Doctor Faustus (Marlowe) 209
   Etrangère, L' 11
   Faust (Béraud, Nodier, Merle) 15, 26, 84, 209–211
   Fille de l'air, La (Cogniard, Raymond) 43, 65, 139
   Fuenta Ovejuna (Vega) 263
   Guerre des servantes, La (Théaulon, Alboize, Harel) 263
   Hamlet (Shakespeare) 111
   Jocko (Gabriel, Rochefort) 9, 10
   Kiss, The (Fitzball) 99
   Kobold, Der (parodies by Told and Nestroy) 45n
   Macbeth (Shakespeare) 16
   Marino Falieri (Delavigne) 16
   Odette, ou la Petite Reine (Octo, Ratier, Saint-Yves) 191
   Ondine, (Pixerécourt, Sauvage) 98
   Petit Carnaval de Venise, Le 6
   Polichinel Vampire (F.A. Blache) 7, 8
   Polichinelle avalé par la baleine (Lefebvre) 7, 8
   Rameau d'or, Le (Lefebvre) 9
   Ruy Blas (Hugo) 51
   Salvator Rosa 159
   Sapajou (Dupetit-Méré) 10, 11
   Sept Heures (Ducange, Anicet) 16
   Zacharie 73
Plunkett, Adeline 92, 99, 102, 110, 121, 128–130, 302, 354
Pochini, Carolina 349
Pougens, Charles-Marie de 9
Pragher, Fanny 144, 145, 354
Pratesi, Gaspare 135, 195, 354, 355
Pratesi, Giuseppina 356
Přemysl, King of Bohemia 263
Prikhunova, Anna 248, 251, 253, 258, 270, 278–280, 282, 284, 297, 299, 306, 308, 309, 356, 357
Proche, Augustine 81
Pugni, Cesare 91, 92, 98, 106–108, 112, 126, 130, 136, 143, 145, 150, 161, 162, 164, 167, 170, 171, 173, 176, 178, 180, 185, 186, 188, 189, 194, 207, 220, 251–254, 257, 261, 268, 272, 277, 288, 290, 299, 305, 310, 322, 337, 353–357
Pusenov 318

Radina, Lyubov 288, 303, 306, 357
Radzivill, Prince Leon 342
Ragaine, Jean 283
Raphael 57, 157
Rappaport, M. 313
Ratier, V. 191n
Raviglia 194, 209
Raymond 43
Razzani, Francesco 195
Reni, Guido 157, 169
Retzsch, Moritz ii, 84, 85
Reuling, J. Wilhelm 43, 352
Richard, Joseph 251, 281
Richard, Zina 248, 251, 280n, 281–284, 291, 295, 302, 327, 328, 333, 337, 340, 341, 356
Ricordi 136n, 185
Robert, Adrien 128
Robert, Elizabeth 241
Robert, Léopold ii, 102, 159, 257, 258
Rochas, André 1
Rochat, F. 3
Roger 3
Roller, Andrei 231, 246, 250, 258, 264, 265, 272, 277, 289–291, 305–307, 310
Romani, Pietro 32
Romano, Giulio 157
Ronchi, Giuseppe 209
Ronzani, Domenico 135, 199, 219, 276, 302n, 328, 349, 354
Roqueplan, Nestor 224
Rosa, Salvator ii, 157, 158, 160, 164, 290
Rosati, Carolina 200–203, 207, 220–222, 226, 304, 355
Rossini, Gioacchino 18, 23, 32, 36, 108, 154, 284, 352
Rota, Giuseppe 328, 329, 332
Royer, Alphonse 320
Ryukhina, Alexandra 269, 280, 294, 356

Saburov, Andrei 309, 316–318
Sacré, Victor 235
Saint-Elme 3
Saint-Georges, Jules-Henri Vernoy de 63, 65, 68, 73, 74, 234, 235, 247, 304, 307, 353, 355
Saint-Julien, Alfred de 235, 356
Saint-Julien, Charles de 283, 292, 293
Saint-Léon, Arthur 15, 91, 96–98, 101, 102, 121, 126, 130–132, 149, 165, 168, 172, 173, 176–178, 232, 261, 276, 278, 292, 294, 303, 316–318, 322, 327, 332–335, 345, 348, 354, 357
Saint-Victor, Paul de 301
Saint-Yves 191n
Salvioni, Guglielmina 346
Samovskaya, Capitolina see Perrot, Capitolina
Samovskaya, Maria 320, 334, 335, 341, 342
Sangalli, Rita 336, 337
Sankovskaya, Ekaterina 249n
Sauvage, Thomas 51, 57, 98, 353
Savoisy 191
Scheffer, Elisa 92, 101, 110, 121, 128, 129, 131, 354
Schiller, Friedrich 39
Schneider, Louis 248
Schultz 310
Scott, Walter 231
Scotti, Maria 301
Scribe, Eugène 158, 235n
Scudo, Paul 235n, 241n
Sergueyev, Konstantin 347
Sergueyev, Nicolai iii, 345
Serkov 277
Serov, A.N. 277
Shakespeare, William 16, 111, 222
Shangine 277
Shiryayev, Alexandre 346, 347
Shishko 265, 305, 310, 311, 314
Shishkov, Matvei 310
Simone, Antone 348
Singier 6
Sloman, D. 84, 100–102, 104
Slonimsky, Yuri iv, 348
Smirnova, Tatiana 230, 231, 246, 282, 354, 356
Snetkova, Maria 270, 279, 280
Sokolov 252
Sokolova, Evgenia 346, 347
Sokolova, Maria 253, 255
Spies, M. de 226, 228, 229
Stapfer, Albert 209
Stepanov notation system iii, 345
Stepanov, Vladimir 345
Stoltz, Rosina 60
Stolyarov 310
Stone, Thomas 93
Stukolkin, Timofei 299, 310, 357
Subra, Julia 337, 341
Surovshchikova, Maria see Petipa, Maria S.
Sutherland, Duchess of 179
Sylvain, James 110

Taglioni, Filippo 27, 31, 262
Taglioni, Louise 162, 165, 172,

382